D0942114

THE
WORLD'S HISTORY

VOLUME 2: Since 1100

HOWARD SPODEK

We Can Do It!

Prentice Hall Inc., Upper Saddle River, NJ 07458

Published 1998 by Prentice Hall Inc.
A Division of Simon & Schuster
Upper Saddle River, New Jersey 07458

Copyright © 1998 Howard Spodek

All rights reserved. No part of this book may be reproduced, in any form or by any means, without permission in writing from the publisher.

ISBN 0-13-079203-9 (paperback)

This book was designed and produced by
Calmann & King Ltd, London

Editorial work by Melanie White and Damian Thompson
Supplementary editorial work by Lydia Darbyshire, Andrew Heritage, Callie Kendall, and Delia Gaze (glossary)
Design by Ian Hunt and Prentice Hall
Maps by Ailsa Heritage and Andrea Fairbrass
Artworks by Dave Kemp
Picture research by Callie Kendall
Printed and bound by R.R. Donnelley & Sons Co., USA

Cover picture: Silk culture and manufacture, seventeenth-century Chinese ink drawing. By courtesy of the Board of Trustees of the Victoria and Albert Museum, London.

Title-page picture: "Rosie the Riveter," symbol of World War II American women workers, on a poster from the War Production Co-ordinating Committee.

PICTURE CREDITS

T = top; B= bottom; R = right; L = left.

The Aga Khan Trust for Culture/J. Bétant 697T/Pascal Marechauy 697B/Yazdi Jahanguir Mazlum 696; AKG, London/Erich Lessing 385; Ancient Art & Architecture Collection 456, 457; Andes Press Agency/Carlos Reyes-Manzo 725, 733L, 771; Associated Press 659; Axiom/James Morris 690; Mark Azavedo Photo Library 552; Bettmann/Reuters 722, 724, 733R; Bettmann/UPI 599T, 674, 683, 720, 756, 759, 757; Bibliothèque Nationale, Paris 366; Daniel Blatt 703; Bridgeman Art Library, London, 411, 421, 435, 465, 473, 479, 527/ Bibliothèque Nationale, Paris 367T/British Library, London 452, 710/Guildhall Library, Corporation of London 505/Giraudon 477/Peter Willi 541/Museo Nacional Centro de Arte Reina Sofia, Madrid+Giraudon (© Succession Picasso/DACS 1998) 598/Prado, Madrid 493T/Prado, Madrid+Index 461, 493B/Private collection+ Index 492/Royal Geographical Society, London 447/Alexander Turnbull Library, N.Z. 446; © British Crown ©/MOD/photo Cambridge University Committee for Aerial Photography 417; Brown Brothers 507, 509T, 524, 543, 553T, 558, 588, 749; Camera Press 593, 692/Romuauld Meigneux 770/Julien Quideau 736; Comstock 1997/Georg Gerster 365; Coo-ee Historical Picture Library 506, 533; Corbis/Bettmann 623, 631, 657/Jimmy Carter Presidential Library 689/Hulton Getty 575, 629, 641, 675/Library of Congress 753/NASA 602/The National Archives 573, 591, 599B, 660/Enzo Ragazzini 677; ET Archive cover, 355, 371, 513, 580, 613/ National Palace Museum, Taiwan 367B; FAO 604; Werner Forman Archive, London/British Museum 363, 413B/courtesy of Christie's 424/India Office Library (British Library), London 423/ Musée d'Art et d'Histoire, St. Denis, Paris+Giraudon 561/Musée des Arts Decoratifs, Paris 413T/Museum für Volkerkunde, Berlin 412; Fotomas Index 402; © Fundacion Dolores Olmedo/photo: Bob Schalkwijk 772; Giraudon 483; The Granger Collection, New York title page, 396, 405, 422, 442, 444, 472, 476, 480, 486, 489, 581, 592; Sonia Halliday Photographs 432; Robert Harding Picture Library 642; Hulton Getty 514, 540, 555, 668; Victoria Hyde 568; Imperial War Museum, London 594, 715; Courtesy of Japan Information & Cultural Centre, London 638; Joel Photograph Library 685; David King Collection 516, 611, 615, 616, 618, 620, 621R+L, 651; Eadweard Muybridge Collection, Kingston Museum/Les Kirkin 508; Wilberforce House, Kingston-upon-Hull City Museums, Art Gallery and Archives 429, 453T+B; Library of Congress 529; Magnum/Rene Burri 764/Jean Gaumy 694/Burt Glinn 765/Susan Meiselas 768/ Marc Riboud 665/Eugene Smith 637/Nicolas Tikhomiroff 701; Mary Evans Picture Library 416, 553B, 560, 566/Fawcett Library 550; The Jacob A. Riis Collection #101, Museum of the City of New York, © Museum of the City of New York 509B; Christine Osborne Pictures/Middle East Pictures 578, 693, 734; courtesy of Peabody Essex Museum, Salem, MA 654; © Pitt Rivers Museum, University of Oxford 737; Popperfoto 671/Reuters 625, 664, 732; © Punch Ltd 536; Roget-Viollet 469; Ann Ronan at Image Select 498, 501, 502; Royal Commonwealth Society Collection 712; Seattle Art Museum, Eugene Fuller Memorial Collection 368; South American Pictures 361, 399/Robert Francis 761/Tony Morrison 748, 750, 751T+B; Spectrum, London 384; Topham Picturepoint 673, 687, 704, 716, 721, 728; TRH/DOD 633/DOD+USAF 600/IWM, London 585; Trip/B. North 688; © 1988 by The Regents of The University of California/ University of California Press, Berkeley and Los Angeles, California 628.

To my wife Lisa, who made this work possible

CONTENTS

PART 5 — *World Trade*

1100–1776 C.E.

CHANNELS OF COMMUNICATION: THE EXCHANGE OF COMMODITIES, DISEASES, AND CULTURE

12 ESTABLISHING WORLD TRADE ROUTES 356

1100–1500 C.E.

THE PATTERNS AND PHILOSOPHIES OF EARLY ECONOMIC SYSTEMS

13 THE UNIFICATION OF WORLD TRADE 394

1500–1776

THE INVISIBLE HAND REACHES OUT: A CAPITALIST WORLD SYSTEM APPEARS

PART 6 *Migration: Free People and Slaves*

1500–1750

"BE FRUITFUL AND MULTIPLY, FILL UP THE EARTH AND SUBDUE IT": DEMOGRAPHIC CHANGES IN A NEW GLOBAL ECUMENE

14 DEMOGRAPHY AND MIGRATION 430

1500–1750

THE MOVEMENT OF PEOPLES AROUND THE EARTH

PART 7

Social Change

1688–1914

WESTERN REVOLUTIONS AND THEIR EXPORTS

15 POLITICAL REVOLUTIONS IN EUROPE AND THE AMERICAS 462

1688–1850

THE BIRTH OF HUMAN RIGHTS IN THE AGE OF ENLIGHTENMENT

16 THE INDUSTRIAL REVOLUTION 497

1740–1914

THE GLOBAL CONSEQUENCES OF INDUSTRIAL EXPANSION AND IMPERIALISM

17 SOCIAL REVOLUTIONS 538

1830–1914

URBANIZATION, GENDER RELATIONS, AND NATIONALISM WEST AND EAST

CONTESTED VISIONS OF A NEW INTERNATIONAL ORDER

18 TECHNOLOGIES OF MASS-PRODUCTION AND DESTRUCTION 574

1914–1990s

19 THE SOVIET UNION AND JAPAN 608

1914–1997

PLAYING TECHNOLOGICAL CATCH-UP
WITH THE WEST

MAPS

ACKNOWLEDGMENTS

After several years of work, at last comes the opportunity to thank publicly the many people who have made this book possible through their encouragement, careful reading of early drafts, comments, and general support. The idea for this text took form in the course of work with many superb teachers in a world history workshop in the School District of Philadelphia. The administrators of that program—Carol Parssinen and Ellen Wylie of the Philadelphia Alliance for Teaching Humanities in the Schools and Jim Culbertson and Joe Jacovino from the School District—set the framework for that program which led to writing this text. I thank them and the many participants who helped make our studies so fruitful. Three of the participants later joined me at Temple University, Philadelphia, in teaching future teachers of history, and I thank Patricia Jiggetts Jones, Gloria Mitchell-Barnes, and Karen Kreider for helping me plan the content and pedagogy of an introductory world history course. Sue Rosenthal reminded me to encourage students to find their own place in history and thus inspired the afterword of this book.

As I prepared a new introductory course in world history at Temple University, I was granted a semester's study leave for which I thank the Temple University Faculty Senate. Throughout this project I received the constant support of Dean Carolyn Adams and department chairs Jim Hilty and Morris Vogel.

Many colleagues have read or discussed parts of this text in manuscript and have made helpful suggestions. Within Temple University's history department these include Barbara Day-Hickman, Ruth Karras, Tim Mixter, Dieu Nguyen, Arthur Schmidt, Teshale Tibebu, and Kathy Walker. Vasiliki Limberis of our religion department and Len Greenfield from anthropology helped with issues outside the immediate discipline. In addition I thank Michael Adas, Al Andrea, Joan Arno, Terry Burke, Tim Burke, Lee Cassanelli, Richard Eaton, Narayani Gupta, Chris Jones, Maghan Keita, Dina Rizk Khoury, Lynn Lees, Alan Mann, David O'Connor, Greg Possehl, Jerry Ruderman, and Gail Vander Heide. Jim Krippner-Martinez' help with Latin America was critical, as was the assistance of Susannah Ruth Spodek on Japan. I trust that all these colleagues and friends will find in the finished book evidence of their contributions, and that they will forgive me for not following their advice even more carefully.

I first used most of the text materials in this book with my students at Temple University. They provided the first indications of what worked well in teaching world history and should be kept in the final product, and what did not and should be scrapped. I thank them both for their patience and for the many suggestions they made.

I owe a great debt to the editors and staff at Calmann and King, London, who saw this book through from its inception to its conclusion. They seemed to know just when to encourage, to support, to understand, and to demand. Rosemary Bradley (now with Prentice Hall) commissioned the book; Melanie White edited and guided the book from beginning to end; Damian Thompson prepared the layout and design and helped select, gather, and caption the illustrations which drive the written text forward; Lee Ripley Greenfield had overall executive charge of the project in its last four years.

The most profound and personal thanks come last. My father and mother, may their memories be a blessing, always encouraged and supported my studies. My father, though a man of business rather than of the academy, always enjoyed historical discussions. Mother, of course, prepared, and presided over, the dinner table at which these discussions took place, often adding her own comments as well.

When I began writing this book, my two older children, Susie and Josh, were already in college. Sarah, the youngest, was still in high school. All three were always in my mind as I wrote. They were my first audience as I asked myself: What should students know about world history? They were usually the first readers of early drafts of each chapter, and their comments were perceptive and helpful. Most gratifying of all: Susie, who spent four years living and working in Japan, graciously provided early drafts of materials on Japan; Sarah, who spent two years with the Peace Corps in Morocco, helped me through issues in the Arab and Berber worlds; and Josh, training as a physicist, reminded me to give proper attention to the importance of science in history. To them I dedicate the first volume of this work.

I met Lisa Hixenbaugh about a year into the writing of this book, and we were married just a few months before its completion. She has enriched and enhanced my life. Graciously and without complaint she gave up time that we might have spent together so that the writing could be completed. She endured interminable monologues on the status of the project. Her support and encouragement helped make the entire task feasible. It is my pleasure to dedicate the second volume to her.

REVIEWERS OF THE TEXT

J. Lee Annis, Jr., Montgomery College; Samuel Brunk, University of Nebraska at Lincoln; Nancy S. Crump, Wayne State College; David L. Ferch, Sierra College; William Jones, Mt. San Antonio College; David L. Longfellow, Baylor University; Mark McLeod, University of Delaware; Eleanor W. McCluskey, Broward Community College; Joseph Mitchell and Oliver B. Pollack, University of Nebraska at Omaha; John Powell, Penn State University at Erie; David K. Robinson, Northeast Missouri State University; Charles R. Sullivan, University of Dallas.

QUOTED EXTRACTS: ACKNOWLEDGMENTS

For permission to reprint copyright material the publishers gratefully acknowledge the following:

AMS Press Inc.: *The Gandhi Reader, No. 1*, ed. Homer Jack (Grove Press, 1956), by permission of AMS Press Inc.

American Historical Association: "Imperialism and History: A Century of Theory, from Marx to Postcolonialism" by Patrick Wolfe from *American Historical Review* (Volume CII, No. 2, April 1997).

Bantam Doubleday Dell Publishing Group Inc.: *My Mission in Life* by Eva Peron, trans. Ethel Cherry (Doubleday, 1952), by permission of the publisher.

Dennis Brutus: "Their Behaviour" from *The Heritage of African Poetry*, ed. Isidore Okpewho (Longman, 1985), by permission of the author.

John Pepper Clark: "Agbor Dancer" from *The Heritage of African Poetry*, ed. Isidore Okpewho (Longman, 1985).

Columbia University Press: *Sources of Chinese Tradition* by William Theodore de Bary, © 1960 by Columbia University Press; *The Autobiography of Yukichi Fukuzawa*, © 1966 by Columbia University Press, by permission of the publisher.

Duke University Press: "Towards an Analogy of City Images" by A.K. Ramanujan from *Urban India: Society, Space and Image*, © 1970, Duke University Program in Comparative Studies on Southern Asia, reprinted by permission of the publisher.

Farrar, Straus & Giroux Inc.: *Night* by Elie Wiesel (Bantam Books, 1962), by permission of Farrar, Straus & Giroux Inc.

Grove/Atlantic Inc.: *The Wretched of the Earth* by Frantz Fanon (Penguin Twentieth Century Classics, 1990), by permission of Grove/Atlantic.

Harcourt Brace & Company: "How Should We Live" by Wislawa Szymborska from *View With a Grain of Sand* (Harcourt Brace, 1995), by permission of the publisher.

The Harvill Press: *The Gulag Archipelago. 3 Volumes*, trans. T. Whitney and H. Willetts (Harvill Press, 1974–78).

Heinemann Publishers (Oxford): *God's Bits of Wood* by Sembene Ousmane, trans. Francis Price (Heinemann, 1970), reprinted by permission of Heinemann Educational Publishers, a division of Reed Educational & Professional Publishing Ltd; "Moroccan Woman's Poem" from *Third World Lives of Struggle*, eds. Hazel Johnson and Henry Bernstein (Heinemann Educational Books, 1982).

Houghton Mifflin Company: *The Human Record: Sources of Global History*, eds. A. Andrea and J. Overfield (1990, 1994).

Macmillan Ltd: *Don Quixote of La Mancha* by Miguel de Cervantes, trans. Walter Starkie (New American Library, 1957), by permission of Macmillan Ltd.

John Murray (Publishers) Ltd: *An Arab Philosophy of History*, trans. Charles Issawi (1950), by permission of the publisher.

Jawaharlal Nehru Memorial Fund: *The Discovery of India* by Jawaharlal Nehru (Asia Publishing House, 1960), by permission of Jawaharlal Nehru Memorial Fund on behalf of Mrs. Sonia Gandhi.

Oxford University Press Ltd: "Prayer to Masks" and "Relentlessly She Drives Me" by Léopold Sédar Senghor from *Selected Poems*, trans. John Reed and Clive Wake, © Oxford University Press 1964, by permission of the publisher.

Penguin USA: "The Doll's House" by Henrik Ibsen, trans. Rolf Fjelde from *Literature of the Western World, Volume II*, eds. Brian Wilke and James Hurt (Macmillan, 1984), by permission of Penguin USA.

Paul E. Sigmund: *The Ideologies of the Developing World*, ed. Paul E. Sigmund (Praeger, 1972), by permission of the editor.

Simon & Schuster Inc.: "The Second Coming" from *The Collected Works of W.B. Yeats, Volume I: The Poems*, revised and edited by Richard J. Finneran, © 1924 by Macmillan Publishing Company, renewed 1952 by Bertha Georgie Yeats, by permission of the publisher.

University of California Press: *Canto General*, by Pablo Neruda, trans./ed. Jack Schmitt, © 1991 Fundacion Pablo Neruda, Regents of the University of California; *Japan, Inc.: Introduction to Japanese Economics (The Comic Book)* by Shotaro Ishinomori, © 1988 The Regents of the University of California; *Unesco, General History of Africa, Volume 1, Methodology and African Prehistory*, ed./trans. J. Ki-Zerbo, © 1993 The Regents of the University of California, all reprinted by permission of the publisher.

The University of Chicago Press: *Africa and the Disciplines*, eds. Robert Bates, V. Mudimbe, and Jean O'Barr (1993), by permission of the publisher.

The University of Wisconsin Press: *The Atlantic Slave Trade* by Philip Curtin (1969), by permission of the publisher.

Verso: *Rigoberta Menchu: An Indian Woman in Guatemala* by Rigoberta Menchu, trans. Elisabeth Burgos Debray (1984), by permission of the publisher.

Every effort has been made to obtain permission from all copyright holders, but in some cases this has not proved possible. The publishers therefore wish to thank all authors or copyright holders who are included without acknowledgment. Prentice Hall Inc./Calmann & King apologizes for any errors or omissions in the above list and would be grateful to be notified of any corrections that should be incorporated in the next edition.

SUPPLEMENTARY INSTRUCTIONAL MATERIALS

The World's History comes with an extensive package of supplementary print and multimedia materials for both instructors and students.

PRINT SUPPLEMENTS

- The *Instructor's Resource Manual* contains chapter outlines, detailed chapter overviews, activities, discussion questions, suggested readings, and information on audio-visual resources.

- The *Test Item File* offers a menu of multiple-choice, true-false, essay, and map questions for each chapter. A collection of blank maps can be photocopied and used for map testing or other class exercises.

- *Prentice Hall Custom Test*, a commercial-quality computerized test management program, available for DOS, Windows, and Macintosh environments, allows instructors to select items from the *Test Item File* and design their own exams.

- A *Transparency Pack* provides instructors with full-color transparency acetates of all the maps, charts, and graphs in the text for use in the classroom.

- The *Study Guide* (Volumes I and II) provides, for each chapter, a brief overview, a list of chapter objectives, study exercises, multiple-choice, short-answer, and essay questions. In addition, each chapter includes two to three pages of specific map questions and exercises.

- *World History: An Atlas and Study Guide* is a four-color map workbook that includes over 100 maps with exercises, activities, and questions that help students learn both geography and history.

- *Documents in World History* (Volumes I and II) is a collection of additional primary source documents that underscore the themes outlined in the text. Organized by chapter, this set for each of the two volumes includes review questions for each document.

- *Reading Critically about History* is a brief guide to reading effectively that provides students with helpful strategies for reading a history textbook. It is available free to students when packaged with *The World's History*.

- *Understanding and Answering Essay Questions* suggests helpful analytical tools for understanding different types of essay questions and provides precise guidelines for preparing well-crafted essay answers. This brief guide is available free to students when packaged with *The World's History*.

- *Themes of the Times* is a newspaper supplement prepared jointly for students by Prentice Hall and the premier news publication, *The New York Times*. Issued twice a year it contains recent articles pertinent to American history. These articles connect the classroom to the world. For information about a reduced-rate subscription to *The New York Times*, call toll-free: 1-800-631-1222.

MULTIMEDIA SUPPLEMENTS

- *History on the Internet* is a brief guide to the Internet that provides students with clear strategies for navigating the Internet and World Wide Web. Exercises within and at the end of the chapters allow students to practice searching for the myriad of resources available to the student of history. This 48-page supplementary book is free to students when packaged with *The World's History*.

- *Digital Art Library World History* is a collection of the maps, charts, and graphs, and other useful lecture material from the text on disk for use with Microsoft Powerpoint™. The material can be used in a lecture, as a slide show, or printed as transparency acetates.

- *The World's History Companion Website* (*www.prenhall.com/spodek*) works in tandem with the text to help students use the World Wide Web to enrich their understanding of world history. Featuring chapter objectives, study questions, new updates, labeling exercises, and much more, it also links the text with related material available on the Internet.

PREFACE

WHY HISTORY?

The professional historian and the student of an introductory course often seem to pass each other on different tracks. For the professional, nothing is more fascinating than history. For the student, particularly one in a compulsory course, the whole enterprise often seems a bore. This introductory text is designed to help that student understand and share the fascination of the historian. It will also remind professors of their original attraction to history, before they began the specialization that has almost certainly marked their later careers. Furthermore, it encourages student and professor to explore together the history of the world and the significance of this study.

Professional historians love their field for many reasons. History offers perspective and guidance in forming a personal view of human development. It teaches the necessity of seeing many sides of issues. It explores the complexity and interrelationship of events and makes possible the search for patterns and meaning in human life.

Historians also love to debate. They love the challenge of demonstrating that their interpretations of the pattern and significance of events are the most accurate and the most satisfying in their fit between the available data and theory. Historians also love the detective work of their profession, whether it is researching through old archives, uncovering and using new sources of information, or reinterpreting long-ignored sources. In recent years historians have turned, for example, to oral history, old church records, files of photographs, cave paintings, individual census records, and reinterpretations of mythology.

Historical records are not simply lists of events, however. They are the means by which historians develop their interpretations of those events. Because interpretations differ, there is no single historical record, but various narrations of events each told from a different perspective. Therefore the study of history is intimately linked to the study of *values*.

To construct their interpretations, historians examine the values—the motives, wishes, desires, visions—of people of the past. In interpreting those values, historians must confront and engage their own values, comparing and contrasting these values with those of people in the past. For example, they ask how various people viewed slavery in the slave-holding societies of the past. In the back of their minds they compare and contrast those older values with values held by various people today and especially with their own personal values. They ask: How and why have values changed or remained the same through the passage of time? Why, and in what way, do my values compare and contrast with values of the past? By learning to pose such questions, students will be better equipped to discover and create their own place in the continuing movement of human history.

This text, therefore, consistently addresses three fundamental questions: What do we know? How do we know it? What difference does it make? It emphasizes **historiography**, the process of creating historical records. Students will see that these records are neither gospel truth nor fabricated fiction, but a first step in understanding and interpreting the past. They will learn how historians frame questions for study and how the questions that are asked determine the answers that are found. They will learn to frame their own, new questions about both the past and the present.

Professional historians consider history to be the king of disciplines. Synthesizing the concepts of fellow social scientists in economics, politics, **anthropology**, sociology, and geography, historians create a more integrated and comprehensive interpretation of the past. Joining with their colleagues in the humanities, historians delight in hearing and telling exciting stories that recall heroes and villains, the low born and the high, the wisdom and the folly of days gone by. This fusion of all the social sciences and humanities gives the study of history its range, depth, significance, and pleasure. Training in historical thinking provides an excellent introduction to understanding change and continuity in our own day as well as in the past.

WHY WORLD HISTORY?

Why specifically world history? Why should we teach and study world history, and what should be the content of such a course?

First, world history is a good place to begin for it is a new field for professor and student alike. Neither its content nor its pedagogy is yet fixed. Many of the existing textbooks on the market still have their origins in the study of western Europe, with segments added to cover the rest of the world. World history as the study of the inter-relationships of all regions of the world, seen from the many perspectives of the different peoples of the earth, is still virgin territory.

Second, for citizens of multicultural, multi-ethnic nations such as the United States, Canada, South Africa, and India, and for those of the many other countries such as the United Kingdom and Australia which are moving in that direction, a world history course offers the opportunity to gain an appreciation of the national and cultural origins of all their diverse citizens. In this way, the study of world history may help to strengthen the bonds of national citizenship.

Third, as the entire world becomes a single unit for interaction, it becomes an increasingly appropriate subject for historical study. The noted historian E.H. Carr explained that history "is an unending dialogue between the present and the past." The new reality of global interaction in communication, business, politics, religion, culture, and ecology has helped to generate the new academic subject of world history.

THE ORIGINS AND DEVELOPMENT OF THIS TEXT

The inspiration for this text was a ground-breaking four-year program in the School District of Philadelphia, 1988–92. Teachers in the District asked for instruction in world history so that they could better teach their ninth-grade course and, indeed, rewrite its curriculum. In the program established to meet their request, some thirty college professors met with about one hundred Philadelphia teachers. I was the academic coordinator, teaching several of the formal courses offered and responsible for staffing the others. From the courses we designed for teachers came the basic framework for the current text. There is no better, more interactive, more critical, yet more helpful audience for new teaching materials than students who are themselves teachers. Together we learned a great deal about the study and teaching of world history at high school, college, and graduate levels.*

Following this schools-based project, twenty college professors from twelve different colleges and universities and twenty high school teachers from fifteen different schools in the Philadelphia metropolitan region were awarded a substantial grant from the National Endowment for the Humanities to pursue further methods of teaching world history—content and pedagogy—at the college level in ways that would best prepare future teachers. I served as project director. Participation in this two-year collaborative project helped me further to refine the content and the method of the current text.†

Finally, in conjunction with these major projects, I began in 1990 to offer a year-long course in world history at Temple University, Philadelphia. The structure of that course is the structure of this text. As each chapter was completed, I included it in the reading materials of the course. So the text has had five years of field testing.

ORGANIZATION AND APPROACH

The text, like the year-long course, links *chronology*, *themes*, and *geography* in eight units of study. The units move progressively along a time line from the emergence of early humans to the present day. Each unit emphasizes a single theme—for example, urbanization or religion or trade—and students learn to use all eight themes to analyze historical events and to develop a grasp of the chronology of human development. Geographically, each unit covers the entire globe, although specific topics place greater emphasis on specific regions.

IMPORTANT SPECIAL FEATURES

To provide the students with direct experience of the historian's craft the text includes:

- Primary sources to illuminate the experiences of an age and place directly. Their analysis is an essential part of the study of history.
- Historians' later interpretations to provide perspective on how historical records were produced and fought over. The analysis of these secondary sources is an essential part of the study of historiography.
- Sidebars to provide more detailed discussions of particular issues beyond the narrative. Such supplements appear in every chapter.
- Extensive, clear, and informative charts and maps to represent information graphically and geographically.
- A wide range of illustrations, many in color, to supplement the written word. Some of the illustrations are grouped into "Spotlights" to illuminate specific issues. These include, for example, at the earliest, a Spotlight on Ban Po, China, which identifies the archaeologist's understanding of prehistoric agricultural villages, to, at the latest, a portfolio of the murals of Diego Rivera, indicating how an individual artist interprets and represents the history of his people through his painting.

Collectively, these materials provide a rich, comprehensive, and challenging introduction to the study of world history and the methods and key interpretations of its historians. Enjoy!

---

* Carol Parsinnen and Howard Spodek, " 'We're Making History': Philadelphia Educators Tackle a National Issue," *The History Teacher* XXV, No. 3 (May 1992), 321–38.
† Howard Spodek, *et al.*, "World History: Preparing Teachers through High School–College Collaboration, The Philadelphia Story, 1993–1995," *The History Teacher* XXIX, No. 1 (November 1995), 1–41.

INTRODUCTION

History will be kind to me, for I intend to write it.

WINSTON CHURCHILL

THE WORLD THROUGH HISTORIANS' EYES

hat's history!" In common usage this phrase diminishes an event as belonging only to the past, implying that it is no longer important and has no further consequence. For the historian, however, history is just the opposite. History records those events that are of greatest importance, of most lasting significance, and of most enduring consequence. History is the assortment of records that humans create, preserve, fight over, revise, and transmit from one generation to the next. It contains the deepest understandings of how we got to where we are now; the struggles fought, won, and lost; the choices made and not made; the roads taken and not taken. We study history to know who we are, who we might have become, and who we might yet become.

HISTORIOGRAPHY

History is not a single, dry record of names, dates, and places. Nor is it a record that somehow, magically, came into being by itself. Historical records are the products of many human choices. From all the events that have occurred, historians choose those they believe worth remembering for inclu-

sion in their accounts and leave out those that are less relevant. Historians differ, however, in their assessment of the importance and significance of events. They debate which events are most significant and which are less so, which should be included in the records and which may be left out. Differences in historians' assessments lead to the writing and preservation of different histories. These differences are important because they represent different understandings of who we have become, and how, and of who we may become, and how. The debates and discussions of historians in forming and arguing about their assessments form part of the historiographical record. **Historiography** is the study of the making of historical records, of the work historians do and how they do it.

Even when historians are in agreement as to which events are most significant, they may differ in evaluating why the event is significant. One historian's interpretation of events may be diametrically opposed to another's. For example, virtually all historians agree that part of the significance of World War II lay in its new policies and technologies of destruction: nuclear weapons in battle and genocide behind the lines. In terms of interpretation, pessimists might stress the continuing menace of these legacies of terror, while optimists might argue that the very violence of the war and the Holocaust triggered a search for limits on nuclear arms and greater tolerance for minorities. With each success in nuclear arms limitation and in toleration, the optimists seem more persuasive; with each spread of nuclear weapons and each outbreak of genocide, the pessimists seem to win.

The study of history is thus an interpretation of significance as well as an investigation of facts. The significance of events is determined by their consequences. Sometimes we do not know what the consequences are; or the consequences may not have run their course; or we may differ in our assessments of the consequences. The play between past events and their current consequences is what historian E.H. Carr had in mind in his famous description of history as "an unending dialogue between the present and the past" (Carr, p. 30).

After historians ask the factual questions of Who, Where, When, What, Why, and How, they reach the "So what?" questions. These affect fundamentally the historians' discussion about what to include in their accounts and what to leave out. In world history, where the subject matter is everything that has ever been done by humans, this problem of selection is fundamental. The problem of interpretation comes with it. These "So what?" questions depend finally on individual interpretation, on the personal values of the historian. Readers, in turn, will evaluate the historians' argument partly by its consistency with the available data, partly by the values implicit or explicit in it, and, finally, partly by comparing the author's values with their own. The study of history thus becomes a dialogue between the values of the historian and the values of the student of history. As you read this text, for example, you should become aware of the values held by the author and of your own values as reader.

As historians present their differing interpretations, each tries to mount the most persuasive arguments, marshaling **primary source** materials, that is, materials from contemporary participants in the events; **secondary sources**, that is, later comments on the consequences of the events; and appeals to the sensibilities of the reader. In turn, the reader will be asking: Does the historians' interpretation sound reasonable? Do people really act as the historian suggests they do? Do the motivations suggested by the historian sound reasonable or is some other interpretation more consistent with the primary and secondary sources and with human motivation? When historians differ in their interpretations of events, readers must judge which argument is more persuasive.

HISTORY AND IDENTITY

History is among the most passionate and bitterly contentious of disciplines because most people and groups locate a large part of their identity in their history. Americans may take pride in their nationality, for example, for having created a representative, constitutional democracy that has endured for over 200 years (see Part 7). Yet they may be saddened, shamed, or perhaps incensed by the existence of 250 years of slavery followed by inequalities in race relations continuing to the present (see Part 6). Christians may take pride in thousands of years of missions of compassion toward the poor and downtrodden, yet they may be saddened, shamed, or perhaps incensed by an almost equally long record of religious warfare and, sometimes, persecution of those whose beliefs differed from their own (see Part 4).

As various ethnic, religious, class, and gender groups represent themselves in public political life, they seek not only to understand the history that has made them what they are, but also to attempt to persuade others to understand that history in the same way. Feminist historians, for example, find in their reading of history that **patriarchy**, a system of male-created and male-dominated institutions, has put women in a position of subordination. To the extent that they weave a persuasive argument from available data and their interpretation of it, or discover new data and create new interpretations, they win over others to their position.

Meanwhile, other historians may present women's position in the world more as a product of biological differentiation than of human decisions. Some may not even agree that women have been subordinated to men, but that both genders have shared in a great deal of suffering (and joy) throughout history (see Parts 1 and 7). The historical debates over the origins and evolution of gender relationships evoke strong emotions because people's self-image, the image of their group, and the perceptions held of them by others are all at stake. And the stakes are high. As historian Gerda Lerner writes in *The Creation of Patriarchy*: "Women's history is indispensable and essential to the emancipation of women" (p. 3).

CONTROL OF HISTORICAL RECORDS

From earliest times, control over the historical records and their interpretation has been fundamental to political rule. The first emperor of China, Qin Shihuang (r. 221–207 B.C.E.), the man who built the concept of a united China that has lasted until today, "discarded the ways of the former kings and burned the writings of the hundred schools in order to make the people ignorant" (deBary, p. 167). So wrote Qia I (201–169 B.C.E.), poet and statesman of the succeeding Han dynasty. Shihuang wished that only his interpretation of China's past, and his place in it, be preserved. Later intellectuals condemned his actions—but the records were irretrievable (see Part 3).

Colonial governments seeking to control subject peoples attempt to interpret their histories by explaining that the conquered people were so backward that they benefited from the conquest. Later historians may be less kind to the colonizers. Some 1900 years ago the historian Tacitus wrote bitterly of the ancient Romans in their conquest of England: "Robbery, butchery, rapine, the liars call Empire; they create a desolation and call it peace" (*Agricola*, 30).

In our own century, the many nations that have won their freedom from colonialism echo similar resentments against their foreign rulers and set out to revise the historical record in keeping with their newly won political freedom. Jawaharlal Nehru, the first prime minister of independent India (1947–64), wrote in 1944, from the cell in which he had been imprisoned for his leadership of his country's independence movement:

> British accounts of India's history, more especially of what is called the British period, are bitterly resented. History is almost always written by the victors and conquerors and gives their viewpoint; or, at any rate, the victors' version is given prominence and holds the field. (Nehru, p. 289)

Philip Curtin, historian of Africa and of slavery, elaborates an equally critical view of European colonial accounts of Africa's history:

> African history was seriously neglected until the 1950s. . . . The colonial period in Africa left an intellectual legacy to be overcome, just as it had in other parts of the world. . . . The colonial imprint on historical knowledge emerged in the nineteenth and early twentieth centuries as a false perspective, a Eurocentric view of world history created at a time of European domination . . . Even where Europeans never ruled, European knowledge was often accepted as *modern* knowledge, including aspects of the Eurocentric historiography. (Curtin, p. 54)

Instead, Curtin continues, a proper historiography must:

> show the African past from an African point of view. . . . For Africans, to know about the past of their own societies is a form of self-knowledge crucial to a sense of identity in a diverse and rapidly changing world. A recovery of African history has been an important part of African development over recent decades. (p. 54)

Even without colonialism, thugs sometimes gain control of national histories. George Orwell's satirical novel *Animal Farm* (published in 1945) presented an allegory in which pigs come to rule over a farm. Among their many acts of domination, the pigs seize control of the historical records of the farm animals' failed experiment in equality and impose their own official interpretation, which justifies their own rule. As full evidence has come to light of the rewriting of history and suppression of alternative records by the Communist Party of the former Soviet Union between 1917 and 1989, the bitter truth underlying Orwell's satire has been fully revealed (see Part 8).

Although the American record on records is much different, in the United States, too, records have been suppressed. Several academic groups are even now trying to use the Freedom of Information Act to pry open diplomatic archives that have been sealed. (Most official archives everywhere have twenty-, thirty-, or forty-year rules governing the waiting period before certain sensitive records are opened to the public. These rules, which are designed to protect living people and certain policies currently in practice from excessive scrutiny, are customary everywhere.)

Religious and ethnic groups, too, may seek to control historical records. The Spanish Catholic Inquisition in the fifteenth, sixteenth, and seventeenth centuries destroyed many historical records both in Spain and in the Americas, and banned access to many more in an attempt to keep alive only officially sanctioned histories and interpretations and to kill off others (see Part 4). More recent-

ly, despite all the evidence of the Holocaust, the murder of 6 million Jews by the Nazi government of Germany during World War II, a few people have claimed that the event never took place. They deny the existence of such racial and religious hatred, and its consequences, and ignore deep-seated problems in the relationships between majority and minority populations.

HISTORICAL REVISION

Interpretations of events may become highly contested and revised even after several centuries have passed. The significance of the voyages of Columbus was once celebrated uncritically in the United States in tribute both to "the Admiral of the Ocean Sea" himself and to the courage and enterprise of the European explorers and early settlers who brought European civilizations to the Americas. In South America, however, where Native American Indians are more numerous and people of European ancestry form a smaller proportion of the pop-

ulation, the celebrations have been far more ambivalent, muted, and meditative.

In 1992, on the 500th anniversary of Columbus' first voyage to the Americas, altogether new and more sobering elements entered the commemoration ceremonies, even in the United States. The negative consequences of Columbus' voyages, previously ignored, were now recalled and emphasized: the death of up to 90 percent of the Native American Indian population in the century after the arrival of Europeans; the Atlantic slave trade, initiated by trade in Indian slaves; and the exploitation of the natural resources of a continent until then little touched by humans. The ecological consequences, which are only now beginning to receive more attention, were not all negative, however. They included the very fruitful exchange of natural products between the hemispheres. Horses, wheat, and sheep were introduced to the Americas; potatoes, tomatoes, and corn to Afro-Eurasia. Unfortunately, the spread of syphilis was one of the consequences of the exchange; scholars disagree on who transmitted this disease to whom (see Part 5).

Lenin addressing troops in Sverdlov Square, Moscow, May 5, 1920. The leaders of the Russian Communist revolution crudely refashioned the historical record to suit the wishes of the winners. After Lenin's death in 1924, his second-in-command Leon Trotsky (pictured sitting on the podium in the left-hand picture) lost to Josef Stalin the bitter power struggle that ensued. Not only was Trotsky banished from the Soviet Union, but so was his appearance in the official archives (see doctored picture on right).

WORLD HISTORY VS. WESTERN HISTORY

Because the study of history is so intimately tied to our sense of identity, as individuals, groups, and citizens of the world, the field is emotionally and bitterly contested. For this reason, the place of world history in the American college curriculum has itself been contested. The contest has been primarily between the advocates of European/ Western history and those favoring a global view. Advocates of Western history wish to educate a student knowledgeable of the central political, cultural, and religious institutions of the Western world, which are the basis of the political life of the United States and the roots of the cultural and religious heritage of its citizens of European ancestry.

Advocates of world history recognize the validity and importance of these claims, but advance countervailing positions:

- Increasingly dense networks of transportation and communication have brought the world, for many purposes, into a single unit. The growth and consolidation of that global unit deserves its own historical study.

- America is increasingly drawn into a world far wider than Europe alone, with the nations and peoples of the Pacific Rim and of Latin America becoming particularly prominent partners.

- The population of America, always at least 15 percent non-European, especially African–American, is now adding large new immigrant

Indians giving Hernán Cortés a headband, from Diego Duran's *Historia de las Indias*, 1547. Bent on conquest and plunder, the bearded Spaniard Cortés arrived on the Atlantic coast of Mexico in 1519. His forces sacked the ancient city of Tenochtitlán, decimated the Aztec people and imprisoned their chief, Montezuma, before proclaiming the Aztec Empire "New Spain." By stark contrast, this bland Spanish watercolor shows local tribesmen respectfully paying homage to the invader as if he were a god; in ignoring the brutality exercised in the colonization of South America, the artist is, in effect, "rewriting" history. (*Biblioteca National, Madrid*)

streams from Latin America and Asia, increasing the need for knowledge of these many cultures and their histories if there is to be a rich, balanced understanding of all the peoples of the United States.

The fierce debate between the advocates of Western history and those favoring world history is thus, in part, a contest for an understanding of the nature of America's population, culture, and place in the world as it has been and as it may become.

The current text is addressed primarily to American students, and many of its references are to American experience, but as global immigration increases the ethnic diversity of most countries of the world, the same need to understand world history in order to understand national history will increase everywhere.

TOOLS

The study of history requires many tools, and this text includes most of the principal ones:

- The core of historical study is a direct encounter with primary materials, usually documents, but including other artifacts from the time—for example, letters, diaries, newspaper accounts, photographs, and artwork. Representative primary materials are included in every chapter.

- Visual images, a strong feature of this book, complement the text, offering non-verbal "texts" of the time.

- Portfolio spreads contain brief essays, linked to the main text, that treat pictures as a springboard for discussion.

- Maps place events in space and in geographical relationship to one another.

- Chronological timelines situate events in time and sequence.

- Brief charts supply summaries as well as contextual information on topics like religion, science, and trade.

▪ Occasional biographical sketches of outstanding individuals, and of average ones, provide personal insights and points of identification.

▪ Various, often conflicting, interpretations demonstrate the existence of multiple perspectives. They help students to challenge their own values and develop their own interpretive criteria.

CHRONOLOGY AND THEME

History is a study of change over time and also of continuities in the face of change. In this text we mark eight turning points in human history, setting each as the focus of a single unit. The choices are somewhat arbitrary, but they do capture fundamental transformations. They also demonstrate how a historian argues for the significance of one turning point over another. Each turning point is marked by the rise to prominence of a new theme in human history and a new focus in the narrative. For example, we move from an emphasis on early human cultures in Part 1 to agricultural and urban "revolutions" in Part 2, to the establishment of the first empires in Part 3. Within each chronological/thematic unit, we stress a single disciplinary or interdisciplinary approach—for example, anthropology in early human cultures, urban studies in the rise of early cities, and political science in the establishment of empires.

We highlight a specific discipline in each chronological unit for teaching purposes, in order to demonstrate the usefulness of each discipline in illuminating historical change. We recognize, however, that all the disciplinary approaches and the realities to which they refer, are relevant in each time period. While our method is somewhat arbitrary, it allows readers to understand how various disciplines, alone and together, help us understand the varied aspects of historical narratives.

The eight turning points by which we mark world history and the specific themes and disciplines we pair with them are:

1 The emergence of the first humans and human culture, 4,500,000 B.C.E. to 10,000 B.C.E. Focus on *anthropology* and *historiography.*

2 The emergence of the first cities and urban civilization following the agricultural revolution, 10,000 B.C.E. to 400 C.E. Focus on *interdisciplinary urban studies.*

3 The emergence of early empires, from Sargon of Assyria and Alexander of Macedon through China, Rome, and India, and the trade routes that linked them, 2000 B.C.E. to 200 C.E. Focus on *politics.*

4 The rise and spread of world religions, focusing on Islam, 622–1500 C.E.; reviewing the Jewish and Christian background and contemporary systems; and comparing the Asia-centered religions of Hinduism, Buddhism, and the ethical system of Confucianism. Focus on *religion.*

5 World trading systems, 1000–1776, with the linkage of eastern and western hemispheres as the fulcrum, about 1500. By the end of this period, capitalism was defined as a new economic system. Focus on *economics.*

6 Migrations, free and slave, 1000–1750. Focus on *demography.*

7 Revolutions, political and industrial, beginning in Europe and spreading globally, 1750–1914. Focus on *social changes*, especially *changes in family and gender roles.*

8 Technological change and its human control, 1914 to the present. Focus on *technological systems.*

COMPARATIVE HISTORY AND HYPOTHESIS TESTING

Because each unit is built on comparisons among different regions and civilizations of the world, the reader will become accustomed to posing hypotheses based on general principles, and then testing them against comparative data from around the world. This method of playing back and forth between general theory and specific case study, testing whether the general theory and the specific data fit each other, is at the heart of the social sciences. For example, in Part 2 we will explore the general characteristics of cities, and then check if the generalizations hold up through case studies of various cities around the world. In Part 3, we will seek general theories of the rise and fall of early empires based on comparisons among China, Rome, and India. In Part 4 we will search for commonalities among religious belief systems through a survey of several major religions.

CONTINUITY VS. CHANGE IN HISTORY: REVISIONIST HISTORY— FEMINIST HISTORY

eminist historian Judith Bennett argues that in the period 1300 to 1700, women's economic and social position did not change much. Further, she argues, the study of women's history in Europe is the study of unchanging economic subordination to men at least from 1300 to the present:

> In the study of women's work . . . we should take as our central question not transformation . . . but instead continuity. We should ask: why has

women's work retained such dismal characteristics over so many centuries? . . . We should ask: why wages for "women's work" remained consistently lower than wages paid for work associated with men? We should ask, in short: why has women's work stood still in the midst of considerable economic change? . . . I think that this emphasis on continuity demands an attention to the mechanisms and operations of patriarchy in the history of women. (p. 164)

Pieter de Hoogh, *A Woman and Her Maid, c.* **1650.** In this Dutch domestic scene, the high walls of the courtyard and the swaggering walk of the paterfamilias as he returns home can be read as emphasizing the separation between the male world of public commerce and the female world of private domesticity. (*National Gallery, London*)

FRAMING QUESTIONS FOR MULTIPLE PERSPECTIVES

The text highlights the importance of multiple perspectives in studying and interpreting history. The answers we get—the narrative histories we write—are based on the questions we ask. Each unit suggests a variety of questions that can be asked about the historical event being studied, and a variety of interpretations that can emerge in the process of answering them. Often there is more than one "correct" way of understanding change over time and its significance. Different questions will trigger very different research and very different answers. For example, in Part 5 we ask about the stages and processes by which Western commercial power began to surpass that of Asia. This question presupposes the fact that at earlier times Asian power had been superior and asks why it declined and why European power advanced. In Part 7 we ask how the industrial revolution affected and changed relationships between men and women; this question will yield different research and a different narrative from questions about, for example, women's contributions to industrialization, which is a useful question, albeit a different one.

FINDING ONE'S PLACE IN HISTORY

We intend that readers will understand world history not as a burden to learn and to live with, but as a legacy within which to find their own place. This text shows people throughout history reckoning with the alternatives available and making choices among them. Their examples should provide some solace, courage, and guidance to readers now making their own choices. History has always been seen as both bondage to the past and liberation from it. We write so that students should understand both potentials, and seek a path of freedom.

BIBLIOGRAPHY

Bennett, Judith M. "Medieval Women, Modern Women: Across the Great Divide," in David Aers, ed., *Culture and History, 1350–1600: Essays on English Communities, Identities, and Writing* (New York: Harvester Wheatsheaf, 1992), 147–75.

Carr, E.H. *What Is History?* (Harmondsworth, Middlesex: Penguin Books, 1964).

Curtin, Philip D. "Recent Trends in African Historiography and Their Contribution to History in General," in Joseph Ki-Zerbo, ed., *General History of Africa*, Vol. I: *Methodology and African Pre-History* (Berkeley: University of California Press, 1981), 54–71.

deBary, William Theodore, *et al.*, comps. *Sources of Chinese Tradition* (New York: Columbia University Press, 1960).

Lerner, Gerda. *The Creation of Patriarchy* (New York: Oxford University Press, 1986).

Nehru, Jawaharlal. *The Discovery of India* (Delhi: Oxford University Press, 1989).

Orwell, George. *Animal Farm* (New York: Harcourt, Brace, 1946).

Tacitus, Cornelius. *Tacitus' Agricola, Germany, and Dialogue on Orators*, trans. Herbert W. Benario (Norman: University of Oklahoma Press, 1991).

THE
WORLD'S HISTORY
VOLUME 2: Since 1100

5
PART

World Trade

1100–1776 C.E.

CHANNELS OF COMMUNICATION: THE EXCHANGE OF COMMODITIES, DISEASES AND CULTURE

In earlier parts of this book we have touched on economic systems and the importance of trade in regional and world economies. Trade linked the oldest centers of urban civilization—Mesopotamia, the Indus valley, and the Nile valley—as we noted in Part 2. In Part 3 we saw that empires sought to secure the principal transportation routes and that the imperial rulers usually controlled a substantial part of their trade. Finally, in Part 4 we noted that world religions spread along the same routes as trade, and that religions were often carried by the merchants themselves as well as by more formal official representations. Both Buddhism and Islam spread to eastern Asia via the overland silk routes, and to southeast Asia via the shipping lanes of the Indian Ocean. The exchange of commodities went hand in hand with the exchange of ideas.

In this part we will look more closely at the traders, the trade routes, and the importance of trade and economics in world history between 1100 and 1776. This part has two chapters, divided about the year 1500, when a series of voyages by Christopher Columbus, Ferdinand Magellan, and other explorer-traders demonstrated conclusively that the world was a globe; revealed that there were continental land masses in both the

The Triumph of Death, French, 1503 (detail).

western and the eastern hemispheres; and linked these hemispheres in continuous relationships of economic and cultural exchange.

The first chapter of this part describes the patterns and the philosophies of world trade prior to this linkage. It indicates the importance of the pre-1500 networks in the establishment of the later systems.

The second chapter examines the changes in world trade patterns and economic philosophies from 1500 up to 1776, when the publication of Adam Smith's *Wealth of Nations* signaled the arrival of a new philosophy of world trade and economics, later called capitalism. Smith applauded the work of private businesspeople who were pursuing their own profit, and proclaimed them the chief engine of progressive change in world history. He opposed governmental and religious control of trade, the pattern we shall most frequently encounter before 1500. Smith's word was not final, and the philosophy of capitalism is still debated today, reviled by some, extolled by others, but significant to virtually all debates over the larger questions of economics and to many questions of politics, culture, and religion as well. Debates over the capitalist system versus other forms of economic organization open this chapter and reappear frequently in Parts 7 and 8.

12
CHAPTER

ESTABLISHING WORLD TRADE ROUTES

"A growing mountain of hard evidence ... indicates indubitably that the whole of Eurasia was culturally and technologically interconnected [by about 1500 B.C.E.]"

VICTOR H. MAIR

"Stadtluft macht frei" — "City air makes one free."

GERMAN PROVERB

1100–1500 C.E.

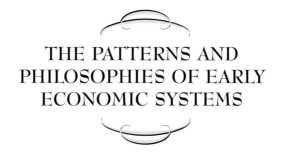

THE PATTERNS AND PHILOSOPHIES OF EARLY ECONOMIC SYSTEMS

TRADE AND TRADERS: GOALS AND FUNCTIONS

Today long-distance, international trade forms a substantial part of the world's commerce and includes even the most basic products of everyday food and clothing. In earlier times, long-distance trade was only a small fraction of overall trade, mostly supplying luxury goods for the upper classes: silks, gold, spices, and the like. Because these goods were valuable relative to their weight, merchants could carry them over long distances and still sell them for handsome profits. The buyers were mostly wealthy, for only they could afford such luxuries. Some commercial goods, like raw wool and cotton, were also traded over medium distances, a few hundred miles. The transportation costs were justified as these goods became more valuable after importation when they were manufactured into finished products.

The largest part of the exchange economy was in local transactions—food crops traded for local hand manufactures or raw materials. These goods were necessities but they had little value in relationship to their weight; the cost of transportation was a substantial part of their final price. They were, therefore, traded only over short distances. Often, they were bartered in exchange for other local goods rather than being sold for money in more distant markets. This exchange of local goods is a fundamental part of local and regional history, but the study of world history focuses on long-distance exchange and its importance in knitting together distant regions of the world. Trade provides an index of economic vitality. It also stimulates economic growth; people produce goods and provide services only if markets exist for them. (Anyone who has ever looked for a job has experienced this. If jobs exist, they work; if jobs do not exist, they remain unemployed and economically unproductive.)

WORLD TRADE: WHAT DIFFERENCE DOES IT MAKE?

Historians studying world trade seek to understand its purposes, conditions, and regulations. We ask about social as well as economic values. For example: What benefits are achieved by each different system of trade? Which systems benefit which members of society? Which systems harm which members of society? What are the trade-offs in benefits and losses under each system?

Some of the most provocative explorations of the history of trade originated in public policy debates in the United States and Europe following the Great Depression. That economic collapse of the

TIMELINE: MEDIEVAL WORLD TRADE

DATE C.E.	POLITICAL/SOCIAL EVENTS	TRADE DEVELOPMENTS	EXPLORATION
1050	▪ Normans under William I invade England (1066) ▪ Seljuk Turks take Baghdad ▪ Franks invade Anatolia and Syria and found Crusader states ▪ Almoravids destroy Kingdom of Ghana (1067)	▪ Venice dominates Adriatic; trading ports set up throughout eastern Mediterranean (1000–1100)	
1100	▪ Alfonso I becomes first king of Portugal (1143)	▪ Age of Great Zimbabwe in southern Africa ▪ Wool trade flourishing between England and Flanders	
1150	▪ Saladin, sultan of Turkish Syria and Egypt, retakes Jerusalem	▪ Market fairs in the Champagne region, France ▪ Paper-making spreads from Muslim world	
1200	▪ Foundation of first Muslim empire in India ▪ Genghis Khan establishes Mongol Empire (1206–1405) ▪ Collapse of Mayan civilization in Central America; rise of Incas in Peru ▪ Rise of Mali, west Africa	▪ Rise of craft guilds in towns of western Europe ▪ German Gothland Society trades between Lübeck, Cologne, Riga, Hamburg, and Novgorod in Russia (c. 1228)	
1250	▪ Osman I founds Ottoman dynasty in Turkey (1290–1326) ▪ Emergence of Empire of Benin, Nigeria	▪ Increasing Venetian links with central Asia and China (1255–95)	▪ Marco Polo arrives in China (1275)
1300	▪ Hundred Years War between England and France (1337–1453) ▪ Height of Mali (Mandingo) Empire under Sultan Mansa Musa Bubonic plague (1348)	▪ Gold from west Africa circulating in two-thirds of the western hemisphere	▪ Ibn Battuta's travels in east Asia and Africa (c. 1330–60)
1350	▪ Ghettoization of Jews in western Europe ▪ Ashikaga Shoguns dominate Japan (1338–1573)	▪ Foundation of Hanseatic League (1369) ▪ Revolt of craftsmen in Flanders	
1400	▪ Ottoman Turks establish foothold in Europe at Gallipoli	▪ Great Chinese naval expeditions reach east coast of Africa and India ▪ China reconstructs and extends Grand Canal	▪ Portugal's Prince Henry the Navigator sponsors expeditions to west Africa
1450	▪ Printing of Gutenberg's Bible (1455) ▪ War of the Roses in England (1453–85) Constantinople falls to the Turks (1453) ▪ Muslims driven from Spain (1492)	▪ Decline of Kilwa and Great Zimbabwe in southeast Africa (c. 1450)	▪ Bartholomeu Dias sails round Cape of Good Hope (1492) ▪ Columbus reaches the Americas (1492) ▪ Vasco de Gama reaches Malabar coast, India (1498)
1500	▪ Zenith of Songhai Empire of the middle Niger region (1492–1529) ▪ Hernán Cortés and Spanish conquistadores defeat Aztecs and seize Mexico (1519–21) ▪ Francisco Pizarro and Spanish conquistadores defeat Incas and seize Peru	▪ Portugal sets up trading post at Goa, in India (1502)	▪ Ferdinand Magellan's voyage round globe (1519–22)

1930s, discussed in Chapter 18, challenged the advocates of market-based, free-trade economies. Traders in a **free market economy** seek personal economic profit for themselves by buying goods at one price and selling them at a higher price. In their quest for economic profit, however, businesspeople also risk economic loss because conditions and prices in the market change constantly. In completely free market economies conditions of trade would not be regulated at all. Prices would vary only in terms of the relationship between the **supply** of goods and the economic **demand** for them, and businesspeople would be free to seek their fortune as they choose. All societies, however, do regulate trade to some degree in order also to serve the non-economic goals of the society. Business may be more or less regulated, but it is never completely unregulated.

The questions asked in the 1930s were: Had the freedom given to private businesspeople been too extensive? Had excessive freedom ultimately devastated the economies of the world in the 1930s? Should governments be given more control over the regulation and planning of national economies? As the debate continued, scholars searched the past for relevant experience.

Karl Polanyi, a historical anthropologist at Columbia University, argued that market economies, private profit seeking, and capitalism were a peculiar and unnatural way of structuring an economy. Market economies had not existed in the distant past. Although they had captured the imagination of many people in Polanyi's own time, they were, in fact, historical oddities. With an interdisciplinary team of colleagues, Polanyi examined the past and found that:

> Prehistory, early history, and . . . the whole history apart from those last centuries, had economies the organization of which differed from anything assumed by the economist. . . . They possessed no system of price-making markets. (p. 241)

> Not before the third century B.C. was the working of a supply-demand-price mechanism in international trade noticeable. (p. 87)

The earlier systems had been different because their goals had been different. In the ancient Mediterranean, at least until the time of Aristotle, not private profit, but "community, self-sufficiency and justice . . . were the frame of reference . . . on all economic matters" (p. 80).

> The human economy . . . is embedded and enmeshed in institutions, economic and noneconomic. The inclusion of the noneconomic is vital. For religion or government may be as important for the structure and functioning of the economy as monetary institutions or the availability of tools and machines. (p. 250)

Polanyi argued that the exchange of goods was not carried out primarily in trade-for-profit, but in reciprocal gift-giving between individuals and in redistribution carried out by government and religious institutions claiming to serve the common good. Exchange for profit had been frowned upon or even forbidden because it requires and engenders unhealthy competitiveness, "an attitude involving a distinctive antagonistic relationship between the partners" (p. 255). Economies were to serve the purposes of establishing social cohesion and satisfying the basic needs of all members of the society-- rather than serving the private interests of a few.

Polanyi and his colleagues backed their argument with a series of accompanying historical sketches of "Marketless Trading in Hammurabi's Time," "Mesopotamian Economic History," and "Ports of Trade in the Eastern Mediterranean," and then added studies of contemporary non-market economies from India and Africa, both north and south of the Sahara. Some recent anthropological studies have supported Polanyi's analyses of early economies. Yale University anthropologist James Scott, for example, has found in many peasant villages a "moral economy," a mandate that everyone within the village be fed before any individual is permitted to sell surplus food outside the village for private profit.

Other scholars disagreed sharply, citing different data from different kinds of economic systems. In *Cross-Cultural Trade in World History*, Philip Curtin, Professor of History at Johns Hopkins University, presents considerable evidence of market economies based on private profit throughout the world from earliest times. Curtin agrees with Polanyi that trade is embedded in deeper political, social, religious, and moral structures of society, but he notes that more independent trade for private profit exists as well, with equally deep historic roots. Long-distance trade for private profit has flourished in major port cities around the world for millennia. The merchants who carried this trade were often foreigners, with some independence from local political and social structures. They tended to occupy marginal positions in the host society,

RIGHTS OF THE POOR: SUBSISTENCE AS A MORAL CLAIM

Following his anthropological research in southeast Asia, James Scott probed farther into other regions and earlier historical times, and found a similar belief in a "moral economy":

> The peasant's perspective as drawn here is very much in keeping with "the moral economy of the poor" as it has appeared historically in other contexts. At the core of popular protest movements of urban and rural poor in eighteenth- and nineteenth-century Europe was not so much a radical belief in equality of wealth and landholding but the more modest claim of a "right to subsistence"—a claim that became increasingly self-conscious as it was increasingly threatened. Its central assumption was simply that, whatever their civil and political disabilities, the poor had the social right of subsistence. Hence, any claim on peasants by elites or the state could have no justice when it infringed on subsistence needs. The notion took many forms and was of course interpreted elastically when it suited, but in various guises it provided the moral indignation that fueled countless rebellions and *jacqueries* [rural revolts] . . . The *"droit de subsistance"* was what galvanized many of the poor in the French Revolution; it was behind *"taxation populaire"* when the public seized grain and sold it at a popularly determined just price; it was also behind the "Jacobin maximum" which tied the price of basic necessities to wage levels. In England it can equally be seen in bread riots and in the ill-fated Speenhamland relief system [which failed in its attempt to help poor people]. The minimal formulation was that elites must not invade the subsistence reserve of poor people; its maximal formulation was that elites had a positive moral obligation to provide for the maintenance needs of their subjects in time of dearth. For the Southeast Asian peasant also, this ethos provided a standard of equity against which the moral performance of elites might be judged.
>
> Scott, pp. 32–4

but central positions in the international trade networks.

> Trade communities of merchants living among aliens in associated networks are to be found on every continent and back through time to the very beginning of urban life. They are . . . one of the most widespread of all human institutions over a very long run of time. (Curtin, p. 3)

These communities were composed of "stranger merchants . . . cross-cultural brokers, helping and encouraging trade between the host society and people of their own origin who moved along the trade routes" (p. 2). They formed "trade diasporas . . . a whole series of trade settlements in alien towns . . . an interrelated net of commercial communities forming a trade network" (p. 2). These trade diasporas appear in the archaeological record as early as 3500 B.C.E. The visiting merchants who carried the trade were marginal to their host societies rather than embedded within them. They were not entirely unregulated by the hosts, but neither were they totally subordinated. They were expected to take at least a reasonable profit; sometimes they took more. "St. Nicholas was the patron saint of thieves and merchants alike" (Curtin, p. 6). To illustrate his argument, Curtin sketches a series of trade diasporas around the world in a variety of time periods.

TRADE NETWORKS: 1250–1500

The historical sociologist Janet Abu-Lughod traces eight interlocking trade circuits connecting the commerce of the eastern hemisphere in the period 1250–1350. Her synthesis, *Before European Hegemony: The World System* A.D. *1250–1350*, analyzes and maps six trade routes based on sea travel, primarily in the Indian Ocean; the thousands of miles of overland silk routes across central Asia; and a comparatively short land and river route within western Europe. In *Europe and the People without History* historical anthropologist Eric Wolf proposes a similar outline of trade linkages, and includes three regions omitted by Abu-Lughod: west Africa south of the Sahara, connected to the Mediterranean by camel caravan; the valley of Mexico with its ties to the Yucatán; and the Andes Mountains of Latin America, with its links to the Pacific coast.

Abu-Lughod and Wolf, separately, reach several conclusions of fundamental importance:

Before 1500 Asian and African trading systems were already well established by the time Europeans sailed into the Indian Ocean to trade in their own ships in 1498.

At 1500 European traders established a permanent connection between the eastern and western hemispheres for the first time after Columbus' four voyages, 1492–1506.

After 1500 As European traders grew more powerful, they attempted to subordinate pre-existing systems to their own centralized control from European headquarters. European control increased as northwestern Europe industrialized after 1750 (see Chapter 16).

WORLD TRADE PATTERNS, 1100–1500: WHAT DO WE KNOW?

THE AMERICAS

In the Andes Mountains of South America, a major hub of civilization grew up after 600 C.E. (see Chapter 4). By the time the Incas consolidated their empire in the early fifteenth century, the mountain peoples generated extensive trade, connecting settlements over hundreds of miles north to south and linking together a political nation of some 32 million people. Trade was important up and down the mountain sides. With peaks rising up to 20,000 feet (over 6000 meters), these mountain slopes hosted several different ecological zones, encouraging product differentiation and trade. The valleys below provided sweet potatoes, maize, manioc, squash, beans, chili peppers, peanuts, and cotton. The hills above produced white potatoes, a cereal grain

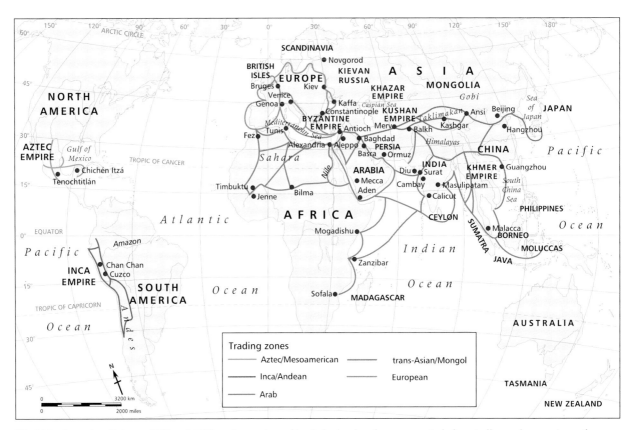

World trade routes Between 1100 and 1500 a relay system of trade by land and sea connected almost all populous regions of Eurasia, as well as north and east Africa. Long-distance traders carried goods along their own segments of these routes, and then turned them over to traders in the next sector. The western hemisphere was still separate, and had two major trade units of its own.

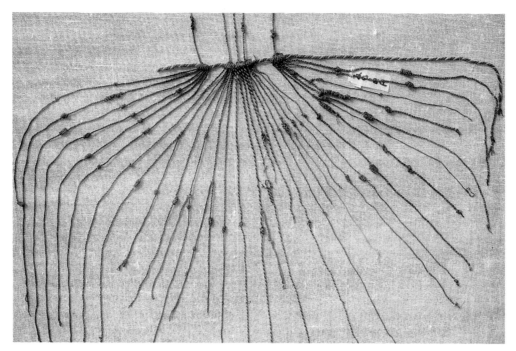

In the Inca empire, which extended from Ecuador to central Chile, trading was facilitated by an extensive road network. This *quipu*, a device of knotted string used to record dates and accounts, would have been a handy aid to the traveling South American businessman of the early 1400s.

called quinoa, coca, feathers, animal skins, and medicines. The highlands people specialized in manufacture and crafts, including gold working. Trade between the ecological zones was controlled by the state and its semi-divine rulers. Under Inca rulers, from the early 1400s until the Spanish conquest in 1533, many of the best of the 15,000 miles (24,000 kilometers) of roads through the Andes were open only to government officials.

In the Yucatán of Central and North America, the Mayan peoples had flourished from 200 B.C.E. to 900 C.E. (see pp. 100–5). Archaeologists Linda Schele and David Freidel tell us that Mayan traders flourished rather independently, amassing a disproportionate share of wealth. "In a culture which regarded the accumulation of wealth as an aberration, this turn of events created unease and social strife" (p. 97). So ultimately the traders were brought under the control of the hierarchical state, creating a new set of unequal relations, which were dominated by kings rather than merchants.

By the time the Spanish arrived in the 1520s, the Mayans had weakened in the Yucatán, and the Aztecs dominated the valley of Mexico. The Spanish conquistadores wrote vivid accounts of the great market place of the Aztec capital, Tenochtitlán. William Prescott's classic *History of the Conquest of Mexico* summarizes:

On drawing near to the . . . great market, the Spaniards were astonished at the throng of people pressing towards it, and, on entering the place, their surprise was still further heightened by the sight of the multitudes assembled there, and the dimensions of the inclosure, thrice as large as the celebrated square of Salamanca [Spain]. Here were met together traders from all parts, with the products and manufactures peculiar to their countries; the goldsmiths of Azcapozalso; the potters and jewellers of Cholula, the painters of Tezcuco, the stone-cutters of Tenajocan, the hunters of Xilotepec, the fishermen of Cuitlahuac, the fruiterers of the warm countries, the mat and chair-makers of Quauhtitlan, and the florists of Xochimilco—all busily engaged in recommending their respective wares, and in chattering with purchasers. (p. 328)

The market met every fifth day, with perhaps 40,000 to 50,000 merchants swarming in, rowing their canoes across the lake in which Tenochtitlán was built. Prescott compares the market to "the periodical fairs in Europe, not as they exist now, but as they existed in the Middle Ages, when . . . they served as the great central marts for commercial intercourse" (p. 331).

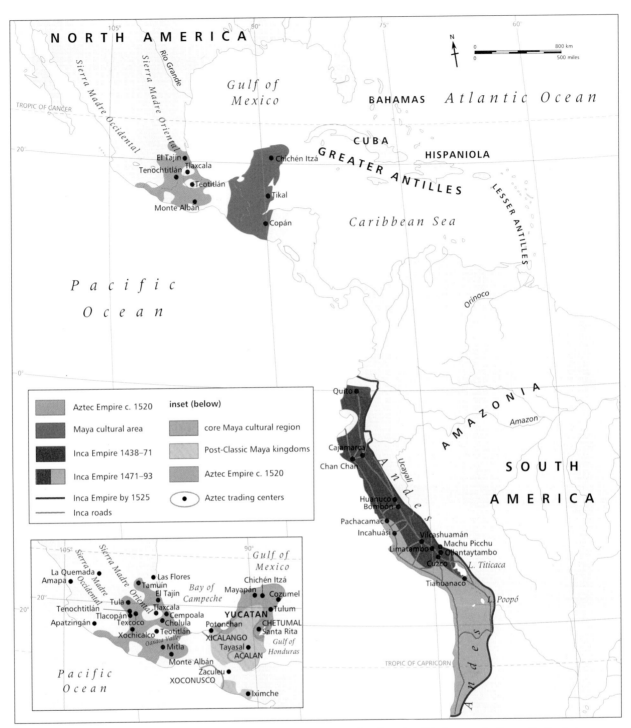

Pre-Columbian America Pre-Columbian America had two great regions of trade and political power. In the north, the Aztec kingdom, centered on Tenochtitlán, dominated. The adjacent Maya of central America were in decline. In South America, about 1500, the Inca dominated the Andes mountain regions, linking them together through an extensive system of roads.

But how independent were these Tenochtitlán merchants? The Spanish described the city's market as being under tight government control. In addition to officers who kept the peace, collected taxes, and checked the accuracy of weights and measures, a court of twelve judges sat to decide cases immediately (p. 331).

A guild of traders, called *pochteca*, carried on long-distance trade, which expanded steadily through the fifteenth century. They led caravans hundreds of miles, carrying city-crafted obsidian knives, fur blankets, clothes, herbs, and dyes, and brought back such raw materials as jade, seashells, jaguar skins, feathers from forest birds, and, in the greatest volume, cotton from the Gulf coast. They were to marry only within the guild, and, though they were commoners, they could send their sons to temple schools and they had their own courts.

To what degree were the *pochteca* independent? The answer is not clear. They often gathered both goods and military intelligence for the ruling families. They were protected by royal troops, and sometimes attacks on traveling *pochteca* were returned by troops, who used the attacks as a justification for punishing the attackers and confiscating their lands. Curtin notes that the *pochteca* lived in their own wards in the towns, had their own magistrates, and supervised the markets on their own. Their main god, Yiacatecutli, seemed akin to the Toltec god Quetzalcoatl, and this, too, suggests that they were to some degree foreigners living in a trade diaspora. Curtin credits the *pochteca* with a high degree of independence from the state and temple (Curtin, 85–7).

As the American Indian nations had not invented the wheel, goods were carried by pack animals and humans. Along the South American coast, near the equator, the Incas sailed boats constructed of balsa wood. The Mayans paddled canoes through the river systems of the Yucatán. The two major civilizational hubs functioned independently of one another and both were, of course, virtually completely cut off from Afro-Eurasia. When Europeans arrived in the sixteenth century brandishing new weapons, commanding new military organizations, and transmitting new diseases, the American residents were unprepared for the challenges.

SUB-SAHARAN AFRICA

West Africa

The introduction of the camel in the second to fifth century C.E. opened the possibility of regular trans-Saharan trade. Oases provided the necessary rest and watering points for their caravans, and produced dates, a major commodity of trade. The earliest written records of this trade begin with the arrival of Islamic traders in the eighth century.

For the most part, African political units were local, but three large empires were forged successively around the northern bend in the Niger, near

Timbuktu, where the **sahel**, the arid fringe of the desert, meets the vast Sahara itself. These three empires were: Ghana, about 700 to about 1100; Mali, about 1100 to about 1400; and Songhay, about 1300 to about 1600, when the kingdom was destroyed in battle by the Beni Marin tribes of Morocco. These kingdoms kept the trade routes open and secure. In contrast with almost all other governments, which amassed their wealth and power by controlling land and agriculture, these empires drew their power from their control over trade, traders, and trade routes.

Gold, slaves, cloth, ivory, ebony, pepper, and kola nuts (a stimulant) moved north across the Sahara; salt, dates, horses, brass, copper, glassware, beads, leather, textiles, clothing, and foodstuffs moved south. Gold was the central attraction. Up to *c.* 1350, the gold mines of west Africa "furnished about two-thirds of the gold circulating in the econ-

Lid of salt cellar, Nigerian, Benin style, early sixteenth century. Complete with anchors, crow's nest, and rigging, this maritime salt cellar was carved from ivory by west African craftsmen and intended for export to Portugal: the boat is a Portuguese caravel.

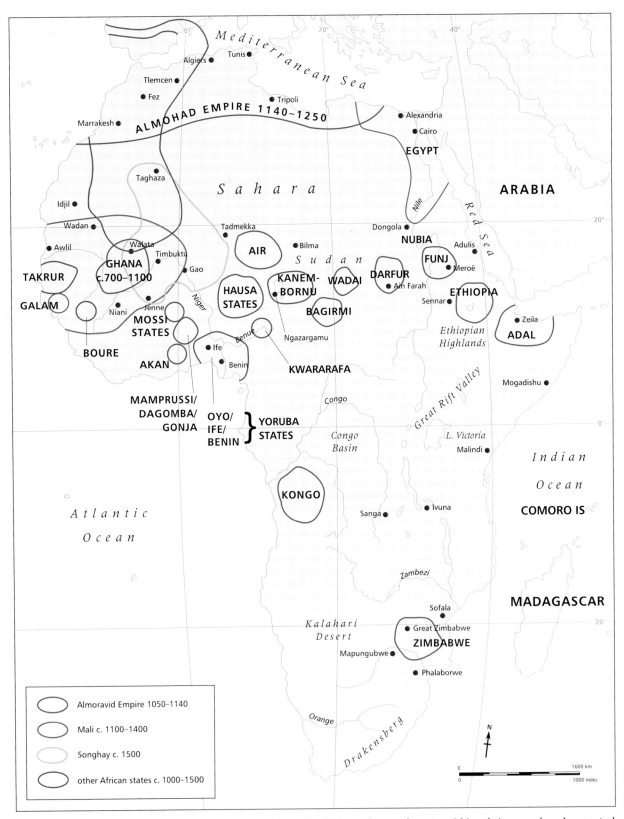

African kingdoms. Numerous states appeared between 1000 and 1500 in northern and western Africa, their power based on control over long-distance trade—gold, ivory, and slaves moving north; metalware, textiles, and salt (from the Sahara) carried south. These states, protected from marauders by the vast Sahara, could usually maintain their independence from northern powers.

Great Zimbabwe is the biggest and most celebrated of several stone enclosures in East Africa dating from the tenth to fifteenth centuries. As well as being a trading post for luxury goods—Islamic pottery and cowrie shells were dug up at the site—Great Zimbabwe provided raw materials for trade at the coastal settlements, especially gold, copper, tin, and iron.

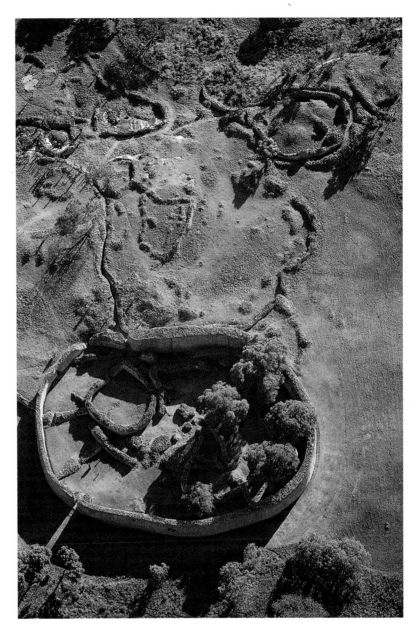

omy of the hemisphere" (Wolf, pp. 38–9). In 1324, when the Muslim emperor of Mali, Mansa Musa (r. 1307–32), passed through Cairo on his way to Mecca, he dispensed so much gold in gifts to court officials and in purchases in the bazaar that the value of Cairo's currency was depressed for many years. A European map of 1375 showing a seated Mansa Musa as ruler of Mali is captioned as follows: "So abundant is the gold found in his country that he is the richest and most noble king in all the land" (see also p. 332).

There were many natural breakpoints for the north–south trade: From the Mediterranean coast to the northern fringe of the desert, trade was borne by pack horse; across the desert, via oases, by camel; across the arid sahel and the grassy **savanna** lands again by pack animal; and finally through the tropical forest, afflicted with the lethal tsetse fly, it was borne by human porters. For the most part, the trade was carried from one market center to the next in short relays by locally dominant trade groups. A few trading communities, however, notably the Soninke and, especially, their Mande-speaking Dyula branch, established trade diasporas, which negotiated with the rulers.

> Thus, Africa south of the Sahara was not the isolated, backward area of European imagination, but an integral part of a web of relations that connected forest cultivators and miners with savanna and desert traders and with the merchants and rulers of the North African settled belt. This web of relations had a warp of gold. (Wolf, p. 40)

East Africa

East Africa, south of the Horn, came into the trade system of the Indian Ocean through the voyages of Arab merchants in the ninth century. The first major port had been Manda, succeeded in the thirteenth century by Kilwa. The ruling Arab dynasty seized control also of the port of Sofala, which lay to the south. Through local African traders they traded with the interior, especially at Great Zimbabwe (Curtin, p. 34).

The gold, ivory, horns, skins, tortoiseshell, and slaves collected from the interior were traded to Arabia and India for spices, pottery, glass beads,

The Ships of Trade

From the late seventh century ships sailed from the Red Sea and Persian Gulf ports all the way to China, returning with silk, porcelain, and jade. Sometimes they traveled part of the way, exchanging their West Asian cargo for Chinese goods at an intermediate port, perhaps in the Malayan archipelago. As trade increased along these routes, the ports grew in size by servicing the ships and crews. They became homes to cosmopolitan business communities that financed and directed the voyages. Al-Masudi, noting the pattern of trans-shipments in his encyclopedia of 916, describes Muslim merchants who had married and settled in the Indian ports.

Regional shipping routes were linked into this oceanic, intercontinental trade, and the Oman–Basra route through the Persian Gulf, connecting Mesopotamia and the Indian Ocean, was one of the most important of them. **Picture 1** depicts a boat that plied this route. The illustration accompanied the twelfth-century *Maqamat*, or tales of

Picture 1 Arab trader, illustration from the *Maqamat* of al-Hariri, twelfth century.

fiction, of al-Hariri and portrays Arab passengers with a crew apparently from India and perhaps Africa.

Europeans bought the silks of China, the spices of south and southeast Asia, and the textiles of India in ports much closer to home, such as Alexandria, where the Arab traders transported them. But travel accounts of more distant civilizations, especially the reports by Marco Polo from his travels across Asia in 1271–95, excited Europe's imagination, as the painting on p. 373 suggests. **Picture 2** is a fanciful depiction of Cambay, the principal port of the northwest coast of India, in an illustration from the *Livre des Merveilles* (*The Book of Wonders*) (1410). Cambay's walls, buildings, and even ships are more European than Indian. The painter had heard wondrous tales, but had not actually seen the port with his own eyes.

Picture 2 Trade in the Gulf of Cambay, India, from the *Livre des Merveilles*, 1410.

With the six official expeditions of Admiral Zheng He between 1405 and 1433, the Chinese government dispatched foreign diplomatic and trade missions all the way to the Persian Gulf and the east coast of Africa. Inland trade, however, was much more typical. China held one-fifth of the world's population and its internal markets were huge. River traffic at festival time in Kaifeng, the capital of the northern Song dynasty (**picture 3**), show well-developed channels of trade plied by a multitude of Chinese junks. The picture is a section taken from a twelfth-century scroll painting by Zhang Zeduan.

Picture 3 Going up River at Qing Ming festival, Kaifeng, by Zhang Zeduan, Song dynasty scroll.

and cloth. Under the Mahdali dynasty, trade became a Kilwan monopoly, but both previously and later it was apparently more open. Arab traders carried most of the Indian Ocean commerce, but there were exceptions. In the early 1400s, the Chinese admiral Zheng He, a Muslim, reached Kilwa several times, seeking tribute for the Ming Empire (see p. 377). More frequently, Chinese goods were shipped via India by intermediary Arab merchants.

INDIAN OCEAN TRADE

Four of Abu-Lughod's routes include Indian Ocean ports. Sea lanes provided alternatives to the overland silk route. They linked eastern, southern, and western Asia and Africa. During the height of its empire, traders from Rome itself plied their trade in these waters, and on rare occasions continued all the way to China. They were not, however, ethnically Italian:

> They were descendants of the same people who had been trading to the East before the Roman Empire came into existence: Jews from Egypt and the Fertile Crescent, Greek-speaking Egyptians, and other Levantines from the ecumenical and Hellenized world of Mediterranean commerce. (Curtin, p. 100)

Roman trade left a permanent heritage of diaspora traders, in the form of small religious communities of Jews and Christians, living along the southwest coast of India long after the fall of Rome.

Jewish Traders

During the period of Tang-Abbasid control over the silk route, Jews had again emerged as a preeminent trading community of the diaspora.

> For a brief period centered on the eighth and early ninth centuries, a Jewish trade diaspora became the most important trade group over the whole network of routes linking Europe and China. The Jews who ran this trade were called *Radaniyya* in Arabic . . . [probably from] Persian *rha dan*, meaning "those who know the way." (Curtin, p. 106)

The religious diaspora of the Jews facilitated their trade connections. Charlemagne's ninth-century empire (see p. 314) used them for carrying trade in France. Babylon, astride many of the key trade routes in western Asia, held the most prominent Jewish community in the world at the time, but there were also small Jewish communities in Calicut and Cochin in south India and in Kai-feng, China. When the Portuguese explorer Vasco da Gama reached Calicut in 1498, a local Jewish merchant was able to serve as interpreter. Cairo, one of the world's great trade centers, also sheltered a very significant Jewish community.

Statuette of Semitic trader, Chinese, tenth century. Traders from the Roman Empire were likely to be Jews from the Fertile Crescent, Greek-speaking Egyptians, and other Levantines. They and their descendants eventually settled along the trans-Asian routes, which most likely explains the Chinese derivation of this glazed porcelain Jewish (?) peddler, made during Tang dynasty times.

Jewish Traders: How do we know? Information on all Middle Eastern cultures from the ninth through the twelfth centuries has come to historians from the Cairo Genizah (Hebrew for a repository of old papers), studied by Solomon Goitein from the 1950s through the 1970s. Jewish law requires that religious writings not be destroyed; the Genizah was the storage point in Cairo for these documents for three centuries. It also included massive bundles of notes and manuscripts on secular and sacred aspects of life, and on society in general as well as the Jewish community in particular. The centuries-old manuscripts have proven to be a gold mine for historians.

Muslim Traders

With the rise of Islam (see Chapter 11), and especially after the Abbasids shifted their capital to Baghdad, Muslim traders, Arabs and Persians, dominated the routes through the Indian Ocean.

> In the broadest perspective of Afro-Eurasian history, in the period from about 750 A.D. to at least 1500, Islam was the central civilization for the whole of the Old World. . . . it was also the principal agency for contact between the discrete cultures of this period, serving as the carrier that transmitted innovations from one society to another. . . . The Muslim religion was also carried as part of a broad process of culture change—largely by traders, not conquerors. (Curtin, p. 107)

Islam encouraged trade. Muhammad himself had been a trader and caravan driver and he came from a trading town. The *hajj* (pilgrimage) encouraged for every Muslim at least once during his or her lifetime, demanded international travel; trade connections flourished with it. A Muslim trade colony had operated in Sri Lanka from about 700 C.E. Arab traders sailed with the monsoon winds first to India, then on to southeast Asia, and some, even on to the southeast coast of China. Catching the proper seasonal winds in each direction, and using their **lateen**, triangular, sails to maximum effect, sailors could complete a round trip from Mesopotamia to China in less than two years. Carried not by military power but by traders, Islam came to be the dominant religion in Indonesia (the largest Muslim country in the world today), and to attract tens of millions of Chinese adherents. The entire length of the Indian Ocean littoral, from east Africa through India and on to Indonesia, housed a Muslim, largely Arab, trading diaspora. The stories of Sinbad the

𝒯RADE, 1100–1500

c. 1147	Wool trade flourishing between England and Flanders
1206–1405	Mongol stability opens up silk routes and fosters greater Eurasian trade
c. 1228	German Gothland Society trades between Lübeck, Cologne, Riga, Hamburg, and Novgorod in Russia
1253–5	Trade mission of William of Rubruck from France to Mongol court of Karakorum
1252–99	Trade war fought between Venice and Genoa
1255–95	Increasing Venetian links with central Asia and China
1300	Gold from West Africa circulating in two-thirds of the western hemisphere
c. 1337–50	Hanseatic League in Germany organizes trade from Baltic to Flanders, centered on Lübeck and Bruges
1405–33	Ming admiral Zheng He undertakes six voyages in Indian Ocean
1480–60	Portugal's Prince Henry the Navigator sponsors expeditions to west Africa
1488	Bartholomeu Dias rounds Cape of Good Hope, opening a new trade route to India

Sailor, preserved in the tales told by Scheherezade in the *Thousand and One Nights*, reflect the importance of this Muslim trade network.

THE MILITARY AND TRADE EMPIRE OF THE MONGOLS

The great central Asian silk route had declined after the ninth century along with the Abbasid and Tang dynasties, which had protected and encouraged it. Under the Mongol Empire, 1206–1405, the largest land empire ever known, it was reborn. The 2 million Mongols who inhabited the plateau region of

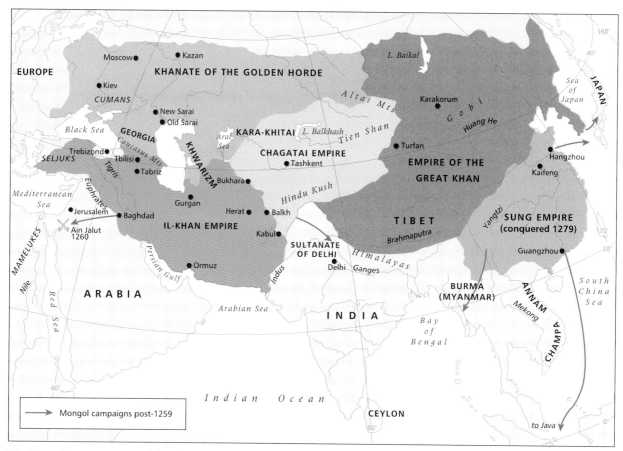

The Mongol successor states After the death of Genghis Khan's grandson Mongke in 1259, the Mongol world devolved into four successor states. Kublai Khan emerged as the most powerful, but only after a long struggle with Song China. In central Asia, the Chagatai dominated the eastern steppe; the Golden Horde became established in southern Russia; and the Il-Khan in Persia ruled from Kabul to Anatolia.

central Asia were divided into several warring tribes, each led by a *khan*. The land was poor and the climate harsh. The Mongols shepherded their cattle, sheep, and goats in a circular pattern of migration called **transhumance**: in the brief summers they moved northward; in winter they turned back south. They spent most of their waking hours on horseback and mastered the art of warfare from the stirrups, with bow and arrow as well as sword by their side.

Genghis Khan

Temujin, later Genghis Khan, was born about 1162 into one of the more powerful and more militant Mongol tribes. His father, chief of his tribe, was poisoned by a rival tribe. About three generations before Temujin's birth, one of his ancestors, Kabul Khan, had briefly united the Mongols, and to reunify them became Genghis' own mission. He conquered the surrounding tribes, one by one, and

united them at Karakorum, his capital. Although skilled at negotiation, Temujin was infamous for his brutality. According to legend, he had declared:

> The greatest joy a man can have is victory: to conquer one's enemy armies, to pursue them, to deprive them of their possessions, to reduce their families to tears, to ride on their horses, and to make love to their wives and daughters.
> (Time-Life, *Mongol Conquests*, p. 13)

Temujin defeated the Tatars and killed all surviving males taller than a cart axle. He defeated the Taichi'ut and boiled alive all their chiefs. In 1206, an assembly of all the chiefs of the steppe regions proclaimed him Genghis Khan ("Universal Ruler"). He organized them for further battle under a pyramid of officers leading units of 100, 1000, and 10,000 mounted warriors, commanded, as they grew older, by his four sons. Promotion within the fighting machine was by merit. Internal feuding among the Mongols ended. A new legal code, based on written and recorded case law, called for high moral standards within the Mongol nation.

Genghis turned east toward China. *En route* he captured the Tangut kingdom of Xixia, and from Chinese engineers he mastered the weapons of siege warfare: the **mangonel** and **trebuchet**, which could catapult great rocks; giant crossbows mounted on stands; and gunpowder, which he could launch from longbows in bamboo-tube rockets. In 1211 he pierced the Great Wall of China, and in 1215 he conquered the capital Zhongdu (modern Beijing), killing thousands. Genghis' officials and successors continued south until they captured all of China, establishing the Mongol dynasty, 1276–1367. They conquered Korea, large parts of southeast Asia as far as Java, and attempted, but failed, to take Japan as well. The planned assault on Japan in 1281 was stopped by *kamikaze*, divine winds, which prevented the fleet from sailing.

Genghis turned west, conquering the Kara-Khitai Empire that included the major cities Tashkent and Samarkand. He turned southward toward India, reaching the Indus River and stationing troops in the Punjab, but he was unable to penetrate further. Turning northwest, he proceeded to conquer Khwarizm. In the great cities of Bukhara, Nishapur, Merv, Herat, Balkh, and Gurgan, millions were reported killed, an exaggeration, but an indication of great slaughter. Genghis went on to capture Tabriz and Tbilisi. When he died in 1227, his four sons continued the expansion relentlessly. In the northwest they defeated the Bulgars along the Volga and the Cumans of the southern steppes and then entered Russia. They took Moscow, destroyed Kiev, overran Moravia and Silesia, and set their sights on the conquest of Hungary. In 1241, Genghis' son Ogedei (Ögödei; 1185–1241) died, and during the succession dispute the Mongols withdrew east of Kiev. They never resumed their westward movement. Central and western Europe remained untouched.

In the southwest, under Genghis' grandson Hulegu (*c.* 1217–65), the Mongols captured and

Genghis Khan's conquests had as much impact on west Asia as they did on China. This Persian illustration of Genghis pursuing his enemies comes from a history, which some consider to be the first world history, written by Rashid al-Din (1247–1318), a Persian administrator employed by Mongol Ilkhans in Iran. (*Seattle Art Museum*)

destroyed Baghdad, ending the five-century-old Abbasid dynasty by killing the caliph. Meanwhile Mongke, Genghis' grandson and the fourth and last successor to his title as "Great Khan," died while campaigning in China and many of the Mongol forces withdrew to attend a general conclave in Karakorum to choose his successor. A small force, however, proceeded to Ain Jalut, in modern day Jordan, and were defeated in battle. The Mongols never pressed further westward. The empire divided permanently into four separate *khanates*, or empires. At their apogee, 1279–1350, the Mongols ruled all of China, almost all of Russia, Iran, Iraq, and central Asia.

Mongol rule was extensive but brief. The Mongols could not govern their empire from horseback, and they were soon absorbed by the peoples they had conquered. They intermarried freely with the Turks who had joined them as allies in conquest. In Russia, Mongols and Turks merged with Slavs and Finns in a new Turkish-speaking ethnic group, the Tartars. In Persia and China they assimilated into local culture, converting to various religions, including Christianity, Buddhism, and Confucianism. In most of the areas inhabited by Muslims, the Mongols and their Turkish allies typically converted to Islam.

After such transformations, the four segments of Genghis' empire went their own separate ways. Slowly they were driven from their conquests. By 1335 the male line of Genghis and his grandson Hulegu died out in the Il-Khan Empire in Persia. The Ming dynasty defeated and evicted the Mongol (or Yuan) rulers in 1367. The Russians pushed out the Golden Horde (named not, as one might think, for their numbers, but for their tents, *Ordu* in Turkish). The last Mongol state in the Crimea was conquered only in the eighteenth century. The Chagatai Khanate was destroyed by Timur the Lame (Tamerlane) after 1369.

Cultural historians credit the Mongols with very little permanent contribution—they were absorbed into other, more settled and sophisticated cultures—but they did establish, for about a century, the "Pax Mongolica," the Mongolian Peace, over a vast region, in which intercontinental trade could flourish across the reopened silk route. Reports from two world travelers, Ibn Battuta (1304–68) of Morocco and Marco Polo (1254–1324) of Venice, give vivid insights into that exotic trade route.

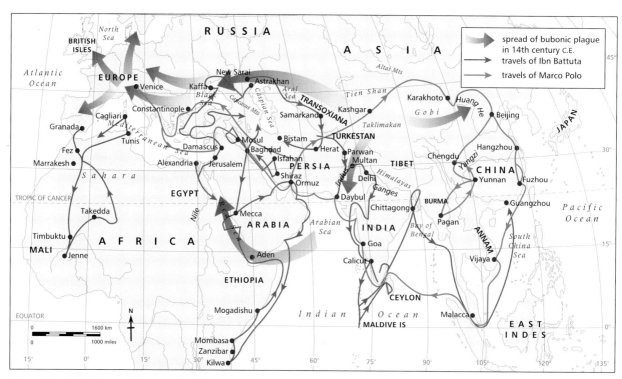

The routes of the Plague The central and east Asian stability imposed by Mongol rule—the "Mongol peace"—brought mixed benefits. Trade flourished, and travelers such as Ibn Battuta and Marco Polo were able to write remarkable accounts of the lands they visited. At the same time, however, vectors for other travelers, such as the rats that carried bubonic plague, also opened up. The Black Death, originating in central Asia, was one of a succession of plagues that decimated parts of Europe and China.

World Travelers: Marco Polo and Ibn Battuta

In Chapter 11 we noted Ibn Battuta's observations on the variety of Islamic practices he encountered during his thirty years and 73,000 miles (117,000 kilometers) of travel (see p. 346). He also commented extensively on conditions of travel and trade. In central Asia Ibn Battuta encountered a military expedition of Oz Beg Khan (d. 1341), the ruler of the khanate of the Golden Horde:

> We saw a vast city on the move with its inhabitants, with mosques and bazaars in it, the smoke of the kitchens rising in the air (for they cook while on the march), and horse-drawn wagons transporting the people. (Dunn, p. 167)

The tents of this camp/city were Mongol **yurts**. Made of wooden poles covered with leather pelt, and with rugs on the floor, the yurts could be disassembled quickly for travel.

Later, Ibn Battuta was granted his request to travel with one of the Mongol princesses along the trade route as she returned to her father's home in Constantinople to give birth to her child. The princess travelled with 5000 horsemen under military command, 500 of her own troops and servants, 200

Marco Polo, from *Romance of Alexander, c.* 1340. The great world traveler is shown setting sail for China from Venice in 1271. Europe was eager for news of the Mongol Empire—potential allies against the ancient Muslim enemy—and a steady stream of intrepid merchants and missionaries brought back amazing reports of the Khan's court. The somewhat fanciful reminiscences of Marco Polo are, however, by far the most famous. (*Bodleian Library, Oxford*)

slave girls, 20 Greek and Indian pages, 400 wagons, 2000 horses, and about 500 oxen and camels (Dunn, p. 170). They crossed from Islamic Mongol territory to Christian Byzantium.

Ibn Battuta addressed his Arabic *rihla* (travel accounts) to a Muslim audience. Marco Polo wrote in Franco-Italian and his travel accounts were soon translated into several European languages, introducing to Christian Europe a new understanding of world trade. In 1260, Marco's father and uncle had traveled from their home in Venice on a trade mission as far as Bogara and Sarai, at the northern end of the Caspian Sea. War broke out, and their route back home was blocked. But the route eastward was open, and the brothers finally traveled as far as Beijing, where Genghis' grandson, Kublai Khan (1215–94), ruled. The Great Khan invited them to return with more information on Christianity and a delegation from the pope. The information and delegation never materialized, but in 1271 the two brothers, with Marco, set out for China, arriving in 1275. They remained for seventeen years, before returning to Venice in 1295. In 1298, captured in war by Genoese sailors, Marco dictated the tales of his travel to fellow-prisoner Rustichello (Rusticiano), and Europe had its most complete and consistent account up to that date of the silk route and of the fabulous Chinese Empire of Kublai Khan.

*T*HE FABULOUS TRAVELS OF MARCO POLO

Marco Polo was a merchant in a family of merchants, and his eye was thus particularly attuned to patterns of trade. His numerous descriptions of urban markets support Curtin's concept of an urban-centered trade diaspora. For example, consider Marco Polo's description of Tabriz in northwest Persia:

> The people of Tabriz live by trade and industry; for cloth of gold and silk is woven here in great quantity and of great value. The city is so favourably situated that it is a market for merchandise from India and Baghdad, from Mosul and Hormuz, and from many other places; and many Latin merchants come here to buy the merchandise imported from foreign lands. It is also a market for precious stones, which are found here in great abundance. It is a city where good profits are made by traveling merchants. The inhabitants are a mixed lot and good for very little. There are Armenians and Nestorians, Jacobites and Georgians and Persians; and there are also worshippers of Mahomet, who are the natives of the city and are called Tabrizis. (Polo, p. 57)

Central Asian routes challenged travelers and their animals:

> For the merchants of these parts, when they travel from one country to another, traverse vast deserts, that is to say dry, barren, sandy regions, producing no grass or fodder suitable for horses, and the wells and sources of fresh water lie so far apart that they must travel by long stages if their beasts are to have anything to drink. Since horses cannot endure this, the merchants use only these [specially selected] asses, because they are swift coursers and steady amblers, besides being less costly to keep. So they fetch a better price than horses. They also use camels, which likewise carry heavy loads and are cheap to maintain. (Polo, p. 61)

Despite the Pax Mongolica, merchants still had to be prepared to defend themselves from attack:

> Among the people of these kingdoms there are many who are brutal and bloodthirsty. They are for ever slaughtering one another; and, were it not for fear of the government, that is, the Tartar lordship of the Levant, they would do great mischief to travelling merchants. The government imposes severe penalties upon them and has ordered that along all dangerous routes the inhabitants at the request of the merchants shall supply good and efficient escorts from district to district for their safe conduct on payment of two or three groats for each loaded beast according to the length of the journey. Yet, for all that the government can do, these brigands are not to be deterred from frequent depredations. Unless the merchants are well armed and equipped with bows, they slay and harry them unsparingly. (Polo, p. 61)

Bubonic Plague and the Trade Routes

In addition to commerce and religion, the bubonic plague also traveled the trade routes. William McNeill's masterly *Plagues and Peoples* argues persuasively that "Mongol movements across previously isolating distances in all probability brought the bacillus *Pasteurella pestis* to the rodents of the Eurasian steppe for the first time" (p. 134). The infection apparently entered China in 1331 and traveled the caravan routes of Asia for fifteen years, reaching the Crimea in 1346. There, the rats boarded ships, disembarking with the disease at all the ports of Europe and the Near East.

In Europe, where the plague was new and people had no natural immunity, one-third of the population died. The ravages of the plague foreshadowed further, even worse, epidemics that would sweep across the continent, as groups of people who had not previously been exposed to one another's diseases began to meet for the first time (see Chapter 14).

CHINA AND THE SOUTH CHINA SEA

When Marco Polo finally arrived in China in 1275 he was overwhelmed. He described its ruler, Kublai Khan, as "the mightiest man, whether in respect of subjects or of territory or of treasure, who is in the world today or who ever has been, from Adam our first parent down to the present moment" (p. 113). Polo correctly informed the West that China in the late 1200s was the richest, most technologically advanced, and largest politically unified country in the world. Certain elements leading to the creation of wealth had been in place for centuries. In the ninth century, under the Tang, wood block printing had been invented. From that time onward, ideas could spread in China more rapidly than anywhere else. One of the first uses of print was to conserve and spread religious concepts; the oldest printed book extant in the world is a copy of the Buddhist *Diamond Sutra* from 868 (see p. 268). The government also used print to spread information on new farming methods.

The great luxury products of China—silk, porcelain, and tea—continued to attract the merchants of the world as they had since Tang times. Foreign merchants were housed in the suburbs of the capital, each nationality with its own accommodations. Lombards, Germans, and French from Europe were among them. A huge service industry grew up to attend them, Polo noted, in particular, an army of prostitutes:

> I assure you that there are fully 20,000 of them, all serving the needs of men for money. They have a captain general, and there are chiefs of hundreds and of thousands responsible to the captain. This is because, whenever ambassadors come to the Great Khan on his business and are maintained at his expense, which is done on a lavish scale, the captain is called upon to provide one of these women every night for the ambassador and one for each of his attendants. They are changed each night and receive no payment; for this is the tax they pay to the Great Khan. (Polo, p. 129)

The international merchants were at the peak of a highly integrated national system of trade and commerce. Market towns sprang up throughout China, enabling virtually every rural family to sell its products for cash and to buy city goods. In turn, the small market towns were linked to larger cities, which provided more specialized products and access to government administrators. At the apex of this national system of urbanization were regional capitals, such as Kai-feng and Hangzhou. Geographer William Skinner's extensive presentation on the geography and functioning of market towns in China demonstrated the significance of this dense network of towns. Here, families could buy and sell, arrange a marriage, determine the latest government rulings, hear about new farming possibilities, learn the dates and the results of academic examinations. "By late traditional times, markets had so proliferated on the Chinese landscape and were so distributed that at least one was accessible to virtually every rural household" (Skinner, p. 6).

At the base of the economic system were the rural families, struggling to survive by producing commodities demanded by the traders. Hand manufacture, especially of cotton cloth, often supplemented farm production in rural areas. The producers were integrated into the market system either through direct, personal access or through brokers who supplied raw materials and bought the finished product through the putting out system. Dong Xianliang's "Weaving Song," written during the Ming dynasty, summarizes the industrial organization:

> He tends his cotton in the garden in the morning,
> In the evening makes his cloth upon the loom.
> His wife weaves with ever-moving fingers;

His girls spin with never-ceasing wheels.
It is the humid and unhealthy season.
When they finish the last of the cotton from their garden.
Prices go up and up, if outside merchants come to buy;
So if warp's plentiful a lack of weft brings grief.
They therefore buy raw cotton and spin it night after night.

(Elvin, p. 273)

Women were the chief producers in this supplemental rural industry. They also took the finished product to market. Conditions both of production and of marketing could be savage. Xu Xianzhong's "Prose Poem on Cotton Cloth" presents the harshness of both aspects:

Why do you ignore their toil? Why are you touched
Only by the loveliness that is born from toil?
. . .
Shall I tell you how their work exhausts them?

By hand and treadle they turn the rollers of wood and iron,
Feeling their fibre in between their fingers;
The cotton comes out fluffy and the seeds fall away.
The string of the cotton bow is stretched so taut
It twangs with a sob from its pillar.
They draw out slivers, spin them on their wheels
To the accompaniment of a medley of creakings.
Working through the darkness by candlelight,
Forgetful of bed. When energy ebbs, they sing.
The quilts are cold. Unheard, the waterclock flows over.
. . .
When a woman leaves for market
She does not look at her hungry husband.
Afraid her cloth's not good enough,
She adorns her face with cream and powder,
Touches men's shoulders to arouse their lust,
And sells herself with pleasant words.
Money she thinks of as a beast its prey;
Merchants she coaxes as she would her father.
Nor is her burden lifted till one buys.

(Elvin, pp. 273–4)

Ink and watercolor print showing silk manufacture, Chinese, early seventeenth century. During the Song dynasty (960–1279), long-distance trade across central Asia dwindled. Maritime trade, with its very much safer and cheaper routes, now offered a viable alternative, and silk, along with porcelain and tea, continued to attract the merchants of the world. Unwinding filaments from silkworm cocoons in order to make yarn was considered women's work, as this Ming dynasty print suggests. (*Victoria & Albert Museum, London*)

From Mongol to Ming: Dynastic Transition

Marco Polo realized that the economy did not serve everyone equally well. In south China especially he saw bitter poverty and class divisions:

> In the province of Manzi almost all the poor and needy sell some of their sons and daughters to the rich and noble, so that they may support themselves on the price paid for them and the children may be better fed in their new homes. (Polo, p. 227)

Polo also understood that the Mongol rulers were resented as foreign colonial masters:

> All the Cathayans hated the government of the Great Khan, because he set over them Tartar rulers, mostly Saracens, and they could not endure it, since it made them feel that they were no more than slaves. Moreover the Great Khan had no legal title to rule the province of Cathay, having acquired it by force. (Polo, p. 133)

Throughout the ninety years of Mongol rule, 1276–1367, China's population plummeted from a high of 100 million to just over 50 million. Revolution ensued, and in 1368 the Ming dynasty replaced the Mongols and ruled for almost three centuries, until 1644.

Under the Ming dynasty, the population picked up sharply. By 1450 it had reached 100 million again, and by 1580 the population was at least 130 million. Mark Elvin estimates it in that year as "somewhere between 160 and 250 million" (p. 129). Plagues and rebellions caused the population to fall back to 100 million by 1650, but from that trough it rose consistently into present times.

The population settled new territories as it grew. The origins of the Chinese Empire had been in the Yellow River valley in the north (see Chapter 4). At the time of the Han dynasty, upwards of 80 percent of the population of China lived north of the Yangzi valley. Under the late Tang dynasty the population was divided about equally between north and south. Warfare in the north drove the migrants south. At the height of the Mongol dynasty up to 90 percent of the population lived in the south. Economically, the south produced rice, cotton, and tea, three of China's most valuable products, not available in the northern climate. Closer to the southeast Asian and Indian Ocean sea lanes, the south also developed China's principal ports for international commerce. After the Mongols were defeated, however, migration began to reverse. By about 1500, 75 percent lived in the south, and northward movement was continuing.

International Trade and Government Intervention

China's ports, as Marco Polo had described them, hosted traders from around the world. Their Chinese counterparts were both private traders and traders in government service. In the early fifteenth century, the Ming Emperor Yongle commissioned a series of seven spectacular ocean voyages under the Mongolian, Muslim, eunuch, Admiral Zheng He. The first voyage set out in 1405 with sixty-two large junks, 100 smaller ships, and 30,000 crew. The largest ships were 450 feet (140 meters) long, displaced 1600 tons, held a crew of about 500, and were the largest ships built anywhere up to that time. They carried silks, porcelains, and pepper. The first expedition sailed as far as Calicut, near the southwest tip of India. In six further missions between 1407 and 1433, Zheng He sailed to ports all along the Indian Ocean littoral, at least twice reaching the east African ports of Mogadishu, Brava, Malindi, and Kilwa. The Emperor Yongle seemed most pleased with a giraffe sent to him by the sultan of Malindi on the fourth voyage, 1416–19.

Why did China halt the voyages? Why did China not dispatch its own missions to Europe, and even to the western hemisphere, rather than only receive voyages from Europeans, beginning with the Portuguese in 1514? Many answers appear possible: The Ming turned their energies inward, toward consolidation and internal development. At first they pushed the Mongols further north from the wall, but an invasion of Mongolia failed in 1449. Thereafter, the Ming limited their military goals, rebuilt the wall, and restricted their forces to more defensible borders.

In 1411 the Ming reconstructed and extended the Grand Canal from Hangzhou in the south to Beijing in the north. The canal was the cheapest, most efficient means of shipping the grain and produce required by the northern capital. The man-made inland waterway also reduced the importance of coastal shipping, enabling the Ming emperors to turn their backs on the seas and ocean. The faction of eunuchs, dedicated court servants like Zheng He, who urged the government to continue its sponsorship of foreign trade, lost out in palace competition to other factions that promoted internal development. International private shipping was also curtailed.

The government limited contacts with foreigners and prohibited private overseas trade by Chinese merchants. The Ming dynasty went further by promulgating a series of acts to curtail overseas private trade. In 1371, coastal residents were forbidden to travel overseas. Then, recognizing that smuggling resulted, the government issued further prohibitions in 1390, 1394, 1397, 1433, 1449, and 1452. The continuing prohibitions reveal that smuggling did continue, but, for the most part, private Chinese sailors were cut off from foreign trade.

The government defined the expeditions of Zheng He as political missions that sought tribute to China from outlying countries. Although products were exchanged on these voyages, officially trade was not their goal. So, while both private and government trade flourished in the interior of China and while thousands of Chinese emigrated to carry on private businesses throughout southeast Asia, China's official overseas trade virtually stopped. The Zheng He expeditions proved to be spectacular exceptions to generally restrictive policies.

The costs of these decisions to limit China's international trade, both official and private, proved enormous. Chinese society became introverted, and although economic growth continued, it was with no "fundamental breakthrough in technique" (Elvin, p. 95). New "invention was almost entirely absent. ... The dynamic quality of the medieval Chinese economy disappeared. This seems to have happened some time around the middle of the fourteenth century" (p. 203).

Military technology improved but then stagnated. China had invented gunpowder before 1000 C.E., but used it only sporadically. Ming cannon in the early fifteenth century were at least equal to those anywhere in the world, but metal was in short supply, limiting development. The Ming fought few battles against fortress cities, where cannon were most useful, so they also saw little need to invest further in developing heavy weaponry. No enemies appeared against whom it would have been useful or necessary. In fighting against invasions from the north, the crossbow was of more importance to the infantrymen, who made up China's armies of a million and more soldiers. At first, when China was itself very advanced, these decisions seemed not so consequential. Later, they rendered the country vulnerable. China rested content with its accomplishments and stagnated in

what Elvin has called a "high level equilibrium trap" (p. 203).

MEDIEVAL EUROPE AND THE MEDITERRANEAN, 700–1500

Marco Polo's accounts of his travels suggest that western Europeans were paying more attention to international trade by the mid-1200s. The remote western fringes of Eurasia were emerging from the agrarian, localized, **manorial economy** and otherworldly spirit which had marked the Middle Ages, the period from about 700 to about 1350 C.E. The Middle Ages were named in the fifteenth century when western Europeans were reviving and reintegrating lost Greek and Roman urban culture back into their lives. They saw this new movement as a **Renaissance** or rebirth, and disparaged the previous era from the decline of Greek and Roman "classical" culture until their own time as an in-between time, medieval, a middle age, between the greatness that had been and the greatness that they felt was now returning. Scholars today, however, are not so dismissive of this rich and innovative period.

The Early Middle Ages

During medieval times, there had been no political force able to protect trade, build and maintain roads, and provide consistent standards of currency and law. Moreover, with the rise of Islam along its eastern and southern coasts, the Mediterranean had become a zone of armed conflict. Trade in western Europe plummeted and cities declined. Rome's population, more than a million during its days as an imperial capital, dwindled to 50,000 in 700 C.E. Even so it was the largest city in western Europe's new era. Charlemagne (742–814) created an empire centered on his capital in Aix-la-Chapelle (Aachen) in northwest Germany, but the structure did not last (see pp. 314–16). Charlemagne's descendants could not preserve it from internal decay and external attack from Norsemen from the north, Magyars (Hungarians) from the east, and Arabs and Berbers from the south, who invaded and plundered throughout the ninth century.

In the absence of central government and of urban administration, two responses emerged. One addressed the need for authority and order across large territories. The other provided a new localized means of production and consumption in the absence of trade and trade networks. Each of these systems of organization, one for government, one for economics, has been called "**feudal**" (having to do with land control) by later historians. Let us examine both, first the governmental, then the economic. Men capable of enforcing law and order by virtue of their military might—their ability to fight as armed horsemen and to gather other armed cavalry under their leadership—ranked themselves by relative military power. They then swore allegiance to one another, those with greater power serving as lords, those with lesser serving as vassals. The

In the feudal system, vassals pledged allegiance to lords in exchange for property and protection: the relationship was invested with religious significance, because the ladder of hierarchy from serfs, vassals, lords, and the king was seen as extending to heaven. This thirteenth-century manuscript shows the girding-on of swords, part of the formal ritual associated with the making of a knight. Hands clasped above the head was the typical posture of prayer in the Middle Ages. (*British Museum, London*)

mounted horsemen among the vassals were called knights. The ranking was hierarchical, but just as those below owed responsibilities to those above, so those above owed (different) responsibilities to those below. The system thus combined and reinforced legal obligations with personal obligations.

But most people were not lords, vassals, or knights. Most life in Christian western Europe—excluding Muslim Spain—centered on rural manors. These relatively self-contained estates, dominated by locally powerful landowners, provided most of their own domestic production and consumption and did very little trading with the outside world. Many of the residents of the manors were **serfs**, people bound to the land by personal status and offering to the lord of the manor their labor and services or a cash rent in exchange for the right to work the land, a share in its product, and protection from outside attack. While the system was hierarchical and restrictive, especially for the serfs, it also gave them some degree of control over the land.

"CAPITULARE DE VILLIS" — FEUDALISM AND THE RULES OF MANOR LIFE

In this list of instructions, Louis the Pious (r. 814–840), son of Charlemagne, outlines the administration of his own estates in Aquitaine. The document dates to about the year 800, and relates to an unusually large and efficiently managed estate, but it provides useful insights into general principles for administering a self-contained rural manor.

1. We wish that our estates which we have instituted to serve our needs discharge their services to us entirely and to no other men.
2. Our people shall be well taken care of and reduced to poverty by no one.
3. Our stewards shall not presume to put our people to their own service, either to force them to work, to cut wood, or to do any other task for them. And they shall accept no gift from them. . . .
4. If any of our people does injury to us either by stealing or by some other offense he shall make good the damage and for the remainder of the legal satisfaction he shall be punished by whipping, with the exception of homicide and arson cases which are punishable by fines. . . .
5. When our stewards ought to see that our work is done—the sowing, plowing, harvesting, cutting of hay, or gathering of grapes—let each one at the proper season and in each and every place organize and oversee what is to be done that it may be done well. . . .
6. We wish our stewards to give a tithe [10 percent] of all our products to the churches on our domains and that the tithe not be given to the churches of another except to those entitled to it by ancient usage. And our churches shall not have clerics other than our own, that is, of our people or our place.
31. They shall set aside each year what they ought to give as food and maintenance to the workers entitled to it and to the women working in the women's quarters and shall give it fully at the right time and make known to us what they have done with it and where they got it.
36. Our woods and forests shall be well taken care of and where there shall be a place for a clearing let it be cleared. Our stewards shall not allow the fields to become woods and where there ought to be woods they shall not allow anyone to cut too much or damage them.
43. For our women's work-shops the stewards shall provide the materials at the right time as it has been established, that is flax, wool, woad, vermilion dye, madder, wool-combs, teasels, soap, grease, vessels and other lesser things which are necessary there.
49. The women's quarters, that is, their houses, heated rooms, and sitting rooms, shall be well ordered and have good fences around them and strong gates that our work may be done well.

Introduction to Contemporary Civilization in the West, pp. 5–13

The other-worldly Christian ethic that was prevalent at the time frowned on such fundamental business practices as trade for profit, interest on loans, and amassing private wealth. St. Augustine's fifth-century observations carried the day: "Business is in itself an evil, for it turns men from seeking true rest, which is in God" (cited in *Introduction to Contemporary Civilization in the West*, Vol. I, p. 65). By the eighth century, Europe had become a trade backwater of relatively self-sufficient rural manors.

The High Middle Ages

By about the year 1000 signs of economic revival had begun in agriculture and population growth.

Lords of the manors began to farm in a three-field system instead of two. That is, each year they left fallow one-third of their land instead of one-half, immediately raising production potential by 33 percent. New harnesses were developed, which could yoke horses more efficiently to heavier plows, which could dig more deeply into the soil, facilitating the expansion of farming into new areas. Up to about 1000, four-fifths of northwestern Europe was covered by dense forests. Peasants then began to clear and cultivate the forests of northeastern France. Germans colonized the Rhineland and Black Forest areas. Scandinavians and East Slavs moved eastward into the great plains of central Europe and even further into

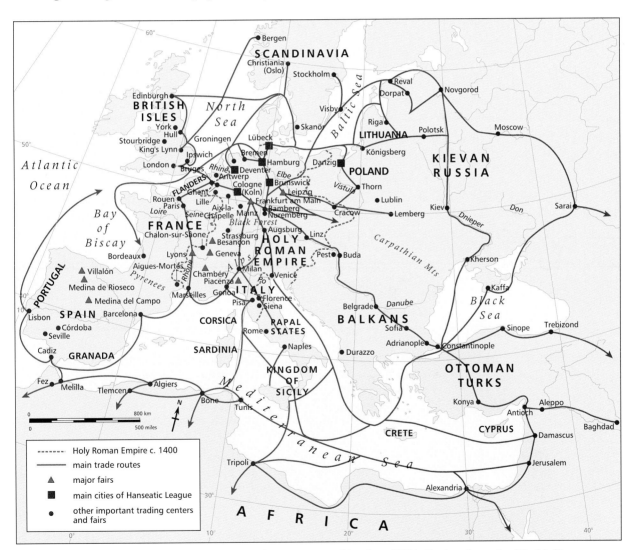

Medieval European trade Four important sets of trade routes emerged by about 1200 in Europe: the ports of the Mediterranean, led by Venice and Genoa; the North Sea and the Baltic, dominated by the Hanseatic League of merchants; a regular system of fairs along the north–south routes between northern Italy and the mouth of the Rhine; and the river systems of Russia, where Scandinavian sailors carried their goods.

the great flat, flowing steppes of Russia. On the basis of such data as the annual growth rings of trees and pollen counts in bogs, historians now believe that the European climate also changed, becoming warmer and promoting greater agricultural productivity. Population increased and spread. The population of Europe is estimated at 30 million in 1000, 40–45 million in 1150, and 70 million in 1300.

The Rise of an Urban Middle Class

In eastern Europe, Mongol raids limited economic growth. In the thirteenth century the Mongols, moving westward, blocked the Slav advance. In the later fourteenth century, although they withdrew as a conquering power, the nomadic Mongols periodically swooped in to plunder. Their presence inhibited the development of urban areas and trade in Russia's eastern regions. In central Europe, eastern Germany in particular, landed aristocrats blocked the rise of new commercial classes, who might have built independent cities of trade. The region's economy and government were dominated by a military aristocracy.

In western Europe, on the other hand, cities and an urban, middle-class business community (the bourgeoisie—from "burg" or "town"), flourished by 1300. The restoration of trade, trade routes, and urban market centers, and the increasing importance of businessmen—and some business women, usually widows—marked the later medieval period. Western Europe increased its concentration of wealth, skills, new leadership groups, and new

philosophies. Commercial exchange with, and Crusades against, neighboring Arab and Islamic civilizations reconnected Europe with the lost heritage of Greece and Rome, which the Arab Muslims had preserved and elaborated. The cities of Italy, preserving some of Rome's urban heritage, and persisting in a measure of Mediterranean trade, never entirely lost their cohesion and their control over the adjacent countryside.

Now, in the cities of northern and coastal Italy—Venice, Genoa, Pisa, Florence, Milan—and along the North Sea coast—Bruges and Ghent—commerce and manufacture combined to propel economic growth. Woolen textile manufacture in Flanders in the north, and cotton and woolen textile production in Florence in the south, began to create industrial classes, comfortable merchants, and thriving markets. Venice, and to a lesser extent Genoa and Pisa, traded across the Mediterranean, bringing to Europe luxury goods from the Middle East and farther Asia.

By 1150 periodic market fairs in the Champagne region provided points for the exchange of Flemish cloth, French wines, and goods from Asia. Henri Pirenne, in his book *Medieval Cities*, hailed the long-distance, traveling merchants who (re)opened these international trade routes as courageous sires of a new age of commerce, wealth, and intellectual cross-fertilization, and the towns they built as homes of innovation and growth. Pirenne notes that these new heroes of commerce often grew from somewhat unsavory roots to positions of distinction through unremitting attention to business matters.

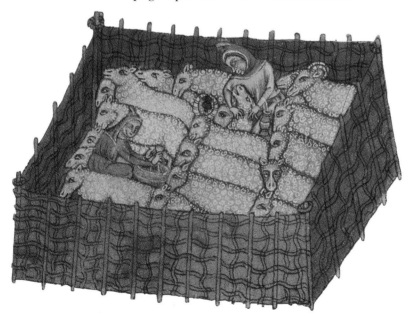

Sheep in pen being milked, Luttrell Psalter, fourteenth century. Woolen-cloth merchants had congregated at Flanders from an early stage, and by the twelfth century the industry there needed English wool to function to capacity. Prior to medieval times overland traders could transport only small and valuable objects over long distances; by the fourteenth century the emergence of sea routes meant that bulk goods, such as wool and grain, could be traded internationally. (*British Library, London*)

THE ORIGINS OF A BUSINESSMAN: ST. GODRIC OF FINCHALE

The Belgian historian Henri Pirenne cites the biography of St. Godric Finchale as "the most characteristic" of the new business class, although his final renunciation was unusual:

> He was born towards the end of the eleventh century in Lincolnshire [England], of poor peasant stock, and he must have been put to it from early childhood to find a means of livelihood. Like many other unfortunates in every age, he was a beach-comber, on the lookout for wreckage cast up by the waves. Next, perhaps following some lucky find, he played the role of peddler and went about the country with a pack on his back. Eventually he accumulated a little capital and, one fine day, he joined a band of merchants met in the course of his peregrinations. With them he went from market to market, from fair to fair, from town to town. Thus become a merchant by profession, he rapidly realized profits big enough to enable him to form an association with his fellows, to load a ship in common with them and to engage in coastal trade along the shores of England, Scotland, Denmark, and Flanders. The company prospered to the fullest. Its operations consisted in shipping abroad goods which were known to be scarce, and there picking up in return merchandise which it took care to dispose of in places where the demand was the greatest and where might be realized, in consequence, the largest profits. At the end of several years this prudent custom of buying cheap and selling dear made of Godric a very rich man. It was then that, moved by grace, he suddenly renounced the life he had led until then, turned over his possessions to the poor, and became a hermit. (pp. 116–17)

(See also the original biographical sketch by Reginald of Durham reproduced in Ross and McLaughlin, pp. 138–44.)

The new towns contained several classes: the church officials, bishops in the largest of the cities, who had continued through the most difficult times to maintain churches, cathedrals, monasteries, and convents; artisans and small-scale manufacturers, who were attracted by markets for both labor and finished products; shopkeepers, who traded mostly in locally produced commodities and everyday necessities; and now the adventurous long-distance merchants. By 1200, the largest of the Italian towns had populations of 50,000 to 80,000; in northern Europe, 25,000 to 30,000.

The merchants, both long-distance traders and local guild members, needing both physical and legal protection from attack and looting, began to organize the townspeople to demand charters of independence from regional rulers. They sought codes of law to safeguard them against arbitrary confiscation and taxation; to provide adequate space for markets; to enforce official standards of weights, measures, coinage, currency, and laws; and the construction of protective walls around the cities. To achieve these institutional goals, the merchants and most other citizens swore oaths of allegiance to one another to protect and defend their new urban institutions, by force if necessary. The early modern western European city, the home of the merchant class, took on an entirely new organizational and institutional structure. It became the incubator, and eventually the powerhouse, of one of the central values of the modern western world: private trade and private profit.

The Church Revises its Economic Policies

In establishing its independent power, the urban, trading, middle-class community was fighting the two most powerful groups of the time, church clergy and landed aristocrats. From its earliest times, the church had taken a dim view of the quest for profit and wealth. St. Augustine, as we noted (see p. 306), perpetuated the disdain. In the High Middle Ages theologians seriously debated whether it was possible for a merchant to attain salvation.

The taking and giving of interest on loans was forbidden to Christians, and for this reason much of the business of moneylending was carried out by Jews, who were so much a part of the merchant classes in early medieval northern Europe that a traditional administrative phrase referred to "Jews and other merchants" (Mundy and Riesenberg, p. 47). Jewish prominence in trade and urban life was, in part, a product of church laws forbidding their ownership of land. By the end of the thirteenth century, Christian rulers were also forcing Jews to live in ghettos, specific areas of the cities to which they were confined each night. Stigmatized four times over as alien by religion, foreign by ancestry, moneylenders by occupation, and segregated by residence, Jews were nevertheless tolerated as an economically vital trade diaspora until local people mastered the intricacies of business. After that, Jews were often persecuted, sometimes murdered, and repeatedly exiled—from England in 1290, from France in 1394, from Spain in 1492, and from many German cities.

As urban commerce flourished, the church built up its urban churches and cathedrals. By the thirteenth century the church itself had become a great property holder and a borrower and lender. Christian art, too, became more worldly; paintings and sculptures of saints took on less austere, more robust forms. As the church also sought the patronage of the rising merchant classes, it began to modify some of its earlier denunciations of business and its practices and to turn a blind eye to the charging of interest. The greatest of the medieval church theologians, St. Thomas Aquinas (1225–74), addressed the issue directly.

In Chapter 11 we noted the religious and political dimensions of the crusades. These expeditions, from 1095 to the fourteenth century, were perhaps

ST. THOMAS RATIONALIZES THE PRACTICES OF BUSINESS

*S*t. Thomas Aquinas, the greatest of the medieval scholastics, or university theologians, attempted in his *Summa Theologica* to reconcile church doctrine with the commercial practices of the rising bourgeoisie. Aquinas justified commerce: "Buying and selling seem to be established for the common advantage of both parties" (*Introduction to Contemporary Civilization in the West*, Vol. I, p. 67). He wrote of a "just" price, determined by negotiation between buyer and seller. Neither church nor government needed to regulate prices: "The just price of things is not fixed with mathematical precision, but depends on a kind of estimate, so that a slight addition or subtraction would not seem to destroy the equality of justice" (pp. 67–8). Profit was allowed if its uses were deemed appropriate: "Nothing prevents gain from being directed to some necessary or even virtuous end, and thus trading becomes lawful." Traders were allowed compensation for their labor: "A man may take to trade . . . and seek gain, not as an end, but as payment for his labor" (p. 74). Aquinas elaborated similar interpretations to allow interest on commercial loans. Even investment in usury seemed permitted, as long as "the usurer to whom one entrusts one's money has other means of practising usury, there is no sin in entrusting it to him that it may be in safer keeping, since this is to use a sinner for a good purpose" (p. 83). Thus the church adapted its otherworldly values to those of the commercial middle class.

Opposite page: This aerial view of present-day Delft, in the west Netherlands, shows gabled medieval townhouses surrounding the bustling market square. Since the late 1500s the town has been famous for its pottery and porcelain known as delftware. Dutch products began to compete in European markets with porcelain imports from China.

Compare today's photograph of a medieval square on market day (opposite) with this view of a cloth market in another Dutch town, 's-Hertogenbosch, painted in 1530. The layout and construction of the stalls are virtually identical.

ESTABLISHING WORLD TRADE ROUTES (1100–1500 C.E.)   **385**

even more important for their economic influence in Europe. In the process of launching the First Crusade in 1095, Pope Urban II not only asserted the military and political importance of the papacy but also promoted the commercial and naval power of the Italian city-states, especially Venice. Fleets from the major commercial cities of Italy boarded commercial cargo along with the crusader soldiers. The expeditions whetted European appetites for the luxury products of Asia, which had been difficult to obtain.

Guilds and City-States Confront Rural Aristocrats

As business increased, local traders and manufacturers organized into trade organizations called **guilds**, which regulated the quality and quantity of production and trade, prices, wages, and the recruitment, training, and certification of apprentices, journeymen, and masters. The guilds also represented their members in town governments and thus helped to keep industrial and commercial interests at the forefront of the civic agenda. Guild members were mostly males, but widowed heads of households and workshops were also included among the voting members. Most guilds were organized locally, within their home towns, but international traders organized international guilds corresponding to their commercial interests. The Hanseatic League, though lacking the social and religious dimensions of a true guild, was founded in 1369 to represent the interests of leading shippers of the cities of Germany and nearby northern Europe. The League dominated the commerce of their region.

West European cities, organized internally through associations of their guilds and often supported by local clergy, won their political independence from surrounding landed aristocrats. The city-states were strongest where commerce was most firmly established—in north Italian cities, such as Venice, Genoa, Pisa, and Florence, and in Flanders, in Bruges, Ghent, and Antwerp. City-states also asserted political control over surrounding suburbs and the nearby rural areas, which were needed for their food and supplies. They claimed personal liberty from the lord of the surrounding countryside and asserted their own right to govern fiscal and judicial matters. In some parts of Germany rural serfs who managed to escape their manors and survive in a city for a year won their freedom from the land. "*Stadtluft macht frei* (City air makes one free)," they declared.

In the face of urban cohesion and organization, territorial princes were often forced to relinquish their control. Sometimes these lords were bought off; occasionally they were defeated in open war-

Italian School, The Oar Makers, eighteenth-century painting of a medieval guild sign. By the thirteenth century, as the advantages of corporate organizations over individual enterprise loomed larger, specific craftsmen's guilds began to appear—in this case, that of the oar makers. Guilds issued regulations that covered everything from protecting the welfare of deceased members' families to ensuring quality of production. (*Museo Correr, Venice*)

fare, as the citizens of Bruges, Ghent, and other Flemish cities defeated the king of France, albeit temporarily, at the Battle of Courtrai in 1302. Clergy, who also stood to gain from the independence of towns in which their major churches were located, often mediated between urban and rural interests, usually in favor of the city. The merchants of the city, and the long-distance merchants who traveled through on business, gained freedom to conduct business and earn profits free from princely interference and exactions. By the early 1300s, traders had achieved an independent political status backed by armed force as well as wealth, a status unknown elsewhere in the world.

Economic and Social Conflict Within the City

In two regions of western Europe, north Italy and Flanders, industrialization in the textile industries had proceeded so far by 1300 that latent class antagonisms between employer and employee occasionally broke out in open conflict. Between 200 and 300 workshops in Florence produced a total of 100,000 pieces of woolen cloth each year and provided a livelihood for one-fourth of the city's population. Other cities of northern Italy, though smaller, had similar industrial patterns. Flanders and the neighboring regions of northern France and Belgium were even more industrialized and felt perhaps the greatest tension between employer and employee. Capitalist traders organized the industry by transmitting the demands for production and supplying the raw materials and equipment to meet it. Below them, the class structure was neither simple nor without the possibility of upward mobility. Guild masters, and the aspiring journeymen and apprentices within the guilds, held the best positions among the manual workers: shearing the sheep; fulling the cloth (that is, shrinking and thickening it by moistening, heating, and pressing it); and dyeing the wool. Weavers, carders, and combers were lower on the pay and social scales, and of these, only the weavers were likely to organize a guild. Below all these, an army of poor people washed, warped, and spun the wool. Female and child laborers, employed at even lower pay and in worse conditions than the men, enabled working families to survive.

Revolts at the end of the thirteenth century broke out in the Flemish cities of Douai, Tournai, Ypres, and Bruges. The leaders were usually craftsmen, and the immediate goal was usually participation in government for members of the craft guilds. The proletariat, the workers outside the guild organizations, could hope only that increased wages, shorter hours, and better conditions of work might follow.

In the fourteenth century, increasingly impoverished workers, suffering also from plagues, wars, and bad harvests, confronted increasingly wealthy traders and industrialists. Workers were forbidden to strike and, in some towns, forbidden even to assemble. Nevertheless, a limited class-consciousness was growing, especially in Florence, the greatest industrial center of western Europe. Finally, the *Ciompi* (named for the neighborhood of Florence in which they lived), the lowest class of workers, who were not affiliated with guilds, joined by lower level artisans, revolted. They understood the risks: in 1345 ten wool-carders had been hanged for organizing workers. In 1378 the *Ciompi* presented their demands to the officials of Florence. They wanted open access to the guilds, the right to unionize, a reduction of worker fines and punishments, and the right "to participate in the government of the City." They gained some of their goals, but the powerful business leaders of the city ultimately triumphed. By 1382 the major guilds were back in control, and soon a more dictatorial government under the Medici family (see below) was installed. Similar revolts occurred in Flanders, but on a smaller scale, and with no more success.

Renaissance: Intellectual and Cultural Transformation

On the basis of merchant wealth in the cities, a Renaissance, a rebirth, in thought, literature, art, manners, and sensibilities, arose throughout central and western Europe. The Renaissance began in the middle 1300s and continued for about two centuries. Proclaiming that the proper study of man is man, Renaissance **humanism** assigned to God a less overwhelming, less intimidating role in human life and concerns. Asserting the importance of the individual, it challenged the monopoly of the church over the interpretation of cultural life. In his *Oration on the Dignity of Man*, Giovanni Pico della Mirandola (1463–94) places in the mouth of God himself the most succinct statement of this humanistic perspective of the Renaissance:

> I have given you, Adam, neither a predetermined place nor a particular aspect nor any special prerogatives in order that you may take and possess

these through your own decision and choice. The limitations on the nature of other creatures are contained within my prescribed laws. You shall determine your own nature without constraint from any barrier, by means of the freedom to whose power I have entrusted you. . . . I have made you neither heavenly nor earthly, neither mortal nor immortal so that, like a free and sovereign artificer, you might mold and fashion yourself into that form you yourself shall have chosen. (Cited in Wilkie/Hurt, p. 1571)

The richest fruits of Renaissance creativity matured in Florence (home of the *Ciompi* revolt), where the illustrious Medici family provided lavish patronage. The family's fortune had been built by the merchant-banker Giovanni de' Medici (1360–1429), and enhanced by his son, Cosimo (1389–1464), and grandson, Lorenzo (1449–92). Here cre-

ative artists like Michelangelo (1475–1564), painter of the Sistine Chapel ceiling; Leonardo da Vinci (1452–1519), scientific experimenter and painter of the *Mona Lisa*; and Niccolò Machiavelli (1469–1527), author of *The Prince*, which proposed a new, harsh, and hard-nosed philosophy of government, developed and expressed their genius. At the same time, the general population of the city enjoyed high standards of literacy and expressiveness.

Creativity flourished in the practical as well as the fine arts and contributed substantially to the rise of merchant power. Many innovations came from amalgamating local techniques with those encountered in the course of trade missions, especially those that brought Europeans in contact with Arab civilization. Improvements in sailing technology included a new design in the ships themselves. In the thirteenth century the caravel of the Mediterranean, with its triangular, or lateen (Latin) sails,

$\mathcal{T}$HE REALPOLITIK OF NICCOLÒ MACHIAVELLI

Humanism included perspectives on how people actually behaved, as well as on how they ought to behave. In political thought this perspective yielded studies in *realpolitik*, a very down-to-earth, even cynical view of human behavior that argued that ends justify means. Its principal exponent, Niccolò Machiavelli, had held several high-ranking posts in the government of his native Florence before the Medici family came to power in 1512 and dismissed him as a potential enemy of the new administration. Until the end of his life, Machiavelli wrote on the philosophy of government, hoping that his instructions on "good" government would guide some future leader to restore Italy to its former glory.

From this arises the question whether it is better to be loved more than feared, or feared more than loved. The reply is, that one ought to be both feared and loved, but as it is difficult for the two to go together, it is much safer to be feared than loved . . . For it may be said of men in general that they are ungrateful, voluble dissemblers, anxious to avoid danger, and covetous of gain; as long as you benefit them, they are entirely yours; they offer you their blood, their goods, their life, and their children, as I have before said, when the necessity is

remote; but when it approaches, they revolt . . . Men have less scruple in offending one who makes himself loved than one who makes himself feared; for love is held by a chain of obligation which, men being selfish, is broken whenever it serves their purposes; but fear is maintained by a dread of punishment which never fails. . . .

A prudent ruler ought not to keep faith when by so doing it would be against his interest, and when the reasons which made him bind himself no longer exist. If men were all good, this precept would not be a good one; but as they are bad, and would not observe their faith with you, so you are not bound to keep faith with them . . . But it is necessary to be able to disguise this character well, and to be a great feigner and dissembler; and men are so simple and so ready to obey present necessities, that one who deceives will always find those who allow themselves to be deceived . . . It is not, therefore, necessary for a prince to have all the above named [virtuous] qualities, but it is very necessary to seem to have them. I would even be bold to say that to possess them and always to observe them is dangerous, but to appear to possess them is useful.

(Machiavelli, pp. 60–65)

used mostly by Arab sailors, was blended with the straight sternpost and stern rudder of northern Europe. The caravel could also be rerigged with a square sail for greater speed in a tail wind. The astrolabe, again an Arab invention, helped determine longitude at sea. The rediscovery in the early fifteenth century of Ptolemy's *Geography*, written in the second century C.E., and preserved in the Arab world, helped to spark interest in proper mapping. An error in longitude in Ptolemy's map led Columbus to underestimate the size of the globe and think he could reach east Asia by sailing across the Atlantic.

Cannon, especially when mounted on ships, gave European merchants firepower not available to others. Although the Chinese had invented gunpowder centuries before (see p. 378) the Europeans applied the invention in the fourteenth century to become the masters of gun-making. By the early 1400s they were using cannonballs. The Ottoman Turks employed Christian west Europeans to build and operate the cannon they used to besiege and conquer Constantinople. By the late 1400s European warring powers were competing energetically in an "arms race" to develop the most powerful and effective cannons and guns. Leonardo and others worked on the mathematics of the projectiles. (So did Sir Isaac Newton in the seventeenth century, and his labors led to his invention of the calculus.) When Portuguese ships first sailed into Asian waters in 1498, claiming the right to regulate commerce, their guns and cannons enabled them to sink all challengers.

The Chinese had also invented the principle of movable type and the printing press, but, again, European technology surpassed them in implementation. Movable type was better suited to Europe's alphabetic languages than to Chinese ideographs. By 1455, in Mainz, Germany, Johannes Gutenburg (1390/1400–68) had printed the first major book set in movable type, the Bible. By the end of the century at least 10 million individual books in some 30,000 different editions had been produced and distributed.

Of specific use to merchants in fourteenth-century Italy, two centuries after the decimal system had been absorbed from India via the Arab world, business people began to develop double-entry bookkeeping. It facilitated accurate recording of transactions and efficient tracking of business profits and losses. In 1494 Luca Pacioli (*c.* 1445–*c.* 1514), a Franciscan friar and mathematician, first published the method in systematic form.

Masaccio, *Trinity with the Virgin, St. John, and Donors,* **1427.** During the Renaissance, people began to rethink their relationship to God and the world around them; at the same time, artists were developing a new means of depicting reality. According to some art history scholars, Masaccio's monumental fresco is the first painting created in correct geometric perspective (the single vanishing point lies at the foot of the cross). (*S. Maria Novella, Florence*)

Ironies of the Fourteenth Century:
Plague and War

The Renaissance in culture and invention seems to have been limited mostly to the upper classes, for in many respects the fourteenth century in western Europe was catastrophic. The area was plunged into famine, plague, and civil, international, and intercontinental warfare, which halted its economic prosperity and population growth for a century. A great famine struck 1315–17 and may have left the population generally so weakened that when bubonic plague reached Europe by way of trading ships in 1348, it killed off a third of Europe's population, reducing it from 70 million in 1300 to only 45 million in 1400. Workers, suffering from natural disaster and also pressured by the exploitation of many of their employers, began to revolt in some of the most industrialized cities. The Renaissance

The Triumph of Death, **French, 1503.** This sixteenth-century work recalls the enormous loss of life caused by the Black Death of 1348. Brought back from east Asia by Genoan merchants, the bubonic plague is estimated to have killed between 20 and 50 percent of Europe's inhabitants. Contemporary medicine was impotent in the face of the disease, whose onset meant certain death.
(*Bibliothèque Nationale, Paris*)

began in the very face of these upheavals and catastrophic losses.

The peasants who survived the plague benefited from the labor shortages that followed, gaining higher wages and access to more land, freedom from labor services, and geographical mobility. They began to form a new class of property-owning peasants. They rioted more frequently and more boldly against kings and nobles, who attempted to raise taxes for the incessant warfare of the time.

England and France fought the so-called Hundred Years War, 1337–1453. During this time, France also experienced civil warfare between the followers of the Dukes of Burgundy and Orleans. England saw its barons fight among themselves, Scotland invade, and Wales revolt. When defeat by the French in 1453 pushed the English from almost all the land they had held on the Continent, a civil war, the War of the Roses, broke out at home, 1453–85. Henry VII won out, establishing the Tudor dynasty (1485–1603). Ironically, the seemingly interminable fighting created a new sense of national identity in both England and France and helped to strengthen their "new monarchies" in centralizing their administrations (see Chapter 13).

THE RISE OF THE OTTOMANS IN EASTERN EUROPE

While western Europe was establishing the frameworks of new economic, cultural, and political organizations, in eastern Europe the Byzantine Empire collapsed. Already weakened internally, it could not withstand the advancing Ottoman Turks. The Turks captured Gallipoli in 1354, Adrianople in 1361, Kosovo in 1389, Nicopolis in 1396, and Constantinople itself in 1453. By the mid-sixteenth century, the Ottomans ruled not only the Balkans and Anatolia, but also Hungary, the Crimea, Mesopotamia, Syria, Egypt, and most of northern Africa.

EXPLORATION AND DISCOVERY

The loss of access to the eastern Mediterranean and its Asian trade pushed western Europeans to explore for alternative routes. Prince Henry the Navigator (1394–1460), a member of Portugal's ruling family, fostered continuous exploration of the west African coast in search of a southern passage around Africa to Asia. Portugal founded small ports and entrepots all along the Atlantic coast of Africa. Portuguese traders carried out extensive trade in slaves and gold, taking some 150,000 slaves

EUROPEAN VOYAGES OF EXPLORATION

Date	Explorer	Journey
490 B.C.E.	Hanno	Around part of coast of Africa
325 B.C.E.	Alexander the Great	With fleet along north Indian coast and up the Persian Gulf
84 C.E.	Agricola	With fleet that circumnavigated Britain
1003 C.E.	Leif Eriksson	To North America and discovered "Vinland" (thought to be Nova Scotia)
1272 C.E.	Marco Polo	Visited China
1433 C.E.	Henry the Navigator	Around Cape Bojadar
1446 C.E.	Alvaro Fernandes	Discovered Cape Verde and Senegal
1488 C.E.	Bartholomeu Dias	Around the Cape of Storms (Cape of Good Hope); new route to India
1492 C.E.	Christopher Columbus	To the New World
1497 C.E.	John Cabot	To coast of Newfoundland
1497 C.E.	Vasco da Gama	Around Cape of Good Hope
1499 C.E.	Amerigo Vespucci	To mouth of Amazon
1500 C.E.	Diego Diaz	To Madagascar
1501 C.E.	Amerigo Vespucci	To coast of South America
1513 C.E.	Vasco Nuñez de Balboa	Across Panama Isthmus; discovered Pacific Ocean
1519–21 C.E.	Ferdinand Magellan	Circumnavigated globe; discovered Magellan Straits, Philippines
1524 C.E.	Giovanni da Verrazano	To New York Bay and the Hudson River
1526 C.E.	Sebastian Cabot	To Rio de la Plata
1531 C.E.	Diego de Ordaz	To River Orinoco
1536 C.E.	Pedro de Mendoza	Founded Buenos Aires and explored Parana and Paraguay rivers
1549 C.E.	St. Francis Xavier	Visited Japan
1580 C.E.	Francis Drake	Circumnavigated the globe
1595 C.E.	Walter Raleigh	To Orinoco River
1610 C.E.	Henry Hudson	To Hudson's Bay
1617 C.E.	Walter Raleigh	To Guiana
1642 C.E.	Abel Janszoon Tasman	To Tasmania and New Zealand
1678 C.E.	Robert Cavelier de Salle	To the Great Lakes
1736 C.E.	Anders Celsius	To Lapland
1761 C.E.	Carsten Niebuhr	To Arabia
1769 C.E.	James Cook	To Society Islands; charted coasts of New Zealand and eastern Australia; Botany Bay
1774 C.E.	James Cook	To Pacific, South Georgia, and South Sandwich Islands

from Africa in the half-century 1450–1500. The Portuguese had already captured Ceuta on the Mediterranean coast of Morocco in 1415, giving her (and later Spain) a toe-hold in Africa.

In 1492 Bartholomeu Dias (*c.* 1450–1500) rounded the Cape of Good Hope and sailed into the Indian Ocean. Pushing further on that route, with the help of local navigators, in 1498 Vasco da Gama (*c.* 1460–1524) reached India's Malabar coast. On a second voyage in 1502, da Gama captained an armed fleet of twenty-one ships and fought against local Arab sailor-merchants who were backed by Egyptians, Turks, and even Venetians opposed to the new interloper. Their ships and guns gave the Portuguese the advantage, and they established their Indian Ocean headquarters at Goa on the west coast of India, and a chain of fortified ports as far as Indonesia and China. By 1504, an average of a ship a month sailed from Lisbon to Asia. In the process the Portuguese earned a reputation for violence and arbitrary authority.

Spain, sharing an Atlantic coast with Portugal, also looked to the Atlantic, but Spain decided to attempt crossing the ocean. The crown and court, convinced by the Italian ship captain Christopher Columbus (1451–1506) that a western passage to China and India was possible across the Atlantic, sponsored his voyages. Most professional cartographers believed that the world was a globe, but their calculations had severely underestimated the size of the globe, and they had no idea that two continents occupied the opposite side. Reaching the Americas in 1492, Columbus did not at first understand that he had not arrived at "The Indies." Ferdinand Magellan (c. 1480–1521) more clearly established the general dimensions of the earth's sphere by a three-year voyage around the globe, 1519–22, a voyage that altered forever the intellectual, commercial, and demographic horizons of the world. (In the process he established the basis of Spain's claim to the Philippines, later named for King Philip II of Spain.)

Ironically, the Spanish had not been among Europe's leading traders. Geographical position, emerging state power, and religious conviction seemed to weigh at least as heavily as the desire for commercial advantage in the Iberian explorations. Both Spain and Portugal have ports on the Atlantic coast, and only the Straits of Gibraltar separate them from Africa. Portugal's royal family, through Prince Henry, actively patronized exploration and trade. Spain's two major regional kingdoms had just united in the 1469 marriage of Ferdinand of Aragon with Isabella of Castille. Both Spain and Portugal were devoutly and aggressively devoted to Roman Catholicism. Spanish forces, strengthened by unification and inspired by the church, completed the *reconquista* in 1492, driving Muslims out of Granada, their last remaining outpost in Spain. In 1493 a proclamation by the pope charged Spain and Portugal with evangelizing their new discoveries, and by the 1494 Treaty of Tordesillas Rome divided the newly accessible worlds of Asia and the western hemisphere between the Spanish and Portuguese. By persuasion and by force Spain and Portugal converted thousands of people all over the world.

Other, more economically advanced European powers did not compete seriously with Spain and Portugal for another century. They were embroiled in their own religious and civil wars and were still integrating their internal economies. By 1600, however, the merchants and rulers of the Netherlands, France, and Britain were ready for new endeavors. They followed the Spanish and Portuguese and, in many areas, displaced them. The interactions of these trading powers among themselves and with the other great powers of the world through the period 1500–1750 are the principal subject of the next chapter.

BIBLIOGRAPHY

Abu-Lughod, Janet L. *Before European Hegemony: The World System A.D. 1250–1350* (New York: Oxford University Press, 1989).

—. *The World System in the Thirteenth Century: Dead-End or Precursor?* (Washington: American Historical Association, 1989).

Adas, Michael, ed. *Islamic and European Expansion* (Philadelphia: Temple University Press, 1993).

Anderson, Bonnie S. and Judith P. Zinsser. *A History of Their Own* (New York: Harper and Row, 1988).

Andrea, Alfred and James Overfield, eds. *The Human Record: Sources of Global History*, 2 vols. (Boston: Houghton Mifflin, 2nd edn, 1994).

Aquinas, St. Thomas, *Suma Theologica* (excerpts) in *Introduction to Contemporary Civilization in the West*, cited below.

Bentley, Jerry H. *Old World Encounters* (New York: Oxford University Press, 1993).

Bloch, Marc. *Feudal Society*, 2 vols. (Chicago: University of Chicago Press, 1961).

Braudel, Fernand. *Capitalism and Material Life, 1400–1800*, trans. from the French by Miriam Kochan (New York: Harper and Row, 1973).

Brown, Elizabeth A. R. "The Tyranny of a Construct: Feudalism and Historians of Medieval Europe," *American Historical Review* LXXIX, no. 4 (October 1974), 1063–1088.

Chaudhuri, K. N. *Asia Before Europe* (Cambridge: Cambridge University Press, 1990).

—. *Trade and Civilization in the Indian Ocean: An Economic History from the Rise of Islam to 1750* (Cambridge: Cambridge University Press, 1985).

—. *Introduction to Contemporary Civilization in the West*, Vol. I (New York: Columbia University Press, 2nd ed., 1954).

Crosby, Alfred W. *Ecological Imperialism: The Biological*

Expansion of Europe, 900–1900
(Cambridge: Cambridge University Press, 1986).

Curtin, Philip. *Cross-Cultural Trade in World History*
(Cambridge: Cambridge University Press, 1984).

Duby, Georges. *The Age of the Cathedrals: Art and Society, 980–1420*, trans. from the French by Eleanor Levieux and Barbara Thompson
(Chicago: University of Chicago Press, 1981).

Dunn, Ross. *The Adventures of Ibn Battuta*
(Berkeley: University of California Press, 1986).

Elvin, Mark. *The Pattern of the Chinese Past* (Stanford: Stanford University Press, 1973).

Frank, Andre Gunder and Barry K. Gills, eds. *The World System: Five Hundred Years or Five Thousand?* (London: Routledge, 1993).

Ghosh, Amitav. *In an Antique Land*
(New York: Knopf, 1993).

Heilbroner, Robert. *The Worldly Philosophers*
(New York: Simon and Schuster, 1972).

Hohenberg, Paul M. and Lynn Hollen Lees. *The Making of Urban Europe, 1000–1950.*
(Cambridge: Harvard University Press, 1985).

Kulke, Hermann and Dietmar Rothermund. *A History of India* (Totowa, NJ: Barnes and Noble Books, 1986).

Levathes, Louise. *When China Ruled the Seas: The Treasure Fleet of the Dragon Throne, 1405–33*
(New York: Oxford University Press, 1996).

Levenson, Jay A. *Circa 1492: Art in the Age of Exploration*
(Washington: National Gallery of Art, 1991).

Lopez, Robert S. *The Birth of Europe*
(New York: M. Evans and Co., 1967).

Machiavelli, Niccolò, trans. by Luigi Ricci. *The Prince and the Discourses* (New York: Modern Library, 1950).

Mair, Victor H., "Mummies of the Tarim Basin," *Archaeology* XLVIII, No. 2 (1995), 28–35.

McNeill, William H. *The Age of Gunpowder Empires, 1450–1800* (Washington: American Historical Association, 1989).

—. *Plagues and Peoples* (Garden City, NY: Anchor Press/Doubleday, 1976).

—. *The Pursuit of Power: Technology, Armed Force, and Society since 1000 A.D.* (Chicago: University of Chicago Press, 1983).

Mirsky, Jeanette, ed. *The Great Chinese Travellers*
(Chicago: University of Chicago Press, 1964).

Mundy, John H. and Peter Riesenberg. *The Medieval Town* (New York; Van Nostrand Reinhold Company, 1958).

Nicholas, David. *The Evolution of the Medieval World*
(New York: Longman, 1992).

Pirenne, Henri. *Medieval Cities* (Princeton: Princeton University Press, 1925).

Polanyi, Karl, Conrad M. Arensberg, and Harry W. Pearson, eds. *Trade and Market in the Early Empires*
(Chicago: The Free Press, 1957).

Polo, Marco. *The Travels*, trans. from the French by Ronald Latham (London: Penguin Books, 1958).

Prescott, William H. *History of the Conquest of Mexico and History of the Conquest of Peru* (New York: Modern Library, n.d.; 1st ed., *c.* 1844–7).

Raychaudhuri, Tapan and Irfan Habib. *The Cambridge Economic History of India.* Vol. I: *c.* 122–*c.* 1750
(Cambridge: Cambridge University Press, 1982).

Reynolds, Susan. *Fiefs and Vassals* (Oxford: Clarendon Press, 1994).

Rorig, Fritz. *The Medieval Town* (Berkeley: University of California Press, 1971).

Ross, James Bruce and Mary Martin McLaughlin, eds. *The Portable Medieval Reader* (New York: Penguin Books, 1978).

Schele, Linda and David Freidel. *A Forest of Kings: The Untold Story of the Ancient Maya*
(New York: William Morrow and Co., 1990).

Scott, James C. *The Moral Economy of the Peasant*
(New Haven: Yale University Press, 1976).

Skinner, G. William, "Marketing and Social Structure in Rural China," *Journal of Asian Studies* XXIV, No. 1 (November 1964), 3–43.

Scheherezade: Tales from a Thousand and One Nights. Trans. by A.V Arberry (New York: New American Library, 1955)

Time-Life Books. *The Age of Calamity: Time Frame AD 1300–1400* (Alexandria, VA: Time-Life Books, 1990).

—. *The Divine Campaigns: Time Frame AD 1100–1200* (Alexandria, VA: Time-Life Books, 1988).

—. *The Mongol Conquests: Time Frame AD 1200–1300* (Alexandria, VA: Time-Life Books, 1989).

—. *Voyages of Discovery: Time Frame AD 1400–1500* (Alexandria, VA: Time-Life Books, 1989).

The (London) Times Atlas of World History ed. Geoffrey Barraclough (London: Times Books Ltd., 1981).

Tuchman, Barbara. *A Distant Mirror: The Calamitous Fourteenth Century* (New York: Knopf, 1978).

Wallerstein, Immanuel. *The Modern World-System I* (San Diego: Academic Press, Inc., 1974).

Wilkie, Brian and James Hurt, eds. *Literature of the Western World*, Vol. I (New York: Macmillan, 1984).

Wills, John E., Jr., "Maritime Asia, 1500–1800: the Interactive Emergence of European Domination," *American Historical Review* XCVIII, No. 1 (February 1993), 83–105.

Wolf, Eric. *Europe and the People without History* (Berkeley: University of California Press, 1982).

Wood, Frances. *Did Marco Polo Go to China?* (Boulder, CO: Westview Press, 1996).

13

CHAPTER

"Civil government, so far as it is instituted for the security of property, is in reality instituted for the defense of the rich against the poor."

ADAM SMITH

THE UNIFICATION OF WORLD TRADE

1500–1776

THE INVISIBLE HAND REACHES OUT: A CAPITALIST WORLD SYSTEM APPEARS

CAPITALISM AND THE EXPANSION OF EUROPE

This chapter opens in 1500, at a time when ocean voyages of exploration and trade were linking the eastern and western hemispheres and initiating a new phase of world history. It closes almost three centuries later as most of the regions of the world begin to enter into a single system of trade and exchange. This emerging system of capitalism was based on the private ownership of wealth and the means of production and on the pursuit of private economic profit. Capitalism allowed private individuals to exchange their products and labor in a free, unregulated market. It had little place for the restrictive rules of church and government. It allowed free market exchange to decide prices of goods and labor by reaching a balance between supply and demand. The free market encouraged private individuals to invest their capital, or accumulated wealth, in economic activities that might earn profits (or suffer losses).

In Chapter 12 we saw that the business people of Europe expanded their enterprises. Trading centers such as Venice, Florence, Genoa, Milan, Bruges, Antwerp, Paris, Lyons, and London grew even larger as the headquarters of the new commerce. After 1500, European enterprise also expanded into already existing networks in Asia and began to restructure them. In the Americas, too, it created new networks. This global expansion of European enterprise provides an important focus for organizing our understanding of the period 1500–1776. The economic encounter of African and Asian societies with the new European commercial practices provides another focus which demonstrates, by comparison, the exceptional powers claimed by the merchant-traders of northwestern Europe, and the extraordinary support they received from their governments.

EUROPEAN COLONIZATION AND THE EXPANSION OF TRADE: <u>WHAT DIFFERENCE DOES IT MAKE?</u>

In earlier chapters we have usually been concerned with the question of "How Do We Know?" and the search for adequate sources of information. By 1500, sources become increasingly abundant, and our concern turns increasingly to selecting interpretive frameworks for understanding the significance of historical events. For example, two fundamentally different interpretive frameworks have inspired fierce debate over the significance of world trade between 1500 and 1776.

The first interpretive framework asks: From whose point of view should we tell the story of the creation of a global trade network? To what degree should we emphasize western European creativity in technology, culture, politics, and commerce as the driving force promoting this increased level of global exchange? Conversely, to what degree should we focus on ancient and proud civilizations of Asia, Africa, and the Americas as they re-examined their own economic, political, and cultural institutions in light of the new arrivals? Each part of the world has its own position in global exchange, and each sees the rest of the world outward from its own vantage point. Is it possible for historians to become polycentric, or multi-centric, holding in our minds multiple perspectives that can encompass the varied ways in which global economic exchange has been seen?

The second interpretive framework focuses on identifying winners and losers in the new, capitalist system of global economic exchange. Advocates of capitalism saw in this new economic philosophy the potential for a world of vastly increased economic productivity and wealth that would ultimately benefit everyone. Even critics acknowledged the increased productivity and wealth, but they feared that business people would hoard these benefits for themselves. The advantages would not "trickle down" to the common people and would result in a wider gulf between the rich and the poor.

Critics also noted that capitalism tended to break the personal, emotional, and social ties that linked upper and lower classes to one another as patron to client, regardless of their economic relationships. These social ties could be restrictive, especially for the client, but they also provided the promise of protection in time of economic difficul-ty. By comparison, capitalism seemed at once more free and more ruthless.

Academics in our own day refer to the first, optimistic perspective, stressing the productivity of capitalist enterprise, as the theory of development or of modernization. They refer to the second, pessimistic theory, stressing the mal-distribution of wealth, as the theory of dependency or the **development of underdevelopment**. We shall be alert to each of these interpretations throughout this chapter and in Chapter 16, which considers the industrial revolution and imperialism.

SPAIN'S EMPIRE

Critics who claim that Europe's wealth was built on the exploitation of people overseas have some jusi-fication, but the experiences of Spain and Portugal demonstrate that exploitation alone was not enough. To build and sustain wealth, countries also must conceive and implement policies of economic growth. To do so they must be able to use wealth effectively and require banks and instruments of exchange to store and transmit money. Countries also need to develop commercial intelligence to enable them to create and evaluate strategies for investing capital sensibly and profitably. Efficient means of transporting goods and people must be developed. Both Spain and Portugal failed in these tasks. Both countries built enormous global empires in the sixteenth century based on their ocean explorations (see Chapter 12), but by the end of the sixteenth century both these empires were on the wane, first challenged and then surpassed by Holland, France, and England, countries that established successful commercial communities.

NEW WORLD CONQUESTS

The four voyages of Christopher Columbus between 1492 and 1504 revealed to the Spanish crown some of the resources in gold and silver to be found in the Americas, the potential for agricultural development, and the millions of souls to be brought into the Roman Catholic Church. Spanish settlers began to colonize the islands of the Caribbean and the north coast of South America. Spanish *conquistadors* marched inland to conquer what they could. In 1519 Hernán Cortés began his expedition from Vera Cruz with 600 Spaniards, joined by hundreds more native Americans from the various states through which he passed, to

	EUROPE	ASIA AND AFRICA	ART AND SOCIAL DEVELOPMENTS
1525	▪ Reformation and Counter-Reformation: ▪ Luther excommunicated (1521); ▪ Calvin begins Presbyterian movement in France; Society of Jesus established (1534)	▪ Suleiman the Magnificent (r. 1520–66) ▪ Battle of Panipat (1526): Babar defeats Delhi Sultan and founds Mughal Empire ▪ Turks capture Tunis, Baghdad, and Mesopotamia (1534) ▪ Songhay destroys Mali Empire (1546)	▪ Cortés captures Tenochtitlán (1521) ▪ Portuguese complete circumnavigation of world (1522) ▪ Pizarro conquers Incas (1531–3) ▪ Miguel de Cervantes (1547–1616) ▪ Luther's German bible (1534)
1550	▪ Charles V (r. 1519–56) annexes the Netherlands (1549) ▪ France seizes Toul, Metz, and Verdun (1552) ▪ Protestants persecuted in England under Mary I (r. 1553–8) ▪ Peace of Augsburg (1555): princes in Holy Roman Empire granted freedom of religion ▪ French Wars of Religion (1562–98) ▪ Seven Years' War (1563)	▪ St. Francis Xavier in Japan (1549–51) ▪ Turkey and Hungary at war (1551–62) ▪ Mughals defeat Vijayanagara Empire (1565) ▪ Nobunaga deposes shogunate (1567)	▪ Tobacco to Europe (1559) ▪ William Shakespeare (1564–1616) ▪ Galileo Galilei (1564–1642) ▪ Claudio Monteverdi (1567–1643)
1575	▪ Netherlands revolt against Spain (1568–1648) ▪ Battle of Lepanto (1571): Turks defeated by Don Juan of Austria ▪ Spain conquers Portugal (1580) ▪ Dutch Republic declares independence (1581) ▪ Spanish Armada against England defeated (1588) ▪ Dutch take over trade in Indonesia (1595)	▪ Akbar the Great conquers Bengal (1575) and completes unification of northern India (1577) ▪ War among Chewa peoples of southeast Africa (1587) ▪ Japan unified under Hideyoshi (1590) ▪ Songhay destroyed by Morocco (1591)	▪ Johannes Kepler (1571–1630) ▪ Great Pharmacopoeia of Li Shih-Chen (1578) ▪ Gregorian calendar introduced into Roman Catholic countries (1582)
1600	▪ English East India Company (1600) ▪ Dutch East India Company (1602) ▪ First English trading post in India (1614) ▪ Thirty Years' War (1618–48) ▪ *Mayflower* sets out for New World (1620)	▪ Tokugawa shogunate (Edo period) in Japan (1603–1867) ▪ Oyo Empire in Nigeria	▪ Rembrandt (1606–69) ▪ Blue Mosque built in Constantinople (1609–16) ▪ Tea from China to Europe (1609) ▪ Molière (1622–73)
1625	▪ Hereditary rule of Habsburgs in Bohemia confirmed (1627) ▪ Russian explorers reach Pacific across Siberia (1638) ▪ Abel Tasman sights Tasmania and New Zealand (1643) ▪ Treaty of Westphalia (1648) recognizes independence of Swiss and Dutch republics	▪ Shimbara uprising and slaughter of Christians virtually ends Christianity in Japan (1638)	▪ William Harvey demonstrates circulation of blood (1628) ▪ Jean-Baptiste Racine (1639–99) ▪ Serfdom established in Russia (by 1649)

overthrow the powerful Aztec empire at Teno-chtitlán, modern day Mexico City. They conquered the capital city in 1521 after a bitter four-month siege and the empire fell to them. In the next few years they captured the Yucatán and most of central America. Cortés became ruler of the Kingdom of New Spain, re-organized in 1535 as the Vice-Royalty of New Spain.

In South America, the Inca Empire of the west coast and Andes Mountains became accessible to Spanish conquistadors after Vasco Nuñez de Balboa found a portage across the Isthmus of Panama in 1513. The Spanish could now transport their ships from the Atlantic coast overland across the Isthmus and then sail south along the Pacific Coast to Peru. Rumors of great stores of gold encouraged these voyages. In 1532, Francisco Pizarro, leading a force of some two hundred men,

	EUROPE	ASIA AND AFRICA	ART AND SOCIAL DEVELOPMENTS
1650	▌England acquires Bombay (1661) ▌Jean-Baptiste Colbert (1619–83) reforms French finances from 1661; introduces mercantilist reforms ▌Hudson Bay Company (1670)	▌China takes Formosa (Taiwan) (1661) ▌Hindus persecuted by Aurangzeb India (1669)	▌Great Plague and Fire of London (1665–6) ▌Newton discovers laws of gravitation (1665)
1675	▌Revocation of Edict of Nantes (1685) ▌"Glorious Revolution" in England (1688)	▌Sikh uprisings in India (1676–8) ▌Treaty of Radzin (1681): Russia gains most of Turkish Ukraine ▌Cheng Chin surrenders Formosa to the Manchus (1683) ▌Chinese ports open to trade (1685) ▌Battle of Mohács (1687): Turks defeated ▌Calcutta founded by British (1690) ▌Treaty of Karlowitz (1699): Austria gets Hungary from Turkey; Poland gets Turkish Ukraine and Podolia	▌Henry Purcell (c. 1659–95) ▌Coffee reaches Vienna (1683) ▌Johann Sebastian Bach (1685–1750) ▌George Friederich Handel (1685–1759) ▌John Locke's Treatises on Government (1690) ▌Stock Exchange founded in London (1698)
1700	▌Great Northern War between Sweden and Russia with Poland and Denmark (1700–21) ▌War of Spanish Succession (1701–4) ▌Swedish-Polish War (1702) ▌Russo-Swedish War (1706) ▌Russo-Turkish War (1710–11) ▌Austro-Turkish War (1716–18) ▌War of Quadruple Alliance (1718)	▌Rise of Ashanti power on Gold Coast (1707) ▌Afghan rising against Persia (1709) ▌Kingdom of Segu founded in west Africa (1712) ▌Persia under Afghan rule (1722–30)	▌St. Petersburg founded by Peter the Great (1703)
1725	▌War of Polish Succession (1733–8) ▌Russo-Turkish War (1736–8) ▌War of Jenkins's Ear (1739) ▌War of Austrian Succession (1740–48) ▌Jacobite Rebellion in Britain (1745–6)	▌Safavids deposed by Nadir Shah (1736) ▌Marahatas extend influence in northern India (1737) ▌Bengal independent (1740–56)	
1750	▌Seven Years' War (1756–73) ▌Russo-Turkish War (1768–74)	▌Carnatic War (Britain against France) in India (1751) ▌Afghan-Maharata Wars (1759–61)	▌Diderot's *Encyclopédie* (1751–80) ▌Wolfgang Amadeus Mozart (1756–91)
1775	▌Spanish-Algerian War (1775) ▌American War of Independence (1775–83)	▌Famine causes rice riots in Japan (1787) ▌American ships trade with Japan for Dutch (1797–1808), ending Japanese policy of isolation	▌*Wealth of Nations* by Adam Smith published (1776) ▌Rosetta stone discovered (1789) enabling Egyptian hieroglyphics to be deciphered

captured the Inca Emperor Atahualpa. Although given a room full of gold as ransom for his life, Pizarro nevertheless feared a revolt and killed the emperor. In 1533 they captured the Inca capital, Cuzco. The Spanish conquistadors fought among themselves for years until Spain established the Vice-Royalty of Peru in mid-century as the South American counterpart to the Vice-Royalty of New Spain in the North.

How had a few hundred Spanish soldiers and their Indian allies succeeded in overthrowing the two largest empires in the Americas? The native Americans had:

🐾 divided and fought among themselves;

🐾 lacked the Spaniards' military technology and organization;

🐾 despaired when their commanders-in-chief, Montezuma in Mexico and Atahualpa in Peru, were captured;

🐾 succumbed to European diseases, such as small-pox (see Chapter 14).

Emperor Atahualpa arrested by Francisco Pizarro in 1532 (*opposite*). When Pizarro landed on the northern coast of Peru on May 13, 1532 he brought with him a force of 200 men with horses, guns, and swords. The Inca Emperor Atahualpa, backed up by thousands of troops, felt he had little to fear from the Spanish and, as this contemporary Peruvian drawing shows, he accepted Pizarro's seemingly friendly invitation to meet accompanied only by his bodyguards. It was a trap, and Pizarro arrested and then executed him.

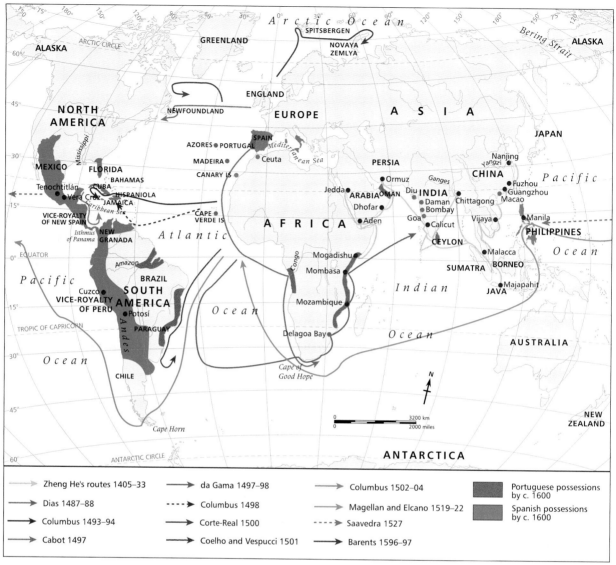

World exploration The closure of sea routes through the Middle East drove the trading nations of Western Europe to seek alternate maritime passages to Asia. European navigators and cartographers rapidly built a map of the globe which included, by sailing west, the "New World" of the Americas and, by sailing south, a passage around Africa, linking with the Arab trading routes of the Indian Ocean. The voyages of the Ming Chinese admiral Zheng He were undertaken to demonstrate China's strength even more than for trade.

Zheng He's routes 1405–33	da Gama 1497–98	Columbus 1502–04	Portuguese possessions by c. 1600
Dias 1487–88	Columbus 1498	Magellan and Elcano 1519–22	Spanish possessions by c. 1600
Columbus 1493–94	Corte-Real 1500	Saavedra 1527	
Cabot 1497	Coelho and Vespucci 1501	Barents 1596–97	

MAKING THE CONQUESTS PAY

After the conquests, the Spanish began to reorganize the economies of the Americas. They established the *encomienda* system, assigning the taxes and the labor of local Indian populations to Spanish colonists who were also to convert them to Roman Catholicism, if possible. The Indians were virtually enslaved under conditions of great cruelty. The *encomienda* system was first established on the island of Hispaniola, where in twenty years the Indian population fell from several million to

29,000. Humane voices, especially of priests such as Bartolomé de Las Casas, opposed the *encomienda* system, but it continued until so many Indians died that it could function no longer. In most of Mexico and Peru the system ended by the late 1500s, but it continued for another century in Venezuela, for another two centuries, until 1791, in Chile, and until the very early 1800s in Paraguay.

The replacement systems were not much more humane. The ***repartimiento*** system in central Mexico and the similar ***mita*** system in Peru forced Indians into low paid or unpaid labor for a portion of each year on Spanish-owned farms, in mines and workshops, and on public works projects. These systems, too, were forms of unofficial slavery. Not all labor was coerced, however. Spanish-owned **haciendas**, agricultural estates producing commercial crops and livestock, employed both free and indentured labor. The haciendas often produced commercially the newly imported products of the eastern hemisphere—wheat, cattle, pigs, sheep, chickens, horses, and mules—in addition to the indigenous local crops of maize, potatoes, and manioc (cassava). Silver mines, too, often used paid labor at very low wages. The immense Potosí mine in Upper Peru (today's Bolivia) employed 40,000 Indian miners in the seventeenth century. On the other hand, as sugar plantations were introduced into the Caribbean islands and into Brazil, Indian laborers were unable or unwilling to perform the gang labor of the cane fields, so slaves were imported by the millions from Africa (see Chapter 14). African slaves also worked the tobacco, cacao, and indigo plantations.

From the Spanish perspective, the most valuable products of the Americas throughout the sixteenth century were gold and silver. The mine at Potosí, discovered in 1545, was the largest silver mine in the world. Smaller mines were opened in Mexico in 1545 and 1558. In 1556 a new method of separating silver from ore by using mercury, available from Almaden in Spain, was discovered. Between 1550 and 1800 Mexico and South America produced more than 80% of the world's silver and more than 70% of its gold. The precious metals were exported each year from Latin America eastward to Europe and westward to the Philippines, where the Spanish had captured Manila in 1571 and established their chief trade center for East Asia. They were ultimately used to pay for European purchases of silks, tea, textiles, and spices from India and China. Between one-third and one-half of all American silver produced between 1527 and 1821 found its way to China. The Mexican peso became legal currency in China.

MERCHANT PROFITS

The gold and silver mines of the Americas brought virtual enslavement to the native Americans, and they benefited the Spaniards

less than the merchants of Antwerp, Genoa, Amsterdam, London, and Paris. The Spanish did not have the commercial infrastructure to employ the new resources in profitable investments, and they lacked the ships to carry the trade generated by the new finds of gold and silver. Indeed, they often lacked even the ships to carry the precious metals themselves in the armed and escorted flotillas that set sail each year from the Caribbean to Europe, and from the west coast of Mexico to Manila.

The experienced merchants of the trade cities of Europe organized the necessary commercial ser-

Plan of Potosí and the Cerro Rico (Rich Hill), Upper Peru. This seventeenth-century painting shows Potosí and the hills in which the lucrative silver mines were located. The mines at Potosí employed some 40,000 poorly paid Indian laborers and tens of thousands of horses—shown in this painting ascending and descending the hills—to transport the material and drive the machinery.

vices. They exchanged the raw metals for cash and bills of exchange, provided loans to tide over the period from the arrival of one shipment of silver to the next, arranged the purchase of goods needed by the Spanish, and supplied the necessary shipping. The most important of these commercial centers was Antwerp (Belgium), with its extraordinarily skilled and wealthy merchant families, such as the Welsers and the Fuggers.

WARFARE AND BANKRUPTCY

Two powerful kings ruled Spain for most of the sixteenth century: Charles V (r. 1516–56) and his son Philip II (r. 1556–98). Both ruled much more than Spain. Many regions of Europe at this time were "owned" by particular families who had the responsibility to protect them, and the right to tax them and to bequeath them to others. Charles inherited from his mother's parents, Ferdinand and Isabella, Spain and the Spanish colonies in Africa, the Americas, Naples, and Sicily. From his father's family, the House of Burgundy, he inherited the Netherlands and the German lands owned by the Habsburg family. Charles was the most powerful ruler in Europe.

Charles V had been raised by his father's family of the House of Burgundy in Flanders. He knew no Spanish, and in his pride and his foreignness he alienated Spain. He appointed foreign courtiers from Flanders to offices in Spain, and he used Spanish wealth to fund his political programs in central European territories. Spaniards revolted. The nobles wanted to stop the drain of money to central Europe and the assignment of offices to foreigners. They wanted Charles to return to Spain. As civil order broke down, artisans and business classes in Castile revolted against the great landholders in the Communero revolt of 1520–21. The revolutionaries held conflicting goals, and as they fought one another to exhaustion, Charles easily retained his hold on government.

But when Charles entered into wars against the Ottoman Turkish empire in eastern Europe and on the Mediterranean, and into the Christian religious wars of Catholic versus Protestant in northern and central Europe (see next section, on the Protestant Reformation and the Catholic Counter– Reformation), he bankrupted even the silver-rich treasury of Spain. After Charles's abdication in 1556, his son Philip II continued the politics of warfare and suffered many of the same results. Even his military victories were financial defeats.

TRADE AND RELIGION IN EUROPE: THE PROTESTANT REFORMATION AND THE CATHOLIC COUNTER-REFORMATION

Charles V and his son Philip II fought against Protestant countries in wars explicitly devoted to matters of faith and commitment to specific religious communities. These wars siphoned off the vast treasures which Spain brought from the Americas, and so diverted her from economic and commercial growth. Here we take a moment to analyze the basis for the schism between Catholics and Protestants that so divided Europe in the sixteenth and seventeenth centuries. We will also consider scholarly arguments over the extent to which specific religious philosophies have direct impact on national economic development.

THE REFORMATION

Roman Catholicism had won the hearts, spirits, and tithes of the overwhelming majority of the population of western and central Europe. By 1500 it had become so wealthy and powerful in the process that several reformers charged the church with straying too far from Jesus' early simplicity and his message of compassion for the poor.

Martin Luther (1483–1546), a pious German monk who lived in a monastery in Wittenberg and taught in the university there, shared these criticisms of the church's wealth and further asserted that it claimed too much power over individual conscience. Luther doubted the importance of church sacraments and authority. He kept his doubts private, however, until in 1517 a friar came to Wittenberg selling **indulgences,** exemption from punishment for sins, in exchange for donations to the church. Outraged, Luther posted on the door of the castle church ninety-five theses asserting the importance of faith and grace alone. Priests, he wrote, were not needed to mediate between humans and God. Pressed to recant, Luther refused, declaring "it is neither right nor safe to act against conscience." Excommunicated by the Pope, Luther was protected by several of the local rulers in Germany, who used the occasion to assert their independence of the Holy Roman Emperor, Charles V. From this time, Lutheranism, as the newly emerging denomination was called, often aligned itself with local rulers. When a revolt of peasants against their landlords swept Germany in 1524, Luther urged the local princes to suppress the revolt by force, and thousands were killed. Lutheranism was adopted by the kings of Denmark and Sweden and many of the princes of Germany, and this region of northern Europe became the heartland of Lutheranism. Printing presses using movable type, introduced into Europe about 1450, helped to spread the new message.

In Geneva, Switzerland, John Calvin (1509–64) preached another doctrine of reform. Like Luther, Calvin spoke of justification by faith and the supremacy of individual conscience, but he denied the authority of the church. Calvin went beyond Luther in arguing that God grants his grace to whomever he chooses, regardless of individual

behavior. Unlike Luther, Calvin rejected alliances with government, although he did create a religious community which dominated the city government of Geneva. Calvinism spread widely without the patronage of any political authority. (In the United States Calvinism is the dominant faith of Presbyterianism, named for its elected leaders or presbyters.)

A third major strand of reform arose in England, where King Henry VIII (r. 1509–47) broke from the church not for reasons of doctrine, but to claim authority for England over the entire Roman Catholic establishment within the country—churches, monasteries, and clergy—and to gain for himself a divorce, which the church had forbidden, from the first of his six wives. Henry had no doctrinal quarrel with Rome. He simply wanted to head

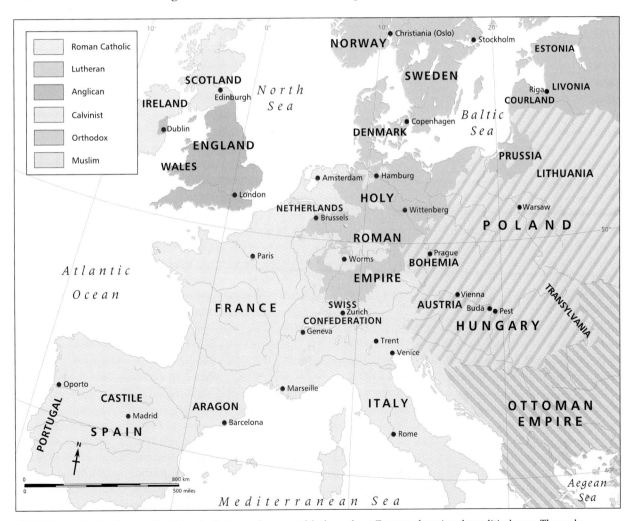

The Reformation in Europe The tide of religious reform was felt throughout Europe, changing the political map. The early commitment of most of northern Europe to Calvinism, Lutheranism, or Anglicanism was counterbalanced by the recovery to Catholicism of France and Poland. Counter-Reformation zeal, combined with political confrontation and dynastic rivalry, culminated in the Thirty Years' War (1618–48), played out at enormous cost across Europe's heartland.

the English church himself, and in 1534 Parliament named him "Protector and Only Supreme Head of the Church and Clergy of England," a title passed on to later English sovereigns. In England, Henry's new church was called Anglican. (Its followers in the United States are called Episcopalians.) Each of the three reform movements permitted their clergy to marry.

THE COUNTER-REFORMATION

Its religious monopoly challenged, the Roman Catholic church countered with the Council of Trent, which met irregularly for eighteen years, 1545–63. The Council reaffirmed the basic doctrines of Catholicism, including the celibacy of the clergy, and encouraged greater religious devotion among the clergy. New religious orders arose to purify the church and transmit its readings. St. Ignatius Loyola (1491–1556) founded the Society of Jesus, which was especially dedicated to education, secular as well as religious, and to carrying the message of the church around the world. St. Francis Xavier (1506–52) carried the Jesuit message to India, Indonesia, and Japan, baptizing thousands of new Catholics. In Paris, St. Vincent de Paul (1581–1660) began his work among the wretched of the slums, a humanitarian mission that continues around the world today.

The Roman Catholic church was fighting for an international, universal vision of the world under its own leadership, while the various Protestant movements encouraged separate national states. In return, several of the new national states encouraged the Protestant movement.

RELIGIOUS BELIEFS AND CAPITALIST PRACTICE

The noted social scientist Max Weber, writing *The Protestant Ethic and the Spirit of Capitalism* in the early 1990s, suggested that Protestantism's emphasis on individual achievement and grace tended to promote economic enterprise and capitalism. Protestants, Weber claimed, would assert and demonstrate their virtue through devotion to thrift, discipline, industriousness and business. Subsequent authors, however, notably the British social historian R.H. Tawney, countered that capitalist thought and practice had preceded Protestantism and that some Catholic areas, such as northern Italy and parts of France, were strongly capitalistic, while some Protestant areas, notably in north Germany, were not. Tawney argued that it was difficult to show any consistent correlation between religious doctrines and economic policy. Nevertheless, debates over the relationship between religious doctrine and business practice continue

John Calvin weighing the Bible against Popish Pomp. Calvin had studied the writings of the first generation of reformers such as Martin Luther and accepted without question the idea of justification by faith alone and the biblical foundation of religious authority. This contemporary woodcut shows him weighing what he saw as the extraneous ceremonial trappings and overweening bishops of the Catholic church against the simple truth of the Bible.

unabated until today in relation to all major religions. (Today when East Asian economies are flourishing, Confucian traditions are praised for encouraging development. During the previous century the same traditions, interpreted differently, had been blamed for a lack of development.)

PROTESTANT CHALLENGES FROM THE DUTCH REPUBLIC AND ENGLAND

Inspired by Protestant doctrines and chafing under Spanish rule, the Netherlands, including today's regions of both Holland and Belgium, rose in revolt. Although geographically small, they were among the wealthiest of Philip's possessions. They were offended by the excessive quantity and deficient quality of the Spanish administrators sent to govern them. They also feared that Philip would extend the Spanish Inquisition and its persecution of non-Catholics to the Netherlands. Many of the peoples of the Netherlands had left Catholicism for new Protestant movements, and many Protestants from other countries had come seeking asylum. Protestants and Catholics had reached an accommodation in the Netherlands, and neither community wished to see that harmony destroyed by the Inquisition. Philip's government refused to pay attention, and the Netherlands erupted in fury. A civil war ensued in which thousands were killed, property was destroyed, and churches were desecrated. By 1576, however, the Netherlands had suffered enough, and representatives of all the Netherlands united across religious lines to expel the Spanish.

In the same year, Queen Elizabeth of England (r. 1558–1603), the daughter of Henry VIII, officially and publicly aligned her country with the rebels in the Netherlands and began to pursue a policy of alliance with Protestant forces throughout Europe.

𝒫ROTESTANT REFORMATION AND COUNTER-REFORMATION—KEY EVENTS

c. 1170	Waldensians in France reject church doctrines including transubstantiation and purgatory
1244	Catholic church crushes Albigensians in southern France
14th century	Lollards dispute church doctrine and want ecclesiastical property put to charitable use
1419	Hussites in Bohemia wage war against the Holy Roman Empire
1517	Martin Luther protests against sale of indulgences at Wittenberg
1519	Ulrich Zwingli leads Reformation in Switzerland
1529	The first known use of the word "Protestant"
1533	Henry VIII of England renounces papal supremacy and proclaims himself head of the "Church of England"
1534	Ignatius Loyola founds Society of Jesus (Jesuits); Luther's German translation of Bible published
1541	John Calvin establishes Presbyterian theocracy in Geneva, Switzerland
1545–63	Council of Trent held by Catholic church to initiate Counter-Reformation
1549–51	St. Francis Xavier travels in Japan
1555	Peace of Augsburg allows princes within the Holy Roman Empire to choose faith (either Catholic or Lutheran) for their realms
1559	John Knox returns from exile to found the Church of Scotland
1562	French Wars of Religion begin
1572	Approximately 25,000 French Huguenots killed in Massacre of St. Bartholomew
1588	Spanish Armada against England fails
1598	Henry IV of France enacts Edict of Nantes, granting religious freedom to Huguenots
1648	Thirty Years' War ends with split between Protestant and Catholic countries of Europe established
1685	Revocation of Edict of Nantes forces some 400,000 French Huguenots to flee to Protestant countries

In reply, Philip II prepared to invade England, the headquarters of the opposition. In 1588 the Spanish Armada set out for England with 130 ships, 30,000 men, and 2400 pieces of artillery. The Armada was destroyed by the English and by a fierce storm, called at the time "the Protestant wind." The northern Netherlands, Holland, was on its way to winning its independence (1609), although the southern half of the region decided to remain allied with Spain as the Spanish Netherlands, only later (1830) becoming the independent country of Belgium.

Spain entered a century-long decline. In 1640 Portugal, which had been united with Spain since 1580, declared its independence once again, and constituent units of Spain, especially Catalonia in the northeast, fought costly, if unsuccessful, wars for independence. Philip III (r. 1598–1621) and Philip IV (r. 1621–65) were incompetent rulers; Charles II (r. 1665–1700) was mentally incapable of ruling. And finally, about mid-century, the stream of silver from the Americas dried up, dwindling from 135 million pesos in the decade 1591–1600 to 19 million in 1651–60. Spain had squandered a fabulous windfall of silver and gold. England and Holland emerged as the rising powers of Europe; their self-confidence and their economies boomed; and their merchant classes organized to travel the world.

DON QUIXOTE OF LA MANCHA

Miguel de Cervantes Saavedra (1547–1616) experienced the heights and depths of Spain's rise and fall. He fought for Spain in its naval victory over the Ottomans in the Battle of Lepanto (1571), although he himself was captured and held prisoner for five years. Later, he helped to provision the ill-fated Spanish Armada against England. Cervantes felt both the majesty of Spain's aspiration to save and rule Europe in the name of Catholicism and the bitterness of its defeats. In *Don Quixote of La Mancha*, often considered the most outstanding novel ever written in Spanish, Cervantes created two figures who represented these two perspectives: Don Quixote, the romantic knight with his head in the clouds, and Sancho Panza, his squire with his feet firmly rooted on earth. The Don's famous encounter with a cluster of windmills—which he mistakes for hostile giants—represents the poignant, if humorous, confrontation between noble aspiration and harsh reality.

Just then they came in sight of thirty or forty windmills that rise from the plain, and no sooner did Don Quixote see them than he said to his squire: "Fortune is guiding our affairs better than we ourselves could have wished. Do you see over yonder, friend Sancho, thirty or forty hulking giants? I intend to do battle with them and slay them. With their spoils we shall begin to be rich, for this is a righteous war and the removal of so foul a brood from off the face of the earth is a service God will bless."

"What giants?" asked Sancho Panza.

"Those you see over there," replied his master, "with their long arms; some of them have them well-nigh two leagues in length."

"Take care, sir," cried Sancho. "Those over there are not giants but windmills, and those things that seem to be arms are their sails, which when they are whirled around by the wind turn the millstone."

"It is clear," replied Don Quixote, "that you are not experienced in adventures. Those are giants, and if you are afraid, turn aside and pray whilst I enter into fierce and unequal battle with them."

Uttering these words, he clapped spurs to Rozinante, his steed … and rammed the first mill in his way. He ran his lance into the sail, but the wind twisted it with such violence that it shivered the lance in pieces and dragged both rider and horse after it, rolling them over and over on the ground, sorely damaged.

"God help us!" cried Sancho. "Did I not tell you, sir, to mind what you were doing, for those were only windmills? Nobody could have mistaken them unless he had windmills in his brain."

"Hold your peace, good Sancho," replied Don Quixote. "The affairs of war are, above all others, subject to continual change."

Cervantes' novel gives us the adjective *quixotic*: impractically idealistic, marked by rash, lofty, romantic ideas.

PORTUGAL'S EMPIRE

When the rulers of Castile and Aragon, Isabella and Ferdinand, married and united their thrones, creating modern Spain in 1492, the western third of the Iberian peninsula, Portugal, remained a separate state. For sixty years, from 1580 to 1640, it was incorporated into Spain, but otherwise it has remained separate until today. In terms of worldwide exploration and trade, Portugal had entered the field earlier and more vigorously than Spain, but it, too, fell under the commercial domination of Genoa and Antwerp. In addition, Portugal's population was too small and diffused to sustain the trading empire it created.

SUGAR, SLAVES, AND FOOD

Portugal sought souls for Christianity, gold for its national treasury, grain and fish to supplement its domestic food supply, and slaves for its new plan-

tations. Recognizing the economic potential of the sugar plantations, which they had seen in the eastern Mediterranean, Portuguese entrepreneurs transplanted them to Madeira and other islands in the Atlantic Ocean. (Spanish landlords and businessmen did the same in the Canary Islands.)

In 1415 Portugal captured Ceuta on the Moroccan coast of North Africa, one of the major points of the trans-Saharan trade in gold and slaves. Then to get closer to the sources of supply, Portuguese ships, supported by the crown, sailed down the coast of West Africa, rounding Cape Bojador in 1434 and continuing on to the Gold Coast in 1472. Bartholomew Diaz reached the Cape of Good Hope and continued northward a few hundred miles up the east coast of Africa in 1498. As the Portuguese explored they also built fortresses—such as El Mina in modern Ghana—as assembly and shipping points for their purchases of slaves and gold. The crown also claimed some of these lands, including Angola, in 1484. By 1500, Lisbon

The fortress of São Jorge da Mina (later called El Mina), African Gold Coast, 1482. Built at the order of King John II of Portugal in 1482, this fortress—like many others—provided a fortified trading post designed to both protect Portuguese trade from rival Europeans and to serve as a supply base. At the beginning of the sixteenth century trade was in gold and kola nuts with imports of American crops such as maize and cassava, and trans-shipment of slaves. It was not until the late seventeenth century that the export of slaves became the main trade on the Gold Coast.

was receiving some 1500 lbs (700 kg) of gold and 10,000 slaves each year from west Africa. The slave trade was of minor importance at the time. In the next century, however, in the New World, the Portuguese would develop an enormous plantation-based sugar industry which would exploit the labor of millions of slaves. The importance of these slaves, in terms of both trade and the enforced migrations of people, is considered in detail in the next chapter.

THE INDIAN OCEAN: ADVANCING PORTUGAL'S COASTAL EXPLORATIONS OF AFRICA

In 1498 Vasco da Gama extended Portugal's voyages of exploration. Departing from Africa with the assistance of a local pilot who knew the route, he sailed into one of the world's liveliest arenas of trade, the Indian Ocean and the west coast of India (see Chapter 12). Almost immediately the Portuguese introduced armed violence into trade relations that had been peaceful. In 1500 a Portuguese expedition under Pedro Alvarez Cabral, on its way to founding a fort at Cochin, India, was instructed to sink Muslim ships on sight. When da Gama returned on his second voyage in 1502 he came with twenty-one armed ships to assert Portuguese power in the Indian Ocean. Seven years later, at the Battle of Diu, Portuguese cannon devastated a combined Egyptian-Gujarati-Calicut fleet. Under Governor Alfonso de Albuquerque (1509–15) Portugal captured Goa in 1510, Malacca in 1511, and Hormuz in 1515. At the height of their Indian Ocean power, Portugal held some fifty ports. Portuguese trade boomed.

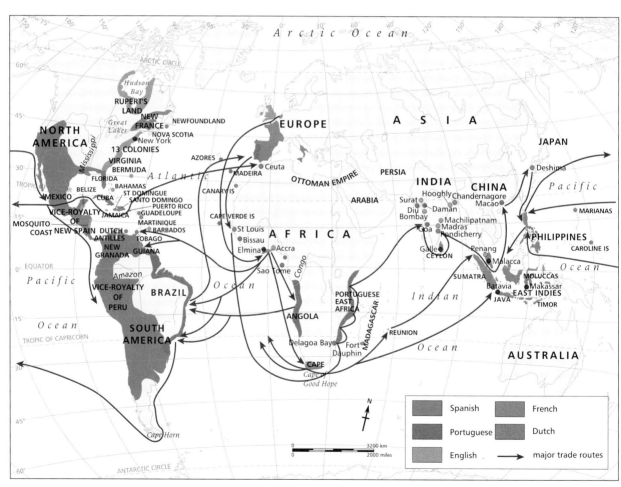

The first European trading empires European seaborne intercontinental trade was dominated by Spain and Portugal in the sixteenth century. The Spanish rapidly colonized Central America, the Andes mountain regions, and the Philippines. The Portuguese concentrated on the coasts of Brazil and east and west Africa. A century later the Dutch, English, and French followed, establishing settler colonies in North America and South Africa and fortified trading posts along the coasts elsewhere.

HOW SIGNIFICANT WERE
THE PORTUGUESE?
A HISTORIOGRAPHIC DEBATE

*H*ow important was Portuguese military and commercial power in the Indian Ocean? The king of Portugal referred to himself as "Lord of Conquest, Navigation, and Commerce of Ethiopia, Arabia, Persia, and India" (Pearson, *India and the Indian Ocean*, p. 84), but what did that title mean? Was it realistic for a country of only one and a quarter million people to assert control of the trade of the Indian Ocean from a distance of 10,000 miles (16,000 kilometers)? Michael Pearson, one of the most careful scholars of Portuguese naval expansion, believes that Portuguese armed shipping introduced a new element into the Indian Ocean trade, but it was not a decisive element. In fact their ports "constituted a drain on Portuguese resources, and were in any case of dubious strategic value … the Portuguese … like many later imperialists, found involvement easy but withdrawal difficult: thus resources drained away on unnecessary forts" (p. 85). Portuguese officials tried to force all ships in the Indian Ocean to purchase transit passes, basically extorting protection money, and to dock at Portuguese headquarters in Goa. These attempts had only limited success. Farther east, "they had very little impact at all" (p. 89). When Portugal tried to control the trade of Canton in 1521–2, the Chinese coastguard fleet drove them away, although in 1557 the Portuguese were given the nearby port of Macao. The Portuguese in Malacca were constantly attacked by neighboring Muslim princes and were finally expelled in 1575.

On the other hand, the distinguished world historian William McNeill argues that the 1509 Battle of Diu, in which Portuguese cannon devastated a combined Egyptian-Gujarati-Calicut fleet, "established European naval superiority in the Indian Ocean for centuries to come" (McNeill, p. 113). And the Indian historian K.N. Pannikar agrees, titling one of his books *The Vasco da Gama Age of World History*. Why do these historians produce such apparently conflicting evaluations? Two possible answers come to mind. First, perhaps McNeill and Pannikar are more willing to accept Portuguese boasting at face value because the only systematic records we have of Indian Ocean trade in the sixteenth century are Portuguese. Countervailing records are virtually non-existent. Significantly, Pearson has conducted his own painstaking research into the Portuguese governmental and commercial records in Lisbon and Goa, and is prepared to evaluate their claims with a more critical eye.

Second, these historians choose very different time frames for their evaluations. Pearson analyzes the actual accomplishments of the Portuguese themselves in the sixteenth century, and finds them limited. McNeill and Pannikar adopt a much longer time frame, including not only the Portuguese in the sixteenth century, but also the Dutch and the British who arrived a century later with much greater force, dramatically altering the structure of Indian Ocean trade. Adopting different time frames, the historians emphasize different outcomes. In fact, these different emphases are compatible with each other. The Portuguese actually accomplished less than they claimed but they opened the route for others to accomplish far more.

THE DUTCH REPUBLIC

In the early seventeenth century, the Dutch had the most efficient economic system in Europe. The Dutch Republic bordered the North Sea, reclaimed land from its waters, and lived from its largesse. Fishing was Holland's great national industry. One out of every four Dutch persons was reliant on the herring industry—catching, salting, smoking, pick-ling, selling—and others depended on cod fishing and whaling. With their windmills and their dikes, the Dutch also reclaimed land from the sea: 364,565 acres (147,539 hectares) between 1540 and 1715 and another 84,638 acres (34,253 hectares) from inland lakes. With such an investment of capital and energy, the Dutch worked their land carefully and efficiently. They developed new methods of crop rotation, planting turnips in the fall to provide winter food for humans and sheep. At other times of year they raised peas, beans, and clover to restore nitrogen to the soil. With these cropping patterns, the Dutch no longer had to leave one third of their land fallow each year. They farmed it all, increasing productivity by 50 percent. In addition, the Dutch built one of the largest textile industries in Europe, based on wool from their own sheep and huge quantities imported from England.

On the sea and in the rivers, the Dutch sailed 10,000 ships as early as 1600, and for the next century they dominated the shipping of northern Europe. From the Baltic they brought timber and grain to Amsterdam and western Europe. In exchange, from the ports of Portugal, Spain, and France they carried salt, oil, wool, wine, and, most of all, the silver and gold of the New World. Often they warehoused the trade goods *en route* to other ports in Amsterdam, earning additional profits on the storage. They used substantial amounts of the timber themselves to build the most seaworthy, yet economical, ships of the day.

The Dutch also developed the commercial institutions to underpin their dominance in trade. The bourse, or stock exchange, was opened in Amsterdam in the mid-sixteenth century as the Dutch were gaining control of the Baltic trade, and it was reopened in 1592 as they captured a dominant role in supplying grain to Mediterranean countries. In 1598 they initiated a Chamber of Insurance; in 1609 the Bank of Amsterdam was established. This bank accepted coins from all over the world, assessed their gold and silver content, and exchanged them for gold florin coins, which were fixed in weight and value and became the standard everywhere. The Dutch government guaranteed the safety of deposits in the national bank, attracting capital from throughout Europe. Depositors were able to draw checks on their accounts. For two centuries, until the French Revolution in 1789, Amsterdam was the financial center of Europe.

The Dutch government actively promoted business. At the time, Holland was a union of seven

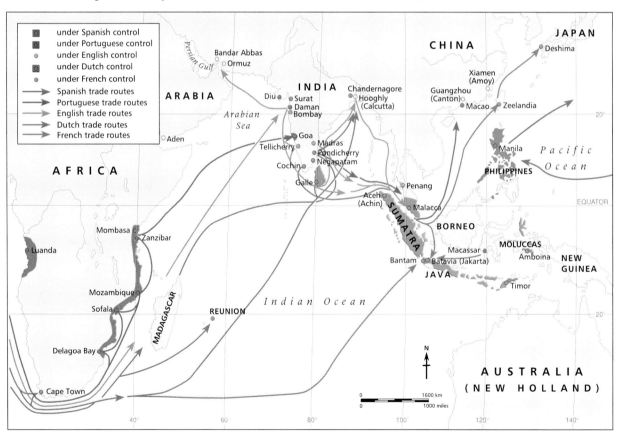

Indian Ocean Trade in the seventeenth century Prior to the sixteenth century, Arabs and other local traders had dominated Indian Ocean commerce. When the Portuguese arrived in 1498, however, European nations entered directly into these trade routes in armed ships. Controlled from headquarters in Europe, they established coastal trade enclaves throughout the region. They began to battle each other for supremacy, projecting European competition into these distant waters and shores.

provinces, each a republic led by prosperous businessmen, and the Dutch Republic won its independence from Spain through more than four decades of warfare, from 1566 to 1609. The basis of the war was both political and religious. The southern ten provinces of the Netherlands were Catholic, and they remained as the Spanish Netherlands, today's Belgium, when the northern seven provinces, predominantly Protestant, declared themselves the Dutch Republic. The war also brought to an end the supremacy of Antwerp, which yielded place to Amsterdam as the leading center of commerce. The Dutch Republic understood the importance of sea-borne trade and of their religious and political relationship to England. The ruling "High Mightinesses the Estates General of the United Provinces" attended these issues, and indeed in 1688, one of them, William of Orange, the husband of Mary, the niece of James II of England, became king of England (see Chapter 15).

In 1602 Dutch businessmen founded the Dutch East India Company, a joint stock company dedicated to trade in Asia. The Company captured several Portuguese ports, but concentrated on the most lucrative of all the East Asian centers, Java and the Moluccas, or the Spice Islands of today's Indonesia. Here "their economic leadership of the world was finally consolidated" (Braudel, vol. 3, p. 211). In

ℛROTESTANT REFORMATION AND COUNTER-REFORMATION—KEY PEOPLE

Peter Waldo	(fl. 1170) Founded the Waldensians, who lived in poverty and rejected transubstantiation, purgatory, and the invocation of saints. Although persecuted, the sect spread throughout France, Germany, and Italy.
John Wycliffe	(c. 1330–84) English reformer. Rejected penances and indulgences. Initiated translation of Bible into English. His followers were known as Lollards.
Jan Hus	(c. 1373–1415) Bohemian reformer, rector of Prague University, and founder of the Hussites. Defended Wycliffe and attacked ecclesiastical abuses. He rejected the pope's authority and was burned at the stake for heresy.
Martin Luther	(1483–1546) German founder of Protestantism and the Reformation. Pinned 95 theses to door of church in Wittenberg, protesting church decadence, including the sale of indulgences. He translated the Bible into German.
Ulrich Zwingli	(1484–1531) Swiss Protestant. The leader of the Reformation in Switzerland, he insisted on the primacy of the scriptures and attacked monasticism and idolatry.
Ignatius Loyola	(1491–1556) Spanish noble and founder (1534) of the Jesuit movement, which sought to protect Catholicism against the Reformation and carry out missionary work, including to Brazil, Japan, and India as well as in Europe.
John Knox	(c. 1505–72) Scottish divine who established the Church of Scotland, and after the English Civil War introduced Presbyterianism in Scotland.
St. Francis Xavier	(1506–52) Spanish Roman Catholic missionary (to India, the East Indies, China, and Japan) who helped to found the Jesuits.
John Calvin	(1509–64) French Protestant and reformer. Established strict theocracy in Geneva, Switzerland. Set out the principles of predestination and rejection of papal authority in *Institutes of the Christian Religion*.

1619 the Dutch East India Company founded Jakarta, which served as its regional headquarters until Indonesia won its independence in 1950. In 1623 the Dutch seized Amboina in the Moluccas, killing a group of Englishmen they found there, and forcing the English back to India, their second choice at the time. In 1600 a group of Dutch traders had reached Japan. Even after all other foreigners were expelled in 1641 (see p. 424), the Dutch were permitted a small settlement on Deshima Island, off Nagasaki, and for two centuries they were the only European traders allowed in Japan. In 1652 the Dutch captured the Cape of Good Hope from the Portuguese and established the first settlement of Afrikaners, South Africans of Dutch descent, who remain powerful there.

In the Americas, the Dutch West India Company raided the shipping of the Spanish and the Portuguese, and then founded their own rich sugar plantations in Caracas, Curaçao, and Guiana. For a few decades they held Bahia in Brazil, but the Portuguese drove them out in 1654. In North America they established New Amsterdam on Manhattan Island; the English conquered it and renamed it New York.

For all their commercial skill and success, the Dutch could not ultimately retain their supremacy. Beginning with the English Navigation Act of 1651, which permitted imports to England only in English ships or in those of the exporting country, the English attempted to restrict Dutch shipping. Years of warfare on land against France also

THE JOINT STOCK COMPANIES IN ASIA

*I*n the early 1600s financiers in the Dutch Republic, England, France, and elsewhere invested in national joint stock companies for trading overseas. They invested in expectation of the great profits that might come from successful shipping ventures, while their potential losses were limited to the value of their investment.

In India, the English, French, and Dutch East India Companies set up trading posts, usually called "factories," within towns. The English, for example, started to trade at Machhilipatnam on the southeast coast, and in 1613 at Surat on the west coast. In 1615 they fortified the Surat position and set up inland trading centers at Agra, Burhanpur, and Patna. The French similarly established themselves at Pondicherry, and the Dutch at Machhilipatnam to the north. Until the end of the century, the Mughals and local government generally welcomed the foreign traders as means of stimulating the economy through trade and enriching the government through taxes.

In the Indian Ocean, pepper was a large part of the companies' trade. Between them, the English and Dutch East India Companies carried 13.5 million pounds (6.07 million kilograms) of pepper to Europe in the peak year of 1670, although a sizeable portion of the Dutch share came from Indonesia. Other goods included indigo, raw silk, saltpeter, and, increasingly,

Indian textiles. By 1684, the English East India Company alone imported 1,760,315 pieces of cotton cloth. There were also large-scale exports of textiles carried by Europeans from India to Africa in payment for slaves going to the Caribbean.

As the companies' ships traveled armed, and as their representatives established fortresses and trading centers on the coasts of Asia and of the Americas, the companies became, in effect, miniature governments. Malachy Postlethwayt's *Universal Dictionary* of 1751 wrote that the Dutch East India Company

> makes peace and war at pleasure, and by its own authority; administers justice to all; ... settles colonies, builds fortifications, levies troops, maintains numerous armies and garrisons, fits out fleets, and coins money. (Cited in Tracy, *The Political Economy of Merchant Empires*, p. 196)

For example, following its victories at Plassey in 1757 and Buxar in 1765, the English East India Company became the *de facto* government of Bengal in India, and continued to expand until it was effectively the ruler of almost all of India. The British government regulated the East India Company from its founding in 1600, but finally disbanded it and took over direct rule of India after the Indian revolt of 1857.

exhausted Dutch resources. In 1700 the Dutch Republic had a population of 2 million people; at this time the population of the British Isles was 9 million, and that of France 19 million. An aggressive small country simply could not continue to compete with two aggressive large countries.

FRANCE AND ENGLAND

With the Dutch worn down by decades of war and maritime competition, France and England competed for dominance in world trade. For two centuries each pursued its own strategy—France by land and England by sea—and leadership finally went to the mistress of the waves.

FRANCE: CONSOLIDATING THE NATION

In the second half of the sixteenth century, France endured four decades of civil warfare because the crown was unable to control the various antagonistic factions, religious groups, and regions of the country. Struggles between Catholics and Protestants, called Huguenots in France, helped to fuel the warfare. So, too, did the desire of the nobles to have more independence from the king. In 1589 Henry of Navarre, a Huguenot, came to the throne as Henry IV (r. 1589–1610). Recognizing the importance of Catholicism to the majority of the French people, he became a Catholic with the apocryphal comment, "Paris is worth a Mass." In 1598 Henry

Andries van Eertvel, *The Return to Amsterdam of the Fleet of the Dutch East India Company,* **1599.** The Dutch East India Company was founded in 1602 to create a monopoly over Dutch trade and to seize control of the Portuguese trade routes in the Indian Ocean. The company owned a fleet of ships armed with cannon which carried pepper, indigo, raw silk, saltpeter and increasingly textiles from India to Western Europe. In the later 1600s, large-scale exports of textiles were also carried from India to Africa in payment for slaves going to the Caribbean. (*Johnny Van Haeften Gallery, London*).

SPOTLIGHT

The European "Other" in Art

Early encounters between peoples of different cultures quickly made their way into art. Artistic representation, like the three examples here, transports us back to earlier times and places, and invites the modern viewer to add contemporary understandings to those of the artist. Here we focus on portrayals of Europeans by indigenous artists from Nigeria, India, and the Andes, respectively. The artworks all date from the middle to the late seventeenth century, by which time the colonial presence was firmly established in all three continents; a strong sense emerges, nevertheless, of the alien, "other" appearance and manners of these Westerners through the eyes of those engaged in depicting them.

Picture 1 shows leopard hunters returning with their catch on a brass plaque typical of the artistic craft of the Benin City in today's Nigeria. The dress, helmets, daggers, and firearms of the hunters, and what we can see of their faces, suggest that they are Portuguese. The plaque itself decorated the palace of the Obas, or rulers, of Benin, and suggests the magnitude of the impact of the early Portuguese traders and visitors. Mostly known to us for their trade in slaves, apparently the Portuguese had other, though similarly violent, interests on the West African coast.

By contrast with our first example, the Indian cotton textile in **picture 2** provides a much more detailed portrayal of Dutch traders greeting each other. Painted on cotton cloth in the late seventeenth century, it suggests that the Dutch have come from far across the seas and trade in a rich array of goods. The

Picture 1 Brass plaque from Benin City (Nigeria), seventeenth century.

whiskers, wide-brimmed hats, ornate doublets and pantaloons, and buckled shoes of the Westerners are painstakingly rendered, and the artist was clearly keen to contrast their appearance with that of the bemused Indian gentleman (far right). The doffing of caps and handshakes must appear strange to this onlooker, who would be accustomed to greeting others by joining his own palms in the "namaste" salute. The Indian artist has painted the faces of the Dutch in careful, realistic detail, suggesting a more intimate knowledge of the European subjects.

The painted Inca ritual drinking vessel made of wood, known as a kero, in **picture 3**, represents people of *three* different cultures: to the left, an Inca dignitary; in the center a Spaniard playing a trumpet; and, on the right, one of the earliest (*c.* 1650 C.E.) depictions of a black African in South America, a man playing a drum. The similar postures, dress, and hats of the Spaniard and the African, as well as their instuments, suggest that they are of roughly similar status, and engaged in a common enterprise. This is not the representation of slavery that contemporary viewers might have expected. In this way the art resulting from cross-cultural encounters reminds us to take nothing for granted but to keep our eyes alert to the unusual.

Picture 2 Indian cotton cloth, late seventeenth century.

Picture 3 Inca–Spanish wooden drinking vessel, Peru, *c.* 1650.

issued the Edict of Nantes, which gave Protestants the same civil rights as Catholics and thus helped to heal the religious schism between them. He was not entirely successful, however, and, indeed, was assassinated by a Catholic militant in 1610. His successor, Louis XIII (r. 1610–43), following the advice of his chief minister, the Cardinal Richelieu, encouraged nobles to invest in trade by land and sea, built up France's armies, and cultivated allies among France's neighbors.

Louis XIV, in an extraordinarily long and forceful reign (1643–1715), "made France the strongest country in Europe" (p. 157), according to R.R. Palmer, a leading historian of France and Europe. Under the Sun King, as Louis was known, France set the standard throughout Europe for administration, war, diplomacy, language, thought, literature, architecture, fashion, cooking, and etiquette. Although they had been slower to enter transoceanic trade, the French now began to trade in India and Madagascar, the American Great Lakes and Mississippi River; to establish colonies in the West Indies; and to stake a claim to Canada. By 1690 Louis XIV had raised an army of 400,000 men, equal to the combined armies of England, the Habsburg Empire, Prussia, Russia, and the Dutch Republic. At this time, the French navy was also larger than the English, with 120 ships of the line compared to the English navy's 100. Also, as we have seen, in 1700, France had a population of 19 million, more than double that of the British Isles.

Louis XIV boasted *"L'état, c'est moi"*—"I am the state"—by which he meant that the powers of the state rested in him alone. His leading religious adviser, Bishop Jacques–Bénigne Bossuet (1627–1704), linked the king's power to divine right, asserting that "Royalty has its origin in the divinity itself" (Columbia University. *Contemporary Civilization*, p. 705). Louis XIV continued the right of the king to appoint the Catholic clergy in France, and he revoked the Edict of Nantes in the belief that a single, dominant religion was more important than the toleration of minorities within his kingdom.

Economically, Louis XIV's chief economic advisor, Jean–Baptiste Colbert (1625–96), pursued a policy of **mercantilism**—fostering the economic welfare of one's own nation against all others—by strengthening the economic power and control of the state over the national economy, even more aggressively than had Richelieu. To facilitate trade, he abolished local taxes on trade throughout central France (a region as large as England), although his government was not powerful enough to do away with these internal tariffs throughout the entire country. Colbert established a Commercial Code to unify business practice throughout the country. To improve communication and transportation, he built roads and canals, including a link between the Bay of Biscay and the Mediterranean. He set quality standards for hand manufacturers to improve their marketability and gave financial incentives to the French manufacturers of such luxury goods as silks, tapestries, glass, and woolens. Meanwhile the needs of the army created huge national markets for uniforms, equipment, and provisions.

The growth of French military and economic strength disturbed the balance of power in Europe and precipitated a series of wars. The War of the League of Augsburg, 1688–97, and the War of the Spanish Succession, 1702–13, reduced France's power and she ceded to Britain the American colonies of Newfoundland and Nova Scotia and all French claims to the Hudson Bay territory. Britain began to pull ahead in overseas possessions.

BRITAIN: ESTABLISHING COMMERCIAL SUPREMACY

(The names of Britain and England are often used interchangeably in everyday usage. Formally, however, before the 1707 Act of Union, England and Wales were one country, Scotland another. By the 1707 Act they were united into the single country of Britain.) In the same wars, Britain won from Spain the *asiento*, the right to carry all the slave cargoes from Africa to Spanish America, plus one shipload of more conventional goods each year to Panama. These officially recognized trading rights also provided cover for British ships to engage illegally in the business of piracy and smuggling, which flourished in the Caribbean. Control of transoceanic colonies and trade had become a prized objective. While most inhabitants of the United States may naturally think of North America as the object of this competition, in reality in the eighteenth century the most valued properties in the Americas were the sugar-producing islands of the Caribbean, and the most valuable trade was in human cargo—that is, the slaves who worked the sugar plantations. In Asia, control of sea lanes and of the outposts established by the various East India companies was the prize; the winner had not yet emerged.

Competition for dominance between the French and the British continued through four more wars in the eighteenth century: the War of Austrian Succession, 1740–48; the Seven Years' War, 1756–63;

the War of American Independence (the American Revolution), 1775–81 (see Chapter 15); and the wars of the French Revolution and Napoleon, 1792–1815 (see Chapter 15). These wars demonstrated the importance of sea power, and here the British triumphed. Paul Kennedy supplies data (p. 99) that demonstrate the supremacy of the French on land but the British at sea: Around 1790, the French population outnumbered the British 28 million to 16 million, and French armies outnumbered the British by an even greater ratio, 180,000 to 40,000. But the British navy had 195 ships of the line compared with France's 81.

Suffering defeats at sea, the French retreated from their colonial positions. In the Peace Settlement at Paris in 1763 at the end of the Seven Years' War, they turned over their immense, but thinly populated, holdings in North America east of the Mississippi to the British and those west of the Mississippi to Spain. They kept their rich, sugar-producing islands in the Caribbean: Saint Domingue (Haiti), Guadeloupe, and Martinique. In India, although they lost out in other locations, they kept Pondicherry on the southeast coast and a few additional commercial locations. The French navy still functioned and was deployed against the British in America during the American Revolution, but it was competely crushed during the Napoleonic Wars. The British, though they lost the thirteen colonies of the United States in 1783, triumphed everywhere else because of the great strength of their navy. They held Canada. They held their islands in the Caribbean. They increased their holdings in India (see p. 410), and they dominated the sea lanes both across the Atlantic Ocean and through the Indian Ocean.

The British Triumph in Overseas Trade and Colonization: What Do We Know and How Do We Know?

How did Britain achieve supremacy in world trade and colonization? How can we understand the process? Fernand Braudel's epic three-volume *Civilization and Capitalism 15th–18th Century*, which surveys the entire process of the rise of capitalism, stresses a comparative approach. He compares, for example, England's early success in achieving a single unified national market throughout its island kingdom with the far more limited success of France, which managed to integrate economically only about one-third of its territories until the

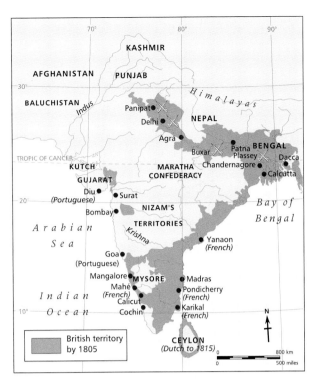

British power in India to 1805 The weakening of the Mughal Empire created a situation which was exploited by the English and French East India companies. They created strategic alliances with local independent princes and competed for power on land and sea. With Clive's victory at Plassey (1757) the English gained Bengal, a power base which allowed them to expand steadily, but their control over India was not secure until their final defeat of the Maratha confederation in 1818.

French Revolution in 1789. A further comparative advantage for England was its geography. As an island with many navigable rivers, England's ports and markets were numerous and easily accessible. More than virtually all other countries, except perhaps Holland, Britain concentrated on building its navy and merchant marine, and, in comparison, Britain was far larger than Holland. Ironically, England chose to concentrate on the sea after it lost its territories on the European continent to France in the Hundred Years' War, 1453–1558. France, by comparison, was the largest power in western Europe and divided its interests between the Continent and the seas.

Institutionally, England surpassed all others, even Holland, in supporting sophisticated economic enterprise. Recognizing the importance of a stable currency, England fixed the value of the pound sterling in 1560–61 at 4 ounces (114 grams) of silver, and maintained that valuation until after World War I. The Bank of England, created in 1694, could transact its business with a currency of fixed value.

Moreover, Britain never defaulted on its debts and so she earned the trust of the international financial community. In times of war as well as of peace, Britain could borrow whatever sums she needed. "England, by dethroning Amsterdam, had become the point of convergence of all the world's trade—and all the world so to speak settled its accounts in London" (Braudel, p. 364). Politically, Britain developed a new system of constitutional monarchy after 1688 which gave strong support to private commercial interests, as we shall see in Chapter 15. The French later ridiculed Britain as "a nation of shopkeepers," but geographically, militarily, institutionally, politically, and agriculturally, the British were building the capacity to become the most effective businessmen in the world.

AGRICULTURE IN ECONOMIC GROWTH

Commercial agriculture underpins the growth of cities and trade networks (see Part 2), and Britain and the Dutch Republic had the most productive and efficient commercial agriculture in the world. Holland, as noted above, farmed with special care, treating its land as a precious resource. Meanwhile British farmers introduced new equipment such as iron plows and Jethro Tull's seed drill. They initiated huge irrigation and drainage projects to make new land available.

New laws regarding land ownership changed fundamentally the relationships between tenants and landlords. In Britain (and Holland) peasants began to pay rent to landowners in a business relationship, rather than performing services for them as client to patron. Moreover, lands that had been held in common by the village community and had been used for grazing sheep and cattle by shepherds and livestock owners who had no lands of their own were now parcelled out for private ownership through a series of enclosure acts. Enclosures had begun in England in very limited measure in the late 1400s. In the eighteenth century the process resumed and the pace increased. In the period 1714–1801, about one-fourth of the land in Britain was converted from community property to private property through enclosures. The results were very favorable to landowners, and urban businessmen now bought land as agricultural investment property. Agricultural productivity shot up; landowners prospered. But hundreds of thousands of farmers with small plots and cottagers who had subsisted through the use of the common lands for grazing their animals were now turned into tenant farmers and wage laborers. Many left the land altogether and headed for the growing cities. The results were revolutionary, and profoundly disturbing, as economic historian Robert Heilbroner explains:

> Where before there was a kind of communality of ownership, now there is private property. Where there were yeomen now there are sheep … As early as the middle of the sixteenth century riots had broken out against it; in one such uprising, 3,500 people were killed. (Heilbroner, p. 30)

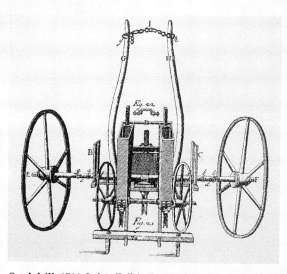

Seed drill, 1701. Jethro Tull (1674–1741) is a key figure of the eighteenth-century agricultural revolution, which saw new technology harnessed to farming techniques. Tull's machine drill employed a rotary mechanism that sowed seeds in rows, permitting cultivation between the rows and thus reducing the need for weeding.

The process continued until the mid-nineteenth century (beyond our time period here):

> In 1820 … the Duchess of Sutherland dispossessed 15,000 tenants from 794,000 acres of land, replaced them with 131,000 sheep, and by way of compensa-

CAPITALISM

By the late eighteenth century, European economies were expanding and had become the subject of discussion and debate not only among businesspeople and political leaders, but among philosophers as well. Adam Smith (1723–90) had already established his reputation as a moral philosopher before he turned to writing what became his most famous work. In 1776 Smith published *The Wealth of Nations*, a book of a thousand pages, the first systematic explanation of a newly emerging philosophy of economics, later called capitalism. In contrast to the mercantilist views of his day, Smith argued that national wealth was not to be measured by treasuries of precious metals, but rather by

tion rented her evicted families an average of two acres of submarginal land each. (Heilbroner, p. 30)

For better and for worse, the capitalist market system had come to the English countryside and to Holland. Other areas of Europe lagged far behind in turning land into commercial property and in transforming the relationships between landowners and those who worked the land into commercial arrangements.

Enclosure Acts. This aerial photograph of the village of Padbury in Buckinghamshire, England, shows the ridge and furrow of former open field agriculture. The straight hedges were established after the Enclosure Acts of the late eighteenth century. Single crops would have been grown in these large fields and exchanged at market for a range of goods. The concentric circles (lower right) mark the site of a former windmill.

EUROPEAN EXPLORATION AND SETTLEMENT 1500–1670

1500	Pedro Alvarez Cabral claims Brazil for Portugal
1501–2	Amerigo Vespucci explores coast of Brazil
1502	Columbus discovers Nicaragua
1505	Portugal establishes trading posts on Malabar coast and discovers Mozambique
1507	Martin Waldseemüller produces first map of the world showing South America and Asia
1509	Battle of Diu gives Portuguese control of Indian seas
1516	Juan de Solis discovers Rio de la Plata
1519–21	Hernán Cortés conquers Mexico
1520	Ferdinand Magellan discovers Tierra del Fuego
1530–8	Francisco Pizarro explores Peru
1534–6	Jacques Cartier explores St. Lawrence River
1535–7	Spanish explore Chile
1541	Hernando de Soto discovers Mississippi River Francisco de Orellana explores Amazon River
1557	Portuguese settle at Macao, China
1586	Francis Drake leads expedition to West Indies
1596	Willem Barents discovers Spitzbergen
1600	English East India Company founded
1602	Dutch East India Company founded
1603–9	Samuel de Champlain explores interior of Canada
1604	French East India Company founded
1607	English colony of Virginia founded at Jamestown by John Smith
1610	Henry Hudson discovers Hudson Bay
1610	Tea introduced to Europe
1616	Willem Schouten discovers Cape Horn
1620	Pilgrim Fathers reach Cape Cod, Massachusetts, in the *Mayflower* and found New Plymouth
1621	Dutch West Indies Company is founded
1624	Virginia becomes a crown colony
1630	Some 16,000 colonists from England begin to settle in Massachusetts
1642	Abel Tasman visits Australia and sights New Zealand
1652	Cape Town founded by the Dutch
1670	Hudson Bay Company founded

quantities of productivity and of trade. He opened his great work with an illustration from a pin factory where a division of labor into specialized tasks of production increased output dramatically. Smith further argued that when workers specialize in what they do best, and then exchange their products in the market, productivity increases. The competitive free market guides production: Goods that consumers demand to buy attract higher prices, and producers supply them in order to earn good profits; unwanted goods earn no profits, and producers stop producing them. This law of **supply and demand** in the market leads to the production of the amounts and kinds of goods that suit the wishes of consumers. According to Smith's Law of Accumulation, profits will then be reinvested in further production.

Smith reached a new and surprising conclusion: wealth comes not by the command of a ruler, nor from the regulations of the clergy, nor from the altruism of members of the community, but as a result of people pursuing their own economic self-interest, and exchanging the fruits of their labor in the market.

> It is not from the benevolence of the butcher, the brewer, or the baker that we expect our dinner, but from their regard to their self-interest. We address ourselves, not to their humanity, but to their self-love, and never talk to them of our necessities, but of their advantages. (p. 14)

Although Smith did not use the term, today we call the system he analyzed capitalism—that is, most wealth, or capital, rests in private, non-governmental hands, and economic decisions on price, supply, and demand are made through the free market rather than by government decision. Critics of this capitalist market system, in which buyer and seller negotiate freely over prices, equated capitalism's self-interest with greed, but Smith explained how competition, like an "invisible hand," transformed self-interest into community benefit. If a greedy producer charges too much for his goods, someone else will undercut him and lower prices will result; if he pays his employees too little, they will abandon him and seek work elsewhere. Out of the conflicting self-interests of individual members of the society, paradoxically, social harmony will emerge. Smith, who was a professor of moral philosophy at the University of Edinburgh, disagreed with those who said that rulers or priests must regulate the economy in order to achieve equity. Like an "invis-

ible hand," he believed, the impersonal market would do the job.

Believing that the market would correct most economic imbalances, Smith opposed government intervention in the market. He argued for a hands-off government policy of *laissez-faire* toward the market—that is, let people do as they choose. But he did recognize that some necessities for economic growth were beyond the powers of any single, small producer. "The erection and maintenance of the public works which facilitate the commerce of any country, such as good roads, bridges, navigable canals, harbors, et cetera, must require very different degrees of expense" (vol. V, p. 1), and therefore Smith urged government to promote these public works. He believed that education was fundamental to economic productivity. Private education, because it was more accountable, was more effective than public education, but government-supported public education was better than none.

Smith recognized, of course, that the market did not always do its work of balancing supply and demand. Huge businesses that formed virtual **monopolies** could control whole industries and manipulate market forces. Their size gave them unfair leverage, and Smith wanted them broken up. *The Wealth of Nations* attacked the East India Company, the joint stock company that monopolized virtually all of Britain's trade in Asia and had even become the acting government of Bengal in India (see p. 410). Smith argued that its monopoly should be broken. His plea, however, failed.

Capitalism was the prevailing economic philosophy in Britain in the years of its economic supremacy in the nineteenth century (see Chapter 16), and the new system spread to many other countries as well. As we shall see in the following chapters, many critics attacked capitalism, blaming it for the inhumanity and cruelty of the slave trade, the seizure of colonies overseas, and the vulnerability of workers at home. Smith understood these problems, but argued that they were corruptions of the market system rather than natural products of it. He condemned slavery as a form of kidnapping and theft of human beings, rather than a free market exchange. Similarly he deplored the European destruction of the native American states and populations as a violation of human ethics:

> The savage injustice of the Europeans rendered an event which ought to have been beneficial to all ruinous and destructive to several of those unfortunate countries. (p. 416)

On the issue of vulnerability of workers, Smith was less understanding. Critics noted that the balance between supply and demand took time to emerge and in the meantime workers suffered. The business cycle was wrenching. Producers increased supplies until the market was glutted and then they stopped. Jobs were plentiful and then were cut back. In the long run balance might result, but in the short run the economy was a roller-coaster. Moreover as the Industrial Revolution began at the end of the eighteenth century, business firms multiplied in size, leaving the individual worker powerless to bargain for wages and working conditions.

DIVERSE CULTURES; DIVERSE ECONOMIC SYSTEMS

The global expansion of western European countries between the sixteenth and the eighteenth centuries provides only one perspective on trade in this period. Now we examine other trading groups around the globe, analyzing differences and similarities among them, and also noting the results of their mutual encounters. African export trade, for example, was reoriented geographically to the coastal ports established by European traders, and the slave trade sent millions of Africans to the western hemisphere as human cargo. These developments, although important in considerations of trade, will be discussed at length in the next chapter on migration patterns. Here we will consider the trade patterns of Russia and Asian powers. The history of the migration of Asian imperial conquerors will also be discussed in the next chapter.

RUSSIA

At the end of the seventeenth century Russia had little direct contact with the market economies of northwestern Europe. The country was geographically remote by land, and by sea the only port was Archangel at the extreme north, on the White Sea, iced in for most of the year. The foreign trade that did exist was carried by foreign ships traveling Russia's river system. Russia belonged to the Greek Orthodox branch of Christianity, so communication with the Church of Rome and its Western European networks was also limited.

Russia had begun to take its modern form only after Ivan III (1462–1505) overthrew the domination of the Mongols in 1480. Muscovy, the territory around Moscow, became the core of an expanding independent state. At first, Russia expanded southeastward, defeating the khanate of Astrakhan in 1556 and capturing the Volga River basin south to the Caspian Sea and its access to the silk trade of Persia. It also expanded eastward to the Pacific (1649), capturing Siberia and its rich population of fur-bearing animals. Russia had only a tiny urban trading class and very few big city markets. As late as 1811, only 4 percent of its population was urban. The overwhelming majority of its people lived in serfdom, a virtual slavery. Occasional serf uprisings, like that led by Stepan Razin (Stenka Razin; d. 1671) in 1667, were brutally suppressed, and the gulf between free persons and serfs increased.

When Peter the Great (r. 1682–1725) became emperor, he saw Sweden as his principal enemy. Sweden already held Finland and the entire eastern shore of the Baltic, bottling up Russia without any Baltic port. Then, in a crushing blow, 8000 Swedish troops defeated 40,000 Russians at the Battle of Narva in 1700. Humiliated, Peter set out to construct in Russia a powerful state based on a powerful army and navy. As a young man, Peter had traveled through western Europe, especially in England and Holland, working for several months as a ship's carpenter in Amsterdam. Impressed by the military strength of the western European countries, Peter invited to Russia military experts from the west to train and lead his troops after he became emperor. He bought the artillery of western Europe and copied it. In 1709, when Sweden invaded Russia, Peter was prepared. He retreated until the Swedes fell from the exhaustion of pursuing him through the severe Russian winter. Then, holding his ground at Poltava in south Russia, he defeated the remainder. The Swedish army was finished as an imperial force, and Russia began to seize Baltic possessions.

By 1703-04 Peter had started to build a new capital, an all-weather port and "window on the West," in St. Petersburg. He promoted mining, metallurgy, and textile manufacture, largely as means of supplying his troops. As labor, he used serfs. He created a new system of administration with himself as head. He subordinated the Eastern Orthodox clergy to his own leadership. He created a new "state service," including both civil and military officials, and made appointments to it completely without regard to family status. The move was revolutionary, but it did not survive long after Peter's death. Peter established and edited the first newspaper in Russia. He forced the westernization of the nobility

Bartolomeo Carlo Rastrelli, *The Founding of St. Petersburg, Russia, 1723.* This bronze relief commemorates the founding of St. Petersburg in 1704. Peter the Great intended his capital to be an all-weather port and a "window on the West." As part of his drive for Westernization he decreed that the aristocracy must abandon their Russian dress in favor of European clothes. The garb of the men depicted here indicates clearly that the edict was already in place. (*Hermitage, St. Petersburg*)

and gentry, established schools for their children, and sent many to study in western Europe. He made them abandon their Russian dress in favor of the clothing of western Europe, and forced the men to shave or trim their beards in Western style.

Peter achieved many of his goals, establishing a strong central administration, a powerful military, some commercial enterprise, international trade connections, and diplomatic contact with the nations of Western Europe. He did not, however, free Russia's merchants to carry on the kinds of independent economic activity characteristic of West European commerce. And he kept the largest enterprises, like weapons manufacture and shipping, in the hands of the state. Considered an enlightened despot—a ruler who advanced new concepts of intellectual inquiry and legal rights, at least for the nobility, but who held on to power for himself—Peter died in 1725. Since he had killed his own son rather than permit him to sidetrack reforms, Peter was succeeded for two years by his wife and then by other family members. In 1762 Catherine the Great assumed the throne and ruled for thirty-four years. At least as despotic as Peter,

Catherine won especially important victories over Poles and Turks, expanding the borders of Russia to the Black Sea. After brutally suppressing a revolt by hundreds of thousands of serfs led by Yemelyan Pugachev (1726–75), she reduced Russia's serfs to a position of virtual slavery.

OTTOMANS AND MUGHALS

At the beginning of our period, two enormous empires, the Ottomans and the Mughals, were rising in Asia just as Spain and Portugal were in Europe. Indeed there was some connection. The Ottoman conquest of Constantinople in 1453, and its control of the eastern Mediterranean trade, forced the Atlantic countries to seek new routes to Asia, inspiring Columbus' and Vasco da Gama's voyages of exploration. The Mughals, a land-based empire, began their rise to power a little later, beginning their invasion of India in 1526.

By 1600 all four empires were approaching the height of their powers. By 1700 all were in severe decline because of overextension, draining warfare, weak state systems and lack of attention to technological improvements, especially in the military. All four also allowed control of their economic affairs to fall into the hands of foreigners. By the end of our period, all were subordinated to greater or lesser degree under the power of the newly risen French and British.

The Ottomans did not control their own trade and its profits. At first, because of political alliances with France, only French ships were allowed to trade with the Ottomans. After 1580 trade opened more widely and the English and Dutch entered the trade, along with Jews, Armenians, Venetians, and Genoese. The situation came to resemble Spain's, in which the empire's new riches went into the hands of foreign merchants. A shift in the balance of trade also weakened the central government. The Ottomans imported more manufactured goods and exported more raw materials, increasing the wealth of the landed estate holders and enabling them to break free of central control.

In India, between 1556 and 1605, the Mughal emperor Akbar established one of the great empires of the world. Akbar's administrative reforms brought change in trade and economies as well. Village India joined the cash economy, and city markets encouraged the production of luxury goods for the court and everyday goods for the common people. A series of studies by scholars of the Mughal period, such as Irfan Habib, Shireen

Moosvi, and Hamida Khatoon Naqvi, and by scholars of the early years of British penetration of the Indian markets, notably Tapan Raychaudhuri and Chris Bayly, have examined the workings of these urban markets.

The markets contained a wide array of craftsmen, shopkeepers, and higher level specialists. Moneylenders and moneychangers were active throughout the urban system, enabling the smooth transfer of funds across the empire. Their *hundis* (bills of exchange) were accepted throughout the empire, and these financial instruments facilitated the work of government officials in collecting and transmitting the land revenue in cash. Indian cities boasted very wealthy business financiers and important guild organizations. The guilds, much like the contemporary European guilds, regulated and supervised the major trades in cities. Contrary to popular beliefs sometimes mistakenly held about India as an other-worldly culture, business flourished and prospered. After all, among the multitude of India's castes (see Chapters 8 and 9), were *baniyas* or *vaishyas* who were charged specifically with carrying on business.

Indian traders were highly mobile, and therefore had some independence from the political fortunes of the rulers of the time. If a particular ruler could not defend his territory against foreign invasion, or maintain internal law and order, or tried to extort excessive taxes, the merchant communities left for other cities more amenable to their pursuits. Conversely, rulers who wanted to improve their commercial prospects lured these footloose merchants with offers of free land and low taxes. Thus, even in the event of political decline or catastrophe, India's business might continue.

Indian businessmen continued to carry on coastal and ocean-going trade, but the imperial government could not support these ventures very effectively. They had no navy. In 1686, for example, the English blocked Indian trade between Bengal and Southeast Asia and even seized ships belonging to the officers and family members of the Mughal rulers. The Emperor Aurangzeb replied by land, forcing the English out of their settlement at Hoogli. But the English relocated at a new town, Calcutta, and continued their maritime commerce and armed competition. Furthermore, despite sophisticated economic institutions developed within family-held firms, Indian merchants did not develop impersonal business firms like the European joint stock companies. When the

Merchants with their camel caravans in Asia, 1575. As this French woodcut indicates, the Ottomans allowed the French to trade with them, and camel caravans were used to transport the raw materials and goods to the ships.

Officers of the British East India Company enjoying Indian musicians and dancers, Indian painting, *c.* 1820. One of the European officers smokes a large hookah or pipe. The British East India Company established a trade triangle between China, India, and Britain which made silk and tea available to the English. Increasingly the trading company assumed military and political powers, and by the middle of the eighteenth century it was the *de facto* government in Bengal.

European joint stock companies arrived on the sub-continent, they opened a new scale of overseas operations (see p. 410).

MING AND QING DYNASTIES IN CHINA

The Ming dynasty in China, as we saw in Chapter 12, had largely closed China to foreign trade in favor of developing the internal economy and of defending the northern borders against Mongol and Manchu attack. They repaired the Great Wall and extended it for an additional 600 miles (965 kilometers). Having limited the size and power of their navy, the Ming were harassed by Japanese and Chinese pirates on their coasts. In reply, they avoided the sea and revived the system of inland transportation by canals instead. The pirate attacks increased and became minor invasions of the mainland, even up the Yangzi River. Japanese unification

at the end of the sixteenth century brought the pirates under control, but then Japan invaded Korea in 1592 with the ultimate goal of invading China. Warfare continued for years, mostly within the Korean peninsula, but also within north China, until Japan finally withdrew in 1598.

The Western presence was very limited at this stage. The few Portuguese who arrived in China after 1514 were mostly Jesuit missionaries whose influence was felt far more in the culture of the court than in the commerce of the marketplace. Matteo Ricci (1552–1610), one of the most prominent of the Jesuit missionaries to China, shared with government officials in Beijing his knowledge of mathematics, cartography, astronomy, mechanics, and clocks, while he mastered the Chinese language and many of the Confucian classics. The Jesuits concentrated their efforts on winning the elites of China, and by 1700 some 300,000 Chinese had converted to Christianity.

Despite the shutdown of most international trade, China's economy boomed, at least until about 1600. China, after all, contained one-fifth of the world's population and generated an immense internal economy. The canal system encouraged north–south trade. Using kaolin clay, Chinese artisans created a porcelain more beautiful and stronger than ever. Weaving and dyeing of silk continued and expanded near Suzhou; cotton textiles flourished at Nanjing; Hebei specialized in iron

Portuguese ships and sailors, lacquer screen, Chinese, seventeenth century. The faces of the sailors and the ship itself are not depicted as hostile, although at the beginning of the previous century the Portuguese had been expelled for aggressive actions and by mid century were restricted to the coastal enclaves.

manufacture. In the late Ming period, private sea-going trade with Southeast Asia began to flourish again, often carried by families who had sent emigrants to the region and thus had local contacts. Within China, this trade was regulated by local authorities on the south China coast. Fascinating research by Wang Gungwu on the overseas Chinese merchants suggests that had the Chinese government supported these traders instead of restricting them, they too might have been effective in building overseas merchant empires:

> There is also the difference between merchants barely tolerated by a centralized empire and those whose rulers and governments used them for their imperial cause ... they could, in terms of entrepreneurship and daring, do everything that the various Europeans could do. But they were helpless to produce the necessary institutional change in China to match European or even Japanese power. They were never the instruments of any effort by Ming or Qing authorities to build merchant empires; nor could they hope to get mandarin or ideological support for any innovative efforts of their own.
> (p. 401)

When Europeans came to trade, the Chinese government restricted them to coastal enclaves. The Ming dynasty limited the Portuguese to Macao in 1557 (where they remain until 1999 under agreement with the current Chinese government). By the time the Dutch and British arrived in the 1600s, the Ming had weakened internally and the Mandate of Heaven (see Chapter 7) passed to the Qing, Manchus from north of the Great Wall, who captured the government of China in 1644. The Qing finally secured the southeast coast in 1683. They established the "Canton system," restricting European traders to the area around Canton (Guangzhou), and entrusting their supervision and control to a monopoly of Chinese firms called the Cohong. Because of these restrictions, and because of the vast size of China, the European merchants had little effect on China. The silver they brought, however, enriched the Chinese economy. As noted above (see p. 399), between a third and a half of all the silver of the New World ultimately went to China to pay for purchases of silk, porcelain, tea, and other products. Merchants became wealthy, but the government did not. The quality of the Ming administration grew weaker, undermining the dynasty and preparing an opening for the succession of the Qing (see Chapter 15).

TOKUGAWA JAPAN

The Japanese experience of Europeans united religious and economic aspects. The first to make a significant impact was the Jesuit priest St. Francis Xavier, who arrived in 1549. Like Matteo Ricci in China, he, too, adapted to local cultural practices in dress, food, residence, and, of course, language. For their religious ideas, their culture, and trade, Europeans were at first warmly welcomed. Among their contributions were tobacco, bread, playing cards, and deep-fat frying, which became the Japanese specialty of tempura. Christianity found a foothold in Japan, and by 1614, as in China, there were over 300,000 converts.

The Japanese government, apprehensive about so large a group of elite converts, and consolidating its own power in a new **shogunate**, or military administration, began to crack down. In 1597, after a Spanish ship captain boasted of the power of his king, and after Spain had colonized Manila, the **shogun** Hideyoshi crucified six Franciscan missionaries and eighteen Japanese converts. In 1606 Christianity was outlawed, and in 1614 the new shogun Tokugawa Ieyasu began to expel all Christian missionaries. Three thousand Japanese Christians were martyred. In 1623 the British left Japan; in 1624 the Spanish were expelled; in 1630 Japanese were forbidden to travel overseas. In 1637–8, in reaction to a revolt that was more a rural economic protest than a religious uprising, 37,000 Christians were killed. The Portuguese were expelled. Only a small contingent of Dutch traders was permitted to remain, confined to Deshima Island off Nagasaki. A limited number of Chinese ships continued to visit Japan each year and some diplomatic contact with Korea continued, but Japan chose to live largely in isolation.

As in China, the suppression of contact with outsiders did not cripple Japan. Its process of political consolidation continued under the three Tokugawa family shoguns from the 1600 battle of Sekigahara until 1651. The country was unified and peaceful. Guns were virtually banned. Agriculture thrived as the area of land under cultivation doubled, and the production of cash crops, such as indigo, tobacco, sugar cane, and mulberry leaves as food for silk worms, increased. The population almost doubled, from 18 million in 1600 to 30 million by the mid-1700s, at which point it stabilized temporarily. The new government was in the hands of the **samurai** warrior classes, who made up about 7 percent of the population. They benefited most from the improved conditions, and there were sometimes violent protests against the increasing disparities in income, but standards of living and of education generally improved. City merchants, *chonin*, emerged as a newly wealthy and powerful class, dealing in the new cash commodities of farm and hand manufacture. They supplied banking, shipping, loans, and other commercial services, and founded family businesses, some of which endure today. The Tokugawa capital Edo (Tokyo) grew to a million people by 1700, among the largest cities in the world at the time.

SOUTHEAST ASIA

Southeast Asia was one of the great prizes of international commerce throughout our period, and foreign merchants from China, Japan, India, Arabia, and Europe were active in its markets. Yet the merchants of the region did not themselves become major factors in the international side of the trade.

Foreign traders began their activities on the coast and then moved inland, taking control of local markets. They also fought among themselves. The Dutch East India Company, for example, ousted from the Indonesian archipelago not only the local merchants but also European competitors by 1640. By this time, the spice trade was beginning to level off, and the Dutch were in the process of restructuring the economies of Southeast Asia, especially Indonesia, to produce such commercial crops as sugar, coffee, and tobacco. In the Philippines, the Spanish asserted similar power.

Local rulers entered into commercial agreements with the foreign traders that enriched themselves, but not their merchant communities. Commercial profits were repatriated from Southeast Asia back to Europe, creating ever more serious imbalances of power and wealth. Capitalist enterprise in the hands of merchants, backed by the state and by military power, was radiating outward from Europe; Southeast Asia had become a participant in this new system, and a victim of it.

BIBLIOGRAPHY

Andrea, Alfred and James Overfield, eds. *The Human Record*. (Boston: Houghton Mifflin, 2nd ed., 1994).

Austen, Ralph A. "Marginalization, Stagnation, and Growth: the Trans-Saharan Caravan Trade in the Era of European Expansion, 1500–1900," in Tracy, *The Rise of Merchant Empires*, 311–350.

Bayly, C.A. *Indian Society and the Making of the British Empire* (Cambridge University Press, 1988).

Braudel, Fernand. *Capitalism and Material Life 1400–1800*, trans. by Mirian Kochan (New York: Harper and Row, 1973).

—. *Civilization and Capitalism 15th–18th Century*. Vol. 2: *The Wheels of Commerce*, trans. by Sian Reynolds (New York: Harper and Row, 1986).

—. *Civilization and Capitalism 15th–18th Century*. Vol. 3: *The Perspective of the World*, trans. by Sian Reynolds (New York: Harper and Row, 1986).

—.*The Mediterranean and the Mediterranean World in the Age of Phillip II*, 2 vols, trans. from the French by Sian Reynolds (New York: Harper Torchbooks, Vol. 1: 1972; Vol. 2: 1973).

Cervantes Saavedra, Miguel de. *Don Quixote of La Mancha*, trans. by Walter Starkie (New York: New American Library, 1957).

Chaudhuri, K.N. "Reflections on the Organizing Principle of Premodern Trade," in Tracy, ed., *The Political Economy of Merchant Empires*, 421–2.

—. *Trade and Civilization in the Indian Ocean* (Cambridge: Cambridge University Press, 1985).

Cipolla, Carlo. *Clocks and Culture 1300–1700* (New York: W.W. Norton, 1978).

Columbia University. *Introduction to Contemporary Civilization in the West*, 2 vols. (New York: Columbia University Press, 2nd ed., 1954).

Cross, Harry E., "South American Bullion Production and Export 1550–1750," in J.F. Richards, ed., *Precious Metals in the Later Medieval and Early Modern Worlds*, 397–423 (Durham, North Carolina: Carolina Academic Press, 1983).

Curtin, Philip, Steven Feierman, Leonard Thompson, and Jan Vansina. *African History from Earliest Times to Independence* (New York: Longman, 2nd ed. 1995).

Curtin, Philip D., ed. *Africa Remembered: Narratives by West Africans from the Era of the Slave Trade* (Madison: University of Wisconsin Press, 1967).

—. *The Rise and Fall of the Plantation Complex* (Cambridge: Cambridge University Press, 1990).

Dale, Stephen Frederic. *Indian Merchants and Eurasian Trade, 1600–1750* (Cambridge University Press, 1994).

Das Gupta, Ashin and M.N. Pearson, eds. *India and the Indian Ocean 1500–1800*

(Calcutta: Oxford University Press, 1987).

Ebrey, Patricia Buckley. *Cambridge Illustrated History of China* (Cambridge University Press, 1996).

—. ed. *Chinese Civilization: A Sourcebook* (New York: Free Press, 2nd ed. 1993).

Elvin, Mark. *The Pattern of the Chinese Past* (Stanford: Stanford University Press, 1973).

Fairbank, John K., Edwin O. Reischauer, and Albert M. Craig. *East Asia: Tradition and Transformation*, revised ed. (Boston: Houghton Mifflin, 1989).

Gungwu, Wang, "Merchants without Empire: the Hokkien Sojourning Communities," in Tracy, *The Rise of Merchant Empires*, 400–21.

Habib, Irfan, "Merchant Communities in Precolonial India," in Tracy, *The Rise of Merchant Empires*, 371–99.

Heilbroner, Robert. *The Worldly Philosophers*, 4th ed. (New York: Simon and Schuster, 1972).

Hirschman, Albert O. *The Passions and the Interests*, 20th anniversary ed. (Princeton: Princeton University Press, 1997).

Kathirithamby-Wells, Jeyamalar, "Restraints on the Development of Merchant Capitalism in Southeast Asia before *c.* 1800," in Anthony Reid, ed., *Southeast Asia in the Early Modern Era*, 123–48.

Kennedy, Paul, *The Rise and Fall of the Great Powers* (New York: Vintage Books, 1987).

Klein, Herbert, "Economic Aspects of the Eighteenth-Century Atlantic Slave Trade," in Tracy, *The Rise of Merchant Empires*, 287–310.

Kulke, Harmann and Dietmar Rothermund. *A History of India* (Totowa, NJ: Barnes and Noble, 1986).

Lapidus, Ira. *A History of Islamic Societies* (Cambridge: Cambridge University Press, 1988).

McNeill, William H. "The Age of Gunpowder Empires, 1450–1800," in Michael Ades, ed., *Islamic and European Expansion* (Philadelphia: Temple University Press, 1993), 103–9.

Mauro, Frederic, "Merchant Communities, 1350–1750," in Tracy, *The Rise of Merchant Empires*, 255–86.

Mintz, Sidney W. *Sweetness and Power: The Place of Sugar in Modern History* (New York: Penguin Books, 1985).

Northrup, David, ed. *The Atlantic Slave Trade* (Lexington, MA: D.C. Heath, 1994).

Palmer, R.R. and Joel Colton. *A History of the Modern World* (New York: Knopf, 6th ed., 1984).

Pannikar, K.M. *Asia and Western Dominance 1498–1945: A Survey of the Vasco da Gama Epoch of Ancient History* (London: Allen and Unwin, 1953).

Parker, Geoffrey, "Europe and the Wider World, 1500–1700," in Tracy, ed., *The Political Economy of Merchant Empires*, 161–195.

Pearson, M.N., "Merchants and States," in Tracy, ed., *The Political Economy of Merchant Empires*, 41–116.

Reid, Anthony. *Southeast Asia in the Age of Commerce 1450–1680*. Vol 1: *The Land Below the Winds*; Vol 2: *Expansion and Crisis* (New Haven: Yale University Press, Vol. 1: 1988; Vol. 2: 1993).

—. ed. *Southeast Asia in the Early Modern Era: Trade, Power, and Belief* (Ithaca: Cornell University Press, 1993).

Richards, John F. *The Mughal Empire* (Cambridge: Cambridge University Press, 1993).

Robinson, Francis, ed. *The Cambridge Illustrated History of the Islamic World* (Cambridge: Cambridge University Press, 1996).

Rothermund, Dietmar. *Asian Trade and European Expansion in the Age of Mercantilism* (Delhi: Manohar, 1981).

Schama, Simon. *The Embarrassment of Riches* (New York: Knopf, 1987).

Schirokauer, Conrad. *A Brief History of Chinese and Japanese Civilizations*. (Fort Worth: Harcourt Brace Jovanovich, 2nd ed., 1989).

Smith, Adam. *An Inquiry into the Nature and Causes of the Wealth of Nations* (New York: Modern Library, 1937).

Spence, Jonathan D. *The Memory Palace of Matteo Ricci* (New York: Penguin Books, 1985).

Steensgaard, Niels. *The Asian Trade Revolution of the Seventeenth Century* (Chicago: University of Chicago Press, 1973).

Tawney, R.H. *Religion and the Rise of Capitalism* (New York: Harcourt, Brace, & Co., 1926).

The [London] Times. Atlas of World History, ed. Geoffrey Barraclough (London: Times Books Ltd., 1981).

Thornton, John. *Africa and Africans in the Making of the Atlantic World, 1400–1680* (Cambridge: Cambridge University Press, 1992).

Tracy, James D., ed. *The Political Economy of Merchant Empires* (Cambridge University Press, 1991).

—. ed. *The Rise of Merchant Empires* (Cambridge: Cambridge University Press, 1990).

Wallerstein, Immanuel. *The Modern World System* 3 vols. (San Diego: Academic Press, Inc., Vol. 1:1974; Vol. 2:1980; Vol. 3: 1989).

Weber, Max. *The Protestant Ethic and the Spirit of Capitalism*. Trans. by Talcott Parsons (London, 1930).

Williams, Eric. *Capitalism and Slavery* (Chapel Hill: University of North Carolina Press, 1994).

Wolf, Eric. *Europe and the People without History* (Berkeley: University of California Press, 1982).

Wrigley, E.A. "A Simple Model of London's Importance in Changing English Society and Economy 1650–1750," in Philip Abrams and E.A. Wrigley, eds., *Towns in Societies* (Cambridge: Cambridge University Press, 1978).

PART 6

Migration: Free People and Slaves

1500–1750

"BE FRUITFUL AND MULTIPLY, FILL UP THE EARTH AND SUBDUE IT": DEMOGRAPHIC CHANGES IN A NEW GLOBAL ECUMENE

From the beginning, historians have chosen most frequently to write about great individuals, major institutions, and the politics and wars of particular peoples. In this century, and especially within the past fifty years, historians have begun to examine demographics, that is, human populations viewed collectively and usually represented in quantitative terms. They ask such questions as: When and why do populations grow and decline? What are the impacts on population of disease, war, famine, and more efficient farming methods? We have already touched on some of these issues beginning with the migration of Homo sapiens around the globe. In this part we shall examine demographic data specifically concerned with migration, the movement of large groups of people across geographical space, from one region to another, and between countryside and city.

New topics in the study of the past are often inspired by new experiences in the present. In our own time, demographic shifts are dramatically altering our world, both in the population explosion which has doubled the earth's population in the last thirty years and in the

François Biard, *The Slave Trade*, 1840. (*Kingston-upon-Hull City Museums and Art Galleries*)

migrations of hundreds of millions of people both from one region to another and from rural areas to cities in the process of urbanization. These demographic transformations evoke comparisons with earlier historical eras, especially the period 1500–1750 when the population of whole continents was restructured as new peoples immigrated and native populations perished. At the same time, great capital cities, some of them newly founded, also experienced enormous population growth.

There is another reason for choosing to study aggregate populations instead of individual lives. This is often the closest we can come to understanding the lives of average people. They may not have left written records—most were not literate—so we are not able to know their individual biographies, but through demographic studies of aggregate groups we may be able to gain a better understanding of the societies in which they lived and died.

Finally, new kinds of research often require new kinds of tools; sometimes the research is motivated by the availability of these new tools. Population history requires quantitative information and the statistical tools to work with it. Within the last generation demographers have made great strides in methodology, some of it as a result of new computers and data processing capabilities.

14

CHAPTER

"The world is divided and organized according to the force of numbers, which gives each living mass its individual significance and fixes its level of culture and efficiency, its biological (and economic) rhythm of growth, and its pathological destiny."

FERNAND BRAUDEL

DEMOGRAPHY AND MIGRATION

1500–1750

THE MOVEMENT OF PEOPLES AROUND THE EARTH

This chapter introduces both important migration events and important scholars who have studied them. Among the events are the migrations of conquering nomadic groups as they swept into new lands: the Ottomans, Safavids, and Mughals who invaded and occupied southeastern Europe and western and southern Asia, and the Manchus who invaded and conquered China. We turn to the Americas to see Europeans invade and settle, and later import millions of people from Africa to work as slaves, while up to 90% of native Americans succumbed to new diseases and died. We will find that similar proportions of the indigenous populations died off when European settlers arrived in Australia and New Zealand. The final event we examine is the construction and reconstruction of great national and imperial capitals which drew to them vast numbers of urban immigrants.

DEMOGRAPHY: WHAT IS IT AND WHAT ARE ITS USES?

In this chapter we will touch on the work of four major demographic inquiries. In looking at the consequences of European expansion we will consider first the work of Fernand Braudel, the great French historian of the *longue durée* (historical change over long periods of time), who examined "the weight of numbers," the overall shift in human population from one area of the world to another. Carl Sauer and others of the "Berkeley School" tried to gauge with greater accuracy the death rates of Amerindians as Europeans invaded and migrated to their lands. In our study of the slave trade from Africa to the Americas we will focus on the quantitative study of Philip Curtin. Finally in our examination of the changing demography of London we will draw on the work of E.A. Wrigley and others of the Cambridge [England] Group for the History of Population and Social Structure, who used available population data to analyze major changes in social structures, especially of Europe.

Demographers such as these examine aggregate human populations in quantitative terms. They ask about total population and its components: age groups, gender, household size. They utilize life expectancy and other "vital statistics" such as birth rates, death rates, and marriage rates. They may analyze the average age at marriage; rates of childbirth, legitimacy and illegitimacy; the quantitative impacts on population of epidemics, natural catastrophes, and war; class size and composition. Through large-scale analyses of such data demographers seek to understand and interpret patterns of change and, although the statistics may sometimes seem dry, they tell stories of fundamental structures and changes in human society. Today, in recognition of the importance of these data, most governments gather the information as a matter of course. To find information on earlier periods which lack such systematic official data collection, historians search for other sources. Church registers of birth and death, travelers' estimates of popula-

tions and of catastrophes, ships' records of passengers and cargo, for example, have all proved valuable sources.

ASIAN MIGRATIONS 1250–1600

Between 1400 and 1750, successive waves of new migrants within Asia created three new empires and several new ruling dynasties within already existing empires. Turkish invaders founded the Ottoman, Safavid, and Mughal Empires, while the Manchus in China and the descendants of Genghis Khan in central Asia introduced new dynasties to existing empires.

THE OTTOMAN EMPIRE 1300–1700

The Ottoman Empire, named for Osman whose military victory in 1301 laid its foundation in northwest Anatolia, grew from his small holding to become a world power. It rose to prominence at the same time as Spain and Portugal did in western Europe (see Chapter 13) and was at its height in 1600. By 1700, however, it was in decline. The

Eurasian empires, 1300–1700 Eurasia on the eve of European expansion was dominated by a complex of huge, interlocking, land-based empire states, linked by overland trade routes such as the Silk Road, and by the Arab trading ecumene of the Indian Ocean. Largely sustained by historic momentum and sheer geographic extent, their dynastic and bureaucratic dynamics were inward-looking and ill-prepared for the challenge of European imperialism which would, over the next four hundred years, effectively destroy them.

Ottomans began by expanding outward from their early home in Anatolia, confronting the Byzantine empire to the west and the Seljuk Turks to the east. Through the thirteenth and fourteenth centuries the Ottomans captured much of Anatolia, crossing into Europe to take Gallipoli in 1354. Three groups led and sustained the Turkish invasions: **gazis**, Turkish warriors inspired by Islam to conquer territories and bring them under Dar-ul-Islam, the rule of an Islamic state; **Sufis**, members of religious orders, often practicing mystical and ecstatic rituals, who accompanied the troops and introduced Islam within the conquered regions; and **janissaries**, slaves captured or bought from among the conquered populations, usually from among the Christians of the Balkans, to be converted to Islam and serve in the elite Turkish armies and, occasionally, in the administration. In 1527 the slave infantry numbered about 28,000. In conquering Anatolia, Turks displaced the local agricultural communities and became the majority population.

Having established a foothold in Europe, the Ottomans invited Turkish warriors into the Balkans and occupied northern Greece, Macedonia and Bulgaria. At the Battle of Kosovo in 1389 they secured Serbia, and established control of the western Balkans. Demographically, however, the invaders were not so numerous in this region nor did they force widespread conversion. A census of 1520–30 showed that about one-fifth of the Balkan population was Muslim, about four-fifths was Christian, and there was a small Jewish minority.

Under Mehemmed (Mehmed) II, "The Conqueror" (r. 1451–81), the Ottomans moved on to conquer Constantinople in 1453 and then the remainder of Anatolia, the Crimean on the north side of the Black Sea, and substantial areas of Venice's empire in Greece and the Aegean. They began the process of rebuilding Constantinople into a great capital city, and by 1600 it had become one of the largest cities in Europe, with 700,000 inhabitants. The capital attracted a great influx of immigrant scholars to its **medresses**, religious schools, and its bureaucratic jobs, which required Islamic learning and knowledge of the law.

Selim I (r. 1512–20) defeated decisively the Shi'a Safavid empire in Persia at the 1513 Battle of Chaldiran. Turning next against the Mameluke Empire of Egypt, he conquered its key cities of Aleppo, Damascus, and its capital in Cairo. These victories gave the Ottomans control of the holy cities of Jerusalem, Mecca, and Medina, and of both coasts of the Red Sea. Suleiman (Süleyman) I, "the Magnificent" (r. 1520–66), returned to battle in Europe, adding Hungary to his empire and pushing to the gates of Vienna. As they entered central

Siege of Beograd by Mehemmed II, sixteenth-century Persian manuscript. After the setback of defeat by central Asian conqueror Tamerlane in 1402, the Ottoman Empire rebuilt, consolidated, and extended their power. A major watershed was passed when Sultan Mehemmed II conquered Constantinople (Istanbul) in 1453, making it the third and last Ottomon capital city. This Turkish empire endured for 600 years (1300–1922) and at its height spanned three continents. (*Topkapi Palace, Istanbul*)

Europe, the Ottomans confronted the Habsburg Empire. Alliances here crossed religious lines, with Catholic France sometimes joining with the Muslim Ottomans in alliance against the Catholic Habsburgs. In a series of battles, which collectively formed a kind of world war, the Ottomans were defeated at sea in 1571 at Lepanto off the coast of Greece, by a coalition of the papacy, Venice, and the Habsburgs. Finally, in 1580, a peace treaty confirmed the informal boundaries that endure in the Mediterranean until today between predominantly Christian Europe to the north and west, and predominantly Muslim North Africa and West Asia to the south and east.

Battles on land continued until 1606, when the peace treaty of Zsitva Torok confirmed Ottoman rule over Romania, Hungary, and Transylvania, but recognized the Habsburgs as their equals. Financially and militarily drained by two centuries of warfare with the Habsburgs in the Balkans and southeastern Europe, the Ottomans halted their expansion into these areas in 1606. In 1683, a last attempt to seize Vienna failed. North of the Black Sea, where Russia, Poland and the Ottomans fought, the empire had greater success, taking con-

trol of substantial parts of the Ukraine in 1676. These victories, however, marked the end of Ottoman dominance in the region. Russia, its military power built under Peter the Great and Catherine the Great, pushed the Ottomans back. Throughout the late 1700s, the Ottomans once again brought in Western European experts to retrain their military, but this effort was too little, too late. The Ottoman Empire had fallen too far behind the Western Europeans and the Russians economically and militarily; they could no longer catch up.

Through both immigration and natural increase, the population of the Ottoman empire seems to have more than doubled, from 12–13 million in 1520–30 in the early years of the rule of Suleiman I (a time when Spain may have had 5 million inhabitants; England 2.5 million; Portugal 1 million) to 17–18 million in 1580, to possibly 30–35 million by 1600 (Braudel, *The Mediterranean*, Vol. 1, p. 410). This doubling, or even tripling, of the empire's population was consistent with the general population increase of the Mediterranean basin, which rose from about 30 or 35 million in 1500 to 60 to 70 million in 1600.

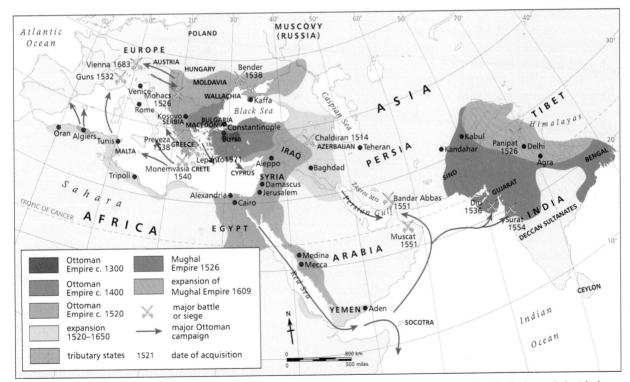

Ottoman and Mughal Empires, 1300–1700 As the Mongols ceased their advance, some of the peoples who had traveled with them began to assert their power. The Ottoman Turks began to establish their new empire, which conquered Constantinople in 1453 and thrust into southeastern Europe as well as the Mediterranean coast. Babur, a Mughal, began the conquest of India in 1526 and his grandson Akbar proceeded to construct one of the largest, most powerful, and most cultured empires of his day.

INDIA: THE MUGHAL EMPIRE
1526–1750

The Mughals, a mixture of Mongol and Turkish peoples from Central Asia, rose to power a little later than the Ottomans, beginning their invasion of India in 1526. Under four generations of commanding emperors—Akbar (r. 1556–1605), Jehangir (r. 1605–27), Shah Jahan (r. 1627–58), Aurangzeb (r. 1658–1707)—they dominated most of the subcontinent, ruling it from splendid capitals which they built in the north, and from mobile tent-cities which they occupied while fighting throughout the subcontinent. Although they continued to rule in name until 1858, the Mughals began to decline as a result of Aurangzeb's extended military campaigns which wasted the financial and human resources of his empire, and also antagonized the Hindu majority population over whom the Mughals, who were Muslims, ruled.

The Mughals were only the most recent of peoples who invaded India. From prehistoric times, India had experienced wave after wave of immigration. Most of the migrants arrived from the northwest, crossing the passes between today's Afghanistan and Pakistan. The Indo-Aryans, who laid the cultural and social foundations of the subcontinent, arrived via this route about 1700 B.C.E. The archaeological evidence as well as their literature suggest that they fought and conquered the resident people of the Indus Valley civilization. Greeks, Scythians, and Huns were among the later immigrant groups who also crossed the passes to make India their home.

In 711–713, in an exception to the usual pattern, Muslim Arabs invaded along the Makran Coast of the Arabian Sea, and conquered and settled Sind. But the great Muslim invasions came overland through the mountain passes from Afghanistan. The Muslim sultan in Afghanistan, Mahmud of Ghazna (971–1030), began the Muslim conquest of India about the year 1000 C.E. A dynasty from Ghur followed in 1186, and one of their generals conquered Delhi in 1206, declaring himself the Sultan of Delhi and beginning three hundred years of the Delhi sultanate. His dynasty and its successors were of the Afghan Turkish elite. The problem for all these rulers, and perhaps for the subcontinent to this day, was how to integrate into a single, stable society the Turkish warlords; the accompanying Muslim scholars, bureaucrats, and holy men; and the Hindu majority population, which often resisted the invaders.

In 1523 Babur (Zahir-ud-Din Mohammad; 1483–1530), a descendant of Timur on his father's side and of Genghis Khan on his mother's side, invaded India and conquered the Delhi rulers. In 1526 he established himself as Sultan. His son, Humayan, was defeated in battles with Afghans and driven out of India, but he fought his way back through Afghanistan and into north India before his death. The task of continuing the conquest and conslidating its administration fell to his son Akbar (1542–1605), perhaps India's greatest ruler.

In a half century of rule, 1556–1605, Akbar established one of the great empires of the world. He extended his dominions over about two-thirds of the subcontinent—from its northwestern base in Afghanistan, Kashmir, Punjab and the upper Ganges, southward to encompass Rajasthan and Gujurat, and eastward all the way through Bengal. His great-grandson, and third successor, Aurangzeb (Alamgir; 1658–1707), continued the conquest almost to the southern tip of the country. But Aurangzeb forsook Akbar's tolerance. He imposed a poll tax on Hindus and desecrated their shrines and statues, antagonizing them and fomenting resentment. Aurangzeb's military adventures in the south overextended his armies and overtaxed the peasantry to the point of revolt. Hindu Marathas in western India and Sikhs in the north, as well as the Afghan Nadir Shah, who invaded from Iran in 1739, rose against the Mughal Empire. By the middle of the eighteenth century, the empire lay weak and open to new invaders from western Europe—the British and the French.

AKBAR'S REIGN:
HOW DO WE KNOW?

A Muslim ruling over a vast Hindu majority, Akbar incorporated into his military leadership many Hindu **rajas**, and brought into his harem the daughters of many Rajput rulers. Two-thirds of his civil and military officers were foreigners: Afghans, Turks, Iranians, Arabs, and others. Between 20 and 25 percent of India's population became Muslim, most through conversion, the rest the product of immigration from outside. The popular religious culture of India, especially of north India, became a mixture of Hindu and Muslim practices. Sufis spread their message in Hindi, a modern derivative of Sanskrit, the sacred language of Hindus. At the same time they inspired the creation of the Urdu (camp) language, which used the syntactical structure of Hindi, the alphabet of Arabic and Persian,

Bullocks dragging siege guns uphill during an attack on Ranthanmbhore Fort, from the *Akbar-Name*, Mughal, 1563. Generally considered the true founder of the Mughal Empire, Akbar recovered the Afghan territory lost by his father and extended his rule over most of the Indian subcontinent. The young emperor laid the foundations for efficient administration, strong economic growth, and the splendid art and architecture of his successors. (*Victoria and Albert Museum, London*)

and a vocabulary of words drawn from Sanskrit, Persian, and Arabic. Akbar, in particular, encouraged cultural **syncretism** and the mixing of groups. In his court, he encouraged representative spokesmen of numerous religions to explain and argue their doctrines; he incorporated Hindus into about one-fourth of his governmental positions; and he himself took Hindu as well as Muslim brides into his harem.

A great conqueror, Akbar spent years on the move with his troops, but he also built new capitals for himself, first at Agra, later at Fatehpur Sikri nearby. With his chief revenue officer, Todar Mal, he established an administrative bureaucracy modeled on a military hierarchy. He surveyed each region of India down to the village level, evaluated its fertility, and thus established the land revenue each was to pay. His administrators collected the payment in cash. These reforms brought village India into a cash economy, while city markets encouraged the production of luxury goods for the court and everyday goods for the common people.

In 1600, at the height of Akbar's rule, the population of India was 140–150 million, with about 110 million contained within the Mughal Empire, about the same population as China and twice that of the Ottoman Empire at its largest. Irfan Habib, Professor of History at the Aligarh Muslim University, arrived at this estimate by analyzing earlier estimates based on land revenue records, which indicated the amount of land under cultivation, as well as other records indicating the tax payments on agricultural production, and then estimating the number of persons needed to cultivate such amounts of land and raise crops of such value. The population increase that occurred all over Afro-Eurasia at this time affected India as well, and Habib estimates the population of the subcontinent in 1800 at about 200 million.

MIGRATION 1370–1930

1370	Tamerlane leads Safavid Persia to victory over Iran, northern India, Anatolia, and northern Syria
c. 1450	Portugal begins to trade in slaves from the West African coast
1500–1770	Around 9.5 million slaves are transported to the Americas
1521–35	Hernán Cortés captures most of Central America and the Yucatán for Spain
1533	Francisco Pizarro defeats Incas; establishes Spanish colony in South America
1565–1605	Akbar establishes Mughal Empire, gaining dominion over two-thirds of India
1600	Ottoman Empire population (c. 30–35 million) has more than doubled in sixty years
1620	*Mayflower* sets sail for New World
c. 1640	Russia gains control over most of North Asia
1652	Dutch settlers set up a base at Cape Town, South Africa
1680–1800	Chinese imperial expansion to most of central Asia
c. 1780	British settlement of Australia and New Zealand begins
1820–1930	50 million Europeans migrate to North and South America, Australia, and New Zealand

SAFAVID PERSIA
1500–1700

In the thirteenth century the Mongols devastated and repopulated Persia. The results were a catastrophic fall in population, income and state revenue. At first they systematically exterminated the populations of the cities they confronted; others, hearing of the massacres, fled. The invading Mongols and Turks settled on the land, reduced to serfdom those who remained behind, and taxed them into poverty. By the end of the century, however, the Mongol forces that remained to settle Persia began to assimilate Persian ways, rebuilding the cities, redeveloping the irrigation works, supporting agriculture and trade, including the silk routes to China, and adopting both the religion of Islam and the culture of Persia, with its monarchical traditions.

In 1370 the successor to the Chaghatay branch of the Mongols, Timur the Lame (c. 1336–1405; Tamburlane or Tamerlane, as Europeans called him), came to power, ruling Iran, and much of northern India, Anatolia, and northern Syria from his capital in Samarkand until his death in 1405.

With this further set of invasions, Turkish peoples came to constitute about one-fourth of Iran's population, which is the ratio today. The Mongol/ Turkish invaders were pastoral peoples, and under their rule substantial agricultural land reverted to pasturage and villagers turned to nomadic existences, farming in valley bottoms and herding sheep in nearby mountain highlands.

Some of the Turks, as well as other ethnic groups in Iran, later came to accept the militantly religious teachings of Shaykh Safi al-Din (1252–1334), whose followers claimed political as well as religious authority. In 1501, after two centuries of Sufi teachings of the word of Safi, Shah Isma'il (1487–1524) declared himself the hidden imam, the long-awaited political/ religious messiah, occupied Tabriz and announced himself the Shah of Iran. Like other Muslim rulers, the Safavids imported slaves from Georgia, Armenia, and Turkish lands to form the core of their armies.

The Safavids found it difficult to bring together the very diverse peoples and interests of Iran. The greatest achievement was by Shah Abbas (1588–1629), who built up the military capacity of the country. He did this, in part, by importing European weapons, equipment, technicians, and advisers, and Asian slave troops. He acquired and built muskets and artillery that were capable of matching the Ottomans'. Abbas also built a great, new capital city at Isfahan. He encouraged trade and commerce there by inviting Armenian merchants as well as many artisans, including ceramicists who could produce "Chinese" porcelains. He invited some Chinese potters to teach Iranians their trade, and some of them remained, settled in Isfahan. Abbas, however, murdered competing religious leaders and groups, including other Shi'a groups as well as Sunnis and Sufis. His successors in the middle of the century gave official sanction to efforts to convert both Jews and Zoroastrians to

Islam by force. But they did not succeed in bringing all the powers of his decentralized realm into a centralized monarchy.

By the end of the seventeenth century, the Safavid army was unraveling, its central administration was failing, regional powers were reasserting themselves, and Iran was in anarchy. Despite the occasional brilliant military conqueror, such as Nadir Shah (1688–1747), another Turkish/ Mongol immigrant who took the throne in 1736, Iran was already moving toward partition, first internally, and later at the hands of Europeans and Russians.

The Defeat of Pir Padishah by Shah Rukh in 1403, Persian, 1420–30. Shah Rukh, son of Timur the Lame, was a direct ancestor of the Safavid Persians. During his reign, he had to deal with several rebellions, including one by the Sarbadars, a brigand community in Khurasan. Leading the decisive charge, Shah Rukh's army commander beheads one of the rebel cavalrymen. (*Victoria & Albert Museum. London*)

CHINA: THE MING AND MANCHU DYNASTIES 1368–1750

In 1211 Genghis Khan invaded and conquered China, destroying the Qin and Song dynasties in the process. His descendants established the Yuan dynasty, which ruled for a century (1271–1368), but the Ming dynasty drove them out and established their own long and successful rule (1368–1644). (See Chapter 12.)

By 1600 China's economy was flourishing and the country contained one-fifth of the world's population, about 150 million people. Ming border policy was to pacify and to accommodate the Mongol peoples of the north. The emperors stationed large numbers of troops there and rebuilt the Great Wall. Ming anxieties were well founded; in 1644 China was again conquered by invaders from the north, and the Jurchen, or Manchus, of Manchuria established a new dynasty, the Qing (1644–1911). The Manchu invasions undercut China's power and sophistication, and contributed—along with natural disasters, virulent epidemics, and the failure of irrigation systems—to a catastrophic fall in China's population. The Mandate of Heaven had surely passed from the Ming.

The Qing expanded the borders of China, more than doubling the size of the country. They conquered and controlled Tibet, Xinjiang, Outer Mongolia and the Tarim Basin, the heartland of the old silk route. One of their most important European contacts was with Russia, and disputes between the two empires were negotiated in the Treaty of Nerchinsk, 1689, the first Chinese–European treaty negotiated in terms of equality. The treaty facilitated trade between China and Russia and delimited their border along the Amur River, although the border between Mongolia and Siberia was not fixed.

The country's population began to grow again in the eighteenth century. This was made possible by the introduction of new crops into China from the New World. Sweet potatoes, for example, were widespread in coastal China by the mid-eighteenth century, while maize and the Irish potato became common in the north and in the southwest at the same time. Peanuts had spread rapidly in south and southwestern China in the late Ming, and were also becoming an important crop in north China by the end of Qianlong's reign (r. 1736–95). All these crops helped to improve the health of China's rural workers and, because the crops also grew well even in poor and hilly land, they enabled the population to increase rapidly.

GLOBAL POPULATION GROWTH AND SHIFT

From 1500–1750 internal developments within Europe itself had begun to shift the balance of

Pirates from the barbarian north. Through the fifteenth and sixteenth centuries, the Ming dynasty was bedeviled by raids and attacks from the Mongols and other barbarian peoples on China's northern frontiers. The Great Wall underwent major reconstruction in this period. Coastal residents, too, were forced to take to their boats to battle the pirates who attacked their settlements. (*Historiographical Institute, University of Tokyo*).

power from Asia to Europe. Many of these developments were discussed in Part 5:

- changing balances of trade;

- increasing powers of the traders in the diaspora cities of trade around the globe;

- increasing power of European nation states and their support for overseas trade;

- shifting of trade to the Atlantic (rather than the Indian) Ocean;

- increasing pace of technological invention in Europe, especially in guns and ships;

- increasing discipline and order within European armies;

- importing of immense quantities of gold and silver from the New World;

- exploiting the labor of millions of slaves taken from Africa to work the plantations of the New World;

- and the inspirational message of aggressive Christianity.

Here, however, our emphasis is on the sheer demographic force of numbers in European expansion, and the creation of "New Europes" worldwide. The shifting weight of numbers helped cause, and also reflected, the shifting power relationships.

Demographers estimate that Europe's population more than tripled between 1000 and 1700, with the greatest growth coming after the Black Plague of 1348–51. The plague killed off perhaps a third of Europe's population, but it soon increased again to its former levels and then continued to multiply. The "New World" provided a new home to some of the increased millions.

Meanwhile, the population of Asia held its own, while that of Africa was reduced, in part by the loss of some 10 million slaves. The native populations of the Americas were decimated, with up to 90 percent of the native Indian populations lost, although numbers were slowly augmented by European migrants. In the most sweeping terms, and based on very high levels of guesswork, the demographic shift in regions of the world is represented by the pie charts below:

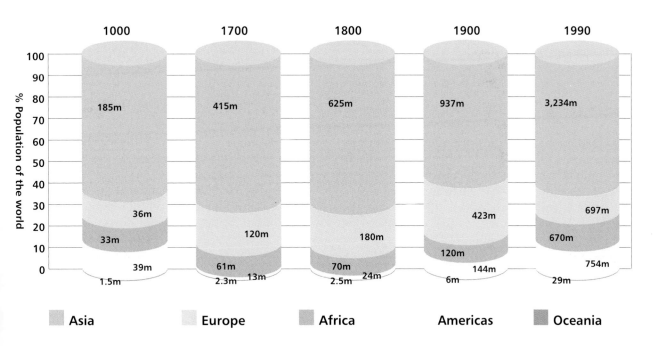

World population growth. From earliest times to around 1600, population growth averaged around 20 per million inhabitants, or 0.002 percent. This growth was far from steady, marked by oscillations dictated by climate, food supply, disease, and war. Between 1650 and 1950, owing to great advances in scientific knowledge, all continents shared in a five-fold population increase. Now crisis looms. Because of greatly increased life expectancy in the developing nations, world population is set to double by the year 2030.

FERNAND BRAUDEL AND THE
ANNALES SCHOOL OF HISTORY

The historian's task of gathering data often requires long hours of solitary research in dusty archives. But in evaluating and interpreting these data, historians engage one another, and sometimes the general public, in discussion and debate. In these processes they sometimes form into "schools," groups of historians who share common perspectives in terms of problems to be addressed or interpretative frameworks to be employed. Some perspectives are so widely shared that they are too large to be labeled as a single school, for example feminist readings that stress the importance of gender relations or Marxist readings that stress the importance of class. Sometimes, however, "schools" form around groups of perhaps five to fifty historians.

In the closing years of the nineteenth century social scientists in France such as the sociologist Emile Durkheim and the geographer Paul Vidal de La Blanche, emphasized the potentials of interdisciplinary study. Each discipline would add its special insights to research on a common problem. Lucien Febvre (1878–1956) and Marc Bloch (1886–1944) built on this perspective in creating the *Annales* school. Both emphasized interdisciplinary study: geography; *mentalités*, the collective perspective of masses of people; and the balance between the individual and the entire society. Both minimized what most other historians of the time considered the core of the discpline:

political history, biography, and international relations.

For example, Bloch's first major work, *The Royal Touch* (1924), examined a belief common in England and France for centuries, until about 1700, that the touch of the king had the power to cure certain diseases. Bloch sought to understand the king's political power in the minds of the people. His most famous work, *Feudal Society*, published in two volumes, 1939–40, synthesized four centuries of European history, 900–1300, examining not only issues of land, hierarchy, and warfare, but also what Bloch called "collective conscience, collective memory, and collective images" in feudal society.

For thirteen years, 1920–1933, Febvre and Bloch served on the faculty of the University of Strasbourg. In January 1929, as joint editors, they founded a new journal of history, from which their "school" took its name, the *Annales d'histoire économique et sociale*. As its name suggests, the journal was dedicated to interdisciplinary history, and included a geographer, a sociologist, an economist, and a political scientist on its editorial committee. The pages of the journal became the intellectual gathering place of the school—a school which soon became the dominant force behind historical studies in France.

Febvre's greatest disciple, Fernand Braudel (1902–85), helped administer the Centre des Recherches

---

Asia held about two-thirds of the world's population, with the proportion actually growing from 63 percent to 69 percent of the total between 1000 and 1800. Europeans, however, increased even faster. They multiplied not only within Europe but, in the words of Alfred Crosby, a leading scholar on the demographic effects of European expansion, they also "leapfrogged around the globe [to found] Neo-Europes, lands thousands of kilometers from Europe and from each other" (Crosby, p. 2). In 1800 North America held almost five million whites, South America about 500,000, Australia 10,000, and New Zealand a few thousand. "These numbers were not yet very large, but they laid the foundation for 'the deluge.' Between 1820 and 1930, well over fifty million Europeans migrated to the Neo-European lands overseas ... approximately one-

fifth of the entire population of Europe at the beginning of that period" (Crosby, p. 5). The number of peoples of European ancestry who settled outside Europe grew from 5.7 million in 1810 to 200 million in 1910. These nineteenth-century figures take us into the times of the Industrial Revolution and its massive transformations, which is covered in the next part, but the demographic spread across the world had already begun by 1800.

The expansion of Europe was not unique in world history, yet it was probably the most numerically sizeable and geographically widespread mass migration ever seen; a migration across vast expanses of water; creating permanent links among continents of the world that had been almost entirely separate; and bringing European dominion over three continents besides its own.

Historiques (set up by Febvre) and publish the journal. After Febvre's death in 1956, Braudel succeeded him in the leadership of both institutions.

Braudel's first great historical work was his study of *The Mediterranean and the Mediterranean World in the Age of Philp II*, in two volumes, first published in 1949. Here Braudel worked out in practice his concept of three time frames always operating simultaneously: most deeply rooted, the *longue durée*, the fundamental conditions of material life, states of mind, natural environment, and geography; the middle time frame of social, economic, and political organization; and the short term, the time of an individual life, the time frame of most conventional historical study of events, or *l'histoire événementielle*. Implementing this concept of diverse time frames, Braudel begins with the physical and human geography of the Mediterranean basin, goes on to its political systems, and ends with the specific policies of Philip II and other rulers of his time. His work revolutionized the way many historians understood their discipline.

For our own purposes in this chapter, Braudel's three-volume study of *Civilization and Capitalism: 15th–18th Century* (1967–1979) is even more important. The first volume sets out such issues of the *longue durée* as global population figures; the everyday food that people ate in different parts of the world; the houses they lived in, the clothes they wore, the fashions they affected; the technology they used; their money and media of exchange; and the cities they built and used. Volume two focusses principally on economic systems, especially in Europe, and, by comparison, elsewhere as well. Volume three follows the transformations of that economy from the establishment of a capitalist system of trade through the beginning of the industrial revolution. Braudel gives us a history of the economy of the world as an integrated whole, though clearly from a European focus. In both of these major works, Braudel omitted the study of popular attitudes, *mentalités*, so important to his mentor Febvre and Bloch, and only in the second edition (1966) did he employ quantification as a significant tool.

Some of the school's influences have already been noted in Chapter 13, for example K.N. Chaudhuri's analyses of Indian Ocean trade, so reminiscent of Braudel's studies of the Mediterranean; Immanuel Wallerstein's studies of the World-System, following Braudel's researches in the global spread of capitalism; and the volumes on merchant trade and empires edited by James Tracy, which build on both studies. Today the school has a multitude of international links with cultural historians such as Peter Burke, Robert Darnton, Natalie Zemon Davis, Carlo Ginzburg, and Lawrence Stone. The influence of the school has spread in the English-speaking world especially since the translation of Braudel's *Mediterranean* in 1972. By now, the contributors to and readers of the *Annales* are so diverse and so integrated with other forms of interdisciplinary history that they have outgrown their distinction as a separate school.

THE EXPANSION OF EUROPE 1096–1750

Some historians trace the modern emigration of Europeans outward for purposes of conquest and settlement back to the series of Crusades that lasted from 1096 until the last crusader kingdom was destroyed in 1291. Those expeditions were declared for religious purposes: to seize and settle the "Holy Land." Trade, however, was an important factor. Along with the military campaigns, Europeans established themselves in commercial centers astride the land and sea silk routes to China; perched on the coast of Africa, where European textiles and metal products were exchanged for gold and slaves; and established trading posts for similar exchanges along the north–south caravan routes crossing the Sahara (see Chapter 12). The spread of Christianity remained a second goal, and most European settlements also housed at least some missionaries.

As we have seen in Chapter 13, in the sixteenth century both Spain and Portugal built enormous global empires based on their sea explorations. The voyages of Columbus revealed to the Spanish crown gold and silver reserves in the Americas. Many Europeans who followed him were prepared to kill native Americans and to take over their lands. Cortés conquered the Aztec nation of Mexico in 1519 and Pizarro the Incas in 1521. The death and destruction were monumental, but warfare was not the greatest killer; disease was even more deadly (see p. 442).

THE COLUMBIAN EXCHANGES OF PLANTS, ANIMALS, AND DISEASE

The peoples of the eastern and western hemispheres had no sustained contact for thousands of years. Columbus's voyages therefore ushered in a new era of interaction. This "Columbian Exchange" brought in its wake both catastrophe and new opportunities. The catastrophe befell the Amerindians who had no resistance to the diseases carried by the Europeans. The new opportunities came with the intercontinental exchange of new plants and animals. Historian Alfred Crosby evaluates both sets of consequences, following the systematic efforts begun by the "Berkeley School" in the 1930s.

Crosby cites the lowest currently accepted estimate of the Amerindian population of 1492 as 33 million, the highest perhaps 50 million. By comparison, Europe at the time had a population of 80 million. The death of millions of Amerindians followed almost immediately after Europeans began to arrive. At their lowest points after the coming of Europeans, the pop-ulations of the western hemisphere dropped to 4.5 million. "The conclusion must be that the major initial effect of the Columbian voyages was the transformation of America into a charnel house" (Crosby, p. 160).

The biggest killers were not guns, but diseases: smallpox, measles, whooping cough, chicken pox, bubonic plague, malaria, diphtheria, amoebic dysentery, and influenza. The populations of the New World, separated by thousands of years and thousands of miles from those of the Old, had little resistance to its diseases. 90 percent of the population died.

Ironically, and more happily, links between the hemispheres also brought an exchange of food sources, which later facilitated the multiplication of human lives. From South America, the cassava spread to Africa and Asia and the white potato to northern Europe. Sweet potatoes traveled to China as did maize, of which China is today the second largest producer after the United States. Today, the former Soviet Union produces ten times more potatoes by weight than does South America; Africa produces almost twice as much cassava as does South America.

The migration of flora and fauna went from east to west as well. Wheat was the leading Old World crop to come to the New World, but perhaps an even greater contribution came in domesticated animals: cattle, sheep, pigs, and goats. Domesticated horses, too, were imported from the Old World to the New. In the long run, these exchanges of food sources did much to increase the population of the world more than ten times, from about 500 million in 1492 to about 5.5 billion today. But not everyone participated in this growth. There were demographic winners and losers. Peoples of the European continent in 1492 were the biggest winners; Asians generally did well; Amerindians were among the biggest losers.

The migration of disease. Aztec victims of the smallpox epidemic of 1538 are covered in shrouds, as two Indians (right) lie dying.

By the early 1600s, however, Spanish supremacy was being challenged by the Dutch Republic, England and France. All three had developed expertise in the construction of high quality ships, and all three fostered business groups skilled in trade and motivated by profit, with strong ties to political leadership. At first, all three concentrated on the Caribbean, and its potential for profits from plantations. They seized and settled outposts: England most notably in the Bahamas and Jamaica, France in Saint-Domingue (today's Haiti), and the Dutch along the Brazilian coast and in Curaçao. Later they turned to the North American mainland. The British founded numerous, thriving colonies along the Atlantic Coast, from Newfoundland to South Carolina, and inland on Hudson's Bay. The French settled, lightly, the inland waterways of the St. Lawrence River, the Great Lakes, and the Mississippi River, as well as Gulf Coast Louisiana. During the global warfare between Britain and France, 1756–63, British military forces conquered the North American mainland from the Atlantic to the Mississippi. Their victory ensured English-speaking North America. French cultural influences and migration, however, continued strong in the region of Quebec, and have maintained a French-speaking province there until today. But attention was also turned to the Antipodes and South Africa, and it is at these countries that we will look in our consideration of European migration and its effects.

EUROPEAN MIGRATION TO NORTH AMERICA

1565	Spanish settle in Florida
1604	Nova Scotia settled by French
1607	First permanent English settlement at Jamestown, Virginia
1608	"New France" in Canada settled by French
1611	Dutch settle on Manhattan Island
1620	*Mayflower* sails from Plymouth, England, with Pilgrim Fathers to found first colony in New England, at Plymouth, Massachusetts
1622	Maine settled by English
1624	New York settled by Dutch
1629	Massachusetts settled by Massachusetts Bay Co.
1634	English Catholics found Maryland
1635–8	Connecticut settled by English
1638	Rhode Island settled by groups from Massachusetts
1638	Delaware settled by Swedes
1663	Carolina settled by English
1670	Rupert's Land claimed by Hudson Bay Co.
1681	Pennsylvania settled by English Quakers
1682	French claim Mississippi area
1713	British sovereignty over Newfoundland recognized

THE ANTIPODES: AUSTRALIA AND NEW ZEALAND 1600–1900

Crossing the Atlantic became relatively quick and easy, but reaching Australia and New Zealand, on the opposite side of the globe, was quite a different matter. Even their neighbors had established only minimal contacts with them. There had been some landings by Asians in the sixteenth century on the north coast. They came in search of a sea slug, which looked like a withered penis when smoked and dried and which was Indonesia's largest export to the Chinese, who valued them as an aphrodisiac.

Spanish copies of Portuguese charts suggest that Portuguese sailors had landed on and mapped the northern and eastern coasts of Australia, and that the Spanish may have known about them, but no continuing contact resulted. In the early 1600s, a few Dutch sailors reached parts of the coast, several wrecking their ships in the process. Between 1642 and 1644, under commission from the Dutch East India Company, the Dutch commander Abel Tasman (c. 1605–59) began the systematic exploration of New Zealand, the island that was later named Tasmania, and the north coast of Australia. He reported "naked beach roving wretches, destitute even of rice … miserably poor, and in many places of a very bad disposition" (cited in Hughes, p. 48). With such unpromising descriptions reaching England, and the general decline of Spanish, Dutch, and Portuguese power, Australia remained virtually untouched by Europeans for a century and a half.

In 1768, the English Captain James Cook (1728–79) set out on a three-year voyage, which took him to Tahiti to take astronomical observations; to Australia to determine the nature of the "Southern Continent" reported by Tasman; to map New Zealand; and, thanks to the zeal of a young amateur botanist, Joseph Banks, to report on the natural resources of all these distant lands. The success of Cook's three-year voyage was made possible by discoveries of proper food supplements to prevent scurvy among the sailors and of new instrumentation to chart longitude and thus establish location at sea. Cook's descriptions of the people he encountered in Australia differed markedly from those of Tasman:

> in reality they are far happier than we Europeans, being wholy unacquainted not only with the superfluous but the necessary conveniencies so much sought after in Europe, they are happy in not knowing the use of them. They live in tranquility which is not disturb'd by the Inequality of Condition. (Hughes, p. 54)

On the basis of Cook's report, the British government decided that Australia could serve as the "dumping ground" it had been seeking for the prisoners who were overcrowding the jails at home. British settlement in Australia thus began in the form of penal colonies, first at Botany Bay and then at other points along the southeast coast, the best watered and most fertile part of Australia. Because mountains flanked close against the coast and fresh water was scarce, progress inland was problematic, and settlement by Europeans was slow, based on commercial agriculture in wool, dairy cattle, and sugar cultivation. In the 1850s and again in the 1890s, however, gold was discovered and newcomers rushed in. The advent of faster shipping stimulated wheat exports, and refrigeration increased the frozen meat trade after 1880. Even so, the population in 1861 was only 1,200,000; by 1901 it had climbed to 3,800,000.

The coming of Europeans, even in small numbers, destroyed the fragile ecology of aboriginal civilization. It survived only in the center and far north. In 1788, when Europeans first arrived to settle Australia, there had been perhaps 300,000 aborigines. By 1990, the 16.6 million inhabitants of Australia were 95 percent European, 4 percent Asian, 1.2 percent aboriginal (*World Almanac*, p. 737). Today, most of Australia's 50,000 full-blooded aborigines, and many of its 150,000 part-aborigines live on reservations in arid inland regions.

The devastation caused by the arrival of British settlers was repeated in New Zealand. The Maori, an East Polynesian people, had arrived and settled New Zealand about 750 C.E. They had lived there for almost a thousand years, probably in isolation, until Tasman, sailing past Australia, reached New

Captain James Cook's crew refitting H.M.S. *Endeavour* **at the Endeavour River on the East Coast of Australia, June 1770.** In the course of his great explorations of the South Pacific Ocean, Cook made the first European landing on Australia, which he claimed for Britain under the name of New South Wales. Convicts were later banished in droves to the new colony to ease overcrowding in British jails.

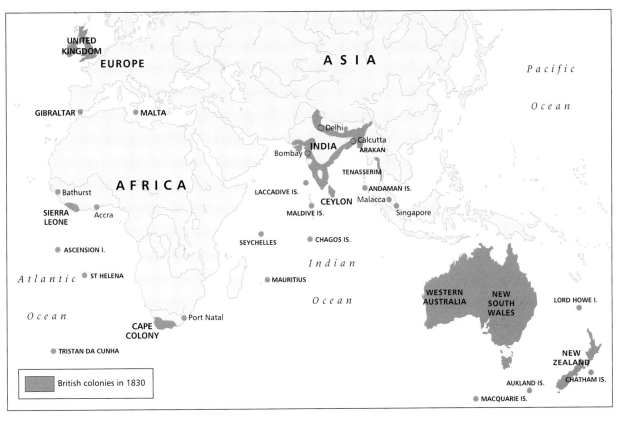

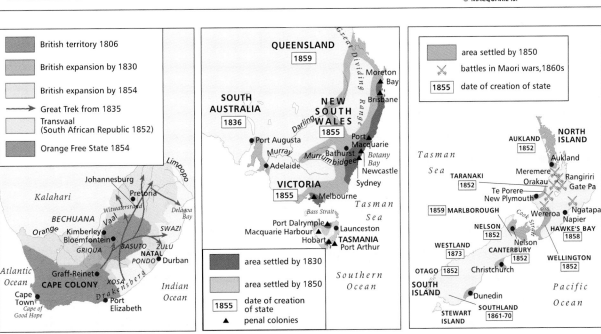

British settlement in Australia, New Zealand, and South Africa British expansion in the scramble for empire, driven by land hunger and mineral wealth, was unparalleled. Outside the riches of India, British colonists ousted the Dutch from Cape Colony, grasped the habitable littoral of southeast Australia (initially colonizing it with prisoners and other social outcasts), and laid claim to the world's most southerly inhabitable territory, New Zealand, as a promised land for its burgeoning early nineteenth-century population.

Zealand's west coast in 1642. The Maori killed four members of his party and prevented his landing. On his voyage more than a century later, James Cook further explored New Zealand for four months and found the Maori brave, warlike, and cannabalistic. Joseph Banks, the botanist who was on the voyage, wrote: "I suppose they live intirely [sic] on fish, dogs, and enemies" (Hughes, p. 52).

The people may have been fierce, but the seals and whales in the coastal waters, and the flax and timber on land, attracted hunters and traders from Australia, America, and Britain. The first missionaries came in 1814 to convert the Maori. Warfare against and among the Maori was made more deadly by weapons introduced by Europeans. Diseases accompanying the European arrival, especially tuberculosis, venereal diseases, and measles, cut the Maori population from about 200,000 when Cook arrived to perhaps 100,000 in 1840 and to 42,000 by the end of the century. In 1840, British settlers signed a treaty with a group of Maori chiefs that gave sovereignty to the British crown. Although they declared equal rights under law for Maoris and Europeans, in practice they enforced racial inequality. The British confiscated Maori lands on North Island and precipitated wars that drove the Maori from some of New Zealand's richest lands.

SOUTH AFRICA 1652–1902

Today, four-fifths of South Africa's 40 million people are non-whites; the remaining 8 million are of European ancestry. The first European settlers were sent by the Dutch East India Company in 1652 to set up a base at Cape Town for shipping between Europe and Asia. The Company soon invited Dutch, French, and German settlers to move inland and to establish ranches in Cape Colony. By 1700, the Europeans held most of the good farmland in the region; by 1795, they had spread 300 miles north (480 kilometers) and 500 miles (800 kilometers) east of Cape Town. The colony then had a total population of 60,000, of which one-third were whites. Most of the African peoples were of two main ethnic groups—the Khoikhoi herdsmen and the San hunters—with some slaves from other African groups, and some peoples of mixed ancestry.

In 1795, the British took control of the Cape Colony from its Dutch settlers to prevent it from falling to France, which had conquered Holland during the Wars of the French Revolution (see Chapter 15). In 1814, the Dutch formally gave the Cape to the British, and the first British colonists came in 1820. The struggle for land and power among the British, Dutch, and Africans is discussed in Chapter 16.

Captain Hobson signing the Treaty of Waitanga with Maori chiefs, 1840. The treaty was intended to secure the annexation of New Zealand to the British government, while securing the constitutional rights of the Maoris. But language difficulties and cultural differences caused misinterpretation of the fine print and the settlers' sense of racial superiority over the "natives" eventually precipitated wars and the forfeiture of Maori lands.

New Sidbury, Cape Province **by Thomas Baines, *c.*1837.** After the British took control of the Cape Colony in 1795, the Boers, or Dutch settlers, became aggrieved when their African slaves were freed (1833) and lands formerly annexed by them were returned to African tribes (1836). To evade British control, Boer families moved north in large groups. This migration—or Great Trek—came to stand as a symbol of their independent spirit, and they view it as one of the most important events in their history.

SLAVERY: ENFORCED MIGRATION 1500–1750

Most of the migrations of Europeans discussed so far were of free peoples, who moved by choice. But throughout the seventeenth and eighteenth centuries, Africa contributed more immigrants to the New World than did Europe. These Africans came as slaves, taken as captives and transported against their will.

The slave trade was not new. As we have seen in Chapter 12, camel caravans had carried gold and slaves northward across the Sahara, and European cotton and woolen textiles, copper, and brass southward from the Mediterranean since about the seventh century C.E. On its east coast, Africa had been long integrated into the Indian Ocean trade by Muslim and Arab traders. They exported from Africa gold, slaves, ivory, and amber and imported cotton and silk cloth.

Portuguese and later European trading re-oriented the trade routes of Africa to the Atlantic coast. Caravans continued to cross the desert, but far more trade now came to the new town fortresses, which were constructed at such places as St. Louis, Cape Coast, El Mina, São Tomé Island, Bonny, Luanda, and Benguela. Here, Africans brought gold and slaves to trade to the European shippers. The number of slaves rose from under a thousand a year in 1451–75, when Portugal began to trade in slaves from the West African coast, to about 7,500 a year in the first half of the seventeenth century, to about 50,000 a year throughout the eighteenth and first half of the nineteenth centuries. In all, the trans-Atlantic slave trade carried some 10 million people from Africa to the Western Hemisphere to work as slaves, generally on sugar, tobacco, and cotton plantations.

The slaves took on economic importance in direct proportion to the expansion of the sugar plantation economy of the Caribbean after 1650. In the 1700s, the plantations reached their maximum productivity and profitability. Between 1713 and 1792 Great Britain alone imported £162 million of goods from the Caribbean, almost all of it sugar. This was half again as much as all British imports from Asia during the same period. France held the richest single sugar colony in the Caribbean, Saint-Domingue in Haiti (see Chapter 15).

HOW MANY SLAVES?
HOW DO WE KNOW?

The landmark study on the demographics of the slave trade remains Philip Curtin's *The Atlantic Slave Trade: A Census*, published in 1969. Curtin read carefully the existing estimate of the number of slaves carried from Africa to the New World and concluded that it had been hastily accepted with little basis in research. Leading authorities on slavery, including Basil Davidson, Roland Oliver, J.D. Fage, and Robert Rotberg, had attributed their estimate of 15 million slaves landed in the Americas to the work of R.R. Kuczynski. Kuczynski, however, had

cited W.E.B. DuBois, who in turn had cited Edward E. Dunbar. And who was Dunbar? Curtin characterizes him as "an American publicist of the 1860s" who had written an article, "History of the Rise and Decline of Commercial Slavery in America, with Reference to the Future of Mexico," combining his concerns with the politics of America on the eve of the Civil War and of Mexico just after its War of Reform. Were Dunbar's figures accurate? Curtin replies, "The estimates were guesses, but they were guesses educated by a knowledge of the historical literature." The problem for Curtin was that none of the eminent scholars who had accepted Dunbar's estimates had ever done the research necessary to

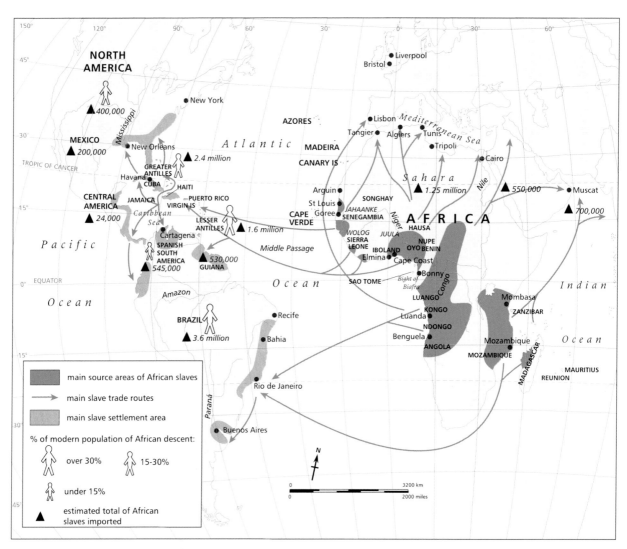

The African Slave Trade A trade in sub-Saharan African slaves dated from the Roman Empire, and had been lucratively developed by Arab merchants from the eighth century. But the impact of Western European entrepreneurs, seeking cheap labor for the Americas, was unparalleled. The millions of Africans who survived the Middle Passage by boat from Africa to the Americas between about 1550 and the late nineteenth century formed a new African diaspora in the New World.

evaluate them. Curtin undertook this task. He limited himself to data already published rather than undertaking original archival searches of his own, but these records did include import records of specific African and American ports, shipping records, and projections based on historical slave populations in the Americas. On this basis, Curtin produced the first systemic analysis of the quantity of slaves from Africa landed in the Americas.

First he analyzed the structure of the plantation economy that produced the sugar, and stresses six key points:

- it relied on slave labor;

- it was organized as an early large-scale capitalist enterprise with gangs of laborers;

- its owners held "feudal," legal rights over the workers;

- it supplied a crop for export to distant European markets but often did not even grow its own food; it was completely reliant on international trade for profits and for necessities;

- "political control over the system lay on another continent and in another kind of society" (Curtin);

- in its organization, the sugar plantation was a forerunner of factory labor.

Curtin begins his analysis with the importation of slaves into Europe, including Sicily, Portugal, Spain, and Italy, as well as to the sugar-producing islands off the coasts of these countries. Evaluating and revising the statistics of previous demographers for the period 1450–1500, Curtin estimates that 50,000 Africans were imported as slaves into Europe and 25,000 into the Atlantic islands of Madeira, Cape Verde, and the Canaries. Another 100,000 were transported off the African coast to São Tomé.

Based primarily on the records of *asientos*, licenses issued to foreign firms between 1521 and 1773 and, later, government records, especially from Great Britain, Curtin estimates that up to 1865 the entire import of Africans to Spanish America was 1,552,000, with 702,000 of these going to Cuba. For the entire period from 1640 to 1807 (when the British outlawed the slave trade), Curtin estimates that 1,665,000 people were imported as slaves to the

British West Indies. To the French West Indies between 1664 and 1838, Curtin estimates that 1,600,200 were imported and that in Portuguese America, these numbers were more than double. To Brazil alone, with its massive sugar plantations in Bahia, Curtin accepts the estimates of two earlier demographers of about 3,646,800. To the Dutch West Indies, 500,000 people were imported as slaves; to the Danish West Indies, now the American Virgin Islands, 28,000. Imports of people as slaves from Africa to the United States and pre-1776 North America totalled about 399,000.

Thus, Curtin's 1969 estimate for the total importation of slaves to the Americas was 9,566,000. Overall, "more Africans than Europeans arrived in the Americas between, say, 1492 and 1770" (p. 87). Curtin noted that, although his estimates could well be off by as much as 50 percent, they are, nevertheless, "correct enough to point out contra-

Slavery—Key Events

1619	First black slaves land in an English colony (Virginia)
1680–1786	Estimated 2 million slaves shipped from Africa to the West Indies
1787–1804	Northern states of US abolish slavery
1790	Estimated 70,000-plus slaves shipped in single year
1791	Insurrection in Haiti against French colonizers led by Toussaint L'Ouverture
1804	Haiti achieves independence from foreign rule
1816–92	Some 22,000 freed slaves from the US settle in Liberia
1833	Slavery abolished in British Empire
1851–2	Harriet Beecher Stowe (1811–96) writes *Uncle Tom's Cabin*, which inspires US abolitionists
1865	Slavery abolished in United States after Civil War
1886	Slavery abolished in Cuba
1888	Slavery abolished in Brazil

dictions in present hypotheses and to raise new questions for comparative demography and social history" (p. 93)

One of Curtin's findings, for example, is that the USA and Canada imported only 4.5 percent of all the slaves imported into the Americas, about 400,000 out of 9,566,000.

> Rather than sustaining the regular excess of deaths over births typical of tropical America, the North American colonies developed a pattern of natural growth among the slaves … By the end of the eighteenth century, North American slave populations were growing at nearly the same rate as that of the settler populations from Europe … Historians have neglected [this] almost completely, even though it has an obvious and important bearing on such recent historical problems as the comparative history of slavery in the New World. Nor have demographic historians yet produced a complete or satisfactory explanation of this phenomenon. (p. 73)

The sex ratio of men to women among African-Americans sustains the argument that North American slave owners must have treated their human property in ways that allowed them to live and reproduce, in contrast to slave owners resident in the Caribbean:

> Since many more men than women were shipped from Africa in the illegal slave trade [a ratio of about two to one], substantial imports would have influenced the sex ratio of the North American slave population. Yet, the census of 1861 actually shows the number of Negro women slightly exceeding the number of Negro men in the United States … Contrary to the parochial view of history that most North Americans pick up in school, the United States was only a marginal recipient of slaves from Africa. The real center of the trade was tropical America, with almost 90 percent going to the Atlantic fringe from Brazil through the Guianas to the Caribbean coast and islands. (p. 74)

Curtin's work initiated continuing statistical research. Paul Lovejoy's careful study, published in 1982, generally supported Curtin. Lovejoy indicated that the distribution of ports of departure and ports of arrival may need some re-examination, but "My synthesis of the partial totals supports Curtin's total estimate for imports into the Americas and the islands of the Atlantic basin" (in

Northrup, p. 55). Joseph Inikori suggests increasing Curtin's estimate to the range of 12 to 20 million, but a reply by David Henige, in his essay "Measuring the Immeasurable," calls into question Inikori's use of suspect estimates and excessive extrapolation from them. The debate continues, but we now have a clear, empirical basis for understanding the dimensions of three centuries of Atlantic trade in human beings.

Two more demographic issues have followed Curtin's *Census*. First, historians seek to locate the geographical source of slaves exports from Africa. Lovejoy, for example, finds that of the 5.5 million exported in the hundred years between 1701 and 1800, the three largest sources were west central Africa, with 2 million, the Bight of Biafra, with 814,000, and the Senegambia, with 201,000 (Lovejoy, p. 50).

After a careful assessment of the locations of the trade along the coast, Curtin sees the law of supply and demand at work, creating cycles of rising and falling prices. When slaves were plentiful, often because of warfare and the seizing of captives who could be sold into slavery, prices fell; then more European slavers arrived to take advantage of the low prices, increasing demand raising prices, and encouraging European slavers to look elsewhere. The marketplace shifted as prices oscillated. The result seems to be that no area was constantly a supplier, but that each area had time to recover some of its population losses. Curtin also points out that only about one-third of the slaves sold overseas were women, so that population losses to the next generation were somewhat limited.

With the second demographic issue historians examine new sources and new methods of obtaining cheap, highly controlled labor employed by plantation owners after the slave trade was abolished and suppressed, beginning with legislation in Great Britain in 1807. As Curtin points out, the British and French developed schemes to coerce Africans to emigrate to the West Indies. Asia also became a source of supply. Between 1845 and 1914, nearly 450,000 contract workers emigrated from India to the British West Indies and French Caribbean. Private planters, with the cooperation of the government of British India, also began developing systems of indentured, contract labor to bring workers from India to the Indian Ocean (French) colonies of Mauritius and Réunion. The Dutch brought Javanese workers to their plantations in Surinam. Cuba imported some 150,000 Chinese contract workers between 1849 and 1875.

REINTERPRETING THE SLAVE TRADE: WHAT IS ITS SIGNIFICANCE?

From the fifteenth to nineteenth centuries, many individual states were taking form on the African continent. The largest, like the Songhay empire of West Africa, was about the size of France or Spain. Medium-sized states, the size of Portugal or of England, were more numerous, including the Oyo Empire in Nigeria, Nupe, Igala, and Benin in the lower Niger Valley, the Hausa states of northern Nigeria, and Kongo, in central Africa. Slavery and the slave trade were important to the rise and decline of these states. First, in a region where land was not privately owned, slaves represented the main form of wealth. A rich state held many slaves. Second, the slaves were a source of labor, a means of increasing wealth. Third, the trade in slaves was a means of still further increasing wealth, either for the state itself or for private traders.

A turn-about in the interpretation of the slave trade is underway. Africans are emerging as active businessmen who helped build up this important trade. John Thornton's revisionist study, *Africa and Africans in the Making of the Atlantic World, 1400-1640*, surveys the early years of the trade, before it became a flood, and stresses this African commercial participation. Long before Europeans arrived on the Atlantic coast, slavery was big business in Africa. When European traders offered new opportunities, African businessmen joined in, continuing to control the trade up to the water's edge.

My examination of the military and political relations between Africans and Europeans concludes that Africans controlled the nature of their interactions with Europe. Europeans did not possesss the military power to force Africans to participate in any type of trade in which their leaders did not wish to engage. Therefore all African trade with the Atlantic, including the slave trade, had to be voluntary. Finally, a careful look at the slave trade and the process of acquisition of slaves argues that slaves had long been used in African societies, that African political systems placed great importance on the legal relationships of slavery for political purposes, and that relatively large numbers of people were likely to be slaves at any one time. Because so much of the process of acquisition, transfer, and sale of slaves was under the control of African states and elites, they were able to protect themselves from the demographic impact and transfer the considerable social dislocations to poorer members of their own societies. (p. 7)

Europeans possessed neither the military strength nor the immunity to disease to enter the interior of the continent. They stayed in coastal enclaves, while Africans captured the slaves and brought them to be purchased. Occasionally, African rulers attempted to limit the trade, but both African and European traders seemed beyond their control.

The lure of profit increased as the demand for slaves multiplied in the next two centuries. Some of the trading communities of Africa, ethnic groups that traditionally facilitated and controlled trade,

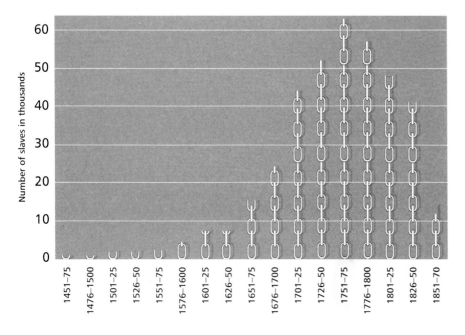

Growth trends of the Atlantic slave trade. Despite fluctuations in the early seventeenth and early nineteenth centuries, the graph shows a remarkably constant long-term average rate of growth—2.2 percent—in the number of slaves imported annually. By the 1790s, slave populations in North America were increasing at the same level as that of settler populations from Europe. (Source: Curtin, *The Atlantic Slave Trade*)

SPOTLIGHT

Slavery:

THE PLANTATION SYSTEM

Artistic representations of slavery and the slave trade carry their own editorial comment. W. Clark's "Ten Views of Antigua" (1823), from which **picture 1** is taken, presents the plantation system under a bright blue sky. Two images predominate: the white gentleman making his rounds upon his horse, benignly tipping one of his charges, and the long line of cane cutters stretching

as far as the eye can see. The healthy-looking workers resemble free employees more than slaves. Harvesting appears as hard, productive labor, performed by strong, surprisingly heavily clothed workers. Two overseers, one in the lower right and another near the center of the painting, convey an impression of careful management and tight, almost industrial organization.

The Slave Trade (**picture 2**), by François Biard, paints a very different, deeply disturbing picture, deliberately emphasizing the sadism of traffic in humans, as people are inspected, purchased, branded, and whipped. To the rear right of the market, located on the African coast, are shackled rows of slaves awaiting their turn on the block. This scene has little to do with economic productivity; to the

Picture 1 W. Clark, *Slaves Fell the Ripe Sugar, Antigua*, 1823.

extent that economics is involved in this view of slavery, it is in the intense bargaining over the price of the slave in the center of the picture who is bound, prodded, and whose teeth are being checked by a crew member. The artist's purpose is to criticize the brutal indifference toward human suffering that was an intrinsic part of the slave trade. Many of the slaves are women, especially those undergoing the most brutal treatment and responding with the most pain, and an overwhelming undercurrent of sadistic sexuality permeates the image. Whites are not alone in enjoying the infliction of pain. Blacks and whites are equally intent on bargaining over the price of the bound slave in the center; and while a white man brands one female slave, a black man whips another. Despite its touches of voyeurism and pornography, the entire system of slavery here stands condemned unequivocally.

To the left of the painting, slaves are forced on board ships that would carry them across the Atlantic to the plantations of the

Picture 2 François Biard, *The Slave Trade*, 1840.

Caribbean and North America. The "tight packing" of the slave ship *Brookes* in 1789, depicted here in a drawing from the time (**picture 3**), condemns the slave trade by straightforwardly exposing a different side of its economics. The desire to use every inch of space for transporting live human cargo saw human beings squashed together so tightly that they hardly had room to turn over. Each man was allowed a space 6 feet long by 16 inches wide, and usually 2½ feet high; each woman 5' 10" by 16"; each boy 5' by 14"; each girl 4'6" by 12". So densely packed were the ships that contagious diseases spread like wildfire, leading to significant loss of life, and later the shippers were forced to reduce the crowding. Objective descriptions of the conditions of the slave trade, such as this one, helped inspire its abolition in England in 1807.

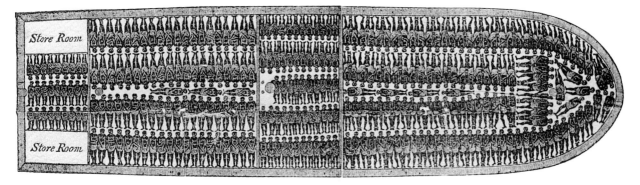

Picture 3 Copper engraving of *Brookes* slave ship, Liverpool, 1789.

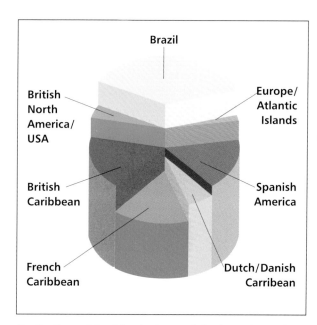

Destinations of the Atlantic slave trade by importing regions 1451–1870. The historian Philip Curtin estimated that 9.5 million slaves were imported to the Americas alone, with the largest number being shipped to Brazil to work its huge sugar plantations in Bahia. (Source: Curtin, *The African Slave Trade*)

probably profited, including the Jahaanke of the Gambia–River Niger region; the Juula of northern Ghana, Côte d'Ivoire, and Upper Niger River; the Wolof of Senegal; and the Awka and Aro of Iboland in Nigeria. A new community of African– Portuguese traders was also born as Portuguese and Africans along the coast bonded and had children.

The effects of the slave trade on the total economy of Africa remain much disputed. Some scholars, following the pioneering work of Walter Rodney in his *How Europe Underdeveloped Africa* (1972), continue to cite dire economic consequences. Some more recent writers, however, like David Eltis, suggest that the slave trade, despite its enormous absolute size, was small relative to the total size of Africa's population and internal economy. This debate over size and significance continues.

No one, of course, can estimate the lost opportunities for African development represented by the export of so many millions of its strongest and most resilient men and women. Crosby points out ironically that, as part of the Atlantic exchange, Africa received new crops such as maize, manioc, and cassava, which became staple foods and may actually have increased the population more than the export of population depleted it. And, of course, slavery established a new population of African Americans throughout the Western Hemisphere.

CITIES AND DEMOGRAPHICS

Studies of population movement analyze not only migration across global regions, but also the movement from rural to urban areas, and from one urban area to another. Because cities serve as centers for rule, administration, economic production, trade, and cosmopolitan philosophy and art, migration into (or out of) the cities tells us something of the transformation of society. Here, we combine demographic data with our information on the nature of the city or cities under study to assess these transformations. The movement from nomadic to urban society is one of the most striking examples.

As we know from Part 2, we expect urban occupations, diversity of population, and rates of innovation to be very different from those of the countryside. What then was happening in the various regions of the world we have been examining in terms of rural–urban movement? Although an examination of capital cities is not decisive, it is informative, especially for an era in which specific accurate population data may not be available. We expect, however, that capitals of strong states will attract large and vibrant populations.

DELHI/SHAH JAHANABAD

Each Mughal emperor built his own capital. The sultans immediately preceding them had ruled from Delhi. Akbar ruled primarily from Agra, about 100 miles (160 kilometers) south of Delhi, but in 1569 he built a new capital, about 20 miles (32 kilometers) away, at Fatehpur Sikri to honor a Sufi saint who had prayed there for a male heir for the emperor. By the end of the century, however, a shortage of water at the beautiful, architecturally eclectic capital forced Akbar to abandon the city and return to Agra. His son, Jahangir, preferred to rule from Lahore and built up that Punjabi city as his capital. Akbar's grandson, Shah Jahan, rebuilt Delhi as his own capital and gave it his own name.

Built in a semicircular shape, with a radius of 10–12 miles (16–20 kilometers), Shah Jahanabad apparently had a population reaching 2 million. As a newly rebuilt city, almost all its residents were economic migrants. The merchant and artisan population, in particular, was composed of foreign merchants such as Armenians, Persians, Central Asians and Kashmiris.

Stephen Blake in his study *Shahjahanabad* describes the Delhi of Shah Jahan as recapturing the spirit of imperial authority vested in it over cen-

IBN KHALDUN ON URBAN LIFE IN THE FOURTEENTH CENTURY

The process of transition from nomadic to sedentary and urban forms, and the "softening" of the invaders that had occurred, had been remarked upon by the great social philosopher Ibn Khaldun of Tunis (1332–1406) in his observations of contemporary Arab life. Ibn Khaldun presents an early philosophy of the flowering and decline of civilization. Although his observations were of a slightly earlier time, they would still have been valid in north Africa at least until the Ottoman conquest in the early fourteenth century.

It is rare that the age of the state should exceed three generations, a generation being the average age of an individual, that is forty years or the time necessary for full growth and development.

We said that the age of the state rarely exceeds three generations because the first generation still retains its nomadic roughness and savagery, and such nomadic characteristics as a hard life, courage, predatoriness, and the desire to share glory. All this means that the strength of the solidarity uniting the people is still firm, which makes that people feared and powerful and able to dominate others.

The second generation, however, have already passed from the nomadic to the sedentary way of life, owing to the power they wield and the luxury they enjoy. They have abandoned their rough life for an easy and luxurious one. ...

As for the third generation, they have completely forgotten the nomadic and rough stage, as though it had never existed. They have also lost their love of power and their social solidarity through having been accustomed to being ruled. Luxury corrupts them, because of the pleasant and easy way of living in which they have been brought up. As a result, they become a liability on the state, like women and children who need to be protected. ...

... the rulers of a state, once they have become sedentary, always imitate in their ways of living those of the state to which they have succeeded and whose condition they have seen and generally adopted.

This is what happened to the Arabs, when they conquered and ruled over the Persian and Byzantine empires ... Up until then they had known nothing of civilization. (Ibn Khaldun, pp. 117–19)

Ibn Khaldun's portrait of the decadence and decay of civilizations does not, however, fit all cases. In India, for example, Aurangzeb provoked fatal rebellions when he tried to rule too strictly over too many people, from too remote a location. Aurangzeb's fatal flaw was not decadence but excessive zeal.

---

turies, most recently by the Delhi Sultanate. It served also as a religious center, a place of pilgrimage revered throughout India for its tombs and graves of saints and holy men. The inner city was encircled by a massive stone wall, 3.8 miles (6 kilometers) long, 27 feet (8 meters) high, 12 feet (3.6 meters) thick. At the convergence of the main streets stood the palace-fort, the home of the emperor, the administrative center of the Mughal Empire. The city had its splendors. The poet Amir Khusrau inscribed on the walls of the private audience hall of the emperor, above the peacock throne: "If there is a paradise on earth, it is here, it is here, it is here". Opposite it, a thousand yards west, set on a small hill, rose the *masjid-i-jami*, the Friday mosque, or chief public mosque of the city. In keeping with Islamic architectural principles, gardens with streams of water running through them to delight the eye and the ear were included in the landscaping.

The larger city housed an assembly of military camps, each under the leadership of one of the emperor's leading generals. M. Gentile, a visiting Frenchman in the mid–eighteenth century wrote: "There are many mansions of the nobles, which one can compare to small towns and in which reside the women, equipment, and bazars (or public markets) of the nobles" (Blake, p. 179). The twentieth-century historian, Percival Spear, referred to Shah Jahanabad's "nomadic court and its tents of stone" (Toynbee, p. 237), the architecture reminding the viewer that the Mughals "had started as nomads in the central Asian steppes, and until their last days they never forgot their origin" (p. 238). Each noble-

Shah Jahan leaving the Great Mosque at Delhi by elephant, seventeenth century. Akbar's grandson Shah Jahan restored and rebuilt Delhi in the 1600s, to serve as the capital of the Mughal Empire. In 1739 the Persian emperor Nadir Shah conquered the city and looted its treasures, including the famous Peacock Throne. Today it is India's third largest city.

man also built his own mosque. But the main function of the city was as the center of administrative and military power. Visitors to India observed that in reality the largest city in India was the military camp led by the emperor in the field. When he went to war, as Aurangzeb did for years at a time, hundreds of thousands of soldiers and camp followers accompanied him; Delhi itself was deserted.

ISFAHAN

In Iran, Shah Abbas (1537–1628) made Isfahan his capital in 1598. One of the largest and most beautiful cities of its time, it contained perhaps a half million people in its 25-mile (40-kilometer) circumference. Its two most monumental features were a 2½-mile (4-kilometer) long elegant promenade, the Chahar Bagh, lined by gardens and court residences encouraged by Shah Abbas and, in the center of the city, the **maidan**, a large public square a third of a mile (536 meters) long by a tenth of a mile (160 metres) wide, was lined on one side by two tiers of shops, on the other sides by the royal palace, the royal mosque, and the smaller Lutfullah mosque. Within its walls the maidan served as marketplace, meeting place, and even as a sportsfield where polo was played.

Shah Abbas fostered increased artisanal production and trade, and Isfahan welcomed merchants and craftsmen from around the world. In the extended bazaar, which stretched for 1½ miles

(2.4 kilometers) from the maidan to the main mosque, were located shops, factories, and warehouses, as well as smaller mosques, medresses (Islamic schools), baths, and **caravanserais** (travellers' hostels). Up to 25,000 people worked in the textile industry alone. Chinese ceramicists were imported to train workers in Chinese porcelain manufacture, and carpets and metalwork were also anchors of Isfahan's craft production.

Despite their differences in religion, Shah Abbas and the European powers shared a common political and military opposition to the Ottoman Empire, which lay between them. In the early 1600s Shah Abbas allowed both the English and the Dutch to open trade offices in Isfahan. He also practiced religious tolerance, perhaps for practical reasons. Augustinian, Carmelite, and Capuchin missions were established. Christian Armenians, forced by Shah Abbas to immigrate from their earlier home in Julfa to expand Isfahan's commerce, built their own suburb called New Julfa, appropriate to their status as prosperous merchants. A Jewish quarter also grew up in the northwestern part of the city, but later in Shah Abbas' reign Jews were persecuted and forced to convert to Islam or to leave.

Shah Abbas maintained absolute command, and imported soldiers who were totally loyal to him. He also kept his forces supplied with up-to-date weapons, for he understood that Iran's status and survival depended upon them, surrounded as it was by the hostile Ottoman Empire on the west, continuing threats from nomads to the north, and a powerful, if friendly, Mughal Empire on the east. In a report of 1605 to Pope Paul V, the friar Paul Simon focused on the Shah's ruthlessness, absolutism, and military preparedness:

> His militia is divided into three kinds of troops: one of Georgians, who will be about 25,000 and are mounted; the second force … is made up of slaves of various races, many of them Christian renegades: their number will be as many again … The third body consists of soldiers whom the great governors of Persia are obliged to maintain and pay the whole year; they will be about 50,000. (Andrea and Overfield, pp. 91–92)

ISTANBUL/CONSTANTINOPLE

Constantinople had been the capital of the much reduced Byzantine Empire when Sultan Mehemmed II captured it and made it his own capital in 1453. He renamed the city Istanbul and began to recast it as the administrative center of the Ottoman Empire, which he was rapidly enlarging. In 1478 Istanbul had about 80,000 inhabitants; betweeen 1520 and 1535, there were 400,000; and some Western observers estimated a population of 700,000 by 1600. Istanbul had become a city of Turks—58 percent of the population in the sixteenth and seventeenth centuries—but there were also Greeks, Jews, Armenians, and Tziganes.

The vast conurbation was composed of three major segments plus numerous suburbs. Central Istanbul housed the government center, with trees, gardens, fountains, promenades, and 400 mosques; sprawling, uneven bazaars where luxuries as well as day-to-day necessities could be purchased; and the Serai, near the tip of the peninsula, where the government officials lived in their palaces and gardens. Across the small waterway, called the Golden Horn, were the ports and major commercial establishments of Galata. Here the Western ships came; here were the Jewish businessmen; the shops and warehouses; cabarets; the French ambassador; Latin and Greek merchants dressing in the Turkish style and living in grand houses. On Galata, too, were the two major arsenals, that of Kasim Pasha and the Topkhana, marking the Ottoman commitment to military power. On the Asian side of the Straits of the Bosphorus was the third part of Istanbul, Uskudar, a more Turkish city, and the terminus of the great land routes through Asia.

Map of Constantinople (Istanbul), late sixteenth century. Byzantine-ruled Constantinople harked back to the great pre-medieval cities of Rome, Athens, and Jerusalem, whose cultural achievements it rivaled. Under the Ottomans, who renamed it Istanbul, it can be viewed as the first of the great early modern centers—a city of diverse peoples and trade in goods and ideas.

Fernand Braudel sees in Istanbul the prototype of the great modern European capitals that would arise a century later. Economically these cities produced little, but they processed goods passing through, and were the "hothouses of civilization" (p. 351), where new ideas and patterns arose and created an order. Braudel remarks that cities that were only capitals would not fare well in the next century; those that were economically productive would. Beginning in the late sixteenth century, the economy of Istanbul was undercut by changes in the world economy. As trade shifted to the Atlantic and to European powers that carried their own commerce around the African continent instead of through the Middle East, the Ottoman Empire and its capital were left as a backwater. Trade deserted them. The vast amounts of silver and gold entering European markets from the Americas in the 1500s also inflated and subverted Istanbul's economy.

LONDON

By comparison with the Asian and East European capitals, London had a very different pattern of immigration and employment. While Peking, Delhi, Isfahan, and Istanbul all declined during the seventeenth century in response to negative political and economic factors, London grew, primarily because of economic factors.

E.A. Wrigley, one of the founding members of the Cambridge Group for the History of Population and Social Structure, has examined the changing demography of London between 1650 and 1750 to analyze the city's relationship with English society and economy. Wrigley begins with London's extraordinary population growth, from 200,000 in 1600, to 400,000 in 1650 and 575,000 by 1700, when it became the largest city in Western Europe, to 675,000 in 1750 and 900,000 in 1800. London dominated the development of all of England. In 1650 London held 7 percent of England's total population; in 1750, 11 percent.

Before the twentieth century, as a general rule, large cities everywhere in the world were so unsanitary that death rates exceeded birth rates. So the extraordinary population growth reflects not only births within the city, but also extraordinary immigration to compensate for high death rates. Wrigley estimates that by the end of the 1600s, 8,000 people a year were migrating into London. Since the entire population of England at this time was only 5 million, London was siphoning half of England's population growth into itself.

With so high a proportion of England's population living in London, or at least visiting the city for a substantial part of their lives, Wrigley suggests that this contact must have had significant influence on the country as a whole. He suggests that the high levels of population growth in London in the seventeenth century may have been a significant factor in giving birth to the industrialization of the eighteenth.

Wrigley suggests several relevant causal relationships. The first group concerns economics: London's growth promoted the creation of a national market, including transportation and communication facilities; evoked increasing agricultural productivity to feed the urban population; developed new sources of raw materials, especially coal, to provide for them; developed new commercial instruments; and increased productivity and purchasing power. Demographically, London's high death and immigration rates kept England's rate of population growth relatively low. Sociologically, London's growth disseminated new ways of thinking about economics and its importance. Londoners placed increasing value on production and consumption for the common person, encouraging higher levels of entrepreneurship throughout the country.

Wrigley does not here discuss the political variables, but without them London's growth could have simply led to parasitism, with the urban people commandeering the production of the countryside for their own good. Such parasitism was common in imperial capitals elsewhere. In London, however, values of production and increased consumption for the common person were reinforced by a government increasingly dominated by commercial classes.

Wrigley's study addresses squarely the relationship between demographic shifts and changes in politics, economics, and social life. In Part 5 we considered the early economic transformation in the trade of England and of the world; now we see how closely this transformation matches the demographic expansion that Wrigley outlines for London. He also makes clear that these transformations have important implications for fundamental political restructuring, industrialization, and social change (see Part 7). Wrigley re-affirms the views of other scholars of historical demography which we have examined—such as Braudel, Curtin, and Sauer—that demographic shifts are fundamental causes of, and reactions to, the great global transformations of history.

BIBLIOGRAPHY

Andrea, Alfred J. and James H. Overfield, eds.,
The Human Record: Sources of Global History, Vol. II
(Boston: Houghton Mifflin Co., 2nd ed., 1994).

Blake, Stephen P. *Shahjahanabad*
(Cambridge: Cambridge University Press, 1990).

Braudel, Fernand. *Capitalism and Material Life 1400–1800*,
trans. by Miriam Kochan
(New York: Harper & Row, 1973)

— . *The Mediterranean and the Mediterranean World in the
Age of Philip II*, 2 vols., trans. by Sian Reynolds
(New York: Harper and Row, 1973).

Crosby, Alfred W. *Ecological Imperialism:
The Biological Expansion of Europe, 900–1900*
(Cambridge: Cambridge University Press, 1986).

Curtin, Philip D. *The Atlantic Slave Trade: A Census*
(Madison: University of Wisconsin Press, 1969).

— . *The Rise and Fall of the Plantation Complex:
Essays in Atlantic History*
(Cambridge: Cambridge University Press, 1990).

Eltis, David, "Precolonial Western Africa and the
Atlantic Economy," in Barbara Solow, ed.
Slavery and the Rise of the Atlantic System
(Cambridge: Cambridge University Press, 1991),
97–119, excerpted in Northrup, pp. 161–173.

Frykenberg, R.E., ed., *Delhi through the Ages:
Essays in Urban History, Culture and Society*
(Delhi: Oxford University Press, 1986).

Habib, Irfan, "Population," in *The Cambridge Economic
History of India*, Vol. 1: c. 1200–c. 1750, eds.
Tapan Raychaudhuri and Irfan Habib
(Cambridge: Cambridge University Press, 1982),
163–171.

Henige, David, "Measuring the Immeasurable:
The Atlantic Slave Trade, West African Population
and the Pyrrhonian Critic," *Journal of African History*
XXVII.2 (1986), 303–13.

Hughes, Robert. *The Fatal Shore. The Epic of Australia's
Founding* (New York: Knopf, 1986).

Ibn Khaldun. *An Arab Philosophy of History*, trans. by
Charles Issawi (London: John Murray, 1950).

Inalcik, Halil. *The Ottoman Empire: The Classical Age*,
trans. by Norman Itzkowitz and Colin Imber
(New York: Praeger Publishers, 1973).

Inikori, Joseph E. and Stanley L. Engerman, eds.,
The Atlantic Slave Trade
(Durham: Duke University Press, 1992).

Keegan, John. *A History of Warfare*
(New York: Knopf, 1993).

Lapidus, Ira M. *A History of Islamic Societies*
(Berkeley: University of California Press, 1988).

Lovejoy, Paul E., "The Volume of the Atlantic Slave
Trade: A Synthesis," *Journal of African History* XXIII
(1982), 473–500.

McNeill, William H. *The Pursuit of Power:
Technology, Armed Force, and Society since 1000 A.D.*
(Chicago: University of Chicago Press, 1983).

Mintz, Sidney W. *Sweetness and Power: The Place of Sugar
in Modern History* (New York: Penguin Books, 1985).

Naqvi, Hamida Khatoon, "Shahjahanabad: The Mughal
Delhi, 1638–1803: An Introduction," in *Delhi through
the Ages*, ed., R. E. Frykenberg
(Delhi: Oxford University Press, 1986), 143–51.

Northrup, David, ed. *The Atlantic Slave Trade*
(Lexington, MA: D.C. Heath, 1994).

Past Worlds: The [London] Times Atlas of Archaeology
(Maplewood, NJ: Hammond, 1988).

Robinson, Francis. *Atlas of the Islamic World since 1500*
(New York: Facts on File, Inc., 1982).

Rodney, Walter. *How Europe Underdeveloped Africa*
(Washington: Howard University Press, 1972).

Sauer, Carl Ortwin. *Sixteenth Century North America:
The Land and People as Seen by the Europeans*
(Berkeley: University of California Press, 1971).

Schwartzberg, Joseph, ed., *A Historical Atlas of South Asia*
(Chicago: University of Chicago Press, 1978).

Spence, Jonathan D. *The Search for Modern China*
(New York: W.W. Norton and Co., 1990).

The [London] Times Atlas of World History ed. Geoffrey
Barraclough (London: Times Books, 1979).

Thornton, John. *Africa and Africans in the Making of the
Atlantic World, 1400–1640*
(Cambridge: Cambridge University Press, 1992).

Tosh, John. *The Pursuit of History*
(New York: Longman, 1984).

Toynbee, Arnold. *Cities of Destiny*
(New York: Weathervane Books, 1967).

Willigan, J. Dennis and Katherine A. Lynch.
Sources and Methods of Historical Demography
(New York: Academic Press, 1982).

Wolf, Eric. *Europe and the People without History*
(Berkeley: University of California Press, 1982).

World Almanac and Book of Facts 1977 (Mahwah,
New Jersey: World Almanac Books, 1996).

Wrigley, E.A. *Population and History*
(New York: McGraw-Hill Book Company, 1969).

— . "A Simple Model of London's Importance in
Changing English Society and Economy 1650-1750,"
Past and Present XXXVII (1967), 44–70.

7

PART

Social Change

1688–1914

WESTERN REVOLUTIONS AND THEIR EXPORT

An unprecedented ferment in global exploration, commerce, and migration began in the thirteenth century (see Parts 5 and 6). By the seventeenth century accommodations to these transformations were needed in political, economic, and social philosophy and organization. These accommodations first took form in Europe and the Americas. Later, through political colonialism, economic imperialism, and Christian missionary activity, they spread to the rest of the world. The new forms percolated into everyday life and consciousness everywhere, but each society adapted in its own way. The results were, as one might expect, diverse and quite often unexpected.

Explosive events, "revolutions," punctuated the changes through the years 1688–1914. One cluster of revolutions—in Britain, America, France, Haiti, and Latin America—promoted new political philosophies and introduced new political structures. Many historians, such as R.R. Palmer, refer to them collectively as constituting "The Age of Democratic Revolution." Beginning about the same time, a series of innovations in

Francisco Jose de Goya, *Execution of the Defenders of Madrid, 3rd May, 1808*, 1814. (*Prado, Madrid*)

economic organization and the uses of machinery dramatically increased the quantity and quality of economic productivity. Most historians name this transformation the "Industrial Revolution." These revolutions in politics and economics were accompanied by equally dramatic social changes, which affected the individual, the family, the neighborhood, and the community. For purposes of analysis, this part will consider these three transformations sequentially: political change in this chapter, industrial change in Chapter 16, and social in change in Chapter 17.

15
CHAPTER

"The aim of every political association is the preservation of the natural and imprescriptible rights of man; these rights are liberty, property, security, and resistance to oppression."

FRENCH DECLARATION OF
THE RIGHTS OF MAN AND
THE CITIZEN

POLITICAL REVOLUTIONS IN EUROPE AND THE AMERICAS

1688–1850

THE BIRTH OF HUMAN RIGHTS IN THE AGE OF ENLIGHTENMENT

POLITICAL REVOLUTION

A revolution is a fundamental and often rapid change in the way systems operate—whether political, economic, intellectual or social. A political revolution, for example, not only removes some people from office and replaces them with others, it also changes the fundamental basis on which the new leaders come to power, the authority they claim, and their mission in office. Leaders of revolutions usually state their goals in terms of high, uncompromisable principles. As revolutionary struggles unfold and as different groups rise and fall, however, they may lurch from one political position to another relatively swiftly and often violently.

In a major revolution several groups may participate and cooperate in the struggle to replace an existing government. Each group may have its own goals, and these goals may be in conflict. As their joint movement appears to be nearing success and it becomes likely that a new government will replace the old, the struggle among the various participating groups will emerge. Each group will seek fiercely to incorporate its own programs and personnel into the new government and even to dominate it. This struggle to control the new government may be even more brutal, violent, chaotic, and unpredictable than the battle to overthrow the old. The stakes are high. Major revolutions can have significant, lasting consequences, not only for participants in that place and time but also for people of following generations and different locations.

The first three political revolutions we will consider all share these characteristics of major revolutions. The "Glorious Revolution" of 1688 in England, the revolt of the American colonies against British rule in 1776, and the French Revolution of 1789 removed one set of rulers and replaced them with another; changed the basis of authority of the state and its relationship to its citizens; and proposed new missions for the state. When we refer here to the "state" we mean the entire mechanism of government, its officers, its institutions, and its organization. All of these revolutions were fought in the name of principle. The English revolution was considered "bloodless," although it was the culmination of a lengthy period of national violence and civil warfare. The American and French Revolutions precipitated lengthy wars.

All three of these revolutions have been characterized as "democratic" because they increased the participation of more (but not all) of the people in government. All of them at some time tried to balance two additional, competing goals: they sought to protect the rights of propertied people while increasing the power of the state (although not of the king). These goals were not, and to this day are not, fully compatible. Individual rights, property rights, and the rights of the state often conflict. So we must be careful in our understanding of the "democracy" that emerged from these revolutions.

Collectively, for Europeans and Americans, the revolutions that occurred in the hundred years between 1688 and 1789:

- situated the authority of government on earth rather than in heaven and thus increased the influence of the secular over the other-worldly;

- rejected the theory that governments were based on a **divine right of king**s in favor of the theory that governments derive their just powers from the consent of the governed;

- encouraged the creation of an effective bureaucracy to administer the affairs of government;

- emphasized the principle of individual merit, of "a career open to talent," rather than promoting people on the basis of personal and hereditary connections;

- helped to solidify the nation-state as the principal unit of government;

- extended effective power over the state to classes of people hitherto excluded, especially to men of the professions and business;

- encouraged the growth of business and industry for private profit;

- inspired the revolutionary leaders to export their new ideologies and methods to new geographical areas, sometimes by force; and

- precipitated wars of heretofore unknown degrees of military mobilization, geographical extent, and human destructiveness.

"Liberty," "equality," "fraternity," "natural rights," "the pursuit of happiness," "property," and "no taxation without representation" were the battle cries of these various revolutions. As frequently happens, the results were often unintended, unanticipated, and ironic. The political forms that actually resulted did increase human freedom for many people in many countries, but they often coexisted with slavery, patriarchy, colonialism, and warfare.

To understand these ironies more fully, we examine two further revolutions, which were inspired in part by these first three. In 1791, the slaves of Haiti, a French colony, revolted and abolished slavery. The French reluctance, and later refusal, to sanction this revolution against slavery demonstrated serious shortcomings in their own revolution. Then, in the first three decades of the nineteenth century, all the colonies of Spain and Portugal in Latin America fought for and won their independence. But the triumphant **creole** elite—the descendants of the European settlers in these colonies—suppressed indigenous peoples, people of mixed Spanish-Amerindian ancestry (*mestizos*), and African-Americans, thereby spreading disillusionment throughout the continent.

ENGLAND'S GLORIOUS REVOLUTION 1688

PHILOSOPHICAL RATIONALES

The philosophy justifying England's "Glorious Revolution" developed over many years. Thomas Hobbes (1588–1679), one of England's leading political philosphers, seemed to justify the enormous, existing power of the king over the citizens. In his most influential work *Leviathan*, of 1651,

	EUROPE	NORTH AMERICA	SOUTH AMERICA
1640	◼ Portuguese revolt against Spain (1640) ◼ Civil Wars in England (1642–6, 1647–9) ◼ Revolts of Fronde in France (1648–9, 1650–3) ◼ Catalan revolt in Spain ends (1652)		◼ Portugal takes Brazil from the Dutch (1654) ◼ England takes Jamaica from Spain (1655)
1660	◼ Treaty of Lisbon (1668): Portugal independent of Spain		
1680	◼ "Glorious Revolution": James II replaced by William III		
1700	◼ Hungarian revolt against Austria (1703–11)		
1720			
1740			
1760		◼ Uprising against British led by Ottawa chief, Pontiac (1763) ◼ Stamp Act (1765) imposes tax in American colonies; repealed in 1766 ◼ Townshend Acts (1767): tax imposed on imports in North America; repealed in 1770, except on tea ◼ Boston Massacre (1770): British troops kill five ◼ Boston Tea Party (1773) ◼ "Intolerable" Acts (1775): repressive measures lead to first Continental Congress at Philadelphia ◼ War of American Independence (1775–83)	
1780	◼ French Revolution (1789) ◼ Rebellion in Ireland by United Irishmen wanting separation from England (1798)	◼ George Washington becomes first president (1789–97)	◼ Peruvian Indians, led by Inca Tupac Amarú revolt against Spain (1780–83) ◼ Toussaint L'Ouverture leads slave revolt against French in Haiti (1791)
1800	◼ Serbian nationalists revolt against Turkey (1804–13) ◼ Serbs revolt against Turkey (1815); Milosh Obrenovich recognized as Prince of Serbia (1817)		◼ Haiti becomes independent (1804) ◼ Paraguay and Venezuela independent (1811) ◼ Argentina independent (1816) ◼ Chile independent (1818) ◼ Simón Bolívar achieves independence of Greater Colombia (1819)
1820	◼ Liberal revolutions in Spain, Portugal, and Italy ◼ Greek War of Independence against Turkey (1821–9) ◼ Miguelite Wars in Portugal (1828–34) ◼ Revolution in Paris (1830): Charles X overthrown in favour of Louis-Philippe (r. 1830–48) ◼ Revolution in Belgium against Dutch (1830); ◼ Belgian independence guaranteed by Britain and France (1831) ◼ Revolution in Poland crushed by Russia (1830) ◼ Uprisings in Modena, Parma, and Papal States overcome by Austria (1831) ◼ Giuseppe Mazzini founds *Young Italy* (1831) ◼ Carlist Wars in Spain (1834–9)	◼ Rebellions in Upper and Lower Canada (1839)	◼ Peru and Mexico declare independence (1821) ◼ Brazil achieves independence from Portugal (1822) ◼ Bolivia independent (1825) ◼ Greater Colombia divided into Colombia, Venezuela, Ecuador, and New Granada (1829)
1840	◼ Year of Revolutions in France, Italy, the Austrian Empire, and Prussia (1848)	◼ Union Act (1840): Upper and Lower Canada united ◼ Webster–Ashburton Treaty (1842): boundary dispute between Canada and US settled	

he declared: "Nothing the sovereign representative can do to a subject, on what pretence soever, can properly be called injustice, or injury." But Hobbes was simultaneously providing a rationale for limiting the king's power. He declared that the king could claim his authority not by virtue of special, personal rights, nor of representing God on earth, but because "Every subject is author of every act the sovereign doth." In other words, the king has authority to the extent that he represents the will of the people.

HOBBES AND "THE STATE OF NATURE"

Hobbes, like others of his time, was trying to understand the English monarchy in terms of its origins. He postulated the myth of a prehistoric, individualistic, unruly, "state of nature," which people had rejected in order to create a society that would protect them individually and collectively. In monarchies the king provided that protection. The "social contract" that had created the society was still in effect. Uncontrolled by law and a king, Hobbes wrote, "the life of man [is] solitary, poor, nasty, brutish, and short … During the time men live without a common power to keep them all in awe, they are in that condition which is called war; and

such a war, as is of every man against every man." To escape such lawlessness, men had exchanged their individual liberties for social and political order. Their (mythical) social contract, not divine appointment, had created monarchy in order to serve the people.

At about the time Hobbes was writing, England was in continuing revolt against its sovereigns. Religion was a burning issue, and it seemed that no sovereign could satisfy all the conflicting wishes of dissenters—Presbyterians and Roman Catholics—and the official Anglican church. Frustrations simmered but had no focus until both James I (r. 1603–25) and his son Charles I (r. 1625–49) ran out of money to administer their governments, especially the naval and military departments, and therefore had convened Parliament to request additional funds. Members of Parliament—landowners, increasingly wealthy city merchants, lawyers, Puritans and other religious dissenters, as well as Anglican clergy—were not inclined to give the kings the money they requested. They challenged royal authority, proposed increased power for an elected legislature, promotion by merit in government jobs, and, most of all, religious tolerance in private and public life. When Charles I nevertheless attempted to levy taxes without its sanction, the Parliament he had convened in 1640 came to open

An Eyewitness Representation of the Execution of Charles I, **by Weesop, 1649.** Charles's belief in the divine right of kings and the authority of the Church of England led eventually to a civil war with Parliament—which he and his supporters lost. At his subsequent trial, the king was sentenced to death as a tyrant, murderer, and enemy of the nation and beheaded at Whitehall, London, on January 30, 1649. (*Private Collection*)

warfare with him and ultimately, under the leadership of Oliver Cromwell (Lord Protector of England, 1653–8), executed him. Cromwell, an ardent Calvinist (see p. 401) and military genius, ruled in rather arbitrary fashion until he died in 1658. Neither Cromwell nor Parliament had been able to achieve a new form of effective government and the monarchy was restored in 1660.

THE BILL OF RIGHTS 1689

Charles II (r. 1660–85) and his brother James II (r. 1685–90) continued to claim more powers than the Parliament wished to sanction. James II, a Catholic, favored Catholics in many of his official appointments. When, in his old age, a son was born to James, several leading nobles began to fear that James and his successors might reinstitute Catholicism as England's official religion a century and a half after Henry VIII had disestablished it in favor of the Church of England (see p. 401). They invited James II's daughter, Mary, and her husband William of Orange, King of Holland, both resolute Protestants, to return to England and assume the monarchy. In 1688 William and Mary arrived in England and confirmed their new rule by defeating the troops still loyal to James II at the Battle of the Boyne in Ireland in 1690.

Although the new king and queen had been invited primarily to resolve religious conflicts, their ascension to the throne also brought resolution to the power conflict between king and Parliament. The Bill of Rights that was enacted by Parliament in 1689 created a kind of contract between the monarchy and people. It stipulated, among other clauses, that no taxes could be raised, nor armies recruited without prior Parliamentary approval; no subject could be arrested and detained without legal process; and no law could be suspended by the king unilaterally. The Glorious Revolution thus not only displaced one monarch in favor of another but also limited the powers of the monarch under constitutional law. After all, this new monarch had been selected by noblemen and confirmed by Parliament. The Anglican church remained the established Church of England, but the Toleration Act of 1689 granted Puritan Dissenters—but not Roman Catholics—the right of free public worship. Parliament did not yet revoke the Test Act which reserved military and civil offices for Anglicans only. These settlements brought some resolution to the issues of religion in politics that had beset England for so long.

MAJOR DISCOVERIES AND INVENTIONS—1640–1830

1640	Theory of numbers: Pierre de Fermat
1642	Calculating machine: Blaise Pascal
1650	Air pump: Otto von Guericke
1656	Pendulum clock: Otto von Guericke
1665–75	Calculus: Isaac Newton and Gottfried Leibnitz (independently)
1698	Steam pump: Thomas Savory
1712	Steam engine: Thomas Newcomen
1714	Mercury thermometer: Gabriel Fahrenheit
1733	Flying shuttle: John Kay Seed drill: Jethro Tull
1752	Lightning conductor: Benjamin Franklin
1764	Spinning jenny: James Hargreaves
1765	Condensing steam engine: James Watt
1768	Hydrometer: Antoine Baumé
1783	Parachute: Louis Lenormand
1785	Power loom: Edmund Cartwright
1789	Combustion: Antoine Lavoisier
1790	Sewing machine: Thomas Saint
1793	Cotton gin: Eli Whitney
1800	Electric battery: Alessandro Volta
1804	Steam locomotive: Richard Trevithick
1815	Miner's safety lamp: Humphry Davy
1816	Bicycle: Karl von Sauerbronn
1822	Camera: Joseph Niepce
1823	Digital calculating machine: Charles Babbage
1824	Portland cement: Joseph Aspdin
1825	Electromagnet: William Sturgeon
1826	Photograph: Joseph Niepce
1828	Blast furnace: James Neilson

LOCKE AND THE ENLIGHTENMENT

This formal, public re-negotiation of the tacit contract between king and people recalls the philosophy of Hobbes, but it went beyond Hobbes' bleak view of human political nature. The philosophical accomplishments of the Glorious Revolution are even more closely associated with the writings of John Locke (1632–1704), who had fled England in 1683 for Holland, returning only after the revolution was complete. While he was in Holland, Locke wrote his most important essay on political philosophy, *Second Treatise on Government*, although it was not published until 1689, after the Glorious Revolution had been implemented and Locke felt it safe to return to England. Since Locke's philosophy parallels not only the British revolution but also many subsequent ones, his arguments deserve attention.

Like Hobbes, Locke argued that government is a secular compact entered into voluntarily and freely by individuals. If there are to be kings, they too must live under the constitution. Locke, like Hobbes, based his argument on a mythical, prehistoric, "state of nature," which people forsook in order to provide for their common defense and needs. He, however, stressed the importance of common consent in the earlier mythical contract. The legitimacy of the contract continues only as long as the consent continues. If they no longer consent to the contract, the people have the right to terminate it. Going beyond Hobbes, Locke explicitly proclaimed the right of revolution in his *Second Treatise on Government*:

> There remains still in the people a supreme power to remove or alter the legislative, when they find the legislative act contrary to the trust reposed in them. For all power given with trust for the attaining of an end, being limited by that end, whenever that end is manifestly neglected, or opposed, the trust must necessarily be forfeited, and the power devolves into the hands of those that gave it, who may place it anew where they shall think best for their safety and security. (p. 92)

Locke postulated the "equal right that every man hath to his natural freedom, without being subjected to the will or authority of any other man" (p. 33). "Absolute monarchy, which by some men is counted the only government in the world, is indeed inconsistent with civil society" (p. 53). Majority rule is Locke's basis of government: "the act of the

John Locke by Sylvester Brounower, 1685. The political theory of Enlightenment philosopher John Locke has inspired revolutions in England and America. Locke argued for the sovereignty of the people over the state and for government being subject to common consent. Revolution, it followed, was not simply a right but often an obligation. (*National Portrait Gallery, London*)

majority passes for the act of the whole, and of course determines as having by the law of nature and reason, the power of the whole" (p. 59).

GOVERNMENT BY PROPERTY OWNERS

Locke was not, however, proposing radical democracy; he was not advocating one person–one vote. For Locke, government was for property owners. "Government," Locke proclaimed, "has no other end but the preservation of property" (p. 57). "The great and chief end therefore, of men's uniting into commonwealths, and putting themselves under government, is the preservation of their property" (p. 75). Indeed, after the initial, mythical social contract had established the government's authority, succeeding generations had signalled their continuing acceptance of that contract by allowing their property to be protected by the government. "The supreme power cannot take from any man any part of his property without his own consent. For the preservation of property being the end of government, and that for which men enter into society, it necessarily supposes and requires, that the people should have property" (p. 85).

Taxes, therefore, cannot be levied unilaterally or arbitrarily. "If anyone shall claim a power to lay and levy taxes on the people, by his own authority, and without such consent of the people, he thereby invades the fundamental law of property, and subverts the end of government" (p. 87).

Hobbes had already indicated the growing importance of property and industry to seventeenth-century England. Without peace and stability, he wrote:

> there is no place for industry; because the fruit thereof is uncertain; and consequently no culture of the earth; no navigation, nor use of the commodities that may be imported by sea; no commodious building; no instruments of moving, and removing, such things as require much force; no knowledge of the face of the earth; no account of time; no arts; no letters; no society. (p. 895)

Hobbes wanted a society of economic productivity achieved through industry, commerce, and invention. Locke saw private ownership of property and private profit as the means to achieving that end. He saw the property-owning classes of England, the men who made the Glorious Revolution, as the nation's proper leaders and administrators, and he asserted the importance of the enclosure acts by which England was dividing up the common lands of each village, turning them into private property, and selling them (see p. 416). These enclosure acts were creating a new, wealthier landlord class, which turned its energies to increasing agricultural productivity. At the same time the acts forced rural people, who had owned no land of their own but who had been grazing their animals on the commons, to give up their independence. Most found work with more prosperous landlords and some moved to the cities in search of new jobs.

Locke is today usually criticized for overlooking the situation of the non-propertied classes. In his mythical state of nature land had been abundant—available for the taking—and anyone could become a property owner. But in both Locke's time and our own, access to unclaimed, unowned property is not so easy. Indeed, when Locke notes that "the turfs my servant has cut … become my property" (p. 19), he credits the labor of the landless servant to his landed master. In practice, Locke's theory justified the government of England by Parliament under constitutional law which limited the power of the king and transferred it to the hands of the propertied classes—the system which was evolving in his time. Locke's is the voice of the improving landlords and the rising commercial classes who made the Glorious Revolution.

UNIVERSAL SUFFRAGE VS. PROPERTY RIGHTS

E.P. Thompson, the twentieth-century British historian, emphasized the contributions of common people to history. In his groundbreaking *The Making of the English Working Class* (pp. 22–3), Thompson cites statements made in 1647 at an army council meeting that attempted to find a constitutional solution to the struggle between the king and Parliament and to determine the role of the common people in electing the Parliament.

Oliver Cromwell's son-in-law, General Ireton, proposed extending the franchise, but only to men of property, fearing that private property might otherwise be abolished: "No person hath a right to an interest or share in the disposing of the affairs of the kingdom … that hath not a permanent fixed interest in this kingdom. … If you admit any man that hath a breath and being, Why may not those men vote against all property?"

The common soldiers replied more democratically and more bitterly. One asserted: "There are many thousands of us soldiers that have ventured our lives; we have had little propriety in the kingdom as to our estates, yet we have had a birthright. But it seems now, except a man hath a fixed estate in this kingdom, he hath no right. … I wonder we were so much deceived." If we are asked to fight on behalf of the government, we should have a voice in its election.

For its time the Glorious Revolution may have been democratic because it placed the king under constitutional rule. But until 1820 fewer than 500 influential men in all of Britain, it has been estimated, could control the election of the majority of the Parliament. The 1832 Reform Act expanded the actual electorate in the British Isles from about a half million to about 800,000. Not until 1867 and 1884 did Reform Acts extend the vote to the middle and lower classes as well as to Catholics, Dissenters, and Jews. By that time the Industrial Revolution had created an entirely new class of occupations and workers who could successfully demand representation, as we shall see in the next chapter. Women got the vote in England only in the twentieth century.

THE *PHILOSOPHES* AND THE ENLIGHTENMENT IN THE EIGHTEENTH CENTURY

In the century between the Glorious Revolution in England and the American and French revolutions, a new movement in philosophic thought emerged called the Enlightenment. Its intellectual center was in France, although important participants lived in America, Scotland, England, Prussia, Russia, and elsewhere. The French leaders of the Enlightenment were called **philosophes**, and their philosophy helped to inspire both the American and the French revolutions.

The *philosophes* believed in a world of rationality, in which collected human knowledge and systematic thought could serve as powerful tools for finding order in the universe and for solving key problems in political and economic life. Their concerns for clarity of thought, combined with the desire to solve practical problems in public life, gave them considerable influence on the restructuring of new political institutions in their age of revolution. The authors of the American Declaration of Independence and of the French Declaration of the Rights of Man and the Citizen drew much of their inspiration from the *philosophes*. The *philosophes* believed in order, but also in freedom of thought and expression. For them, public discussion and debate were the means toward finding better ideas and solutions. Indeed, the *philosophes* were in constant dialogue and debate with one another.

Travel influenced the *philosophes'* thought, opening them to a wider range of ideas. Charles de Secondat, the Baron de Montesquieu (1689–1755), traveled widely himself and presented satiric criticism of French institutions, including the monarchy and the Catholic church, in the form of *Persian Letters*, supposedly dispatched by two visitors to France writing their observations to readers at home. Twenty-seven years later, in 1748, Montesquieu wrote his most influential work, *The Spirit of Laws*, in which he recognized that different coun-

The Philosophers at Supper by Jean Huber, 1750. Voltaire (1), Condorcet (5), and Diderot (6) are among the figures depicted in this engraving, a visual checklist of important Enlightenment thinkers. Seeing the Western world as emerging from centuries of darkness and ignorance, these Frenchmen promoted reason, science and a respect for humanity— ideas that would underpin the intellectual case for the French Revolution of 1789. (*Bibliothèque Nationale, Paris*)

tries need different kinds of governments, and advocated a separation of powers based on his (mis)understanding of the British system. The authors of the United States constitution later acknowledged their debt to Montesquieu's thought.

In terms of spiritual and religious beliefs, most *philosophes* were deists. They allowed that the world may have required an original creator, like Aristotle's prime mover, but once the processes of life had begun, he had withdrawn. Their metaphor was of a watchmaker who built the mechanism, started it moving, and departed. Humanity's fate thereafter was in its own hands.

In contrast to such Catholic doctrines as original sin and the authority of the church over human reason, the *philosophes* argued that human progress was possible through the steady and unrestricted expansion of knowledge or "enlightenment." Jean-Antoine-Nicolas de Caritat, Marquis de Condorcet (1743–94), author of the *Sketch of the Progress of the Human Mind* (published in 1795), proclaimed "the perfectibility of humanity is indefinite" (Andrea and Overfield, p. 153). The most famous academic product of the *philosophes* and the Enlightenment was the *Encyclopedia, or Rational Dictionary of the Arts, Sciences, and Crafts*, compiled by Denis Diderot (1713–84) and containing articles by leading scholars and *philosophes*. The *Encyclopedia* reaffirmed this faith in human progress based on education:

> The aim of an Encyclopedia is to collect all the knowledge that now lies scattered over the face of the earth, to make known its general structure to the men among whom we live, and to transmit it to those who will come after us, in order that the labors of past ages may be useful to the ages that will follow, that our grandsons, as they become better educated, may become at the same time more virtuous and more happy, and that we may not die without having deserved well of the human race. (Columbia University, *Contemporary Civilization*, pp. 988–9)

Diderot called for further social and political revolution. "We are beginning to shake off the yoke of authority and tradition in order to hold fast to the laws of reason" (p. 992). Challenging authority meant being open to multiple perspectives rather than holding a single truth, and Diderot built this concept into the structure of his volumes.

THE ENLIGHTENMENT—KEY FIGURES

Thomas Hobbes   (1588–1679) English political philosopher who, in *Leviathan* (1651), advocated a social contract, as the only way of ensuring order and security for citizens, and absolutism for monarchs.

John Locke   (1632–1704) English writer on philosophy, politics, economics, and theology, who maintained that the experience of the senses rather than philosophical speculation was the source of knowledge. As for politics, he argued that governments derive their authority from popular consent.

Voltaire   (François-Marie Arouet; 1694–1778) French writer of histories, political analysis, essays on science and literature, poems, plays, and philosophy. He attacked organized religion, oppression, and civil injustice with wit and style.

David Hume   (1711–76) Scottish philosopher and historian who argued that human knowledge was restricted to the experience of ideas and impressions and that it was impossible ultimately to verify the truth.

Jean-Jacques Rousseau   (1712–78) French writer, philosopher, educationalist, and champion of liberty. His works include *Social Contract* (1762), which emphasized, ambiguously, the rights of people over those of government and the rights of government over the people.

Denis Diderot   (1713–84) French philosopher and chief editor of the 28-volume *Encylopédie* (1751–72). Written by a group of French scholars, the work was notable for its religious skepticism and concerns for social and political issues.

Jean le Rond d'Alembert   (1717–83) French philosopher, mathematician, and theoretical physicist. He put forward several theorems and principles in dynamics and celestial mechanics, and was responsible for devising the theory of partial differential equations.

By giving cross-references to articles where solid principles serve as foundation for the diametrically opposed truths we shall be able to throw down the whole edifice of mud and scatter the idle heap of dust. ... If these cross-references, which now confirm and now refute, are carried out artistically according to a plan carefully conceived in advance, they will give to the Encyclopedia the ... ability to change men's common way of thinking. (p. 996)

The *Encyclopedia* ultimately filled seventeen volumes of text and eleven of illustrations.

Another *philosophe*, François-Marie Arouet, better known as Voltaire (1694–1778), spoke out with courage and wit. His *Elements of the Philosophy of Newton* (1738) explicated new scientific evidence of the rational order and the human ability to comprehend the universe; *Philosophical Letters on the English* (1734) argued for freedom of religion, inquiry, and the press; *Essai sur les moeurs* (1756), translated as *Universal History*, gave a humanistic context to historical development and placed responsibility in human hands. Voltaire cried *"Ecrasez l'infame!"*— "crush the infamy" of superstition, intolerance, and the power of the clergy.

The *philosophes* were not, however, committed to popular democracy. Voltaire preferred benevolent and **enlightened despotism** to badly administered self-rule. In the best of all possible worlds, there would be an enlightened ruler like Frederick II, the Great, of Prussia (r. 1740–86), at whose court Voltaire lived for several years, or Catherine II, the Great, Empress of Russia (r. 1762–96), of whom he was a close friend, or Joseph II, Emperor of Austria (r. 1765–90). All three ruled countries in which the administration was efficient, taxes were reasonable, agricultural and handicraft production was encouraged, freedom of expression and religion was allowed, the military was strengthened, and from which powerful empires resulted. The enlightened despot acted in disciplined ways, subject in his or her mind to the law of nature. But the population at large had no say or vote in the administration.

Skepticism regarding democratic government was carried further in the works of Jean-Jacques Rousseau (1712–78), perhaps the most enigmatic and ambiguous of all of the eighteenth-century French thinkers. Rousseau questioned the primacy of intellect and human ingenuity. Like Hobbes and Locke, he wrote of the "state of nature," but, unlike them, he seemed, in some ways, to wish actually to return to it. His *Social Contract* (1762) lamented "Man is born free; and everywhere he is in chains."

In his *Discourse on the Origin of Inequality* (1755) he wrote:

There is hardly any inequality in the state of nature; all the inequality which now prevails owes its strength and growth to the development of our faculties and the advance of the human mind, and becomes at last permanent and legitimate by the establishment of property and laws. (Columbia University, *Contemporary Civilization*, p. 1147)

Rousseau proposed a democracy far more radical than that of the other *philosophes* yet he also seemed to justify a repressive tyranny of the majority. Like Locke and Hobbes, Rousseau mythologized an original social contract transforming a state of nature into a community, but he attributed great power to that community: "Each of us puts his person and all his power in common under the supreme direction of the general will" (Columbia University, *Contemporary Civilization*, p. 1151). "Whoever refuses to obey the general will shall be compelled to do so by the whole body. This means nothing less than that he will be forced to be free" (p. 1153). Political philosphers have argued for two centuries over the paradox of Rousseau's "general will." How is the citizen "forced to be free"? Is this a proclamation of freedom, justification for suppressing minorities, or a proposal for creating a totalitarian state?

Adam Smith, whose economic ideas we have already examined (see p. 417), is sometimes grouped with the *philosophes*, with whom he carried on extensive discussions and correspondence. Smith's economic theory rests on a set of optimistic and humanistic philosophical beliefs, including the belief that humans are most productive when they work for their own benefit: "Every man ... is much more deeply interested in whatever immediately concerns himself, than in what concerns any other man." Like Locke, Smith believed it was normal for people to want to "better their condition" materially. He saw that this attempt was not always successful, but suggested:

it is well that nature imposes upon us in this manner. It is this deception which rouses and keeps in continual motion the industry of mankind. It is this which first prompted them to cultivate the ground, to build houses, to found cities and commonwealths, and to invent and improve all the sciences and arts, which ennoble and embellish human life. (*Moral Sentiments*, IV. 1.10)

SCIENTIFIC REVOLUTIONS

*S*cience promotes three different kinds of revolution. First, in alliance with technology, science provides new tools which change the way we live and work. We have seen this revolutionary alliance repeatedly in this text—for example in the new guns, ships, and navigational equipment created from the fifteenth century onward—and, of course, we see it in everyday life. More fundamentally, science provides a method of thought and research which constantly challenges conventional thinking and stands ready to overthrow it. Thomas Kuhn's *The Structure of Scientific Revolutions* (1970) argues that in most cases scientists are pursuing "normal science" in which accepted theories hold up in practice. But in some cases, so many exceptions appear that the accepted theory, or model, or "paradigm" is rejected. A scientific revolution begins as researchers seek new paradigms. Scientific method demands that the procedures, usually observations and experiments, be open to examination and verification by everyone. It promotes honesty.

In an earlier book, Kuhn demonstrated revolutionary science in the astronomical researches of Nicholas Copernicus (1473–1543), who, against received opinion, proposed a **heliocentric** (sun-in-the-center) model of the solar system. But Copernicus was writing for a highly specialized audience, and his discoveries made a relatively minor impact in his own time. Galileo Galilei (1564–1642) issued a far more public message and introduced a new scientific apparatus, the telescope, which he did not invent but which he did improve and popularize. In 1610, in "The Starry Messenger," Galileo reaffirmed and expanded Copernicus' finding: the earth was not the fixed center of a series of fixed spheres of planets and stars, but a "wandering body" (p. 45) in a starry universe.

Galileo demonstrated all three revolutionary potentials of science: 1) He introduced new technology. 2) He tested the accepted paradigms of his day and, when they proved inadequate, proposed new ones. 3) He collided with powerful, hostile interests outside the scientific community. Under increased pressure from Protestant fundamentalists, the Church attacked. Galileo was forced to recant his truths publicly in 1633 and was placed under house arrest near Florence until his death. In the short run the church had its way, but scientific investigation could not be stopped. Intelligent (and brave) people could not be forbidden to believe what their eyes, their experiments, and their calculations told them was true.

The scientific method of systematic experimentation and testing of theories became an important, even dominant, way of understanding the world. In 1622, King Charles II of England chartered the Royal Society, the first national academy of science. In 1665 it published *Philosophical Transactions*, the world's first scientific journal. Sir Isaac Newton (1642–1727), its president for twenty-five years, brought unparalleled prestige to scientific method by formulating and testing universal laws of optics and motion, and by formulating the calculus. Scientific method was institutionalized as a permanent intellectual revolution.

A page from Sir Isaac Newton's manuscript *Philosophiae Naturalis Principia Mathematica*, 1687. Newton, the forefather of modern physics and mathematics, was one of the driving forces behind the scientific revolution of the Enlightenment Age. Now most celebrated for his discovery of the law of gravity, he also solved mysteries of light and optics, and along with German philosopher Gottfried Leibnitz, invented calculus, a branch of mathematics.

Smith believed in the beneficial effects of private initiative and the rewards of private profit. The desire to please others, he suggested, would balance the desire for private enrichment, leading to "the most effectual means for promoting the happiness of mankind." Nevertheless, much less optimistically, Smith recognized that private enrichment would engender jealousy and envy. Private property, therefore, needed to be protected and this, he agreed with Locke, was the task of government:

> Civil government, so far as it is instituted for the security of property, is in reality instituted for the defense of the rich against the poor, or of those who have some property against those who have none at all. (Smith, *The Wealth of Nations*, p. 674)

Smith wanted the government to protect property and even to promote it through large-scale public projects that were beyond the scope of the individual businessman, such as the construction of major roads, ports, and education systems. He wanted government to prohibit monopolies, so that free trade and market competition could flourish among producers and consumers. He thought that government regulation or control of the marketplace would only impede the working of the "Invisible Hand."

At the time of the American and French revolutions these powerful arguments for enlightenment, rationality, experimental science, secularism, private profit and ownership, "fellow feeling," and limitations on the power of government all clamored for major changes in politics, economics, and social life. But what would be the substance and direction of those changes? How would they be implemented and by whom?

REVOLUTION IN NORTH AMERICA 1776

As English settlers began to colonize North America, Australia, and South Africa in the seventeenth and eighteenth centuries, they assumed that they shared in the rights of all Englishmen. By the 1760s, however, North American settlers were beginning to resent the control over their political and economic life exerted by rulers in Britain. British control over American trade, restrictions on

Signing of the Declaration of Independence, July 4, 1776 by John Trumbull, 1786–97. What began as a protest against colonial trade restrictions and the limiting of political liberty grew into a revolutionary struggle and the birth of a nation. The Declaration of Independence enshrined the principles underlying the new United States and later influenced freedom-fighters all over the world. (*Capitol Collection, Washington*)

the development of American shipping, and the resulting limitations on the development of certain kinds of manufacture, were as galling as the issue of taxation. The 1763 British victory over the French in the Seven Years' War in North America, concluding a global cluster of wars between the two powers for commercial and naval supremacy (see p. 415), ended the threat of attacks by French or Indians and freed the American colonists from further need of British troops. However, the British decided to maintain a large army in North America and to tax the colonies directly to pay for it. The 1765 Stamp Act levied taxes on a long list of commerical and legal documents. It was vigorously protested by the colonists and only reluctantly repealed by Parliament because of serious rioting and boycotting of British goods.

Additional grievances against further imperious decrees of King George III built up until finally the Americans declared themselves an independent country in 1776 and fought to end British rule over them. The American Declaration of Independence set out a list of these "injuries and usurpations." It reflected the American resolve to secure the same legal rights as Englishmen had won at home almost a century earlier. It declared that the king had refused to pass laws "unless those people would relinquish the Right of Representation in the Legislature, a Right inestimable to them, and formidable to tyrants only. ... He has dissolved Representative Houses repeatedly. ... He has kept among us, in Times of peace, Standing Armies, without the consent of our Legislatures." It charged King George III with "abolishing the free system of English Laws in a neighbouring Province [Massachusetts] establishing therein an arbitrary Government ... taking away our Charters, abolishing our most valuable Laws, and altering fundamentally the Forms of our Governments." It declared the social contract that bound the colonies to England had been broken. It declared, ultimately, the right of revolution.

The American Revolution went further in establishing political democracy than had the Glorious Revolution in England. It abolished the monarchy entirely, replacing it with an elected government. Having declared that "all men are created equal," with unalienable rights not only to life and liberty, but also to the vague but seductive "pursuit of happiness," the revolutionaries now set out to consolidate their commitments in a new legal structure. Their leaders, men like George Washington, Benjamin Franklin, Thomas Jefferson, and James

Madison, were soldiers, entrepreneurs, and statesmen of considerable erudition, common sense, restraint, and balance.

THE CONSTITUTION AND THE BILL OF RIGHTS 1789

After the Authorities won their war for independence, 1775–81, and, in 1783, achieved a peace treaty with Britain, political leaders of the thirteen colonies that had fought met in Philadelphia to establish a framework for their new nation. They drafted a new Constitution in 1789, and a Bill of Rights, which was ratified in 1791. The American Bill of Rights, the first ten amendments to the Constitution, guaranteed to Americans not only the basic rights enjoyed by the British at the time, but more: freedom of religion (and the separation of church and state), press, assembly, and petition; the right to bear arms; protection against unreasonable searches and against cruel and unusual punishment; and the right to a speedy and proper trial by a jury of peers. The Americans established a federal system of government. The states individually set the rules for voting and many, but not all, removed the property requirements. By 1800 Vermont had instituted universal manhood suffrage, and South Carolina, Pennsylvania, New Hampshire, and Delaware extended the vote to virtually every adult white male taxpayer.

Historians of the early United States situate the more radical American approach to political liberty in at least four factors: cultural, economic, social and philosophical. First, a disproportionate share of the settlers coming to America from England and Europe were religious dissenters seeking spiritual independence outside the established churches of their countries. Their widespread, popular beliefs in the importance of individual liberties carried over from religion into politics.

Second, the availability of open land presented abundant individual opportunity to Americans, and they ratified this in law. Later, the historian Frederick Jackson Turner would extend this "frontier thesis," arguing that the relative freedom and openness of American life was based psychologically as well as materially on the presence of seemingly endless open frontier land. Third, the absence of landed and aristocratic privilege, and the strength of artisan classes in the urban population increased the demand for democracy. Finally, eighteenth-century political thought had generally grown more radical, especially among the

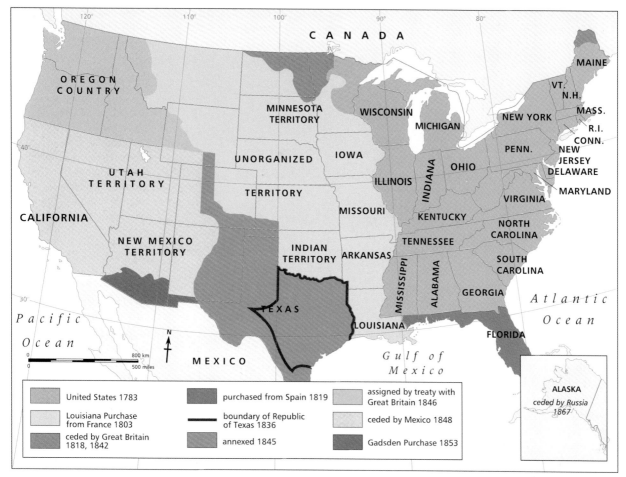

The growth of the United States The westward expansion of the United States was effected by territorial cession, acquisition, and conquest. Following independence in 1783, the Louisiana Purchase from France (1803), and the annexations of West and East Florida from Spain, doubled the nation's size. Another doubling occurred with the annexation of Texas (1845), the acquisition of Oregon (1846), and victory over Mexico (1848), which brought the southwest. Alaska was purchased from Russia (1867). In all cases, European immigrants displaced Native Americans, and in less than a century the United States had become one of the world's largest nations.

philosophes in France. By the time the Americans wrote their Bill of Rights, the French Revolution was well underway.

THE FIRST ANTI-IMPERIAL REVOLUTION

The American Revolution, in addition to securing British rights for Americans, was also, and perhaps more importantly, the first modern anti-colonial revolution. The trade and taxation policies imposed by Britain had pushed businessmen and artisans into opposition to British rule. Other nations, notably France, eager to embarrass Britain and to detach its most promising colonies, provided financial and military support, which helped the Americans to win their independence.

One of the goals of the Revolution was to open the North American continent west of the Appalachian Mountains to settlement. The British prohibition on this westward movement had stood in stark contrast to Spanish and Portuguese settlement policy in Latin America. As the newly independent Americans migrated westward, annexing land as they went, they began to develop imperial interests that were expressed in the mystique of "Manifest Destiny." This popular belief in America's natural growth across the continent was consolidated with the huge Lousiana Purchase from France in 1803. Texans were encouraged to assert their independence from Mexico in 1836 and were then absorbed into the American Union in 1845. Warfare with Mexico in 1846–8 ended in victory for the United States and the annexation of the

An anonymous engraving of the Boston Tea Party, 1796. On December 16, 1773, a group of American firebrands, who objected to the importation of highly taxed cheap British tea, disguised themselves as Native Americans, boarded the offending ships in Boston Harbor and tipped the cargo into the sea. The protest, an emblem of colonial hostility to British rule, is captured in this earliest-known depiction of the event.

southwest. Other annexations of land in North America took place more peacefully, with negotiations with Britain for the Oregon country in 1844 and with Russia for the purchase of Alaska in 1867.

Over the centuries America continued to serve as an inspiration to anti-colonial forces. Jawaharlal Nehru, leading India's twentieth-century struggle for independence from Britain, cited the American Revolution as a model for his own country: "This political change in America was important and destined to bear great results. The American colonies which became free then have grown today [1932] into the most powerful, the richest, and industrially the most advanced country in the world" (p. 355).

The American Revolution, however, did not bring democracy to everyone. The greatest shortcoming was the American perpetuation of slavery. The system was finally ended only by the American Civil War, 1861–5, the bloodiest in the history of the nation. Even afterward, racial discrimination characterized American law until the 1960s and continues to mark American practice up to the present. The status of the Native American population actually worsened after the Revolution, as settlers of European extraction headed west, first by wagon train and later by railroad. They slaughtered American Indians, pushed them out of the way, confined them to remote, semi-barren reservations, destroyed the buffalo herds on which their nomadic existence depended, yet discouraged the preservation of their separate cultures and languages. For the indigenous Indians the effects of the Revolution were exactly opposite to those of the settlers: expansion became contraction, democracy became tyranny, prosperity became poverty, and liberty became confinement.

The hypocrisy of democratic statements, on the one hand, and atrocities against Indians, on the other, peaked in the presidency of Andrew Jackson (1829–37). Jackson fought against economic and political privilege and to extend opportunity to the common man, yet he ordered the United States Army to evict the Cherokee Indian Nation from their lands in Georgia and to drive them to the "Great American Desert" in the west in direct defiance of the Supreme Court of the United States. About one-fourth of the 15,000 Indians forced onto this "Trail of Tears" died *en route*.

How did America reconcile its ideals of equality and liberty with the enslavement of blacks and the confinement of Indians at home? It did so by considering non-whites and non-Europeans as "other" —that is, as not quite equal biologically. Race was often used as a definition, usually made by a quick, if approximate and sometimes inaccurate, visual measure, and often as a legal standard. The fixing of legal identity by race, which had been heretofore a flexible category, became especially common in the southern United States in dealing with slaves, ex-slaves, and free blacks. For many years, racial definition was used as a legal standard in excluding Asians from immigrating as well. If non-whites were considered not quite equal biologically, the unalienable right to liberty could be abridged. Once the revolutionary principle of equality was accepted in America and elsewhere, the battle was drawn between those who wished to narrow its application to an "in-group" while excluding "others" and those who wished to apply it to all peoples. That battle continues today, in law and in practice, in the United States and around the globe.

THE FRENCH REVOLUTION AND NAPOLEON 1789–1812

The American Revolution, with its combined messages of colonial revolt, constitutional government, individual freedom, and equality under law, inspired many peoples at the time and over the centuries. But in comparison with European countries and their experiences, America and its Revolution were unique. In the eighteenth century, America was a country of three million people on the fringes of a continental wilderness, without traditions of class and clerical privilege, and founded in large measure by dissidents. Building on already existing British freedoms and fighting a war (with several international allies) against a distant colonial government, the leaders of the Revolution were an educated, comfortable elite. The French Revolution, on the other hand, was an internal revolt against entrenched feudal, clerical, and monarchical privilege within the most populous (24 million people) and most powerful European state of its time. It unleashed powerful, combative internal factions, none of which could control the direction or the velocity of revolutionary events inside or outside of France. The French Revolution immediately affected all of Europe, most of the Western Hemisphere, and indeed the whole world. Some would argue that the battles over its central principles continue even today. The twentieth-century Chinese leader Chou En-lai, when asked to assess the effects of the French Revolution, allegedly replied: "It's too soon to tell."

ORIGINS OF REVOLUTION

The French Revolution, like the English Civil Wars of the 1640s, was triggered by the king's need for funds. Much like Charles I, King Louis XVI (r. 1774–92) decided to solicit these funds by convening leaders of the French people through the "Estates General" in 1789.

From this point on, political, social, and ideological change proceeded very rapidly as political institutions, social classes, and philosophical beliefs challenged one another in a continuous unfolding of critical events. France was divided, hierarchical-

The Oath of the Tennis Court by Jacques-Louis David, 1790. In this dramatic composition, David captures the moment when the Third Estate asserted their sovereignty as the elected representatives of France. The merchants, professionals, and artisans who attended the hastily convened meeting swore to remain in session until they had drawn up a new constitution—one that would end the vested interests of the nobility and clergy. (*Musée Carnavalet, Paris*)

THE HISTORIOGRAPHY OF THE FRENCH REVOLUTION

The study of the French Revolution remains the pre-eminent subject of French historiography, producing a seemingly endless variety of interpretations. Three approaches, however, have predominated. The first emphasizes the importance of ideas, stressing the *philosophes* as the precursors of revolution. This interpretation tends to focus on the first three months of the Revolution and the significance of the "Declaration of the Rights of Man and the Citizen." R.R. Palmer's *The Age of the Democratic Revolution* (1959), for example, favors this reading. A second interpretation stresses the significance of class interests in the Revolution, and tends to highlight the next chronological stage, as urban workers and rural peasantry escalated their protests and demonstrations. George Lefebvre's *The Coming of the French Revolution* (1939) represents this position. A more recent interpretation (influenced by literary theory) speaks of the revolution as "discourse," an interplay of ideas and interest groups that constantly shifts, or "skids," as events unfold. As the direction of the Revolution changed irrevocably with each new event, for example the execution of Louis XVI, ideas were reassessed and classes reshuffled themselves into new alignments. François Furet's *Interpreting the French Revolution* (1978) is the leading statement of this point of view. Our narrative, including the discussion of the *philosophes* on pp. 469–73, incorporates elements of all three interpretive perspectives.

ly, into three "Estates": the clergy, numbering about 100,000 and controlling perhaps 10 percent of the land of France; the nobility, perhaps 300,000 men, who owned approximately 25 percent of the land; and everyone else. This third estate included a rising and prosperous group of urban merchants and professionals (estimated at 8 percent of the total population), as well as working-class artisans, and the four-fifths of France who were farmers. The wealth that the king wished to tap was concentrated in the first two estates and the **bourgeoisie**, or leading urban professional and commercial classes, of the third.

The Estates General had not been convened since 1614 and the procedures for its meeting were disputed. In addition all three estates had grievances. The first two wished to resist taxation and did not wish to relinquish any power to the king. The third resented the special privileges of the first two. Some within the third estate, especially, were inspired by the *philosophes* to demand a more accountable government. Others, hit hard by a series of poor harvests, felt that the government, church, and nobility should do more to help them. The clergy and nobility wanted each estate to meet separately, but the third estate, whose numbers equalled the other two combined, argued for joint meetings. A few of the clergy and nobility agreed to join with them and together they swore the "Tennis Court Oath" to maintain themselves as a true National Assembly and to draft a constitution for a new government of France.

The leaders of the third estate and its allies took inspiration from the British and, even more so, from the American revolutions. Their local spokesman and leading pamphleteer was actually a clergyman, the Abbé Emmanuel-Joseph Sieyès (1748–1836), who wrote *What Is the Third Estate?* (1789), which opened with a catechism of three political questions and answers: "(1) What is the third estate? Everything. (2) What has it been in the political order up to the present? Nothing. (3) What does it demand? To become something." The leaders of the third estate began to ask for an end to the multitude of feudal privileges that had enriched and empowered the clergy and the nobility while reducing the opportunities available to everyone else and impoverishing the French Crown.

THE REVOLT OF THE POOR

Louis XVI, more fearful of the newly assertive third estate than of the clergy and nobility, called up some 18,000 troops to defend himself from possible attack at his palace in Versailles, where all these events were taking place. Meanwhile, in Paris, 12 miles (19 kilometers) away, and throughout France, mobs of people were rising against organized authority. The harvest had been poor, and the price of bread in 1789 was near record heights. Some

The Hall of Mirrors, Palace of Versailles, c. 1725. This opulent royal palace, 12 miles (19 kilometers) southwest of Paris, is closely associated with Louis XIV, the Sun King. His belief in the absolute power of kings finds its expression at Versailles. Its aristocratic splendor fueled the anger of the poor peasants and revolutionaries.

farmers refused to pay their taxes and their manorial dues, and many city people were hungry. Beggars and brigands began to roam the countryside and move toward Paris.

In the capital, mobs stormed the Bastille, which was a combination of jail and armory. Meeting violent resistance, they murdered the governor of the Bastille, the mayor of Paris, and a number of soldiers. In an attempt to contain these revolutionary disorders, the king recognized the National Assembly, the new group formed by the third estate and its allies, as representatives of the people and authorized it to draft a new constitution.

The National Assembly abolished what was left of feudalism and serfdom, the tithe for the church, and the special privileges of the nobility. It issued the "Declaration of the Rights of Man and the Citizen" with seventeen articles, including:

1. Men are born and remain free and equal in rights; social distinctions may be based only upon general usefulness.

2. The aim of every political association is the preservation of the natural and inalienable rights of man; these rights are liberty, property, security, and resistance to oppression.

3. The source of all sovereignty resides essentially in the nation. ...

6. Law is the expression of the general will. ... All citizens, being equal before it, are equally admissible to all public offices, positions, and employments, according to their capacity, and without other distinction than that of virtues and talents. ...

13. For the maintenance of the public force and for the expenses of administration a common tax is indispensable; it must be assessed equally on all citizens in proportion to their means. ...

15. Society has the right to require of every public agent an accounting of his administration.

Contemporary colored engraving showing women marching to Versailles on 5 October 1789. Angered by reports of a luxurious banquet staged by the king, a large crowd of Parisians, mostly women, stormed Versailles and laid siege to the royal palace. Louis XVI and his family, though later executed, were at this point saved only by the intervention of the French general the Marquis de Lafayette.

The Declaration further affirmed freedom of thought, religion, petition, and due process under law. It represented a triumph for the doctrines of the *philosophes*.

Meanwhile, hungry mobs in Paris continued towards insurrection. In October, led by a demonstration of housewives, market women, and revolutionary militants protesting the high price of bread, 20,000 Parisians marched 12 miles (19 kilometers) to the royal palace in Versailles. The "March of the Women" broke into the palace, overwhelmed the National Guard, and forced the royal family to return to Paris where they could be kept under surveillance. In the meantime, in the countryside, peasants felt an (unfounded) "Great Fear" that landlords were attempting to block reform by hiring thugs to burn the harvest. In response, peasants attacked the estates of the nobility and the clergy, and their managers.

Over the next two years, the National Assembly drew up a constitution, which called for a constitutional monarchy; did away with titles and perquisites of nobility and clergy; introduced uniform government across the country; disestablished the Roman Catholic clergy and confiscated the property of the church; and convened a new Legislative Assembly, for which about one-half of adult, male Frenchmen were entitled to vote, essentially by a property qualification. Protestants, Jews, and agnostics were admitted to full citizenship and could vote and run for office if they met the property qualifications. Citizenship would be based not on religious affiliation but on residence in the country and allegiance to its government. Except for the radical—and polarizing—anti-clerical position, the actions of the French Revolution thus far seemed quite similar to those of Britain and America. They were consistent with the optimistic and activist world-view of the *philosophes*.

INTERNATIONAL WAR, THE "SECOND" REVOLUTION, AND THE TERROR 1791–99

In June 1791 Louis XVI and his queen Marie-Antoinette attempted to flee France but were apprehended and, thereafter, held as virtual prisoners in the royal palace. Shocked and frightened, thousands of aristocrats emigrated to neighboring countries which were more respectful of monarchy and aristocracy. News of the abolition of feudal privilege and of the Civil Constitution of the Clergy filled the nobility and clergy across Europe with dread. Leopold II, the Habsburg Emperor (r. 1790–92) and brother of Marie-Antoinette, entered into discussions with other rulers to consider war against the new French government. The French National Assembly began to mobilize both in response to this threat and in anticipation of extending the revolution. In April 1792 they declared war on the Austrian monarchy, and for the next 23 years, France would be at war with several of the major countries of Europe.

Events careered onward at a revolutionary pace. The war went poorly and mobs stormed the royal palace attempting to kill the king. He sought pro-tection in the National Assembly and was impris-oned; all his official powers were terminated. The Legislative Assembly disbanded and called for a new National Convention—to be elected by univer-sal male suffrage—to draw up a new constitution. The new Convention met in September 1792. All the representatives were *Jacobins*, members of a nationwide network of political clubs named

FRENCH REVOLUTION—KEY EVENTS

1789

May Meeting of Estates-General called by Louis XVI to discuss financial reforms; nobles oppose reform

June Third Estate (commoners) demand end to system by which First and Second Estates (nobles and church) can outvote them; Louis rejects request

Third Estate declares themselves to be a National Assembly and resolves not to dissolve

July Threat to dissolve Assembly angers mob

Storming of the Bastille

August Abolition of privileges; peasants no longer pay tithes

1790

June National Assembly abolishes hereditary titles; other reforms passed include centralization of government and dissolution of religious orders

July Civil Constitution requires election of priests

1791

June Louis XVI escapes from Paris but is captured at Varennes

September King swears allegiance to Constitution

October New legislative assembly meets but is divided between Jacobins and Girondins

1792

January Girondins form government but are undermined by Jacobins

April Frances declares war on Austria

August Monarchy is overthrown

September National Convention, dominated by Jacobins, elected on basis of universal suffrage; proclaims a republic

1793

January Louis XVI guillotined

April National Convention establishes Committee of Public Safety, which is dominated by Maximilien Robespierre

October Marie-Antoinette guillotined

Reign of Terror begins

1794

July Robespierre and 21 supporters guillotined

Moderate Thermidoreans take control of Convention and create Directory of five members

1795–9 Directory fails to resolve France's internal and external problems

1799 Directory overthrown by coup, after which Consulate of three members, including Napoleon, is established

(ironically) for a former convent in Paris where they had first met. They divided into the more moderate *Girondins*, named for a region of France and in general representing the provinces, and the *Montagnards*, representatives mostly from Paris, who drew their name from the benches they occupied on the uppermost left side of the assembly hall. By 361 to 359 votes, the Convention voted to execute the king in January 1793. The "Second Revolution" was well underway.

Outside the Assembly, the Paris Commune, the government of Paris, represented the workers, merchants, and artisans of the city, who were generally more radical than the Convention. They were called the *sansculottes*, "without breeches," because the men wore long trousers rather than the knee breeches of the middle and aristocratic classes. In June 1793, the Commune invaded the National Convention and forced the arrest of thirty one *Girondins* on charges of treason, leaving the more radical *Montagnards* in control.

To govern in the midst of the combined international and civil warfare, the Convention created a Committee of Public Safety, which launched a Reign of Terror against "counter-revolutionaries." It executed about 40,000 people between mid-1793 and mid-1794. At Nantes, in the Vendée region of western France, the center of the royalist counter-revolution, the Committee intentionally drowned 2000 people. To wage war abroad it instituted a *levée en masse*, or national military draft, which raised an unprecedented army of 800,000 men, and mobilized the economic resources of France to support it.

The Committee intensified the campaign against feudal privilege, rejecting the payment of compensation for the one-time manor lords, who lost their special rights over their tenants. It promoted instruction in practical farming and craft production, spoke of introducing universal elementary education, and abolished slavery throughout France's colonies. It introduced a new calendar, counting Year 1 from the founding of the French Republic in 1793, giving new names to the twelve months, and dividing each month into three weeks of ten days each. The most important leader of the Committee, Maximilien Robespierre (1758–94), introduced in 1794 the Worship of the Supreme Being, a kind of civic religious ritual that alienated the Catholic majority in France.

By July 1794, however, French armies were winning wars against the other European powers, and the domestic economy seemed to be recovering.

The members of the Convention, partly out of fear for their own lives, managed to end both the mob-inspired violence and the official Terror. The Convention outlawed and guillotined Robespierre. It relaxed price controls and, when working-class mobs threatened the Convention, called in the troops and suppressed the revolt. In 1795 it instituted yet another constitution, this time calling for a three-stage election of a representative government. Almost all adult males could vote for electors who, in turn, chose a national legislative assembly composed of men who did have to meet property qualifications and who, in turn, chose an executive of five Directors. When the 1795 elections were threatened by insurrection, the Convention called upon General Napoleon Bonaparte (1769–1821) to protect the process.

The Directory, as it was called, governed from 1795 to 1799. With the execution of the monarch, the manorial system and the privileges of the nobility and clergy had come to an end, and the Directory ratified the new peasant and commercial landowners in the possession of their new property. However, the Directory itself was unpopular and unstable, and the greater freedom benefited its opponents while at the same time enabling the Catholic church to make a strong comeback. The elections of Directors in 1797, 1798, and 1799 were disputed, and on each occasion army officers were called in to dismiss the Directors, until, in 1799, Bonaparte, acting with the Abbé Sieyès, staged a *coup d'état* and had himself appointed First Consul. In 1802 his position was upgraded to consul for life and, in 1804, to emperor. Losing the right of free elections, France itself became a benevolent despotism. The process that historians usually call the French Revolution was over.

NAPOLEON IN POWER 1799–1812

As head of government, Napoleon consolidated and even expanded many of the innovations of the Revolution. To maintain the equality of classes and to systematize the administration of justice, he codified the laws of France. The Code Napoléon or Civil Code, which was issued in 1804, pressed for equality before the law and the principle of a "career open to talents," that is, all people should have access to professional advancement according to their ability, rather than by birth or social status. Uniform codes of criminal, commercial, and penal law were also introduced. The administration was

Napoleon Crossing the Alps by Jacques-Louis David, c. 1800. Having chronicled the Revolution with his brush, David became Napoleon's official painter. The heroic style of the portrait matches the Emperor's enormous confidence as he heads for military glory in the Italian campaigns of 1796–7. The truth of the journey was rather different: Napoleon crossed the Alps on a docile but footsure mule, not a fiery stallion. (*Palace of Versailles, near Paris*)

POLITICAL REVOLUTIONS IN EUROPE AND THE AMERICAS (1688–1850)   483

organized into a smoothly functioning service throughout France.

Fearing a counter-revolution led by the church, Napoleon reached a **Concordat** with the Pope. The French government continued to hold the former church lands, but agreed in exchange to pay the salaries of the clergy (including Protestants and others) and to allow the Pope to regain authority over the appointment and discipline of the Roman Catholic clergy. Protestants, dissenters, Jews, and others were reaffirmed in full citizenship, with all the rights and obligations that such status entailed, as long as they swore their allegiance to the state. In many conquered cities, including Rome and Frankfurt, French armies pulled down the ghetto walls that for centuries had segregated Jews. The government hired a large bureaucracy to adminis-

ter the state. It selected personnel mostly on the Revolutionary principle of a "career open to talent," hiring the best qualified personnel rather than those with personal or hereditary connections.

This openness of opportunity suited Napoleon very well. He had come from Corsica, of a modest family, and made his mark as a military officer. He had no respect for unearned authority. Nor was he formally religious. He earned his power through his military, administrative, and leadership skills. In a striking exception to the principle of advancement by merit, however, Napoleon appointed his brothers as kings of Spain, Holland, and Westphalia, his brother-in-law as king of Naples, and his stepson as viceroy of the kingdom of Italy. He himself continued to lead the forces of France in military victories over the powers of Europe.

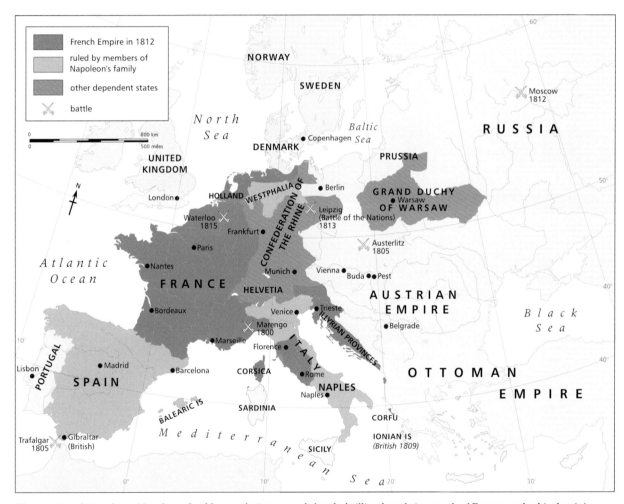

The empire of Napoleon Napoleon, fired by revolutionary zeal, fought brilliantly to bring much of Europe under his dominion, often installing relatives as rulers. Napoleonic institutions were introduced to Italy, the Low Countries, Germany, and then Poland by force of arms. By 1812 Napoleon seemed invincible, but Britain's strength at sea and Napoleon's disastrous losses on land in his invasion of Russia (1812) led to his downfall.

NAPOLEONIC WARS AND THE SPREAD OF REVOLUTION 1799–1812

As a son of the Revolution, Napoleon sought to spread its principles by force of arms. By 1810 he had conquered or entered into alliances with all the major powers and regions of Europe except Portugal, the Ottoman-held Balkans, and Britain. In each conquered state, Napoleon introduced the principal reforms of the Revolution: an end to feudal privilege, equality of rights, religious toleration, codified law, free trade, and efficient and systematic administration, including statistical accounting, registration of documents, and the use of the metric system. In many areas of Europe, Napoleon was welcomed for the reforms he brought.

There were, however, flaws in Napoleon's policies, and they finally brought his rule to an end. First, Napoleon attempted to conquer Britain, and ultimately the naval power of that island nation and the land forces of its allies, especially those of Russia, proved too strong. Napoleon could not break the British hold on continental shipping and was defeated at sea by Lord Nelson at the Battle of Trafalgar in 1805. When the Russian emperor supported Britain, Napoleon invaded Russia in 1812 and mired his army irretrievably in the vastness of that country during the bitterness of its winter. During that campaign, 400,000 of Napoleon's troops died from battle, starvation, and exposure; another 100,000 were captured.

Finally, the nations Napoleon conquered began to experience the stirrings of nationalism and the desire to rule themselves. Haiti, which had achieved virtual independence in the 1790s, resisted Napoleon's attempt to re-impose French rule and re-institute slavery in the island (see p. 486). Some 50,000 French troops perished in Haiti, most by diseases such as yellow fever, but many at the hands of revolutionary slaves. European peoples, too, did not want their countries to be colonies of France. By 1813 Napoleon had been defeated by his disastrous losses in Russia and by a coalition of European armies; the French were driven back to their borders. In 1814 Napoleon abdicated and Louis XVIII (r. 1814–15; 1815–24) assumed the throne of France. Napoleon escaped from exile on the Mediterranean island of Elba only to be defeated and exiled again in 1815, this time to St. Helena in the South Atlantic. The Napoleonic era was over. Political conservatism enveloped France and Europe for a generation.

HAITI: SLAVE REVOLUTION AND RESPONSE 1791

The formal philosophy and rhetoric of enlightenment and revolution (see p. 463) proclaim the natural desire of all humans to be free. In the slave plantations of the Caribbean, slave revolts on a small, local scale were common, feared, and ruthlessly suppressed. In the western sector of the island of Hispaniola in the colony of Saint-Domingue (modern Haiti), French planters had established one of the most brutal of the slave plan-

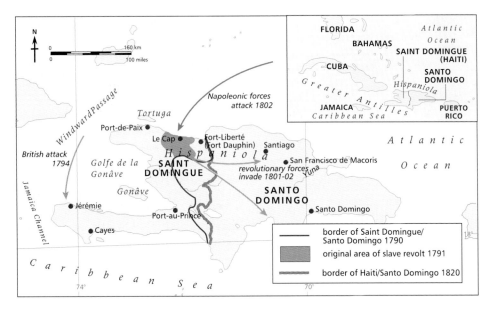

The revolution in Haiti
One of the most dramatic revolutions occurred on the Caribbean island of Hispaniola. A slave revolt in 1791 in the French region, Saint Domingue, spread rapidly, briefly penetrating and uniting with the Spanish sector, Santo Domingo. Despite interventions by French and British forces, and the incarceration of its leader, Toussaint L'Ouverture, in 1803, Haiti gained its independence from France in 1804, the first successful slave revolt in history.

tation systems. By 1791, 500,000 black slaves formed the overwhelming majority of the population, with 40,000 whites, many of them owners of plantations and slaves, and 30,000 free people of color, both **mulatto** and black. For decades, the slaves had escaped psychologically and culturally through the practice of **voodoo**, a religion that blended the Catholicism of their masters with religious practices brought from Africa. Physically, they had escaped through *maroonage*, flight from the plantations to the surrounding hills. Sometimes the escaped slaves, maroons, established their own colonies. In the 1750s one of the maroons, François Makandal, built among the maroon colonies a network of resistance to slavery. Inspired to independence by voodoo beliefs and using poison to attack individual plantation owners, Makandal apparently planned to poison the water supply of Le Cap, the main town of northern Saint-Domingue, but he was captured and burned at the stake in 1758.

French lithograph of Pierre Dominique Toussaint L'Ouverture, early nineteenth century. The colony of Saint-Domingue (present-day Haiti) in the West Indies had made a fortune for the French through sugar plantations worked by African slaves. In the 1790s, under the leadership of Toussaint L'Ouverture, it became the site of a black liberation movement that would eventually lead to independence. The one-time slave acquired his surname because of the ferocity with which he made an opening ("ouverture") in the enemy ranks.

In 1791, slave revolts broke out across Saint-Domingue. The inspiration seems to have been the natural desire for freedom, perhaps abetted by news of the American and French Revolutions. One of the earliest rallying cries, delivered by the poet Boukman Dutty in Haitian-French patois, *"Coute la liberté li pale nan coeur nous tous"*—"Listen to the voice of liberty which speaks in the hearts of all of us," implied no knowledge of the European and American revolutions.

The revolt spread. From guerrilla warfare by maroon bands, it grew to general armed struggle and civil warfare. In the western part of Saint-Domingue, white planters welcomed the support of British troops, who came as allies to suppress the slave revolt but also to drive out the French. The mulattoes—those of mixed race parentage—were free people, and some of them owned slaves. They now sought their own rights of representation and were divided over the issue of slavery. In the eastern part of Saint-Domingue, a new leader, Toussaint L'Ouverture (c. 1743–1803), a freed black, established an alliance with the Spanish rulers against both the slave system in Saint-Domingue (but not in the Spanish part of the island!) and the French. Toussaint incorporated the rhetoric of the French Revolution into his own. In 1794, under Robespierre, the French National Assembly abolished slavery in all French colonies. In response, Toussaint linked himself to France as he continued his war against slaveowners, who were now aligned with the British and who resisted the new French decree. By May 1800 Toussaint had become the effective ruler of Saint-Domingue.

When Napoleon came to power in 1799 he reversed French policy on slavery. He dispatched 20,000 French troops to recapture the island and, presumably, to reinstitute slavery as he did in Guadeloupe in 1802. Napoleon's representative deceived Toussaint into suspending his revolution. Toussaint was imprisoned in 1802 and exiled to France, where he died the next year. Nevertheless, unified black and mulatto armies, now under many different cooperating leaders rather than the single command of Toussaint, continued the struggle against France, drove out its forces, and, once again, abolished slavery. As many as 50,000 French troops died of yellow fever, and thousands more became military casualties. On January 1, 1804, Saint-Domingue at last proclaimed its independence and its new name of Haiti, the Carib name for mountain. This completed the only known successful slave revolution in history.

ABOLITION OF SLAVERY AND THE SLAVE TRADE: HISTORIANS DEBATE THE CAUSES

Initially, the British tried to assist in putting down the slave rebellion in Haiti. When they failed, their subsequent decision to limit the spread of slavery by abolishing the slave trade in 1807 reflected, in part, their fear of further revolts. In 1833 Britain abolished slavery throughout its Empire. The United States, a slave-holding country which feared that the Haitian slave revolt might spread northward, prohibited all trade with Haiti in 1806. In 1808, following Britain's lead, America outlawed participation in the international slave trade, although it abolished internal slavery only after the Civil War (1861–5). It recognized Haiti as an independent country also during that war, in 1862.

Even as late as the 1840s, however, the slave trade continued at about three-quarters of its highest volume. Revolution in Haiti and civil war in the United States indicated the depth of passions surrounding the issue. However, the Atlantic slave trade did not end effectively until slavery was abolished in 1876 in Puerto Rico, in 1884 in Cuba, and in 1888 in Brazil.

Why was the slave trade, and then slavery itself, abolished in the Atlantic countries? To what extent was the spread of democratic revolution responsible? Analyses differ. Historians who emphasize the significance of the Haitian Revolution, as C.L.R. James and David Nicholls do, stress the fear that it engendered among slave owners. In the lands of the Caribbean, including northeastern Brazil, black slaves working the high-mortality plantations formed up to 90 percent of the population. Local rebellions already occurred frequently, and large-scale revolution now appeared as a real possibility. The abolition of the slave trade provided some limit on the slave population, although total abolition— a much more expensive act for the slave owners— came only later.

A second school of thought, shared by historians such as David Brion Davis and Orlando Patterson, stresses the importance of compassion as a motive. Davis emphasizes the increasing influence of humanitarian sentiment in European Christian thought from the seventeenth century:

The philosophy of benevolence was a product of the seventeenth century, when certain British Protestants, shaken by theological controversy and the implications of modern science, looked increasingly to human nature and conduct as a basis for faith. In their impatience with theological dogma, their distaste for the doctrine of original sin, their appreciation for human feeling and sentiment, and their confidence in man's capacity for moral improvement, these Latitudinarians, as they were called, anticipated the main concerns of the Enlightenment, and laid an indispensable foundation for social reform. (pp. 348–49)

Paradoxically, the emphasis on compassion increased in reaction against the immense scale and unprecedented cruelty of slavery in the New World. Among Christian groups opposing slavery, Quakers and Methodists stood out. The birth and growth of both these denominations—Quakerism under the leadership of George Fox (1624–91) and Methodism under John Wesley (1703–91)—were contemporary with the development of mass slavery in the Americas. Other branches of Christianity

William Wilberforce by George Richmond, 1833. An evangelical Christian and social reformer, Wilberforce was elected to Parliament in 1780, after which he devoted his energies to abolishing slavery. His ultimate goal—the Emancipation Bill—was finally passed in 1833, one month after his death. (*National Portrait Gallery, London*)

had long since made peace with the institution of slavery, contenting themselves with promising a gentler existence in life after death. Quakers and Methodists, however, had to confront the reality of slavery for the first time in one of its cruelest, New World, forms. In Britain, William Wilberforce (1759–1833), a philanthropist and member of the Clapham Sect—a group of well-to-do Evangelicals—played a major part in the antislavery movement. As a Member of Parliament, he led the campaign to abolish the slave trade and to emancipate existing slaves.

The *philosophes* argued a third, similar but more intellectual position against slavery. They argued that slavery violated the law of nature; it was inconsistent with the nature of humankind. Montesquieu

(1689–1755), in his assessments of the nature of laws and government, argued that "the call for slavery was the call of the wealthy and the decadent, not for the general welfare of mankind" (cited in Davis, p. 408).

Finally, an economic critique began to develop in the eighteenth century. Slavery was not profitable to the society, certainly not to the slave, and not to the development of a more productive economy in the long run. In *The Wealth of Nations* Adam Smith argued that slavery, like all examples of monopoly and special privilege, inhibited economic growth. Lacking the opportunity to acquire wealth and property for himself, the slave would find it in his interest to work as little as possible. Slave-owners advocated their system not so much

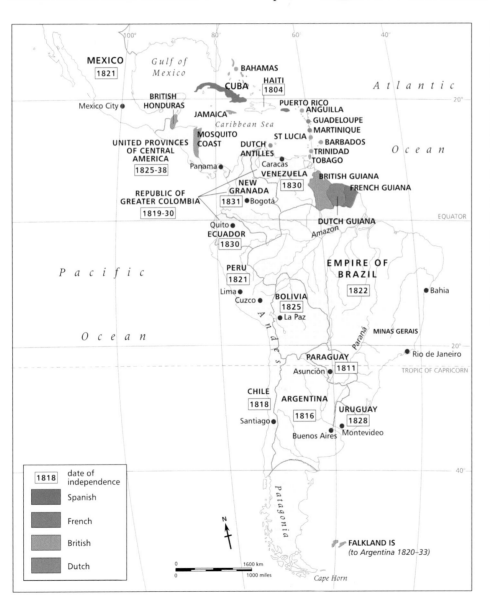

Liberation movements in Latin America The collapse of Iberian rule in Latin America was virtually complete by 1826. Sustained campaigns by Simón Bolívar and Antonio José de Sucre demolished Spanish control of Venezuela, Colombia, and Peru while, from the south, José de San Martin led the Argentine and Chilean Army of the Andes north to Lima. But liberation brought many internal power struggles and divisions, leaving the present-day South American map comprising some twenty republics.

for its economic benefits but for the power it gave them over others, despite economic losses! The leading exponents of this economic rationale for abolition in recent times have been Marxists, led by Eric Williams in his classic *Capitalism and Slavery* (1944). Many economic historians disagreed with this analysis, most notably Robert Fogel and Stanley Engerman, who published *Time on the Cross* in 1974, an elaborate two-volume statistical study linking economics with statistics (**econometrics**) to show the profitability of slavery. Seymour Drescher argued bluntly (1977) that abolition was "econocide," economic disaster, for Britain. Drescher sided with the humanitarian assessment: abolition was implemented despite its economic costs.

What to do without slaves? The successor system to slavery was not free labor. Indentured labor, supplied in large part by vast contract immigration from India and China, filled the labor needs of the post-slavery Caribbean as well as those of new plantation economies in the Indian Ocean in Fiji, Mauritius, and Réunion, and in south and east Africa. Although not quite slaves, indentured servants traded many of their basic economic and political rights for a number of years in exchange for employment.

Finally, with the export of slave labor from Africa banned, European entrepreneurs began in the later 1800s to explore the possibilities of shifting the production of primary products to Africa itself and to employ on-site personnel to perform the necessary work. Although this system sounded like free labor, in fact the wages were so low and conditions so abysmal, that many observers saw these economic initiatives as a newer form of slavery.

Anonymous painting of *Simón Bolívar Crossing the Andes*, early 19th century. After a youth spent in Europe, Bolívar returned to Latin America and devoted the rest of his life to securing its liberation from Spain. His military campaigns led to the independence of Venezuela, Colombia, Ecuador and Peru, and in 1825, he established a new republic in southern Peru, which was named Bolivia in his honor. (The painting is an obvious homage to David's *Napoleon*, see p. 483.)

THE END OF COLONIALISM IN LATIN AMERICA: INDEPENDENCE AND DISILLUSIONMENT 1810–30

In the period 1810 to 1826 virtually all the countries of Latin America expelled their European colonial rulers and established their independence. Latin Americans drew inspiration from the intellectual and political legacies of the American, French, and Haitian revolutions, although few wanted to move so far toward democratic rights as the Europeans had done, and many were frightened by the events in Haiti.

The revolts of the early nineteenth century were led, for the most part, by creole elites, American-born direct descendants of Spanish settlers. A series of earlier revolts, however, had been led by Amerindians and *mestizos*. In 1780, in Cuzco, Peru, Tupac Amaru, a *mestizo* with Inca ancestors, led 70,000 rebels against Spanish rule. Creoles did not join in this revolt and Tupac Amaru was captured and executed in 1783. The entire revolt was brutally crushed. The Comunero Revolt in Bogotá, Colombia in 1781, drove the viceroy from Bogotá, but ended with some concessions by the Spanish and internal fighting among the rebels. A conspiracy among bureaucrats, intellectuals, and miners in Minas Girais, Brazil, was discovered in 1788, and its leaders were arrested and hanged. Mulattoes led a revolt in Bahia, Brazil, in 1798. At the time of all these revolts, Spain and Portugal were still independent, powerful countries and, with the aid of creoles and *mazombos* (American-born direct descendants of Portuguese settlers), they suppressed the revolts. In general, the creoles and *mazombos* saw their fate linked more to the Spanish and Portuguese rulers than to the Amerindians or to those of mixed parentage. The Napoleonic wars in Spain, however, gave the colonies the opportunity to declare their independence, with the creoles leading the way. The revolts were bloody and successful.

In virtually every revolt, leadership was provided by a creole elite. Such men as Father Miguel Hidalgo (1753–1811) in Mexico, Simón Bolívar (1783–1830) in Venezuela and northern South America, and José de San Martín (1778–1850) in Argentina and southern South America, were all creoles, as were their leading generals, administrators, and supporters. They were familiar with European traditions and events, and many of them had studied in Europe. Indeed many of the revolutions seemed to be fought for the benefit of the creoles, who actually formed less than 5 percent of the total population. Other Latin Americans, *mestizos* and Amerindians, gained little. On the Caribbean islands of Cuba and Puerto Rico there were no rebellions. Here the elites, frightened lest the slave revolt of Haiti be repeated on their own islands, remained loyal to Spain.

MEXICO

Father Miguel Hidalgo led the first wave of Mexico's revolt until he was executed in 1811. Father José María Morelos (1765–1815), then took command of the revolutionary movement. Morelos sought to displace the Spanish and creole elites, to abolish slavery, and, unlike Hidalgo, to revoke the special privileges and landholdings of the church. The Spanish captured and executed him in 1815. By the time Mexico finally won its independence in 1821, its revolution had passed to the hands of its most conservative creole elite. For two years Mexico was ruled as a monarchy, but in 1823 it was proclaimed a republic. Military leaders, businessmen, and foreign powers all struggled for control and Mexico remained unstable for decades. Its size

was also reduced by half. Central American regions, after years of rebellions, broke away from Mexico and formed a union. The resentment of Guatemala, the largest country in the region, combined with regional antagonisms, led to the dissolution of this union in 1838. Texas, with waves of immigrants entering from the United States, and encouraged by the United States government, declared its independence from Mexico in 1836. Nine years later the United States annexed Texas, precipitating the Mexican-American war. In the peace settlement, America gained the territories of its current southwestern States.

BRAZIL

Brazil, the largest country in Latin America in terms of both geography and population, had a different method of achieving independence, and this helps to explain why it did not break apart after independence. When Napoleon invaded Portugal in 1807, the Portuguese royal family, assisted by Britain, fled to Rio de Janeiro and ruled the Portuguese Empire from the Brazilian capital for thirteen years. King Dom João (John) VI (r. 1816–26) raised Brazil's legal status to equal that of Portugal and expanded Rio as a center of trade, administration, education, and cultural institutions.

In 1821 João returned with his court to Lisbon, but left his son and heir, Prince Pedro, in Rio. When the Parliament, or Cortes, in Lisbon attempted to cut Brazil and Rio back to size, the American-born Brazilian elite, the *mazombos*, counseled defiance. In 1822 Pedro declared Brazil independent, and Portugal did little to stop the move. Pedro was soon crowned "Constitutional Emperor and Perpetual Defender of Brazil," but the effective rulers of Brazil were its *mazombo* elites. Brazil was thus spared the warfare, disintegration, and *caudillismo*, or rule of local strongmen, characteristic of Spanish Latin America, but it was ruled by very similar American-born descendants of Iberian families. While the former Spanish colonies became republics, Brazil became a monarchy under a member of the Portuguese royal family.

PARAGUAY: THE NEW HISTORIOGRAPHY

Tiny landlocked Paraguay, with a population of 150,000, declared its independence in 1810–11 from the viceroyalty of La Plata as well as from Spain and defeated an Argentine army which had been dispatched to subdue it. Paraguay's Dictator, José Gaspar Rodríguez de Francia, who governed until his death in 1840, has been characterized very negatively by historians of several nations, including his own. But new revisionist studies by historians such as Richard Alan White portray Francia as a revolutionary who led his country to a period of exemplary economic and cultural independence. They suggest that Francia's negative evaluations resulted from his harsh treatment of creole elites, and his autocratic policies, but that his concern for economic development helped the Amerindians of Paraguay by keeping them isolated from exploitative world markets.

Paraguay based its revolution on self-government and land redistribution. For a half century, rulers redistributed lands of the government, the church, and private large-scale landowners to the masses of *mestizo* and Indian cultivators. Paraguay became self-sufficient in food production. The government established a simple but effective education system which virtually eliminated illiteracy. The state established an iron works, textile mills, and livestock industries. It did not accept foreign investment or entanglement. Paraguay's achievements in political independence, economic growth, self-reliance, and raising the standards of its native and *mestizo* populations, engendered envy in its neighbors and apprehension among foreign financiers.

From 1865 to 1870 Argentina, Brazil, and Uruguay, backed by loans from England, fought against Paraguay to destroy its populist policies. After the invaders won, they killed off the majority of Paraguay's adult male population, dismantled its political institutions, and opened its economy to foreign investment and control. Paraguay's unique experiment was over.

AN EPIC VERSE HISTORY OF LATIN AMERICA

The Chilean writer Pablo Neruda (1904–73), a recipient of the Nobel Prize for Literature in 1971, advanced a critical and disillusioned vision of Latin America in its first century of independence. In *Canto General* (1950), Neruda's epic poem of Latin American history, he paints the Spanish settlement of the land as a harsh and tawdry process.

> The land passed between the entailed estates,
> doubloon to doubloon, dispossessed,
> paste of apparitions and convents
> until the entire blue geography was
> divided into haciendas and encomiendas.
> The mestizo's ulcer, the overseer's
> and slaver's whip
> moved through the lifeless space.
> The Creole was an impoverished specter
> who picked up the crumbs,
> until he saved enough
> to acquire a little title
> painted with gilt letters.
> And in the dark carnival
> he masqueraded as a count
> a proud man among beggars,
> with his little silver cane. ...

The *conquistadores* of the sixteenth century had been expelled by the *libertadors* of the early nineteenth century, but the infrastructure of shopkeepers, clergy, administrators, and hangers-on that had become established in Latin America remained in place as the real inheritors of the revolution. Neruda scowled:

> Soon, undershirt by undershirt,
> they expelled the conquistador
> and established the conquest
> of the grocery store.
> Then they acquired pride
> bought on the black market.
> They were adjudged
> haciendas, whips, slaves,
> catechisms, commissaries,
> alms boxes, tenements, brothels,
> and all this they called
> holy western culture.

Neruda singles out the petty businessmen as the new, but unworthy, elite of Latin America. In more enterprising regions bigger businessmen and investors occupied the leadership positions. These men of practical affairs combined with craftsmen on the one hand, and with government policy makers on the other, to introduce limited industrial development in the twentieth century (see Chapter 23).

Francisco Goya:
REVOLUTIONARY REALITY AND RHETORIC

The *philosophes* of the Enlightenment proclaimed that human reason and learning could initiate a new age of peace, prosperity, happiness, and personal development. Many radicals put their faith in the French Revolution to usher in this new era, although its leaders admitted that the process might, unfortunately, be bloody. The Spanish painter Francisco Goya (1746–1828), while siding with the revolutionary cause, created dazzling, cynical critiques of these claims that continue to trouble us two centuries later.

Later to become one of the great artistic geniuses of his age, Goya studied painting in Madrid. In the 1790s he produced a series of etchings, "Los Caprichos," which are considered among the most powerful since those of Rembrandt van Rijn (1606–1669). One of them, *The Sleep of Reason Produces Monsters* (**picture 1**), created a terrifying scene that apparently challenged a key tenet of the Enlightenment. The title is included within the painting itself and would seem to suggest that when the mind's defenses are down, as

in sleep, we are prey to internal monsters. These psychological insights into the frailties of the human mind precede Sigmund Freud's (1856–1939) concept of the unconscious (see p. 596) by a century. Goya later added a subtitle echoing the faith of the Enlightenment: "Imagination abandoned by reason produces impossible monsters; united with her, she is the mother of the

Picture 1 Francisco Goya, *The Sleep of Reason Produces Monsters*, 1799.

arts." But the etching itself continues to question whether reason will ever be powerful enough to subdue all the demons which beset us.

Goya did not, however, defect to the side of traditional inherited privilege. Commissioned to paint the family of the Spanish King Charles IV, who had joined with other European monarchs in war against the young French republic, Goya produced a canvas of psychological revelations just as devastating in its own way as *The Sleep of Reason*. In *Charles IV and His Family* (**picture 2**), painted in 1800, the clothing of the royal family is regal enough, as is the setting in one of the picture galleries of the palace; Goya's techniques of illuminating his subjects is incandescent and the medium is an enormous, opulent, 9-by-11-foot oil painting. But the vulgar postures and faces of the subjects betray an unimaginative, harsh, hollow, and frightened family. Royalty was no more exempt from Goya's attacks than reason.

Goya's *Execution of the Defenders of Madrid* (**picture 3**)

Picture 2 Francisco Goya, *Charles IV and His Family*, 1800.

depicts yet another betrayal of high aspirations. Many Spaniards had hoped that Napoleon's victory over Spain would bring a new era of enlightenment and progress. But the French troops were barbaric, and the Spanish resistance savage. The crushing of the rebellion culminated in the execution of Spanish martyrs on May 3, 1808. In another huge canvas, Goya illuminated this defeat with the intensity of a religious martyrdom, focussed on the Christlike pose of the firing squad's victim. For Goya, royal power had been a sham, but neither had reason or revolution fulfilled their promise of creating an enlightened world.

Picture 3 Francisco Goya, *Execution of the Defenders of Madrid, 3rd May, 1808*, 1814.

AFTER INDEPENDENCE

The continent had been wrested from Spain by the sword. The greatest of the leaders, Simón Bolívar of Venezuela in the north, José de San Martín of Argentina in the south, Antonio José de Sucré of Ecuador, and Bernardo O'Higgins of Chile combined military excellence with intellectual, administrative, and diplomatic accomplishments; many others had been essentially military figures. Once the Spanish were defeated, the generals began to fight among themselves.

Bolívar grew disillusioned and bitter as "Gran Colombia" dissolved into Colombia, Venezuela, and Ecuador. Further south, the Spanish viceroyalty of La Plata dissolved into Argentina, Paraguay, Uruguay, and Bolivia. For a decade, 1829–39, under General Andrés Santa Cruz, a *mestizo*, Peru and Bolivia were united, but then broke apart, to the relief of some of their neighbors. Chile, isolated by the Andes mountains to its east, and open to the outside world via the Pacific Ocean to its west, also became a separate, independent nation. In total, 18 separate nations emerged from Spanish America.

Warfare between many of the new states and violent repression of the Indian and African-American populations (one-fourth of Brazil's population in 1850 were slaves) gave prominence and power both to national armies and to private military forces throughout Latin America. The military strongmen, or *caudillos*, came to control local areas and even national governments. Personal rule, only minimally controlled by official codes of law or by formal election procedures, prevailed in many countries up to the last decades of the twentieth century.

RELIGIOUS AND ECONOMIC ISSUES

Many of the new nations of Latin America wished to increase their own power by breaking the authority and wealth of the Catholic church. Many confiscated church lands, refused the official collection of tithes to fund the church, demanded a voice in the selection of church clergy, and limited church control over educational facilities. To some degree, these crusades against church power reflected also Indian pressures for a greater appreciation of indigenous cultures, both outside of Christianity and in syncretic movements to join Christian practices to existing indigenous beliefs and rituals. Mexico, which had a large Indian and *mestizo* population, was most eager to limit church power, and its continuing struggles were the bloodiest. Over time, in

AN EARLY CRITIQUE OF ECONOMIC DEPENDENCE

*L*atin Americans believed that with political independence would come economic independence. In 1815, while in temporary exile in Jamaica, Simón Bolívar wrote of the indignity as well as the impoverishment brought upon Latin America by foreign control.

Americans today, and perhaps to a greater extent than ever before, who live within the Spanish system occupy a position in society no better than that of serfs destined to labor, or at best they have no more status than that of mere consumers. Yet even this status is surrounded with galling restrictions, such as being forbidden to grow European crops, or to store products which are royal monopolies, or to establish factories of a type the Peninsula [Spain] itself does not possess. To this add the privileges, even in articles of prime necessity, and the barriers between the American provinces, designed to prevent all exchange of trade, traffic, and understanding. In short, do you wish to know what our future held?—simply the cultivation of the fields of indigo, grain, coffee, sugar cane, cacao, and cotton; cattle raising on the broad plains, hunting wild game in the jungles; digging in the earth to mine its gold—but even these limitations could never satisfy the greed of Spain. So negative was our existence that I can find nothing comparable in any other civilized society. … (Letter of January, 1815)

Ironically, even after political independence became a reality, the economy of Latin America remained subject to the control of foreign investors.

each country, individual accommodations were made between church and state, and to this day they continue to renegotiate their positions.

Economically, until at least 1870, Latin America remained overwhelmingly agrarian, with the hacienda, a kind of feudal estate, continuing as the principal institution for organizing production and labor. The vast majority of the hacienda owners were creole, while the peasant workers were overwhelmingly Indian and *mestizo*. Many Indians remained in villages, where their participation in any larger, external, national economy was marginal. Because ancestry counted so profoundly for each group, the ethnic and racial composition of the population, whether native-born or foreign-born, whether Indian, African, *mestizo*, or Caucasian, in large measure determined the fate and the culture of each colony.

As production for foreign markets increased, new forms of foreign domination, "**neo-colonialism**," arose. The principal new power was Britain, and its method was economic investment and control. By 1824, there were 100 British commercial firms functioning in Latin America staffed by 3000 British citizens. Shipping to and from Latin America was carried primarily by British ships. Britain's economic domination of Latin American economies increased with the growing productivity and profitability of its industrial revolution at home.

In the mid-nineteenth century, Latin America was home to a mixed amalgam of philosophies and practices. From the United States and France, it inherited a legacy of revolution in the name of representative democracy and individual freedom. It inherited from Spain and Portugal a loyalty to more conservative, religious, hierarchical traditions and, from its own history of settlement, a diverse mix of peoples from three continents, often in uneasy relationship to one another. From the international economy Latin America inherited a subordinate position, dependent on outside supply, demand, and control.

This chapter began with the relatively clear voices of liberal, individualistic philosophies of revolution as they were expressed in northwestern Europe and the United States, although the actual revolutions which resulted remained far from achieving these goals. It ends with Latin America and its diverse array of cross-cutting philosophies, peoples, and interests—both internal and external to the region—as they struggled to assert their own direction and identity. In the next chapter we see how the advent of a different kind of revolution—one in industrial production and organization—intersected with these already complex trends.

BIBLIOGRAPHY

Andrea, Alfred and James Overfield, eds.
   The Human Record, 2 vols.
   (Boston: Houghton Mifflin Co., 2nd ed, 1994).

Archer, Leonie, ed. *Slavery and Other Forms of Unfree Labor* (London: Routledge, 1988).

Bayly, Christopher Alan. *Indian Society and the Making of the British Empire* (Cambridge: Cambridge University Press, 1988).

Boorstin, Daniel. *The Discoverers* (New York: Random House, 1983).

Burns, E. Bradford. *Latin America* (Englewood Cliffs, NJ: Prentice Hall, 5th ed, 1990).

Curtin, Philip. *The Rise and Fall of the Plantation Complex* (New York: Cambridge University Press, 1989).

Columbia College, Columbia University. *Contemporary Civilization in the West*, Vol 2. (New York: Columbia University Press, 1954).

Davis, David Brion. *The Problem of Slavery in the Age of Revolution*, 1770–1823 (Ithaca: Cornell University Press, 1975).

de Bary, Wm. Theodore, *et al. Sources of Indian Tradition* (New York: Columbia University Press, 1960).

Drescher, Seymour. *Econocide* (Pittsburgh: University of Pittsburgh Press, 1977).

—. *The Problem of Slavery in Western Culture* (New York: Oxford University Press, 1966).

Fick, Carolyn E. *The Making of Haiti* (Knoxville: University of Tennessee Press, 1990).

Fogel, Robert William and Stanley L. Engerman. *Time on the Cross*, 2 vols (Boston: Little, Brown, 1974).

Foner, Eric, ed. *The New American History* (Philadelphia: Temple University Press, 1990).

Foucault, Michel. *Discipline and Punish: The Birth of the Prison*, trans. by Alan Sheridan (New York: Vintage Books, 1979).

Furet, François. *Interpreting the French Revolution*, trans. by Elborg Foster (Cambridge: Cambridge University Press, 1981).

Galilei, Galileo. *Discoveries and Opinions of Galileo*, trans. by Stillman Drake (New York: Anchor Books, 1957).

Genovese, Eugene. *From Rebellion to Revolution* (Baton Rouge: Louisiana University Press, 1979).

Halévy, Élie. *England in 1815* (New York: Barnes and Noble, 1961).

Hanke, Lewis and Jane M. Rausch, eds. *People and Issues in Latin American History* (New York: Markus Weiner, 1990).

Hobbes, Thomas. *Selections*, ed. Frederick J.E. Woodbridge (New York: Charles Scribner's Sons, 1958).

Hobsbawm, Eric. *The Age of Empire 1875–1914* (New York: Vintage Books, 1987).

—. *The Age of Revolution 1789–1848* (New York: New American Library, 1962).

James, C.L.R., *The Black Jacobins* (New York: Random House, 1963).

Kolchin, Peter. *American Slavery 1619–1877* (New York: Hill and Wang, 1993).

Kuhn, Thomas S. *The Copernican Revolution* (Cambridge: Harvard University Press, 1957).

—. *The Structure of Scientific Revolutions* (Chicago: University of Chicago Press, 2nd edn, 1980).

Lefebvre, Georges. *The Coming of the French Revolution*, trans. by R.R. Palmer (Princeton: Princeton University Press, 1947).

Locke, John. *Second Treatise on Government* (Arlington Heights, IL: Crofts Classics, 1982).

Mintz, Sidney W. *Sweetness and Power: The Place of Sugar in Modern History* (New York: Viking Penguin, 1985).

Murphey, Rhoads. *A History of Asia* (New York: HarperCollins, 1992).

Nash, Gary B., *et al.*, eds. *The American People*, 2 vols. (New York: Harper and Row, 1986).

Nehru, Jawaharlal. *Glimpses of World History* (New Delhi: Jawaharlal Nehru Memorial Fund and Oxford University Press, ed. 1982).

Neruda, Pablo. *Canto General*, trans. by Jack Schmitt (Berkeley: University of California Press, 1991).

Nicholls, David, "Haiti: Race, Slavery and Independence (1804–1825)," in Archer, ed., *Slavery*, pp. 225–38.

Northrup, David, ed. *The Atlantic Slave Trade* (Lexington, MA: D.C. Heath and Company, 1994).

Palmer, R.R. *The Age of Democratic Revolution* (Princeton: Princeton University Press, 1959).

Patterson, Orlando. *Freedom in the Making of Western Culture* (New York: Basic Books, 1991).

Raychaudhuri, Tapan. *Europe Reconsidered: Perceptions of the West in Nineteenth-century Bengal* (Delhi: Oxford University Press, 1988).

Rousseau, Jean-Jacques. *The Social Contract*, trans. by Maurice Cranston (New York: Viking Penguin, 1968).

Smith, Adam. *The Theory of Moral Sentiments* (Charlottesville, VA: Lincoln-Rembrandt Publishers, 6th ed., 1986).

—. *The Wealth of Nations*, Books I–III (New York: Viking Penguin Classics, 1986)

Spear, Percival, ed. *The Oxford History of India* (Oxford: Clarendon Press, 3rd ed., 1961).

Thompson, E.P. *The Making of the English Working Class* (New York: Vintage Books, 1966).

Thompson, Vincent Bakpetu. *The Making of the African Diaspora in the Americas 1441–1900)* (New York: Longman, 1987).

The [London] *Times Atlas of World History* ed. Geoffrey Barraclough (London: Times Books, 1981).

Tocqueville, Alexis de. *The Old Regime and the French Revolution*, trans. by Gilbert Stuart (Garden City, New York: Doubleday Anchor Books, 1955).

Turner, Frederick Jackson. *The Frontier in American History* (New York; Henry Holt, 1920).

Ward, David. *Cities and Immigrants* (New York: Oxford University Press, 1971).

Weinberg, Albert Katz. *Manifest Destiny* (Chicago: Quadrangle Books, 1963).

White, Richard Alan. *Paraguay's Autonomous Revolution, 1810–1840* (Albuquerque: University of New Mexico Press, 1978).

Wilentz, Sean. *Chants Democratic: New York and the Rise of the American Working Class, 1788–1850* (New York: Oxford University Press, 1984).

Williams, Eric. *Capitalism and Slavery* (Chapel Hill: University of North Carolina Press, 1944).

16
CHAPTER

"Our wealth has gone into the hands of foreigners. ... Introduce industry from countries abroad and achieve mastery of the modern machinery."

DALPATRAM KAVI

THE INDUSTRIAL REVOLUTION

1740–1914

THE GLOBAL CONSEQUENCES OF INDUSTRIAL EXPANSION AND IMPERIALISM

THE INDUSTRIAL REVOLUTION: WHAT WAS IT? WHAT WAS ITS SIGNIFICANCE?

The industrial revolution which took place in the eighteenth and nineteenth centuries changed far more than the machinery we use and the organization of our work. It also changed the locations of our workplaces and homes, the size and composition of our families and the quality and quantity of the time we spend with them, the educational systems we create, the wars we fight, and the relationships among nations. This chapter examines the industrial revolution as a process with deep roots and lasting consequences—a process extending backward and forward in time, and touching most areas of life. It also views the industrial revolution as a global process, exploring not only the workshops of production, but also the procurement of raw materials in the

fields and mines of the world, and the sales of manufactured products in far-flung marketplaces. The masters of the new industrial productivity took this comprehensive view, and it often led them into global ventures, which sometimes became imperial in their scope. This chapter therefore begins with the invention of new machinery and concludes with an analysis of the relationship between the industrial revolution and imperialism. The social effects of the industrial revolution on urbanization, gender and family relationships, and new personal and national identities are considered in the following chapter.

BRITAIN 1740–1860

The industrial revolution began in Britain and 1740–1860 is usually considered the crucial era of its arrival. In this period the British cotton textile industry grew into the world's most productive; its railway network became the nation's principal means of inland transportation and communication; and a new fleet of steam-powered ships enabled Britain to project its new productivity and power around the globe.

A REVOLUTION IN TEXTILE MANUFACTURE

Until the mid-eighteenth century, the staple British textile had been woolens, but then India's light, colorful, durable cotton textiles began to displace woolens in the market. Britain responded by manipulating tariffs and import regulations to ban Indian cottons, while British inventors began to produce new machinery which enabled Britain to surpass Indian production in both quantity and quality. In 1733, John Kay (1704–64) invented the "flying shuttle," which allowed a single weaver to send the shuttle forth and back across the loom automatically, without the need of a second operator to push it back. The spinners could not keep up with the increased demand of the weavers until, in 1764, James Hargreaves (d. 1778) introduced the spinning jenny, which could spin yarn mechanically. His first jenny ran eight spindles at once; by 1770, 16; by the end of the century, 120. Machines to card and comb the cotton to prepare it for spinning were also developed.

Thus far, the machinery was new, but the power source was still human labor, and production was still concentrated in rural homes and small workshops. In 1769, Richard Arkwright (1732–92) patented the "water frame," a machine that could spin several strands simultaneously. Powered by water, it could run continuously. Samuel Crompton (1753–1827) patented a "mule," a hybrid that joined the principles of the spinning jenny and the water frame to produce a better quality and higher quantity of cotton thread. Now British cloth could rival that of India.

Meanwhile, in the coalfields of Britain, mine owners were seeking more efficient means of pumping water out of mine shafts, enabling deeper digging. By 1702, Thomas Newcomen (1663–1729) had mastered the use of steam power to drive these pumps. In 1763, James Watt (1736–1819), a technician at the University of Glasgow, was experimenting with improvements to Newcomen's steam engine, when Matthew Boulton (1728–1809), a small manufacturer, provided him with the capital necessary to develop larger and more costly steam engines. By 1785 the firm of Boulton and Watt was manufacturing new steam engines for use in Britain and for export. In the 1780s Arkwright substituted a new Boulton and Watt steam engine in place of water power. From this point, equipment grew more sophisticated and more expensive. Spinning and weaving moved from the producer's home or small workshop adjacent to a stream of water, to new steam-powered cotton textile mills, which increased continuously in size and productivity.

James Hargreaves's spinning jenny, c. 1780. Named for his daughter, Hargreaves's invention was a carding machine that prepared natural fibers for spinning. It thus made possible the automatic production of cotton thread. Despite protests by hand workers, spinning became a crucial element of the English factory system.

	BRITAIN		REST OF EUROPE	
1700	▮ Act of Settlement (1701): ▮ Hanoverian succession established Queen Anne (r. 1702–14) ▮ Act of Union (1707) unites England and Scotland as Great Britain ▮ George I (r. 1714–27) ▮ First Jacobite Rebellion (1715–16)		▮ Great Northern War Russia and Sweden vie for power in Baltic ▮ War of the Spanish Succession (1701–13) ▮ Frederick I of Prussia (r. 1701–13) ▮ Joseph I, Holy Roman Emperor (r. 1705–11) ▮ Charles VI, Holy Roman Emperor (r. 1711–40) ▮ Frederick William I of Prussia (r. 1713–40) ▮ Treaty of Utrecht (1713) ▮ Pragmatic Sanction (1713) ▮ Louis V of France (r. 1715–74)	▮ Papal bull condemns Jansenists (1713)
1720	▮ George II (r. 1727–60) ▮ War of Jenkins's Ear (1739)	▮ South Sea Bubble (1720) causes financial panic ▮ Robert Walpole first prime minister (1721–42) ▮ John Kay invents flying shuttle loom (1733) ▮ John Wesley founds Methodist movement (1739)	▮ Catherine I of Russia (r. 1725–7) ▮ War of Polish Succession (1733–5)	▮ John Law's Mississippi Company collapses in France (1720)
1740	▮ Second Jacobite rebellion (1745–6)		▮ Frederick II of Prussia (r. 1740–86) ▮ Maria Theresa, Empress of Austria (r. 1740–80) ▮ War of Austrian Succession (1740–48) ▮ Charles VII, Holy Roman Emperor (r. 1742–5) ▮ Francis I, Holy Roman Emperor (r. 1745–65) ▮ Treaty of Aix-la-Chapelle (1748) ▮ Seven Years' War (1756–6)	▮ Voltaire at court of Frederick II (1751–3) ▮ Earthquake in Lisbon kills 30,000 people (1755)
1760	▮ George III (r. 1760–1820)	▮ James Hargreaves invents spinning jenny (1764) ▮ James Cook's voyage to Australia (1767–71) ▮ James Watt and Matthew Boulton produce first commercial steam engine ▮ Adam Smith publishes *The Wealth of Nations* (1776) ▮ Anti-Catholic Gordon Riots in London (1778)	▮ Catherine II of Russia (r. 1762–96) ▮ Joseph II, Holy Roman Emperor (1765–90); co-regent with Maria Theresa until 1780 ▮ Louis XVI of France (r. 1774–92) War of Bavarian Succession (1778–9)	▮ Jean-Jacques Rousseau publishes *Du Contrat social* (1762) ▮ Carl Scheele discovers oxygen (1771) ▮ Clement XIV suppresses Jesuits (1773) ▮ Catherine the Great reorganizes local government in Russia (1775)
1780		▮ First convicts transported to Australia (1788)	▮ Assembly of Notables in France dismissed after refusing to reform finances (1787) ▮ French Revolution begins (1789) ▮ Leopold II, Holy Roman Emperor (r. 1790–92) ▮ Francis II, Holy Roman Emperor (1792–1806) ▮ Reign of Terror in France (1793–4) ▮ Paul I of Russia (r. 1796–1801)	▮ Joseph II introduces religious toleration in Austria and abolishes serfdom (1781) ▮ Joseph and Jacques Montgolfier make first successful hot-air balloon (1783)
1800	▮ Act of Union (1801) unites Great Britain and Ireland ▮ George III declared insane (1811) ▮ Prince of Wales rules as Prince Regent	▮ Richard Trevithick built first steam locomotive (1804) ▮ Slave trade abolished in British Empire (1807) ▮ Luddites riot against mechanization of textile industry (1811–20) ▮ Peterloo Massacre (1819)	▮ Bonaparte becomes Napoleon I, Emperor of the French (1804); abdicates and is exiled to Elba (1814) then St. Helena (1815) ▮ Alexander I of Russia (1810–25) ▮ Louis XVIII of France (r. 1814–24)	▮ Political activity in Germany suppressed (1819) ▮ *Zollverein* begins in Germany at Prussia's instigation (1819)

	BRITAIN		REST OF EUROPE	
1820	∎ George IV (r. 1820–30) ∎ William IV (r. 1830–37) ∎ Victoria (r. 1837–1901)	∎ Cato Street Conspiracy to kill cabinet members fails (1820) ∎ Combination Acts repealed (1824): trade unions allowed ∎ Catholic Emancipation Act (1829) ∎ Reform Act (1832): extends franchise to middle class ∎ Factory Act (1833): prevents employments of children under nine ∎ Slavery abolished in Empire (1833) ∎ Tolpuddle Martyrs transported for forming union (1834) ∎ Chartism begins (1836) ∎ Anti-Corn Law League (1839)	∎ Charles X of France (r. 1824–30) ∎ Nicholas I of Russia (1825–55) ∎ Decembrist rising in Russia against czar (1825) ∎ Louis Philippe of France (r. 1830–48)	
1840	∎ Crimean War (1854–6) ∎ Fenian Society founded in US (1858)	∎ Penny post (1840) ∎ Potato famine in Ireland leads to repeal of Corn Laws (1846) ∎ Great Exhibition, Crystal Palace (1851)	∎ Year of Revolutions in Europe (1848)* ∎ Louis Napoléon of France (1848–52) ∎ Switzerland introduces federal constitution (1848) ∎ Revolutions in Italy and Hungary crushed (1849) ∎ Napoleon III, Emperor of France (r. 1852–70) ∎ Spanish government overthrown (1854) ∎ Alexander II of Russia (r. 1855–81)	∎ *Communist Manifesto* written by Marx and Engels (1848)
1860	∎ Irish Land League founded (1879)	∎ Karl Marx founds *First International* in London (1864) ∎ Second Reform Act (1867) ∎ Trades unions legalized (1871)	∎ Italy (except for Rome and Venice) united under Victor Emmanuel (1861) ∎ Bismarck declares German Empire (1871) ∎ Frederick of Germany (r. 1888) ∎ William II of Germany (r. 1888–1918)	∎ Serfs freed in Russia (1861) ∎ North German Confederation formed (1867) ∎ Franco-Prussian War (1870–71) ∎ First republic in Spain (1873–4) ∎ First Impressionist exhibition held (1874)
1880		∎ Third Reform Act (1884) Independent Labour founded (1893)	∎ Alexander III of Russia (r. 1881–94) ∎ Nicholas II of Russia (r. 1894–1917)	∎ Illness insurance in Germany (1883) ∎ Louis Pasteur gives first inoculations against rabies (1885) ∎ Financial scandal in France caused by collapse of Panama Canal Company ∎ General strike in Belgium (1893) ∎ Dreyfus affair (1894)

* Year of Revolutions – 1848
Revolution in Paris: Louis Philippe abdicates; Second Republic established, with Louis Napoleon as president
Revolutions in Milan, Naples, Venice, and Rome easily suppressed
Revolutions in Berlin, Vienna, Prague, and Budapest initially successful
Uprising in Wallachia (Romania) suppressed by Russia

New power-looms, invented to cope with increased spinning capacity, had became commercially profitable by about 1800, and were introduced on a large scale after the Napoleonic wars of 1812–15.

The new productivity of the machines drove the economy of Britain. Hand spinners in India required 50,000 hours to produce 100 pounds (45 kilograms) of cotton yarn. Crompton's mule could do the same task in 2,000 hours; Arkwright's steam-powered frame, available by 1795, took 300 hours; and automatic mules, available by 1825, took 135 hours. Moreover, the quality of the finished product steadily increased in strength, durability, and fine texture. The number of mule spindles rose from 50,000 in 1788 to 4.6 million in 1811. Cotton textiles became the most important product of British industries by 1820, making up almost half of Britain's exports.

The new productivity and structure of the cotton textile industry had effects that are sometimes overlooked on the millions of spinners and weavers who continued to work at home on much simpler machines. As late as 1815 owners of new weaving mills also continued the putting-out system, providing weavers with cotton thread and paying them for the finished, woven product. When cutbacks in production were necessary, the home workers could be cut, while the large factories continued to run. The burden of recession could be shifted to the shoulders of the home producer, leaving the factory owners and laborers relatively unscathed. In 1791, home-based workers in the north of England burned down one of the new power-loom factories in Manchester. Machine-wrecking riots followed for several decades, culminating in the Luddite riots of 1810–20. Named for their mythical leader, Ned Ludd, the rioters wanted the new machines banned. Thousands of soldiers were called in to suppress these riots.

The textile revolution also generated spin-off effects around the world. Britain's new mills required unprecedented quantities of good quality cotton. The invention of the cotton gin by Eli Whitney (1765–1825) in 1793 meant that a worker could clean 50 pounds (23 kilograms) of cotton in the time it had taken to clean one. This solved part of the problem. The plantation economy of the United States revived and expanded, providing the necessary raw cotton and giving slavery a new lease on life. American cotton production rose from 3,000 bales in 1790 to 178,000 bales in 1810; 732,000 bales in 1830; and 4,500,000 bales in 1860 (Fogel and Engerman, p. 44). India's industrial position was reversed as she became a supplier of raw cotton to Britain and an importer of machine-manufactured cotton textiles from Britain. Industrialization in Britain was reshaping the world economy.

CAPITAL GOODS: IRON, STEAM ENGINES, RAILWAYS, AND STEAMSHIPS

The textile industry began with a consumer product that everyone used and that already employed a substantial handicraft labor force; it mechanized and reorganized the production process in factories. Other industrial innovations created new products. Many were in the capital goods sector of the economy—that is, they produced tools to expand production rather goods for private consumption. Britain's iron industry, which had been established since the mid-1500s, at first used charcoal to heat iron ore, but by about 1750 new processes of mining provided coal more abundantly and cheaply. About 1775, the iron industry relocated to the coal and iron fields of the British Midlands. A process of stirring the molten iron ore at high temperatures was introduced by Henry

COLLIERIES.

Pit-head scenes, including horse windlass (bottom) and weighing coal, by William Henry Payne, mid eighteenth century. Coal was the fuel needed to power the industrial revolution, as factory owners grew to realize that mechanization held the key to bigger profits. Ironically, James Watt invented his steam engine from a prototype invented to pump water out of mine shafts. This colored engraving gives us a sense of the back-breaking labor required of the pre-industrial miner.

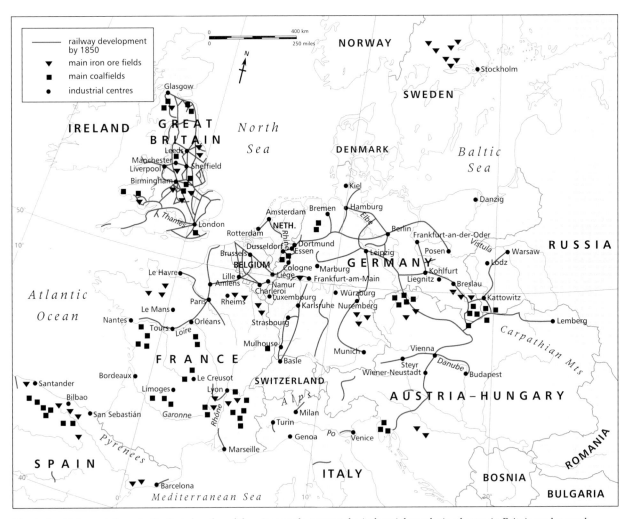

Map legend:

- railway development by 1850
- ▼ main iron ore fields
- ■ main coalfields
- • industrial centres

400 km
250 miles

NORWAY

• Stockholm

SWEDEN

IRELAND

GREAT BRITAIN

• Glasgow

North Sea

DENMARK

Baltic Sea

• Leeds
• Manchester
• Liverpool • Sheffield
• Birmingham

• Kiel

• Danzig

50°

• London

Rotterdam • Amsterdam Bremen • Hamburg
NETH.

Berlin
Frankfurt-an-der-Oder

RUSSIA

10°

Dusseldorf • Dortmund
Brussels • Essen
BELGIUM Cologne
Liège • Marburg
Namur
Charleroi • Luxembourg • Frankfurt-am-Main

Leipzig
Posen
• Warsaw
Kohlfurt • Lódz
GERMANY
Liegnitz • Breslau
• Kattowitz

Atlantic Ocean

Le Havre
Lille
Amiens
Paris Rheims

Würzburg
• Karlsruhe Nuremberg

• Lemberg

Le Mans
Nantes
Tours Orléans
Loire
Strasbourg

Carpathian Mts

FRANCE
Mulhouse
Munich
Vienna

Bordeaux
Limoges Le Creusot
Lyon
SWITZERLAND
Basle

Steyr
Wiener-Neustadt
Danube • Budapest

AUSTRIA–HUNGARY

Santander
Bilbao
San Sebastián
Garonne
Rhône

Alps
Milan

Po
Turin
Genoa Venice

ROMANIA

Marseille

SPAIN

Barcelona

Mediterranean Sea

ITALY

BOSNIA

BULGARIA

40°

The industrial revolution In the first decades of the nineteenth century the industrial revolution began in Britain and spread throughout the entrepreneurial trading nations of Western Europe (and enmeshed their colonies, which provided both raw materials and markets). The earlier use of water power gave way to steam engines; coal became the power source. Similarly canal transportation was superseded by railways, driven by steam.

Cort (1740–1800) in the 1780s. This "puddling" encouraged the use of larger ovens and integrated the processes of melting, hammering, and rolling the iron into bars of very high quality. Productivity increased dramatically. As the price of production dropped and the quality increased, iron was introduced into building construction. The greatest demand for the metal came, however, with new inventions: the steam engine, railroad track and locomotives, steamships, and new urban systems of gas supply and solid and liquid waste disposal all depended on iron for their construction. Britain produced 25,000 tons of pig iron in 1720, 125,000 tons in 1796, and 250,000 tons in 1804. Its world market share was 19 percent in 1800 and 52 percent in 1840—that is, Britain produced as much manufactured iron as the whole rest of the world.

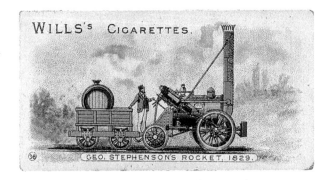

George Stephenson's locomotive *Rocket*, 1829, from a chromolithographic cigarette card of 1901. On October 14, 1829, the *Rocket* won a competition for an engine to haul freight and passengers on the Manchester–Liverpool Railway. The success of Stephenson's invention stimulated a boom in locomotive construction and track laying around the world.

CONFLICTING IMAGES OF EARLY INDUSTRIAL LIFE: THE ENGLISH ROMANTIC POETS

In the century 1750–1850, Britain was transformed by industrialization. Factories, cities, and the working classes all multiplied. One response to the turmoil created by these changes was Romanticism, a new international movement in literature and the arts, which opposed the rationalism of the Enlightenment and which glorified emotion. Poets in Britain, such as William Wordsworth (1770–1850) and Samuel Taylor Coleridge (1772–1834), turned away from the belief in modern progress through science and rational knowledge toward nature, history and their own feelings. They saw a great vision of a new aesthetic beauty emerging. Others, such as the poet William Blake (1757–1827), who were closer to the lives of working-class people, saw the great suffering caused by industrialization. Devoutly religious and nationalistic, Blake nevertheless condemned the people, the government, and the Church of England, for tolerating "a land of poverty" in the very midst of "a rich and fruitful land."

The following two conflicting perspectives are based on views of London about 1800.

Upon Westminster Bridge, September 3, 1802

Earth has not anything to show more fair:
Dull would he be of soul who could pass by
A sight so touching in its majesty;
This City now doth, like a garment, wear
The beauty of the morning; silent, bare,
Ships, towers, domes, theatres, and temples lie
Open unto the fields, and to the sky;

All bright and glittering in the smokeless air.
Never did sun more beautifully steep
In his first splendour, valley, rock, or hill;
Ne'er saw I, never felt, a calm so deep!
The river glideth at his own sweet will:
Dear God! the very houses seem asleep;
And all that mighty heart is lying still!

William Wordsworth

London

I wander thro' each charter'd* street,
Near where the charter'd Thames does flow,
And mark in every face I meet
Marks of weakness, marks of woe.

In every cry of every Man,
In every Infant's cry of fear,
In every voice, in every ban,
The mind-forg'd manacles I hear.

How the Chimney-sweeper's cry
Every blackning Church appalls;
And the hapless Soldier's sigh
Runs in blood down Palace walls.

But most thro' midnight streets I hear
How the youthful Harlot's curse
Blasts the new-born Infant's tear+,
And blights with plagues the Marriage hearse.

William Blake

*charter'd = licensed by the government, controlled, owned
+the infant is blind at birth, from venereal disease transmitted by the parent

With the new steam engine and the increased availability and quality of iron, the railroad industry was born. The first reliable locomotive, George Stephenson's *Rocket*, was produced in 1829. It serviced the Manchester–Liverpool route, reaching a speed of 16 miles (26 kilometers) per hour! By the 1840s a railroad boom swept England and crossed the Atlantic to the United States, where it facilitated the westward expansion of that rapidly expanding country. By the 1850s most of the 23,500 miles (37,820 kilometers) of today's railway network in Britain were already in place, and entrepreneurs found new foreign markets for their locomotives and tracks in India and Latin America.

The new locomotives quickly superseded the canal systems of Britain and the United States which had been built mostly since the 1750s as the favored means of transporting raw materials and bulk goods between industrial cities. Until the coming of the steam-powered train, these canals had been considered the transportation wave of the future. (The speed with which the newer technology displaced the older provides one reason why historians resist predicting the future. Events do not necessarily proceed in a straight-line process of development, and new, unanticipated developments frequently displace older patterns quite unexpectedly.)

Steamships, using much the same technology as locomotives, were introduced at about the same time. The first transatlantic steamship lines began operation in 1838. World steamship tonnage multiplied more than 100 times, from 32,000 tons in 1831 to 3,300,000 tons in 1876. With its new textile mills, iron factories, and steam-driven transportation networks, Britain soon became the "workshop of the world."

WHY DID THE INDUSTRIAL REVOLUTION BEGIN IN BRITAIN? HOW DO WE KNOW?

Historians have long debated the origins of the industrial revolution. The term "industrial revolution" itself was coined by the historian Arnold Toynbee (uncle of the twentieth-century historian Arnold Toynbee) in a set of lectures delivered in 1880–81. Toynbee identified 1760 as the beginning of the process. He chose this date in recognition of the inventions we have been discussing here. In 1934, John Nef, economic historian at the University of Chicago, argued that the iron industry had already been in place by the mid-sixteenth century and that date was a more appropriate choice. More recent historians, such as Fernand Braudel, have seen the roots of the industrialization process stretching back for centuries in many of the areas we have discussed in the last few chapters. All these processes coalesced in the British economy in the late eighteenth century to create the industrial revolution:

꿈 increasing productivity in agriculture;

꿈 new merchant classes in power, and the evolution of a capitalist philosophy of economics which justified their power;

꿈 a powerful state that supported economic development, despite the pure capitalist doctrine of *laissez-faire* that called for the state to stay out of business;

꿈 the rise of science, with its new, empirical view of the world, and of technology, with its determination to find practical solutions to practical problems;

꿈 a social structure that allowed and even encouraged people of different classes to work together, especially artisans who worked with their hands and financiers, who provided capital;

꿈 more intense patterns of global trading;

꿈 an expanding population which increased both the labor supply and the demand for more production;

꿈 slave labor in plantation economies, which brought more than a century of exceptional capital accumulation;

꿈 the discovery of massive deposits of gold and silver in the New World, which also increased capital accumulation; and

꿈 "proto-industrialization"—that is, early forms of industrial organization that introduced new skills to both management and labor, paving the way to large-scale factory production.

Is this question of the origins of the industrial revolution purely academic, simply one of those debates over dates that historians enjoy? In fact, the debate carries serious implications for planning industrial development in today's world. As many newly independent nations with little industry seek to industrialize, they ask: Does industrialization mean simply the acquisition of machinery and the adaptation of advanced technology? Or must a nation also experience a much wider range of agricultural, economic, philosophical, scientific, political, and social changes? How, and under what terms, can it raise the capital necessary to begin? What are the tasks confronting a government wishing to promote industrialization? We shall examine these twentieth century questions in Chapters 19 through 23. Those countries that have achieved high levels of industrialization—mostly the countries of Europe and their daughter civilizations overseas; Japan; and now some of the countries of East Asia (see Chapter 19)—have experienced a wide range of fundamental changes, akin to many of those that Britain experienced.

Interior of Crystal Palace, designed by Joseph Paxton for the Great Exhibition of 1851 in London. This glass-and-iron exhibition hall, a landmark of early modern architecture, was a celebration of the powerful Victorian economy and an expression of British technological accomplishment and imperial might.

THE SECOND STAGE OF INDUSTRIALIZATION 1860–1910

NEW PRODUCTS AND NEW NATIONS

Between 1860 and the outbreak of World War I in 1914, a "second industrial revolution" further transformed world productivity, the ways in which humans lived their lives, and the power balances among the major nations and regions of the world. The principal technological advances came in steel, chemicals, and electricity, and these were supported by organizational breakthroughs in shipping, banking, and insurance.

Steel and Chemical Industries

The invention of new technologies—the Bessemer steel converter (1856) in Britain followed by the Siemens–Martin open-hearth method of produc-tion (1864) in Germany—soon allowed iron ore to be converted to steel cheaply and abundantly. Germany, united as a country in 1871 under Otto von Bismarck (see p. 560), forged ahead. By 1900 it was producing more steel than Britain, 6.3 million tons to 5.0 tons; in 1913, on the eve of World War I, Germany's lead had grown to 17.6 million tons against 7.7 tons. Germany also led in the invention of a number of additional new technologies, especially the internal combustion engine, the diesel engine, and the automobile.

Chemical industries grew especially after 1870 as synthetic substances, notably derivatives from coal, began to augment and replace the earlier reliance on natural substances from the vegetable world, such as alkalis and dyes. Now, synthetic, aniline dyes were made from coal tar. Both fertilizers and explosives could be made from synthetic nitrogen and phosphates. Artificial fertilizers added to a revolution in agricultural productivity, while explosives helped in the construction of engineering feats, such as the new tunnels through the Alps in Europe, the Suez Canal in North Africa, and

A canal connects two oceans. The construction of the Panama Canal in 1905, linking the Atlantic and Pacific Oceans, ranks as one of the greatest engineering feats of all time. The task involved removing around 175 million cubic yards (143 million cubic meters) of earth and sanitizing the entire area, which was infested by mosquitoes that spread yellow fever and malaria.

the Panama Canal in Central America. Soda, made from the coal by-product of ammonia, was used in manufacturing both soap and glass. New drugs, insecticides, perfumes, and cosmetics were produced and made their way to the marketplace. Plastics, produced from coal tar acids, became available in the late nineteenth century.

Electricity

Electrical inventions sparked one another throughout Europe and across the Atlantic to the United States, as well. In 1831 Michael Faraday (1791–1867) in Britain first demonstrated the principle of electromagnetic induction by moving a metal conductor through a magnetic field to generate electricity, a process repeated regularly today in high school classrooms. By 1850 several companies were producing simple electric generators. In the 1860s Ernst Werner von Siemens (1816–92) in Germany developed a practical dynamo. In the United States in the 1880s Nikola Tesla (1856–1943) invented methods to transmit the power effectively over long distances, patenting the alternating current generator in 1892.

The best-known inventor of the age was the American Thomas Alva Edison (1847–1931), who acquired more than one thousand patents for new innovations, 225 of which were patented between 1879 and 1882, for incandescent light bulbs, fuses, sockets, switches, circuit breakers, and meters. Others included an early form of telegraph in 1864; the stock ticker in 1870; the phonograph based on a metal cylinder in 1877; and the wax cylinder recorder in 1888, forerunner of the vinyl record player; and the kinetoscope in 1889, a forerunner of the moving picture. More important than any single invention, however, was Edison's establishment in 1876 of (probably the first) private industrial development laboratory in Menlo Park, New Jersey, a rural area halfway between New York and Philadelphia. Until this time, invention had been largely an individual phenomenon, based on the skills and luck of the individual inventor. Edison's new research facility institutionalized the process of invention.

FACTORY PRODUCTION

Production, too, was concentrated into immense, impersonal corporations. The second industrial revolution corresponded to the era of big business. In Germany, the rising power in Europe, two large **cartels**, collaborative business associations, were formed for the production of electronic equipment: Siemens–Schuckert and Allgemeine Elektrizitäts Gesellschaft (AEG). Two others, specializing in chemical production, later merged into I.G. Farben (1925). For steel production, each major producing country had its own examples: Krupp in Germany, Schneider–Creusot in France, Vickers–Armstrong in Britain, and, largest of all, the United States Steel Corporation. These huge corporations integrated the entire process of production from raw material to finished product. They owned their own coal and iron mines, produced steel, and manufactured such final products as ships, railway equipment, and armaments.

Industrial concentration displaced the artisan in favor of mass-production and mass-consumption. In these mass-market innovations, the United States was frequently the leader, producing the sewing machine (invented by Elias Howe in 1846); the typewriter (1867); clocks and watches, the everyday timekeepers of the new office and factory routines; the telephone, phonograph, and cinema; the bicycle, invented in its modern form in Britain by James Starley in 1885; and small arms, like the

Machine shop, West Lynn works, USA, c. 1898. The United States led the way in mass production of household goods. In the nineteenth century, people flocked to the big cities to work in factories—often for low pay, with long hours and in hot, noisy conditions. The factory system expanded hugely after 1913 when Henry Ford introduced assembly-line technologies to motor-car production.

SPOTLIGHT

Through the Camera's Lens

Photography has dramatically altered the way we see and represent our world. The earliest photographic processes, developed by Louis J.M. Daguerre (1787–1851) and then by William Henry Fox Talbot (1800–77), pioneered the process and later inventions brought photography to ever wider audiences. Faster lenses (1840s), the changeover from "wet" (1851) to "dry" (1871) glass and metal plates, and then the use of film (about 1900) as the medium for the exposure process were key technical developments.

In 1888 George Eastman invented the "Kodak," the first camera which could be mass-produced. Amateurs could now simply take their own photographs, leaving the processes of developing and printing them to commercial laboratories. Photography became a mass hobby.

The invention of more sensitive plates and faster shutter speeds enabled the photography of rapid motion. In 1878 Eadweard Muybridge captured the beauty of a galloping horse in twelve shots from a racetrack (**picture 1**), and invalidated forever the classical representation of horses racing with all four legs extended off the ground. By providing exact images of what the eye could see, photography also challenged the fine arts, especially painting; photographers could capture scenes with an accuracy that no artist could hope to match. In creative response, painters sought new ways of representing reality: impressionism and, later, the various schools of abstract art evolved in large part because the camera had usurped the traditional role of painting.

Photography also became a medium for telling stories, and the power of photo-journalism was realized at a very early date. In 1855 the British government dispatched Roger Fenton to photograph the Crimean War and bring home pictures that might disprove reports of blundering military commanders. The American Civil War was widely photographed, most strikingly by Mathew Brady and his corps of about twenty cameramen. They chose to show the horrors and the grimness of the war (**picture 2**) rather than its heroism. Brady hoped to turn

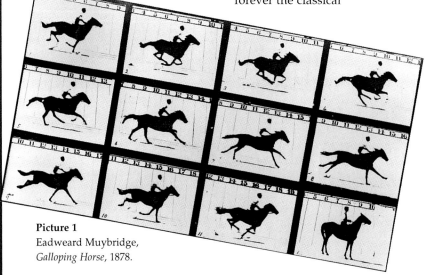

Picture 1
Eadweard Muybridge,
Galloping Horse, 1878.

Picture 2 Mathew Brady, Battery ready for action at Richmond, Virginia, 1864.

the North even more solidly against the South for having precipitated the war, but time has blunted the overt political message. His pictures are now read as a general testimony to the universal hardships of war.

Jacob Riis turned his camera on the slums of New York City (**picture 3**) to create his book *How the Other Half Lives*. Riis's images of the crowding, poverty, and harshness of tenement life served as a powerful voice in campaigns for social reform. Some critics noted, however, that the pictures were too composed and self-consciously "artistic" to evoke genuine horror on the part of the viewer, and while the camera could blankly record images of urban blight, it could neither explain their causes nor formulate their cures.

Picture 3 Jacob A. Riis, *Bandits' Roost, New York*, 1888.

revolver, invented by Samuel Colt in 1836, and the rifle, invented by Oliver Winchester, and improved to a repeating rifle by Christopher Spencer in 1860.

WARFARE AND INDUSTRIALIZATION

Warfare and industrialization went hand-in-hand. In the United States, for example, the Civil War (1861–5) not only preserved a political union but also marked the victory of the industrializing, urban, free-labor north against the rural, plantation economy, slave-holding south. It marked a transformation that soon placed the United States among the leaders of world industrialization. Wars of white immigrants against native American Indians, which soon turned into slaughters and forcible relocations into reservations, accompanied the new cross-continental railroads. Wars against Mexicans completed the borders of the contiguous United States, and wars against the Spanish brought the United States its first overseas colonies.

The machine gun, invented by Richard Gatling in 1861, was improved several times. In 1883 it took on the name of Maxim gun, for the American Hiram Maxim who created a gun that had a range of almost 1½ miles (2.4 kilometers) and could shoot eleven rounds per second. The Maxim won its greatest fame in Africa, where Europeans found it indispensable in their colonization efforts (see p. 530). In Germany, the Krupp family of steel manufacturers concentrated on producing the heavy armaments that enabled Prussia to defeat France in 1870, to forge a united Germany (see Chapter 17), and to prove a formidable combatant in both World Wars (see Chapter 18).

THE EFFECTS OF THE SECOND INDUSTRIAL REVOLUTION WORLDWIDE

Profits from all these businesses, civilian and military, spilled over into finance capital, the purposeful re-investment of capital into new business to reap new profits. Financiers sought new opportunities in more far-flung regions of the world. The industrial development of the Americas offered huge opportunities, and Britain became the largest investor. From the 1840s, for example, the railway networks of both North and South America were in large part financed by British investors. The availability of such investment capital made the task of industrial and urban development easier in the Americas, because the needed sums could be borrowed and repaid later.

These borrowings, and the industrialization and urbanization that came from them, encouraged the immigration that helped increase the population of North America from 39 million in 1850 to 106 million in 1900, and that of South America from 20 million to 38 million in the same period. The United States absorbed these investments without losing political control of its own internal development and became the most industrialized of all countries. South America, however, became an early example of **neo-colonialism**—attracting foreign economic control without direct foreign political control.

Canada enjoyed internal self-government within the British Empire from 1840 and became a unified Dominion, including Ontario, Quebec, Nova Scotia, and New Brunswick, in 1867. It attracted increasing immigration and investment, especially after the United States' frontier was filled in with its own immigrants. Nova Scotia and New Brunswick had joined the original provinces of Quebec and Ontario on condition that a railroad be built to link them with Quebec. More dramatically, spanning all of Canada from east to west, the Canadian Pacific Railway was completed in 1885. Between 1900 and 1916, 73 million acres (29.5 million hectares) of land were occupied with wheat and other commercial agriculture. $400 million per year was invested in this sector and in the mining of coal, gold, lead, zinc, nickel, and copper.

In Russia and the Ottoman Empire, the largest investments came from France. For the six decades leading up to World War I, Russia's industrial output grew at the rate of 5 percent per year. It produced more steel than France, Italy, or Japan and by 1914 it had 46,000 miles (74,000 kilometers) of railroad track and was the world's fourth largest industrial power. It could not, however, keep up with the industrial advances of the United States and Germany. Similarly, Russia's railway mileage seems less than adequate when the immense expanse of the country, by far the largest in the world, is considered. The proportion of Russian industrial production remained at about 8 percent of the world total from 1880 to 1914, and most of its heavy industry was owned by foreigners.

Total foreign investment in the Ottoman Empire was much less, about $1.2 billion in 1914, and the empire's industrial base became progressively less competitive than those of Western European nations. Increasingly, the Ottoman Empire was seen as "the sick man of Europe" (see p. 522).

Overall global investments were immense, with Britain far in the lead. By 1914 Britain had invested some $20 billion, France about $8.7 billion, and Germany about $6 billion. The global age of finance capital was in full swing.

SOCIAL CHANGES: THE CONDITIONS OF WORKING PEOPLE

WHAT DO WE KNOW AND HOW DO WE KNOW IT?

So far we have concentrated on the immense new productivity of industrialization, of the abundance and the wonders of new products. But how did the workers fare? What were the conditions of life for those who worked the machines that produced this new wealth? Reports from the early years in Britain, the birthplace of the industrial revolution, relate with horrifying regularity the wretchedness of the conditions of the working class. These reports, which include popular literature, official government reports, political tracts, and the cries of labor organizers, repeat the same theme: In the midst of increasing national wealth, workers lived lives of immense poverty and degradation. On the other hand, by the end of our period (1914), the condition of working-class people in Western Europe and the United States, at least, was becoming comfortable. What had happened? How? What is the significance of the change? These questions remain important today as increasingly powerful machines continue to produce more abundant and more sophisticated products and more anxiety in the life of workers.

EUROPEAN SOCIAL REFORMERS AND PHILOSOPHERS OF THE 1800s

Jeremy Bentham	(1748–1832) English philosopher, founder of Utilitarianism, and legal and social reformer, who believed that the object of all legislation should be "the greatest happiness for the greatest number."
William Wilberforce	(1759–1833) English politician and philanthropist, who played a major part in the abolition of the slave trade within the British Empire, introducing a first bill into Parliament in 1807 and founding the Anti-slavery Society in 1823. He was also a leading member of the "Clapham Sect," which supported the extension of missionary activity in India.
Georg Wilhem Friedrich Hegel	(1770–1831) German philosopher who is regarded as one of the most significant idealist philosophers and whose work has influenced such disparate groups as Marxists, Positivists, and Existentialists. He believed that humans are capable of absolute knowledge.
Elizabeth Fry	(1780–1845) English philanthropist, who, in 1817, formed an association for the improvement of the conditions in which women prisoners were held.
Auguste Comte	(1798–1857) French philosopher, who is seen as the founder of sociology. In *Cours de philosophie positive* (1830–42) he argued that society would evolve toward a new "golden age" of science, industry, and rational morality.
Edwin Chadwick	(1800–90) English reformer and author of the Poor Law Report (1834). Through his influence measures were enacted to eradicate cholera, improve sanitation in urban areas, and clear city slums.
John Stuart Mill	(1806–73) Liberal English philosopher and economist, who eventually abandoned the extreme individualism of the Utilitarians and began to recognize differences in both the quality and quantity of pleasure, humanizing the philosophy by introducing an element of idealism.
Karl Marx	(1818–83) German political philosopher, economist, and social theorist. He began a life-long collaboration with Friedrich Engels in 1844. *The Communist Manifesto* (1847–8) and *Das Kapital* (1867) analyze the economics of capitalism and the necessity of revolutionary class struggle. His account of change through conflict has continued to influence thinkers.

DEMOGRAPHIC CAUSES AND EFFECTS OF THE INDUSTRIAL REVOLUTION

Many demographic shifts suggest that levels of population and industrialization increased together. The population of Europe almost doubled between 1750 and 1850, from 140 million to 265 million, and then jumped another 50 percent to 400 million by 1900. At the same time, emigration carried an additional 50 million people overseas, especially to the Americas, Australia, and South Africa. Much of this increase occurred before the introduction of machinery. Also, the increase seems to have been worldwide; China's population multiplied four times between 1650 and 1850. Historians now believe the main cause was the availability of new foods, such as maize, provided by the "Columbian exchange" (see p. 442).

Demographers note two waves of change that followed the industrial revolution: first, death rates fell as people ate better and kept cleaner, and as public health measures increased the safety of the water supply, improved the sanitation of cities, combatted epidemics, and taught new standards of personal hygiene. Then birth rates went down. Parents began to realize that improved health increased the likelihood that their children would live to adulthood, and that they did not need to produce numerous children to insure that two or three or four would survive. They began to practice family planning. The old "Iron Law of Wages," had argued that as income increased people would simply use the surplus to have more children; this did not happen. Population growth in industrialized countries began to stabilize.

WINNERS AND LOSERS IN THE INDUSTRIAL REVOLUTION

New entrepreneurs, men creating successful new industrial enterprises, often profited handsomely in this era. Their literary representative was Samuel Smiles (1812–1904), whose *Self Help*, published in 1859, advocated self-reliance as the key to "a harvest of wealth and prosperity." Smiles described the careers of many of these self-made new men, the "industrial heroes of the civilized world," including Josiah Wedgwood, a potter, son and grandson of potters, who created a new form and quality of pottery that bears his name till today. Wedgwood pottery transformed the British industry, earning great profits for Wedgwood and

providing employment in his own factories for 20,000 workers. As industries of all sorts expanded, each nation had its own examples of "captains of industry"—for example, four generations of the Friedrich Krupp family in Germany; Andrew Carnegie and J. Pierpont Morgan in the USA.

On the other hand, not everyone benefited. Handicraft workers were displaced by the new mechanization. In 1820 there were 240,000 hand-loom weavers in Britain; in 1840, 123,000; in 1856, 23,000. Some of these workers found jobs running the new power-looms, but many could not make the transition and fell into poverty.

While attending his father's factory in England, Friedrich Engels (1829–95) compiled devastating accounts of *The Condition of the Working Class in England* (1845). Engels' description of the St. Giles slum in London demonstrates the moral outrage that led him to join with Karl Marx in calling for revolution:

> Heaps of garbage and ashes lie in all directions, and the foul liquids emptied before the doors gather in stinking pools. Here live the poorest of the poor, the worst paid workers with thieves and the victims of prostititution indiscriminately huddled together … [T]hey who have some kind of shelter are fortunate in comparison with the utterly homeless. In London fifty thousand human beings get up every morning, not knowing where they are to lay their heads at night.

Government reports, although more restrained in tone, sustained these horrific views. They called for, and got, remedial legislation. Official committees studied working-class conditions in the factories and neighborhoods of Britain's growing industrial cities and in its mines. In 1831, a committee chaired by the Member of Parliament Michael Thomas Sadler (1780–1835) investigated the conditions of child labor in cotton and linen factories. It found children beginning work at the age of six, usually for twelve- and thirteen-hour days. They were often given food so wretched that, despite their hunger, they left it for pigs to eat. Workplaces were cramped and dirty all year long, and were especially damaging to health during the long nights of winter, when gas, candles, and oil lamps added their soot and smoke to the air of the factory. Still worse conditions were revealed by the Committee on the Conditions in Mines, which was appointed in 1842 and was chaired by Anthony Ashley Cooper, 7th Earl of Shaftesbury. Children worked

Putters or trolley boys, from *Mines and Miners* by L. Simonin, early nineteenth century. Until the reforms of the 1870s, owners of factories and mines were able to force children as young as five and six to work up to sixteen hours a day—often in hazardous conditions. Orphans and pauper children were especially vulnerable since capitalists merely had to keep them fed and sheltered in return for their services. The resulting disease, industrial injury, and illiteracy tended to make poor families even poorer.

for fourteen hours underground each day. Legally, they could work from the age of nine, but parents needing extra income frequently brought even younger children.

Sir Edwin Chadwick (1800–90), an investigator for the Royal Commission on the Poor Laws, issued his *Inquiry into the Condition of the Poor* in 1842 after taking abundant testimony from workers in factories and mines, homes and workplaces:

> The frequency of cases of early deaths, and orphanages, and widowhood amongst one class of labourers, the journeymen tailors, led me to make some inquiries as to the causes affecting them; and I submit the following evidence for peculiar consideration, as an illustration of the operation of one predominant cause; bad ventilation or overcrowding, and the consequences on the moral habits, the loss of healthful existence and happiness to the labourer, the loss of profit to the employer, and of produce to the community, and the loss in expenditure for the relief of the destitution, which original cause (the bad ventilation) we have high scientific authority for stating to be easily and economically controllable.

Chadwick noted that the British government had already begun legislating the conditions of child labor and of tenement construction. He now urged further legislation to provide for sewage, drainage, sanitation, and a clean water supply. His Report suggested that not only the poor workers but also their employers, the community, and the govern-

ment would benefit. Chadwick's report helped inspire broad public support for the Public Health Act of 1848 and the creation of a Board of Health.

POLITICAL REACTION IN BRITAIN AND EUROPE 1800–1914

POLITICAL RESPONSES IN BRITAIN

Britain had a growing urban, industrial population, which started to demand political change. The government, recognizing that industrialization was transforming Britain and fearful of the consequences, responded initially by trying to repress the movement for reform. The *Peterloo Massacre* at St. Peter's Fields in Manchester in 1819 demonstrated the government's position. A huge, but peaceful demonstration by 80,000 people called for universal male suffrage, the annual election of the House of Commons in Parliament, and the abolition of the Corn Laws. The Corn Laws had raised the tariff on grain to levels that effectively banned importation, thus keeping the price of basic foodstuffs high, favoring landowners and farmers at the expense of the growing urban, industrial population. Soldiers fired on the demonstrators, killing eleven and wounding some 400. The government applauded the soldiers and passed further legislation to restrict free expression.

The mood of Parliament had changed by 1832, partly because of revolutions on the European continent, and partly because of riots in England. Fearing the possibility of revolution, the Whig party in Parliament forced through the Reform Bill of 1832. Its most significant provision was to shift 143 seats in Parliament from rural constituencies, which were losing population and were often dominated by single families, to expanding urban constituencies. The number of voters increased about 60 percent but still numbered only about 800,000 in all of Britain. A far greater proportion of these men, however, were professionals: doctors, lawyers, businessmen, and journalists. Thus far, the benefits went to the middle classes, but soon the two main parties, conservative Tories and more liberal Whigs, jockeying for power, began to craft new programs benefiting urban working people in an attempt to gain more votes.

Parliament abolished slavery in the British Empire in 1833 (see p. 487) and passed a new Poor Law in 1834, which provided assistance just adequate to sustain life. The law required that recipients live in a government workhouse and participate in government-created work projects, but this provision was not usually enforced. In 1835 it enacted a Municipal Corporations Act, which reformed both elections and administrations in large cities, enabling them to cope more successfully with the problems of growth and industrialization. Legislation of direct concern to labor was passed: the Factory Act of 1833 not only forbade the employment of children under the age of nine in textile mills, it also, for the first time, provided for paid inspectors to enforce the legislation. In 1842 the employment of women and of children under the age of ten was forbidden in the coal mines. The Ten Hour Act of 1847 extended this ruling to cover factories and, in practice, men's hours were also soon reduced.

But Parliament moved slowly and sometimes it refused to move at all. The Chartist movement presented a Charter with more than a million signatures to Parliament in 1838. The Charter called for universal male suffrage, an end to property qualifications for members of parliament, and equal electoral districts. Despite, or perhaps because of, a wave of violence instigated by some of the Chartists, the House of Commons rejected the petition. When it was resubmitted in 1842, with more than 3.3 million signatures, the Charter was rejected again, overwhelmingly, by 287 votes to 49. Parliament feared that universal suffrage would

bring an end to the sanctity of property and the capitalist economic system.

In 1846, however, under a Tory government led by Robert Peel, Parliament did repeal the Corn Laws, signalling the victory of the urban constituencies and the triumph of free trade. Britain gave up its policy of self-sufficiency in food and entered fully into the international trade system to purchase its food and sell its manufactured goods. A second Reform Bill in 1867, passed by the Tory government of Benjamin Disraeli, doubled the electorate to about 2 million, about one-third of all adult males. The Bill enfranchised most urban working men.

The two major political parties, Liberals and Tories, now competed directly for the favor of the industrial workers. In 1870, the Liberal government of William Gladstone began to provide universal, state-supported education and, in the next year, it formally legalized labor unions. The Tories, under Disraeli's second administration, 1876–80, extended the acts regulating public sanitation and conditions of labor in factories and mines. They also

The Chartists. As this contemporary cartoon implies, the sheer weight of support received by the Chartists was a powerful argument in favor of voting rights being extended to all men (though not yet women). Parliament rejected increasingly large charters, or petitions, on three occasions and it was not until 1918 that universe male suffrage was adopted in Great Britain.

regulated the conditions of housing for the poor. In 1884, under Gladstone, a third Reform Bill doubled the electorate again. In 1918 Great Britain adopted universal male suffrage and extended the vote to women over the age of 30.

LABOR ORGANIZATION

British workers had been forbidden to unionize under the Combination Act of 1799, but in 1824 these laws were repealed. Small trade unions took root, usually finding their greatest success among the better-off "aristocracy of labor," the machinists, carpenters, printers, and spinners. Sometimes they would go on strike; politically they organized for suffrage campaigns; and some helped organize cooperative enterprises. Only under the Trade Union Act of 1871 was the right to strike recognized officially. Unskilled workers began increasingly to join into unions, with miners and transport workers usually in the lead. They drew encouragement from the Fabian Society, a group of intellectuals centered in the Bloomsbury section of London, which sought to make government and society more receptive to

LABOR ORGANIZATION AND PARLIAMENT: TWO VIEWS OF THEIR RELATIONSHIP

Social historian E.P. Thompson identifies the London Corresponding Society founded in 1792, as perhaps "the first definitely working-class political organisation formed in Britain" (Thompson, p. 20). A century later, Britain had between 1.5 and 2 million trade union members. They organized to form Britain's first avowedly Labour Party. The Party won only two seats in the 1900 elections, but in 1906 it captured twenty-nine seats and began its permanent role in parliamentary politics in Britain.

The growth of an organized labor movement had a great influence on Parliament, yet different historians discuss this relationship between labor and Parliament from very different perspectives. Most stress the wisdom and flexibility of Parliament in yielding increasing power to a wide variety of new urban industrial interest groups, including laborers, even as early as 1832. Compare, for example, R.R. Palmer writing on the Reform Bill:

Great Britain in 1830 was probably nearer to real revolution than any country of Europe—for the revolutions of 1830 on the Continent were in reality only insurrections and readjustments. In Britain a distressed mass of factory workers, and of craft workers thrown out of employment by factory compettition, was led by an irate manufacturing interest, grown strong by industrial changes and determined no longer to tolerate its exclusion from political life. Had these elements resorted to general violence a real revolution might have occurred. Yet there was no violent revolution in Britain. The reason probably lies first of all in the existence of the historic institution of Parliament, which, erratic though it was before the Reform Bill, provided the means by which social changes could be legally accomplished and continued, in principle, to enjoy universal respect. (p. 462)

The 1832 Bill did not, however, actually vest power with industrial laborers, and Thompson charges that the working classes felt betrayed. They had struggled heroically and now would have to continue their struggle.

Again and again in these years working men expressed their resentment: "they wish to make us tools", or "implements", or "machines". A witness before the parliamentary committee enquiring into the hand-loom weavers (1835) was asked to state the view of his fellows on the Reform Bill:

Q: Are the working classes better satisfied with the institutions of the country since the change has taken place?

A: I do not think they are. They viewed the Reform Bill as a measure calculated to join the middle and upper classes to Government, and leave them in the hands of Government as a sort of machine to work according to the pleasure of Government. (pp. 831–2)

working-class interests without violence. They supported the London Dock strike of 1889, which demonstrated working-class strength by closing that great port. They formed the core constituency of the new Labour Party. By 1914, 4 million Britons held membership in trade unions.

LABOR ORGANIZATION OUTSIDE BRITAIN

Karl Marx and Theories of Worker Revolution

In Britain workers created their own organizations and pulled political party leaders in their wake. Elsewhere, political leaders and intellectual theoreticians attempted to give leadership in organizing much smaller groups of workers. Foremost among the theoreticians was Karl Marx (1818–83). A well-educated and trained German journalist of Jewish ancestry, Marx called for a worker-led revolution. He organized revolutionary socialists through active campaigning, polemical tracts calling for revolution, such as the *Communist Manifesto*, which he wrote with Friedrich Engels, and three volumes of scholarly analysis and critique of the capitalist system called *Capital*.

Marx began his studies in Berlin at a time when western and central Europe were alive with revolutionary sentiments—both of workers seeking new rights and of nationalists seeking greater political representation. In 1848, many of these revolutionary pressures came to a head—and were crushed. In France, a revolt against the monarchy of Louis Philippe (r. 1830–48) and the proclamation of a provisional republic was followed by the establishment of government-sponsored workshops to provide employment for the poor. A new, far more conservative government was elected in April, however, and it closed the workshops in Paris. The poor people of the city took to the barricades, and the army was called out. More than ten thousand people were killed or injured in the street riots which followed.

In Austria, protesting students and workers took control of Prague and Vienna and were crushed in both cities by regular forces of the Austrian army at the cost of thousands of casualties. In Prussia, in the same year, worker demands for more democracy and more worker rights joined with demands for a new constitution which would lead toward the merger of Prussia with the many small German-speaking states of the former Holy Roman Empire into a new country of Germany. At first it appeared that the Prussian king Frederick William IV (r. 1840–61) would grant these demands, and a Constituent Assembly was convened in Frankfurt to write a new German constitution. In the end, however, the king reasserted his divine right to rule and rejected the constitution. Under these circumstances the smaller states refused to join in a unified government. With conservative forces in the ascendant, Marx moved to London where he spent the rest of his life, much of it in active scholarship in the British Museum.

Marx believed that wealth is produced not so much by capitalists, who control the finances, but by the **proletariat**—the laborers—who do the actu-

Poster commemorating "The Internationale", the rallying anthem of the Communist movement. Karl Marx (left) and Friedrich Engels (right), who appear at the top of this poster, collaborated in developing the theoretical principles underlying "scientific socialism" and in organizing a working-class movement dedicated to revolting against capitalism.

al physical work of production. Because this is not recognized, workers do not receive proper returns for their contributions. Violent revolution is the only recourse "to raise the proletariat to the position of ruling class, to establish democracy" (*Communist Manifesto*, p. 30). In a stirring call to this revolution, Marx and Engels declare the Communist party as its leader:

> Let the ruling classes tremble at a Communist revolution. The proletarians have nothing to lose but their chains. They have a world to win. Workingmen of all countries, unite! (p. 44)

Until the revolution would take place, Marx and Engels called for many shorter term legislative goals, which they shared with many other labor groups at the time and which were subsequently adopted in virtually all industrialized countries, including: "a heavy progressive or graduated income tax, ... free education for all children in public schools ... and ... abolition of child factory labor in its present form."

After the revolution would occur, Marx and Engels called for the establishment of a very powerful, worker-led government to assume control of the economy, and they looked forward to a still later time when the state would be unnecessary and would wither away. They identified the state as "the organized power of one class for oppressing another," so when workers ruled the state, there would be no need for further oppression, and the state would vanish. Marx and Engels gave no further description of this utopia, but it finally rested on their most central and most radical tenet:

> The theory of the Communists may be summed up in the single sentence: Abolition of private property. (p. 23)

Marx's theory included a view of history that saw class struggle as perpetual: "The history of all hitherto existing society is the history of class struggles." The current form of the struggle was bourgeoisie vs. proletariat. The bourgeoisie themselves had created the proletariat by organizing the new factories which employed them. Marx condemned the sexual ethics of the bourgeoisie. Despite their official reverence for the family, Marx accused them of sexual abuse of their workers, economic perpetuation of prostitution, and wife-swapping among themselves: "Our bourgeois, not content with having the wives and daughters of their proletarians at their disposal, not to speak of common prostitutes, take the greatest pleasure in seducing each other's wives." Marx heaped scorn on religion, charging the bourgeoisie with using it as an opiate to divert the proletariat from its fundamental economic concerns. Marx was a materialist, arguing that economics is the fundamental basis of life; ideas and intellectual life are derivative of economic status: "Man's consciousness changes with every change in the conditions of his material existence, in his social relations and in his social life. ... The ruling ideas of each age have ever been the ideas of its ruling class."

The proletarian revolution predicted as inevitable by Marx and Engels did not take place in the nineteenth century. (In Chapter 19 we will consider the extent to which the 1917 Russian revolution was proletarian and Marxist.) As we have seen in Britain, three factors worked toward a different resolution of class tensions. First, workers' unions began to win their demands for higher pay, shorter hours, and better working conditions. Second, political institutions expanded to assimilate the new worker organizations and accommodated many of their demands. Third, legislation favorable to workers was passed, the franchise was extended, and a labor party took its place in Parliament.

In retrospect, some of Marx and Engels' most enduring interpretations have been cultural even more than economic. They identified:

- the challenge of coping with rapid change, announcing in the *Communist Manifesto* that "all that is solid melts into air";

- the alienation of factory workers from their work, as they became insignificant cogs in great systems of production; and

- the alienation of workers from nature, as farmers left the countryside to find jobs in urban industries.

Germany 1870–1914

A wave of labor unrest and strikes swept across Europe in the late 1860s and early 1870s, signaling the growing strength of labor. In Germany chief minister Otto von Bismarck (1815–98) pursued diverse and sometimes conflicting strategies to keep working people allied to his government. He extended universal male suffrage to the North German Confederation in 1867 and then to all of

Germany when he unified the country in 1871, but he limited the power of the legislature and diluted the power of the vote since the government ministers were responsible to the king, not to Parliament. When Germany's opposition Social Democratic Party became Europe's first political party based on the working classes in 1875, Bismarck sharply restricted its organizational activities. On the other hand, declaring "I too am a socialist," he passed legislation providing workers' disability and accident insurance and, in the 1880s, the first compulsory social security system in Europe. This legislation, however, covered only male industrial workers, not women or children. Because of government policies, worker militancy, and its opportunity to learn from Britain's earlier painful experiences, Germany did not repeat the worst conditions of child and female labor, and of excessive hours and brutal conditions of industrial work.

The United States 1870–1914

In the United States, labor began to organize especially with the industrialization that began after the Civil War (1861–5). A number of craft unions joined together to form the National Labor Union in 1866, but although it claimed 300,000 members by the early 1870s, it did not survive the depression of 1873. The Noble Order of the Knights of Labor, founded as a secret society in 1869, grew into a mass union, open to all workers, with a membership of 700,000 in 1886. The leadership of the Knights of Labor could not control its membership, however, and various wildcat strikes broke out, some of them violent, alienating much of the rest of the membership. America's most successful labor organization was the American Federation of Labor, a union of skilled craft workers, which was founded in 1886 by Samuel Gompers (1850–1924). Its membership grew to 1 million by 1900 and 2 million by 1914. Women were not allowed to join, but in 1900 the International Ladies Garment Workers Union (ILGWU) was formed—with males dominating its leadership!

A series of strikes in America throughout the 1890s led to violence. Hired detectives, local police, and even army troops attacked strikers and were attacked in return. Near Pittsburgh, steel workers lost the Homestead Steel strike in 1892 as the Governor of Pennsylvania sent in 8000 troops. The American Railway Union under Eugene Debs lost a strike at the Pullman Palace Car Company in Chicago when the Governor of Illinois obtained a court injunction to force the workers back to their jobs. Violence ensued, leaving scores of workers dead. In resolving a 1908 strike of hat makers, the United States Supreme Court ruled that trade unions were subject to the Sherman Anti-Trust Act, leaving their members personally liable for business losses suffered during strikes. Until this ruling was reversed in the 1930s, militant unionism was virtually dead, although the small Industrial Workers of the World (IWW), representing a radical perspective on labor organization, did form in 1905.

Labor organization in the United States was fragmented into craft-specific unions. In this nation of immigrants, workers also held multiple identities; their ethnic identities frequently interfered with their concerns for building union solidarity with those of other ethnic groups. Many immigrants came to America to earn money and return home; these workers did not usually have a commitment to active unionization. Pay scales and working conditions in the United States were significantly better than in Europe, further muting worker grievances. Finally, the capitalist ideology of the country discouraged class divisions, and the government restricted labor organization. The United States did develop powerful labor organizations, mostly in the twentieth century, but it never produced a significant political party based primarily on labor.

France 1870–1914

In France, much of the potential leadership of a workers' movement was wiped out in 1870 by the massacre of the Paris Commune, an uprising in Paris of urban leaders. At least 20,000 people were killed by the French national government and another 10,000 were exiled. Ten years later, when some of the exiles from the Paris Commune returned, organization began again. In 1884 *syndicats*, labor unions, were legalized. Two competing federations were formed, one calling primarily for mutual help, the other for political action. Together, they numbered 140,000 members in 1890, a figure that more than tripled to 580,000 by the end of the century. By 1909, an umbrella group, the Confederation Génerale de Travail, numbered nearly a million. In 1890, May 1 was recognized as an annual "Labor Day." French politics, however, was dominated by the wealthier business leaders. Industrial workers organized, but they commanded less influence than farmers, shopkeepers, and small businessmen.

Massacre of the Paris radicals. The slaughter meted out to the Paris Commune of 1871 is graphically depicted by the Post-Impressionist painter Edouard Manet. Left-wing urban leaders tried to set up their own state-within-a-state, but the communards were put down brutally by the national government. At least 20,000 were summarily executed and over 40,000 were taken prisoner. (*Museum Folkwang, Essen*)

COMPETITION AMONG INDUSTRIAL POWERS: THE QUEST FOR EMPIRE

Britain pioneered the industrial revolution, but by the mid-nineteenth century rivals had begun to appear. The United States emerged from its Civil War in 1865 with a rapidly growing immigrant population moving westward by railway across a continent that was abundant in resources, and, removing Indians that blocked its mobility, overtook British industrial production by 1900. Germany unified its constituent states into a single country under Kaiser Wilhelm and Prime Minister Otto von Bismarck in 1871, and also surpassed Britain in the early years of the twentieth century. In addition, Germany's population at 67 million was almost 50 percent greater than Britain's, and was growing faster. France produced only half the industrial output of Britain or Germany, but nevertheless ranked third among European powers.

The greatest competition took place overseas, beyond the borders of Europe, in the quest for imperial power. Empires were not new, of course,

but the use of advanced technology and new strategies of financial and economic dominance gave them new power over others in the late nineteenth and early twentieth centuries. By 1914, peoples of Europe and of European ancestry had settled and ruled, directly or indirectly, 85 percent of the earth's land surface: Canada, the United States, large parts of Latin America, Siberia, Australia, New Zealand, and substantial parts of South Africa by settlement and conquest; most of India, Southeast Asia, and Africa by direct rule over indigenous populations; China by indirect rule. Much of Latin America, although politically independent, was dominated internally by elites of European ancestry and externally by European financial investors and their governments. Some states, like Russia and the Ottoman Empire, were dominated in large part by capital from northwestern Europe, but also held their own colonial areas. In terms introduced by the historian Fernand Braudel and the sociologist Immanuel Wallerstein, northwest Europe and the United States had become the core regions of world economic and political power; most of the rest of the world, excepting Japan, was incorporated and subordinated into its periphery.

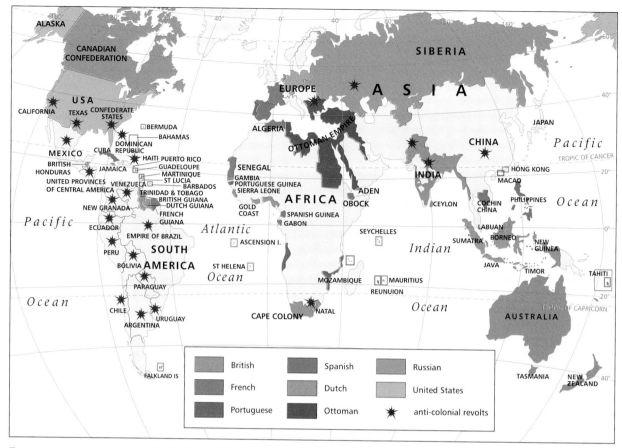

European imperialism 1815–1870 By the middle of the nineteenth century, revolutions had brought independence to most of the Americas. With Africa largely impenetrable, European imperialists now focussed on Asia. Russia had spread across Siberia to the Pacific, and the United States extended from the Atlantic to the Pacific, while Britain controlled India, South Africa, Australia, and New Zealand. In 1867 Canada achieved "dominion" status, virtual political independence.

The leading states of Western Europe had achieved their power through their "dual revolutions," political and industrial. Politically and socially they had achieved, or seemed to be in the process of achieving:

🐾 consolidated nation-states;

🐾 parliamentary democracies;

🐾 bureaucratic administrations;

🐾 freedom of the press, assembly, and religion;

🐾 freedom from wrongful arrest and torture;

🐾 increased levels of literacy and general, public education;

🐾 high levels of trade and international exchange;

🐾 high levels of economic entrepreneurship and legal protection of property;

🐾 humanitarian perspectives;

🐾 thriving artistic life.

Economically and industrially, they had achieved or seemed to be in the process of achieving:

🐾 high levels of productivity;

🐾 competence in new methods of science and technology;

🐾 relatively high levels of health and of medical care;

🐾 an integrated world economy; and

🐾 powerful weaponry.

Western Europeans, especially Britons, began to define themselves as people who had mastered these qualities; in contrast to the peoples whom they were colonizing and dominating, who lacked them. Soon after Charles Darwin published *On The Origin of Species* in 1859, the philosopher Herbert Spencer (1820–1903) (mis)represented the concept of "survival of the fittest" as a doctrine explaining and justifying the rule by the strong over the weak. Spencer's "social Darwinism" argued that those who were strong deserved their superiority, the weak deserved their inferiority. Spencer also believed that the European races were more advanced than those of other regions. The social-political order that confirmed wealthy, powerful, white, male Europeans in positions of dominance was as it ought to be.

ASSERTIONS OF EUROPEAN SUPREMACY AND OBLIGATION

Rudyard Kipling's famous poem, "The White Man's Burden," proclaims Britain's superiority—racial, moral, political, economic, and religious—over the peoples it conquered. Kipling represents the breach between the white colonial and the sullen, "Half-devil and half-child" peoples he governed as unbridgeable. He laments the plight of the poor white man, who gives his all to help ungrateful heathen peoples. In the hey-day of imperialism, Kipling does not note any benefits to the colonizers nor does he suggest the role of military power and violence in producing and maintaining the empire. Kipling dedicated the poem to the United States as a warning as it began its colonial rule of the Philippines in 1899.

The White Man's Burden

Take up the White Man's burden—
Send forth the best ye breed—
Go bind your sons to exile
To serve your captives' need;
To wait in heavy harness,
On fluttered folk and wild—
Your new-caught, sullen peoples,
Half-devil and half-child.

Take up the White Man's burden—
In patience to abide,
To veil the threat of terror
And check the show of pride;
By open speech and simple,
An hundred times made plain,
To seek another's profit,
And work another's gain.

Take up the White Man's burden—
The savage wars of peace—
Fill full the mouth of Famine
And bid the sickness cease;

And when your goal is nearest
The end for others sought,
Watch Sloth and heathen Folly
Bring all your hope to nought.

Take up the White Man's burden—
No tawdry rule of kings,
But toil of serf and sweeper—
The tale of common things.
The ports ye shall not enter,
The roads ye shall not tread,
Go make them with you living,
And mark them with your dead.

Take up the White Man's burden—
And reap his old reward:
The blame of those ye better,
The hate of those ye guard—
The cry of hosts ye humor
(Ah, slowly!) toward the light:—
"Why brought ye us from bondage,
Our loved Egyptian night?"

Take up the White Man's burden—
Ye dare not stoop to less—
Nor call too loud on Freedom
To cloak your weariness;
By all ye cry or whisper,
By all ye leave or do,
The silent, sullen peoples
Shall weigh your Gods and you.

Take up the White Man's burden—
Have done with childish days—
The lightly proferred laurel,
The easy, ungrudged praise.
Comes now, to search your manhood
Through all the thankless years,
Cold, edged with dear-bought wisdom,
The judgment of your peers!

	OTTOMAN EMPIRE	CHINA	INDIA	AFRICA
1700	▌Ottomans lose battle at Peterwardein, Serbia, to Prince Eugene of Savoy (1716)		▌Weakening of Mughal Empire after death of Aurangzeb (r. 1658–1707)	
1720	▌Russia and Austria at war in Turkey (1736–9)	▌Qing army enters Lhasa (1720)	▌Hyderabad achieves independence from Mughals (1724) ▌Maratha government rises to power (1730–35) ▌Nadir Shah of Persia (r. 1736–47) conquers Afghanistan and invades northern India (1738) and sacks Delhi (1739)	▌Revival of ancient empire of Borno (central Sudan) (c.1730)
1740		▌Tribal rebellions in western Sichuan (1746–9) ▌China invades and conquers Tibet (1752)	▌Ahmad Shah ruler of Afghanistan (1747) ▌Robert Clive seizes Arcot, southern India (1751) ▌Black Hole of Calcutta: Siraj-ud-Daulah, Nawab of Bengal, captures Calcutta (1756) ▌Battle of Plassey: Clive defeats Nawab of Bengal and establishes British rule (1757)	▌Usman Dan Fodio born, founder of sultanate in northern and central Nigeria (1754)
1760	▌Russia and Turkey at war (1767–74) ▌Russia conquers the Crimea (1771) ▌Treaty of Kuchuk Kainarji (1774): Russia gains Black Sea ports and right to represent Greek Orthodox Church in Turkey		▌Battle of Panipat: Afghan forces defeat Maratas (1761) ▌Warren Hastings (1732–1818) appointed first governor-general of Bengal (1774) ▌War between Britain and Maratas (1775) ends with Treaty of Salbai (1782)	▌End of Funj sultanate in eastern Sudanic region (1762)
1780	▌Russia annexes Crimea (1783) ▌Russia and Turkey at war (1787–92) ▌Aga Mohammed founds Qajar (Kajar) dynasty in Persia (1794–1925)	▌Uprising by Chinese Muslim minority in Gansu (1781–4) ▌China invades Nepal when Gurkhas threaten Tibet's borders (1792) ▌White Lotus Society rebellion (1796–1804)	▌India Act (1784): British government controls political affairs in India ▌Governor-general, Lord Cornwallis, stabilizes revenues and reorganizes legal system (1793) ▌Britain captures Ceylon from the Dutch (1796) ▌Tippoo Sahib (last ruler of Mysore) killed (1789): British control extends over southern India	▌Britain takes Cape of Good Hope from Dutch (1795) ▌Mungo Park (1771–1806) explores Gambia River and reaches Niger River (1795) ▌Bonaparte leads expedition to Egypt (1798–99)
1800	▌Mohammad Ali appointed governor of Egypt by Selim III of Turkey (1805) ▌Mamelukes massacred in Cairo by Mohammad Ali (1811)	▌Singapore founded by Sir Stamford Raffles (1819)	▌Kashmir conquered by Janjit Singh (1819)	▌Portuguese explorers begin to cross Africa from west (Angola) to east (1802), reaching Tete in Mozambique (1811) ▌Fulanis conquer Hausa (1804) ▌Zulu Empire founded by Chaka (1818)
1820	▌Persia and Turkey at War (1821–3) ▌Egyptian forces invade Greece (1825) and capture Missolonghi (1826)	▌Opium war between Britain and China (1839–42)	▌First Anglo-Burmese War (1824–6): Britain begins to annexe Burma ▌War between Britain and Afghanistan (1839)	▌Egypt conquers Sudan (1820–22) ▌Liberia founded as colony for freed slaves from US (1822)

THE OTTOMAN EMPIRE: THE "SICK MAN OF EUROPE" 1829–76

As the colonizing powers of the world built their empires, they surveyed the weaknesses in many of the formerly powerful empires around them. The closest geographically, the Ottoman Empire, had been in continous decline since it had lost control of Hungary in 1699. With the joint backing of the British, French, and Russians in 1829, Greece won its independence, and three Balkan states—Serbia, Wallachia, and Moldavia—were recognized as

	OTTOMAN EMPIRE	CHINA	INDIA	AFRICA
1820	■ War between Russia and Turkey (1828–9) ■ Greece independent (1830) ■ War between Egypt and Turkey (1832–3) ■ Convention of Kuytahia (1833): Mohammad Ali gains Syria			■ War between Britain and Asante in Gold Coast (1824–7) ■ Great Trek (1835–7): Boers found Transvaal ■ Battle of Blood River (1838): Boers defeat Zulus in Natal ■ Britain occupies Aden (1839)
1840	■ Treaty of London (1840): Egyptian expansion limited by European powers ■ Convention of Alexandria: Mohammad Ali confirmed as hereditary ruler of Egypt ■ Straits Convention (1841): Dardanelles and Bosporus closed to foreign ships in peace ■ Turkey declares war on Russia (1853) ■ Crimean War (1854–6)	■ Treaty of Nanking (1842): Hong Kong ceded to Britain ■ Taiping rebellion (1850–64): revolt against the Manchu dynasty ■ Anglo-Chinese war (1856–60) ■ Treaty of Aigun (1858): Russia gains Amur region ■ Treaties of Tientsin (1858): 11 Chinese ports opened	■ Britain withdraws from Kabul (1842) ■ Anglo-Sikh wars (1845–8): Britain annexes Punjab ■ Second Burmese War (1852–3) ■ Persia captures Herat (1856): leads to war with Britain ■ Indian Mutiny (1857–8) ■ India Act (1858): government of India passes to Crown from East India Company	■ Britain and Boers at war (1842) ■ Natal a British colony (1843) ■ Britain and Bantus at war (1846–7) ■ Zulu reserves established in Natal (1846) ■ Sand River Convention (1852): Transvaal independent ■ David Livingstone (1813–73) begins exploration (1853) ■ Orange Free State established (1854) ■ Ethiopia reunited by Emperor Tewodros II (c. 1855)
1860	■ Rising against Turkey in Herzegovina and Bosnia (1875) ■ Anti-Turkish rising in Bulgaria brutally put down with thousands killed (1876) ■ Serbia and Montenegro at war with Turkey (1876) but are defeated ■ Russia and Turkey at war over Balkans (1877) ■ Treaty of San Stefano (1878): Montenegro, Serbia, Bulgaria, and Romania independent	■ British and French occupy Peking (1860) ■ Zuo Zongtang suppresses Muslim rebellion in northwest and regains central Asia (1862) ■ France establishes protectorate over Cochin-China (1862–7) ■ French establish protectorate in Cambodia	■ Victoria proclaimed Empress of India (1877) ■ Second Afghan War (1878–80): Britain gains control of Afghanistan	■ British expedition to Ethiopia (1868) ■ Suez Canal opened (1869) ■ Second Ashanti War (1873–4) ■ Britain and France assume control of Egypt's finances (1876) and country (1879) ■ Britain annexes the Transvaal (1877) ■ Zulu War (1879): Britain defeats Zulus
1880	■ Ottoman Society for Union and Progress formed, calling for constitutional government (1889) ■ Armenians massacred in Constantinople (1895)	■ France gains protectorates over Annam and Tonkin (1885) ■ Sun Yat-sen founds first revolutionary society (1894) ■ China recognizes Korean independence (1895) ■ Anglo-French agreement on boundaries of Siam (1896) Germany occupies Kiaochow (1887) ■ China cedes Port Arthur to Russia (1898) ■ Chinese leaders attempt governmental and educational reform (1898) ■ Boxer Rebellion (1900)	■ Third Anglo-Burmese War (1885–6): Britain annexes Upper Burma	■ Boer victory (1881) over British ■ Britain occupies Cairo; France withdraws (1882) ■ Berlin Congress (1884): European powers divide up Africa ■ Germany occupies Togoland, Cameroons, and South-West Africa (1884) ■ Congo Free State set up under Leopold II of Belgium (1885) ■ Britain establishes protectorates over southern Nigeria and Bechuanaland (1885) ■ German East Africa founded (1885) ■ French protectorate over Côte d'Ivoire (1893) ■ Rhodesia so named (1895) ■ France annexes Madagascar (1896) ■ British protectorates in Sierra Leone and East Africa (1896) ■ Boer Wars (1889–1902)

autonomous, although still formally under the Ottoman Empire. In the aftermath of these imperial defeats, Mehmet Ali seized his opportunity to make Egypt effectively independent in 1832 (see p. 530); the Saud family had already won for Arabia similar autonomy; and the French began their occupation of Algeria in 1830. The Ottoman Empire had become the "Sick Man of Europe."

The Ottoman Empire ruled its subjects, in large part, through their religious communities. Each community administered its own legal system and even collected its own taxes. Different religious groups within the empire looked outward for protection, if necessary, by their co-religionists in other countries. The Greek Orthodox, in particular, looked toward Russia; the Roman Catholics looked to France; Protestants to Britain. Religious missions from these countries received special protection within the Ottoman Empire, and often served as bases for trade and intelligence-gathering as well. Moreover, foreigners trading within the empire were permitted the right to trial by judges of their own nation. Ottoman theory and practice of the state was quite different from that of Western Europe, where the unified nation-state was becoming the norm. In addition, the Ottomans had not kept up with the industrial development of the rest of Europe. In the 1840s Sultan Abdul Mejid enacted the *Tanzimat* (Restructuring) reforms to bring the Ottoman legal code and its social and educational standards into closer accord with those of Western European states, but with very limited success.

The Crimean War of 1853–54 demonstrated the weakness of the Ottoman system. Here on the north shore of the Black Sea, the major powers of Europe confronted one another in a conflict which tested their abilities both to fight and to negotiate settlements. The war began as Russia tested Ottoman strength by attacking Turkey in the Crimean peninsula. Turkey was saved only through the assistance of France and Britain, which pushed back the Russian assault, restoring Crimea to the Ottomans. Austria seized the opportunity to occupy Wallachia and Moldavia, and the final peace treaty recognized both Romania and Serbia as self-governing principalities, under the protection of other European powers.

In an attempt to remedy its weaknesses, the Ottoman government issued the Hatt-i Humayun edict in 1856. This ushered in numerous changes to conform to Western European standards, including equality under a common law for all citizens, tax reform, security of property, the end of torture, more honest administration, and greater freedom of the press. The "Young Turks," a group of modernizing intellectuals, were delighted, and nationalistic Armenians, Bulgars, Macedonians, and Cretans hoped for greater autonomy. A change of sultan in 1876, however, brought a reverse of all these policies and aspirations. The Young Turks went into exile, and Bulgarian and Armenian nationalists were massacred.

A weak Ottoman Empire left a power vacuum in southeast Europe, which invited continuing foreign intervention and competition. A new Russian attack through the Balkans reached Istanbul itself in 1877. Britain threatened to go to war with Russia, but Bismarck convened an international conference in Berlin in 1878 to resolve the conflict through diplomacy. Warfare was averted for the moment, but

Florence Nightingale, Turkey, c. 1854. During the Crimean War "the Lady of the Lamp" established and supervised efficient nursing departments at Scutari and Balaklava. Her unflagging efforts ensured that the mortality rate among the injured was greatly reduced. The effect of her reforms would transform nursing from the realm of the menial drudge into a skilled medical profession with high standards of education.

the mixture of Ottoman weakness, aggressive expansionism on the part of other European countries, assertive nationalism in the Balkans, and increasing militarization with increasingly powerful weapons threatened a later, larger war. It arrived in 1914 (see pp. 583–6).

SOUTHEAST ASIA AND INDONESIA 1795–1880

In Southeast Asia, the colonial competition that had marked the period from 1500 to 1750 continued sporadically. The British established a settlement at Penang, Malaya; took Malacca from the Dutch in 1795; and, under Sir Stamford Raffles, established Singapore in 1819. In a series of wars, the British took control of Burma and turned it into a major exporter of rice, timber, teak, and oil, and developed the port of Rangoon to handle the trade. Tin was discovered in Malaya, and its rubber plantations became the world's largest producer.

France began its conquest of Indochina in 1859, completing the takeover by 1893, ostensibly to protect French Catholic missionaries. In dislodging Vietnam from China's tributary sphere, the French interrupted a centuries-old relationship. Vietnam's leading products for export were rice and rubber. Germany, entering late into the colonial competition, annexed Eastern New Guinea and the Marshall and Solomon Islands in the 1880s.

Sharing in the expansionist spirit of the times, Holland decided to annex the entire Indonesian archipelago, building on its administrative center at Batavia (Jakarta) in Java and the trading posts it already occupied. The Dutch wished to dissuade other European powers from intruding and to add the profits from rubber, oil, tin, and tobacco from the other islands to those from sugar, coffee, tea, and tobacco from Java. The Dutch ruled through violence and cruelty. The Java War, 1825– 30, had many background provocations and finally erupted when the Dutch built a highway through property housing the tomb of a Muslim saint. In five years of brutal combat between Dutch and Javanese, 15,000 government soldiers were killed, including 8000 Dutch. Some 200,000 Javanese died in the war and in the famine and disease that followed.

INDIA 1858–1914

The British East India Company had come to India in the seventeenth century to buy spices and hand-made cotton textiles in exchange for bullion, wool, and metals. As a result of British commercial policies in the eighteenth century, the importation of Indian textiles was stopped, and as a result of the British industrial revolution, British machine-made cotton textiles flooded India's markets. India had been transformed into the model colony, importing manufactured goods from Britain's industries and exporting raw materials, such as cotton, jute (mostly for making bags), leather, and enormous quantities of tea. India displaced China as the leading provider of tea to Europe. Two-thirds of India's imports from Britain throughout the second half of the nineteenth century and the first years of the twentieth century were machine-manufactured textiles. Iron and steel goods came second. About one-fifth of all overseas British investment in the late nineteenth century was in India. India's own taxes, however, paid for the building and maintenance of the Indian railway system. By 1914 the subcontinent had 35,000 miles (56,000 kilometers) of track. The railway made possible increased commerce, the movement of troops, the relief of famine, the spread of political dissidence, and pilgrimage visits to religious shrines.

India began its own industrial revolution with cotton textiles, primarily in Bombay. This textile industry was started by local Gujaratis, who had long family histories of involvement in business. (In Calcutta, where jute textiles were produced, industry was largely pioneered by British investors.) Mining began in the coal fields of Bengal, Bihar, Orissa, and Assam, and in 1911 the Tata family of Bombay built India's first steel mill at Jamshedpur, Bihar. At the start of World War I, factory employment in all of India had reached about 1 million (out of a total population of about 300 million). While employment in large, mechanized factories was increasing, many hand craftsmen were being displaced, so the actual percentage of people earning their living by manufacturing of all sorts stayed approximately the same, at about 10 percent of the workforce (and has continued about the same till today).

The British ruled India directly, and therefore British influence was felt throughout the administrative and educational systems of the country. Concepts based on European political revolutions were introduced, and imperialism confronted its internal contradiction: How could an imperial power teach the values of self-rule and democracy while maintaining its own foreign rule? Finally, as we shall see in Chapter 20, this contradiction forced Britain to leave India in 1947.

Communities in India that were already active in business provided many of the new industrialists. Indian financiers became industrialists by importing the new industrial machinery ready-made from Europe. In Ahmedabad, the capital of Gujarat, local businessmen, led by an administrator with close ties to British entrepreneurs, followed Bombay in establishing a local cotton textile industry in 1861. A few years earlier Dalpatram Kavi, a local poet and intellectual leader, had called on his fellow countrymen to recognize the importance of industry to their future. His Gujarati poem, "Hunnarkhan-ni Chadayi"—"The Attack of King Industry," presents a far-reaching agenda for reform centering on industrial change but proposing social restructuring as well. It suggests that the British had brought much of value to India and that Indians were prepared to absorb and implement some of this legacy, but without the British imperial presence and its costs.

> Fellow countrymen, let us remove all the
>   miseries of our country,
> Do work, for the new kingdom has come, its
>   king is industry.

> Our wealth has gone into the hands of
>   foreigners. The great blunder is yours
> For you did not unite yourselves—fellow
>   countrymen.

> Consider the time, see for yourselves, all our
>   people have become poor,
> Many men of business have fallen—fellow
>   countrymen.

> Put away idleness and fill the treasuries with
>   knowledge.
> Now awake and work new wonders—fellow
>   countrymen.

> With kith and kin keep harmony, do not enter
>   into debt;
> Diminish the dinners for your caste—
>   fellow countrymen.

> Introduce industry from countries abroad and
>   achieve mastery of the modern machinery.
> Please attend to this plea from the Poet Dalpat—
>   fellow countrymen.

(trans. by Chimanbhai Trivedi and Howard Spodek)

India's reception of British imperialism was quite ambivalent. In 1857 a revolt swept across north India. The British called it an army mutiny but later Indian historians designated it "The First War for National Independence." In fact, the 1857 revolt involved far more than mutinous troops, but far less than the masses generally; it lacked unified leadership and direction. When more organized movements for independence began in the late nineteenth century, their leaders first had to evaluate British rule and to find a balance between acceptance and rejection of its political, economic, social, and cultural models. By the early twentieth century, most politically conscious Indians had come to believe that the British should go home and allow India to choose its own direction.

CHINA 1800–1914

China was already a colony and also possessed colonies of its own at the time Europeans began to challenge its power. The Qing dynasty, which governed China from 1644 to 1911, was headed by Manchu invaders from southeastern Manchuria. Even before they invaded and ruled China, the Manchus had established a state in Manchuria, made Korea a vassal state, and made Inner Mongolia a dependency. After establishing their rule in China, the Qing expanded westward. In the eighteenth century they annexed new lands equal to the size of China itself in Outer Mongolia, Dzungaria, the Tarim Basin, Eastern Turkestan, Tsinghai, and Tibet. They also subordinated the peoples of southeast Asia into tributary relationships. Revolts broke out against Manchu rule, but until 1800 they were mostly at the periphery of the empire and posed no serious threat to the dynasty.

By the early 1800s, however, a continuously rising population put pressure on resources and government administrative capacity. The 100 million people of 1650 tripled to 300 million by 1800 and reached 420 million by 1850. More land was needed. Allowing the settlement of Manchuria seemed a suitable reply to the problem, but the Manchus would not permit Chinese settlement in their homeland. Nor did the Manchus increase the size of their bureaucracy to service the rising population, preferring to delegate administrative responsibilities to local authorities, a response that was inadequate. Finally, the Europeans trading with China, especially the British, had discovered that China would accept opium in payment for its tea, silk, and porcelains. Indeed, the opium trade was another example of the growth of multinational commerce: the British had the crop grown cheaply in their Indian colony and carried it from the ports of Bombay, Calcutta, and Madras to Canton in China. The centuries of paying for Chinese exports with silver and gold came to an end. By the 1820s China was purchasing so much opium that it began to export silver!

The Opium Wars 1839–42 and 1856–60

Seeking to staunch the drain of silver and to stop the importation of opium, the Chinese attempted to ban and resist its the import in 1839. It was too late.

By now the British proclaimed the ideology of "free trade," and in support of this position British shipboard cannon destroyed Chinese ships and port installations in the harbor at Canton. This Opium War of 1839–42 was no contest. China ceded to Britain the island of Hong Kong as a colony and opened five Treaty Ports in which foreigners could live and conduct business under their own laws rather than under the laws of China—a condition known as **extraterritoriality**. France and the United States soon gained similar concessions. Foreign settlements were established in the new treaty ports and became the centers of new industry, education, and publishing. The focus of international trade began to relocate from Canton to Shanghai, at the mouth of the Yangzi River, a more central location along the Chinese coast.

Still China did not establish the formal diplomatic recognition and exchange that European powers had demanded. A second set of wars followed in 1856–60, and these led to the occupation of Beijing by 17,000 French and British soldiers and the sacking of the imperial Summer Palace. More treaty ports were opened, including inland centers along the Yangzi River, now patrolled by British gunboats. Europeans gained control over the

The steamer *Nemesis* destroying eleven Chinese junks at Cherpez Canton, China, by E. Duncan, 1843. The two separate wars fought between Britain and China in the 1840s and 1850s began when the Chinese government tried to halt British merchants from illegally importing opium. The victorious British, here recording an early harbor skirmish, exacted harsh commercial penalties and annexed Chinese territory, including Hong Kong. (*National Maritime Museum, Canada*)

administration of China's foreign trade and tariffs. The opium trade continued to expand. Christian missionaries were given freedom to travel throughout China. Some Chinese worked with the foreigners as *compradors*, or colleagues in business and administration.

As the Manchu government weakened in the last decades of the nineteenth century, revolts broke out, foreign powers continued to seize parts of the country and its tributaries, and there were more calls for internal reform. (The Chinese situation showed similarities with events in the Ottoman Empire at about the same time.) The greatest of the internal revolts, the Taiping Rebellion, began in 1850 led by Hong Xiuquan, a frustrated scholar who claimed visions of himself as the younger

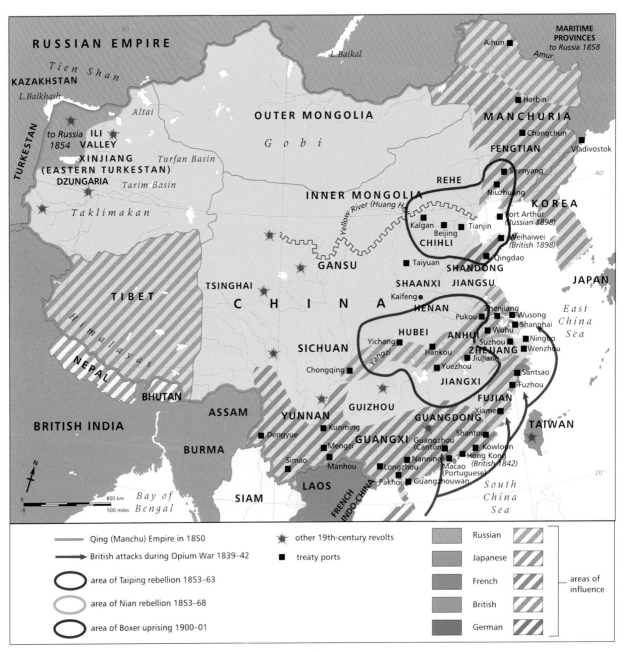

The decline of the Qing dynasty During the course of the nineteenth century, the authority of the Qing (Manchu) dynasty in China was undermined. Beset by the aggressive actions of European colonial powers, extensive trade and territorial concessions were granted. Internally, a series of increasingly violent rebellions, both among subject (often Muslim) peoples and in the Chinese heartland itself, brought the dynasty to the verge of collapse by the turn of the century.

brother of Jesus Christ. The main demands of the Taiping leaders, however, were quite concrete: an end to the corrupt and inefficient Manchu imperial rule, an end to extortionate landlord demands, and alleviation of poverty. Beginning in the southwest, the Taiping came to dominate the Yangzi valley and established their capital in Nanjing in 1853. The imperial government was unable to respond effectively, but regional military leaders, equipped with more modern weapons, finally defeated the revolt and won more power for themselves. By the time the Taiping Rebellion was suppressed in 1864, some 20 million people had been killed. At about the same time, additional rebellions broke out among tribal peoples near Guangzhou (Canton), among the Miao tribals in Guizhou, and among Muslims in Yunnan and Gansu. The largest of all the rebel groups, the Nien, controlled much of the territory between Nanjing and Kaifeng. Collectively, these rebellions cost another 10 million lives.

With the central government fully occupied with these internal revolts, foreign imperialists began to establish their territorial claims as well. Russians seized the Amur River region (1858), the Maritime Provinces (1860), and, for 10 years, the Ili valley in Turkestan (1871–81). France defeated Chinese forces in a local war and seized all of Indo-China (1883–84). Most humiliating of all, Japan defeated China in warfare in 1894–5. China ceded Taiwan to Japan, granting it the right to operate factories in the treaty ports, and paid a huge indemnity. Korea passed to Japanese control, although formal colonial rule did not follow until 1910. The historic relationship of China as teacher and Japan as disciple, which dated back at least to 600 C.E., had been abruptly reversed. The new industrial age had introduced new values and new power relationships.

The Boxer Rebellion 1898–1900

In the last years of the nineteenth century, China was in turmoil. In Beijing, a group of nationalists, called "Boxers" by the Europeans, enraged by foreign arrogance in China, burned Christian missions, killed missionaries, and put siege to the foreign legations for two months. The imperial powers of Europe and the United States put down this revolt and exacted yet another exorbitant indemnity. The Europeans and Americans did not, however, wish to take over the government of China directly. They wanted to have a Chinese government responsible for China. They wanted to preserve China as a quasi-colony, and they therefore supported the Manchus in the formalities of power, even as they steadily hollowed out the content of that power.

Boxers on the march. The mostly poor peasants who formed the Boxer Rebellion of 1898–1900 blamed hard times on foreign interference and Christian missionaries. Renowned for the ferocity of their attacks, the rebels terrified Western residents as they marched into Tianjin (pictured). A 20,000-strong force, comprising soldiers from different colonial powers, finally crushed the revolt in Beijing.

A group of Chinese modernizers began to organize new industries, beginning with textiles, but the government, now in the hands of an aging dowager empress who controlled the heir apparent until she died in 1908, blocked their reform. Frustrated nationalists called for revolution. Their leading organizer was Sun Yat-sen, a Cantonese educated in Honolulu, where he became a Christian, and in Hong Kong, where he became a doctor. Sun called for a two-fold anti-colonial revolution: first, against the Manchus and then against the European, American, and Japanese powers. Only after the first revolution was successful in overthrowing Manchu rule in 1911 did Sun begin to push the Western powers and Japan to leave China. The story of that struggle is told in Chapter 20.

AFRICA 1652–1912

Once equipped with the technology to enter and subdue the continent of Africa, Europeans began to covet it for many diverse reasons. Napoleon invaded Egypt in 1798 because he saw it as a route to India, and a way of dislodging the British from that colony. The hinterlands behind the trading ports offered good lands for farming and South Africa, first desired as a port on the long routes between Europe and Asia, soon became a comfortable and fruitful farming colony. Discovered by outsiders only in the second half of the nineteenth century, the mineral wealth of central and southern Africa—diamonds, gold, and copper—soon became one of its richest attractions for capitalists. Equatorial Africa was also rich in tropical products. Finally, as the possession of colonies began to be seen in Europe as a status symbol of nationalism, the major nations of Europe carved up the continent of Africa, each taking a share.

EGYPT 1798–1882

The earliest European expansion into Africa in modern times, beyond the coastal enclaves that had been established for trade, took place at the extreme north and south of the continent. Napoleon's forces invaded Egypt in 1798 and held it until British forces drove them out in 1801. After both European powers had withdrawn, Muhammad Ali took over actual rule in 1807, even though he was nominally a viceroy of the Ottoman Empire. He built new irrigation works, encouraged the cultivation of cotton for Europe's booming textile industry, and introduced some new industries, including Egypt's own textile mills. He modernized the army and administration, and built a system of secular state schools to train administrators and officers. He introduced a government printing press, which in turn encouraged translations into Arabic. Militarily, he marched his newly equipped armies up the Nile, captured the Sudan, and built the city of Khartoum to serve as its capital in 1830. He also gained control of the holy cities of Mecca and Medina in Arabia to counter the power of the militantly Islamic Wahabi movement there. He occupied Syria and Palestine and threatened Istanbul itself until Britain and France stood in his way, offering him, instead, recognition as the hereditary ruler of Egypt. Muhammad Ali's son commissioned a French firm to build the Suez Canal, which was opened in 1869. His grandson expanded Egyptian territorial holdings both along the coast of the Red Sea and inland toward the headwaters of the Nile.

Egypt entered the international economy based in Europe, but soon was spending more on imports, military modernization, and beautification projects in Cairo than it was earning in exports. As Egyptian debts rose, European creditors pressured their governments to force the *khedive* (the title given to Muhammad Ali and his successors) to appoint European experts as Commissioners of the Debt in 1876. In 1878 the *khedive* was forced to add a French and a British representative to his cabinet. Even so, in 1881 the European powers had the Ottoman sultan dismiss the *khedive*, Muhammad Ali's grandson. When an Egyptian military revolt then seized power, Britain sent in its forces, primarily to protect the Suez canal, and stayed on as the power behind the throne until the 1950s. For Egypt, entanglement with Europe had proved a two-edged sword.

ALGERIA 1830–71

The French invaded Algeria in 1830 to suppress piracy, as the Americans had done at Tripoli, and to collect debts. Once arrived, they remained in control of Algiers and two other ports. Resistance swelled under Abd al-Qadir, head of a rural Muslim brotherhood, who began to build a small state with its own administration and a modernized army of 10,000 men trained by European advisers. At first, the French avoided confrontation with al-Qadir, who stayed south of their holdings, but in 1841 bitter warfare broke out. Before the French won, they had committed 110,000 troops to the war and had attacked neighboring Morocco to block reinforcements to their enemy. Revolts continued to simmer, with the last and largest repressed in 1871. French armies took over rural areas, opening them for French settlement.

SOUTH AFRICA 1652–1910

The Dutch had established a colony at the Cape of Good Hope in South Africa in 1652 as a waystation *en route* to India and the Spice Islands. The settlement grew slowly, and immigrants from other European countries also joined it. The expansion of the European Cape Colony further destabilized a region already passing through an *mfecane*, or time of troubles.

In 1816, Shaka (c. 1787–1828), seized the leadership of his small Zulu kingdom just to the north and east of the Cape Colony. Shaka organized a standing army of 40,000 soldiers, rigorously trained and disciplined, housed in stockades separate from the rest of the population, and armed with newly designed short, stabbing spears, which gave them enormous power over their enemies in hand-to-hand combat. By 1828, when Shaka was assassinated by two half-brothers, his kingdom had expanded, forcing the Soshagane, Nguni, Ndebele, Sotho, Ngwane, and Mfengu peoples to flee their lands. Some moved into the Cape Colony, but the vast majority turned north and west, displacing other peoples in turn.

European expansion at the Cape had similar disruptive effects on local populations. As the Dutch and the British set out to the rural areas to farm, they displaced the Khoikhoi people who had been resident in the area. The Khoikhoi chiefdoms dissolved in the face of warfare, displacement, and catastrophic smallpox epidemics that decimated their numbers. Some of the Khoikhoi, along with other African peoples, were taken as slaves to fill the labor needs of the Europeans.

As a result of their victories in the Napoleonic Wars, military and legal control of the Cape Colony passed to the British. British laws and social practices were instituted, including freedom of the press and of assembly, the development of representative government, the abolition of the slave trade, and the emancipation of slaves. Nevertheless, Europeans controlled the best land of the region, leaving their former slaves to be wage workers rather than land-owners and farmers. Property restrictions on voting effectively kept Africans out of power, and the Masters and Servants Act limited the freedom of movement of black workers.

In a great migration, some 8000 people of Dutch descent, unhappy with the increasingly British customs of the colony, and seeking new land for farming, departed on a great march, or trek, northward in the years between 1834 and 1841. These people, usually called Boers (meaning farmers in Dutch), or Afrikaners (for the African dialect of Dutch they spoke), ultimately founded two new republics, the Orange Free State and the Transvaal. Meanwhile, the Cape Colony expanded eastward, annexing Natal in 1843, partly to keep the Boers out. As they migrated, the Boers fought, displaced, conquered, and restricted to reservations the African peoples they encountered. Seeking labor to harness the land, they often captured and virtually enslaved Africans living around them.

When the Suez Canal restructured the shipping routes between Asia and Europe in 1869, South Africa might have become a quiet colonial backwater. But in the 1870s diamonds were discovered at Kimberley, and in the 1880s the world's largest known deposit of gold was discovered, at Witwatersrand. Competition for this new wealth intensified the general hostility between the Boers and the British into full-scale warfare. The British army of 450,000 men finally defeated the Boer army of 88,000 in the three-year-long Boer War, 1899–1902. In 1910, the British consolidated their own two colonies (Cape and Natal) with the two Boer republics into the Union of South Africa, which became a self-governing country. After 1913 South Africa had the same sorts of political institutions and rights that Australia and Canada did. It was considered a white settler colony despite its black majority.

Labor Issues:
Coercion and Unionization

Throughout Africa, Europeans confronted the problem of finding labor for their new farms and enterprises. By confiscating African land and redistributing it among themselves, Europeans took farms away from Africans and produced a new wage-labor force. The 1913 Natives Land Act of South Africa closed 87 percent of South African land to African ownership; the remaining 13 percent was the most marginal land. The newly displaced labor force was especially vital for the new coffee plantations in the highlands of east Africa. In the farming areas of Kenya, Northern Rhodesia, Nyasaland, and Angola a system of tenancy without wages developed, a kind of share-

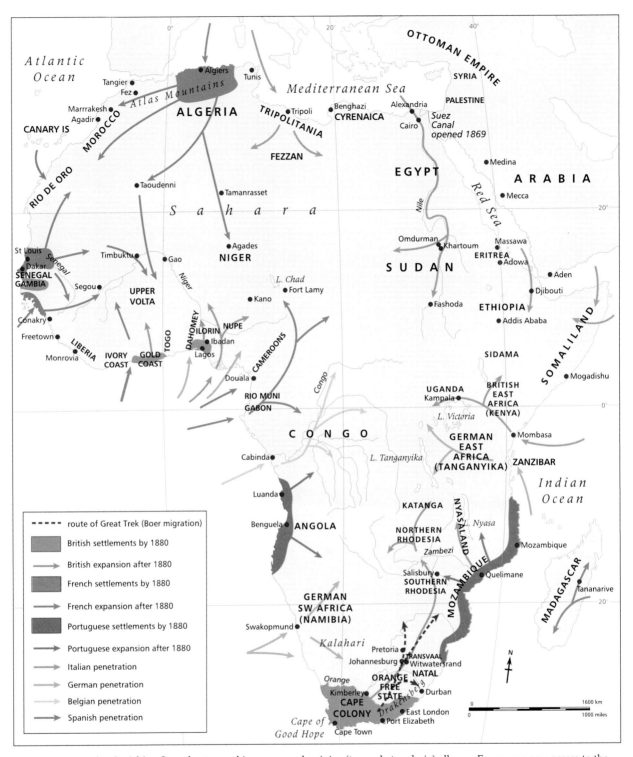

European expansion in Africa Steamboats, machine-guns, and quinine (to combat malaria) all gave Europeans new access to the interior of Africa in the later nineteenth century, and they intensified their nationalistic competition. The British pursued the dream of linking their possessions from Cape Town to Cairo, while France seized much of North and Central Africa. Bismarck's Berlin Convention of 1884 tried to apportion the spoils among all the competing powers.

cropping system. Within their colonies in Angola and Mozambique, the Portuguese used intimidation to coerce labor, but the Africans often fled or otherwise subverted the plans of their colonizers. The British colonies, which used the carrot of (low) wages seemed more successful in eliciting production. Along the coast, indentured laborers from India, China, and southeast Asia were imported by the thousands to work in the sugar plantations.

The greatest problem was finding labor for the South African diamond and gold mines (and later for the great copper mines in the Congo as well). Taxation was introduced that had to be paid in cash, forcing all Africans to find some way of raising the money. Jobs in the mines were one alternative. Because the Europeans feared the revolutionary potential of a stable African labor force in the mines, they usually recruited workers on contracts for only one or two years at a time. They split up families, housing the male workers in barrack-like accommodations near the mines and their families on distant reservations, where the women and children could carry on limited farm-ing and craft production. The mine owners did not pay the workers enough to support their families so the farming and handicrafts of the women in effect subsidized the workers' salaries.

Trade unions in the mines organized only the white skilled workers, and kept Africans out of these jobs. In 1906, when the mines employed 18,000 whites, 94,000 Africans, and 51,000 Chinese indentured laborers, the white skilled workers went on strike to protest their being squeezed out by the Chinese and the Blacks. Owners broke this strike through the use of Afrikaner strike breakers, but ultimately the Chinese miners were repatriated and the skilled jobs were reserved for whites. Race thus trumped both the free markets of capitalism and the solidarity of labor unions.

EUROPEAN EXPLORERS IN CENTRAL AFRICA

The area of the continent least known to Europeans was central Africa. David Livingstone (1813–73), a Scottish missionary who was fascinated by explo-

Stanley tracks down explorer. "Dr Livingstone, I presume?" Before journalist Henry Stanley tracked down the Scottish missionary in the heart of the African interior, the latter had been feared dead. Livingstone, who campaigned against slavery, was the first European explorer to reach Lake Tanganyika, the great Victoria Falls, and parts of Zaire.

ration and eager for the opportunity to provide medical assistance, landed at Luanda along the Angola Coast in 1841 and crossed equatorial Africa to Quelimane, spending fourteen years in this expedition. Two subsequent trips in Equatorial Africa lasted a total of thirteen years, until Livingstone died in the course of his explorations. Livingstone captured the imagination of Europe, and in 1871, the *New York Herald* dispatched Henry Morton Stanley (1841–1904) to try to find him on his third expedition. Not only did Stanley locate Livingstone, he also carried out expeditions of his own through the Lake District of East Africa and along the Congo River. On Stanley's return through Europe, King Leopold II of Belgium engaged him to establish trading stations along the Congo River. Unlike Livingstone, Stanley was motivated by personal profit and he accepted the king's proposal. The colonization of Central Africa was beginning.

Stanley, representing the king and his International Association for the Exploration and Civilization of Africa, negotiated treaties with hundreds of local chiefs. The treaties gave him the power to establish a Confederation of Free Negro Republics, an estate of some 900,000 square miles (2.3 million square kilometers), which functioned as a kind of slave plantation within Africa for the economic benefit of King Leopold. In this enterprise, Leopold was actually acting as a private investor rather than as King of Belgium.

THE SCRAMBLE FOR AFRICA

As European powers colonized central Africa, they came into direct competition with each other. Fearing the consequences of this competition, Bismarck again employed diplomacy to defuse European conflict, as he had done a few years earlier in the Balkans. He convened a conference in Berlin in 1884–5 to determine the allocation of Congo lands and to establish ground rules for determining borders among European colonies in Africa. The Berlin Conference assigned the administration of the Congo, an area one-third the size of the continental United States, to Leopold II personally as a kind of company government. The Congo became, in effect, his private estate, eighty times larger than Belgium itself. Its economic purpose was, first, the harvesting of natural rubber, the sap of the rubber tree, and, later, the exploitation of the Congo's rich mineral reserves, especially copper. Laborers were forced to work as slaves at the point of a gun. Company agents freely killed and

MAJOR DISCOVERIES AND INVENTIONS—1830–1914

1831	Dynamo: Michael Faraday
1834	Reaping machine: Cyrus McCormick
1836	Revolver: Samuel Colt
1837	Telegraph: Samuel Morse
1839	Vulcanized rubber: Charles Goodyear
1852	Gyroscope: Léon Foucault
1853	Passenger elevator: Elisha Otis
1855	Celluloid: Alexander Parkes Bessemer converter: Henry Bessemer Bunsen burner: Robert Bunsen
1858	Refrigerator: Ferdinand Carré Washing machine: Hamilton Smith
1859	Internal combustion engine: Etienne Lenoir
1862	Rapid-fire gun: Richard Gatling
1866	Dynamite: Alfred Nobel
1876	Telephone: Alexander Graham Bell
1877	Phonograph: Thomas Edison
1879	Incandescent lamp: Thomas Edison
1885	Motorcycle: Edward Butler Electric transformer: William Stanley Vacuum flask: James Dewar
1887	Motorcar engine: Gottleib Daimler/Karl Benz
1888	Pneumatic tire: John Boyd Dunlop Kodak camera: George Eastman
1895	Wireless: Guglielmo Marconi X-rays: Wilhelm Roentgen
1896	Radioactivity: Antoine Becquerel
1897	Diesel engine: Rudolf Diesel
1898	Submarine: John P. Holland
1902	Radio-telephone: Reginald Fessenden
1903	Airplane: Wilbur and Orvile Wright
1905	Theory of relativity: Albert Einstein
1911	Combine harvester: Benjamin Holt
1914	Tank: Ernest Swinton

maimed workers who offered resistance. In 1908, recognizing both the cruelty and the economic losses of the Congo administration, the Belgian Parliament took over control of the colony from the king, but the Congo remained one of the most harshly administered of all the African colonies.

The Conference also divided up the lands of Africa on paper, generally apportioning inland areas to the European nations already settled on the adjacent coast. But these nations were then required to establish actual inland settlements in those regions, and they quickly did so, dispatching settlers in a "scramble for Africa." Portugal added to its domains in Angola and Mozambique. Italy captured a piece of Somaliland at the horn of Africa and Eritrea on the Red Sea. It also attempted to conquer proud Ethiopia, but Italy's soldiers were defeated in bloody warfare at Adowa in 1896. Italy did succeed, however, in taking Libya from the weakened Ottoman Empire in 1911. Germany established colonies in German East Africa (Tanganyika), the Cameroons, Togo, and German Southwest Africa (Namibia). The Germans, like the British and French before them, established treaties with African chiefs, who often did not understand the significance of the documents they ratified, but nevertheless found their power over their people strengthened. The chiefs frequently became, in effect, the agents of Europeans for recruiting labor and collecting taxes. In exchange, the Europeans protected the chiefs from resistance and rebellion.

A decade after the Berlin conference, France and Britain, the two largest colonial powers, found themselves on a collision course in the Nile valley. From the north, British troops were moving up the Nile valley to fight the troops of a Muslim militant state, which challenged them near Khartoum. Muhammad Ahmed had proclaimed himself as the **Mahdi**, "the guided one of the Prophet," and began to build a state in the Sudan. In 1885 he defeated an Egyptian force commanded by British General Charles Gordon at Khartoum. For some time Britain did not respond, but a decade later, it sent another force under General Horatio Herbert Kitchener to retake the Sudan for Egypt. At Omdurman, Kitchener's army destroyed the Mahdists, killing 11,000 men and wounding 16,000 more in a single battle on 2 September 1898, while losing just 40 of its own soldiers.

As English forces began to connect the north–south route, French forces were proceeding from their huge holdings in west Africa to link up with their small toehold in the east at French Somaliland. In 1898 General Kitchener confronted French Captain Jean-Baptiste Marchand at Fashoda. War threatened, as provocative correspondence and news accounts were issued on both sides. In the end, the heavily outnumbered French backed down, and France retreated to its substantial holdings in western Africa, Algeria, and to Morocco, which it later divided with Spain in 1912.

MOTIVES FOR EUROPEAN COLONIZATION: DIFFERING HISTORICAL INTERPRETATIONS

The industrial revolution in western Europe and the United States ushered in an era of imperialism that brought most of the world's land under European political control. Why did the industrializing nations assert their powers in this way? To some extent, the answer seems obvious: They relished the power, wealth, and prestige that apparently came with imperial possessions. Sometimes, on the other hand, they claimed to welcome the opportunity to serve others. Further, the industrial system that they were building seemed to take on a life of its own, requiring ever-increasing sources of raw materials and more markets in which to sell. But why was trade alone not enough? Why did the industrialists feel it was necessary to take political control as well? Were there additional motives behind imperialism? And did the results of imperialism match the aspirations of the imperial rulers?

We cannot answer all these questions fully, but a very recent (April 1997) article by Patrick Wolfe in *The American Historical Review*, "History and Imperialism: A Century of Theory, from Marx to Postcolonialism," helps us to review and sort out some of the most prominent attempts.

Karl Marx deplored the exploitation of colonialism, but, as a European, he valued some of its contributions. Britain, he emphasized, brought to India a new economic dynamism, with railroads, industrial infrastructure, and communication networks. Ultimately this transformation would lead to capitalism and then socialism. Marx wrote in 1853: "Whatever may have been the crimes of England, she was the unconscious tool of history in bringing about that revolution" (Marx and Engels, *First Indian War*, p. 21).

J.A. Hobson, a British economist writing in 1902, and V.I. Lenin, the leader of the Communist revolu-

THE RHODES COLOSSUS
STRIDING FROM CAPE TOWN TO CAIRO.

The Rhodes Colossus. Cecil John Rhodes became one of the main champions of British rule in southern Africa, promoting colonization "from Cape Town to Cairo." The statesman and financier divided his time between diamond mining and annexing territories to British imperial rule. Rhodesia (now Zimbabwe and Zambia) was named for him in 1894.

tion in Russia (see Chapter 19), writing in 1916, both agreed that the desire to control raw materials and markets drove imperialism. Hobson pointed out that the profits of the imperial system went mostly to the rich. He believed that if imperialism were ended overseas, a concentration on investment and industry at home would provide greater opportunities to the working classes in Europe. M.N. Roy, a founder of the Communist Party of India, disagreed with Hobson, arguing that the profits of imperialism did provide workers at home in Europe with a feeling of economic gain. The revolt against the imperial, and capitalist, system would begin among the workers in the colonies who were more exploited.

Several analysts have tried to grasp the imperial system as a whole, understanding the impact of colonizer and colonized upon one another. Some, like Marx, above, saw the system introducing valuable modernization into the colonies. Most, like Immanuel Wallerstein and the American economists Paul Baran and Paul Sweezy, argued that the imperial power would always seek to keep the colonies in a position of dependency and underdevelopment. In effect the imperial power might introduce some technological innovations, such as railways that were necessary for their trade, but they had no interest in enabling the colonies to become economic and technological rivals. Indeed, one reason for imposing imperial domination was to prevent the colony from taking control of its own economic policies.

Ronald Robinson and John Gallagher, British historians writing in the 1960s, and French anthropologist Louis Althusser, writing in the 1970s and 1980s, stressed the need to evaluate imperialism on a case-by-case basis. British imperialism in Egypt, for example, was quite sophisticated and benign compared with the raw cruelty of Belgian imperialism in the Congo. Even within individual colonies, imperialists treated different regions and groups differently, for example incorporating educated urban groups into the administration while treating plantation workers almost like slave labor. Imperial rule also varied considerably depending on the administration in power in the imperial country and also on the local imperial representatives on the scene at any given time. All three scholars eschew generalizations and emphasize the complexity of the imperial enterprise.

Finally, some of the most recent scholarly analyses of imperialism—often referred to as postcolonial analyses—have stressed the cultural impact of imperialism on both colony and colonizer. Imperial rulers usually drew a sense of pride from their conquest and exalted their own culture for possessing colonies. Colonized peoples, on the other hand, had to re-examine their historic cultural traditions and identities in light of the fact that they had been conquered by foreigners. The postcolonial literature that analyzes this cultural confrontation is expanding rapidly at present, with contributions by literary critics such as Edward Said, Homi Bhabha, and Gayatri Chakravorty Spivak. Indeed, as industrialization has brought peoples of the world into ever closer contact, and political philosophies have collided with one another, questions of personal and group identity have increased everywhere. In the next chapter we examine three areas of cultural identity—urban identity, gender identity, and national identity—in the age of revolution.

BIBLIOGRAPHY

Abu-Lughod, Janet and Richard Hay, Jr., eds., *Third World Urbanization* (Chicago: Maaroufa Press, 1977).

Adas, Michael, ed. *Islamic and European Expansion* (Philadelphia: Temple University Press, 1993).

—. *Machines as the Measure of Men* (Ithaca: Cornell University Press, 1989).

Andrea, Alfred and James Overfield, eds., *The Human Record*, Vol. 2, (Boston: Houghton Mifflin, 1994).

Bairoch, Paul. *Cities and Economic Development*, trans. by Christopher Braider (Chicago: University of Chicago Press, 1988).

Braudel, Fernand. *Civilization and Capitalism 15th–18th Century: The Perspective of the World*, trans. by Sian Reynolds (New York: Harper and Row, 1984).

Briggs, Asa. *A Social History of England* (New York: Viking Press, 1983).

Burns, E. Bradford. *Latin America: A Concise Interpretive History* (Englewood Cliffs: Prentice Hall, 1990).

Cameron, Rondo. *A Concise Economic History of the World* (New York: Oxford University Press, 1989).

Chadwick, Edwin. *Inquiry into the Condition of the Poor*, in Kishlansky, Mark A., ed. *Sources of the West* (New York: HarperCollins, 1991), pp. 94–98.

Cobban, Alfred. *A History of Modern France*, Vol. 2: *1799–1945* (Harmondsworth: Penguin Books, 1961).

Curtin, Philip, *et al. African History from Earliest Times to Independence* (Longman: London, 2nd ed., 1995).

Dalpat-Kavya Navnit (Selections from Dalpat the Poet), in Gujarati, ed. Deshavram Kashiram Shastri (Ahmedabad: Gujarat Vidyasabha, 1949).

Davis, Lance E. and Robert A. Huttenback. *Mammon and the Pursuit of Empire* (New York: Cambridge University Press, 1989).

Deane, Phyllis. *The First Industrial Revolution* (Cambridge University Press, 2nd ed., 1979).

Fogel, Robert and Stanley L. Engerman. *Time on the Cross*, 2 vols (Boston: Little, Brown, 1974).

Grinker, Roy Richard and Christopher B. Steiner, eds. *Perspectives on Africa* (Oxford: Blackwell, 1997).

Hanke, Lewis and Jane M. Rausch, eds. *People and Issues in Latin American History* (New York: Markus Wiener Publishing, 1990).

Headrick, Daniel R. *The Tools of Empire* (New York: Oxford University Press, 1981).

Hobsbawm, Eric. *The Age of Capital 1848–1875* (New York: Vintage Books, 1975).

—. *The Age of Empire 1875–1914* (New York: Vintage, 1987).

—. *The Age of Revolution 1789–1848* (New York: New American Library, 1962).

Hughes, Thomas P. *American Genesis* (New York: Viking, 1989).

Kennedy, Paul. *The Rise and Fall of the Great Powers* (New York: Random House, 1987).

Laslett, Peter. *The World We Have Lost* (New York: Charles Scribner's Sons, 1965).

Lenin, V.I. *Imperialism, the Highest Stage of Capitalism* (Peking: Foreign Languages Press, 1965).

Magraw, Roger. *France 1815–1914: The Bourgeois Century* (Oxford: Oxford University Press, 1983).

Marx, Karl and Frederick Engels. *The Communist Manifesto* (New York: International Publishers, 1948).

—. *The First Indian War of Independence 1857–1859* (Moscow: Foreign Languages Press, n.d., c. 1960).

Moore, Barrington, Jr. *The Social Origins of Dictatorship and Democracy* (Boston: Beacon Press, 1966).

Murphey, Rhoads. *A History of Asia* (New York: HarperCollins, 1992).

Palmer, R.R. and Joel Colton. *A History of the Modern World* (New York: McGraw Hill, 8th ed., 1995).

Perlin, Frank. *The Invisible City: Monetary, Administrative and Popular Infrastructures in Asia and Europe, 1500–1900* (Brookfield, VT: Variorum, 1993).

Perrot, Michelle. *Workers on Strike; France, 1871–1890*, trans. by Chris Turner with Erica Carter and Claire Laudet (Leamington Spa: Berg, 1987).

Revel, Jacques and Lynn Hunt, eds. *Histories: French Constructions of the Past*, trans. by Arthur Goldhammer *et al.* (New York: New York Press, 1995)

SarDesai, D.R. *Southeast Asia Past and Present* (Boulder: Westview Press, 3rd ed., 1994).

Seal, Anil. *The Emergence of Indian Nationalism* (Cambridge: Cambridge University Press, 1968).

Stearns, Peter N. *The Industrial Revolution in World History* (Boulder, CO: Westview Press, 1993).

Thompson, E.P. *The Making of the English Working Class* (New York: Vintage, 1966).

Time-Life Books. *Time Frame AD 1850–1900: The Colonial Overlords.* (Alexandria, VA: Time-Life Books, 1990).

Wallerstein, Immanuel. *The Modern World-system 1: Capitalist Agriculture and the Origins of the European World-economy in the Sixteenth Century* (San Diego: Academic Press, 1974).

Wilentz, Sean. *Chants Democratic: New York City and the Rise of the American Working Class, 1788–1850* (New York: Oxford University Press, 1984).

Wolf, Eric R. *Europe and the People without History* (Berkeley: University of California Press, 1982).

Wolfe, Patrick, "Imperialism and History: A Century of Theory, from Marx to Postcolonialism," *American Historical Review* CII, No. 2 (April 1997), 388–420.

17

CHAPTER

"Social progress and historic changes occur by virtue of the progress of women toward liberty, and decadence of the social order occurs as the result of a decrease in the liberty of women."

CHARLES FOURIER

SOCIAL REVOLUTIONS

1830–1914

URBANIZATION, GENDER RELATIONS, AND NATIONALISM WEST AND EAST

People's everyday lives and the social structures in which they lived changed dramatically as a result of the political and industrial revolutions. The increasing authority of the nation-state, struggles for participatory democracy, abundant increases in productivity, changing demands within the labor market, and the shifting international power relationships were not remote abstractions. They changed the day-to-day lives of ordinary people. In this chapter we examine three areas of that transformation: urban life, gender relations, and nationalism. We conclude the chapter with special attention to the transformation of Japan in the second half of the nineteenth century. Japan was the first non-European country to industrialize successfully, alter its internal political structures, and enter the international competition in conquering colonies. At the farthest eastern edge of Eurasia, Japan seemed to be following, in its own way, patterns established at the farthest west.

NEW PATTERNS OF URBAN LIFE

Cities from the eighteenth century began a period of growth that has continued without break until today. In the largest cities this process included large-scale suburbanization, which was made possible by the new railroad transportation systems for goods and passengers. Automobiles later enlarged the system to ever-greater dimensions. Growth was both geographic and demographic. Cities grew because they served new functions for more people. One of these functions, which brought about much of the early growth, was the increasing importance of centralized government. The political and administrative function of many cities has continued and is evident not only in the great capitals of industrialized nations like Washington, Canberra, and Paris, but also in the capitals of nations that are not heavily industrialized such as New Delhi, Beijing,

Jakarta, Lagos, and Abidjan. Nevertheless, most economists believe that urbanization based primarily on government jobs is economically and socially problematic. Cities tend to grow on the basis of economic productivity.

Indeed, much of the urban growth in the nineteenth century (unlike that of the late twentieth century) was a direct result of industrialization. The steam engine, which could be constructed anywhere, made the location of industries more flexible. Factories sprang up near port facilities, at inland transportation hubs, in the heart of raw materials resource centers like the Midlands of Britain, or Silesia in central Europe, and in large concentrations of consumers, like the great cities of Paris and London. New industrial metropolises dotted the map.

Immigrants streamed into the new cities for jobs. Farmers became factory workers and the balance between urban and rural populations tilted continuously cityward. Within cities, the children of artisans became factory workers. Both farmers and artisans found the new industrial city shocking. They were exchanging the styles of life of farm and workshop for negative regimes of routinization, standardization, and regulation, and the skills that they had previously mastered were of little use. At the same time, opportunities beckoned: cultural, educational, recreational, social, and, most important, economic. In the early years of the industrial revolution, conditions of labor and of public health were abysmal, but, as productivity increased, workers organized, employers and governments paid heed, and conditions started to improve. "City lights" began to appear more attractive. The nineteenth century began the global age of urbanization.

THE CONDITIONS OF URBANIZATION: HOW DO WE KNOW?

Primary Documents of the Time

"The most remarkable social phenomenon of the present century is the concentration of population in cities." These words made up the opening sentence of Adna Ferrin Weber's *The Growth of Cities in the Nineteenth Century*, published in 1899, the first comprehensive quantitative study of the subject. Weber's research began as a Ph.D. dissertation in demographic statistics in 1898 at Columbia University and was published the next year in book form. A century later it remains an invaluable introduction to the central issues.

In Chapter 16 we saw a small sampling of the poetry, political polemics, and government reports tracking the phenomenon of nineteenth-century urbanization as it was occurring. Here, we will examine a few of the scholarly approaches to the subject that were also appearing, and Weber's book is a good starting point. He called attention to the breakdown of boundaries between city and country. Institutionally, cities were becoming the cockpits of modern life; geographically, they were already spawning suburbs that would later be derided as "urban sprawl."

> In the last half-century [1848–98], all the agencies of modern civilization have worked together to abolish this rural isolation; the cities have torn down their fortifications, which separated them from the open country; while the railways, the newspaper press, freedom of migration and settlement, etc., cause the spread of the ideas originating in the cities and lift the people of the rural districts out of their state of mental stagnation. Industry is also carried on outside of the cities, so that the medieval distinction between town and country has lost its meaning in the advanced countries. (pp. 7–8)

To critics of urbanization, Weber replied that cities and industry were needed to absorb the surplus growth of rural population. In most of Europe, except France, he writes, "the rural populations, by reason of their continuous increase, produce a surplus which must migrate either to the cities or foreign lands" (p. 67). Without cities and industrial jobs, what would happen to this surplus population? This rhetorical question implied by Weber continues to our own day.

As befits his discipline, Weber began with a statistical summary and an analysis of levels of urbanization in his own time, and traced it back through the nineteenth century. As part of his doctoral research, Weber attempted global coverage and he gathered his data from official government publications as well as unofficial population estimates from around the world. In general, he found industrialization the main reason for city growth. England and Wales, 62 percent urban, were by far the most industrialized and the most urbanized countries on earth. The next closest were Australia, at 42 percent, and the various parts of Germany, at about 30 percent. In general, the largest cities were growing fastest. London, the world's largest city in 1890, held 4.2 million people; New York, the second largest, 2.7 million. The least industrialized countries were the least urbanized, below 10 percent—but most of these countries did not maintain statistical records! Besides industry, Weber cited other important reasons for the growth of cities:

- the general improvement in public health regulation, which improved longevity, especially in densely crowded cities;

- the agricultural revolution, still taking place before Weber's eyes, which was freeing an enormous workforce to migrate to cities, and supplying adequate food to nourish them all;

- the growth of government, centralized in cities;

- the growth of commerce, the life blood of cities;

- rising standards of living and attractive personal opportunities in education, amusements, and social interaction and stimulation.

In contrast to the poverty and oppression pictured by Marx and Engels a half century earlier, Weber radiated optimism. Weber's projection included increasing collective action, achieved through peaceful means, and increasing levels of domesticity and personal comfort.

> But there will still be left a large field for private associations, whose activities have already added to the comforts of city life. Consider the conveniences at the disposal of the *fin de siècle* [end of the century] housewife: a house with a good part of the old-fashioned portable furniture built into it, e.g., china cabinets, refrigerators, ward-robes, sideboards, cheval glasses [full-length, swivel mirrors], bath tubs, etc; electric lights, telephones and electric buttons in every room, automatic burglar alarms, etc....[Weber than quotes another urban advocate:] Thus has vanished the necessity for drawing water, hewing wood, keeping a cow, churning, laundering clothes, cleaning house, beating carpets, and very much of the rest of the onerous duties of housekeeping, as our mothers knew it. (pp. 218–20)

A judicious scholar, Weber did not omit the many negative aspects of city life at the end of the nineteenth century. Although death rates in the city had been declining steadily, urban death rates in 1899 remained higher than rural ones in most countries. In one of the worst examples, during the decade 1880–90, when the expected length of life at birth for all of England and Wales was forty-seven years, in Manchester, one of the greatest centers of the early Industrial Revolution, it was twenty-nine!

18 Back Queen Street, Deansgate, Manchester. As this *Illustrated London News* drawing of housing conditions of the Manchester Cotton Operatives in 1862 shows, accommodation in this city could be grim. Manchester in particular, with its high mortality rate, desperately needed the attentions of voluntary agencies that were attempting to better living conditions of those who had been drawn to work in the new industries. Despite the fact that many workers emigrated to the United States or to British colonies overseas, the population continued to grow at a great rate, with adverse consequences for public health and housing.

Industrialization exacted its costs. Nevertheless, Weber reviewed the public health measures such as water and sewage systems and the provision of clinics that had already been effective in other places, strongly advocated more of them, and remained optimistic—if urbanites could cooperate for the common good.

Weber's pioneering work gives us a flavor of the end of the nineteenth-century view of urbanization. His work finds a place among a multitude of other studies and meditations on the industrial city, for this was one of the most critical areas of study of the time. For example, Charles Booth (1840–1916) led a team of researchers in London, which produced the seventeen volumes of *Life and Labour of the People in London*. Between 1886 and 1903, Booth and his colleagues systematically visited thousands of homes throughout London, interviewing workers to discover how the working people of the metropolis labored and lived. An enterprising English businessman, with interests in the United States as well, and a political and social reformer, Booth funded the survey himself in order to understand from on-the-ground investigation what might be done to resolve the persistent problem of poverty in the midst of wealth.

Paris, a Rainy Day **by Gustave Caillebotte, 1876–77.** An Impressionist's-eye-view of life in an urban setting. Although a number of studies suggest that the burgeoning urban development of the turn of the century was detrimental to the health of the poor, this painting presents a more sanitized picture: for the bourgeoisie, with leisure time on their hands, cities, despite their anonymity, could provide a backdrop for pleasant diversions. (*Musée Marmottan, Paris*)

Although not an academic, Booth plunged into the empirical research with a zeal born from the methods of his business affairs and the influence of the newly emerging discipline of sociology. His investigations, which earned world-wide attention, found that 30.7 percent of London's population lived below the poverty line—that is, they received incomes too low to support themselves and their families in health. Poverty was especially severe among the elderly, and Booth began to lobby intensively for old-age pensions (introduced by the Liberal Party in 1906). Although he never developed a theoretical framework for understanding his data, Booth was a pioneer in understanding the actual workings of the metropolis.

Not all studies of the city were so empirically based. Philosophical speculation on the nature of the city also flourished. In Germany, Max Weber (1864–1920), began a series of essays and books attempting to understand the world changing around him, helping also to establish the new discipline of sociology. His essay, "The City," published in 1922, a decade after our period, analyzed the modern industrial city as a new creation. Weber was less interested in the economics of urban life than in its institutional structure. He contrasted the new urban institutions with those of earlier European cities, especially medieval cities (see Chapter 12). Weber concluded that the sprawling industrial city, open to any immigrant who wished to come, embedded within a nation-state that controlled its life and politics, was not the city of earlier times. Europe, at least, was living in a new era.

Georg Simmel (1858–1914), a social psychologist in Germany, wrote in 1903 of the destabilizing effects of these new cities:

> The individual has become a mere cog in an enormous organization of things and powers which tears from his hands all progress, spirituality, and value in order to transform them from their subjective form into the form of a purely objective life. … the metropolis is the genuine arena of this culture which outgrows all personal life. Here … is offered such an overwhelming fullness of crytallized and impersonalized spirit that the personality, so to speak, cannot maintain itself under its impact. (Sennett, pp. 58–9)

Two factors were breaking down the individual personality. First, the division of labor was turning the individual into a specialist and leading to the loss of a sense of personal or community whole-ness. Second, the sheer multitude of people and experiences in the city was also forcing the individual to retreat into a small, private niche. The urban dweller was evolving into a person swift of intellect but lacking integration.

Based on a similar conception of nature and the city, Oswald Spengler (1880–1936), philosopher of history, went the next step and declared that the enormous "world-cities" of his day were inevitably destroying the spirit of the folk peoples that had built them. He titled his famous book *The Decline of the West* (1918–22). The cycle had occurred before in other civilizations:

> This, then, is the conclusion of the city's history; growing from primitive barter-center to culture-city and at last to world-city, it sacrifices first the blood and soul of its creators to the needs of its majestic evolution, and then the last flower of that growth to the spirit of Civilization—and so, doomed, moves on to final self-destruction. (cited in Sennett, p. 85)

Spengler's writing, and others like it, had painful consequences, for in the cultural contest between city and countryside, it stigmatized the cosmopolitan life and people of the city. German cities had not experienced the same rise and liberation of the merchant classes as had England, the Netherlands, and France. German traditions of urban freedom and creativity were weaker and less valued (despite the fact that its cities were becoming industrial powerhouses). A generation after Spengler, Germany would be filled with praise for the traditional values of "the Volk, the People," meaning the native, rural people, and condemnation of the more diverse, cosmopolitan urbanites.

In the United States the formal study of cities lagged. The "Chicago School of urban ecology" was just getting underway about the time of World War I. Sociologists Robert Park (1864–1944) and Louis Wirth (1897–1952) guided interdisciplinary teams of scholars at the University of Chicago in studying their own city, the world's fastest-growing industrial metropolis of the day. To some degree, they philosophized and speculated as did the Germans. To a much larger degree they launched empirical studies of conditions in the city, similar to those carried out by Booth, and they studied neighborhoods within the city as well as the metropolis as a whole.

Most urbanites did not live their lives downtown, as so many previous scholars had implied, but in local neighborhoods, each of which had its own characteristics. These neighborhoods provided the homes of the city residents. People's lives were not so disconnected, isolated, or alienated as it might appear. At the end of the day, most people went back to their own homes in their own neighborhoods, places where they had a strong sense of self and community. These neighborhoods interacted with each other, and with the commercial areas of the city, in their own ways. The variety of social and economic lifestyles multiplied with the size of the city and the diversity of its functions. Neighborhoods reflected this diversity.

The commercial areas themselves were also increasing in size, complexity, and facilities. By the 1870s, department stores, coffeehouses, pubs, and restaurants had added urbanity to the central business district, attracting retail shoppers, window shoppers, and people with some leisure time. Theaters, concert houses, museums, the press and publishing houses, libraries, clubs, and a multitude of new voluntary associations provided culture and entertainment. They also created a "public sphere"—a setting in which the people of a nation form and circulate their most influential civic ideas, goals, and aspirations. Here was the modern analogue of the ancient Greek agora.

A new transportation system made possible this specialization of commercial, cultural, industrial, and residential neighborhoods within the city. London opened its first underground railway system in 1863, the first major subway system in the world, and others followed. From the 1870s, commuter railways began to service new suburbs, and electric trolleys came into service after 1885. The first skyscrapers rose in the 1880s, beginning with ten-story buildings in Chicago. The availability of steel at commercial prices made their construction possible, and the invention of elevators made them accessible.

Guaranty Building in Buffalo, New York, designed by Louis Henry Sullivan, 1894–6. Sullivan's designs for steel-frame construction of large buildings—made possible because steel was now readily available and the elevator had been invented—were the forerunners of today's skyscrapers. A glance at the skyline of any large American or European city will confirm that Sullivan greatly influenced twentieth-century architecture, particularly in the United States. Sullivan's working principle that form follows function applied to the tall buildings (up to ten stories in the late nineteenth century) that he designed. It was important to maximize the limited space in city centers, and the idea of carrying buildings upward instead of outward was a brilliant concept.

POETS OF THE CITY: BAUDELAIRE AND WHITMAN

The nineteenth-century city attracted not only scholars with empirical data, and philosophers with speculations, but also poets with profound feelings. In the last chapter we cited the English Romantic poets Blake and Wordsworth. Here we compare two very different poets. Charles Baudelaire (1821–67) lived a difficult life emotionally and financially. He observed with melancholy and resignation the life of Paris and the Parisians, and yet identified with and loved what he saw. Here, as in most of his poetry, Baudelaire observes the worn, little people to be seen under the surface glitter of Europe's most cultured city.

The Twilight of Dawn

Here and there chimneys begin to smoke.
Women of pleasure, their eyelids bleary,
Their mouths open, sleep only half awake;
Beggar women, their thin, cold breasts sagging,
Breathe onto burning embers, then onto their
    fingers.

It was the hour when, amidst the cold and the
    grind,
The pain of women in childbirth deepens;
Like a sob cut short in a clot of blood,
The crow of a rooster, far off, cuts through the
    hazy air.
A sea of fog bathes the buildings.
Men in agony in the workhouses
Heave their dying breath in undignified gasps.
The debauched return home, broken by their
    work.
The shivering dawn robed in pink and green
Advances slowly along the deserted Seine,
And somber, aging Paris, rubbing its eyes,
Picks up its tools, and sets to work.

(trans. by Howard Spodek)

In the United States, Walt Whitman (1819–92) sang a more optimistic, vigorous song of American life and its seemingly endless immigrant variety. A few of his poems touch on city life. Here he exults in the growth of Manhattan, abounding in human creations but still set in nature. Whitman calls the island by its native American name.

Mannahatta

I was asking for something specific and perfect
    for my city,
Whereupon lo! upsprang the aboriginal name.

Now I see what there is in a name, a word,
    liquid, sane, unruly, musical, self-sufficient,
I see that the word of my city is that word from
    of old,
Because I see that word nested in nests of water-
    bays, superb
Rich, hemm'd thick all around with sailships and
    steamships, an island sixteen miles long,
    solid-founded,
Numberless crowded streets, high growths of
    iron, slender, strong, light, splendidly uprising
    toward clear skies,
Tides swift and ample, well-loved by me, toward
    sundown,
The flowing sea-currents, the little islands, larger
    adjoining islands, the heights, the villas,
The countless masts, the white shore-steamers,
    the lighters, the ferry-boats, the black sea-
    steamers well-model'd,
The down-town streets, the jobbers' houses of
    business, the houses of business of the ship-
    merchants and money-brokers, the river-streets,
Immigrants arriving, fifteen or twenty thousand
    in a week,
The carts hauling goods, the manly race of
    drivers of horses, the brown-faced sailors,
The summer air, the bright sun shining, and the
    sailing clouds aloft,
The winter snows, the sleigh-bells, the broken ice
    in the river, passing along up or down with
    the flood-tide or ebb-tide,
The mechanics of the city, the masters, well-
    form'd, beautiful faced, looking you straight
    in the eyes,
Trottoirs throng'd, vehicles, Broadway, the
    women, the shops and shows,
A million people—manners free and superb—
    open voices—hospitality—the most
    courageous and friendly young men,
City of hurried and sparkling waters! city of
    spires and masts!
City nested in bays! my city!

URBAN SPRAWL: HOW DO WE KNOW?

One of the central problems of the industrializing city of the early nineteenth-century was crowding. Poor ventilation, inadequate sanitation, unclean water, alienation from nature, poor health, and tuberculosis resulted as densities in urban cores reached, and even surpassed, 100,000 people per square mile (2.5 square kilometers). By the last decades of the century the electric trolley cars and commuter railways offered the means to suburbanize, and the city expanded in area as never before. At first the densities in the center did not appear to diminish, for the stream of new immigrants to the city matched and even exceeded those who were suburbanizing. Slowly, however, the highest densities did come down.

We know that urban sprawl had become a problem by the late 1800s because town planners began seeking solutions to the new problem: How to provide space for population increase, allow for geographical expansion, yet continue to provide green space, while fostering participation in both the local community and the metropolis as a whole? The British reformer Ebenezer Howard (1850–1928) provided one of the first proposals in his book *Tomorrow: A Peaceful Path to Real Reform* (1898), later revised and reissued under its more common name, *Garden Cities of Tomorrow* (1902).

Howard's schematic plan for a "Group of Slumless Smokeless Cities" illustrates his provocative concept of a region of about 250,000 people on 66,000 acres (26,700 hectares). This would be far too miniature to cope with the problems of a London or a New York. Its intense control over the planning process also demanded political decisions that might not be possible within a participatory democracy. Nevertheless, the **garden city** concept of a core city ringed by separate suburbs, each set in a green belt, linked to one another by rapid transit, provided provocative, creative, somewhat utopian, thinking for one of the new urban problems dawning with the century.

THE NON-INDUSTRIAL, NON-EUROPEAN CITY

The cities of Europe were different from those of Africa and Asia even before industrialization. Asian and African cities usually functioned primarily as political, religious, and cultural capitals, and they were controlled by leaders of those sectors, while Western European cities, beginning in the twelfth century, began to give greater emphasis to economics and were controlled far more by leaders of commerce. The rise of industrialization in Western Europe intensified that contrast.

What kind of new colonial cities did European businessmen and governments establish in Asia

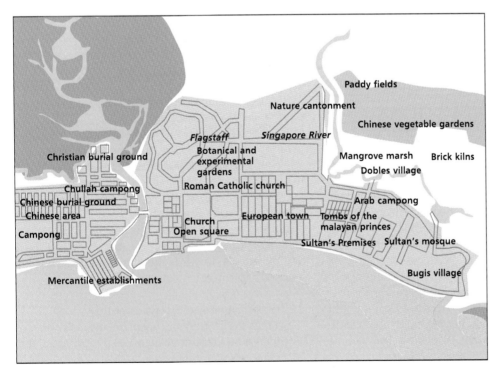

A map of the town and environs of Singapore, from an actual survey by G.D. Coleman, 1839. Singapore was not an indigenous town that gradually grew up around a bustling port; it was purposely founded in 1819 on the site of a fishing village by Sir Stamford Raffles, who saw its potential as a trading center. The British actively encouraged immigration to the new port, and divided the thriving city into separate areas for the different ethnic groups that lived and worked there. Divisions can be seen clearly on the map.

and Africa, in Bombay and Calcutta, Singapore and Hong Kong, St. Louis (Senegal) and Dakar? First, these cities grew beyond their early role as centers for export trade, increasingly emphasizing government and administration. Second, to the extent that new commerce or industry was introduced, it was usually initiated and held by European colonialists. These foreigners ran the businesses for the benefit and profit of their countries and themselves. Third, the urban plan usually encouraged a segregation of populations by ethnicity. European residents lived in sections of the cities largely reserved for them. In the Chinese port cities—beginning with Shanghai, Canton, Amoy, Fuzhou, and Ningbo—each colonizing power—British, French, German, Japanese, American—had a sector in which its own law ruled. They also segregated local populations by ethnicity. The British rulers of Singapore, for example, established separate areas of the city for British and other Europeans, Chinese, Malays, Indians, and Bugis.

Rather than promoting integration and national development, such cities fostered local political fragmentation, low levels of industrial development, and increased European profits. Yet these cities were also the entry point for European business, industry, education, philosophy, manners, and culture, in however limited and restricted a way. Throughout the Asian and African worlds, these segregated, controlled, profit-taking cities were also windows on another world, repulsive to some, but seductive and attractive to others. As we shall see in Part 8, these cities were both the centers of the colonial enterprise and the incubators of anticolonial movements.

GENDER RELATIONS: THEIR SIGNIFICANCE IN AN AGE OF REVOLUTIONS

Many events in history are "gendered"—that is, they affect men and women differently. Increasingly historians analyze these differences to enrich our understanding of the past. In addition, people in search of new forms of relationships between men and women, different from those that exist at present, study past events to find possible alternatives. The knowledge that relationships are not fixed and inevitable, not governed by biological determinism, can be very liberating for people attempting to fashion new ways of living.

THE MOVEMENT TOWARD EQUALITY

The political and industrial revolutions that occurred between 1688 and 1914 were certainly "gendered" events. The Enlightenment and the political revolutions, especially in Britain, the United States, and France, stressed individualism. The individual was to be seen on his or her own merits, rather than in terms of hereditary or group identities. Careers were to be open to merit, not restricted to particular families, classes, or castes. But women did not gain such recognition as individuals, and many commentators remarked on this discrepancy between revolutionary goals for men, and more modest aspirations for women. In Britain, for example, the *Commentaries on the Laws of England* (1765–9) prepared by the jurist William Blackstone (1723–80), which served for more than a century as the basic introduction to the English legal system, explained:

> By marriage, the husband and wife are one person in law: that is, the very being or legal existence of the woman is suspended during the marriage, or at least incorporated and consolidated into that of the husband: under whose wing, protection, and cover, she performs every thing. ... (Bell and Offen, p. 33)

Blackstone expressed the prevailing principle that a married woman was represented by her husband. All important decisions for her are made by him. Nevertheless, under civil law, she might hold property in her own name.

In France, the Revolution challenged man's control over woman in marriage and family, but by the time Napoleon issued the Civil Code in 1804, article 213 declared: "A husband owes protection to his wife; a wife obedience to her husband" (Bell and Offen, p. 39). In principle, husbands controlled property held jointly by the couple, but the two could enter into separate contracts to allow wives to control property of their own, and many did so.

The French Revolution did not achieve legal equality between the genders, but it did encourage feminism, a word coined by the French merchant and philosopher Charles Fourier (1772–1837) to denote efforts towards gender equality. In 1808, Fourier urged reform, and argued that:

> The best nations are always those that accord women the greatest amount of liberty. ... Social progress and historic changes occur by virtue of the progress of women toward liberty, and decadence of

the social order occurs as the result of a decrease in the liberty of women. … In summary, the extension of women's privileges is the general principle for all social progress.

In the midst of the tumult of the French Revolution, in July 1790, the Marquis de Condorcet (1743–94), a philosopher and an elected member of the Legislative Assembly, had proposed "The Admission of Women to the Rights of the City":

[Philosophers and legislators] have they not every one violated the principle of the equality of rights, in tranquilly depriving the half of the human race of that of assisting in the making of law; in excluding women from the right of citizenship? … Now the rights of men result only from this, that men are beings with sensibility, capable of acquiring moral ideas, and of reasoning on these ideas. So women, having these same qualities, have necessarily equal rights. Either no individual of the human race has genuine rights, or else all have the same; and he who votes against the right of another, whatever the religion, color, or sex of that other, has henceforth abjured his own. (Bell and Offen, p. 99)

*W*OMEN'S EMANCIPATION 1790–1928

c. 1790	Olympe de Gouges writes the polemical *Declaration of the Rights of Woman and the Citizen*
1792	Mary Wollstonecraft writes *A Vindication of the Rights of Women*, regarded as the first manifesto of the women's movement in Britain
1794	Condorcet writes of desirability of establishing equality of civil and political rights for men and women in *Progrès de l'esprit*
1829	*Sati* (ritual suicide by Hindu widows) banned in India
1848	Elizabeth Cady Stanton (1815–1902) and Lucretia Mott (1793–1880) organize first women's rights convention at Seneca Falls, New York
1850	Beginnings in Britain of national agitation for women's suffrage
1857–72	Married Women's Property Acts allow British women to keep their own possessions on marriage
1866	Mott founds American Equal Rights Association
1868	First public meeting of women's suffrage movement held in Manchester, England
1869	In Britain women rate-payers may vote in municipal elections; Cady Stanton is first president of US National Woman Suffrage Association
1890	Footbinding beginning to die out in China
1903	Emmeline Pankhurst founds Women's Social and Political Union
1906	Pankhurst and her daughters launch militant campaign in Britain
1913	Suffragettes protest in Washington, D.C.; International Women's Peace Conference held in the Netherlands
1914–18	Women assume responsibilities outside the home during World War I
1919	Constance de Markiewicz the first woman elected to Parliament in Britain
1920	19th amendment to the Constitution gives US women the vote
1918	British women householders over 30 years granted the vote
1928	British women over 21 years granted the vote

Condorcet's call for civic equality for women and men, for equal participation in political life, for women's right to vote, and for equal education ("Instruction should be the same for women and men") was rejected by the Assembly. Nevertheless, it helped to enlarge the discussion of women's rights and of men's responsibilities.

Writing under the pen name Olympe de Gouges, Marie Gouze (1748–93) directly appropriated the language of the Revolution's *Declaration of the Rights of Man and Citizen* (1789). Her *Declaration of the Rights of Woman and Citizen* exposed its lack of concern for the rights of women:

Article I. Woman is born free and remains equal in rights to man. Social distinctions can be founded only on general utility. ...
Article XVII. The right of property is inviolable and sacred to both sexes, jointly or separately. ...
(Bell and Offen, pp. 105–6)

Gouges addressed this document to the French queen, Marie-Antoinette, urging her to adopt this feminist program as her own and thus win over France to the royalist cause. In 1793 the radical Jacobins in the Assembly, condemning Gouges for both royalism and feminism, had her guillotined.

"DECLARATION OF SENTIMENTS" SENECA FALLS CONVENTION, JULY 1848

A half century later, in 1848, at Seneca Falls, New York, a small group of women led by Lucretia Mott (1793–1880), one of the many Quakers active in the movement for women's rights, and Elizabeth Cady Stanton (1815–1902) appropriated the language of the American Declaration of Independence in a similar way, to call attention to the lack of women's rights in the United States. They, too, began with a demand for political rights, but went much farther to call for equality in marriage and divorce, in custody of children, in employment, in education, and in religion.

We hold these truths to be self-evident: that all men and women are created equal. ... The history of mankind is a history of repeated injuries and usurpations on the part of man toward woman, having in direct object the establishment of an absolute tyranny over her. To prove this, let facts be submitted to a candid world.

He has never permitted her to exercise her inalienable right to the elective franchise.

He has compelled her to submit to laws, in the formation of which she had no voice. ...

He has made her, if married, in the eye of the law, civilly dead.

He has taken from her all right in property, even to the wages she earns.

In the covenant of marriage, she is compelled to promise obedience to her husband, he becoming, to all intents and purposes, her master ...

He has so framed the laws of divorce, as to what shall be the proper causes, and in case of separation, to whom the guardianship of the children shall be given, as to be wholly regardless of the happiness of women ...

He closes against her all the avenues to wealth and distinction which he considers most honorable to himself. As a teacher of theology, medicine, or law, she is not known.

He has denied her the facilities for obtaining a thorough education, all colleges being closed against her.

He allows her in Church, as well as State, but a subordinate position, claiming Apostolic authority for her exclusion from the ministry, and, with some exceptions, from any public participation in the affairs of the Church.

He has endeavored, in every way that he could, to destroy her confidence in her own powers, to lessen her self-respect, and to make her willing to lead a dependent and abject life. ...

In entering upon the great work before us, we anticipate no small amount of misconception, misrepresentation, and ridicule; but we shall use every instrumentality within our power to effect our object. We shall employ agents, circulate tracts, petition the State and National legislatures, and endeavor to enlist the pulpit and the press in our behalf. We hope this Convention will be followed by a series of Conventions embracing every part of the country. (Bell and Offen, pp. 252–4)

In Britain, Mary Wollstonecraft (1759–97) wrote *A Vindication of the Rights of Woman* in 1792 in which she argued for equal opportunites for all in education. She insisted that women should have the right to participate in economic and political life on an equal basis with men. Over 60 years later, the distinguished economist and political philosopher John Stuart Mill (1806–73) brought to Parliament in 1866, as part of the debate over the extension of voting rights, a petition asking that women, too, be granted the right to vote. Although Parliament approved the petition, Prime Minister Gladstone rejected it. Mill nevertheless persisted in his efforts. In addition to *On Liberty* (1859), his most famous argument for freedom generally, he wrote extensively on behalf of women's equality in particular, notably *The Subjection of Women* (1869). Mill based his argument for equality not only on legal and moral principles, but also on the assertion that equality among adults was essential to warm emotional ties of mutuality, the basis of rewarding family life and of all civilized life.

FEMINIST FRUSTRATIONS: LIVING IN "A DOLL'S HOUSE"

A Doll's House (1879), by Norwegian playwright Henrik Ibsen (1828–1906), catapulted feminist frustrations onto the public stage. A student of human behavior and a moralist, Ibsen was concerned with social problems and contemporary issues. In his prose dramas, many of which shocked the public with their controversial subjects, Ibsen explored the themes of conflict between the individual and society, between husband and wife, and between love and duty. *A Doll's House* traces a middle-class woman's realization that her role in life is meaningless. At the climax of the play, as the heroine Nora walks out of her home, leaving her husband and children, she explains to her husband:

> You've always been so kind to me. But our home's been nothing but a playpen. I've been your doll-wife here, just as at home I was Papa's doll-child. And in turn the children have been my dolls. I thought it was fun when you played with me, just as they thought it fun when I played with them. That's been our marriage, Torvald. … There's another job I have to do first. I have to try to educate myself. You can't help me with that. I've got to do it alone. And that's why I'm leaving you now … I have to stand competely alone, if I'm ever going to discover myself and the world out there. So I can't go on living with you.

Asked by her husband about her marriage vows, Nora continues:

> I have other duties equally sacred. … Before all else, I'm a human being, no less than you—or anyway, I ought to try to become one. … I have to think over these things myself and try to understand them.

Asked about her religious convictions, Nora replies:

> I only know what the minister said when I was confirmed. He told me religion was this thing and that. When I get clear and away by myself, I'll go into that problem too. I'll see if what the minister said was right, or, in any case, if it's right for me.

Asked about her moral conscience, Nora concludes:

> It's not easy to answer that. … I simply don't know. I'm all confused about these things. I just know I see them so differently from you. I find out, for one thing, that the law's not at all what I'd thought—but I can't get it through my head that the law is fair.

The women's movement pursued many goals, especially property rights, access to education, access to jobs and fair pay, and rights in divorce and child custody. At first suffrage was just one of these goals, but soon feminists came to believe that without the vote, women could not easily achieve any of their other goals. On the other hand, they feared that the majority of women were more religious and more conservative than they were. If women had the vote, feminists feared, the majority would vote conservatively. By the turn of the century in Britain, however, as the Labour Party began to form and, as workers became increasingly active politically, the women's movement grew larger and more militant. In the early 1900s, up to World War I, feminist leaders, such as the barrister Emmeline Goulden Pankhurst (1858–1928) and her daughters, adopted the tactics of direct action: breaking windows, destroying mail, cutting telegraph wires. When arrested, they went on hunger strikes, which the government countered with force feeding.

Despite the fact that these tactics brought immense public attention to the suffragettes, they did not win the vote before the war. During the war suffragettes suspended their activities, plunging themselves into supporting the war effort. The quality and devotion of their work in factories, as nurses, as ambulance drivers, won the admiration of British political leaders, and in 1918, British women over the age of thirty who had higher educational degrees or some property were granted the vote, and, after 1928, it was extended to all women aged twenty-one and older. Norway had been the first European country to grant female suffrage in 1910; Germany, in 1918; the United States in 1920; France in 1945. By the time these victories came, they seemed almost anti-climactic. For many years, women voted more or less as did men of the same class. The vote did, however, give women more leverage in addressing other issues. The area of greatest feminist concern shifted to the workplace and the home.

The Great Procession, June 18, 1910. Not only women campaigned for their right to vote: in this procession of the WSPU (Women's Social and Political Union) a hunger strikers' banner is hoisted aloft by male supporters. Emmeline Pankhurst, an English barrister frustrated that politicians would not pass legislation to allow women to vote, organized the WSPU and began a militant campaign to secure women's suffrage in Britain. She was not afraid to use violent means if necessary, and spent time in prison where she and other jailed suffragettes went on hunger strike.

GENDER RELATIONSHIPS AND THE INDUSTRIAL REVOLUTION

By creating factories, the industrial revolution drove a wedge between the home and the workplace that dramatically affected both. Wives who had been accustomed to working alongside, or at least in proximity to, their husbands on the farm or in the shop or workshop now found that the major source of employment was away from home. The industrial revolution, perhaps even more than the political revolutions, forced redefinitions of identities. What should the woman's role and place be now? How should motherhood and work be balanced? In a world that expected most females to be under the protection of males, how were single women to define, and fend for, themselves? In what voice should the feminist movement address these complex issues?

As the industrial revolution began in semi-rural locations, its labor force was drawn primarily from young, (as yet) unmarried women, frequently daughters of local farmers. Some of the early factory owners built boarding houses for the women and treated them protectively, as young wards. Francis Cabot Lowell (1775–1817) built his mills at Waltham, Massachusetts, on this principle. He promised the women, and their parents, hard work, with pay adequate to help their families and to save towards marriage. After Cabot's death, his partners extended his example by establishing a new town, Lowell, with the largest cotton mill built to that date. By the 1840s, about half the mills in New England followed this model. Factory work had its demands of order, discipline, and the clock, and the dormitory-boarding houses were somewhat crowded, but labor historian Alice Kessler-Harris quotes approvingly the very warm assessment of the Lowell experience from one of its workers in the 1830s: It was "the first field that had ever been open to her outside of her own restricted home. ... the first money they earned! When they felt the jingle of silver in their pocket, there for the first time, their heads became erect and they walked as if on air" (Kessler-Harris, p. 34).

As new machinery became heavier, as factory work became more prevalent, and as economic depression pressed down on both American and British economies, the workforce shifted. Men, often farmers and immigrants, moved into the factories, displacing the women. The men demanded higher pay, which factory owners had previously-hoped to avoid by hiring women. The culture of the industrializing world of that time, primarily in Britain, called for men to support their families. A young, unmarried woman might earn just enough for herself and that would be adequate. A man required a "family wage." The rising productivity of constantly improving machinery made this "family wage" possible, and it became the baseline standard for industry.

Women were thus displaced from factory work and brought back to the home. By the second half of the nineteenth-century, "domesticity" became the norm for middle- and even working-class women and their families. As we noted above (see p. 540), at just this time living standards began to rise and generally continued to rise into the early twentieth-century. Life expectancy for women, a basic index of well-being, rose in Britain from forty-four years in 1890, to fifty-two years in 1910, to sixty years in 1920! At the same time family size decreased. Child-bearing became less frequent, safer thanks to antisepsis, less painful with the use of anesthesia, and safer with the professionalization of the practice of medicine. Free, compulsory education in the 1830s and 1840s began to take children out of the home. Some women began to use their time to enter into the array of white collar jobs that were opening. The most respectable jobs provided satisfying work which also fit the cultural value of women as care givers and nurturers: teaching in the new school systems and nursing in the new hospitals. Other women worked as secretaries and clerks in the new offices, although this was primarily a male occupation in the nineteenth century, and sales personnel in the new department stores (where they also shopped). A very few went on to professions.

Most women spent a great deal of time caring for their families and homes. The industrial revolution, with its new productivity and its new systems of ventilation, central heating, lighting, indoor plumbing, and running hot and cold water, contributed to domestic comfort and made life easier for those who could afford these services.

While domestic concerns and new technological wonders engaged the middle classes, and were desired by the working classes, for a great number of people they were out of reach. The 15-20 percent of adult females who had to work as principal breadwinners for themselves and their families confronted more basic problems of earning a living. The value placed on domesticity as the proper role for females, and the concommitant view that men should earn a "family wage" but that women needed only supplementary income, made the plight of

Women's Bodies and Reform

In the nineteenth century, four separate movements combined to introduce deep reforms in the way women's bodies were presented, viewed, and treated: rationalism, which subjected numerous traditional habits and practices to greater scrutiny; humanitarianism, which encouraged greater kindness and compassion in social relations; feminism, which demanded better, more egalitarian, treatment for women; and colonialism, which often sought changes in the treatment of women in colonized areas, partly in order to improve the women's lives, partly in order to underline the alleged superiority of the status of women in Europe.

Picture 1 shows a woman on a funeral pyre, prepared to commit her body to flames in order to accompany her husband in his death. This act of ritual suicide, called *sati* (suttee), had been practiced by a very small group of upper-caste women in India for centuries. In the late eighteenth century, the British government began to campaign against the practice, finally banning it in British India in 1829 Many Indians, like Raja Rammohun Roy (1772–1833), supported the British and urged them to enact the legislation, but others resented the colonizers' interference. The British presented their motives as simply humanitarian, but more recently historians have suggested that the British emphasis on outlawing *sati* served as a means of proclaiming their own moral superiority over the Indians and justifying imperialism. These historians note that the British were introducing very little structural change in the lives of Indian women, by providing education or jobs for widows for example, that might encourage them to go on living. British legislation against *sati* was generally effective, but not completely. The act of *sati* in picture 1 took place in 1946, and the practice still occurs on rare occasions in today's India.

Footbinding in China had been practiced among the upper

Picture 1 *Sati* ceremony, Allahabad, India, 1946.

Picture 2 Bound feet, compared with a shoe and a tea cup, late nineteenth century.

In "A Correct View of the New Machine for Winding up the Ladies" (**picture 3**), the cartoonist ridicules the practice of waist-binding among European women in the nineteenth century. Upper-class women wore corsets, devices made of whalebone which constricted the waist painfully, making it appear as tiny as possible and, by contrast, accentuating the hips, buttocks, and breasts. The corsets were often so tight that they interfered with women's ability to breathe properly and encouraged "swooning." Still, the practice of corseting continued until around the end of the century, at which time gains in female emancipation forced it out of fashion.

classes since the tenth century. Parents tightly bound the feet of their girl children at about the age of five so that they did not grow longer than five or six inches. The tiny foot that resulted (**picture 2**) was regarded as beautiful and the restrictions on mobility were considered a mark of upper-class elegance. The majority of Chinese women, peasants, were not subjected to footbinding; they had to work the fields. Under the influence of foreign colonial powers in China, anti-footbinding societies began to arise in the 1890s, and the image of the bound foot changed from delicate to grotesque. By the 1930s footbinding was no longer practiced in China, except in isolated cases. Once again foreign pressure had been a combination of rationalism, humanitarianism, feminism, and a desire to assert European moral superiority.

Picture 3 Anon., "The New Machine for Winding up the Ladies," English cartoon, *c.* 1840.

the working woman doubly difficult. These women, often immigrants, desperately poor, and without male support, were no longer seen, as the first industrial women workers had been, as proud and independent, but as unfortunate objects of sympathy and pity.

They found jobs where they could. Domestic service was most common, employing two to three times as many women as industry, even in industrialized countries. On the margins of society, other women earned a living through prostitution. In the second half of the nineteenth-century, censuses in the largest cities, London and Paris, routinely reported tens of thousands of prostitutes walking the streets, serving in brothels, or, occasionally, employed in more elegant settings by more prosperous clients. These women were often condemned by more conventional society, but at the same time they earned some respect for their independence. Most of them worked only until about the age of twenty-five, by which time they usually found other work or were married.

The socialist wing of the feminist movement understood that class differences often inhibited solidarity among women. Karl Marx spoke of the difference between the bourgeois and the proletarian family. He wrote of the conflict between roles of mother and of worker. With Engels, Marx condemned the "double oppression" of women by both capitalism and the family, but he praised capitalism for freeing women from being regarded as property. He encouraged women in their struggle for citizens' rights and economic independence. In *The Origin of the Family, Private Property and the State* (1884), Engels argued that the form of the family was not fixed. It had evolved substantially in the past, and he proposed further, revolutionary change:

> The peculiar character of the supremacy of the husband over the wife in the modern family, the necessity of creating real social equality between them and the way to do it, will only be seen in the clear light of day when both possess legally complete equality of rights. Then it will be plain that the first condition for the liberation of the wife is to bring the whole female sex back into public industry, and that this in turn demands that the characteristic of the monogamous family as the economic unit of society be abolished.

In Germany, the Social Democratic Party (SPD) created a separate organizational structure for women, which enlisted 174,751 women members by 1914, the largest movement of women in Europe. The number reflects, however, not only women seeking independent expression, but also women who sought to ally themselves with their husbands who were members of the party. Working women's organizations were undercut by the opposition of male unionized workers, who feared that the women would take away their jobs or, at least, increase the labor pool and thus drive wages down.

GENDER RELATIONSHIPS IN COLONIZATION

The Europeans who travelled overseas to trade beginning in the sixteenth-century were almost invariably males and they frequently entered into sexual liaisons with local women. As the men stayed longer, these relationships became increasingly important for business and administration as well as for social and sexual pleasure. One example was the **signares**, concubines of French traders in the Senegambia, present-day Senegal and Gambia. As the Senegal Company forbade its traders to marry locally, the men found concubines among the local Wolof and Lebou peoples. These women helped the men to negotiate local languages, customs, and health conditions.

In India, the **nabobs**, the successful traders who became wealthy, frequently took local women in much the same way. Not forbidden to marry, they fathered Anglo-Indian children who came to form a small but important community of their own, especially in the large port cities of Bombay, Madras, and Calcutta.

As Europeans began to establish colonies, and as women began to travel to these colonies, usually with husbands or in search of husbands, they began to draw inward, establishing more rigid boundaries between themselves and the local populations. Earlier historians had attributed this increasing distance to the restrictive attitudes of the European women who wished to prevent their husbands' mixing with the local women. More recent, feminist scholarship has attributed the responsibility for the increased distance to both husband and wife. Both exhibited racism. Both usually wished to keep local men from intimate contact with European women. As colonial settlements increased in size and stability, each family tended to view itself as a representative of the rulers, a colonial outpost in miniature.

Christmas in India, a sketch by E.K. Johnson, *The Graphic*, 1881. Just as, for the most part, European men did not socialize or form a solidarity with the men whose country they had colonized, the women kept themselves apart and their lives centered on their families and their European friends. The wife would oversee the running of the household as she was accustomed to doing at home. Here the *ayah* looks after the youngest child in much the same way that Nanny would have back in England.

Did the colonizing women form a solidarity with their colonized sisters? Most contemporary historians think not. The colonizers tended to fasten on flaws in the gender relations among the colonized peoples, and then set out to introduce reforms. In India the British outlawed *sati*, the practice of widows burning themselves to death on their deceased husbands' funeral pyres; they introduced a minimum age of marriage; they urged widow remarriage despite upper-caste Hindu resistance. In Africa they sought to end polygamy. In each case, the colonial government emphasized the superiority of their own practices, and the good fortune of the colonized to have the Europeans there to save them from themselves. The European colonizers pointed to their interventions in gender relations to justify and praise their own colonial rule. The colonial women did the same.

The colonial presence did, however, introduce new patterns of gender relations into the colonies, based on the European models. At least some of the colonized peoples chose to move toward a more European style of gender relations, including more education for women, more freedom of choice in marriage, more companionate marriage, an end to *sati* in India, to polygamy in parts of Africa, and to footbinding in China. (As children, upper-class women in China had their feet bound so that they did not fully develop. Various reasons are given, the most common being that this was considered a mark of beauty, a sexual fetish, or a demonstration that the woman's future husband would be wealthy enough to support a woman who could hardly walk.) Sometimes new paths were adopted because they seemed better, sometimes because they won favor for the colonized peoples with the colonizing masters. (Later, as nationalism took root, foreign practices were sometimes rejected because of their colonial associations.)

NATIONALISM: WHAT DO WE KNOW?

For most people in today's world, nationality is an important part of personal identity and historians have turned to nationalism as a central issue. Some stress the significance of particular forms of nationalism, others argue that national identity is, and can be, constantly shaped and reshaped. In this sense historians of national identity are similar to historians of gender identity; they not only wish to understand where we have been, they also want to consider alternative futures.

One of the first historians and philosophers of nationalism, the Frenchman Joseph-Ernest Renan (1823–92), in his 1882 lecture "What is a Nation?", captured the two-fold nature of nationalism. Nationalism requires fundamental shared elements in the lives of the citizen, but these alone are not enough for constructing a nation. That task requires also a vision of what the nation might become, and a political commitment to constructing such a future. Further, in considering the nation as a "spir-

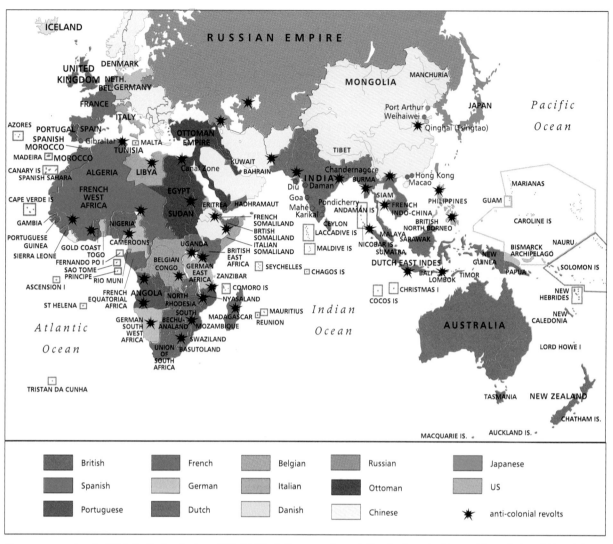

European empires in 1914 By the beginning of World War I, European imperialism had reached its zenith, with four-fifths of the globe under European colonization or direct political control. Only Antarctica remained unclaimed. Although this power was sustained by technological, naval, and military superiority, insurrections were widespread and increasingly well organized. Imperial trade established a global economic system and spread European cultural values.

itual principle," Renan asserted his belief that in his time nationalism was displacing religion as a central concern:

> A nation is a spiritual principle, the outcome of the profound complications of history; it is a spiritual family not a group determined by the shape of the earth. We have now seen what things are not [by themselves] adequate for the creation of such a spiritual principle, namely, race, language, material interest, religous affinities, geography, and military necessity. What [else] then is required? …
>
> A nation is therefore a large-scale solidarity, constituted by the feeling of the sacrifices that one

has made in the past and of those that one is prepared to make in the future. It presupposes a past; it is summarized, however, in the present by a tangible fact, namely, consent, the clearly expressed desire to continue a common life.

In this essay, Renan overlooked two additional elements that later historians added to their concept of modern nationalism. First, at least since the French Revolution, the modern nation exists in a world of nations, frequently competitive with one another. Second, at least since the French Revolution and the industrial revolution, the nation has been the vehicle for the spread of trade networks and capitalism throughout the world.

FRENCH NATIONALISM

The ideology and actions of the French Revolution gave a new definition to the concept of the nation, and introduced new political and cultural loyalties. In 1789, the members of the National Assembly, declaring themselves "The representatives of the people of France," proclaimed in the *Declaration of the Rights of Man and Citizen*: "The source of all sovereignty is located essentially in the nation; no body, no individual can exercise authority which does not emanate from it expressly." This Declaration encapsulated ideas that had been present in France for decades. It proclaimed that the people of France were forging a social contract, swearing allegiance not to a ruler, religion or language/ethnic group but to all the people of the nation—a common political group. The Declaration seemed to take for granted the primordial elements of French nationality—a common language, history, and geography—and with the vision of what the French people might become, they ratified a new national identity for France.

As we have seen (pp. 480–5), the power of France's new nationalism swept across Europe with its armies between 1791 and 1815, not only to conquer others, but also to promote its idea of nationalism. The French state took to itself new, unprecedented powers. It had the authority to tax in the name of the nation, the very authority that Louis XVI had sought for himself when he had convened the Estates General. Having the authority to draft virtually the entire adult male population of the country for the army in the new *levée en masse*, France conscripted an army numbering millions. French armies imposed their imperial governments on the nations they conquered, and, after the promulgation of the Napoleonic codes in 1804, they imposed their legal system as well. The new message seemed clear: A people organized under a national banner of its own making could act with unprecedented power, to tax, to fight, to legislate, to conquer, and to rule.

NATIONALISM IN THE UNITED STATES

The United States had also established itself as a nation based on an oath binding citizens to the common good. Americans declared in their Constitution:

We, the People of the United States, in Order to form a more perfect Union, establish Justice, insure domestic Tranquility, provide for the common defence, promote the general Welfare, and secure the blessings of Liberty to ourselves and our Posterity, do ordain and establish this Constitution for the United States of America.

The American Constitution also illustrated the degree to which a nation was constituted by the will of its leaders, rather than by primordial historical legacies. Indeed, foreign observers like Alexis de Tocqueville (1805–59) commented on the newness of America and its lack of history. A substantial proportion of America's institutions, and of its population, was drawn from Britain, but immigrants came from all over the world. Some were excluded from full citizenship: African-American slaves, native American Indians, and women lacked civil liberties. But the pattern for future inclusion was also being set. New immigrants could join this nation, and, after slaves were freed, so could they, although racism remained powerful. Native Americans remained torn between allegiances to Indian nations and the American nation. At least in theory, the United States declared that the nation was not necessarily an array of people who shared a common history, geography, language, race, ethnicity, religion, and language. A nation could be formed on the basis of a new vision of the present and future and adherence to a common law.

Nationalism in the United States maintained itself by force of arms in the face of secession by eleven Confederate States of America in 1861. The Confederacy claimed greater rights for constituent states, especially the right to sanction slavery, and it favored agrarian rather than industrial economic policies. Some 500,000 men were killed in the Civil War on both sides. Immediately following the war, the victorious central government instituted policies favoring reconciliation (often at the expense of the recently freed ex-slaves), although later these policies became more punitive. After the war, the industrial and economic expansion of the United States set a pace exceeding that of any other nation.

NATIONALISM ON THE PERIPHERY OF WESTERN EUROPE

Nationalists elsewhere also attempted to implement the new message. At first they succeeded only on the periphery of Western Europe. In Chapter 15 we noted the revolutions in Latin America, and their transformation from transcontinental revolts into individual national movements, destroying the unifying visions of Simón Bolívar and José de San Martín. The Latin American events underscored the dominant importance of leadership. Nationalism spoke in the name of the people, but it spoke in the voice of specific leaders and classes of leaders: lawyers, journalists, teachers, military officials.

In Canada, the Report to the British government by the Earl of Durham in 1839 led to the unification of mostly English-speaking Upper Canada, today's Ontario, with mostly French-speaking Lower Canada, today's Quebec. Durham urged the rapid development of railways and canals to consolidate the nation and responsible government over domestic affairs. The Durham Report was quickly accepted and implemented. In 1867 the Dominion of Canada was established, increasing the scope of parliamentary democracy and adding the eastern maritime provinces to the core of Quebec and Ontario. Tensions between the British and French regions of Canada diminished, but they did not disappear and have continued to surface periodically to the present.

Also on the periphery, but within Europe, revolts in the Balkans broke out from 1815 onward in the name of individual nationalities. The first successful revolt was of the Greek peoples against the Ottoman Empire. Greece won its independence in 1829 with the backing of military forces dispatched by England, France, and Russia. At the same time, other Ottoman possessions also gained autonomy: Serbia, Wallachia and Moldavia in present-day Romania, and Egypt. The European powers supported this aggressive nationalism in the Balkans and northeast Africa because it diminished the power of the Ottoman Empire, while increasing their own leverage within the region.

Nationalism always had two faces. As a positive force, it promised to empower the masses of a nation with freedom and evoke their collective participation in building new futures. As a negative power, it threatened to force the masses to serve the state and to turn one nation against another in destructive warfare. The Balkans saw both these faces. Some nationalist movements won independence and the possibility of greater freedom and creativity. On the other hand, a century of simmering nationalism throughout the region climaxed in 1914 when a Serbian nationalist assassinated the Crown Prince of Austria-Hungary in Sarajevo. The major powers of Europe soon took sides and World War I began (see Chapter 18).

THE RISE OF ZIONISM IN EUROPE

One of the last of the nationalist movements to arise in nineteenth-century Europe was Zionism, the movement to recreate a Jewish homeland. Jews had been dispersed into Europe even during the time of the Roman Empire. By the turn of the twentieth century, their principal European locations were in Poland, Russia, and the Ukraine. Through the centuries, the Jewish religion had preserved a cultural foundation for Jewish nationalism, in prayers for a return to Zion, the ancestral homeland in modern Israel. In the second half of the nineteenth century, under the influence of various European nationalist movements, some philosophers proposed going beyond prayer. They looked forward to an actual return and the establishment of a state.

The move from philosophical speculation to political organization took thirty-five years. On

Forefather of Israel. Theodor Herzl was the founder of modern Zionism, the movement which sought to return the Jewish people to their historic homeland of Palestine (Eretz Israel). Herzl also worked to obtain sovereign state rights over the territory in question. Although the Jewish state was successfully established in 1948, Zionism lives on in an effort to relocate the remaining diaspora Jews to Israel. The word "Zion" appears in Jewish literature in various contexts, referring sometimes to the hills in Jerusalem, to the Temple on the Mount, and sometimes to Israel as a whole.

assignment in Paris to report on the trial of Alfred Dreyfus, a Jewish officer in the French army accused of treason, the Viennese Jewish journalist Theodor Herzl (1860–1904) encountered fierce anti-Semitism. Shocked to find such ethnic and religious hatred in the capital of the liberal world, Herzl concluded that Jews could be free, independent, and safe only in a country of their own. In 1897 he founded the Zionist movement. Because Palestine, the goal of most of the early Zionists, was already the home of 600,000 Arabs, Jewish nationalism simultaneously took the form of a colonizing movement originating in Europe. The consequences of this nationalistic/colonizing effort are traced in Chapter 21.

ITALY AND GERMANY

Before 1870 neither Italy nor Germany existed as we now know them. Each was divided up into many regions under the control of different rulers. In Italy, the largest single state was the kingdom of Sardinia-Piedmont, but other states were controlled by other rulers. The area around Venice was controlled by Austria and the region around Rome by the Pope. Most of the small states of Germany had been included within Charlemagne's empire, founded in 800 C.E., and then within its successor institution, the Holy Roman Empire. Each of these states had its own ruler and even its own system of government. The largest, Austria, was in itself a significant state. The smallest had only a few thousand inhabitants. In addition, to the east, lay Prussia, a powerful state which was beginning to think of itself as the leader of the German-speaking peoples. As nation-states began to form in Western Europe, and to demonstrate the economic, political, military, and cultural power that came from unity, regional leaders in Italy and Germany also sought unification for themselves. A common language

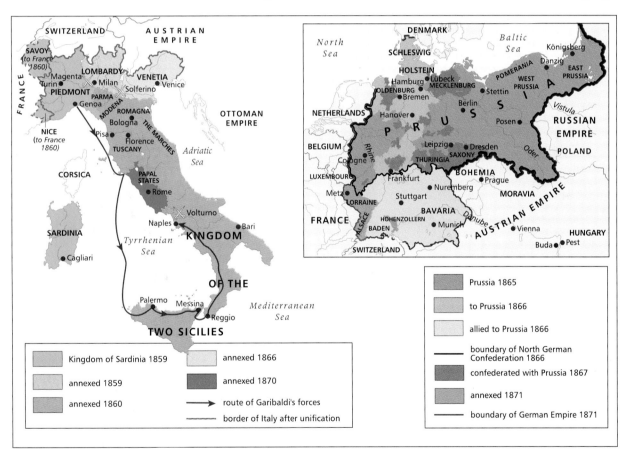

The unification of Italy and Germany The middle years of the nineteenth century saw popular forces drawing together the disparate territories of central Europe into modern nation states. In Germany the political, military, and economic strength of Prussia had been growing for over two centuries, and Bismarck's wars with Denmark (1864), Austria (1866), and France (1870) eventually secured the union. In Italy the expansion of Piedmont–Sardinia into Lombardy, the Veneto, and Rome, and Garibaldi's march through the south, united the nation.

and clearly demarcated geographical borders were considered vital elements in national unity, and were helpful to Italy in consolidating its peninsular nation. Germany, however, lacked clear natural geographic boundaries and faced a serious question as to which German-speaking states would be included within the new country and which would be excluded.

In the heart of Europe, nationalism grew in hard soil. At first, the great powers of Austria, Prussia, Russia, France, and Britain suppressed new national uprisings by peoples within their empires. At their meeting to draft the peace settlements at the Congress of Vienna in 1814–15 after the Napoleonic Wars, they set limits on national movements in central Europe. Led by Prince Clemens von Metternich (1773–1859), foreign minister of Austria, they were successful for a generation, quelling powerful uprisings in Poland, Prussia, Italy, and Hungary between 1846 and 1849. (Belgium did gain national independence, from the Dutch, in 1830.) Only in the 1850s did nationalism win major victories in lands under these empires. Then Italy and Germany began successfully to unite their several divided regions to form new nations. In each country, cultural nationalism came first.

Giuseppe Mazzini (1805–72) provided a prophetic vision for Italy. In 1831 he founded Young Italy, a secret association urging Italian unification and independence from foreign control by the French, Austrians, and Spanish. Mazzini's *On the Duties of Man* expressed his nationalistic, democratic, and humanistic views:

> O my brothers, love your Country! Our country is our Home, the House that God has given us, placing therein a numerous family that loves us, and whom we love; a family with whom we sympathize more readily, and whom we understand more quickly, than we do others; and which, from its being centred round a given spot, and from the homogeneous nature of its elements, is adapted to a special branch of activity.

When Mazzini's cultural view was joined by the political organization of Camillo Cavour (1810–61), who was appointed Prime Minister of Sardinia-Piedmont in 1852 by King Victor Emmanuel II, the nationalist movement was poised for political victory. Cavour formed a brief alliance with Napoleon III of France against Austria, which enabled the annexation of Lombardy. The adjacent regions of Parma, Modena, and Tuscany joined by plebiscite.

Giuseppe Garibaldi (1807–82) led 1150 followers, wearing red shirts, into the south Italian Kingdom of the Two Sicilies, which collapsed and subsequently also joined Piedmont after a **plebiscite**. The Veneto was added after a war, in which Italy allied with Prussia against Austria. Finally Rome was annexed in 1870 after French troops were withdrawn to fight against Prussia. Through the various contributions of Mazzini, Cavour, Garibaldi, Victor Emmanuel II, Napoleon III, war and popular votes, Italy had become a unified nation.

At about the same time, Prime Minister Otto von Bismarck of Prussia (1815–98) was unifying the multitude of small German states into a single country of Germany under William I (King of Prussia 1861–88, Emperor of Germany 1871–88). The cultural basis of German unity was even more solidly established than that of Italy. The brothers

Cartoon of Giuseppe Garibaldi by Gill, 1879. After joining Mazzini's Young Italy movement aged twenty-six, Garibaldi devoted the rest of his life to the struggle for Italian unification and independence. In 1860 he marched his force of 1150 Red Shirts from Genoa to Sicily, which he conquered, setting up a provisional island government.

BISMARCK

French cartoon portraying Prince Otto Eduard Leopold von Bismarck, Prime Minister of Prussia, 1870. Political figures have traditionally been treated irreverently by cartoonists, but this caricature is savage. The French were outraged by Bismarck's ambitions to get the Prussian prince Leopold on to the Spanish throne—a key factor in the war between the two countries.

Jakob and Wilhelm Grimm, founders of the modern science of linguistics, analyzed the various dialects of German and collected fairy tales from all parts of the region, publishing them in 1812 as a unifying folklore for the nation. A series of philosophers and historians, including J.G. von Herder (1744–1803), J.G. Fichte (1762–1814), Georg Wilhelm Friedrich Hegel (1770–1831), Leopold von Ranke (1795–1886), and Heinrich von Treitschke (1834–96) urged Germany to fulfill its natural destiny, just as Mazzini had urged Italy to fulfill its.

From 1828 a series of customs unions had already established an economic foundation for unification. Increasing industrialization provided the financial and military underpinnings for it.

Now Bismarck instituted a policy of "Blood and Iron." Two wars were the key. In 1866 Bismarck defeated Austria and formed the North German Confederation without her. In 1870 he defeated France, annexing Alsace and Lorraine. In light of these victories the southern states of Germany also joined the newly formed nation.

CHINA 1856–1911

European nationalism grew out of competition and warfare among nations. Especially in the 1800s, after the Napoleonic wars, European nations attempted to achieve a balance of power among themselves. In this view, to be a nation was to participate in an international system of nations. Imperial China was, by contrast, considered to be a nation in isolation—until European and American intervention brought her into the global arena of contesting powers in the mid-nineteenth century.

Despite China's powerful historical tradition, linguistic homogeneity, and folkloric and religious traditions, many historians have omitted China from discussions of nationalism. Partly, this omission arises from a **Eurocentricity**, which has overlooked non-European countries. Partly, it represents a view that Chinese nationalism was different from that of Europe. But China did create its own nationalism, as earlier segments of this text have argued and as Prasenjit Duara has emphasized in his recent study *Rescuing History from the Nation*. Throughout its history, China did face hostile neighbors, especially to the north. It negotiated with them; it fought them; it built and rebuilt the Great Wall to keep them out. Nevertheless, China was periodically invaded and conquered by foreigners. Marco Polo found a descendant of Genghis Khan sitting on the throne in Beijing (see p. 374). From 1644 to 1911, during the height of European penetration of China, the country was ruled by Manchus, foreigners from the north. China did have international relations, sometimes tributary, often hostile, with its neighbors. China's genius was its ability to assimilate the foreigners to its own culture so fully that 95 percent of China's population considered themselves "People of Han"—that is, descendants of that early Chinese dynasty. The Chinese sense of national identity was one of the most powerful in the world, and it was the result of purposeful political and cultural decisions implemented over 2000 years.

Nevertheless, the series of defeats at the hands of the Europeans in the Opium Wars (see p. 527), the devastating loss of Korea and Taiwan to the Japanese in the war of 1894–5, and the crushing of the Boxer Rebellion in 1898 (see p. 529) profoundly disturbed China's sense of identity. European and Japanese powers controlled her port cities and became focuses for the introduction of foreign culture, education, commerce, and industry. In response, many Chinese intellectuals began to propose changes in such fundamental, historic Chinese institutions as the examination system, the centrality of Confucian learning, the non-industrial economic system, and even the system of imperial rule. As the Manchu government appeared unwilling to implement these changes, Chinese reformers turned to revolution, seeking the overthrow of the Manchus as the first step toward evicting the European and Japanese foreigners. The revolution of 1911 achieved this first goal, and opened the way to the next two tasks: removing European power over China and charting new paths for the Chinese nation consistent both with its past and with the new military, political, and economic challenges and opportunities facing it.

ANTI-COLONIAL REVOLTS 1857–1912

By 1911, the authors of the Chinese revolution looked forward to modernizing the country. A series of earlier revolts throughout the world colonized by Europe had, however, mostly looked backward to their own traditions. Colonized peoples had revolted to throw out the foreigners and return to the pre-colonial past. The 1857–8 revolt in India took this position; as did the Mahdist revolt on the upper Nile (1881–98); so, too, did Shamil, "ruler of the righteous and destroyer of the unbeliever," against Russia in the Caucasus (between 1834 and 1859); Emilio Aguinaldo against the United States in the Philippines (1898–1902); peasant warfare against the Dutch in Bali and Lombok, Indonesia (1881–94), and in Sumatra (1881–1908). Throughout sub-Saharan Africa local ethnic groups fought European invasion and occupation: Ethiopia defeated Italy at Adowa in 1896; the Bunyoro resisted the British in Uganda (1890–98), as did the Matabele and Mashona in Rhodesia (1896); the Maji-Maji revolt opposed German rule in Tanganyika (1905–7); the Mande under Samori fought the French in west Africa (1884–98); and the Asante fought the British in the Gold Coast (1900). Revolts against the Portuguese in Angola broke out in 1913.

Later, armed revolts and non-violent political movements against colonial rule became more forward-looking. Their leaders sought not a simple return to the past, but a newly restructured nation, usually incorporating significant elements of the past with new goals based in part on examples introduced by colonial powers. In India, the Indian National Congress, founded in 1885, proposed a pattern of parliamentary democracy for India, often (but not always) with an admixture of Hindu reformism. In 1907, in Egypt, Saad Zaghlul (1857–1927) founded the Hizb al-Umma or People's Party, which, in turn, became the core of the nationalist Wafd party after 1919. The Young Turk party, formed in 1878 in patriotic anger against the Ottoman defeats in the Balkans, grew into a revolutionary party by 1908. The Young Turks, like the Chinese nationalists, saw as their first task the removal of the ruling government, the Ottomans, before going on to further reforms. Indonesia's first nationalist association, the Budi Utomo, was formed in 1908; South Africa's National Congress in 1912; and Viet Nam's Viet Nam Quang Phuc Hoi in 1913.

Each of these organizations had a different conception of the future nation it was constructing, modelled in part on European military, economic, political, and administrative forms, but also incorporating its own individual cultural, religious, and social dimensions.

JAPAN: FROM ISOLATION TO EQUALITY 1867–1914

In terms of nationalism, Japan was unified by race, with a national mythistory that goes back to the founding of the nation in the seventh century and a single dynasty of emperors that also stretches back to this beginning, a single national language, an integrated national political structure, and an island-based geography. Japan's insular nature was intensified in the early 1600s when the government closed the country to foreign, especially European, contact. Rather than accept the European model of contesting nation-states, Japan at this point chose relative isolation. With the challenge from Western nations in 1853, however, Japan recognized the need to transform itself militarily, economically, diplomatically, politically and culturally. The history of Japan after 1853 charts its move from isolation to full, prominent participation in this world of nation-states.

THE END OF THE SHOGUNATE

By 1641, Japan had shut down commerce and contact with the European world, except for a Dutch outpost, virtually quarantined on Deshima Island in Nagasaki harbor, which was allowed to receive one ship each year. The Chinese were also permitted to trade, at Nagasaki, but only under severe restrictions. Some trade could also pass through the Ryukyu Islands to China, under the guise of "tribute," and Korea could trade through the islands of Tsushima. Otherwise, Japan was isolated. In the late 1700s and early 1800s, an occasional European ship would attempt to establish contact, but they were turned away.

In 1853, however, Commodore Matthew Perry (1794–1858) was dispatched from the United States with a small squadron, including three steam frigates, to force Japan open to trade as China had been opened in the Opium War a decade before. Japan lacked the means to resist both the Americans and the European powers that soon followed into Japanese waters, and over the next few years she opened more ports, at first on the periphery, but then at Nagasaki, Kobe, and Yokohama. Japan opened Edo (Tokyo) and Osaka to foreign residence, and then granted the foreigners extraterritorial legal rights. Foreigners were permitted to stipulate Japan's tariff policies. In 1863 and 1864, in the face of firing on their ships, British, French, Dutch, and American naval forces demolished Japanese coastal forts and and supplies and forced Japan to pay an indemnity. Like China, Japan seemed headed toward control by foreigners.

Unlike China, however, young, vigorous leaders seized control of the government of Japan, forcing a dramatic restructuring of the nation's politics, administration, class structure, economy, technology, and culture. These leaders, for the most part young **samurai** warriors in the *hans* (feudal estates) of Choshu and Satsuma at the southern extreme of Japan, decided that Japan's current government was not capable of coping with the European threat. Great diversity of opinion flourished among the approximately 250 different *han* in Japan, but the most powerful regional leaders felt that the **shogun**, who ruled Japan in the name of the emperor, should be removed and the emperor himself should be restored as the direct ruler of Japan. The young samurai, members of Japan's hereditary military elite, should formulate the policies of the new administration.

The young samurai were able to employ some of the technological information introduced by the Dutch from their station in Nagasaki harbor. "Dutch learning" had been available for a century. Indeed, in 1811 the shogunate had established an office for translating Dutch material, and it was expanded into a school for European languages and science in 1857. Some of the *han* did the same, including Satsuma, Choshu, and Mito. By 1840, some Japanese were already casting Western guns and artillery. Sakuma Shozan (1811–64), one of the advocates of adopting Western military methods, coined the motto of the movement: "Eastern Ethics; Western Science." Japan could adopt western technology, he counseled, especially military technology, while still maintaining its own culture.

Sakuma believed that opening the country was both necessary and beneficial. Not everyone agreed, however, and in 1860 a group of samurai from the conservative *han* of Mito, argued a contrary position: "Revere the Emperor; Expel the Barbarian." The lines of conflict were sharpening. Political violence increased as exponents of the positions attacked each other. Sakuma was assassinated in 1864 by Mito loyalists, who then assassinated yet another leader and committed ritual suicide. Attacks on foreigners taking up residence and conducting business in Japan also increased.

In 1865 a group of young samurai in Choshu attacked and defeated their *daimyo*, the ruler of their *han*, establishing control of the government of Choshu. Next year, the armed forces of Choshu confronted and defeated those of the shogun while the other *daimyo* sat out the contest. In 1868 the forces of Choshu and Satsuma, joining with those of several other more remote *han*, seized control of the emperor's palace in Kyoto and declared the shogunate ended, the lands of the shogun confiscated, and the emperor restored to imperial power. Most of the fighting was over by November, although naval battles continued into early 1869. The Meiji restoration ended the power of the shogunate forever and brought the *daimyo* and their young samurai to power in the name of the Emperor Meiji (r. 1867–1912). The emperor assumed the throne at the age of fourteen and reigned over one of the most rapid transformations of any country.

POLICIES OF THE MEIJI GOVERNMENT

On April 8, 1868, the revolutionary leaders issued a Charter Oath in the name of the emperor. The fifth

THE MEIJI RESTORATION AND INDUSTRIALIZATION IN JAPAN

1853	Commander Perry sails into Edo Bay, ending 250 years' isolation
1854	Treaty of Kanagawa gives US trading rights with Japan
1860s	Series of "unequal treaties" gives US, Britain, France, Russia and Netherlands commercial and territorial privileges
1868	Tokugawa shogun forced to abdicate and executive power vested with emperor in Meiji restoration
1871	Administration is overhauled; Western-style changes introduced
1872	National education system introduced, providing teaching for 90 per cent of children by 1900 First railway opened
1873	Old order changed by removal of privileges of samurai class
1876	Koreans, under threat, agree to open three of their ports to the Japanese and exchange diplomats
1877	Satsuma rebellion represented last great (unsuccessful) challenge of conservative forces
1879	Representative system of local government introduced
1884	Western-style peerage (upper house) is created
1885	Cabinet government introduced
1889	Adoption of constitution based on Bismarck's Germany
1889	Number of cotton mills has risen from 3 (1877) to 83
1894–5	War with China ends in Japanese victory
1902	Britain and Japan sign military pact
1904–5	War with Russia ends in Japanese victory
1914	Japan joins World War I on side of Allies

and last article proved the most important: "Knowledge shall be sought throughout the world so as to strengthen the foundations of imperial rule." The new goal was "A rich country and a strong military." The new leaders had already begun to search the world for new political, economic, and military models that might be adapted to Japan's needs.

After treaty agreements were signed in 1858, the shogun had dispatched embassies to the United States in 1860 and to Europe in 1862, beginning official exchanges of information. A two-year overseas goodwill mission, headed by Prince Iwakura Tonomi (1825–83), set out in 1871 to deepen relationships with the heads of state of the treaty powers, to discuss later treaty revisions, and to enable Japanese leaders to experience the West at first hand. Fifty-four students accompanied the mission. A ministry of education was established in 1871 and its first budget (1873) included funds for sending 250 students abroad to study. Many of these students became leaders in the new Japan. Foreign instructors were also brought to Japan. The late shogun's government had employed some foreigners in industrial enterprises, but the Meiji rulers imported far more. They set out to develop Hokkaido and brought in American experts, who introduced large-scale farming practices to the northern island. By 1879 the ministry of industry employed 130 foreigners. Doctors were brought from Germany to teach medicine, and from America to teach natural and social sciences. After a few years, however, the cost of importing foreign experts outweighed the benefits, and fewer were employed. Missionaries, who came at their own expense, were an important exception.

RESTRUCTURING GOVERNMENT

The emperor was brought from his home in Kyoto to Edo, the former capital of the Shogun, which was renamed Tokyo ("Eastern Capital") in 1868. In 1869, the *daimyo* of four of the most important *han*—Choshu, Satsuma, Tosa and Hisen—turned over their estates to the emperor, setting the pattern for other *daimyo*. At first they were appointed governors, but two years later their domains were abolished and reorganized among the other prefectures of Japan. The *daimyo* retained certain rights of tax collection, which kept them financially well off, and stipends were paid to the samurai to avoid outright revolt. Nevertheless, a decade of samurai revolts in

FUKUZAWA YUKICHI: CULTURAL INTERPRETER

orn into the lower levels of the feudal aristocracy in Kyushu, Fukuzawa Yukichi (1834–1901) had a thirst for knowledge that took him to Osaka, Nagasaki (for Dutch learning), to the United States in 1860 with the very first Japanese official mission (and again in 1867), and to Europe in 1862. Fukuzawa rejected government office, the usual alternative, in favor of private life as a journalist and teacher. He earned a reputation as the foremost interpreter of the West to Japan and his books describing the West as he understood it sold in the hundreds of thousands to a nation hungry for such observation and interpretation. He founded a school in Tokyo that later became Keio University, the training ground of many of Japan's business leaders. The following excerpts are from Fukuzawa's *Autobiography,* published in 1899. He states his goal of interpreting the West fairly, even though he knows that he will face opposition.

> The final purpose of all my work was to create in Japan a civilized nation, as well equipped in both the arts of war and peace as those of the Western world. I acted as if I had become the sole functioning agent for the introduction of Western culture. It was natural then that I would be disliked by the older type of Japanese, and suspected of working for the benefit of foreigners. ... I regard the human being as the most sacred and responsible of all orders, unable in reason to do anything base. ... In short, my creed is that a man should find his faith in independence and self-respect. (p. 214)

He investigates the style of Western institutions:

> For instance, when I saw a hospital, I wanted to know how it was run—who paid the running expenses; when I visited a bank, I wished to learn how the money was deposited and paid out. By similar first-hand queries, I learned something of the postal system and the military conscription then in force in France but not in England. A perplexing institution was representative government. ... For some time it was beyond my comprehension to understand what they [political parties] were "fighting" for, and what was meant, anyway, by "fighting" in peace time. "This man and that man are 'enemies' in the House," they would tell me. But these "enemies" were to be seen at the same table, eating and drinking with each other. (p. 134)

Choshu, Kyshsu, Hizen, and, by far the largest, in Satsuma did challenge the new government. In Satsuma 40,000 troops, under the reluctant leadership of Saigo Takamori, confronted the government and were crushed. Japan's national government held firm.

The core of the central government's new army, 10,000 men drawn from Satsuma, Choshu, and Tosa, was established in 1871. In 1878, the army was reorganized and money was invested in modern equipment, much of it manufactured in Japan. An army staff college began to train an officer corps along a German model, while the navy adapted an English model, often purchasing its ships from England. Service in the armed forces introduced Japanese conscripts to new ways of life, some travel, reading and writing, shoes, Western-style uniforms, nationalism, and reverence for the emperor. Japan was becoming the most powerful nation in east Asia.

RESTRUCTURING THE ECONOMY

Recognizing an economic principle that underlay the industrial revolution in England, Japan first built up its agriculture. It needed the profits, and it needed the food and manpower which an effective agriculture would make available for urban industry. New seeds, fertilizer, and methods were introduced throughout the islands and Hokkaido was opened to farming. Agricultural colleges spread the new techniques and information. In the 1880s, agricultural production went up by about 30 percent, and from 1890 to 1915 by 100 percent. This production included not only food crops but also tea, cotton, and silk, mostly for the export market. The profits from increased agricultural production did not go to the peasants but to the landlord, who invested them in commerce or industry. Poorer peasants were squeezed off the land by high rents and

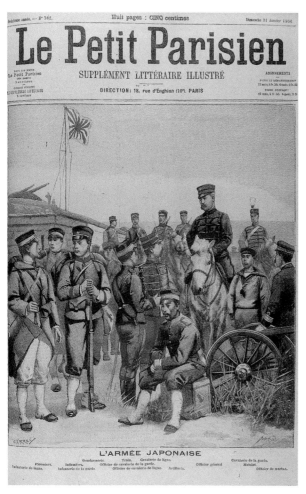

East wears West. The Japanese troops pictured on the front of this French magazine are a perfect example of the lengths to which the government of Japan was willing to go in an effort to fit into the modern world of early twentieth-century politics.

all peasants were heavily taxed to fund the large expenses of industrialization and militarization.

In large-scale industrialization, the government was the entrepreneur. It built the first railway line, between Tokyo and Yokohama, in 1872. In two decades about 2000 miles (3200 kilometers) of track followed. Within the cities, trolleys and *rikishas* (rickshaws) supplemented the train lines. Telegraph lines linked all the major cities by 1880. The government financed coal mines, iron mines, a machine-tool factory, cement works, glass and tile factories, wool and cotton textile mills, shipyards, mines, and weapons manufacture. In 1873 it established the Imperial College of Engineering. But the industry that contributed the most, silk, which accounted for more than 40 percent of all of Japan's exports, was developed largely by private entrepreneurs.

URBANIZATION

In Tokugawa times, each *daimyo* had his own capital. As a result, Japan had a rich array of administrative towns and cities spread throughout the country. During the Meiji Restoration, they provided the network for the diffusion of new cultural patterns. Some cities stood out. Kyoto, the home of the emperor, was the center of traditional culture; Osaka was the most important business center; and Edo (Tokyo) was, by the mid-1800s, the largest and most flourishing of the major cities, with a population of a half million to a million people.

Tokugawa urban culture had mixed strains. At the center of business life were merchants dedicated to making money. Yet they liked entertainment and found it outside their homes. Homes were for wife, children, and household duties. The amusement quarters of the city were for restaurants, theater, artistic culture, the female companionship of *geisha* personal entertainers, and prostitutes.

Social networks based on neighborhoods, shrines, guilds, and civic needs such as firefighting provided a sense of community, and cities grew relatively slowly in the first generation of the Restoration. By 1895 only 12 percent of Japan's population of 42 million lived in cities. Industrialization in large factories had barely begun. In 1897 only 400,000 workers in all of Japan were working in factories employing more than five workers. By the turn of the century, however, the institutional and economic changes of the Restoration were taking effect, and urban populations multiplied, so that by the mid-1930s 45 percent of the 69 million people of Japan were living in cities. The industrial labor force reached 1.7 million in 1920 (and 6 million by 1936).

The culture of parts of the cities changed dramatically. Japanese cities, crowded and subject to fire and earthquake, changed not only with cultural and technological innovations, but also with the necessity to rebuild from time to time. Edward Seidensticker's remarkable study of Tokyo between 1867 and 1923, *Low City, High City*, describes a double transformation. The old heart of Tokyo, the low city, developed bigger businesses, more raucous entertainment, and newer fashions, but it remained rooted in the plebeian culture of the Tokugawa period of Edo. The high city, built literally on somewhat higher ground, was developed later, with modern buildings, more refinement of a Western sort, and a more modernist culture.

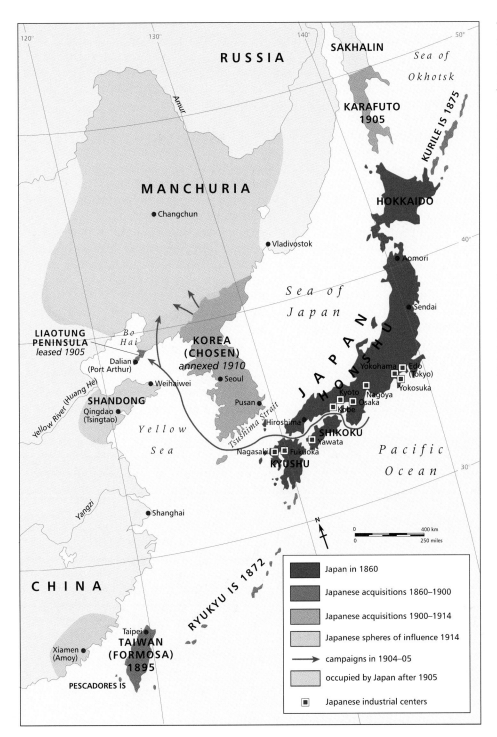

The expansion and modernization of Japan
Responding to the threats of foreign gunboats, Japanese samurai leaders overthrew the long-established Tokugawa Shogunate and restored imperial power under the Emperor Meiji in 1868. Within fifty years, industrial development, growing international trade, and territorial expansion made Japan a world power. Initially asserting its control of neighboring islands, and then taking advantage of Manchu decline, its victories over China (1894–95) and Russia (1904–05) established Japanese control over Taiwan, Korea, Manchuria, and northeast China.

Legend:
- Japan in 1860
- Japanese acquisitions 1860–1900
- Japanese acquisitions 1900–1914
- Japanese spheres of influence 1914
- → campaigns in 1904–05
- occupied by Japan after 1905
- ▣ Japanese industrial centers

CULTURAL AND EDUCATIONAL CHANGE

Western cultural styles, superficial and profound, proliferated in Meiji Japan. The Gregorian calendar and the seven-day week, with Sunday as a holiday, were adopted in 1882, and the metric system in 1886. Samurai men began to prefer Western haircuts to the traditional shaved head and topknot. The military dressed in western-style uniforms, and in 1872 Western dress became mandatory at all official ceremonies. Meat eating was encouraged, despite Buddhist ethics, and *sukiyaki* was developed as part of Japanese cuisine.

Japanese readers turned avidly to Western texts. Western philosophers of the Enlightenment drew attention to individual rights, and Utilitarians, such as John Stuart Mill (see p. 549) were read and appreciated. The more combative social Darwinism of Herbert Spencer (see p. 521) proved attractive as a justification for Japan's sense of its growing power and coming imperialism and Samuel Smiles' emphasis on *Self Help* (see p. 512) also found a receptive readership.

Tokugawa Japan had valued formal education. Samurai had attended Confucian-based schools run by the *han*; commoners studied in schools located in Buddhist temples. At the time of the Restoration, an estimated 45 percent of adult males and 15 percent of adult females could read and write, about the same proportions as in advanced European countries. Building on this base, the government introduced a highly centralized system of education and then mandated compulsory attendance. By 1905, over 90 percent of both boys and girls of primary school age were attending school. The schools were recognized for high quality, for providing public education superior to private schools, and for helping move

Japan from the feudal, hierarchical society of Tokugawa Japan to a more egalitarian system than that of most European countries. At the university level, a series of excellent institutions were established throughout Japan, beginning with Tokyo University in 1886.

GENDER RELATIONS

The Meiji Restoration opened up entirely new arenas of public life and achievement for Japanese men, and, for a few years before marriage, some women also found new opportunities in education, factory employment, and a handful of new cultural opportunities. For the most part, however, women's public options were restricted. As the emperor's position was restored, so was male dominance in the home reinforced. Police Security Regulations of 1890, Article 5, prohibited women and minors from joining political organizations and holding or attending meetings in which political speeches or lectures were given. (The vote was granted to women only after World War II; see p. 634.) The 1898 Civil Code reinforced patriarchy within the family, granting the male head of the

Advertising throwaway from the Mitsui dry-goods store (later Mitsuoki Department Store), Tokyo, *c*. 1895. Retail outlets were obvious signs of the drive to embrace industrialized Western culture, as this "before" and "after" picture aptly demonstrates. The traditional first floor (bottom), with its legions of clerks haggling over material, has been supplanted by the new-fangled second floor (top), whose serene atmosphere and slick glass-display cases proclaim a new, more stylish era.

family unquestioned authority. Women had few legal rights. At marriage, control over her property passed to her husband. Fathers held exclusive right to custody over children. Concubinage was abolished in 1880, but society sanctioned prostitution and the discreet keeping of mistresses. As high school education was extended to women, the Girls' High School Law of 1899 declared its goal to be "good wives and wise mothers." Within the home, women held great authority and respect, but they were allowed virtually no place in the public life of Japan.

WAR, COLONIALISM, AND EQUALITY IN THE FAMILY OF NATIONS

From the beginning of the Meiji Restoration, Japan sought an end to the demeaning provisions of extraterritoriality and also to regain control of its own tariffs. These goals provided the rationales for introducing new legal systems, more consistent with those of Western countries. If Japan's laws were in accord with those of Europe, there would be no justification for continuing extraterritoriality. The British relinquished extraterritoriality in 1899 when the new legal codes took effect. Other nations agreed, and Japan reciprocated by allowing foreigners to establish residences outside the treaty ports. Additional treaties returned full control over tariffs to Japan in 1911.

War and colonization also seemed important to full membership in the European community of nations. Yamagata Aritomo (1838–1922), the chief proponent of the law of universal conscription in 1873 and chief architect of Japan's new army, argued this position, and turned his attention to the conquest of Korea. Japan had forced the establishment of a legation in Korea in 1876. As political leaders in that country divided over policy issues, some sought support from more conservative China, others from more progressive Japan. When fighting between the groups broke out in 1894, both China and Japan sent in troops and war began between the two powers. On land, Japanese armies seized all of Korea and pushed on into Manchuria. At sea, they defeated the Chinese fleet, captured Port Arthur, the naval base in southern Manchuria, and the port of Weihaiwei on Shandong. Peace negotiations gave Japan Taiwan and the Pescadores Islands, and Japan supplanted China as the dominant nation of East Asia. Korea was recognized as independent, but Japan held sway there nonetheless. Japan was also to receive control over the Liaotung Peninsula, but an international diplomatic consortium led by Russia forced it to withdraw, despite Japan's resentment.

In the first years of the twentieth century, two further engagements with the West ratified Japan's arrival among the nationalist powers of the world. First, in 1902, Britain and Japan signed an alliance, the first military pact on equal terms between a

*R*USSO-JAPANESE WAR 1904–5—KEY EVENTS

The war arose from conflicting ambitions in Manchuria and Korea, in particular the Russian occupation of Port Arthur (1896) and Amur province (1900).

May 1904	Battle of Yalu River: the Russians are defeated by the Japanese in the vicinity of Antung (now Dandong), Manchuria. The river forms the border with Korea, and the Japanese army forces a crossing against light opposition. Quickly overcoming the Russians, who retreat north, the Japanese move to besiege Port Arthur (Lushan).
May 1904–January 1905	Siege of Port Arthur: the Japanese fleet blockades the harbor, keeping the Russian fleet bottled up, while the army launches a series of minor attacks. Japanese eventually overcome garrison, which surrenders, after heavy losses. Japanese lose some 58,000 men.
February–May 1905	Battle of Mukden (Shenyang): Japanese defeat Russians outside the capital city of Manchuria, in the last major engagement of the war, in which 41,000 Japanese were killed and wounded and the Russian dead and wounded totalled more than 32,000. The czar is finally persuaded to accept US mediation. Russia's Baltic Fleet is annihilated in the Tsushima Straits.
August 1905	Peace agreement: Russia surrendered its lease on Port Arthur, ceded South Sakhalin to Japan, evacuated Manchuria, and recognized Japanese interests in Korea.

European and a non-Western country. It brought together the most powerful navies of Europe and of East Asia. It blocked Russian aspirations, and it further secured semi-colonial control over China. Second, in response to continuing Russian penetration of Manchuria and increasingly hostile diplomacy, Japan attacked the Russian fleet in Port Arthur in 1904 and declared war. Fighting far from the center of their country, the Russian army was defeated. A Russian fleet dispatched from the Baltic was intercepted and annihilated by the Japanese as it crossed the Straits of Tsushima.

An Asian power had defeated a European power for the first time since the victories of the Ottomans in eastern Europe in the seventeenth century. (In Russia, the defeat precipitated the revolution of 1905.) In the peace conference convened by American President Theodore Roosevelt, Japan was given a protectorate over Korea, predominant rights over southern Manchuria (including the Liaotung Peninsula) and control of the southern Sakhalin Island. In 1910, with no European power protesting, Japan formally annexed Korea. Japan had reached the international status it had desired—less than a half century after embarking on its quest. Nationalism, technological innovation, and imperialism had become supreme in Japan as in Europe.

BIBLIOGRAPHY

Abu-Lughod, Janet and Richard Hay, Jr., eds. *Third World Urbanization* (Chicago: Maaroufa Press, 1977).

Adas, Michael, ed. *Islamic and European Expansion* (Philadelphia: Temple University Press, 1993).

Anderson, Bernard. *Imagined Communities* (London: Verso, 1983).

Anderson, Bonnie and Judith Zinsser. *A History of Their Own*, 2 vols. (New York: Harper and Row, 1988).

Andrea, Alfred and James Overfield, eds. *The Human Record*, Vol 2 (Boston: Houghton Mifflin, 2nd ed. 1994).

Bairoch, Paul. *Cities and Economic Development*, trans. by Christopher Braider (Chicago: University of Chicago Press, 1988).

Baudelaire, Charles. *Les Fleurs du Mal*, trans. by Richard Howard (Boston: Godine, 1983).

Bell, Susan Groag and Karen M. Offen, eds. *Women, the Family, and Freedom*, Vol. 1, 1750–1880 (Stanford: Stanford University Press, 1983).

Bernstein, Gail Lee, ed. *Recreating Japanese Women, 1600–1945* (Berkeley: University of California Press, 1991).

Braudel, Fernand. *The Identity of France*, trans. by Sian Reynolds (New York; Harper and Row, 1988).

Bridenthal, Renate, Claudia Koonz, and Susan Stuard, eds. *Becoming Visible: Women in European History* (Boston: Houghton Mifflin, 2nd ed., 1987).

Booth, Charles. *On the City*, ed. by Harold W. Pfautz (Chicago: University of Chicago Press, 1967).

Burton, Antoinette. *Burdens of History* (Chapel Hill: University of North Carolina Press, 1994).

Casey, James. *The History of the Family* (Oxford: Blackwell, 1989).

Chatterjee, Partha. *The Nation and Its Fragments* (Princeton: Princeton University Press, 1993).

Collcutt, Martin, Marius Jansen, and Isao Kumakura. *Cultural Atlas of Japan* (New York: Facts on File, 1988).

Columbia College, Columbia University. eds. *Contemporary Civilization in the West* (New York: Columbia University Press, 2nd ed., 1954).

Cooper, Frederick and Ann Laura Stoler, eds. *Tensions of Empire* (Berkeley: University of California Press, 1997).

Di Giorgio, Michela, "The Catholic Model," in Fraisse and Perrot, eds. *Emerging Feminism*, pp. 166–197.

Duara, Prasenjit. *Rescuing History from the Nation* (Chicago: University of Chicago Press, 1995).

Eley, Geoff and Ronald Grigor Suny, eds. *Becoming National* (New York: Oxford University Press, 1996).

Fairbank, John K., Edwin O. Reischauer, and Albert Craig. *East Asia: Tradition and Transformation* (Boston: Houghton Mifflin, rev. ed., 1989).

Fraisse, Genevieve and Michelle Perrot, eds. *A History of Women in the West: Emerging Feminism from Revolution to World War*, Vol. IV (Cambridge: Belknap Press, 1993).

Frederick, Christine. *The New Housekeeping* (Garden City, NY: Doubleday, 1914).

Fujimura-Fanselow, Kumiko and Atsuko Kameda, eds. *Japanese Women* (New York: Feminist Press, 1995).

Gluck, Carol. *Japan's Modern Myths* (Princeton: Princeton University Press, 1985).

Hibbert, Christopher. *London* (Harmondsworth, Middlesex: Penguin Books Ltd., 1977).

Hertzberg, Arthur, ed. *The Zionist Idea* (New York: Meridian Books Inc. and Philadelpia: Jewish Publication Society, 1960).

Hirschmeier, Johannes. *The Origins of Entrepreneurship in Meiji Japan* (Cambridge: Harvard University Press, 1964).

Hobsbawm, Eric. *The Age of Capital, 1848–1875* (New York: Vintage Books, 1975).

—. *The Age of Empire, 1875–1914* (New York: Vintage, 1987).

—. *The Age of Revolution, 1789–1848* (New York: New American Library, 1962).

Hohenberg, Paul M. and Lynn Hollen Lees. *The Making of Urban Europe, 1000–1950* (Cambridge: Harvard University Press, 1985).

Hutchinson, John and Anthony D. Smith, eds. *Nationalism* (New York: Oxford University Press, 1994).

Ibsen, Henrik. *A Doll's House*, trans. by Rolf Fjelde in *Literature of the Western World Vol. II: Neoclassicism Through the Modern Period*, ed. by Brian Wilkie and James Hurt (New York: Macmillan Publishing Co., Inc., 1984), pp. 1304–57.

Kaneko, Sachiko, "The Struggle for Legal Rights and Reforms: A Historical View," in Fujimora-Fanselow and Kameda, eds. *Japanese Women*, pp. 3–14.

Kennedy, Paul. *The Rise and Fall of the Great Powers* (New York; Random House, 1987).

Kessler-Harris, Alice. *Out to Work* (New York: Oxford University Press, 1982).

Knibiehler, Yvonne, "Bodies and Hearts," in Fraisse and Perrot, eds., *Emerging Feminism*, pp. 325–68.

Marx, Karl and Frederick Engels. *The Communist Manifesto* (New York: International Publishers, 1948).

Morris-Suzuki, Tessa. *The Technological Transformation of Japan* (Cambridge: Cambridge University Press, 1994).

Mumford, Lewis. *The City in History* (New York: Harcourt Brace & World, 1961).

Procida, Mary A. "Married to the Empire: British Wives and British Imperialism in India, 1883-1947" (University of Pennsylvania: Ph.D. dissertation, 1997).

Renan, Ernest, "What is a Nation?" in Eley and Suny, pp. 42–55.

Restoring Women to History (Bloomington, In: Organization of American Historians, 1988).

Rousseau, Jean-Jacques. *The Social Contract*, trans. by Maurice Cranston (Harmondsworth, Middlesex: Penguin Books, 1968).

Rybczynski, Witold. *Home* (New York: Penguin Books, 1987).

Said, Edward W. *Culture and Imperialism* (New York: Vintage Books, 1993).

Schirokauer, Conrad. *A Brief History of Chinese and Japanese Civilizations* (Fort Worth: Harcourt Brace Jovanovich, 2nd ed., 1989).

Scott, Joan Wallach. *Only Paradoxes to Offer* (Cambridge: Harvard University Press, 1996).

—. "The Woman Worker," in Fraisse and Perrot, eds., *Emerging Feminism*, pp. 399–426.

Seidensticker, Edward. *Low City, High City* (Cambridge: Harvard University Press, 1991).

Sennett, Richard, ed. *Classic Essays on the Culture of Cities* (Englewood Cliffs: Prentice Hall, 1969).

Spivak, Gayatri Chakravorty, "Subaltern Studies: Deconstructing Historiography," in Ranajit Guha and Gayatri Chakravorty Spivak eds., *Selected Subaltern Studies* (New York: Oxford University Press), pp. 3–32.

Strobel, Margaret, "Gender, Sex, and Empire," in Adas, pp. 345–375.

Thomas, Ray and Peter Cresswell. *The New Town Idea* (Walton Hall, Milton Keynes: Open University Press, 1973).

Tilly, Louise, "Industrialization and Gender Inequality," in Adas, pp. 243–310.

Times [London] *Atlas of World History* (London: Times Books, 1981).

Tocqueville, Alexis de. *Democracy in America*, 2 vols (New York: Knopf, 1945).

Tsunoda, Ryusaku, Wm. Theodore de Bary, and Donald Keene, comps. *Sources of Japanese Tradition* (New York: Columbia University Press, 1958).

Uno, Kathleen S., "Women and Changes in the Household Division of Labor," in Gail Lee Bernstein, ed., *Recreating Japanese Women, 1600–1945* (Berkeley: University of California Press, 1991), pp. 17–41.

Wakakuwa, Midori, "Three Women Artists of the Meiji Period (1868–1912): Reconsidering Their Significance from a Feminist Perspective," in Fujimura-Fanselow and Kameda, eds., *Japanese Women*, pp. 61–74.

Walkowitz, Judith, "Dangerous Sexualities," in Fraisse and Perrot, eds., *Emerging Feminism*, pp. 369–98.

Warner, Sam Bass, Jr. *The Private City* (Philadelphia: University of Pennsylvania Press, 1987).

Weber, Adna Ferrin. *The Growth of Cities in the Nineteenth Century* (Ithaca: Cornell University Press, reprint 1963).

Weber, Max. *The City*, trans. by Don Martindale and Gertrud Neuwirth (New York: Free Press, 1958).

Whitman, Walt. *Complete Poetry and Collected Prose* (New York: The Library of America, 1982).

Woolstonecraft, Mary. *Vindication of the Rights of Woman* (London: Penguin Books, 1975).

Yukichi, Fukuzawa. *The Autobiography of Yukichi Fukuzawa*, trans. by Eiichi Kiyooka (New York: Columbia University Press, 1966).

8
PART

Exploding Technologies

1914–1990s

CONTESTED VISIONS OF A NEW INTERNATIONAL ORDER

This part, beginning about the time of World War I, brings us to our own era, and this creates special challenges—and excitement—for the historian. Contemporary history challenges our ability to be objective, to evaluate the consequences of events still in process, and to make sense of data so abundant that we cannot absorb all of it. One of the most important criteria used by the historian—the consequences of the events—is not available to us in evaluating events in the twentieth century. Consider, for example, the effect of the collapse of the Soviet Union since 1991 on our understanding of the significance of the 1917 Communist revolution (see Chapter 19). In what ways will future events similarly change our understanding of the events we are living through? Finally, the historical record must always balance data and interpretation. For earlier eras a scarcity of data often turns interpretation into guesswork. For our own time, the problem is reversed. An abundance of information often indicates many different directions at once, suggesting varying and often conflicting interpretations.

In this part on the twentieth century we must, therefore, be especially clear in our historical method of charting change over time. Two of the greatest changes in this century have been, first, the increasing power of technology to alter the patterns of human life and death and even to affect the entire ecological balance of all life on earth, and, second, the increasing responsibility of humans to decide the development and use of that technology, a responsibility most often discharged politically through the expanding of state powers.

Atomic weapons test in the Marshall Islands, 1950.

The six chapters in this part narrate and analyze in detail the global transformations and legacies brought about by the increasing power of technology. Chapter 18 examines some of the fundamental technological changes of the era, the quality of life, war and peace, and national and international institutional planning. Chapter 19 compares the efforts of the USSR and Japan to catch up technologically with the industrialized worlds of Western Europe and the United States. Chapter 20 examines the technological choices of the two huge billion-population states, China and India, both of which are largely agricultural. Chapter 21 looks at the intersection of technological development, religious policy, and international relations in the Middle East. Chapter 22 looks at the nations of Africa as they have emerged from colonialism (and apartheid) and sought technologies appropriate to their resources and skills. Chapter 23 analyzes the policies of the different nations of Latin America as they have alternated between integration into the world economy and going it alone, and between satisfying their elites and their common people.

Throughout each chapter, the reader must engage contemporary history—and this text—with his or her own values, understanding of human nature, and appreciation of interpretive themes in order to assess the present century—and their place within it.

18
CHAPTER

"Our twentieth century was going to improve on others... A couple of problems weren't going to come up anymore: hunger, for example, and war, and so forth."

WISLAWA SZYMBORSKA

TECHNOLOGIES OF MASS-PRODUCTION AND DESTRUCTION

1914–1990s

WHAT IS A TECHNOLOGICAL SYSTEM AND WHY IS IT IMPORTANT?

TECHNOLOGICAL SYSTEMS

*I*n general, the first part of this chapter will introduce technology in its more benign mode—that is, those developments that encourage life and make it more productive, enjoyable, and perhaps meaningful. The second part will introduce the destructive aspect of technology, manifest especially in violence and warfare. The final segments discuss attempts, often frustrating and frustrated, but nevertheless continuing, to build institutions to harness technology for humane uses.

"Technology" includes not only inventions but also the systems that produce and sustain them. Thomas Hughes, a historian of science and technology, explains this comprehensive definition:

In popular accounts of technology, inventions of the late nineteenth century, such as the incandescent light, the radio, the airplane, and the gasoline-driven automobile, occupy center stage, but these inventions were embedded within technological systems. Such systems involve far more than the so-called hardware, devices, machines and processes, and the transportation, communication, and information networks that interconnect them. Such systems consist also of people and organizations. An electric light-and-power system, for instance, may involve generators, motors, transmission lines, utility companies, manufacturing enterprises, and banks. Even a regulatory body may be co-opted into the system. (p. 3)

The technological enterprise has continued to grow as the most pervasive characteristic of the twentieth century. It has dramatically altered:

- 🍃 the number, longevity, and health of the people who inhabit the globe;

- 🍃 the size and organization of our families;

- 🍃 the location, design, and equipment of our homes, neighborhoods, and workplaces;

- 🍃 the nature and organization of the work we do and the training necessary to do it;

- 🍃 the clothes we wear;

- 🍃 our travel for business and pleasure;

- 🍃 the quantities and varieties of food we eat as well as the regions of the globe from which they come;

- 🍃 the forms of our recreation;

- 🍃 the strategies and destructive potentials of the wars we wage;

- 🍃 the complexity and structure of our economic, social, and governmental organizations; and

- 🍃 the ecology, that is, the interaction of the life systems, of the earth.

DEMOGRAPHIC SHIFTS

Improvements in technology have changed our relationship to life and death, health and sickness. Biological and health advances have included new drugs such as sulfa-based medicines (1930s), penicillin and antibiotics (from the 1940s), hormonal and mood-altering chemicals (from the 1950s), and new methods of contraception, especially the birth control pill (1950s) which have changed sexual attitudes and practices around the globe.

Public health services, the fortunate linking of medical knowledge with government responsibility, have increased, especially in the provision of safe drinking water and sewage offtake (although not always and everywhere as quickly as new needs have arisen). An increasing variety of vaccines has eliminated the fear of many childhood diseases. Polio was tamed in the 1950s, and through the international activities of the World Health Organization in achieving the vaccination of virtually all humans in areas of the world infected with the disease in the 1960s and 1970s, smallpox, a disease of historically epidemic proportions, has been totally eradicated. The last known case was in Somalia in 1977. The once-feared smallpox virus lives today only in laboratory specimens kept for research purposes.

The progress of technology and its application often collided with other ecological constraints. For a time in the 1950s and 1960s, for example, the chemical insecticide DDT seemed to offer a weapon

New farm technology. The American Burger tractor, invented in 1889, was the first to install an internal-combustion engine. With the introduction of automated farm machinery huge tracts of land around the world were brought under cultivation and food productivity soared. Here, in 1917, a woman from Vassar College in Poughkeepsie, New York, plows a field as part of the war effort.

	POLITICAL	SOCIAL	CULTURAL
1900	■ Boer War (1899–1902) ■ Germany enters arms race with Britain (1900) ■ Labour Party founded in Britain (1900) ■ Russo-Japanese War (1904–5) ■ Old Age Pensions in Britain (1909)	■ Guglielmo Marconi transmits signal across the Atlantic (1901) ■ Wright brothers make first powered air flight (1903) ■ Boy Scout movement founded (1907) ■ Henry Ford begins assembly-line manufacture of motorcars (1909) ■ Robert Peary reaches North Pole (1909)	■ Jean-Paul Sartre (1905–81) ■ Dmitri Shostakovitch (1906–57) ■ Cubist painters (Pablo Picasso, Georges Braque) exhibit in Paris (1907–10) ■ *Der Rosenkavalier* by Richard Strauss (1909–10)
1910	■ World War I (1914–18) ■ Treaty of Versailles (1919) ■ Benito Mussolini founds Fascist Movement (1919)	■ Roald Amundsen reaches South Pole (1911) ■ *Titanic* sinks (1912) ■ Igor Sikorsky builds first four-engined airplane (1913) ■ Panama Canal opened (1914) ■ Birth control clinic opens in New York (1916)	■ Marcel Proust publishes *À la recherche du temps perdu* (1913–27) ■ Igor Stravinsky's *Rite of Spring* performed (1913) ■ Sigmund Freud's *Totem and Taboo* published (1913) ■ Benjamin Britten (1913–76) ■ Albert Camus (1913–60) ■ Albert Einstein publishes *General Theory of Relativity* (1915) ■ D.W. Griffith's *Birth of a Nation* (1915) ■ Dadaism founded (1915)
1920	■ League of Nations meets (1920) ■ Adolf Hitler founds National Socialist (Nazi) Party (1923) ■ Locarno Conference (1925) ■ Germany becomes member of League of Nations (1926) ■ Kellogg-Briand Pact (1928)	■ General strike in Britain (1926) ■ Alexander Fleming discovers penicillin (1928) ■ US stock market collapses (1929), leading to worldwide recession	■ John Logie Baird invents television (1925) ■ *The Jazz Singer*, first talking picture (1927) ■ *Plane Crazy*, first Mickey Mouse cartoon (1928)
1930	■ Hitler becomes chancellor and Germany withdraws from League of Nations (1933) ■ Hitler denounces Treaty of Versailles and Germany re-arms (1935) ■ Spanish Civil War (1936–9) ■ Edward VIII of Britain abdicates (1938) ■ World War II (1939–45)	■ Prohibition in US ends (1933) ■ Robert Watson-Watt develops radar system (1935) ■ Persecution of Jews begins in Germany (1935) ■ Sikorsky builds first successful helicopter (1939)	■ *King Kong* (1933) ■ Carl Jung publishes *Modern Man in Search of a Soul* (1933) ■ Elvis Presley (1935–77) ■ *Gone with the Wind* (1939)
1940	■ Nuremberg Trials (1946) ■ War in Indochina between French and nationalists led by Ho Chi Minh (1946–54) ■ Marshall Aid program (1947) ■ NATO formed (1949) ■ France recognizes independence of Cambodia and Vietnam (1949)	■ Frank Whittle invents the jet engine (1941)	■ *Citizen Kane* (1941) ■ Abstract Expressionist movement in painting develops in USA (after 1945) ■ George Orwell publishes *Nineteen Eighty-Four* (1949) ■ Simone de Beauvoir writes *Le Deuxième sexe* (1949)

against the malaria-bearing anopheles mosquito, but DDT proved toxic to humans and animal life and was generally banned from use. Quinine continued as the principal defense and treatment.

Food productivity multiplied. More land was brought under cultivation. New machinery, notably the tractor and combine, facilitated the opening of the American and Canadian Midwest, the Argentinian pampas, the steppe land of the Soviet Union, and the economically developing continent of Australia. By the end of the twentieth century, although some scientists questioned the wisdom of manipulating the basic designs of life, new biotechnology and genetic engineering were creating breakthroughs in kinds and totals of crop production. In 1997 scientists succeeded in cloning a sheep and were experimenting with producing blood in the bodies of animals that could be used for human transfusions. Scientists, clergy, ethicists, and political leaders continue to grapple with the implications of these discoveries.

In the developing nations of the **third world**, beginning in the 1960s, new seeds and fertilizers, engineered in part under the auspices of the philanthropic Rockefeller Foundation, increased the productivity of land under wheat cultivation by up to five times. Experimentation with additional crops, such as rice, is under way. Land that was

	POLITICAL	SOCIAL	CULTURAL
1950	▪ Korean War (1950–53) ▪ Schuman Plan (1951): France, West Germany, Italy, Belgium, Netherlands, and Luxembourg agree on open market for coal and steel ▪ Greece and Turkey join NATO (1952) ▪ Geneva Conference (1954): Vietnam divided, with communist North under Ho Chi Minh ▪ SEATO formed (1954) to prevent spread of communism in Southeast Asia ▪ Warsaw Pact agreed (1955) ▪ Treaty of Rome (1957): Belgium, France, West Germany, Italy, Luxembourg and Netherlands establish EEC	▪ Joseph McCarthy heads inquiry into "un-American activities" (1950) ▪ Contraceptive pill becomes available (1952) ▪ Conquest of Everest (1953) ▪ Jonas Edward Salk develops vaccine against polio (1954) ▪ USSR launches *Sputnik I* (1957) ▪ US launches *Explorer I* (1958); space race begins	▪ *The Catcher in the Rye* by J.D. Salinger (1951) ▪ Theater of the Absurd movement, founded by Eugene Ionesco and Samuel Beckett (1953–60) ▪ Elvis Presley dominates rock music after release of *Heartbreak Hotel* (1956) ▪ Beginning of the Pop Art movement in the USA (after 1956)
1960	▪ Berlin Wall is built (1961) ▪ Fighting between Greeks and Turks in Cyprus (1964) ▪ US troops increasingly involved in Vietnam War (1964–8) ▪ Britain sends troops to Northern Ireland (1969)	▪ Crick, Wilkins, and Watson identify DNA molecular structure (1962) ▪ Rachel Carson writes *Silent Spring* (1963) attacking over-use of pesticides ▪ Neil Armstrong is first man on the moon (1969)	▪ Beatles pop group formed (1960) ▪ *2001: A Space Odyssey*, directed by Stanley Kubrick (1968)
1970	▪ Britain, Eire, and Denmark join EEC (1973) ▪ Coup in Portugal ends dictatorship of Premier Caetano (1974) ▪ Spanish dictator Franco dies; monarchy is restored (1975) ▪ Russian forces in Afghanistan (1979–89)	▪ Greenpeace founded (1971) ▪ John Paul II becomes first non-Italian pope for 450+ years (1978)	▪ *The Female Eunuch* by Germaine Greer (1970) ▪ *Sexual Politics* by Kate Millet (1970) ▪ *The Gulag Archipelago* by Alexander Solzhenitsyn (1975) ▪ *Star Wars*, directed by George Lucas (1977)
1980	▪ Falklands War (Britain v. Argentina; 1982) ▪ US invades Grenada (1983) ▪ Lockerbie air crash kills 270 people (1988) ▪ "Solidarity" in Poland (1989) ▪ Communist rule ends in Poland, Hungary, Czechoslovakia, Bulgaria, and East Germany (1989)	▪ *Voyager* spacecraft flies by Saturn (1980) ▪ AIDS virus identified (1983) ▪ Greenpeace vessel *Rainbow Warrior* sunk by French in South Pacific (1985) ▪ Stock market crashes in New York, Tokyo and London (1987) ▪ Piper Alpha oil rig in North Sea explodes, killing 166 (1988)	▪ *Gandhi*, directed by Richard Attenborough (1983) ▪ Live Aid raises money globally for famine relief (1985) ▪ *Bonfire of the Vanities* by Tom Wolfe (1987) ▪ *Satanic Verses* by Salman Rushdie (1988)
1990	▪ Soviet republics claim independence from Russia (1990) ▪ War in Yugoslavia (from 1991) ▪ Gulf War (1991) ▪ Bill Clinton elected president of USA (1992)	▪ Global warming threat recognized (1990) ▪ Internet system links 5 million users (1993) ▪ Bomb destroys federal building in Oklahoma City, killing 100+ people (1995)	▪ Euro Disney opened in Paris (1992) ▪ Aids quilt exhibited in Washington D.C. (1992) ▪ *Schindler's List*, directed by Steven Spielberg (1993)

already fully populated and under intense cultivation became increasingly productive.

For example, although India's population doubled between 1966 and 1991, the "green revolution" enabled the country to achieve self-sufficiency in food during those years. Distribution and equity, however, presented problems. Many critics noted the increasing income disparities created by the revolution in productivity. Wealthier farmers could most easily afford the new seeds and the additional fertilizer and irrigation water required to cultivate them. The green revolution made the rich richer as it increased productivity. Did it make the poor poorer? Survey results thus far are not conclusive.

New farm machinery reduced the need for labor, however, and rural population ratios dropped sharply—in America from 72 percent in 1900 to 36 percent in 1980; in Europe, quite similarly, from 70 percent to 36 percent; for the world as a whole from 84 percent to 62 percent. Farmers left the countryside in droves to search for urban jobs.

Developments in health and food technology facilitated a population explosion. More people were born and they lived longer. Life expectancy at birth in the USA rose from fifty-four years in 1920 to seventy-five years in 1990. In India it increased from thirty years at Independence in 1947 to fifty-four years in 1981 to sixty-two years in the 1990s. In

TECHNOLOGIES OF MASS-PRODUCTION AND DESTRUCTION (1914–1990s)   **577**

Indian squatter settlement. In the huge cities of the underdeveloped world, shanty towns have sprung up—a makeshift solution to endemic poverty and overcrowding. This squatter settlement in Bombay (population: 11.5 million) might be unsightly, but represents one answer to the acute housing shortage in urban India.

China it reached sixty-nine years and in Japan seventy-nine years in the 1990s. From 1900 to 1990, the population of the world multiplied three and one-half times from about 1.5 billion to approximately 5.3 billion, although the population growth around the globe was not uniform, as may be seen in the chart on p 439. The population *added* between 1980 and the year 2000 is predicted at 1.5 billion, almost the total population of the earth in 1900.

Demographers, seeking to explain the differential population growth, postulate two successive demographic shifts. First, as health conditions and food supply improved, death rates dropped while birth rates remained high and population increased. This has happened all over the world. Later, as parents saw that the mortality rates had fallen and that their children were likely to survive to adulthood, they chose to plan their family size through the use of contraception. Birth rates then dropped, as death rates had earlier. This second stage, of family planning, has occurred in the wealthier regions of the world, where death rates were lowest. In some of these countries, birth rates have actually dropped below death rates and the overall populations of some countries in Europe—Germany in the late twentieth century, France periodically—is actually declining. In poorer countries where death rates are still relatively high, however, the second stage of declining birth rates has not (yet) occurred, and population continues to rise. Demographers suggest, contrary to expectation, that the best way to reduce population growth is to improve health measures to help assure parents that their babies and children will live; then parents will plan fewer of them.

In addition to voluntary programs of birth control within individual families, many nations have undertaken official population policies. Many European countries, like France, in light of declining birth rates, have adopted policies that encourage more births by extending economic support to families with young children. On the other hand, many less wealthy and more crowded countries have promulgated policies to discourage large families. Most drastically, China since the 1980s has attempted to limit families to just one child. Implementation, however, has been difficult. A family wanting a male child, the usual preference, may break the law in attempting a second child if the first is a female, or may even kill a first-born female. In India, ruthless and thoughtless enforcement of rigid sterilization quotas by the government of Indira Gandhi cost her the 1977 elections. Government family planning programs have been restrained ever since. The powerful state and the individual family have clashed here over values and implementation; policies that may benefit the state and the society may not be regarded as beneficial by any individual family.

URBANIZATION AND MIGRATION

The growing population has been moving steadily into cities. We have seen (p. 416) that mechan-ization of agriculture is one of the factors pushing people away from the countryside. In addition, jobs in manufacture, bureaucracy, and service industries pull them to the cities. At the beginning of the century, urbanization was still linked to industrial growth; by the end of the century, the most rapidly growing cities, and, increasingly, the largest of them, are in the poorer, less industrialized areas of the world—for example, Mexico City and São Paulo each with about 20 million in 1990; Bombay and Calcutta in India and Buenos Aires, Argentina, each with about 11.5 million; and Manila, Cairo, and Jakarta, each with about 10 million.

In many of the richer countries, however, in a process termed **counterurbanization**, cities have turned inside out, and central city populations are actually declining. Poorer citizens remain in the center as the richer avail themselves of the new means of transportation and of communication via phone, fax and the World Wide Web to relocate to

CITIES AND CROWDS: ANTS AND INDUSTRY

A poem composed by the Marathi language poet Mardhekar, who comes from Bombay, captures what his translator, A.K. Ramanujam, calls "the vision (or cliché) of the modern city-dweller's city, the city as nightmare, its crowds, its faceless anomie, its clock-bound materialism":

I am an ant,
He is an ant, you are an ant, she is an ant,
A handful are foreign, a handful native;
A thousand have crowded, a million, a billion,
Trillions and trillions of ants;
Innumerable uncountable all have crowded here,
Many from the anthills, many others fugitive!
Some are fat and black, some red, some white;
Some are the winged ants of the monsoon,
Some are the big bold ones of summer,
Some are careful and walk in a file;
Some are silly and eat sugar wherever they find it;
Some stick and sting;
Some live feeding honey to others;

And some fertilize the Queen,
Smart enough to please!
Who will usurp
All these ants
One by one
To become King?
Who will carry
The summa of matter
To the spiritual realm?
—Ants, ants, cheaper by the dozen, ants for sale ...
This flood of ants comes, open the gates!
The suburban train
Of ten past ten
Has arrived emptying its sigh ...

Ramanujam notes a modern transformation in this image of the city and its population squeeze: "Premodern ants were extolled for their industry, not denigrated." And as we saw in Chapter 4, pre-industrial cities had been proclaimed as centers of religious and cultural life. (p. 227)

the suburbs. Businesses, too, recognizing a new freedom of movement, are leaving the central cities, partly to reduce their overhead costs. Multinational corporations cross international boundaries to relocate their factories, removing them from high-wage urban centers in the **first world** to new sites offering cheaper labor in the third.

Since the building of the first aircraft in 1903 by Wilbur and Orville Wright, and the first solo flight across the Atlantic in 1927 by Charles Lindbergh, international and intercontinental travel has become commonplace. Flights are taken for business and pleasure, and tourism has become one of the world's largest industries. In 1989, 38 million people visited the USA, spending $43 billion. Students, in particular, travel around the globe for formal and informal study and work opportunities.

In contrast, many others travel out of economic necessity and fear of repression—often on foot. Millions of political refugees from Vietnam, Afghanistan, Tibet, Iraq, Mozambique, Ethiopia, and numerous other African states, central America, and the USSR seek refuge and asylum in neighboring countries. "Guest workers," also by the millions, travel in search of jobs from southern Europe, North Africa, and Turkey to northern Europe; from the entire world to the oil-rich Persian Gulf areas; and, often illegally, from Latin America to the United States.

DOMESTIC CHANGE

Twentieth-century technology has transformed the quality of daily life as well as its location and density. The automobile, bus, truck, train, airplane, and jet affect transportation for almost all citizens of the world. The revolution in the means of communication—telegraph, telephone, copier, fax machine, modem, internet, radio, phonograph, various kinds of sound reproduction, photography, motion pictures, television, satellite transmission, and cable—have opened visions of the whole world to potentially all its citizens.

They have totally transformed work and play as well as the distribution of these activities in geographical space. Airconditioning has not only changed standards of comfort, but has opened many warmer areas of the world (including the southern United States) to increased immigration and development.

First developed after World War II, early computers were room-filling machines, designed to solve mathematical problems. Nowadays, they are found in homes and offices worldwide and are small enough to be easily portable. The computer has not only affected each one of the above revolutions in transportation and communication, but also has transformed data processing, office work, and the further development of both large-scale

Civil aviation. A steward serves passengers on board a KLM Fokker F18 in 1932. In the 1920s, the popularity of aerial circuses and flying clubs, run by former World War I pilots, combined with rapid improvements in technology, heralded a new age of civil aviation. By the 1930s a worldwide network of commercial routes had developed.

organizations and of science. With the advent of the World Wide Web it is now quite conceivable that future generations may never have to leave their homes to work, shop, bank and communicate with friends and family.

New technological systems such as the automated assembly line production of Henry Ford's automobile factories, the more recent introduction of robotics, and the management techniques of Frederick Taylor have changed the way we work and the efficiency of our production. Scientific research facilities have been established by private industry, like Bell Laboratories, by philanthropic corporations, like the Rockefeller Foundation, and, most of all, by national governments all over the world. They have changed our concept and mode of creativity. No longer needing to rely on experienced, gifted artisans tinkering in small shops, twentieth-century technology has systematized invention and promoted an increasing demand for ever more sophisticated and more expensive research facilities.

Synthetic fabrics and dyes have changed our wardrobes. Plastics have been the most important new, man-made material of the twentieth century and have replaced metals, rubber, and glass in innumerable uses. They have also increased the world's reliance on petroleum, a non-renewable fossil fuel, from which plastics are synthesized.

ENERGY

Twentieth-century technology has demanded ever-increasing supplies of inanimate energy. Among its most central symbols are the electric power generator, the internal-combustion engine, the hydroelectric dam, the oil well, and the nuclear reactor. Gaining access to energy resources has been a key issue for all countries. Some are richly endowed and begin with a large advantage. Others, such as Japan, have few energy resources and must find ways of seizing or buying them, or of tapping the natural energy of sun, wind and water, or of generating new forms of energy by unlocking the atom. Many countries of Western Europe have been seriously dependent on oil throughout the century, although they have other energy resources, especially coal, and are introducing new forms of more accessible energy. The United States, despite vast natural resources, has relied in large part on energy imports to build and support its economy.

Some countries, especially those in the Middle East, have fossil fuel energy resources (oil) far beyond their current needs. Because of the need for oil, the five countries in the world with the largest known crude oil reserves—Saudi Arabia, Iraq, the United Arab Emirates, Kuwait, and Iran—have all been subject to greater or lesser degrees of foreign competition for control and colonization.

Before the silicon chip. Immediately after World War II, when the first practical computers were constructed, advances in information theory and the invention of the transistor gave birth to such hulking monsters as ENIAC, developed at the University of Pennsylvania in 1946.

They are even now at the center of international power struggles for control of that oil wealth. Since 1973, they have banded together with other oil-rich member states of the Organization of Petroleum Exporting Countries (OPEC) to gain better economic terms and more political power for their oil, restructuring the terms of world trade and power in the process. The **geo-politics** of oil supply and demand have therefore been critical issues in twentieth-century history (see p. 691).

Atomic power was first developed for military uses, but it now also provides significant amounts of the world's commercial energy supply. Despite the ecological problems of safety and of nuclear waste disposal, the meltdown of the Russian nuclear reactor in Chernobyl, Ukraine, in 1986, and the near meltdown in 1979 of the American reactor at Three Mile Island in Pennsylvania, many countries continue to expand their nuclear generating capacities. In France, for example, 75 percent of electricity production is supplied by nuclear power.

The hunger for energy drives technological development and vice versa. The increasingly sophisticated technology generates increasing demands for investment capital and skilled personnel. These demands have forced increased educational requirements on labor forces everywhere, and sometimes have led to tensions and even violent competition among nations. The desire to be competitive technologically has, in part, fostered warfare; and much modern technology, in turn, is devoted to the design and production of arms.

WARFARE

Technology has altered our warfare and, conversely, military needs have driven technological development. The presence of new weapons systems has not, however, increased the feeling of human security, but rather has heightened a sense of insecurity, terror, and dread. Nuclear weapons and the delivery systems that make them a universal threat have left everyone, everywhere always aware of the possiblity—whether through intention or accident—of total destruction. Paradoxically, some would argue, the MAD (mutually assured destruction) balance of terror between the two superpowers of America and Russia kept them from war for four decades. Both countries have implemented encouraging, even startling, new programs for arms reductions, which have allayed at least some fears for the moment. Biological and chemical warfare also threaten unimaginable destruction, and the nations of the world negotiate to try to limit or ban them.

WORLD WAR

Two world wars dominated the first half of the twentieth century. Competition among nations over technological advances, productivity, and markets helped to instigate both conflicts. From the late eighteenth century, Britain's technological supremacy was unchallenged, and, from her position of industrial and military strength, she imposed a Pax Britannica, which kept the world safe from major war for more than half a century. By the turn of the century the United States had begun to catch up with, and even surpass, Britain, but distance and American isolationism muted the competition. As Germany also began to approach and surpass Britain in technological capacity, however, competition for industrial markets and prestige brought increasing tension.

WORLD WAR I
1914–18

This economic competition was embedded in still larger issues of nationalism, a powerful force in early twentieth-century Europe (see Chapter 17). People's reverence for their nation-states, and for their shared language, history, and ethnicity within those states, had become so passionate that they were willing to fight and die for them. Cynics argued that the masses of the population were being manipulated to the battle-front by industrialists in each country who stood to profit from war production, but the national feelings were powerful in themselves. Indeed they seemed strongest among smaller, newer states with little economic base in military production.

The more powerful nations also believed that their security could be strengthened by forming defensive alliances. In the closing decades of the nineteenth century these countries joined with their geographic or ideological neighbors to create a system of alliances which led in the early years of the twentieth century to a Europe divided into two potentially hostile camps—the Triple Alliance of Germany, Austria-Hungary, and Italy; and the Triple Entente of France, Russia, and Britain.

BUILD-UP AND EARLY EVENTS OF WORLD WAR I

1882	Triple Alliance among Italy, Germany, and Austria-Hungary
1891–1905	German Schlieffen Plan
1894	Formation of Franco-Russian alliance
1898	Germany starts building a High Seas Fleet, generating Anglo-German naval armaments race
1902	Anglo-Japanese Alliance
1904	Anglo-French Entente
1906	British launch *Dreadnought*, first all-big-gun battleship
1907	Anglo-Russian Entente
1911	Moroccan Crisis; tension between Germany and France over Morocco
1914:	
June	Serbian nationalist assassinates Archduke Ferdinand, heir to the Austro-Hungarian throne
July	Austria invades Serbia; Russia mobilizes and Germany declares war on Russia and France
August	Germany invades Belgium on way to France; Britain declares war on Germany; Battle of Tannenburg: Russia defeated by Germany
September	Battle of the Marne: Allies halt German advance on Paris; Russia retreats from east Prussia; All German colonies in Africa in Allied hands
Oct–Nov	First battle of Ypres: Allies lose more than 100,000 men, but Germans fail to reach Channel ports; Trench warfare (lasts till end of war); Turkey enters war on side of the Central Powers

World War I (called the Great War until World War II surpassed it in magnitude) began on June 28, 1914 when a Serbian nationalist, eager to gain from the Austro-Hungarian empire certain territories with heavily Serbian populations, assassinated Archduke Ferdinand, heir to the Austro-Hungarian throne. A month later, Austria-Hungary declared war on Serbia, triggering a domino effect among other European powers and the Ottoman Empire. Under the system of alliances built up over the preceding three decades, countries now came to the aid of one another. Russia mobilized its armies to defend Serbia. Germany declared war on Russia and France, and invaded Belgium. Britain declared war on Germany.

In November, the Ottoman Empire joined Germany and the Austro-Hungarian Empire in an alliance called the Central Powers. The British, French, and Russians on the other side formed an alliance called the Allied Powers (Allies). At the start of the war, the Central Powers won early victories in Belgium and Poland but in September the German advance was stopped by the Allies at the first Battle of the Marne. Along the western front the opposing armies then continued to fight in two facing trenches which stretched 500 miles (805 km) from the English Channel to the border of Switzerland. On the eastern front Russian armies lost over a million men in combat against the combined German and Austrian forces.

The United States stayed neutral until 1917, selling weapons and material to both sides. In 1917, with Russia in collapse, Germany turned its attention to the western front. To choke off American supplies to the British and French, Germany began intensive submarine warfare against American shipping. Germany gambled that the Allies would collapse before the United States responded—and lost. When German submarines began sinking unarmed passenger ships the United States decided to aid the Allies. Once the United States entered the war in April 1917, providing supplies and troops, the Allies moved toward victory. The fighting finally ended with an armistice in November 1918.

The war introduced new weapons. The machine gun, first used extensively in this war, and the tank, invented in 1914, helped define the nature of World War I. Hundreds of thousands of soldiers dug into trenches on each side, faced each other with very little movement for months at a time and then charged in human waves, in which tens and even hundreds of thousands were slaughtered by machine guns. In addition, Germany introduced poison gas in World War I, leading to subsequent international bans against its use, although it continues to be stored in the armories of many nations. Submarine warfare and aerial bombardment, initiated at the end of World War I, also marked the military campaigns. None of the combatants had expected a war like this, so long and so deadly. By its end a total of 10 million soldiers and civilians had been killed.

The victory of the Allies—primarily Britain, France, and America—over the Central Powers—Germany, the Austro-Hungarian Empire, and the Ottoman Empire—seemed at first to promise lasting peace in a new world order in which colonialism would give way to the independence of all national groups. The American President Woodrow Wilson declared that the goal of the Allies was to "make the world safe for democracy." The voices of all peoples should be heard. Allied war aims, as expressed by Wilson, called for:

> A free, open-minded, and absolutely impartial adjustment of all colonial claims, based upon a strict observance of the principle that in determining all such questions of sovereignty the interests of the population concerned must have equal weight with the equitable claims of the Government whose title is to be determined. (cited in Hofstadter, pp. 224–5)

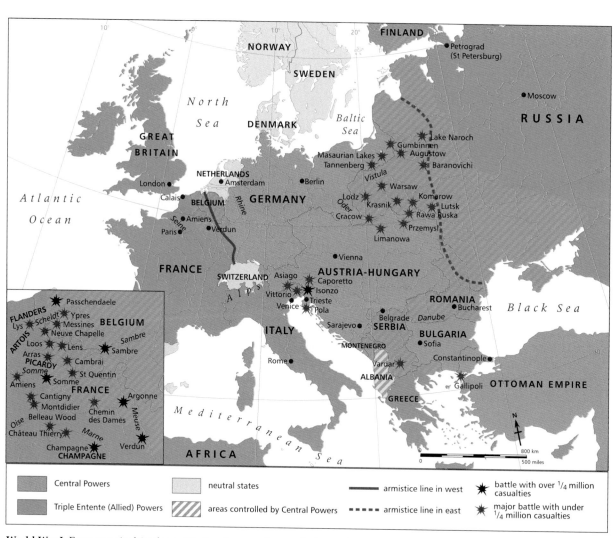

World War I European rivalries for political and economic superiority, within Europe and throughout its imperial holdings, erupted in 1914. A fragile system of alliances designed to contain the ambitions of Germany and Austria-Hungary (the Central Powers) collapsed, resulting in a conflict of horrific proportions. Turkey joined the Central Powers. In France and Italy a stalemate war of attrition developed, but in the east a war of thrust and counter-thrust caused enormous popular dissent and exhaustion, eventually bringing the collapse of the Turkish, Russian, and Austrian empires alike. In all, 10 million people died.

The Treaty of Versailles 1919

Many combatants came to the peace conference in Versailles, including Japan, an ally of Britain, that had seized Germany's possessions in East Asia during the war. Prince Faisal of Jordan represented Arabs who had contributed to victory over the Ottoman Empire. W.E.B. DuBois, an American scholar and political activist, called for social justice on behalf of the Pan-African Congress. In the end, the American, British, and French delegations were most critical to the post-war negotiations.

Two empires, the Austro-Hungarian and the Ottoman, were dissolved. Austria-Hungary was reduced and divided into two separate states. The Ottoman Empire disappeared; its core region in Anatolia and the city of Istanbul became the new nation of Turkey. From their former territories Poland, Czechoslovakia, and Yugoslavia were created; Romania and Greece were expanded. Syria and Lebanon were created as new proto-nations, temporarily **mandated** by the victors to France for tutelage until they could stand on their own independently; Palestine and Iraq were similarly created and mandated to Britain. The negotiators hoped the new borders would protect hostile ethnic groups from each other and from external domination. Legal safeguards for minorities were also enacted in new state constitutions.

Germany lost the region of Alsace-Lorraine to France, large areas in the east to Poland, and small areas to Czechoslovakia, Lithuania, Belgium, and Denmark. Germany was ordered to pay severe **reparations**, although in practice these were later negotiated to more realistic levels. Most gallingly for Germany, it was forced to accept responsibility for causing all the loss and damage of the war. Germany left Versailles humiliated, resentful, but, despite the loss of lands and the financial reparations, potentially still very powerful.

Life in the trenches. World War I became notorious for its trench warfare, in which combatants dug themselves into positions but made few territorial gains. The horrifying drudgery, the cold, the wet, the shelling, the nervous tension, the smell of corpses and mustard gas lasted for years. By 1918, the end of the conflict, around 8 million soldiers had lost their lives.

WAR EXPERIENCES
SUBVERT COLONIALISM

*C*olonial powers employed their colonial armies in fighting both World Wars, transporting them from one battle front to another. Military service overseas often transformed the soldiers, making them skeptical of the advantages of European civilization. Some European soldiers came to realize that at least some of the people they colonized did not respect them but rather feared and hated them. A young journalist from India, serving briefly as a World War I correspondent in Iraq, wrote of his growing realization of the resentment Arabs felt for British colonization. He saw Arab women in particular transmitting their resentment by asserting their religious and cultural conventions. He began to understand more fully the opposition to colonialism that both peoples shared:

We understood ... that in the entire region Arabs regarded the English as their enemies. Bitter antagonism dripped from their eyes. They moved about like lost undertakers, joking among themselves but stopping the moment they saw the British. They talked with the foreigners mechanically, speaking only when it was completely unavoidable. They took their few cents in pay, and otherwise behaved like defeated and dependent enemies. Their dignified women hid themselves in burkhas, which covered them from head to foot. The white soldiers must have sensed their independent temper, however, and therefore their military superiors issued strict orders not to talk with the local women. (Yagnik, p. 262, translated from the Gujarati by Devavrat Pathak and Howard Spodek.)

The League of Nations was founded by the European powers in 1920 in the hope of eliminating warfare and fostering international cooperation. But disillusionment soon followed. The League was crippled by two congenital defects. First, its principal sponsor, the United States, refused to join. The world's most powerful technological, industrial, financial, and military power, the United States withdrew back into the isolation of its ocean defenses.

Second, the League reneged on its promise to end European colonialism in Asia and Africa. On the contrary, the peace treaty written in Versailles in 1919 perpetuated and enlarged foreign colonial rule through the grant of mandatory powers to Britain and France over Middle Eastern lands conquered from the Ottoman Empire and to Britain and others over Chinese lands previously held by Germany. In India, the British fell short on their wartime promise to expand self-rule and instead restricted freedoms of the press and assembly. The League died completely when it failed to counter Italy's invasion of Ethiopia, Germany's re-armament, and the outbreak of the Spanish Civil War in 1936. The war in Spain, 1936–9, saw right-wing insurgent forces led by General Francisco Franco, supported by troops dispatched by Germany and Italy, overthrow the liberal constitutional government, which received little organized support from democratic countries. Many analysts saw this confrontation, which turned Spain into a dictatorship for a generation, as a dress rehearsal for World War II. President Woodrow Wilson's visionary goal of making the world safe for democracy was deferred indefinitely.

ECONOMIC DEPRESSION BETWEEN THE WARS 1920–39 AND THE EXPANSION OF THE WELFARE STATE

Worldwide economic depression in the 1920s further destabilized domestic and international politics. Depression is a severe economic downturn in production and consumption which continues over a significant period of time, at least several months. Depression was considered normal in a free market economy as the forces of supply and demand periodically fell out of step and then came back into line. But the Great Depression was far more extreme in its extent and duration. On October 24, 1929—"Black Thursday"—the New York stock exchange crashed, ending five years of relative prosperity and marking the beginning of a worldwide economic depression which would continue until the outbreak of World War II in 1939.

The United States had emerged from World War I as a creditor nation. The payment of reparations from the war had crippled the German economy and a less rigorous schedule of payments was negotiated. It depended on loans from several nations, especially the United States. With the crash of the stock market, however, American financiers called in these loans, undercutting the European economy. In addition, agriculture, which had produced at record levels during the war, had difficulty cutting back production, resulting in huge, unsold surpluses and a depression in agriculture. In times of such economic difficulty, each country, and especially the United States, acted to close its borders to imports so that it could sell its own products internally without competition. But as each country raised its barriers, international markets dwindled, increasing the depression.

Mass unemployment swept Britain, America and Germany. Latin American countries, notably Argentina, which had been approaching a European living standard, found their economies devastated, turned away from European economic connections, and sought to salvage what they could through domestic development (see pp. 756–7). Communist Russia, also standing somewhat apart from the world economy, had introduced centralized national planning in 1928, emphasizing heavy industrialization. Its economy flourished, mocking the capitalist economies locked in depression (see pp. 614–19).

In 1921 there had been 2 million unemployed in Britain. They collected unemployment insurance in accord with an act that had been passed a decade earlier. The government also implemented an old age pension system, medical aids, and subsidized housing. But the world depression increased this unemployment to almost 3 million. Unemployment payments multiplied, while tax collections dropped. The welfare state expanded and government remained stable, but the depression ground on.

America, the country most dedicated to private capitalism and "rugged individualism," and therefore most reluctant to expand government social

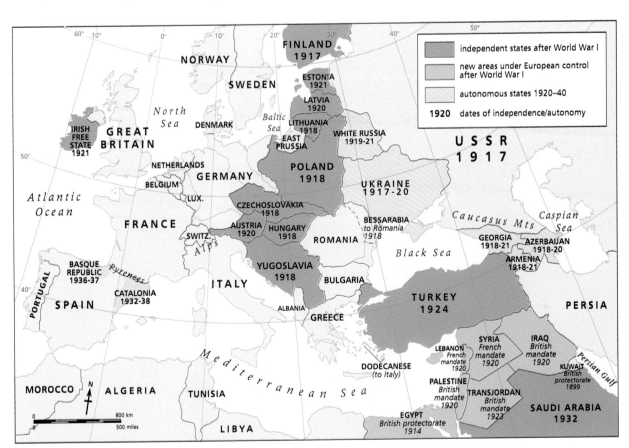

The new post-war nations In the wake of World War I, old empires fell and new states and colonies (called mandates and protectorates) were created. The Austro-Hungarian and Ottoman Empires were eradicated. A belt of nation states was established throughout Central and Eastern Europe; some had very brief lives and were soon annexed by Russia. The core of the Ottoman Empire became Turkey, while other segments were mandated to Britain and France as quasi-colonies.

welfare programs, saw national income drop by half between 1929 and 1932. Almost 14 million people were unemployed. Elected in 1932, in the midst of national despair, Democratic President Franklin Delano Roosevelt rallied the nation with charismatic optimism. Declaring that "The only thing we have to fear is fear itself," he immediately instituted social welfare programs as a means of preserving the capitalist foundation. He provided financial relief for the unemployed, public works projects to create construction jobs, subsidies to farmers to reduce production and eliminate surpluses, and federal support for low-cost housing and slum clearance. A Civilian Conservation Corps was established, ostensibly to promote conservation and reforestation, but mostly to provide some 3 million jobs to youth. The Tennessee Valley Authority created an immense hydroelectric program, combining flood control with rural electrification and regional economic development.

Roosevelt increased the regulation of business and promoted unions. The Securities and Exchange Commission, created in 1929, regulated the stock exchange. The National Recovery Administration encouraged regulation of prices and production until it was judged unconstitutional in 1935. The Social Security Act of 1935 introduced unemployment, old age, and disability insurance—policies already in place in Western Europe well before World War I. Child labor was abolished. Forty hours of work was set as the weekly norm. Minimum hourly wages were fixed. Union organization was encouraged and union membership grew from 4 million in 1929 to 9 million in 1940. The most capitalist of the major powers thus accepted the welfare state. Throughout the century, the scope of welfare expanded and contracted with different governments, philosophies of government, and budgetary conditions, but the principle that the state had a major role in protecting and advancing the welfare of its people persisted.

In Germany, the world depression followed on the heels of catastrophic inflation. In the 1920s the payment of very expensive war reparations wiped out the savings of the middle classes and amplified resentment over the punitive Versailles treaty, including its emphasis on German war guilt and insistence on Germany's disarmament. By 1924 industrial production had recovered but then the Depression wiped out the gains. The new government, located at Weimar, was perceived by many as a noble but weak and precarious experiment in constitutional democracy in a nation that had been led into war by a monarchy. Exciting new movements in art and architecture that were responsive to new technological potential for creativity, notably the Bauhaus, were threatened and ultimately driven out of the country. Anti-democratic forces and political ideologies triumphed over aesthetic and cultural creativity.

FDR's New Deal. "This nation asks for action, and action now." Thus President Franklin D. Roosevelt launched his New Deal in March 1933 in an effort to beat the Depression. Bringing banks and industry under state control, Congress set up the National Recovery Administration to oversee works programs, like this road-widening scheme in New York. Some 13 million Americans were unemployed when FDR took office.

WORLD WAR II 1939–45

The strains of the 1930s ultimately triggered World War II. Germany, Italy, and Japan all sought to alleviate the suffering of the Depression by building up armaments and seeking new conquests. In Germany, Adolf Hitler (1889–1945) led a new party, the National Socialists, or Nazis. The party used strong-arm tactics to cow the opposition, but finally came to power legally on a platform of extreme nationalism, construction of public works, expansionism, and virulent anti-Semitism, all of which Hitler had spelled out in his manifesto, *Mein Kampf, "My Struggle."* Some business and military leaders supported him as a counter-weight to communism. As leader of the largest party in the German parliament in 1933, Hitler became Chancellor. He acted quickly to suppress all other parties, to revoke citizenship from Jews, and to arm Germany. He intensified each of these programs over the next few years and in 1936 he moved troops into the Rhineland (the region around the Rhine River) in violation of the Versailles Treaty. In 1938 Hitler invaded the German-speaking areas of Czechoslovakia. On September 1, 1939 he invaded Poland, and finally met resistance from the great powers who until this time had appeased his aggressions. Britain and France declared war.

In Italy, Benito Mussolini (1883–1945) had become prime minister in 1921 as leader of a party of 300,000 members who threatened to march on Rome if he were not appointed. His party was called fascist, meaning that it represented extreme nationalism, the power of the state over the individual, the supremacy of the leader over the party and nation, and a willingness to use intimidation and violence to achieve his goals:

> War alone brings up to its highest tension all human energy and puts the stamp of nobility upon the peoples who have the courage to meet it. … Thus a doctrine which is founded upon this harmful postulate of peace is hostile to Fascism … all the international leagues and societies … as history will show, can be scattered to the winds when once strong national feeling is aroused by any motive. (Columbia College, p. 1151)

In 1935, preceding Hitler's moves, Mussolini invaded and took over Ethiopia while other nations sat by and did not act, not even by closing the Suez Canal to Italy's troops. Mussolini did not share Hitler's anti-Semitism, but in many other respects

WORLD WAR II—KEY EVENTS

July 7, 1937	Japanese troops invade China
September 1939	Nazi-Soviet Pact: Germany invades Poland. Britain and France declare war. Poland partitioned between Germany and Russia
Mar–Apr 1940	German forces conquer Denmark, Norway, the Netherlands, and Belgium
May–June	Italy declares war on Britain and France; German forces conquer France
June 21, 1941	German forces invade USSR
Dec 7	Japanese bomb US Navy, Pearl Harbor
Jan-Mar 1942	Indonesia, Malaya, Burma and the Philippines are conquered by Japan
April 1942	US planes bomb Tokyo
June	US Navy defeats Japanese at the Battle of the Midway
1942–43	End of Axis resistance in North Africa; Soviet victory in Battle of Stalingrad
1943–44	Red Army slowly pushes Wehrmacht back to Germany
June 6, 1944	Allies land in Normandy (D-Day)
Feb 1945	Yalta conference: Churchill, Roosevelt, and Stalin discuss post-war settlement
May 7, 1945	Germany surrenders
August 6	US drops atom bomb on Hiroshima, Japan, and then on Nagasaki
August 14	Japan surrenders

he was an appropriate junior partner in Hitler's aggressive plans. When civil war broke out in Spain in 1936, both Hitler and Mussolini sent assistance to the right-wing Nationalists. At this point their two nations formed an alliance called the Axis.

In East Asia, as we shall see in the next chapter, Japan also moved aggressively against its neighbor, China. Following the successes of the Meiji Restoration (see p. 564), Japan had become the strongest military power in East Asia, and had cultivated political philosophies to justify invading and taking over neighboring countries. Like Germany, it too had a rapidly rising population, reaching 62 million by 1928, and felt confined. Japan needed to import most of its raw materials but it was technologically more sophisticated than its neighbors. In 1931, Japanese military forces seized Manchuria. The Japanese government had forbidden this action, but acquiesced after the fact. The League of Nations condemned the invasion but imposed no real sanctions, and the condemnation moved Japan to ally with Germany and Italy. In 1937 Japan invaded China, and the Pacific War, as the Japanese call World War II, had begun (see p. 630). Japan became a member of the Axis powers from December 1941.

Until Germany's invasion of Poland the democratic nations which had been victorious in World War I had observed all these separate aggressions and done nothing. The League of Nations had collapsed in the wake of Italy's invasion of Ethiopia. England and France had acquiesced in all of Germany's earlier moves. America had retreated to isolation. These nations had not caused World War II, but by their inaction they had done nothing to prevent it. After their declaration of war, France

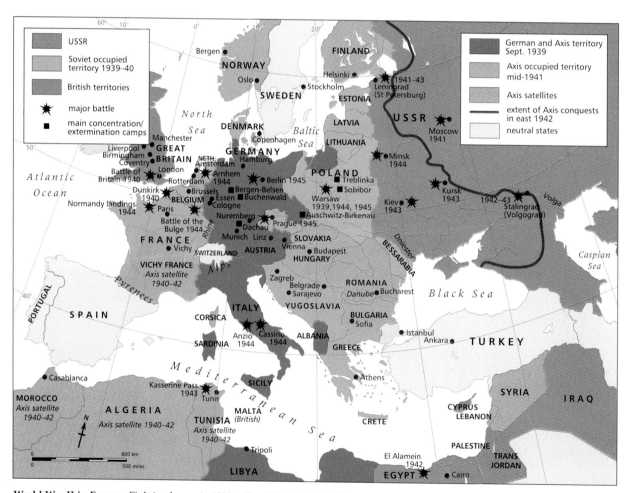

World War II in Europe Fighting began in 1939 with a "blitzkrieg," or lightning war, by Germany and her Italian ally. By late 1942 they controlled most of Europe. But Germany's invasion of Russia in 1941 brought the power of that huge state into opposition and enmeshed Germany into exhausting land war. Britain held out defensively and then began to fight back, especially after the United States entered the war, bringing in air power and material support. By early 1944, the tide had turned.

Nazi Party rally. Over 750,000 Nazi Party workers, soldiers, and civilians greeted Adolf Hitler at the 1934 Nuremberg conference. Against the backdrop of a giant swastika, the German chancellor proclaimed that the Third Reich would last for the next thousand years. Ironically, the trial of Nazi war criminals by the victorious Allied powers would take place in the same city eleven years later.

and Britain took no immediate military action against Germany and a brief period of "phony war" followed during the winter of 1939-40. In April 1940 Hitler again went on the offensive and Germany invaded Denmark and Norway. On May 10 it invaded Belgium and advanced into France. Allied forces were evacuated from France at the end of May and on June 22 the French signed an armistice with Germany. Germany now turned its attention to Britain, and heavy bombing of London and other strategic cities in England took place throughout the autumn.

From Europe the war spread to Africa and by 1942 Germany and its allies had conquered most of western and central Europe, almost half of European Russia and much of north Africa. Battles took place on sea, land, and in the air. As the war progressed the Grand Alliance of Britain, the Free French (an exile government based in London), and the Soviet Union slowly evolved. With the Japanese bombing of the American naval base in Pearl Harbor in December 1941, America entered the war sending combat forces to both Europe and the Pacific. America also joined the other powers of the Grand Alliance (and the larger coalition of twenty other countries) to defeat the Axis powers, and the war in Europe finally ended at the beginning of

May 1945 with the fall of Berlin and the German collapse in Italy and on the Western Front. In the Pacific the United States dropped an atomic bomb on the city of Hiroshima, Japan, on August 6 and three days later another atomic bomb on the city of Nagasaki (see p. 634). On August 14 Japan surrendered and the Pacific war was also over.

World War II is called a "total war" because it involved more nations than had ever before engaged in armed combat and destroyed large numbers of both military and civilians. It is estimated that about 45 million people died—30 million of them civilians. The heaviest fighting was in the Soviet Union and it lost more people than any other country—around 20 million. Japan lost about 2 million people and Germany just over 4 million. Britain lost 400,000 people and the United States about 300,000. Over 6 million Jews died in Nazi concentration camps.

Technology in the War

World War II witnessed a dramatic increase in the use of technology—tanks, submarines, and aircraft—as well as the number of troops. Winston Churchill (1874–1965), prime minister of Britain, captured the significance of this increase in a broadcast to America. After commanding the Battle of Britain, in which the Royal Air Force, aided by the newly invented radar, defended Britain against the bombing runs of Germany's Luftwaffe (airforce), he requested equipment and technology: "Give us the tools and we shall finish the job."

The mobilization of so many personnel and so much equipment opened new visions of life. People who served overseas and who saw for the first time new modes of life, as well as death, were changed in the process. Most affected by the process were women. The demands of keeping factories running full blast during the war while putting millions of soldiers under arms required a larger labor force. During World War I millions of women began to work outside the home for pay, and the stereotypes of "men's work" and "women's work" started to erode. This experience contributed to the achievement of women's suffrage in the United States after World War I and in Western Europe after World War II. After World War I the majority of women did not remain in the workforce, but after World

War II women continued in unprecedented numbers to work in industrial and unconventional jobs. The mobilization of women was, however, culturally specific: German and Japanese women were encouraged to continue to stay at home, despite the exigencies of war; women served actively in Russian factories; Britain conscripted some women in World War II.

Horrors of the War

Two horrors distinguished World War II from all others that came before. Massive warfare had been known before. So too had individual leaders setting out to conquer the known world, from Alexander and Genghis Khan to Napoleon. But the decision by the ruling National Socialist (Nazi) party of Germany to obliterate an entire people—the Jews—from the world, without any ostensible economic or territorial goal, and mobilizing the full resources of the state against the unarmed opponent to carry out the task, constituted a new goal, one executed by new technology.

Anti-Semitism was not new in Europe, but the Nazi program was unprecedented. First, it reversed the trend of acceptance and civic equality introduced a century and a half earlier by the French Revolution. Second, it targeted Jews as an ethnic or racial group rather than as a religion. This was not a policy for conversion or even for exile. Anyone with a Jewish grandparent was considered Jewish under Nazi laws and marked for death.

Although born of an Austrian father and raised in Vienna, Adolf Hitler, the leader of Germany, declared the "Aryan" Germans at the top and the Jews at the bottom of a hierarchy that included the British and other northern Europeans near the top, Poles and other Slavs in the middle, and Africans and other peoples of color near the bottom. Intending to exterminate these "lesser peoples," he built concentration camps where prisoners were used as slave labor before being gassed and cremated. Millions of Jews were brought to the camps by a railway network specially constructed for this

"Rosie the Riveter," symbol of World War II American women workers, on a poster from the War Production Co-ordinating Committee.

purpose. Even in the closing days of the war, when Germany clearly had been defeated, Hitler ordered the trains and the crematoria to continue operations. By 1945, some 6 million Jews accompanied by millions from other "inferior" races, especially gypsies and Poles, joined also by homosexuals and handicapped people, had been murdered. The Holocaust, as this butchery was named, made World War II into a conflict of good versus evil even in the eyes of many Germans after the war. The moral crisis and the appalling devastation of the Holocaust are impossible to fully comprehend, but the writing of survivors such as Elie Wiesel (see p. 597) helps us to understand them. (See also the importance of the Holocaust experience in the founding of the State of Israel on p. 701.)

The atomic bombs dropped by America on Hiroshima and Nagasaki, Japan, introduced a new weapon ultimately capable of destroying all life on earth, changing both the nature of war and peace as well as humanity's conception of itself. At the first test of the bomb, as the fireball rose over the Alamogordo, New Mexico, testing grounds, J. Robert Oppenheimer, appalled architect of the bomb and director of the $2 billion Manhattan Project that produced it, quoted from the Hindu *Bhagavad Gita*: "I am become as death, the destroyer of worlds." Of the 245,000 people living in Hiroshima on 6 August, 75,000 died that day, perhaps another 100,000 thereafter, while still others suffered various kinds of radiation poisoning and genetic deformation. Three days later, a second bomb was dropped on Nagasaki, and on 14 August Japan submitted its unconditional surrender. Today, despite years of continuing efforts towards arms control, there are tens of thousands of nuclear bombs and warheads on missiles, submarines, and airplanes capable of destroying human life many times over.

In retrospect, debate has raged over the wisdom and purpose of using the atomic bomb to end the war in the Pacific. Critics see the act as racist, pointing out that this weapon was not used in Europe (although the bomb was not prepared by the time

The liberation of Belsen. Shocked British soldiers liberating Belsen concentration camp in 1945 found 40,000 Jews and other victims of the Holocaust dying of starvation, typhus, and tuberculosis. Many prisoners had been used for medical experiments. Framed by an open grave, a Dr Klein is shown speaking to Movietone News. His experiments included injecting benzine into his victims to harden their arteries. He was responsible for thousands of deaths.

Germany surrendered in May, 1945). Cynics suggest that its real purpose had less to do with defeating Japan than with demonstrating American power to Russia on the eve of the Cold War (see p. 602). Those who justify the use of the bomb suggest that losses of life on both sides would have been higher had the Allies invaded Japan's home islands instead. The casualties in the battles for Pacific Islands had been in the hundreds of thousands, and war in Japan itself might cost a million more Allied troops and even more Japanese. The use of the bomb certainly saved Allied lives, and even may have saved Japanese lives. Finally, they argue, in a war of such scope and brutality, combatants inevitably use the weapons that are available.

Some of the war technology had by-products of use to civilians as well. Radar, which Britain developed to protect its island kingdom from Germany in the Battle of Britain, 1940, was valuable in commercial aviation. Nuclear energy could be employed under careful supervision for peaceful uses in power generation and medicine. Drugs, such as sulfa and penicillin, entered the civilian pharmacopeia. But the technology of warfare drew the lion's share of the scientific and technological budgets of many nations, including the largest industrial powers, the USA and USSR, and of many developing countries, as well.

Following World War II, the temporary alliance between the United States, Britain, and France on the one hand and the Soviet Union on the other completely shattered. A period of "cold war" began (see p. 602), ending only in 1991 with the break-up of the Soviet Union (see Chapter 19).

Bombers on a raid. By World War II aircraft of all kinds were poised for aerial combat. Here an SAAF/BAF Beaufighter fires three-inch RPs during an attack on German positions in the Yugoslavian town of Zuzemberg in 1945. The astronomical cost of bombs and aircraft contributed to the Allies' wartime expenditure of $57,000 million.

The division of Europe between the western, democratic, capitalist or mixed-economy states and the eastern states under communist governments ended. A new re-unification of Europe had already begun in the late 1980s as many of the USSR's satellite states in eastern Europe became independent. In 1990 East and West Germany were reunified. As the Cold War had siphoned enormous amounts of money and creative energy into military concerns, so the end of the Cold War promised to make more funds and energies available for peaceful uses.

THE LEVIATHAN STATE

THE MILITARY STATE

The twentieth century invested the nation-state itself with unprecedented powers. War was often

the justification. Conscription (the draft) gave governments the power to send soldiers off to war and possible death. During the years of World War I the Allies mobilized 40,700,000 people, the Central Powers 25,100,000; of these 10 million were killed. In World War II, the Allies mobilized 62 million men and women, the Axis powers 30 million; in the war, 16 million soldiers were killed, and approximately 30 million civilians died.

In warfare the state took over increasing control of the economy and technology, and bureaucracies mushroomed. Total war expenditures of the Allies in World War I (in 1913 dollars) was $57,700 million; of the Central Powers, $24,700 million. The state determined levels of production, the allocation of raw materials, rationing of consumer goods, including food, and the regulation of international trade. To pay for the war, states sold huge bond issues, which bound them for years with unprecedented levels of debt. They further destabilized their economies by printing money. The available technologies of communication were commandeered for spreading government propaganda, both officially and unofficially. The press, the movies, and the public schools told the government's side of the war, and did not report that of the enemy. Governments in this way limited the freedom of speech.

World War II, much greater in scope, repeated and intensified the administrative experiences of 1914–18, and increased the powers of government still more. Total costs of the war were estimated at $1,150,000,000,000. The Cold War, sometimes breaking into regional, localized "hot wars" on the territory of subordinate allies—as in Korea, 1950–54; Vietnam, 1954–75; and Ethiopia, Angola, and Mozambique in the 1980s—demanded enormous expenditures and continued the relentless build-up of state power.

People everywhere were alarmed by such a massive concentration of power in the military. In his 1961 farewell address as President of the United States, Dwight Eisenhower, a five-star general who had served as Supreme Commander of Allied Forces in Europe during World War II, now warned his nation against dangers of the "military industrial complex:"

> In the councils of government, we must guard against the acquisition of unwarranted influence, whether sought or unsought, by the military-industrial complex. The potential for the disastrous rise of misplaced power exists and will persist. We must never let the weight of this combination endanger our liberties or democratic processes. We should take nothing for granted. Only an alert and knowledgeable citizenry can compel the proper meshing of the huge industrial and military machinery of defense with our peaceful methods and goals, so that security and liberty may prosper together. (cited in Johnson, p. 424)

Eisenhower's warning went unheeded. The military build-up continued. Military expansion and the concomitant expansion of the state after World War II proceeded, proportionately, even more rapidly in the less developed nations in Latin America, Asia, and Africa. While public expenditures for the military doubled in the **developed world** of North America and Europe from $385

DEFENSE EXPENDITURE*						
	USA	USSR	China	Germany	UK	Japan
1930	.699	.722	–	.162	.512	.218
1938	1.13	5.43	–	7.41	1.86	1.74
1950	14.5	15.5	2.5	–	2.3	–
1970	77.8	72.0	23.7	6.1	5.8	1.3
1987	293.2	274.7	13.4	34.1	31.5	24.2

* In billions of current dollars

Defense expenditure. Fueled by the 1945–49 conflict and the Cold War, massive expenditure by the USA and USSR on military hardware has kept them neck and neck. But the new trend, since 1960, has been the rapid militarization of the developing nations.

billion in 1960 to $789 billion in 1988, in the **developing world**, they multiplied almost five times from $28 billion to $134 billion. Between 1960 and 1988 the number of soldiers in the developing nations rose from 8 million to 16.5 million, though in the developed nations it remained stationary at 10 million.

THE IMAGE OF HUMANITY

Until the eve of World War I, the Western idea of human progress through rationalism, science, and technological progress had been widely accepted. There had been no major international war since the 1871 conflict between France and Germany, and even that had been relatively small and contained (although 250,000 people died). Democracy seemed both progressive and in the ascendant. Life expectancy and quality seemed steadily improving.

The dominance of Europe over ancient Asian and African civilizations had the effect of reaffirming Europeans' belief in the supremacy of their technology and political systems, the "White Man's Burden," and *mission civilisatrice.* Students from all over the world were coming to Europe's universities to study Western sciences and arts. If machines were "the measure of man," European civilization measured best of all, and was still pulling away from the competition.

Some contrary voices, however, were already breaking through the self-congratulation. Mohandas Gandhi (1869–1948) of India, writing in 1906, caricatured and re-evaluated Western accomplishments from a different perspective.

> Formerly when people wanted to fight with one another, they measured between them their bodily strength; now it is possible to take away thousands of lives by one man working behind a gun from a hill. This is civilization. Formerly, men worked in the open air only as much as they liked. Now thousands of workmen meet together and for the sake of maintenance work in factories or mines. Their condition is worse than that of beasts. They are obliged to work, at the risk of their lives, at most dangerous occupations, for the sake of millionaires. Formerly, men were made slaves under physical compulsion. Now they are enslaved by temptations of money and of the luxuries that money can buy. ... This civilization takes note neither of morality nor of religion. Its votaries calmly state that their business is not to teach

religion. Some even consider it to be a superstitious growth. Others put on the cloak of religion, and prate about morality. ... Civilization seeks to increase bodily comforts, and it fails miserably even in doing so. ... This civilization is such that one has only to be patient and it will be self-destroyed. (Gandhi).

New, non-representational, or abstract, art also seemed to question the significance of rationality. The most innovative and honored of its creators, Pablo Picasso (1881–1973), drew from African "primitive" art in creating new forms of his own. Through these African-inspired innovations, he demonstrated that the technologically oriented West had much to learn from the more naturalistic and spiritual cultures that they dominated politically, economically, and militarily.

At about the same time in Vienna, in the heart of central Europe itself, Sigmund Freud's (1856–1939) new study of psychoanalysis ascribed humanity's most profound moving force not to rationality, the pride of European science and technology, but to sexuality. He argued that people did not understand their own deepest drives; these were hidden in the unconscious. He, too, questioned the ability of European civilization to survive:

> There are two tenets of psychoanalysis which offend the whole world and excite its resentment ... The first of these displeasing propositions of psychoanalysis is this: that mental processes are essentially unconscious . ... [the] next proposition consists in the assertion that ... sexual impulses have contributed invaluably to the highest cultural, artistic, and social achievements of the human mind. ... Society can conceive of no more powerful menace to its culture than would arise from the liberation of the sexual impulses and a return of them to their original goal. (*General Introduction*, pp. 25–7)

World War I confirmed the apprehensions of these critics. Freud feared for human life itself, and questioned its meaning and direction. In 1930 he wrote:

> During the last few generations mankind has made an extraordinary advance in the natural sciences and in their technical application and has established his control over nature in a way never before imagined. ... But ... this subjugation of the forces of nature, which is the fulfilment of a longing that goes back thousands of years, has not increased the amount of pleasurable satisfaction which they may expect

from life and has not made them feel happier. (*Civilization*, p. 34–5)

He saw a great struggle between Eros and Thanatos, Love and Death, and remained apprehensive about the future results:

Men have gained control over the forces of nature to such an extent that with their help they would have no difficulty in exterminating one another to the last man. They know this, and hence comes a large part of their current unrest, their unhappiness and their mood of anxiety. And now it is to be expected that the other of the two "Heavenly Powers," Eternal Eros, will make an effort to assert himself in the struggle with his equally immortal adversary. But who can foresee with what success and with what result? (*Civilization*, pp. 34–5)

Voices of despair multiplied. Consider "The Second Coming," written in 1921 shortly after World War I and the Russian Revolution (see pp. 612–14) by the Irish poet and playwright William Butler Yeats (1865–1939):

Turning and turning in the widening gyre
The falcon cannot hear the falconer;
Things fall apart; the centre cannot hold;
Mere anarchy is loosed upon the world,
The blood-dimmed tide is loosed, and everywhere
The ceremony of innocence is drowned;
The best lack all conviction, while the worst
Are full of passionate intensity.

Yeats held out hope no longer in rationality, nor in science, nor in progress, but rather in mystical religious experience:

Surely some revelation is at hand;
Surely the Second Coming is at hand.

His only hope was for an unknown, very different future, no continuation of twentieth-century ways, and he, too, closed in speculation:

And what rough beast, its hour come round at last,
Slouches towards Bethlehem to be born?
(cited in Wilkie and Hurt, p. 1655)

With the far greater destruction of World War II and its atomic bombs and programs of genocide, humanity apparently touched rock bottom. At the age of twelve, in 1941, Elie Wiesel had immersed himself in the practices of **chasidic**, orthodox, devotional Judaism in Sighet, Hungary, and in answer to the question, "Why do you pray?" he had replied, "Why did I pray? A strange question. Why did I live? Why did I breathe?" But in 1944, after three years in a Nazi-built ghetto, he arrived in Birkenau, the gateway to Auschwitz, the hungriest of the concentration camps.

Not far from us, flames were leaping up from a ditch, gigantic flames. They were burning something. A lorry drew up at the pit and delivered its load—little children. Babies! Yes, I saw it—saw it with my own eyes … those children in the flames. (Is it surprising that I could not sleep after that? Sleep had fled my eyes.)
So this was where we were going. A little farther on was another and larger ditch for adults.
I pinched my face. Was I still alive? Was I awake? I could not believe it. How could it be possible for them to burn people, children, and for the world to keep silent? No, none of this could be true. It was a nightmare.

Wiesel soon becomes aware of someone reciting the Kaddish, the Jewish prayer for the dead.

For the first time, I felt revolt rise up in me. Why should I bless His name? The Eternal, Lord of the Universe, the All-Powerful and Terrible, was silent. What had I to thank Him for?

Long-cherished images of humanity and of the gods it had held sacred perished in the holocaust. Yet Wiesel somehow found the courage to make of his experiences in the death camps the stuff of literature and the basis of a new morality:

Never shall I forget that night, the first night in camp, which has turned my life into one long night, seven times cursed and seven times sealed. Never shall I forget that smoke. Never shall I forget the little faces of the children, whose bodies I saw turned into wreaths of smoke beneath a silent blue sky.
Never shall I forget those flames which consumed my faith forever.
Never shall I forget that nocturnal silence which deprived me, for all eternity, of the desire to live. Never shall I forget those moments which murdered my God and my soul and turned my dreams to dust. Never shall I forget these things, even if I am condemned to live as long as God Himself. Never. (*Night*, pp. 41–3)

SPOTLIGHT

Icons of War

Twentieth-century wars have been the bloodiest in history. Ten million civilians and soldiers died in World War I; forty-five million in World War II; tens of millions more in local wars and civil wars, conventional wars and guerrilla wars, around the globe. Weapons of mass destruction have multiplied in number and power, including lethal gas, chemical and germ weapons, as well as nuclear weapons, which threaten all human existence.

How can an artist desiring peace focus world attention on the destructiveness of these weapons? Pablo Picasso (1881–1973), probably the twentieth century's most influential painter, faced this problem after German squadrons supporting the royalist side in the Spanish Civil War (1936–39) carried out the first aerial bombardment against unarmed civilians in history at the unprotected Basque village of Guernica on April 28, 1937. Picasso replied with *Guernica* (**picture 1**), a painting in black and white depicting the anguish, pain, and suffering of men, women, children, and animals. The exact symbolism is not entirely clear even today, but the vision of terror includes a fallen warrior, a despairing woman carrying a wounded child, maimed individuals, and a horse writhing in agony. From the moment of its creation in 1937, *Guernica* has commanded a unique position in anti-war protest. The republican Spanish government immediately displayed the painting in its official pavilion at the Paris International Exhibition of 1938 to call for support against the opposition royalist forces and their German allies. After the royalist–fascist forces won the

Picture 1 Pablo Picasso, *Guernica*, 1937.

Picture 2 Children fleeing from Trang Bang, South Vietnam, June 8, 1972.

civil war, Picasso refused to allow the picture to hang in Spain. It was placed in the Prado Museum in Madrid only after the fall of Francisco Franco's fascist government in 1975.

Picasso brought a single remote air attack to global attention. By contrast, during the American involvement in the war in Vietnam, a multitude of photo-journalists captured the horror vividly and transmitted it around the world instantaneously. Perhaps the most wrenching image to emerge from the fighting—one that had a critical influence in turning Western opinion against America's involvement in the conflict—came from Trang Bang village, when an accidental napalm bombing forced residents to flee, and a little girl was photographed running away from the flames, naked, her flesh burning (**picture 2**).

The atomic bomb posed a new problem for human comprehension. Hiroshima (see p. 600) and Nagasaki revealed the destructiveness of its explosive power and poisonous radiation. **Picture 3**, from an atomic test in the Marshall Islands in 1950, ignores those bitter realities for a moment, glorifying in the bomb's awesome power and even beauty. It recalls the subtitle of Stanley Kubrick's brilliant anti-war film *Dr. Strangelove: or How I Learned to Stop Worrying and Love the Bomb* (1964).

Picture 3 Atom bomb test in the Marshall Islands, 1950.

To transmit this horrible personal history, to warn humanity of its own destructiveness, and to proclaim the need to preserve life became Wiesel's consuming passion. The award of the Nobel Peace Prize in 1986 recognized his mission.

From Japan, which suffered from the world's first and only nuclear explosions used in war, came similar meditations of anguish and despair, followed later by a commitment to prevent such catastrophe in the future. A student in Hiroshima Women's Junior College, Artsuko Tsujioka, remembered the atomic attack on her city in which 78,000 people were killed instantaneously and tens of thousands lingered on to die later or to be misshapen and genetically damaged from the persistent radiation:

> It happened instantaneously. I felt as if my back had been struck with a big hammer, and then as if I had been thrown into boiling oil. … That first night ended. … My friends and the other people were no longer able to move. The skin had peeled off of their burned arms, legs and backs. I wanted to move them, but there was no place on their bodies that I could touch … I still have the scars from that day; on my head, face, arms, legs and chest. There are reddish black scars on my arms and the face that I see in the mirror does not look as if it belongs to me. It always saddens me to think that I will never look the way I used to. I lost all hope at first. I was obsessed with the idea that I had become a freak and did not want to be seen by anyone. I cried constantly for my good friends and kind teachers who had died in such a terrible way.
>
> My way of thinking became warped and pessimistic. Even my beautiful voice, that my friends had envied, had turned weak and hoarse. When I think of the way it was then, I feel as if I were being strangled. But I have been able to take comfort in the thought that physical beauty is not everything, that a beautiful spirit can do away with physical ugliness. This has given me new hope for the future. (cited in Andrea and Overfield, pp. 417–19)

On a national scale, Japan's peace parks at both Hiroshima and Nagasaki record the nuclear destruction as well as subsequent commitments to seek-

A-bomb devastation. On August 6, 1945, the "Enola Gay" Super-Fortress aircraft released the first atom bomb ever used in warfare over Hiroshima, an important Japanese military base and seaport. Over 130,000 people were killed or injured and the city was largely flattened. The USA took the action—and again, three days later at Nagasaki—in a (successful) bid to end the Pacific War.

ing international peace. Japan is now among the least armed of the world's powers, committed to keeping nuclear arms out of Japan and intensely involved in the efforts of the United Nations to work for peace. (Japan's increasing wealth and regional and world economic power, coupled with the decline of the United States, especially as a military power in the Pacific, are, however, putting stresses on Japan's anti-militaristic patterns in the closing years of the century.)

The French **existentialist** author Albert Camus (1913–60), perhaps the most influential voice in European literature in his time, wrote in 1940, the year France fell to Germany: "There is but one truly serious philosophical problem, and that is suicide. Judging whether life is or is not worth living amounts to answering the fundamental question of philosophy." Perhaps, however, rock bottom had been reached, or perhaps hope is part of the human condition, even in conditions of apparent hopelessness, for Camus answered his own question in *The Myth of Sisyphus* (1942) with an affirmation, which he repeated in 1955:

> This book declares that even within the limits of nihilism it is possible to find the means to proceed beyond nihilism. ... Although *The Myth of Sisyphus* poses mortal problems, it sums itself up for me as a lucid invitation to live and to create, in the very midst of the desert. (p. 3)

"HOW SHOULD WE LIVE?"

The Polish poet Wislawa Szymborska, winner of the Nobel Prize for Literature in 1996, also reflects upon the disillusionment of the twentieth century, and also assumes that life should and must go on nevertheless. But "How should we live?" she asks at the close of one of her most poignant poems, written in the 1970s. In this poem, however, she offers no answers:

Our twentieth century was going to improve on
the others.
It will never prove it now,
now that its years are numbered,
its gait is shaky,
its breath is short.

Too many things have happened
that weren't supposed to happen,
and what was supposed to come about
has not.

Happiness and spring, among other things,
were supposed to be getting closer.

Fear was expected to leave the mountains and
the valleys.
Truth was supposed to hit home
before a lie.

A couple of problems weren't going
to come up anymore:

hunger, for example,
and war, and so forth.

There was going to be respect
for helpless people's helplessness,
trust, that kind of stuff.

Anyone who planned to enjoy the world
is now faced
with a hopeless task.

Stupidity isn't funny.
Wisdom isn't gay.
Hope
isn't that young girl anymore,
et cetera, alas.

God was finally going to believe
in a man both good and strong,
but good and strong
are still two different men.

"How should we live?" someone asked me in a
letter.
I had meant to ask him
the same question.

Again, and as ever,
as may be seen above,
the most pressing questions
are naive ones.

INTERNATIONAL AND NATIONAL INSTITUTIONAL PLANNING 1945–1990S

The founding of the United Nations was a life-affirming political response to humanity's horror at its own destructiveness. In 1945, fifty-one nations, mostly of Europe and the Americas, recognizing that "disregard and contempt for human rights have resulted in barbarous acts which have outraged the conscience of mankind," joined together to establish the United Nations Organization to prevent world conflict. The UN sought to establish among all nations mutual commitments to world peace and human rights, to arbitration and negotiation rather than arms in the resolution of conflict, and to the promotion of health, welfare, and the advancement of education and science.

COLD WAR 1945–91

The United Nations has experienced three major stages of development. The first was mediation during the Cold War. In the first years after the massive destruction of World War II in Europe and Asia, the United States provided a kind of Pax Americana to a war-weary world. Through the $12 billion investment of the Marshall Plan it encouraged the reconstruction of Western Europe along democratic and mixed capitalistic–socialistic patterns. During seven years of military and political occupation in Japan, America outlawed the divine status given to the emperor, promulgated a democratic constitution and educational system, and introduced new concepts of business management.

Despite the devastation it suffered during the war, the USSR, as leader of the communist world, feared and challenged American military, technological, and political supremacy. Forty years of Cold War between the two superpowers began. The United States had exploded the world's first atomic bomb in 1945; the USSR followed in 1949 (and Britain in 1952, France in 1960, China in 1964, and India in 1974). The USA's first hydrogen bomb in 1952 was matched by the USSR the next year. The heavens, too, became a field of contest as Russia put the first missile, the *Sputnik*, in space orbit in 1957 followed by the first manned satellite in 1961. America landed the first man on the moon in 1969.

Between 1950 and 1953, the competition erupted in regional warfare between two client, or dependent states, North and South Korea. The North, allied with the USSR and the great Asian communist power of China, attacked the South, whose principal ally was the USA. Subsequently United

"A great step for mankind ..." Edwin ("Buzz") Aldrin, the second man on the moon, clambers down the ladder of the Apollo II lunar module "Eagle" in July 1969. Neil Armstrong set foot on the moon moments earlier. The race for supremacy in space between the superpowers was fueled by the cold war.

Nations troops also joined on behalf of South Korea. By war's end, 115,000 soldiers had been killed fighting for the South and one million civilians had died. The North did not release its statistics. In 1962, a face-off between the USA and the USSR over the Soviet placement of nuclear weapons and delivery systems on Cuba brought the world to the brink of nuclear warfare until the USSR agreed to remove them.

The costs of this military-technological competition were astronomical. In 1960 the governments of the world spent slightly under $300 billion for military expenses; in 1970 and 1980, about $340 billion. Expenditure peaked at almost $500 billion in 1987 before coming down to $410 billion by 1994, thanks to the end of the Cold War. (All figures are given in constant 1987 dollars to adjust for inflation. The actual 1994 figure is $700 billion.)

The United Nations' second phase began around 1960 as scores of formerly colonized, newly independent countries began to enter the organization and attempted to refocus its agenda on issues of decolonization and economic development. The new nations consistently condemned European colonialism and its American support. Frequently they were drawn into the diplomatic orbit of the USSR. Their voices dominated the UN proceedings.

UNITED NATIONS TODAY

In 1985, unable to continue the massive spending required by the arms race, the Soviet Union under Mikhail Gorbachev began new policies of **perestroika**, restructuring its politics and economics, and of **glasnost**, greater openness in domestic and international affairs (see p. 624). The Warsaw Pact, the political-military alliance in eastern Europe led by the USSR, dissolved and its member nations became independent. East and West Germany were re-unified. By 1991 the Soviet Union itself began to disintegrate into independent nations (see p. 624). In response, the American-led North Atlantic Treaty Organization (NATO) softened its military edge. The Cold War seemed over. Despite the extraordinary armaments, sabre rattling, and confrontations, the superpowers had avoided direct warfare for four decades.

As the USA and USSR have moved closer together, the United Nations seems to be entering a third stage, serving as a forum for international action in containing regional conflicts in Ethiopia, Somalia, Angola, the Persian Gulf, Southeast Asia, Haiti, and Bosnia, and in helping negotiate *ad hoc*

international crises, such as hostage situations. But the United Nations, which Gorbachev called a "unique instrument without which world politics would be inconceivable today," lacks the sovereignty of a government. It commands only such *ad hoc* powers as its constituent members choose to vest in it.

The primary focus of attention in the United Nations has been on peace and war, but its other functions, many concerned with technology, have provided forums for the resolution of other issues and the promotion of international welfare. The United Nations' key agencies are:

- the Food and Agriculture Organization (FAO), for improving food supply and distribution;

- the World Trade Organization (WTO), the major body for overseeing international trade, settling trade disputes, and negotiating trade liberalization;

- the World Bank and the International Development Association, for providing assistance to developing nations;

- the United Nations Educational, Scientific, and Cultural Organization (UNESCO), which sponsors research and publication;

- the United Nations Children's (Emergency) Fund (UNICEF), which establishes programs for family welfare;

- the World Health Organization (WHO), which monitors and researches health conditions;

- the International Labor Organization (ILO), which promotes employment and seeks to improve labor conditions and living standards; and

- the World Intellectual Property Organization, which protects the interests of the producers of literary, industrial, scientific, and artistic works.

With some 160 sovereign nation members, and commensurately diverse ideologies, the United Nations' decisions and activities are subjected to a constant stream of criticism from one point or another on the political spectrum. Yet, within that highly politicized framework it goes on with its work providing a forum where nations can meet,

ECOLOGY

*E*cology refers to the relationship of plants, animals, and humans to their environment and to one another. Throughout history, humans have stood in terror and supplication before potentially destructive forces of nature: flood, fire, storm, earthquake, volcano, disease, famine. But from the earliest historical times we have also recognized our capacity for inflicting damage on the eco-system. The 5000-year-old *Epic of Gilgamesh*, which we noted in Chapter 2, described the resentment of Humbaba, the supernatural Lord of the Forest, at the arrogance of Gilgamesh and Enkidu, who chopped down his trees for their urban construction projects in Uruk. The industrial revolution, beginning in the late eighteenth century, as we have seen in Chapter 16, introduced a new dimension of human intervention in the world's ecology as industrial wastes polluted air and water so thoroughly that life spans were cut short and disease flourished. Many nations and localities responded in self-defense with legislation to protect the natural environment and safeguard human health and welfare. In our own century, the potential of humans destroying the ecological balance has reached startling proportions, transcending local and national borders.

Rachel Carson's *Silent Spring* (1962) exposed the devastating effects on humans, wildlife, and plants caused by the use of toxic chemicals—pesticides, fungicides, and herbicides—in everyday farming and insect control throughout America and, by extension, throughout the world. By virtue of its combination of scientific rigor and journalistic vividness, *Silent Spring* is frequently credited as the founding statement of the ecological movement in the twentieth century.

> The most alarming of all man's assaults upon the environment is the contamination of air, earth, rivers, and sea with dangerous and even lethal materials. This

The UN's Food and Agriculture Organization sponsors ecological projects in poor regions of the world. In Senegal, West Africa, a father and son plant seedlings to protect their village's multipurpose garden from the wind and sun. The blue plastic (collected from village waste) covers the soil near the roots, helping to retain the moisture.

discuss common goals, and negotiate disagreements. It does not always succeed, but such a forum is invaluable.

Ecological Issues

By 1990 the United Nations was also involved in organizing against global ecological destruction. Many concerns dominate the agenda, but the main ones are:

- the depletion of the ozone layer through the introduction into the environment of chlorofluorocarbons, a principal chemical in aerosol sprays and in most coolants, such as refrigeration and air conditioning units;

pollution is for the most part irrecoverable; the chain of evil it initiates not only in the world that must support life but in living tissues is for the most part irreversible. In this now universal contamination of the environment, chemicals are the sinister and little recognized partners of radiation in changing the very nature of the world—the very nature of its life....Chemicals sprayed on croplands or forests or gardens lie long in the soil, entering into living organisms, passing from one to another in a chain of poisoning and death. Or they pass mysteriously by underground streams until they emerge, and through the alchemy of air and sunlight, combine into new forms that kill vegetation, sicken cattle, and work unknown harm on those who drink from once-pure wells. (Carson, pp. 23–4)

Carson's powerful voice evoked responses. For example, after she revealed that DDT, one of the most powerful chemicals used to combat mosquitoes and, thus, malaria, was also poisonous to humans, governments thoughout the world generally banned its use. "Green" parties, with strong platforms on ecological issues, began to organize in many countries, especially in Western Europe. Although the "greens" captured few parliamentary seats, more mainstream parties began to adopt some of their programs. Citizens founded organizations such as the World Wildlife Fund and Greenpeace in order to protect the environment. Some farmers began to use natural means of pest control in place of chemicals, and consumers began to seek out "natural" or "organic" foods raised without the use of chemical fertilizers and pesticides.

As the ecological movement grew it emphasized the unity of the global environment and thus the need for coordinated global action. Ecological issues transcended national borders. In 1972 the United Nations Conference on the Human Environment met in Stockholm and moved to establish the United Nations Environment Program (UNEP) to "protect the environment by distributing education materials and by serving as a coordinator and catalyst of environmental initiatives." In 1983 the United Nations General Assembly established a World Commission on Environment and Development (WCED), chaired by Norway's prime minister Gro Harlem Brundtland The WCED was to propose political and technological plans for achieving a healthier environment consistent with greater economic growth which would also preserve the natural environment. Its recommendations covered the challenges of population growth; food security; species and ecosystems (the original concerns of ecologists like Rachel Carson); energy; industry; and urbanization. In addition, it made recommendations for institutional and legal changes to achieve these goals. The political issues were thornier than the technological:

The Earth is one but the world is not. We all depend on one biosphere for sustaining our lives. Yet each community, each country strives for survival and prosperity with little regard for its impact on others. Some consume the Earth's resources at a rate that would leave little for future generations. Others, many more in number, consume far too little and live with the prospect of hunger, squalor, disease, and early death. (Carson, p. 28)

To prepare for implementation, the United Nations sponsored a conference on Environment and Development (UNCED), the "Earth Summit" in Rio de Janeiro, 1992, which was attended by delegates from over 175 countries, including 100 heads of state, the largest such gathering in history. Ecology had become a permanent part of the international agenda.

- global warming, or the greenhouse effect, caused primarily by the introduction into the environment of carbon dioxide, which traps heat in the earth's lower atmosphere, raising temperatures around the globe;

- The destruction of the marine environment through ocean dumping, ship pollution, and the absorption of chemicals into the water table;

- acid rain, the pollution of the atmosphere with chemical pollutants that descend with rainfall;

- deforestation, especially in the tropics, where at least 25 million acres of trees are cut down each year.

In general, more developed countries tended to place the blame for ecological problems on the increase in global population, an increase most marked in the less developed countries. The less developed countries, in response, blamed the more developed as the source of the industries which created the pollution. On the issue of world hunger, the developed countries again pointed to population pressures on food supplies in the less developed countries, while the less developed blamed flaws in the world economy and food distribution mechanisms, both controlled by the wealthier countries. Agreement, however, began to emerge on the need to achieve international cooperation in a stronger UN Environment Program. The problem for the United Nations here, as in its other work, has been its lack of sovereign power. It can gather information, carry out research, make recommendations, hold conferences, and provide counsel, but it has no powers of enforcement. Implementation depends upon the decision of member nations.

THE NATION-STATE, INTERNATIONAL ORGANIZATION, AND THE INDIVIDUAL

As problems of ecology, arms control, and economic regulation transcended national borders, pressures for international organization grew. The post-war period has seen the emergence of regional international organizations with common aims, such as the League of Arab States (1945), the Organization of American States (1948), the Organization of African Unity (1963), the Association of Southeast Asian States (1967), the South Asian Association for Regional Cooperation (1983), and the Commonwealth of Independent States (1991), which was formed by twelve of the fifteen former members of the USSR immediately after its dissolution.

Important inter-regional coalitions for specific purposes also took shape, and two of the most important of these helped to change the direction of the world economy. The Organization of Petroleum Exporting Countries (OPEC) cartel, founded in 1960, shocked the industrial world by successfully forcing sudden, sharp rises in oil prices in 1973 and for several years thereafter, but it splintered internally and disintegrated as a major economic force

by 1980. The so-called Group of 77 (which now includes over 100 members) formed around the United Nations First Conference on Trade and Development (1964) to present the agenda of the lesser developed nations, and it continues in that function today.

Ironically, in light of its wars, Europe set the most promising example of regional cooperation and even unification. In 1947, Winston Churchill had described Europe as "A rubble heap, a charnel house, a breeding ground for pestilence and hate." But by 1997 the organized European Union (EU) had grown to include fifteen member nations living in considerable harmony and enjoying prosperity equal to that of any part of the world. From the first tentative steps taken in the early 1950s, the European nations had worked successfully to bind up the wounds of war and establish cooperative, formal agreements on economic development, trade, and political action. Ancient enemies, such as France, Germany, Britain, and Italy, shared in joint military exercises. Western Europe was richer, more populous, more democratic, and more internally integrated than at any time in its history. Political leaders speculated and spoke seriously of some form of United States of Europe. More recent landmark steps along the way have included: the re-unification of East and West Germany in 1991; the abolition of restrictions on the movement of goods, services, capital, workers, and tourists within the EU; and agreement on common policies on agriculture, fisheries, and nuclear research. Still underway are discussions on a common currency, and common policies on foreign affairs, immigration, defense, and social welfare.

Individuals still felt the need for a political organization that could protect and advance their safety and interests but not overwhelm and coerce them. The growth of "totalitarian" states in fascist wartime Italy and Germany, and in China and the USSR (which we shall examine in the next chapter) had alarmed the world. Some citizens of the western democracies had reservations at the growing power of the state, even in their benign welfare modes, fearing possible losses in individual liberty and autonomy as well as inefficiency and corruption in bloated bureaucracies. The multiplication of single-party governments in the 1970s and 1980s in the emerging new nations of Africa and Asia (discussed in Chapters 20 and 22) spread disillusionment, especially as "enemies of the people" were jailed or driven into exile and the numbers of refugees swelled into the millions.

The search continued for a proper triangular balance between the need for control and guidance of the power of technology, the legitimate activities of government, and the freedom and creativity of the individual. Changes in the government of many democratic countries, beginning with the election of Margaret Thatcher in Britain (1979) and Ronald Reagan in the United States (1980), coupled with the disintegration of the USSR in 1991, and the move toward multi-party democracies in Latin America and Africa in the 1980s and early 1990s, suggested that in many parts of the world (although not yet in China, in light of the Tiananmen Massacre of dissidents in 1989), the search was leading, for the moment, toward the limitation of big, authoritarian government. Indeed even Reagan's more liberal Democratic successor Bill Clinton announced "the day of big government is over," and the first Labor Party successor to Margaret Thatcher in England, Tony Blair, elected in 1997, seemed to adopt a similar philosophy.

In the remaining chapters of this part we shall examine in more detail some of the major issues only touched on in this introduction.

This opening chapter has viewed the events of the twentieth century primarily through the prism of the experiences of the United States and Western Europe. Succeeding chapters will broaden that perspective by focussing on each major region of the world. These chapters will discuss the key issues of the century as seen from these regional perspectives. Here issues such as colonialism and independence, neocolonialism and economic independence, national cultural and economic integration, and regional cooperation will be more important. We shall also discuss the kinds of technology these regions are choosing, and have the capacity to choose, as they confront these issues.

BIBLIOGRAPHY

Andrea, Alfred and James H. Overfield, eds. *The Human Record*, Vol 2 (Boston: Houghton Mifflin, 1994).

Camus, Albert. *The Myth of Sisyphus* (New York: Vintage Books, 1959).

Carson, Rachel. *Silent Spring* (New York: Penguin Books, 1965).

Chafe, William H. and Harvard Sitkoff, eds. *A History of Our Time* (New York: Oxford University Press, 3rd ed., 1991).

Columbia College, Columbia University. *Introduction to Contemporary Civilization in the West: A Source Book*, Vol. 2 (New York: Columbia University Press, 2nd ed., 1954).

Fox, Richard G., ed. *Urban India: Society, Space and Image* (Durham, NC: Duke University Program in Comparative Studies on Southern Asia, 1970).

Franck, Irene and David Brownstone. *The Green Encyclopedia* (New York: Prentice Hall, 1992).

Freud, Sigmund. *Civilization and its Discontents* (New York: W.W. Norton and Co., 1961).

—. *A General Introduction to Psychoanalysis* (New York: Pocket Books, 1952).

Gandhi, Mohandas Karamchand. *Hind Swaraj or Indian Home Rule* (Ahmedabad: Navajivan Press, 1938).

Hofstadter, Richard, ed. *Great Issues in American History: A Documentary Record* (New York: Vintage Books, 1959).

Hughes, Thomas. *American Genesis* (New York: Viking, 1989).

Johnson, Paul. *Modern Times* (New York: Harper and Row, 1983).

Kennedy, Paul. *The Rise and Fall of the Great Powers* (New York: Random House, 1987).

Pickering, Kevin T. and Lewis A. Owen. *An Introduction to Global Environmental Issues* (New York: Routledge, 1994).

Ramanujan, A.K. "Towards an Anthology of City Images," in Fox, ed., *Urban India*, 224–42.

Sivard, Ruth Leger. *World Military and Social Expenditures 1996* (Washington: World Priorities, 16th ed., 1996).

Szymborska, Wislawa. *View with a Grain of Sand* (San Diego: Harcourt Brace, 1995).

United Nations. *Declaration of the Universal Rights of Man.*

Wiesel, Elie. *Night* (New York: Bantam Books, 1962).

Wilkie, Brian and James Hurt, eds. *Literature of the Western World*, Vol. II (New York: Macmillan, 1984).

World Almanac and Book of Facts 1991 through 1997 (Mahwah, NJ: World Almanac Books, 1991 through 1997).

World Bank. *World Development Report 1992: Development and the Environment* (New York: Oxford University Press, 1992).

World Commission on Environment and Development. *Our Common Future* (New York: Oxford University Press, 1987).

Yagnik, Indulal. *Autobiography*, Vol. 1 (in Gujarati) (Ahmedabad: Ravaani Publishing House, 1955).

19

"We must no longer lag behind."

JOSEPH STALIN

"Europe is not the only model. We can be a model too."

NATSUME SOSEKI

THE SOVIET UNION AND JAPAN

1914–1997

PLAYING TECHNOLOGICAL CATCH-UP WITH THE WEST

THE CONTRASTING EXPERIENCES OF THE SOVIET UNION AND JAPAN

Throughout the twentieth century, two powerful countries dedicated themselves to catching up with, and even surpassing, the technological power of Western Europe and North America. Russia and Japan began from very different geo-political and cultural–religious bases. Russia had expanded over several centuries to become the largest country in the world in geographical terms, with access to all the natural resources of eastern Europe and northern Asia. Japan was a small island nation, about the size of California, with few natural resources and a rapidly growing population pressing on available land. Culturally, Russia was the home of the Eastern Orthodox Christian Church, as well as the recipient of important influences from its earlier waves of Mongol immigrants from the east and Scandinavian immigrants from the west. Japan maintained a homogeneous population, united in

its dedication to emperor and nation, and had reached a peaceful accommodation between its Shinto, Buddhist, and Confucian cultural and religious heritages.

The encounters of Russia and Japan with western technology had also been quite different. Following the eighteenth century example of Peter the Great (see p. 420), some of Russia's czars had embraced the new technology, but others had not. Japan had kept western technology and culture out of its islands for more than two centuries (see pp. 424–6), but both nations were forced to confront the increasingly aggressive Western Europeans once again in the mid-nineteenth century. Russia had attacked the Ottoman Empire in the Crimea, and was defeated by the coalition of Britain, France, and their allies. Japan was threatened by the gunboats of the United States fleet under Matthew Perry in 1853. These two events made Russia and Japan realize their need to catch up with Western European and North American military technology and both saw that government initiatives were required to achieve this. But how should they go about it? The two governments developed rather different policies demonstrating different ways to play the technological game. The two halves of this chapter trace their separate trajectories.

RUSSIA
1914–1990s

The Russian Revolution of 1917 challenged the capitalist order by instituting communism. As we noted in Chapter 16, communism advocated the abolition of private property and control of the economic resources by the state. It argued that the communist party should lead the way to this system by the use of violence if necessary. Leaders of the party believed that Russia could telescope the development process and catapult itself into the ranks of the wealthy and powerful. The Bolshevik Party, renamed the Communist Party in 1918, asserted the importance of its own official dominance over the politics, economy, and society of Russia. Through the worldwide organization of the Communist International, it proposed itself as a model for, and leader of, colonized and backward countries in overthrowing foreign control and capitalist economic development. It argued that poor nations had been intentionally "underdeveloped" by, and for, the rich. The new communist system established by the Russian Revolution endured

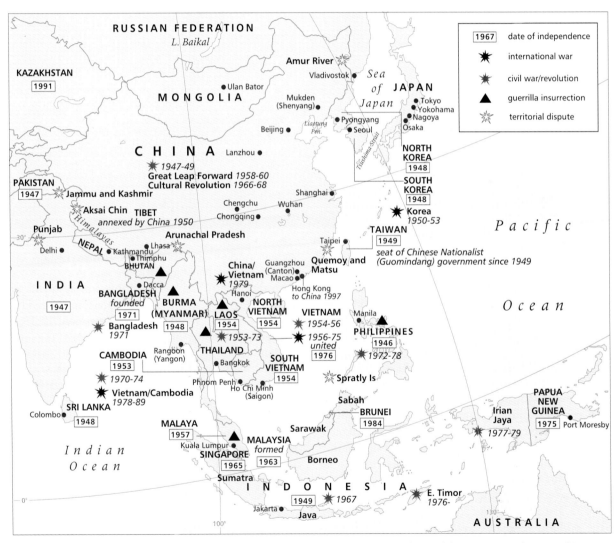

East Asia since 1945 China, the largest nation in East Asia, and in the world, completed one of the greatest revolutions in history, as a communist government displaced an empire which had endured for two millennia and then reunified the country after forty years of civil war. Japan recovered from catastrophic war losses and became rich and powerful. Most nations of the region emerged from Japanese wartime colonialism and claimed independence from European colonialism as well. In such tumultuous times, stability was constantly threatened by war and insurrection.

	SOVIET UNION	JAPAN
1900	▪ Formation of Socialist Revolutionary Party (1901) ▪ Split in Social Democratic Party into Bolsheviks and Mensheviks (1903) ▪ Russo-Japanese war (1904–5): Japan victorious ▪ "Bloody Sunday"; insurrection ruthlessly repressed (1905)	▪ Meiji restoration emphasizes process of catching up with the West (1867)
1910	▪ Declaration of war with Central Powers (1914) ▪ Revolution (1917) ▪ Treaty of Brest-Litovsk (1918): end of war with Central Powers but territory lost ▪ Civil war (1918–22) between Red Army (led by Trotsky) and White Russians; Red Army victorious	▪ Alliance with Britain (1902) ▪ War with Russia (1904–5): Japan annexes Formosa (Taiwan) ▪ Japan formally annexes Korea (1910) ▪ Joins Allies in World War I (1914), attends Versailles Conference (1919), is assigned Germany's Pacific possessions
1920	▪ New economic policy inaugurated, marking retreat from socialism (1921) ▪ Constitution of USSR adopted (1922) ▪ Death of Lenin (1923) ▪ Power struggle sees Stalin oust Trotsky and emerge as leader (1928) ▪ First five-year plan (1928): forced collectivization and industrialization	▪ Earthquake in Tokyo (1923) ▪ Universal male suffrage (1925) ▪ Earthquake in Yokohama kills 140,000 (1925) ▪ Radical nationalism takes hold of country (1927) ▪ Economic depression: 3 million unemployed (1929–31)
1930	▪ Stalin purges opposition in series of show trials; millions sent to gulags (1936–8) ▪ Non-aggression pact with Germany gives USSR eastern Poland, Baltic states, and Bessarabia (1939)	▪ Prime Minister Osachi Hamaguchi assassinated (1931) ▪ War with China (1931–2): Manchuria invaded and placed under Japanese control as Manchukuo Invasion of China (1937): Shanghai and Peking captured; Rape of Nanjing ▪ All political parties under one banner; military government (1938) ▪ Defeated in undeclared border war with USSR (1939)
1940	▪ Estonia, Latvia, Lithuania annexed (1940) ▪ "Great Patriotic War" against Germany (1941–5) ▪ Siege of Stalingrad (1942–3) ▪ Alexander Solzhenitsyn imprisoned and exiled (1945–57) ▪ Yalta agreement recognizes Soviet field of interest in east and southeast Europe ▪ Cold War begins (1947) ▪ Comecon (Council for Mutual Economic Assistance) established (1949); Warsaw Pact	▪ Occupies French Indochina on fall of France (1940) ▪ Japan attacks US fleet at Pearl Harbor and attacks British, US, and Dutch possessions in Pacific (1941) ▪ World War II ends with Japanese surrender after atomic bombs dropped on Hiroshima and Nagasaki; General MacArthur installed as supreme commander of Allied Powers in Japan (1945) ▪ "Peace" constitution issued; emperor becomes a figurehead (1947) ▪ Universal female suffrage (1949)

through years of hardship and of war, both civil and international. After World War II, Russia forced its own example on many of its neighbors by military invasion. At about the same time, elements of the Russian example were accepted more willingly by many other nations—most notably China—and those new nations emerging from colonial rule at about the same time. But since the early 1990s, ironically, the most powerful of Russia's own leaders have chosen to repudiate the philosophy of state-run communism. The new revolutionary changes that have been taking place in Russia since the late 1980s provide an opportunity for re-examination and re-evaluation of the rhetoric and reality of communist rule.

Geographically and politically Russia has one foot in Europe, another in Asia. As we have seen (see p. 420), Peter the Great (r. 1682–1725) turned westward, founding St. Petersburg as his capital, port, and window on the west. Catherine II, the Great (r. 1762–96) further nurtured the European Enlightenment at the Russian court. Stunned by his defeat in the Crimean War (1853–6) by Britain and France in alliance with Turkey and Austria, Czar Alexander II (r. 1855–81) adopted a more liberal policy. He freed Russia's serfs in 1861, instituted the **zemstvo** system of local self-government in 1864, reduced censorship of the press, reformed the legal system, encouraged industrialization, and promoted the construction of a nationwide railway system. Czar Nicholas II (r. 1894–1917) furthered heavy industrialization under two progressive ministers, Count Sergei Yulievich Witte (1849–1915) and Peter Stolypin (1862–1911), and allowed the birth of some representative political institutions, but he rejected the democratic reforms demanded by intellectuals, workers, and political organizers.

THE BUILD-UP TO REVOLUTION 1914–17

On the eve of World War I, Russia lagged far behind the Western European countries economically and industrially. Its population of 175 million was about

	SOVIET UNION	JAPAN
1950	▮ Stalin dies; Beria removed; "collective leadership" in power (1953) ▮ Nikita Khrushchev secretary general of Communist Party (1953–64); denounces Stalin's tyranny ▮ Nikolai Bulganin prime minister (1955–8) ▮ Hungarian uprising against Soviet occupation (1956) ▮ *Sputnik* in orbit (1957) ▮ Boris Pasternak's *Dr. Zhivago* (1957) banned in USSR ▮ "Anti-party" group and Bulganin ousted (1958) ▮ Khrushchev premier (1958–64)	▮ Japan's economy grows 10.5 percent every year (1950–73) ▮ Korean War (1950): Japan benefits from US army contracts ▮ Full sovereignty regained (1952) ▮ Mercury poisoning at Minimata kills 43 and maims many others (1953–6) ▮ Joins United Nations (1958)
1960	▮ Sino-Soviet rift ▮ Cuban missile crisis (1962) ▮ "Collective leadership" takes power (1964) ▮ Czechoslovakia invaded (1968) ▮ Sino-Soviet border war (1969)	▮ Bullet train inaugurated (1964) ▮ Hosts Olympics (1964) ▮ Joins OECD organization (1964) ▮ Bonin and Volcano Islands regained (1968)
1970	▮ Arms limitation agreements with US (1972, 1979) ▮ Leonid Brezhnev president (1977–82) ▮ Afghanistan invaded (1979)	▮ Ryukyu Island regained (1972) ▮ Oil crisis (1973) leads to cuts in economic output; government decides to invest in high-technology industries ▮ Prime Minister Tanaka resigns over Lockheed bribes scandal (1974)
1980	▮ Crisis in Poland (1980–81) ▮ Yuri Andropov president (1982–3): instigates moderate economic reforms ▮ Konstantin Chernenko president (1984–5) ▮ Mikhail Gorbachev president (1985–91): introduces wide-ranging reforms, beginning of *perestroika* ▮ Chernobyl nuclear disaster (1986) ▮ Nationalist uprisings in Kazakhstan, Baltic republics, Georgia, Armenia, and Azerbaijan ▮ Troops withdraw from Afghanistan (1989)	▮ Yasuhiro Nakasone prime minister (1982–7) ▮ Noboru Takeshita prime minister (1987–9) ▮ Recruit Corporation scandal (1988): politicians and members of cabinet involved in insider trading ▮ Emperor Hirohito dies; succeeded by Akihito ▮ Sosuke Uno prime minister (1989) ▮ Tshiki Kaifu prime minister (1989–91) ▮ Trade frictions with USA and Europe
1990	▮ Gorbachev opposes nationalist movements (1990) ▮ Yeltsin elected president of Russia (1991) ▮ Unsuccessful coup against Gorbachev but he resigns and USSR dissolves into constituent republics (1991) ▮ Russian military action in Chechnya (1994) ▮ Communists successful in elections for *duma* (1995)	▮ Kiichi Miyazawa prime minister (1991–4); resigns after being accused of corruption ▮ Worst recession of post-war period (1993) ▮ Tsutomyu Hata prime minister (1994–6) ▮ Earthquake in Kobe kills 5000+ (1995) ▮ Ryutar Hashimoto prime minister (1996)

Distribution of Bolshevik leaflets in Petrograd, Russia, 1917. The seeds of revolution germinated with astonishing speed in the 35-degree-below Soviet winter: long-suffering bread queues suddenly erupted and bakeries were looted; workers, whose factories lacked coal, went on strike; and demonstrators carried banners saying "Down with the German woman"—a reference to Czar Nicholas's wife. Lenin called for "Peace, Land, Bread," seeking withdrawal from war. The Russian monarchy abdicated on March 16, 1917.

THE SOVIET UNION AND JAPAN (1914–1997)   611

75 percent more than that of the United States, more than two and a half times that of Germany, and four times that of Britain; its energy consumption was one-tenth the USA's, 30 percent of Germany's, and one-fourth of Britain's. Its share of world manufacturing was 8 percent compared with America's 32 percent, Germany's 15 percent, and Britain's 14 percent.

Nicholas II had made great strides in increasing industrial production. Energy consumption had increased from 4.6 metric tons equivalent in 1890 to 23 million in 1913; railway mileage from about 22,000 miles (35,400 kilometers) in 1890 to 31,000 miles (50,000 kilometers) in 1900 to 46,000 miles (74,000 kilometers) in 1913; and the per capita level of industrialization doubled from 1880 to 1913. But during that same period, 1880–1913, the USA's per capita level of industrialization quadrupled, Germany's rose three and one-half times, and France's, Italy's, Austria's, and Japan's all slightly more than doubled (Kennedy, p. 200). In a rapidly industrializing world, Russia had to race much faster just to keep up.

Since Russia lacked the capital to build the industries it wanted, it invited foreign investment.

> Foreign investors by 1914 owned 40% of the railway mileage, 40% of the chemical industry, 50% of the coal and oil output, 60% of the copper and iron ore output and 80% of the coke output. Of a total of £500 million invested in Russian industry in 1917, just over one third comprised foreign investments. Also, foreigners held almost 50% of the Russian national debt … making Russia Europe's largest debtor. (Stavrianos, p. 342)

Russia's agriculture was unproductive and its technology was primitive, but economic productivity had little bearing on the power over land and peasantry held by Russia's wealthy elites. An exploited peasantry living in *mirs* (village collectives) had neither the economic incentive nor the technical training to produce more. The small parcels of land they farmed privately were subdivided into tiny plots, as sons in each generation shared equally in dividing the inheritance of their fathers. Finally, the government forbade the sale of village land to outsiders. This did prevent exploitation by absentee landlords, but it blocked the investment from outside the village that might have funded agricultural improvement through new technology. Productivity stagnated. The sharp class divisions between the peasants and the gentry persisted,

THE RUSSIAN REVOLUTION— KEY EVENTS

1898	Social democratic Party (SDP) formed by George Plekhanov (1857–1918) and Vladimir Ilyich Lenin (1870–1924)
1903	Split in SDP at party's second congress into Bolsheviks and Mensheviks
1905 January	"Bloody Sunday" when repression of workers at St. Petersburg leads to strikes and "1905 Revolution"
1917 March	Riots in St. Petersburg; czar abdicates; provisional government under Prince Lvov; power struggle between government and soviet in St. Petersburg
April	Lenin in St. Petersburg demands transfer of power to soviets, end of war, handing over of land to peasants, and control of industry by workers
July	Bolsheviks try to seize power in St. Peterburg; Leon Trotsky (1879–1940) arrested and Lenin goes into hiding
November	Bolshevik revolution: Red Guards seize government offices and the Winter Palace; all members of provisional government arrested; Council of Peoples Commissars established as new government, led by Lenin, with Trotsky as commissar for war and Joseph Stalin (1879–1953) as commissar for national minorities; decree passed distributing land to peasants; banks nationalized; national debt repudiated
July	Czar Nicholas II and family murdered at Yekaterinburg

marked by differences not only in wealth and education, but in carriage, dress, and manners. Moreover, the costs of industrialization and the repayment of foreign loans had to be squeezed out of the agricultural sector. The result was a mass of peasants impoverished, technologically backward, despised by the wealthy elite, and suffering under the weight of a national program of industrialization for which they were made to pay.

LENIN AND THE BOLSHEVIK REVOLUTION

Several revolutionary groups attacked these conditions, each offering a different plan. The Social Democrats followed George Plekhanov (1857–1918), an orthodox Marxist thinker, who saw the need for more capitalist development in Russia to create new urban working and middle classes. Plekhanov's party would then organize the new industrial workers to overthrow the bourgeoisie. A lawyer, Vladimir Ilyich Ulyanov (1870–1924), later calling himself Lenin, joined Plekhanov on the editorial board of *Iskra* ("the Spark"). In the first issue Lenin stressed the need for the party to provide leadership dedicated to the goals of revolution:

> Not a single class in history has reached power without thrusting forward its political leaders, without advancing leading representatives capable of directing and organizing the movement. We must train people who will dedicate to the revolution, not a spare evening but the whole of their lives. (Kochan and Abraham, p. 240)

In 1902, in a pamphlet entitled "What Is to Be Done?", Lenin again underlined the need for an absolutely dedicated core of leaders to carry out the revolution: "Give us an organization of revolutionaries and we will overturn Russia!" (cited in Andrea and Overfield, p. 396). In January 1905, with revolutionary feelings running high, some 200,000 factory workers and others in St. Petersburg, led by a priest, Father Gapon, assembled peacefully and respectfully to deliver to the czar a petition for better working conditions, higher pay, and some institutions of representative government. On that "Bloody Sunday," January 22, troops fired on the demonstrators, killing several hundred and wounding perhaps a thousand. The government's lack of moral authority was unmasked. By the end of the month almost 500,000 workers were on strike, joined by peasant revolts, mutinies of soldiers, and protests by the intelligentsia of doctors, lawyers, professors, teachers, and engineers.

Partly to distract attention from this domestic turmoil, the czar had committed Russia to war with Japan but, in May, shocking losses at sea at the Straits of Tsushima and on land at Mukden (see p. 570) further revealed Russia's inadequacies in both technology and government organization. This defeat in the Russo–Japanese war, domestic tax revolts in the countryside, and strikes in the industrializing cities forced the czar to respond. Yielding as little as possible, he established the first *duma*, or parliament, representing peasants and landlords, but allowing workers only scant representation. The czar limited the powers of the *dumas*, frequently dismissed them, sometimes jailed their members, and chose their class composition selectively in order to divide the principal revolutionary constituencies, workers and bourgeoisie. Thus, paradoxically, the *dumas* endured as a focus for democratic organization and aspiration, but they were unable to work cooperatively, and the czar was able to stave off revolution for a decade.

Small pockets of revolutionary fervor flared up prior to 1917. In 1905, the year these peasants are depicted looting bosses' houses, twenty officers and 230 guards were arrested in St. Petersburg when a plot to assassinate the czar was uncovered.

World War I, with its 2 million casualties, finally united the many forces of opposition and brought down the monarchy. In the first revolution of March 1917, the *duma* forced the czar to abdicate, but the war persisted, encouraged by the aristocracy. The turmoil of mutiny and desertion in the army, food shortages, farm revolts, and factory strikes ground on. More radical groups sought to seize control. Lenin, with the assistance of Germans who wanted to sow discord in Russia, returned from Siberia where he had been exiled for three years for socialist agitation. He called for an immediate withdrawal from the war, the redistribution of land, and a government-run food distribution system. "Peace, Land, Bread," was his motto. Lenin organized an armed takeover of the government headquarters, the railway stations, power plants, post offices, and telephone exchanges. On November 7 (October 25 on the old, Julian calendar), this revolutionary coup succeeded, and the communists seized power. In March 1918, signing the Treaty of Brest-Litovsk with Germany, the communist government took Russia out of the Great War.

Civil war between communist revolutionary "Red" and anti-revolutionary "White" forces enveloped the country. Small contingents of troops from fourteen countries (including a small number of Americans in the Baltic and 8000 at Vladivostok) joined the Whites. The Bolshevik government took over ownership of land, banks, the merchant marine, and all industrial enterprises. It confiscated all holdings of the church and forbade religious teaching in the schools. It established the **Cheka** (security police) and instituted a reign of "Red Terror" against its opponents' "White Terror." In Yekaterinburg, the local soviet executed the czar, his wife, and their children. By 1920 the communists, as the Bolsheviks now called themselves, were victorious in the civil war. In 1921 they banned all opposition, even dissenting voices within the party, and made the central committee, under Lenin's leadership and control, the binding authority in the government.

World war, followed by civil war, followed by even more devastating drought, famine, and economic dislocation convinced Lenin of the need for economic stability and an incentive to produce. He implemented the New Economic Policy (NEP) in 1921, by which peasants were allowed to sell their products on the open market and middlemen to buy and sell goods at a profit. The central government, however, controlled the "commanding heights" of the economy: finance, banking, international trade, power generation, and heavy industry.

STATE PLANNING 1920–53

Lenin sought the industrial transformation of Russia. In 1920, as he established the State Commission for Electrification, he declared: "Communism is Soviet power, plus electrification of the whole country." Lenin invited foreign technical personnel to Russia, first from Germany and then from America, to improve productivity by harnessing capitalist means to communist goals. In 1918 he said:

> The task that the Soviet government must set the people in all its scope is—learn to work. The [Frederick] Taylor system [of scientific management], the last word of capitalism in this respect, like all capitalist progress, is a combination of the subtle brutality of bourgeois exploitation and a number of its greatest scientific achievements in the field of analyzing mechanical motions during work. The elimination of superfluous and awkward motions, the working out of correct methods of work, the introduction of the best system of accounting and control, etc. The Soviet Republic must at all costs adopt all that is valuable in the achievements of science and technology in this field. (cited in Hughes, p. 256)

Lenin's death in 1924 ushered in a bitter power struggle, from which Joseph Stalin (1879–1953) emerged triumphant over Leon Trotsky (1879–1940)—and then adapted his programs. Trotsky, a brilliant, ruthless man, who had organized the Red Army, had argued that through careful but bold planning a technologically backward country could leapfrog stages of growth and, through the "law of combined development," quickly catch up to the more advanced. Having defeated Trotsky, Stalin now implemented Trotsky's program. He declared his driving nationalist passion that Russia must no longer lag behind the more developed nations. Russia must no longer be beaten by others.

> To slacken the tempo would mean falling behind. And those who fall behind get beaten. But we do not want to be beaten. No, we refuse to be beaten! One feature of the history of old Russia was the continual beatings she suffered for falling behind, for her backwardness. She was beaten by the Mongol Khans. She was beaten by the Turkish beys. She was beaten by the Swedish feudal lords.

Lenin and Joseph Stalin at Gorky, Russia, 1922.
After Lenin's premature death two years after this photograph was taken, Stalin battled to eliminate his rivals (Leon Trotsky was banished to Mexico) before emerging as supreme dictator of the Communist Party in 1929. He soon abandoned Lenin's New Economic Policy in favor of a series of brutal five-year plans to enforce the collectivization of agriculture and industry.

She was beaten by the Polish and Lithuanian gentry. She was beaten by the British and French capitalists. She was beaten by the Japanese barons. All beat her—for her backwardness: for military backwardness, for cultural backwardness, for political backwardness, for industrial backwardness, for agricultural backwardness. She was beaten because to do so was profitable and could be done with impunity. ...

That is why we must no longer lag behind. (Andrea and Overfield, p. 398)

Stalin's rhetoric would appeal not only to his immediate audience in Russia, but also to a more global audience of poorer states and colonies beginning to protest against their subordination and to seek independence and development.

To achieve this "combined development," Stalin in 1928 instituted nationwide, state-directed five-year plans that covered the basic economic structure of the whole country. In place of capitalism, in which market forces of supply and demand determine production goals, wages, profits, and the flow of capital, labor, and resources, Stalin instituted government planning to make those decisions from the large-scale national macro-level to the small-scale local micro-level.

Where could Russia find capital to invest in industrial development, especially with most world capital markets closed to the communist state? Stalin turned to his own agricultural sector and peasantry. By artificially lowering the prices for agricultural production and raising the prices for agricultural tools and materials, Stalin used his planning apparatus to squeeze both capital and labor out of agriculture into industry. But he squeezed so hard that agricultural productivity fell, and peasants withheld their crops from the artificially deflated market. State planning was not working.

Nevertheless, in 1929 Stalin increased the role of the state still further. He **collectivized** agriculture. More than half of all Soviet farmers were compelled to give up their individual fields and to live and work instead on newly formed collective farms of 1000 acres (approximately 400 hectares) or more. The communist government increased the use of heavy machinery and large-scale farming operations, stipulated the goods to be produced and their sales prices, encouraged still more millions of peasants to leave the farms for work on the state's new industrial enterprises, and eliminated large landowners and middlemen.

Although many farmers were living better in 1939 than 1929, many others were not. The most industrious and talented farmers were killed or imprisoned. Hundreds of thousands of larger landowners, **kulaks**, who refused collectivization were murdered; millions were transported to labor camps in Siberia. Peasants who owned animals preferred to slaughter them rather than turn them over to collectives. There had been over 60 million head of cattle in the USSR in 1928; by 1933 there were fewer than 35 million. Initiative shrivelled as the more entrepreneurial farmers were turned into a

Class struggle. "Liquidate the Kulaks as a Class" reads this banner held aloft by farm workers in 1930. Between 1929 and 1933, Stalin aimed to convert the whole of the Soviet rural economy to collective farms and agricultural co-operatives. Kulaks were wealthier peasants who had benefited under the former system and were now regarded as oppressors and class enemies.

kind of rural proletariat. The government continued to collect high proportions of the agricultural production to pay for the imports of foreign technology and machinery for its industrial programs. Although few developing countries today are willing to reduce private consumption below 80 percent of the national product, Russia reduced it to little over 50 percent. The political coercion and chaos introduced by these policies, combined with bad harvests in southeast Russia, led to the tragic and wasteful deaths of between 2 million and 3 million peasants by 1932.

While the peasants who survived suffered enormous hardship, industry flourished as never before. At first, Russia hired foreign technology and imported foreign machinery. Despite ideological differences with the United States, Stalin saw the necessity of importing materials, machinery, and even some organizational programming from there. In 1924 Stalin declared:

American efficiency is that indomitable force which neither knows nor recognizes obstacles; which continues on a task once started until it is finished, even if it is a minor task; and without which serious constructive work is inconceivable. ... The combination of Russian revolutionary sweep with American efficiency is the essence of Leninism. (Hughes, p. 251)

Meanwhile, the Russian government was training its own personnel and learning to construct its own massive industrial plants. At the falls of the Dnieper River, the communist state constructed Dnieprostroy, which, when it opened in 1932, was the largest hydroelectric power station in the world. In the early 1920s, the USSR had imported tens of thousands of tractors, most of them Fords and International Harvesters from the United States. By the 1930s, however, Russia constructed a giant plant at Stalingrad to manufacture its own tractors. At Gorki the government built a plant based on the American Ford model at River Rouge, Michigan. At Magnitogorsk, in Siberia, they constructed a steel complex based on US Steel's plant in Gary, Indiana.

From 1928 to 1938, the per capita level of industrialization nearly doubled. From 1928 to 1940, the production of coal increased from 36 to 166 million tons, of electricity from 5 to 48 billion kilowatt hours, and of steel from 4 to 18 million tons. Stalin explained: "The independence of our country cannot be upheld unless we have an adequate industrial basis for defense" (Kochan and Abraham, p. 368). By placing most of their new plants deep in the interior of the country, the planners simultaneously protected them from foreign attack—as World War II loomed on the horizon—and helped develop untouched regions. The planners began to convert a nation of peasants into a nation of industrial workers, as the urban population of the country increased three and one-half times from 10.7 million in 1928 to 36.5 million in 1938, from 7 percent of the country's population to 20 percent.

Most dramatically, the Soviet increases came when the rest of Europe and North America were reeling under world depression. The communist system won new admirers in the West. The American political comedian Will Rogers commented: "Those rascals in Russia, along with their cuckoo stuff have got some mighty good ideas. ... Just think of everybody in a country going to work." Journalist Lincoln Steffens wrote: "All roads in our day lead to Moscow." British political critic and historian John Strachey exclaimed: "To travel from the capitalist world into Soviet territory is to pass from death to birth."

WOMEN WORKERS IN THE SOVIET UNION

For women, too, the Soviet system led to great change, but perhaps less thorough than promised. As elsewhere, World War I brought women into factories, fields, and even the armed forces, and the civil war continued the pattern. Over 70,000 women served in the Red Army. In 1921, 65 percent of Petrograd's factory workers were women. In 1917, the first Soviet marriage law constituted marriage as a civil contract and provided for relatively easy divorce and child maintenance procedures.

The government ordered equal pay for equal work, but the provision was not enforced. To bring law into line with practice, and recognizing the lack of availability of effective birth-control methods, abortion on demand was granted as a right; so was maternity leave with full pay. When the men returned from the wars, they wanted their jobs back and their women at home, but Russian women retained most of the benefits they had won and "legally speaking, Russian women were better off

*S*TALIN'S SOVIET UNION— KEY EVENTS

1912 Stalin is appointed by Lenin to the Bolshevik central committee

1922 Becomes general secretary of central committee

1924 Lenin's death leaves Stalin and Trotsky in power struggle

1928 Stalin engineers Trotsky's exile and achieves supreme power, which he exercises with brutality

1928–38 First two five-year plans involve forced industrialization to develop heavy and light industry and collectivization of agriculture, policies that required deportation and caused famine

1932–4 Famine causes deaths of millions in Ukraine and Kazakhstan

1936–8 Great Purge carried out, in which opposition in both party and army is eliminated in show trials; millions sent to gulags in Siberia and elsewhere

1939 Pact with Hitler gives USSR Baltic states, eastern Poland and Bessarabia, but Stalin taken by surprise when Hitler invades USSR (1941)

1941–5 Russia withstands German invasion, despite 20 million dead

1945 Victory in war encourages Stalin to take the cult of personality to new lengths and the policy of terror continues

1945–8 Eastern Europe consolidated into Warsaw Pact

1953 After Stalin's death his role is denounced by Khrushchev and other members of ruling elite

than women anywhere in the world" (Kochan and Abraham, p. 337). Over the next decades women entered professions so rapidly that they became the majority in medicine and teaching—care-giving occupations—and a substantial minority in engineering, technical occupations, and law.

In practice, however, women bore the "double burden" of continuing the major responsibility for running their homes and caring for their families at the same time they worked full time. With the introduction of state-planned heavy industrialization after 1929, the double burden on women increased. The factories invited their labor, while shortages of foodstuffs forced them to spend more time and energy in ration lines and in the search for food. Abortion became so common that it was once again outlawed for a time after 1936. The struggle to balance the new legal equality and protection with older social and family traditions continues.

Political leaders of countries under European colonial control saw the Russian example—telescoped development, state planning, rapid industrialization, the transformation of the peasantry

This Russian poster for the women chemical workers (1930) appears to idealize full-time employment combined with raising a family. Despite the government's difficulties in enforcing "equal pay for equal work," women's rights improved markedly under the Communist system.

into an urban labor force, emphasis on education and health services, national enthusiasm in rebuilding a nation along scientific lines—as just what they needed. As a political prisoner in British India in July 1933, Jawaharlal Nehru, future first prime minister of independent India, wrote to his daughter:

> People often argue about the Five Year Plan. ... It is easy enough to point out where it has failed. ... [but] One thing is clear: that the Five Year Plan has completely changed the face of Russia. From a feudal country it has suddenly become an advanced industrial country. There has been an amazing cultural advance; and the social services, the system of social, health, and accident insurance, are the most inclusive and advanced in the world. In spite of privation and want, the terrible fear of unemployment and starvation which hangs over workers in other countries has gone. There is a new sense of economic security among the people ... further ... this Plan has impressed itself on the imagination of the world. Everybody talks of "planning" now, and of Five-Year and Ten-Year and Three-Year plans. The Soviets have put magic into the word. (*Glimpses of World History*, pp. 856–7)

EXPORTING THE REVOLUTION?

Soviet leaders wished to spread their revolution throughout the world and had established in 1919 the Third Communist International, or Comintern, to serve that function. Indeed, the succession struggle of 1924, at Lenin's death, had partly turned on the question of how quickly to spread the revolution. Leon Trotsky, who lost, had argued for its rapid export. Joseph Stalin, who won, argued for securing the revolution at home before projecting it abroad. To some nations devastated by World War II, and to others just emerging from colonialism and seeking a model for rapid, government-sponsored modernization, Russia's successes appeared attractive. Russia's ability to survive ferocious punishment in World War II, to fight back, and to win through despite the deaths of some 20 million people—the most severe losses of any combatant nation—and untold material damage earned its people and its government great respect in the world community.

On the other hand, Russia turned to building an empire of its own by armed force. In the first three years after the war Russia imposed communist governments controlled from Moscow on six nations in Eastern Europe—Czechoslovakia, Romania, Bulgaria, Poland, Hungary, and Eastern Germany—adding them to the northern nations of Lithuania, Latvia, and Estonia, which Russia had annexed in 1940. Russia then ordered the economies of these satellite nations to serve their own, having them produce goods needed by Russia and selling them to Russia at artificially low prices. Despite its anti-imperial rhetoric, Russia was constructing its own empire in eastern Europe.

Leaders of the Western European nations and the United States condemned these actions. Britain's Winston Churchill deplored Russia's construction of an "iron curtain" separating Europe into two mutually hostile ideological/political/economic/military blocs. But many nations newly emerging from imperial rule themselves, and fearing American military and economic dominance in the post-war world, were willing to overlook Russian suppression of her neighbors—and of internal opposition—and instead applauded the Russians for providing some balance of power. From 1947 until 1991 much of the world was entan-

gled in the Cold War between the Western nations, which formed the North Atlantic Treaty Organization (NATO), and Russia and its allies organized in the Warsaw Pact. The costs of that Cold War were discussed on p. 603. Some observers saw limited benefits in the Cold War: an opening for new, poor, recently independent nations to play one side against the other for aid and assistance. Most neutral observers, however, criticized the sheer volume of military expenditure, and they blamed both NATO and the Warsaw Pact for encouraging the new nations, too, to waste their resources and energies in unnecessary military exercises.

RUSSIAN STATE POWER AND OPPRESSION

Weighing most heavily against the considerable communist accomplishments within the Soviet Union, however, were some catastrophic failures. The extraordinary power of the party left no room for opposition, for discussion and debate. It

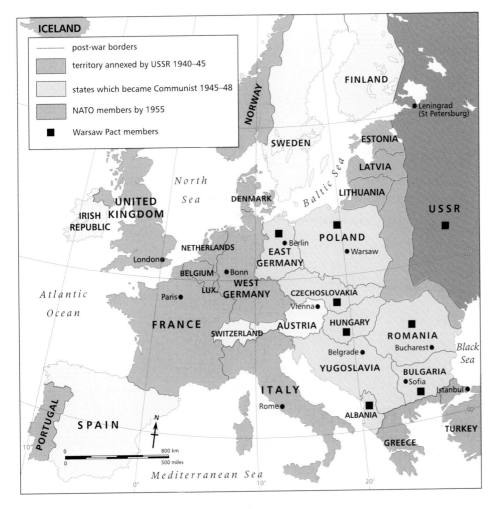

Post-war Europe Western and eastern bloc competition, following their alliance in crushing Nazi Germany, crystallized in the Cold War. The Soviet Union annexed invaded territories in the Baltic states and eastern Poland and set up a string of puppet Communist states as the Warsaw Pact alliance, from East Germany to Bulgaria. The Western Allies formed the countervailing NATO alliance. The stalemate continued for forty years.

THE SOVIET UNION AND JAPAN (1914–1997)   619

SPOTLIGHT

Soviet Socialist Realism

Every state has its own policy for culture, expressed in such elements as school curricula, support for artists and the arts, exhibitions in public museums and galleries, and rules on what may and may not be broadcast through the media and printed in the press. These policies reflect the values and goals of the state, and have enormous influence on the cultural messages received by citizens, on what they get to read, hear, see, and evaluate. In countries where individual expression is protected, the arts and culture will flourish in many forms and directions and artists feel free to produce what they wish, although even here they are alert to emphases suggested by funding resources. In countries where the state imposes its will, at least by controlling the financial supports, at most by forbidding certain expression altogether, the arts and culture are highly controlled. In severe cases, the punishment for breaking with official policy may range from the cut-off of state funding, to restrictions on the right to exhibit cultural productions, to imprisonment or exile, and even to execution.

The art of revolutionary Russia began by glorifying its

Picture 1 Russian poster, "Industrialization Is the Path to Socialism," 1928.

socialist goals, yet official freedom of expression allowed a wide variety of forms. In 1928, the Communist Party instituted the Cultural Revolution to "proletarianize" the arts, that is to create expressions which would be understood immediately by the masses and inspire them to carry out the goals of the revolution. In 1932, all artistic groups other than those sanctioned by the government were smothered, and in 1934 Socialist Realism was left as the only officially sanctioned approach. Avant-garde or "progressive" art was decried as bourgeois and irrelevant to the people, and painters were instructed to depict real events and people in an idealized, optimistic way that provided a glimpse of the glorious future of the Soviet Union under communism. The three posters in this spotlight demonstrate the results.

In a visual pun with the gauge in the center, **picture 1**, "Industrialization Is the

Path to Socialism" (1928), celebrates the tenth anniversary of the October Revolution in 1917 and shows a worker pulling the switch to inaugurate the first Five Year Plan. Few would call this important art according to the usual canons of artistic expression, but it uses artistic forms to send its message to the masses.

Picture 2, "Transportation workers," is a factory poster from 1932 designed to inspire workers to redouble their efforts. The banners call to achieve the Five Year Plan in just four years.

It draws attention to the importance of the railway network to the success of Russia, by far the largest country in the world in terms of geographical size. The poster also proclaims the engineering accomplishments of the Soviets and celebrates the importance of the union of mental and physical labor.

Picture 3 declares "Long live the great banner of Marx, Engels, and Lenin" and attempts to inspire the Soviet people in the forthcoming war against the Allies (Stalin had just signed a

pact with the Nazis). Set in Moscow, it musters many of the central icons of Russian history and the Revolution—the walls of the Kremlin, St. Boris' cathedral, Lenin's tomb—and it reassures the people that Russian military might will be adequate to the coming battle. Most of all it establishes Joseph Stalin as the leader who will ensure victory. Many critics would regard these posters as propaganda rather than art, for aesthetic values take a back seat to the need to excite and persuade the viewer of the truth of the political message.

Picture 2 Russian poster, "Transportation Workers…," 1932.

Picture 3 Russian poster, "Long Live the Great Banner of Marx, Engels, and Lenin," 1939.

allowed no political freedom. As early as 1902, Lenin had called for the party to be "the vanguard fighter … guided by the most advanced theory." The party now controlled the state, the army, the Cheka (later the KGB), or secret police, and the Gosplan or planning commission. Its control stretched into the deepest recesses of the economic, political, social, and cultural life of the country.

Through the party "purges" of the 1930s, Stalin smothered any potential opposition to him and his policies. In 1933, a third of the members of the Communist Party were expelled. Dozens were tried and, after submitting forced confessions, executed or imprisoned. In private thousands more were executed and millions sentenced to the many prison camps located throughout the Soviet Union—designated the *Gulag Archipelago* by Alexander Solzhenitsyn, who first revealed their existence publicly in the 1960s.

KHRUSCHEV, BREZHNEV, AND GORBACHEV

After Stalin's death in 1953, Party General Secretary Nikita Khrushchev (1894–1971) began to disclose and reject some of the coercive powers of the state. At the Twentieth Party Congress in 1956, Khrushchev exposed officially the extent of Stalin's tyranny:

> Arbitrary behavior by one person encouraged and permitted arbitrariness in others. Mass arrests and deportations of many thousands of people, executions without trial and without normal investigation created conditions of insecurity, fear, and even desperation. (Kochan and Abraham, p. 447)

In 1961, at the Twenty-second Party Congress, Khruschev denounced Stalin more fully and had

*T*HE GULAG ARCHIPELAGO

Alexander Solzhenitsyn (b. 1918) spent years in Soviet prison camps and characterized them as the crucial institution in perpetuating Stalin's totalitarian rule. The core of the camps was torture, which reached a peak when prisoners were interrogated.

> But the most awful thing they can do with you is this: undress you from the waist down, place you on your back on the floor, pull your legs apart, seat assistants on them (from the glorious corps of sergeants!) who also hold down your arms; and then the interrogator (and women interrogators have not shrunk from this) stands between your legs and with the toe of his boot (or of her shoe) gradually, steadily, and with ever greater pressure crushes against the floor those organs which once made you a man. He looks into your eyes and repeats and repeats his questions or the betrayal he is urging on you. If he does not press down too quickly or just a shade too powerfully, you still have fifteen seconds left in which to scream that you will confess to everything, that you are ready to see arrested all twenty of those people he's been demanding of you, or that you will slander in the newspapers everthing you hold holy. (pp. 127–8)

Jailers as well as prisoners were dehumanized in the process, though in dramatically different ways:

> If you could just get one of them to resist! "I love strong opponents! It's such fun to break their backs!" said the Leningrad interrogator Sitov to G. G——v.
>
> And if your opponent is so strong that he refuses to give in, all your methods have failed, and you are in a rage? Then don't control your fury! It's tremendously satisfying, that outburst! Let your anger have its way; don't set any bounds to it! Don't hold yourself back! That's when interrogators spit in the open mouth of the accused! And shove his face into a full cuspidor! That's the state of mind in which they drag priests around by their long hair! Or urinate in a kneeling prisoner's face! After such a storm of fury you feel yourself a real honest-to-God man! (p. 150)

For revealing these horrors, Solzhenitsyn was exiled from the Soviet Union. But he was also awarded the Nobel Prize for Literature. His accounts of official government torture resonated in many other countries, as we shall see below.

Moscow power parade. At the height of the Cold War, the arms race against the West saw Russian premiers Khrushchev and Brezhnev pouring colossal sums of money into military hardware. This parade shows tanks moving through Red Square, Moscow, to mark the sixtieth anniversary of the 1917 October Revolution. Note the huge poster of Lenin overseeing the proceedings.

his body removed from Lenin's Mausoleum. Khrushchev released a number of political prisoners of conscience, permitted publication of many politically banned works, and moderated Stalin's plans for heavy industrialization in favor of greater production of consumer goods. The Soviet government itself gradually began to portray Stalin as a political monster.

Under Khrushchev, the Soviet Union continued to attempt to catch up to the West—and in some competitions even to surpass it. The Soviet space program put the first rocket, the Sputnik, into orbit around earth in 1957 and developed far more of the "virgin lands" of Kazakhstan and Siberia. Agriculture continued to lag and consumer goods continued to be very limited, but Russia seemed on a par with the United States militarily and industrially. The question would later arise whether the relatively backward economy could continue to support the national investment in heavy military industries. At the time, however, the Russian government felt surrounded and threatened by the United States and its allies, and, having endured

two world wars, saw no choice but to continue preparing its defenses.

Khrushchev maintained Russia's domination of its neighbors. Brooking no revolt in the Eastern European satellites, he crushed the Hungarian uprising of 1956. He stationed nuclear-tipped missiles in Cuba, Russia's ally in the Caribbean—until forced to withdraw them in 1962 in confrontation with the USA. He built the Berlin Wall in 1961 to close escape routes to the West. The Soviet Party leadership removed Khrushchev from power in 1964. He was followed by almost two decades of bureaucratic administration under Leonid Brezhnev (1906–82).

Brezhnev ruled the Soviet Union from 1964 to 1982 as head of the government and General Secretary of the Communist Party. In 1968 Czechoslovakia attempted to escape Russian control and establish an independent government. Brezhnev ended the hopes of this "Prague Spring" by declaring that the Soviet Union would intervene in the affairs of its satellites to prevent counter-revolution, a policy later named the Brezhnev doctrine. He sent in Soviet troops to crush the Czech revolt. In the first years of his administration, Brezhnev built up the armed forces of the USSR, although later he made cutbacks.

Only in 1985, with the coming to power of Mikhail Gorbachev (b. 1931) and his policies of *glasnost* (political and cultural openness) and of *perestroika* (economic restructuring), were fundamental reforms of the Soviet system undertaken. The USSR could no longer afford the costs of the arms race. Its economy was neither producing nor distributing goods effectively. Its growing professional classes protested the restrictions on freedom of exchange of ideas inside and outside the country. The churches continued to seek greater freedom of expression. In the satellite countries of Eastern Europe and in the non-Russian states of the USSR itself—especially the states of Central Asia which were culturally, linguistically, and religiously very different from Russia—nationalist groups sought greater independence. In its haste to industrialize the Russians had allowed technology to get out of control, as evident in the massive pollution of air and sea, most frighteningly at Lake Baikal, and in the partial meltdown of the nuclear power plant at Chernobyl, Ukraine, in 1986, which spread radiation over several European nations.

Gorbachev withdrew the USSR from the arms race and began a fundamental reorganization of its technological institutions and economic priorities. He terminated control over the governments of Eastern Europe, which Russia had put into place and supported militarily during and after World War II. With the removal of Russian armies, all six nations—East Germany, Poland, Hungary, Czechoslovakia, Bulgaria, and Romania—became independent. Divided by the Allied occupying powers at the end of World War II, East and West Germany re-united, tearing down the Berlin Wall that had marked their division. Gorbachev resisted the right of constituent republics of the USSR to declare independence and leave the union, but many seized the opportunity and declared their independence: the restive Baltic states of Estonia, Latvia, and Lithuania; the highly productive Slavic states of Belarus and Ukraine; the peripheral, non-Slavic states of Armenia and Georgia, and the Muslim majority states of Azerbaijan, Kazakhstan, and Uzbekistan. With government control uncertain, historic ethnic tensions re-emerged within and between these states, and violent clashes marked the end of the empire.

In some ways the Russia of 1985–91 was, ironically, similar to that of 1914–17. In both cases Russia was ruled by an autocratic ruler surrounded by hand-chosen followers and bureaucrats, who received special treatment and were elevated over the rest of the country. Its peasantry farmed collectivized villages. It looked to Western Europe and the United States, which it trailed by similar ratios in both periods, with both fear and admiration, maintaining arms for defense but hungry to devote its technology to more productive uses. To compete, the state built giant industrial enterprises. It

"THE RETURN OF HISTORY"

*G*orbachev understood that reform must rest on a clear understanding of the roots and origins of the problems to be solved, on a clear understanding of history. He encouraged new, honest research in, and publication of, the history of communist Russia as a means of lancing many boils. David Remnick captures the new spirit and its implications in *Lenin's Tomb: The Last Days of the Soviet Empire:*

> After some initial hesitation at the beginning of his time in power, Gorbachev had decreed that the time had come to fill in the "blank spots" of history. There could be no more "rose colored glasses," he

said. At first, his rhetoric was guarded. He spoke of "thousands" instead of tens of millions of victims. He did not dare criticize Lenin, the demigod of the state. But despite Gorbachev's hesitation, the return of historical memory would be his most important decision, one that preceded all others, for without a full and ruthless assessment of the past—an admission of murder, repression, and bankruptcy—real change, much less democratic revolution, was impossible. The return of history to personal, intellectual, and political life was the start of the great reform of the twentieth century and, whether Gorbachev liked it or not, the collapse of the last empire on earth. (p. 4)

spoke to the demands of the common people for more "Peace, Land, Bread," but could not effectively satisfy them. International military and strategic competition was bankrupting the nation, finally leading it to withdraw from warfare—hot in 1917, cold in 1985—and to chart a new course. The old order was in the process of being overthrown by revolutionary forces, but neither the new order nor the dominant forces that would lead it had been determined.

Gorbachev had introduced many of the changes, but they proceeded out of his control and he was no longer able to govern. In 1991 he resigned. The elected President of the largest state, Boris Yeltsin of Russia, created and led the Commonwealth of Independent States (CIS), a new voluntary, non-sovereign federation, which included twelve of the fifteen member states of the former Union of Soviet Socialist Republics (USSR). Together, these states coordinated the dissolution of the Soviet Union, including the allocations among its former member states of its technological and military assets and the control of its nuclear weapons. Many of these weapons were destroyed under new international agreements for disarmament and Russia continued to move forward with a series of agreements on arms reductions.

Economically, Yeltsin continued to privatize much of the economy, selling state enterprises to private business interests. In response to the dislocations in the economy that resulted and the soaring prices of many staple commodities, Yeltsin later limited some of this economic reorganization. Russia seems to be developing not only a more open, less regulated economy, but also a pattern of

INDEPENDENT COUNTRIES OF THE FORMER USSR

Republic	Population (1995)	Capital
Armenia	3.6 million	Yerevan
Azerbaijan	7.6 million	Baku
Belorussia (Belarus)	10.1 million	Minsk
Estonia	1.5 million	Tallinn
Georgia	5.5 million	Tbilisi
Kazakhstan	17.1 million	Alma-Ata (Almaty)
Kirgizia (Kyrgyzstan)	4.7 million	Frunze (Bishkek)
Latvia	2.6 million	Riga
Lithuania	3.7 million	Vilnius
Moldavia	4.4 million	Kishinev (Chisinău)
Russian Federation	147 million	Moscow
Tadzhikistan (Tajikistan)	6.1 million	Dushanbe
Turkmenistan	4.1 million	Ashkhabad (Ashgabat)
Ukraine	51.4 million	Kiev
Uzbekistan	22.8 million	Tashkent

The Russians in Chechnya. Most of the former Soviet satellite states gained independence through peaceful means, but the remote province of Chechnya faced a military invasion when it attempted to secede. Here Russian servicemen drive warily through the war-torn streets of Grozny, the Chechen capital, on the lookout for snipers.

The break-up of the Soviet Union The Soviet experiment with Marxist ideology crumbled, after seventy years, at the end of the 1980s. President Gorbachev's policy of *glasnost* (1988) allowed the nations of Eastern Europe to move, largely bloodlessly, toward independence and economic reform, but in the Caucasus mountains and Central Asia reform was often accompanied by an insurgence of nationalism, organized crime, and power struggles. In 1991 President Yeltsin allowed these nations, too, to become independent—except for Chechnya, where fighting continued for years.

democratic multi-party elections, which includes participation by the discredited but still active Communist Party. In 1996 Yeltsin was elected in nationwide elections to continue as president; his closest opponent ran on the communist ticket.

Many problems persisted. One of Yeltsin's greatest embarrassments was the continuing war in the remote breakaway province of Chechnya. The once proud Russian army could not defeat the rebels. Russia agonized publicly over the future directions for its economy and technology, although both seemed headed toward greater privatization and consumer orientation and away from state control and military mobilization. With a freer economy, a small class of entrepreneurs became much richer, and found the stores stocked with merchandise previously unavailable. But the average person did not find much increase in the general standard of living. Crime became commonplace in Russia, and highly organized criminal organizations flourished in an environment of political corruption and police complicity. Meanwhile Yeltsin's most active challenger was a military general, Alexander Lebed, who did achieve a peace agreement in Chechnya in 1996, but was unclear on his politi-

cal, economic, and technological policies. New directions for Russia's government and economy continued to emerge. In 1997, the Czech Republic, Poland, and Hungary—Russian satellites—were inducted as NATO members, and Russia was accorded associate status in this organization of its former enemies. None could predict the next developments in Russia's astonishing transformation.

JAPAN: FRAGILE SUPERPOWER 1914–1990s

BEFORE WORLD WAR I

Like Russia, Japan feared domination by the nations of Western Europe and the United States. Confronted by foreign gunboats in the mid-nineteenth century (see pp. 563–70), the Japanese responded with the restoration program of the Emperor Meiji, an astonishingly rapid reorganization of government, administration, economy, industry, and finances. Japan was not "Western" but neither was it "backward."

As we have seen in Chapter 17, Japan, following Western examples, asserted a sphere of influence in China and seized colonies for itself. Japan defeated China in Korea in 1895 and became the dominant nation of east Asia, reversing the previous teacher-student relationship between them. Japan also gained increased influence in Korea and received two colonies, the island of Taiwan and the Liaotung Peninsula in Manchuria. Russia, alarmed at the new Japanese presence on the mainland, became increasingly hostile and in 1904–5, two years after signing a military alliance with Britain, Japan attacked Russian positions at Port Arthur, destroyed the Russian fleet in the Straits of Tsushima, and defeated the Russian army in Manchuria. For the first time in modern history, an Asian country had defeated a European one.

World War I touched East Asia only slightly. Nevertheless, Japan sat as one of the victorious Five Great Powers at the 1919 peace conference at Versailles, the only non-Western nation accepted as an equal at the proceedings, and was assigned control over Germany's Pacific colonies, including the Liaotung Peninsula, which Japan had seized in the course of the war.

World War I had presented Japan with an unprecedented economic opportunity. While other industrialized countries were occupied with war in Europe, Japan developed its industries free from the usual international competition. Between 1914 and 1918 Japan's gross national income rose by 40 percent. For the first time Japan began to export more than she imported. Heavy industry showed particularly impressive growth—manufacturing increased 72 percent, with an increase in the labor force of only 42 percent, indicating the increasing introduction of mechanization. Transport increased 60 percent. Between 1914 and 1919 Japan's merchant marine almost doubled, to 2.8 million tons. Consumer goods production and exports also advanced. In the first decades of the twentieth century, Japan's greatest exports were textiles, primarily silk, of which 80 percent was produced by women. During the war, silk cocoon output increased by 60 percent, spurred on partly by increased American demands for silk and facilitated by new technologies, such as an automatic loom patented in 1916 by Toyoda Sakichi, whose son founded the Toyota Motor Company in 1937. (Morris-Suzuki, p. 117)

As a late-comer, Japan could take advantage of technology already developed in the West (the path that Trotsky was preaching in Russia). Japanese industries practiced three different patterns in importing that technology. Some signed agreements with foreign firms to establish branches in Japan; some negotiated for licenses to use the new technologies; and some practised "reverse engineering," disassembling machinery and reproducing it with adaptations appropriate to Japanese needs. Adaptation was standard procedure—for example, applying chemical research to agricultural and even ceramics production. Most of the foreign technology was imported by private firms, but the government also encouraged research by funding state universities, laboratories, and the development of military technology.

Japan bridged the "dual economy," the separation between large-scale and cottage industries which has inhibited growth in many countries. In a "dual economy," one sector consists of large, highly capitalized, technically advanced factories employing thousands of workers producing modern products; the other sector includes small-scale workshops, with relatively low capitalization and less up-to-date equipment, often employing fewer than thirty workers, producing traditional goods. In most countries, the small-scale sector tends to shrivel, its workers consigned to low wages and poor conditions, as larger firms achieve economies of scale and put it out of business. Governments, too, as we have seen in Russia, often invest their resources in large industries, neglecting the small sector. But in Japan, the smaller factories adopted appropriate scale, new technologies, and began to produce new goods needed by the larger industries. From the early years of the century, Japan evolved systems of subcontracting between the large and small sectors which made them interdependent and complementary.

Today, even the largest Japanese industries rely on small factories to supply parts of their final, assembled products (a process of "outsourcing" increasingly adopted today in the United States). Particularly under the pressure of war, 1937–45, Japanese business developed very cost-effective systems of precisely timed (kamban, "just in time") deliveries so that large firms did not need to keep large inventories of parts, but ordered and received them just when they were needed. Under this "just-in-time" system, needed changes in production are usually carried out by the smaller industries. The strain of industrial change is borne disproportionately by the individual small factories, affecting relatively few people, while the larger industries and the economy as a whole are spared.

ECONOMICS IN THE COMIC BOOKS

In Japan, the comics, like television, have become a powerful medium for entertainment, for the transmission of knowledge, and for the diffusion of values. Indeed the term "comics" is a misnomer. Most *manga* (the generic term for cartoons, narrative strips, and animated films), are not at all funny. The most ambitious strive to achieve artistic and intellectual responsibility.

With these words, Peter Duus, Professor of History at Stanford University, introduces *Japan Inc.: An Introduction to Japanese Economics (The Comic Book)* published in translation in 1988 by the University of California Press from the 1986 Japanese original by Shotaro Ishinomori. Weekly "comic books" sell in the hundreds of thousands of copies; the record is 4 million. Some 550,000 copies of *Japan Inc.* were sold in less than a year. The six chapters of the *manga*, "comic," include quite serious issues: Trade Friction, Countering the Rise of the Yen, Industrial Structure, Deficit Finance, Monetary Revolution, and an Epilogue, which stresses the importance of human and humane relations in business. The two pages reproduced here depict a debate between two executives with very different perspectives within a single company as they weigh the effects on small subcontractors of the company's decision to close a local automobile factory and relocate its production to the United States. In the end, Kudo's more compassionate position does win out. (*Japan Inc.* pp. 12–13)

A spread from *Japan Inc.: An Introduction to Japanese Economics* by Shotaro Ishinomori.

Samurai warriors. The ancient and proud warrior class of the samurai worshipped athletic prowess, swordsmanship, and fierce loyalty to the emperor. In 1877 the last 400,000 samurai were pensioned off to become *shizoku*, Japanese gentry, but their virtues lived on in the country's psyche. In times of crisis, the warriors' values turned Japanese nationalism into a potent force.

SOCIAL CONSEQUENCES OF WAR-TIME INDUSTRIAL GROWTH

Because of poor harvests in 1918 the price of rice, Japan's staple food, rose sharply. In response, massive urban riots broke out in hundreds of cities and towns, involving some 700,000 people, lasting fifty days, and resulting in 25,000 arrests and 1,000 deaths. The government responded by importing rice and other staples from its colonial territories in Korea and Taiwan. The riots represented the growth of Japan's urban voice as the urban percentage of the population rose from over 10 percent in 1890 to close to 50 percent in the 1920s (to 78 percent in the 1990s). Labor was increasingly organized and the citizenry politicized. A few weeks later, the government fell, and in 1919 the new government liberalized voting requirements, tripling the eligible electorate to 3 million. In 1925 all male subjects over the age of twenty-five, 12.5 million people, were given the vote.

The riots also reminded Japan of its increasing dependence on its colonies for daily commodities. In the later 1920s Taiwan and Korea provided four-fifths of Japan's rice imports and two-thirds of its sugar. For industrial raw materials, such as minerals, metals, petroleum, fertilizers, and lumber, Japan had to shop further afield, and later this would lead it into extravagant, and fatal, colonial adventures.

At home, in the 1920s, the economy registered mixed results. As the prices of both rice and silk dropped sharply, rural Japan was hard hit. Rural tenants organized unions to contest landlord control. But industrial production increased by two-thirds during the decade. The **zaibatsu** (huge holding companies or conglomerates) came to control much of the Japanese economy. The four largest—Mitsui, Mitsubishi, Sumitomo, and Yasuda—were controlled by individual families, and each operated a bank and enterprises in a variety of industries, ranging from textiles to shipping and machinery. A Mitsubishi mining company, for example, would extract minerals, which would then be made into a product by one of the Mitsubishi manufacturing companies. This product would be marketed abroad by a Mitsubishi trading firm and transported in ships of another Mitsubishi affiliate. The whole process would be financed through the Mitsubishi bank.

The *zaibatsu* combined large size with an ability to shift production to meet demands. The *zaibatsu* families also held considerable influence in government, both through the money they wielded and their close family links with prominent politicians. Government policies helped the *zaibatsu*, often in promoting military industrialization. The Major Industries Control Law of 1931, for example, encouraged large companies in key industries to join in cartels to regulate production and prices. (Morris-Suzuki, p. 139)

MILITARISM

International respect, growing wealth, rising urbanization, increasing industrialization, high rates of literacy, universal male suffrage, and the institutionalization of political parties suggested that Japan was embracing liberal democracy. But countervailing pressures also emerged. The political power of the *zaibatsu* undermined people's faith in democratic practise, and the military held extraordinary power, both under law and in popular opinion. In contrast to most democratic countries, in which the military is under the control of the civilian government, the Japanese constitution of 1889 specified that the ministers of war and of the navy had to be active generals or admirals. Conversely, the formal powers of the Diet were restricted. In theory, the emperor held the ultimate political authority for the country and, although he never did govern actively, political leaders speaking in his name often had great influence on public policy. Japan's traditional Shinto religion (see Chapter 9) emphasized the emperor's divinity and asserted the leading role of Japan's samurai warrior elite.

Many of these military elites began to claim expanded powers for the armed forces. They wished to protect Japan, a resource-poor island nation, especially vulnerable to shifts in international trade and its regulation. The world depression shocked the Japanese economy as the value of exports dropped 50 percent between 1929 and 1931. Unemployment rose to 3 million, with rural areas hardest hit. The future would look brighter if Japan could reorganize and control the economy of east Asia for its own benefit. Many civilians seemed to agree with the military. When Prime Minister Osachi Hamaguchi over-rode his navy and accepted a 1930 international agreement with the United States and Britain, effectively limiting the size of the Japanese navy, a right-wing fanatic shot him to death in 1931. In the next few years similar assassinations would follow.

THE RUN-UP TO
THE PACIFIC WAR 1930–37

On the night of September 18, 1931 members of the Japanese army blew up a section of the South Manchurian Railroad, deliberately provoking military confrontation. While claiming that the Chinese were responsible, the Japanese army dispatched reinforcements and by the next day they controlled all of Mukden. With the "Manchurian incident" the Japanese army began to set its own agenda, without regard to Tokyo's instructions.

The army sought to control all of Manchuria both for its mineral wealth and for its geo-political position as a buffer against Russia. After completing the military takeover, Japan established a puppet state, Manchukuo, and installed its hand-picked emperor, Pu Yi. When the League of Nations censured the Japanese, Japan quit the organization. Mired in economic depression, the major powers did nothing. The Japanese civilian government, which had attempted to rein in the army, lost public support and fell. The next prime minister, the last pre-war leader, was assassinated.

Strategic and commercial concerns began to converge. As Morris-Suzuki notes, Japan's "technologies of peace and war were, above all else, interrelated" (p. 125). The government encouraged and protected infant industries, especially those that could be quickly converted to military production: chemicals, automobiles, aircraft, and shipping. In the two decades from the end of World War I to 1937, Japan's industrial production tripled. Technological advances included the production of new artifical fibers, such as rayon, of which Japan became a major exporter; chemical improvements in fertilizers; improved machine tools; and new techniques in brewing, reducing the time needed to produce *sake* (rice wine). By 1935, 89 percent of Japanese households had access to electric lighting (compared with 68 percent in the United States). By 1936, Japan was the world's third largest consumer of electricity, although most of the production was designated for industry. Consumer goods, such as refrigerators, which were becoming common in the wealthier Western countries, were priced beyond the means of the average Japanese consumer. Okochi Masatoshi, director of Japan's Institute for Physical and Chemical Research, saw clearly the link between commercial and military industrialization. He wrote in 1937: "In the final analysis future wars will not be wars of military might versus military might. They will be wars involving the entire nation's scientific knowledge and industrial capacity" (Morris-Suzuki, p. 127). With the onset of World War II, Japan's industries shifted from civilian to military production.

THE PACIFIC WAR 1937–45

In 1937 a clash between Chinese and Japanese troops at the Marco Polo Bridge near Beijing triggered a full-scale war with China, which marked the beginning of the Pacific War (World War II). The Japanese had not expected the fierce resistance of the Chinese. Planning to end the "China probem" with a single quick victory that would terrify the enemy into suing for peace, the Japanese army launched a full-scale attack on Nanjing (Nanking), capturing the city in December. Japanese troops murdered, raped, and pillaged in what is now generally known as "the Rape of Nanjing." Twelve thousand noncombatant Chinese were killed in the first two or three days after Nanjing was captured, and about 20,000 cases of rape were reported in the first month. In the first six weeks after the fall of Nanjing, as many as 200,000 civilians and prisoners of war were killed in and around the city. The atrocities set an ugly precedent for later Japanese cruelty toward many of the peoples it defeated throughout Asia during the war.

Humiliated and infuriated, the Chinese fought on. In the face of repeated Japanese advances, the Chinese government retreated to Chongqing (Chungking), on the upper Yangzi River deep in the interior of the country. The Chinese, like the Russians retreating before the Germans, followed a scorched-earth strategy, leaving little in their wake that would be of use to the enemy. The war in China dragged on in a stalemate until 1945. Even as Japan extended the war to Southeast Asia and the Pacific Ocean, it did not, and later could not, retrieve its forces from China. Even in 1945, when Japan itself was under attack, about a million Japanese soldiers were still fighting in China, and another 750,000 in Manchuria. China's sheer persistence helped wear out the Japanese.

In September 1940, Japan signed the Tripartite Pact, aligning itself with Germany and Italy as the "Axis Powers." Japan could have joined in their war against the USSR, opening a second front from Manchuria, as Germany wished, but instead, it signed a neutrality pact with the Soviet Union in April 1941. Japan then turned southward to capture French Indo-China, putting it on a collision course with the USA. Isolationist pressure in America had thus far kept the USA out of armed warfare, but America did respond to Japanese aggression in China and Southeast Asia by placing an embargo on trade with Japan and by freezing its assets in July 1941. Resource-poor Japan, fearing for its supplies of oil and other raw materials, now had to choose between pulling back or confronting the United States in open warfare. On December 7, Japan bombed the American Pacific fleet at Pearl Harbor, Hawaii. America declared war the next day. In Britain, Winston Churchill immediately understood the consequences:

> Hitler's fate was sealed. Mussolini's fate was sealed. As for the Japanese, they would be ground to powder. All the rest was merely the proper application of overwhelming force. (Kennedy, *Rise and Fall*, p. 347)

Until American industrial power and troop mobilization could move into high gear, however, Japan moved forward in Southeast Asia, conquering the Philippines, Borneo and the Celebes, the Malay peninsula and Singapore, Sumatra, Java, parts of New Guinea, Indochina, Thailand, and Burma. In the Pacific, it captured the Solomon, Ellice, and Gilbert Islands, reaching almost to Australia.

Summary executions in the Pacific. Japanese soldiers were notoriously brutal in their treatment of prisoners during World War II. Many British servicemen captured in the Pacific theater were forced to construct the Burma Railway and many died of starvation and disease in the process. Some were murdered in cold blood, as here, the imminent execution of three Allied fighters before open graves.

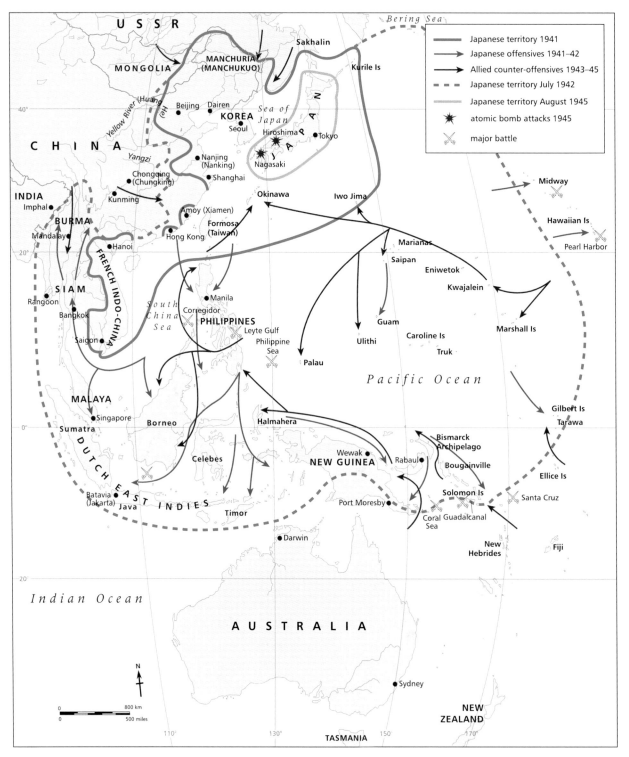

World War II in the Pacific Japan mounted combined operations in 1941 in East Asia, Southeast Asia, and across the Pacific, opening a war front from the borders of India to Hawaii. This supremely aggressive move was meant to secure the resources and markets needed to sustain the "Greater East Asian Co-Prosperity Sphere." It proved impossible to defend: Chinese resistance, a daring US island-hopping campaign in the Pacific—culminating in the explosion of atomic bombs over Hiroshima and Nagasaki—and Soviet assaults on Manchuria defeated Japan completely.

Designating the conquests as the "Greater East Asia Co-Prosperity Sphere," Japan attempted to build a colonial empire that would provide it with raw materials for its industries and markets for its finished products and that would begin to adopt Japanese cultural practices as well. The imperial plan did not work. The colonial economies could not produce and deliver what Japan wanted, and, more crucially, Japan could not absorb the products they could produce. Market structures based on the previous integration of world trade systems were not easily displaced. Instead of implanting its culture, Japan's occupations generally evoked nationalistic opposition to the Japanese conquerors. Japan's treatment of conquered peoples was notably harsh and earned it a reputation for cruelty. For example, Japan's brutalizing of thousands of Korean women to serve as "sex slaves" for Japanese soldiers came to international attention, along with the demand for financial reparation and public apologies, half a century after the war was over.

Japan also encouraged opposition to the European colonial powers, which had preceded the Japanese. After the war, when the European colonizers attempted to return—the British to Burma and Malaya, the French to Indochina, the Dutch to Indonesia, the Americans to the Philippines—local nationalist groups rose in protest, sometimes armed, and achieved independence. In this sense, the Japanese victories were responsible for the ending of European colonialism in the Pacific region after the war.

Once America, with its full industrial and technological strength, entered the war, the tide turned. America's main thrust was against Germany, but it turned also to the Pacific theater. In June 1942, American forces won their first battle at Midway Island. Then, from bases in Australia, they moved northwestward, taking Guadalcanal and New Guinea, recapturing the Philippines and the island chains of the Gilberts, the Marshalls, the Carolines, and the Marianas. In the spring of 1945 they captured Okinawa in three months of brutal fighting. As early as March 1944 the Americans had begun firebombing Japanese cities. Japan had expected Americans to grow tired of the war and negotiate a peace; instead America demanded nothing short of unconditional surrender.

The firebombing intensified. On March 9, 1945, 83,793 people were killed, 40,918 injured, and 267,000 buildings destroyed in Tokyo alone. Burning and starving—caloric intake had dropped from a daily standard of 2200 to 1405 by 1944—Japan fought on. Finally, wishing to prevent the Allied casualties that would certainly have resulted from a land invasion of Japan, and probably also wishing to send a warning to post-war Russia, America dropped the atomic bomb on Hiroshima

US servicemen in the Pacific. Landing in Higgins boats from a base in Australia, American troops of the 163rd Infantry Regiment, 41st Division, hit the beach running during the invasion of Wake Island, 18 May 1944. Two months prior, the United States had begun firebombing Japanese cities.

on August 6, 1945 (see p. 600). On August 8, the USSR entered the Pacific theater with an invasion of Manchuria and Korea. On August 9, America dropped a second atomic bomb, this time on Nagasaki. On August 15, 1945 Japan offered its unconditional surrender.

In August 1945, Japan lay in ruins. Some 3 million Japanese had died in the war, a fourth of Japan's national assets were destroyed, industrial production was at barely 10 percent of normal pre-war levels, millions of homes had been destroyed, and Japan was dispossessed of all colonial holdings. Mass starvation was prevented only by food imported by the occupation authorities.

THE OCCUPATION 1945–52

Japan awaited an uncertain future under American occupation, headed by Supreme Commander for the Allied Powers (SCAP), General Douglas MacArthur. The occupation lasted until 1952, proved benign, and focused on four goals: punishing Japanese leaders as war criminals; establishing democratic institutions and practices; re-starting the devastated Japanese economy; and enlisting Japan as an ally in the new Cold War against the USSR and its allies. All four goals were achieved.

In terms of punishment, some 200,000 wartime leaders in government, the military, and business were barred from office. Twenty-five of the top leaders were tried for starting the war; seven, including General Tojo, were hanged; and most of the rest were sentenced to long prison terms. The emperor was no longer to be regarded as sacred, nor would he wield actual political power. His role would be as a constitutional monarch. The preservation of the emperor as a symbol probably made Japanese acceptance of the occupation somewhat less difficult.

The empire was dissolved, and 5.5 million expatriate Japanese were returned to Japan. The military was completely demobilized. State support for Shinto was ended. Police authority and power were reduced. Freedom of speech was reintroduced. Political prisoners were freed. A new constitution, issued in 1947, granted universal adult suffrage to everyone over the age of twenty, including women for the first time. The Diet became an elected, British-style Parliament, with two houses. The judiciary was independent, headed by a supreme court. Guarantees of freedom of assembly, the press, "life, liberty, and the pursuit of happiness," and the "right to maintain the minimum standards of wholesome and cultural living" were also written into the constitution. (Fairbank, p. 821)

Economically, the Occupation Authority pushed ahead on four fronts. First, it redistributed agricultural land. Land held by absentee landlords and land in excess of 10 acres (4 hectares) per family had to be sold to the government at low rates, and the government, in turn, sold it to tenants. Land worked by tenants dropped from 46 percent to 10 percent. Land rents were also limited. The new class of small farmers prospered and felt strong allegiance to the government.

Second, the largest *zaibatsu* were dissolved into their constituent companies and anti-monopoly legislation was passed. Over the next decades, new conglomerates, called *keiretsu*, grew up with many qualities of the *zaibatsu*, but they were less restrictive, and they allowed more scope for the start-up of new companies.

Third, the Occupation Authority encouraged the formation of labor unions, legalizing the right to organize, bargain, and strike. Within three years the unions had grown to several million members, and had begun to turn communist! The Occupation Authority passed new laws to restrict the unions and purge their communist leaders. Unionization and the number of strikes declined, but labor unions, which work closely with management, remain an important feature in Japan's socio-economic life.

Finally, the Occupation Authority restructured the educational system, encouraging dramatic growth. The numbers of middle school students increased from 2.4 to 4.3 million; high school students from 380,000 to 1.2 million by 1952 to 4.3 million by 1975. By 1995, 90 percent of the appropriate age group graduated from high school. University students have increased from 84,000 to 1.73 million in 1975 to 2.5 million in 1995, one-third of the university-age group.

Ironically, within five years of the end of World War II, the United States enlisted Japan as its ally in the Cold War against China and Russia. Japan's post-war constitution did not allow it to build up its military, but a United States–Japanese Security Treaty did allow the United States to maintain military bases throughout Japan and to retain Okinawa until 1972. Under this treaty Japan was protected militarily by the United States.

Meanwhile, Japan became a principal supplier of materials and support services to the Americans fighting in neighboring Korea. The Korean War (1950–53) proved to be an economic boon to Japan,

HISTORICAL REVISIONISM IN JAPAN

The study of history was transformed under American occupation:

The contents of school textbooks were dramatically revised to remove much of the emperor-centered, nationalistic wartime ideology. Even today, older Japanese can vividly recall their shock and disbelief at being directed by their teachers, on occupation orders, to take a brush and black ink to wipe out whole pages of their textbooks, until new books were available. (Spodek, p. 15)

History is still being revised as Japan attempts to decide how to tell the story of its participation in World War II. Does it stress only the end of the war, and the atomic bombing of Hiroshima and Japan's suffering? Or should it also discuss the beginning of the war and Japan's aggression? Should stress be placed on the American embargoes that forced Japan to choose between retreat and war, or Japan's choice of war? These questions are still very live both in educational circles and in public debate in Japan, in Japanese museum displays at Hiroshima and Nagasaki, and in television serials on the war.

---

providing a jump-start to the new growth. During the course of the war, America bought $4 billion worth of military manufactures and tens of thousands of American troops were stationed in Japan. Between 1950 and 1973, Japan's economy grew at a phenomenal average rate of 10.5 percent a year. The gross national product grew from $24 billion in 1955, to $484 billion in 1975, to $4.3 trillion in 1994.

The American occupation introduced to Japan many management training experts. The most influential was W. Edwards Deming, who brought the concept of quality control systems, or "TQM," Total Quality Management, involving all workers throughout the entire process of production. Japanese businessmen adopted this concept more fully than Americans did. Japanese workers were encouraged to feel themselves a valued part of the production process, their suggestions solicited and taken seriously, their job security ensured to the extent possible, their pay and benefits kept at high levels. A senior Toyota official explained the consequences for measuring success:

In Japan the process is the thing. We rate the efficiency of a company by the way its people do things. How they work together is the important thing. For in the end it is their way of working that determines the success of their product. The process is what counts. (Gibney, p. 349)

Japanese consumer goods, produced through this system of personal care and dedication combined with the highest technological efficiency, earned a reputation for excellent quality and began to take over large shares of the world market, challenging more established producers, including the Americans. In addition, the dissolution of the *zaibatsu*, although replaced in part by the *keiretsu*, left space for new companies to grow.

Although labor unions established in the first few years of the occupation had challenged managerial authority, and a fifteen-month strike at Toyota in 1949–50 had almost destroyed the company, later unions were restrained both by their own internal discipline and by government-imposed discipline, and came to work together with management to achieve the common goals of high levels of production and of worker compensation and treatment.

CONTINUITIES 1952–73

By charging government with the coordination of the national economy, Japan set a path different from both the *laissez-faire* American pattern and the state-control of the USSR. Japan's Ministry for International Trade and Industry (MITI) had charge of national tax and investment policies and encouraged industries in allied fields to share technological information. MITI decided which industries would have access to capital for investment and, in the early post-war years, to imports of scarce foreign machinery, materials, and technology.

Japan had found a way of development that was neither fully capitalist and competitive nor fully state-controlled. It blended private enterprise with state guidance in a competitive, high-technology economy, manufacturing exports for a global

CONTROLLING POLLUTION

*R*apid industrialization and urbanization brought problems of pollution to Japan. By the 1960s, daytime skies in Tokyo were grey, Tokyo Bay was filled with industrial sludge, and traffic policemen suffered from lead poisoning, even though they worked on two-hour rotations. Specific cases of industrial pollution drew worldwide attention. In the small city of Minamata, on the island of Kyushu, mercury dumped into the bay by a large chemical plant was leading to deformities and deaths among the local population. As early as 1926 the fish catch was reduced and local fisherman received compensation from the company.

By the early '50s, a number of Minamata fishermen and their families were experiencing the disquieting symptoms of a previously unknown physical disorder. Robust men and women who had formerly enjoyed good health suddenly found their hands trembling so violently they could no longer strike a match. They soon had difficulty thinking clearly, and it became increasingly difficult for them to operate their boats. Numbness that began in the lips and limbs was followed by disturbances in vision, movement, and speech. As the disease progressed, control over all bodily functions diminished. The victims became bedridden, then fell into unconsciousness. Wild fits of thrashing and senseless shouting comprised a later stage, during which many victims' families, to keep the afflicted from injuring themselves or others, resorted to securing them with heavy rope. About forty percent of those stricken died. (from Norrie Huddle and Michael Reich *Island of Dreams: Environmental Crisis in Japan* (New York: Autumn Press, 1975), pp. 106–7, cited in Upham, p. 338)

By 1958 government research pointed to mercury poisoning as the cause of the disease, but the report was not publicly released. In 1959 the Chisso Corporation, source of the pollution, agreed to pay minimal "sympathy payments" to the victims. Still, government and industry attempted to cover up the case. Then, in 1964, a similar outbreak occurred in Niigata Prefecture on the main Japanese island of Honshu, and although the government tried to cover up this information also, it was publicized by a research team from the Niigata University Medical School in 1967. In 1968 and 1969 lawyers filed four separate suits against polluters: in Minamata, in Niigata, in

economy. Until the 1970s, Japan still imported and adapted much of its new technology. Sony, for example, acquired a patent to produce the newly invented transistor in 1954, solved the problem of broadcasting the human voice, and began to produce transistor radios. The number of researchers employed by private companies multiplied seven times between 1952 and 1975. Japan's research capacity, especially in adaptation, was dispersed throughout Japan in numerous small research centers, which gave the country enormous flexibility in research and production. (In the 1980s some twenty-five industrial research towns, called **technopolises**, were added to the mix.)

Japan gained increasing international recognition for its economic and technological gains. In 1964, a number of symbolic events marked this coming of age. In April, Japan was admitted to the Organization for Economic Cooperation and Development (OECD), which until then had included only European and North American governments. Later in the year, the Shinkansen, or "bullet train," began carrying passengers between Tokyo and Osaka at speeds of 125 miles (200 kilometers) an hour, the fastest in the world. In the same year, Tokyo played host to the summer Olympics, winning universal praise for its new architecture, stadia, hotels, and ability to accommodate and please both the participants and the throngs of spectators.

In the 1960s, in recognition of its increasing economic strength, Japan began to produce more consumer goods. From 1957 to 1965 the percentage of non-agricultural homes with black-and-white television sets rose from 7.8 percent to 95 percent; and the homes with refrigerators from 2.8 percent to 68.7 percent. Consumer demand increased in sophistication and in buying power. In the 1950s people had aspired to "three sacred treasures," no longer the mirror, jewels, and sword of ancient Japan, but a television, refrigerator, and washing machine. By the early 1960s these had become the

Yokkaichi, where the issue was air pollution, and in Toyama, where the problem was cadmium poisoning. These "Big Four" cases progressed through the courts for the next few years. "By 1973, when the Minamata plaintiffs won the largest tort award in Japanese history, the antipollution movement ignited by the Big Four was being described as a radically new form of Japanese political action." (Upham, p. 342)

The issue of industrial pollution, underlined by these cases, had moved to the top of Japan's political agenda. Ruling and opposition parties together agreed on legislation and implementation to produce a clean Japan. "Japan went from being clearly the most polluted of the major industrial countries to comparing favorably on those indexes of pollution related to human health." (Upham, p. 343)

Legacy of pollution.
In Minimata, mercury poisoning killed forty-three people and maimed many others between 1953 and 1956. The disease, causing tumors, paralysis, and bone deformities, was contracted by eating fish contaminated by dimethyl mercury seeping from a local PVC factory. In this famous image, Eugene Smith captured the poignancy of a mother washing her stricken son.

three Cs: car, color television, and air conditioner; and by the later 1960s the three Vs: a villa, a vacation, and a visit overseas.

THE OIL SHOCKS OF 1973 AND 1979

Japan's response to the "oil shocks" of 1973 and 1979 demonstrated both Japan's vulnerability and her flexibility. In October 1973, as war broke out between Israel and its Arab neighbors (see p. 704), Arab oil producers raised the price of oil worldwide by two-thirds and restricted its availability (see p. 698). All industrial nations were hard hit, but Japan, which imported 86 percent of its energy needs, mostly oil from the Middle East, was especially affected. In response, Japan intensified the search for reducing energy uses, and through increased industrial efficiency reduced its dependence on oil by 25 percent; it sought oil imports from new sources; and it began to shift into

even more knowledge-intensive industries, such as electronics and computers, which are much less energy-dependent.

When Arab nations again raised the price of oil dramatically in 1979, Japan was better able to cope than other industrial countries. Its productivity did not decline significantly. From the oil shock of 1973 until 1988, Japan's technology and its economy tell two stories: on the one hand, the rate of growth has declined, averaging 5 percent a year (Ito, p. 3), less than half that of the previous two decades; on the other hand, this performance was better than that of any other major power.

INTERNATIONAL INVESTMENT FINANCE 1989–1990s

Japan continued to earn colossal trade surpluses, reaching $96 billion in 1987 and $95 billion in 1988. Much of this surplus was invested overseas. For example, all the major Japanese automobile manufacturers established production plants in the United States between 1980 and 1985: Nissan in Tennessee; Honda in Ohio; Toyota in California; Mazda in Michigan. Cars produced in these plants are sold in America without import or tariff restrictions, although their profits are sent to Japan. Additional overseas investment is placed in developing countries, especially in nearby Asian countries. Japan became the world's largest donor of foreign aid, giving about $14 billion in 1994. The aid helps the recipient and also provides a climate for Japanese business and investment.

On the other side, forces inhibiting growth include three major problems. First, Japan's enormous trade surpluses have created "trade frictions" with debtor countries. For example, the American trade deficit with Japan in 1986 reached $62 billion and, despite increasing competitiveness from America, it was still $59 billion in 1995. Western nations have urged Japan to impose "voluntary self-restrictions" on exports, to open its own markets to increased imports, and to consume more. Japan agreed, and by 1985 these voluntary restrictions had cut 40 percent of potential exports. Nevertheless, the balance of trade continues dramatically in Japan's favor. The United States and some European countries claim that unfair trade practices keep foreign products out of Japanese markets. The Japanese point out the problems of the Americans and Europeans themselves. Edwin

Reischauer, former United States Ambassador to Japan, summarizes:

They point out that Americans allowed their industrial enterprises to stagnate, let shortsighted concern over quick profits eclipse concern for healthy long-term growth, developed a less well-educated, less diligent, and less loyal work force and an overpaid, top-heavy managerial superstructure, and paid little attention to foreign markets until they found themselves hopelessly behind in them. … They failed to develop goods designed for overseas purchasers, did not study foreign business practices, and did not learn foreign languages. A simple example is that they did not produce righthand-drive cars for Japan, where, as in England, cars drive on the left. Similarly, they made refrigerators that would not fit into Japanese apartments. Up until a few years ago, virtually no foreign businessmen spoke Japanese. As Japanese love to point out, if they had approached the American market the way Americans approached Japan's, their trade with America would consist primarily of things like paper fans. (Reischauer, p. 378)

Second, the off-shore investments in nearby countries—Korea, Taiwan, Hong Kong, Singapore, Thailand, and China—will lead both to increased competition from their new products and to a loss of jobs to their lower-wage economies. Japan is

In this fully automated factory owned by Toyota, robots fit windscreens to a production-line car.

experiencing the same "hollowing out of industry" as did the United States, as industries close at home and factories and jobs are moved off-shore. Meanwhile, the Asian nations receiving the investment appear to be going through the same processes of technological development as Japan did in its post-war years. They compete with Japan internationally and even within the Japanese home market in industries such as textiles, chemicals, iron and steel, and electrical products.

Finally, in 1989 an economic "bubble" burst in Japan, and the country slipped into an unexpected recession. In a "bubble" economy, prices for stocks and investments rise as investors bet on the future, anticipating continually improving economic performance. If these expectations outrun reality, however, prices will suddenly collapse. In Japan in 1989–90 land values plummeted as the total land of Japan, which had been valued at four times the total value of land in the United States, dropped to more realistic levels. The Nikkei stock market index followed, plummeting from 35,000 in 1989 to 14,000 in 1992. Billions of dollars in paper wealth were wiped out, and Japan fell into a long-term depression. This depression curtailed Japan's economic and technological growth and its power in the international economy and raised the question: Will Japan be able to recover and become a leader in the world of global finance as it did in global industry?

SOCIAL-ECONOMIC-TECHNOLOGICAL PROBLEMS WITHIN JAPAN

An Aging Society

Japan's population is aging. Its life spans are the longest in the world. At birth, women's life expectancy is eighty-three years, that of men is seventy-seven. With the aging population, social security benefits become more costly and the proportion of working people to retired people becomes much smaller. All industrialized countries will face this prospect; Japan is confronting it now. One of the solutions has been robotics, in which Japan is far-and-away the world's leader, with more industrial robots than the entire rest of the world combined. Japan has developed whole factories run by computers, lasers, and robots, which almost eliminate the need for human workers. Another solution is the importation of foreign workers, but Japan has

not wanted these foreigners to remain as citizens and ultimately serious frictions may emerge (as they have in Europe) with "guest workers."

An Overworked Society

Devotion to work and the workplace, and high rates of saving, which have produced Japan's high levels of productivity, may also present social problems. People's personal lives and their enjoyment of the products of their hard work have been restricted. Despite the longest life-expectancies in the world, the Japanese have begun to fear *karoshi* (literally death from overwork), high levels of stress-related illness among senior businessmen.

WOMEN IN THE WORKFORCE: DIFFERING PERSPECTIVES

In a recent essay on the status of women in postwar Japan, historian Kathleen Uno speculates that the Meiji ideal of "Good Wife, Wise Mother" was changing. "This ideal defined women as managers of domestic affairs in households and nurturers of children" (Uno, p. 294). By the 1980s, most women still saw their primary role in the household while men's was outside, but perspectives on gender roles were changing, as more women worked outside the home and more shared in housework.

Sandra Buckley, Professor of East Asian studies at McGill University, Montreal, agrees. Economic pressures on the family, the extraordinary long life-expectancy of Japanese women, and the fact that most women have only one or two children, encourage women to enter the labor force. Nevertheless, the overwhelming majority seem to view their primary responsibility as the home, and most work part time rather than full time. Japanese women tend to follow an M-curve of employment, taking jobs after schooling, quitting at the birth of their children, returning when they are grown, and perhaps quitting again when their aging parents (and their husband's parents) need care.

The legal system supports this emphasis on the wife/mother at home. When Japan passed an Equal Employment Opportunity Act (EEOA) in 1986, Buckley argues, "the most significant change under the new law was the removal of all protection clauses" (p. 369). Women could now work at night, at part-time employment and low-wage jobs, just like men. Moreover, Buckley writes, Japanese women seemed to view higher education as a means to a better marriage rather than a better job:

The more educated a woman was, the less likely she was to enter full-time employment and the shorter her average periods of stay in the work force. The reason behind this trend appears to have been the differing value attached to education for men and women. For the male each educational achievement was a qualification for future employment, whereas for the female each educational achievement was a potential qualification for a better marriage match. The more economically secure the marriage she made, the less likely a woman was to need to enter or remain in the workplace to supplement family income. The higher the social and economic status of her partner, the more pressure a woman was under to leave full-time employment. Certain specializations were seen as better qualifications for a particular category of future spouse. Pharmacology was popular in the 1980s as a possible entree to a marriage match with a doctor. Certain women's universities regularly supplied graduating lists to hospitals. One well-known Tokyo women's college was renowned as a source of wives for career diplomats. (p. 362)

Frank Upham, Professor at Boston College Law School, on the other hand, attributed the low employment rate of university-trained women to the employers rather than to the women. With the passage of the EEOA, the employment rate for female university graduates reached 75.2 percent, compared with the male rate of 78.8 percent. Before EEOA, employers had indeed discriminated against university-trained women because they were likely to stay on as full-time employees; the employers preferred women who would quit during child-bearing ages and could, therefore, be kept as part-time, lower paid employees. Conceding that the changes were still small, Upham nevertheless notes that women's work opportunities were increasing. (Upham, p. 337)

TOWARD THE FUTURE

Japan's prime minister during the occupation, Yoshida Shigeru, had set Japan's economic and political policies on three pillars, which lasted until the late 1980s: bureaucratic governance; the dominance of the Liberal Democratic party; and the Cold War alliance of Japan and the United States. Forty years later, Frank Gibney, President of the Pacific Basin Institute, noted: "all three of Yoshida's premises were in ruins" (p. 388). Regulation had restricted the growth of the economy; the Liberal

Democratic party was repudiated for corruption and incompetence and defeated in 1993 for the first time in thirty-eight years; and the Cold War was over, putting into question the need for the Japan–US alliance. Meanwhile, Japan could no longer be passive in foreign affairs. In December 1996, guerrilla rebels in Lima, Peru, seized the home of the Japanese ambassador and hundreds of his guests to evoke Japanese intervention in the policies of the Peruvian government. Japan was perceived as an important player in global politics and diplomacy as well as economics.

JAPAN AS A MODEL

The Asian Tigers

Since Japan's former colonies, Taiwan and Korea, were freed of colonial rule in 1945, they have been among the world's fastest-growing economies. Many observers attribute their success to their following a Japanese pattern, first imposed under colonial rule and later adopted voluntarily. The city states of Singapore and Hong Kong, although colonized by Japan for only a few years during World War II, also seem to follow Japan's example and to grow wealthy. We examine the development of these four Asian "Tigers" as a completion of our assessment of Japan as a model for others to follow.

*E*CONOMIC GROWTH IN EAST ASIA

(Japan and other Asian countries compared by projected 1996 GDPs—amounts in billions of dollars)

China	$739	Japan	$5,252
South Korea	$491		
India	$363		
Taiwan	$287		
Indonesia	$184		
Thailand	$177		
Hong Kong	$167		
Malaysia	$97		
Singapore	$87		
TOTAL	$2,592		$5,252

The three states and one former colony (Hong Kong) are quite different in size and history. South Korea has some 45 million people and has been independent but often under the sway of its powerful neighbors. At the end of World War II it was detached from communist North Korea as a separate country. Taiwan has half that population, 21 million, and is an outlying island of China, beginning to assert its independence as a state only in very recent years. Singapore, founded as a British colony and port in 1819 and remaining in the empire until 1963, is a city-state of 3 million people. Hong Kong, another port and city state, with 6 million people, was also founded as a colony of Britain in 1842 and returned to China in July 1997. All four have experienced rates of industrial and financial growth among the very highest in the world since 1960. Between 1960 and 1994, the gross national product in constant dollars has increased thirty times in Korea; twenty times in Taiwan; fifteen times in Singapore; and about the same amount in Hong Kong.

All four have dramatically developed their technological bases as part of their economic growth, with Korea specializing in large heavy industries, such as automobiles and shipbuilding; Taiwan in textiles, clothing, and electronics; Singapore in shipbuiding, petroleum refining (of the oil of nearby Indonesia and Malaysia), and electronics; and Hong Kong in textile spinning mills. The last three, especially, are also vital financial centers for investments all over the world.

These four East Asian countries have become the envy of the world for their extraordinary economic and technological growth. Do they share common patterns in their development? To what extent has their growth been related to Japan's growth? Does a model for technological growth and its humane use emerge from their experience? Ezra Vogel, Professor of Social Sciences at Harvard University, believes it does. Among the commonalities he cites are:

- aid from the United States in the 1940s and 1950s;

- the destruction of the old order in the wake of World War II and the ending of Japanese and British colonialism;

- land reform in both Korea and Taiwan, and urban sprawl into rural areas in Hong Kong and Singapore;

- a hard-working labor force (previously, at low wages);

- an elite based on merit selected through a formal examination system, a legacy of the Confucian ideal (see Chapter 7);

- the Japanese model, which included "forced intimate contact" (Vogel, *Four Little Dragons*, p. 91) through colonial control, especially in Taiwan and Korea; languages written in Chinese characters; dense population; scarce natural resources; and high levels of literacy.

Problems with the East Asian Model

To what degree does East Asia provide a model to others? There are clearly problems. First, the governments that had guided economic growth had also put limits on political freedoms. William Greider, national editor of *Rolling Stone* magazine, wrote cynically of:

> authoritarian state capitalism that fosters economic prosperity by requiring citizens to forego such decadent Western luxuries as free speech, free press, free assembly and other liberties. (p. 36)

In east Asia, however, by the 1990s political movement was favoring more democracy. Japan had adopted full parliamentary democracy immediately after the war ended. The Four Tigers were beginning to hold regular elections and to allow freedom of political expression. Even Greider recognized the trend:

> South Korea and Taiwan are frequently cited as proof that authoritarian regimes did indeed evolve into more open and democratic societies, though civil rebellions were required to force matters and neither has yet accepted a genuinely open economy and society. (p. 37)

Second, the cutting edge of East Asia's economies seemed to be moving from high-tech industrial production to investment finance, but they had not yet mastered this transition. Many of Japan's overseas investments in the United States and Europe suffered losses, and the "bubble" in domestic land and stock prices burst.

Third, as noted above, the enormous surpluses in balance of payments that Japan and the others were earning, caused problems for their trading partners. Resolving these trade frictions remains a critical issue.

Edwin Reischauer's observation from 1988 remained valid:

> The greatest single problem the Japanese face today is their relationship with other peoples. ... The country's narrow emphasis on its own economic growth, which has been its chief policy ever since World War II, has become positively dangerous. Japan as a world leader must adopt broader aims, which embrace the other nations of the world.

The four Tigers were facing similar problems.

CONCLUSION

Both Russia and Japan had set out to chart new paths of technological development not only for themselves but for others as well. The paths had been quite different. Russia's had imploded, with many of its methods discredited: government control of the total economy, comprehensive medium range (five year) planning, suppression of individual rights for the good of the state, concentration on heavy industry to the detriment of both medium-sized industry and agriculture, industrial development without adequate concern for ecology, and direct control over smaller neighbors to sub-ordinate their economies for the benefit of the imperial power. Russia had also invested immense resources in the technology of military development and space research. The Russian government saw this investment not in economic terms but as a necessity of living in a world of aggressive states. It had cost Russia dearly, but it also enabled the country to survive the German invasion of World War II and to combat American capitalism and imperialism, the perceived enemy, during the Cold War. Russia's technological accomplishments were impressive, and had enabled the country to achieve its goals as it understood them. At the century's end, however, Russia did not seem to be an example to any other country, and it was itself trying to find new paths of development.

Japan's economy, on the other hand, had become a startling success and its methods were studied and sometimes copied by other countries, especially its East Asian neighbors: state guidance and coordination of the economy, concentration on appropriate scale technologies, integration of large, medium, and small sectors of the economy, concentration on export markets, high standards of educa-

tion, quality control at all levels of production. Japan, too, had embarked on periods of imperial expansion, and of subordination of individual rights to those of the state, and these policies had backfired. An island nation with a long history of isolation, Japan had become a world economic and technological leader that was learning to integrate its economic and technological needs with those of others. It was also a pioneer in developing international investment policies, but these had not all worked out well. Japan's methods were, as we have said, emulated by a few other nations. In the end, however, it appeared that no nation, no matter how successful, could provide a ready-made model for others. Each nation had its own history, culture, geography, and range of goals. Technological policies would have to be individually tailored. In the next chapters we will examine alternative courses chosen by other countries and regions.

East Asian cityscape. Neon, symbol of the hi-tech economy, rises vertically into the night sky above a teeming city street in the Ginza district of Tokyo, Japan.

BIBLIOGRAPHY

Andrea, Alfred and James Overfield. *The Human Record*, Vol. 2 (Boston: Houghton Mifflin, 2nd ed., 1994).

Beasley, W.G. *Japanese Imperialism 1894–1945* (New York: Oxford University Press, 1987).

Buckley, S. "Altered States: The Body Politics of 'Being-Woman'," in Gordon, ed., *Postwar Japan*, 342–72.

Buruma, Ian. *God's Dust: A Modern Asian Journey* (New York: Farrar, Straus and Giroux, 1989).

Clark, Ronald. *Lenin: The Man behind the Mask* (London: Faber and Faber, 1988).

Fairbank, John K., Edwin O. Reischauer, and Albert M. Craig. *East Asia: Tradition and Transformation* (Boston: Houghton Mifflin, rev. ed., 1989).

Fitzpatrick, Sheila. *The Russian Revolution* (Oxford: Oxford University Press, 1984).

Gibney, Frank. *Japan: The Fragile Superpower* (Tokyo: Charles E. Tuttle, 3rd rev. ed., 1996).

Gordon, Andrew. *Labor and Imperial Democracy in Prewar Japan* (Berkeley: University of California Press, 1991).

—. ed. *Postwar Japan as History* (Berkeley: University of California Press, 1993).

Greider, William. *One World, Ready or Not* (New York: Simon and Schuster, 1997).

Hane, Mikiso. *Modern Japan: A Historical Survey* (Boulder, CO: Westview Press, 2nd ed. 1992).

Harris, Nigel. *The End of the Third World* (New York: Viking Penguin, 1987).

Hosking, Geoffrey. *A History of the Soviet Union* (London: Fontana, 1985).

Hughes, T. *American Genesis* (New York: Viking, 1989).

Ishinomori, Shotaro. *Japan Inc.: An Introduction to Japanese Economics*, trans. by Betsey Scheiner (Berkeley: University of California Press, 1988)

Ito, Takatoshi. *The Japanese Economy* (Cambridge: MIT Press, 1992).

Johnson, Chalmers, *MITI and the Japanese Miracle* (Stanford: Stanford University Press, 1982).

Kamata, Satoshi. *Japan in the Passing Lane* (New York: Pantheon, 1982).

Kennedy, Paul. *Preparing for the Twenty-first Century* (New York: Random House, 1993)

— . *The Rise and Fall of Great Powers* (New York: Random House, 1987).

Kochan, Lionel and Richard Abraham. *The Making of Modern Russia* (London: Penguin Books, 1983)

Lewin, Moshe. *Russian Peasants and Soviet Power* (New York: W.W. Norton, 1968).

Malia, Martin. *The Soviet Tragedy* (New York: The Free Press, 1994).

Morris-Suzuki, Tessa. *The Technological Transformation of Japan* (Cambridge University Press, 1994).

Myers, Ramon H. and Mark R. Peattie, eds. *The Japanese Colonial Empire, 1895–1945* (Princeton: Princeton University Press, 1984).

Nehru, Jawaharlal: *Glimpses of World History* (New Delhi: Oxford University Press, 1982).

Reed, John. *Ten Days That Shook the World* (London: Penguin Books, 1960).

Reischauer, Edwin O. *The Japanese Today* (Cambridge: Harvard University Press, 1988).

Remnick, David. *Lenin's Tomb: The Last Days of the Soviet Empire* (New York: Vintage Books, 1994).

Samuels, Richard J. *The Business of the Japanese State* (Ithaca: Cornell University Press, 1987).

—. *"Rich Nation, Strong Army"* (Ithaca: Cornell University Press, 1994).

Sivard, Ruth L. *World Military and Social Expenditures, 1991.* (Washington: World Priorities, 4th ed., 1991)

—. *World Military and Social Expenditures, 1996* (Washington: World Priorities, 16th ed., 1996).

Smith, Dennis B. *Japan since 1945: The Rise of an Economic Superpower* (New York: St. Martin's Press, 1995).

Smith, Headrick. *The New Russians* (New York: Random House, 1990).

Solzhenitsyn, Alexander. *The Gulag Archipelago*, 3 vols. (New York: Harper and Row, 1974–78).

Spodek, Susannah R. "On the History of Japan: World War I to the Present," (unpub. manuscript, 1996).

Stavrianos, L.S. *Global Rift* (New York: W. Morrow, 1981)

The [London] *Times Atlas of World History*. Ed. Geoffrey Barraclough (London: Times Books Ltd, 1981).

Trotsky, Leon. *The Russian Revolution* (Garden City, New York: Doubleday Anchor Books, 1959).

Tsunoda, Ryusaku, Wm. Theodore de Bary, and Donald Keene, comps. *Sources of Japanese Tradition* (New York: Columbia University Press, 1958).

Uno, Kathleen S. "Women and Changes in Household Division of Labor," in Gail Lee Bernstein, ed., *Recreating Japanese Women, 1600–1945* (Berkeley: University of California Press, 1991), 17–41.

Upham, Frank K. "Unplaced Persons and Movements for Peace," in Gordon, ed., *Postwar Japan*, 325–46.

Vogel, Ezra. *The Four Little Dragons: The Spread of Industrialization in East Asia* (Cambridge: Harvard University Press, 1991).

— . *Japan as Number One* (Cambridge: Harvard University Press, 1979).

World Almanac and Book of Facts 1997 (Mahwah, New Jersey: World Almanac Books, 1996).

World Bank. *World Development Report 1992: Development and the Environment* (New York: Oxford University Press, 1992).

— . *World Development Report 1995: Workers in an Integrating World* (New York: Oxford University Press, 1995).

— . *World Development Report 1996: From Plan to Market* (New York: Oxford University Press, 1996)

20
CHAPTER

"All power to the Peasant Association"

MAO ZEDONG

"Hunger is the argument that is driving India to the spinning wheel."

M.K. GANDHI

CHINA AND INDIA

1914–1997

THE GIANT AGRARIAN NATION-WORLDS

ome to some of the most ancient and influential civilizations, China and India are so huge that they are are almost worlds in themselves. Both are vast and densely populated countries: China, with 1.2 billion people, contains about one-fifth of the world's total population, and India, with nearly a billion inhabitants, contains one-sixth. Each is four times larger than any other country on earth. (The United States is the third largest country in terms of population, with "only" about 270 million inhabitants.) Although their urban populations are growing rapidly, both China and India remain predominantly agricultural countries; China's current (1997) population is 71 percent rural, India's is 74 percent.

Politically, in this century, until 1947, India was administered as a colony of Britain, and British India included the regions that became the independent states of Pakistan and Bangladesh. China was not administered directly by foreign powers, but Britain, France, Russia, Germany, and Japan had great economic and cultural influence over the huge nation. Between 1931 and 1945 Japan seized huge areas of China in war (see pp. 630–1).

Because of British colonial policies, India has been, despite its diverse ethnicities, languages, religions, and castes (see Chapters 8 and 9), partially unified as a political unit throughout the century, with the enormous exceptions of the partitions of Pakistan and Bangladesh into separate countries. China, on the other hand, despite the relative unity of its culture and ethnicity, was without a central government through most of the first half of the century. China suffered both civil war and invasion from Japan. Both India and China attained modern statehood at about the same time. India won independence from England in 1947. After Japan was defeated in World War II and withdrew, China continued its nationwide communist revolution that drove out foreign powers and unified almost the entire country in 1949 (except for Taiwan).

The two countries then chose very different strategies of development. Influenced by British colonial legacies and by its own heterogeneity, India chose democratic electoral politics and a mixed socialist-capitalist economy. China, on the other hand, was dominated both politically and economically by its victorious communist army and government. Since the 1980s, both countries have chosen to introduce more capitalistic economies that are more open to participation in the global economy, and both countries have developed a variety of technological policies in response to the varied needs of their immense populations and their status as both regional and world powers.

FIRST WORLD, SECOND WORLD, THIRD WORLD

In the period after World War II, many commentators spoke of three worlds, or styles of development: the first world consisted of the wealthy, capitalist, democratic countries of Western Europe and the United States; the second world of Russia and its eastern European allies, with their Communist Party states; and the third world of poorer nations, just emerging from colonization and now seeking their appropriate place in the world.

Today the term "third world" is frequently used with a negative, and much resented, connotation to designate poor, technologically backward, inefficiently organized nations. When the term first came to be used in the 1950s, however, it carried more inspirational connotations. In the first wave of decolonization following World War II, newly independent nations emerged into a world bitterly and expensively polarized into two hostile, belligerent blocs. The United States mobilized a group of Western European nations, which were mostly wealthy or in the process of regaining their wealth after the war, following primarily capitalistic free-market economic principles, and practicing democratic politics. The USSR mobilized an opposing group of nations in Eastern Europe; these were less wealthy but possessed the basic material necessities of life under an economy commanded by the state, which was ruled by the Communist Party. These two blocs, the North Atlantic Treaty Organization (NATO) and the Warsaw Pact, respectively, confronted each other, heavily armed and actively competing in developing and testing nuclear weapons and delivery systems. They competed, too, for the support and alliance of the newly independent nations.

Many of the newly independent nations, however, advocated a third alternative, a "third world." Many wished to be non-aligned, to avoid taking sides. They felt that Europe and America put little value on human life, as two world wars had demonstrated. They urged disarmament, especially nuclear disarmament, at a time when the first two worlds were locked in an arms race to build first the atomic bomb, then the hydrogen bomb, and ever more powerful rockets to launch them. They advocated state investment in such basic human needs as food, clothing, shelter, medical care, and small, "appropriate" scale technology, often through international assistance, rather than in the purchase of weapons.

With independence, each of these former colonies entered the United Nations (see p. 603), changing the size and complexion of that organization. Although race was not usually mentioned overtly in third world advocacy, almost all members of the "third world" were peoples of color, while the overwhelming majority of both first and second world groups were white. In 1955, third world representatives convened by Jawaharlal Nehru (1889–1964) of India, Gamal Abdel Nasser (1918–70) of Egypt, and Marshall Tito (1892–1980) of Yugoslavia met at Bandung, Indonesia, to launch their collective entry into international politics.

Some first and second world leaders, especially the American Secretary of State John Foster Dulles (1888–1959), saw these third world positions as immoral refusals to take sides in what they regarded as the great ideological, quasi-religious struggles of the Cold War. But, generally, in the 1950s the term "third world" had a very positive connotation. The French academic Alfred Sauvy claimed to have coined the term as a parallel to the Third Estate in the French Revolution, which claimed to represent the vast majority of the nation that up to then had been ruled only by the first and second estates of clergy and nobility (see pp. 477–82). The French journal of international economic and political development, *Cahiers du Tiers Monde* ("Journal of the Third World"), established in 1956, also chose its title as a proud call to a new global order.

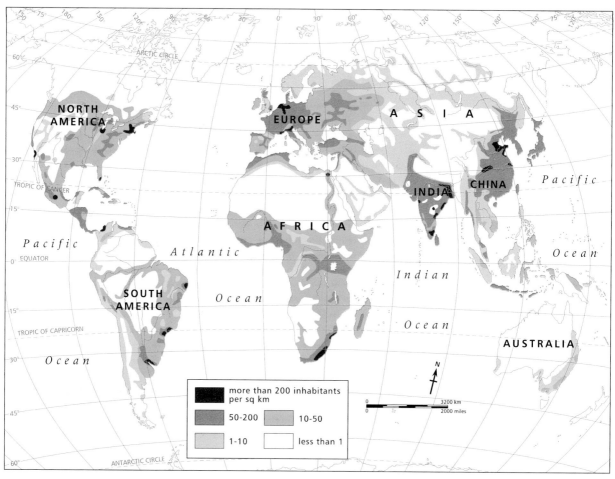

World population distribution today While the bulk of the world's population lives, as always, in coastal regions or along river valleys, the rapid rise in urbanism over the last century has created enormous imbalances as cities attract economic migrants from their hinterlands and from abroad. Some areas, like Europe, are so urbanized that their entire surface has high densities; others like China and India are so packed that even rural areas house urban densities. The only areas with quite low densities are those ecologically difficult for human life—deserts, mountains, frozen regions.

CHINA 1911–1990s:
THE PRELUDE TO
REVOLUTION

The 1911 revolution that ended China's 2000-year-old empire climaxed the nation's first set of responses to Europe's nineteenth-century military and technological invasions. As we have seen in Chapter 16, Britain's gunboat assaults in the opium war of 1839–42 had forced open the sea and river ports of China to opium and western manufactures, imposed unequal treaties established foreign concessions, and granted extraterritorial legal rights to Europeans (see p. 527). Following further defeats and dismemberment in the Arrow War of 1859–60, the Sino-Japanese war of 1894–5, and the Boxer Rebellion in 1899–1900 (see p. 529), China lay supine before European and Japanese control.

With the central government in confusion, peasant revolt simmered. To suppress the Taiping peasant revolt of 1850–64, the empire had required fourteen years of counter-revolutionary warfare in which millions died.

Imperial officials attempted to shore up the government by adopting two methods from the west: a "self-strengthening" of industrial and military capacities and restructuring of the official civil service examinations, with greater infusions of science and technology. Both movements encouraged more hopes for change than they could satisfy. China was industrializing, but only very slowly; in 1911 there were one million industrial workers—of a total population of 400 million. Most industry was small-scale, much of it in textiles. Faith in the viability of Confucian traditions and in the government that was to implement them was dying. After seventy years of military defeat, colonial subordination, peasant revolt, and intellectual contentiousness, China was ripe for revolution. The Mandate of Heaven passed from the Manchu dynasty.

THE 1911 REVOLUTION

A bomb explosion in the Wuhan area in October 1911 had triggered a series of army mutinies and civilian revolts. Within a month, the Manchu government had promulgated a civil constitution and convened a provisional national assembly. Yuan Shihkai (1859–1916), the most powerful military official in China, was elected premier. In January 1912, the boy emperor, P'ui (r. 1908–12), abdicated, ending 2000 years of China's imperial tradition, and Yuan received full powers to organize a provisional republican government. But he exceeded his mandate. In January 1916 Yuan took the title of emperor, provoking widespread revolt. Under severe military attack and critically ill, Yuan died in June. With no governing center, China entered a decade of rule by **warlords**, regional leaders who controlled their own independent militias.

Some of the warlords controlled whole provinces, others only a few towns or segments of railway line; some had formal military training, others were simply local strongmen; some looked forward to playing a role in the formation of a powerful national government, others to continuing division. Many were rapacious. In many parts of China, old, painful proverbs took on new reality: "In an age of chaos, don't miss the chance to loot during the fire" and "In the official's house, wine and meat are allowed to rot, but on the roads are the bones of those who starved to death." (Ebrey, pp. 374–5)

Two groups emerged as the most powerful and the most likely to subdue the warlords and consolidate a national government: the Guomindang (GMD, National People's Party) and the Communists. Both looked to Sun Yat-sen (1866–1925) as a founding mentor. Although raised in a peasant household, Sun received his secondary education in a missionary school in Hawaii and his medical training in Hong Kong. He spent most of his adult life in China's port cities or abroad.

In 1895, Sun's attempt at a coup in Canton failed and he was exiled, returning to China only in 1911. He was in the United States organizing for revolution when the 1911 uprising began. He returned to help found the GMD and to be elected first president of the United Provinces of China, but then was exiled by a jealous and fearful Yuan in 1913. He returned to Guangzhou (Canton) in the 1920s, and led his movement from that port city, but he never regained ruling power.

Sun's "three principles" included a heavy admixture of western thought. The first, nationalism, called for revolution against foreign political control, beginning with the ousting of the Manchus from China, and against foreign economic control, which had rendered China

the colony of every nation with which it has concluded treaties; each of them is China's master. China is not just the colony of one country, but the colony of many countries. We are not just the slaves

Founder of the GMD. Sun Yat-sen (Yixian), photographed here in Western dress as was his custom, is considered to be "father of the nation," even though he spent much of his life abroad and never successfully achieved his own political ambitions. He was a revolutionary and helped to found the Guomindang, and although unable to stay in power himself, he influenced China's most important figures in post-warlord-controlled China: Jiang Jieshi and Mao Zedong.

	INDIA	CHINA
1900	▪ Swadeshi movement (1905) ▪ Inauguration of All-India Muslim League (1906) ▪ Moderates and extremists split in Congress (1907) ▪ *Hind Swaraj* (1909)	▪ War with Japan: China loses Formosa (Taiwan), southern Manchuria, and Korea (1894) ▪ Boxer Rebellion against western influence is suppressed by European troops (1900)
1910	▪ Capital transferred from Calcutta to Delhi (1911) ▪ Gandhi returns from South Africa (1915) and begins first *satyagraha* (1917); reorganizes Congress (1919) ▪ Rowlatt Acts passed (1919), leading Gandhi to start first civil disobedience ▪ Amritsar (Jalianwala Bagh) massacre (1919) ▪ Montagu–Chelmsford reforms; dyarchy (1919)	▪ Japan formally annexes Korea (1910) ▪ Revolution breaks out and the child emperor is deposed (1911-12) Republic declared (1912); Yuan Shik-Kai is premier ▪ Chinese Communist Party formed (1919) ▪ May 4th Movement (1919)
1920	▪ Gandhi launches non-cooperation movement (1920-2) ▪ First airmail letters arrive in India from England (1926) ▪ Nehru committee drafts constitution; accepted by Congress and All-India Convention, but Jinnah leaves Congress (1928)	▪ Sun Yat-Sen dies (1925) ▪ Guomindang and Communists vie for power (1925–49) ▪ Mao's report on Hunan peasant movement (1927) ▪ Jiang Jieshi slaughters Communist industrial workers (1927)
1930	▪ Gandhi arrested; Congress outlawed (1931) ▪ Elections held for provincial assemblies, and Congress ministries formed in Bihar, Orissa, Central Provinces, United Provinces, Bombay, and Madras (1937)	▪ Long March (1934–5) ▪ Mao in Yan'an (1935) ▪ Xi'an incident (1936)
1940	▪ Jinnah declares western democracy unsuitable for India (1940) ▪ Congress demands complete independence; Muslim League demands division of India (1940) ▪ Fall of Rangoon and Singapore (1942) ▪ Congress demands withdrawal of British and begins mass struggle under Gandhi (1942) ▪ Muslim majority provinces under control of Muslim League (1943) ▪ Royal Indian Naval Mutiny (1946) ▪ Second Simla Conference prepares constitutional plan, which is accepted by Muslim League but not by Congress (1946) ▪ Muslim League starts "direct action" (1946) ▪ Congress accepts principle of partition (1947) ▪ India and Pakistan become separate on 15 August 1947	▪ Jiang Jieshi publishes *China's Destiny* (1943) ▪ Civil War continues to 1949 ▪ People's Republic of China proclaimed by Mao Zedong (1949) ▪ Foreigners expelled (1949–50)
1950		▪ Korean War (1950–3) ▪ Soviet-style constitution adopted (1954)

of one country, but the slaves of many countries … Today we are the poorest and weakest nation in the world, and occupy the lowest position in international affairs … other men are the carving knife and serving dish; we are the fish and the meat … we must espouse nationalism and bring this national spirit to the salvation of the country. (de Bary, pp. 769)

His second principle, democracy, emphasized a predominantly Western political model: "Since we have had only ideas about popular rights, and no democratic system has evolved, we have to go to Europe and America for a republican form of government." He did, however, claim the separation of powers as an ancient Chinese tradition. (Andrea and Overfield, p. 350)

The third principle, under the heading "livelihood," revealed Sun's ambivalence toward Western technology and organization. He proclaimed the need for new technology:

First we must build means of communication, railroads and waterways, on a large scale. Second we must open up mines. Third we must hasten to develop manufacturing. Although China has a multitiude of workers, she has no machinery and so cannot compete with other countries. Goods used throughout China have to be manufactured and imported from other countries, with the result that our rights and interests are simply leaking away (de Bary, p. 778)

But Western-style industrialization was not his chosen model:

With the invention of modern machines, the phenomenon of uneven distribution of wealth in the West has become all the more marked. … On my tour of Europe and America, I saw with my own eyes the instability of their economic structure and the deep concern of their leaders in groping for a solution. (Andrea and Overfield, p. 351)

	INDIA	CHINA
1950		▊ "100 Flowers Campaign" criticizes government (1956–7) ▊ Great Leap Forward commune experiment to achieve "true communism" (1958-60)
1960	▊ Indira Gandhi (1917-84) prime minister (1966-77)	▊ Sino-Indian border war (1962) ▊ Economic recovery program under Liu Shaoqi; Maoist "socialist education movement" rectification campaign (1962-5) ▊ China explodes atomic bomb (1964) ▊ Cultural Revolution; Liu Shaoqi overthrown (1966-9) ▊ Ussun River border clashes with USSR (1969)
1970		▊ Reconstruction under Mao and Zhou Enlai (1970-76) ▊ Joins United Nations (1971) ▊ President Nixon visits China (1972) ▊ New state constitution; Zhou's "Four Modernizations" program initiated (1975) ▊ Deaths of Zhou Enlai and Mao Zedong; Hua Guofeng becomes prime minister and party chairman; Deng Xiaoping in hiding; ▊ "Gang of Four" in hiding (1976) ▊ Deng Xiaoping rehabilitated (1977) ▊ Economic reforms introduced; diplomatic relations opened with US; invasion of Vietnam (1979)
1980	▊ Indira Gandhi prime minister again (1980-4); assassinated in 1984 by Sikhs protesting at use of troops to clear Sikhs from Golden Temple at Amritsar ▊ Rajiv Gandhi (1944-91) prime minister (1984-9) ▊ Gas leak at Union Carbide plant in Bhopal kills 2000+ people and harms thousands more; company subsequently pays $470 million reparations	▊ Zhao Ziyang become prime minister (1980) ▊ Hu Yaobang becomes party chairman; "Gang of Four" arrested (1981) ▊ New constitution adopted (1982) ▊ Industrial sector reformed (1984) ▊ Student pro-democracy demonstrations (1986) ▊ Zhao Ziyang becomes party chairman, Li Peng prime minister (1987) ▊ Yang Shangkun becomes president; economic reforms run into problems; inflation soaring (1987) ▊ Tiananmen Square demonstration with 2000+ killed (1989)
1990	▊ Rajiv Gandhi killed by bomb (1991) while campaigning for re-election	▊ Sanctions imposed by EEC and Japan lifted (1991) ▊ Trials of pro-democracy activists continue (1992-5) ▊ Deng Xiaoping, paramount leader, dies; Hong Kong handed back (1997)

Fearing "the expansion of private capital and the emergence of a great wealthy class with the consequent inequalities" in China, Sun called for a different path: state ownership and "state power to build up these enterprises." But he thought Marxism irrelevant for China: "In China, where industry is not yet developed, Marx's class war and dictatorship of the proletariat are impracticable" (de Bary, pp. 778–9). China's economic problem was not unequal distribution but lack of production.

Chinese of all political parties revered Sun, but they could not implement his plans. Sun, however, inspired the two leaders who contested for dominance in China for a quarter century following his death in 1925: the GMD's Jiang Jieshi (Chiang Kai-shek) (1887–1975) and the Communists' Mao Zedong (1893–1976). Jiang began as a military commander and later sought to build a government; Mao began as a Communist Party organizer and later built an army. Both learned that "in a country ruled and plundered by marauding warlord armies, it was naked military power that was crucial in determining the direction of political events" (Meisner, p. 21). In Mao's blunt words: "political power grows out of the barrel of a gun."

POWER STRUGGLES 1925–37

Jiang had studied in a Japanese military academy, fought for the 1911 revolution, and rose to command China's own new military academy, established with Russian financing, on the island of Huangpu, off Canton. After Sun's death, he succeeded to the leadership of the GMD. A staunch advocate of the neo-Confucian New Life movement in the 1930s, Jiang wrote *China's Destiny* in 1943 to re-affirm the conservative virtues of China's indigenous, hierarchical, genteel culture. Yet he also became a Methodist, as Sun had. For both men, Christianity marked their marriage ties to Chinese Christian women (each married a sister of T.V. Soong, one of China's wealthiest industrialists), and an appreciation of the role of foreign Christians in China's economic modernization.

Jiang maintained close personal, professional, and financial connections with Shanghai underworld figures, Russian Comintern agents, Western businessmen, and Christian missionaries. As China dissolved into warlordism, Jiang was named commander-in-chief of the GMD's National Revolutionary Army, and for a quarter of a century he fought to unify China under his own control against three powerful enemies: the warlords; the Japanese, who seized Manchuria in 1931 and went on to invade China proper in 1937 (see p. 630); and the Communists.

Foreign powers in the treaty ports monitored the shifting fortunes of all four contenders for power with considerable self-interest. In 1931, foreigners had a total of US$3,243 million invested in China, slightly more than double the amount of 1914; which was, in turn, slightly more than double that of 1902. Foreign loans financed Chinese railways and heavy industry, and foreigners held three-fourths of all investments in shipping, almost half of the cotton spindles, and 80–90 percent of the coal mines. Through the early 1920s politicization and unionization of industrial workers encouraged many strikes, and the employers, many of them foreigners, often responded with violence. They wanted a compliant government that would help break the strikes. Most of the foreign investors aided, and sought to manipulate, Jiang as the leader closest to their interests. During the period from 1929 to 1937, they lent him much of the money needed to cover the GMD government's annual deficits of 12 to 28 percent a year.

Foreign-based Christian missionaries and educational institutions also supported the GMD, attracted partly by Jiang's own Christian affiliation. The YMCA movement claimed 54,000 members in 1922. In the early 1920s, some 12,000 Christian missionaries, slightly more Protestants than Catholics, served in China. Christian and foreign colleges enrolled 4,000 of the 35,000 students in Chinese colleges in 1922, and 9 percent of their students were women. Much of Western culture and literature was incorporated in the new curricula of China's universities. Chinese students and intellectuals were eager to hear voices from the West and East, and such luminaries as Bertrand Russell, John Dewey, Albert Einstein and Rabindranath Tagore visited and lectured widely.

With the support of Western business and cultural leaders, and the Russian Comintern as well,

Jiang undertook to defeat the warlords and to re-establish a viable central government. Through the great northern expedition from Guangzhou, Jiang captured Beijing in 1927–8, established his own capital in Nanjing on the lower Yangzi River, and began to consolidate GMD power over China. Despite these early military victories, however, Jiang ultimately failed. His government, permeated by corruption, alienated the peasantry by forging alliances with exploitative landlords. High officials sold off provisions intended to feed and clothe its starving armed forces. When the Japanese invasion of 1937 forced Jiang's retreat into the remote mountainous reaches of Chongqing (Chungking), the communists successfully persuaded the Chinese peasants that they, not the GMD, could best fight off the Japanese and best represent peasant interests in a free China.

MAO ZEDONG AND THE RISE OF THE COMMUNIST PARTY FROM 1921

The Communist leader, Mao Zedong (1893–1976), Sun's other principal successor, shared the goals of a strong, united, independent China and the improvement of the people's livelihood, but his background differed. First, the 1911 revolution, in which he participated, was over by the time he was eighteen, and was therefore no longer an issue. Second, Mao's personal experience was limited to China. Although he read widely in Western as well as Chinese literature and philosophy, Mao's first travel outside China, a visit to Russia, came only in 1949. He had helped other Chinese students travel to Europe during World War I, but for himself, he later told reporter Edgar Snow, "I did not want to go to Europe. I felt that I did not know enough about my own country, and that my time could be more profitably spent in China." (Snow, p. 149)

Third, Mao had little experience of the Western business and missionary establishments in China. His own formative experiences were in the countryside and in educational institutions. Compared with both Sun and Jiang, Mao cared little for China's reputation in the West but much for the quality of life of the Chinese peasant. Mao had grown up on his father's farm in Hunan province, where he learned at first hand of the exploitation of the peasant, sometimes, he said, through the oppressive strategies of his father, who rose from poverty to become a middle-level farmer and small-scale trader. Mao later recounted that he left this life to become an athletic, serious, politically committed student, reading widely, and consolidating a core group of similarly inclined young men: "My friends and I preferred to talk only of large matters—the nature of men, of human society, of China, the world, and the universe! … We also became ardent physical culturists." (Snow, p. 146)

By 1919, Mao's educational quests had brought him to Beijing (Peking) University, just as China's resentment against foreign colonialism was boiling over. The peace treaties of World War I assigned Germany's holdings in the Shandong Peninsula of north China to Japan rather than returning them to China. At Versailles, Chinese protestors physically blocked their nation's delegates from attending the signing ceremonies, and thus China never did sign the peace agreements. Within China, protests against the treaties by students and others began on May 4, 1919, engendering a continuing critique of China's international humiliation, the apparent bankruptcy of its historical traditions, and the content of its cultural links to the West. The "May Fourth Movement" also helped to sow the seeds of the Chinese Communist Party (CCP), which came to fruition in 1921 following discussions between Chinese revolutionaries and representatives of the newly formed Comintern of the USSR (see p. 614). At that time, Mao was a participant in the study group of Li Dazhao, chief librarian of Peking University and one of the founders of the CCP.

Li had already proclaimed the importance of the peasantry and called on the university students to help mobilize them:

> Our China is a rural nation and most of the laboring class is made up of peasants. If they are not liberated, then our whole nation will not be liberated … Go out and develop them and cause them to know [that they should] demand liberation, speak out about their sufferings, throw off their ignorance and be people who will themselves plan their own lives. (Spence, p. 308)

Poster from 1960 showing Mao Zedong and supporters of the Cultural Revolution, each holding a copy of Mao's teachings, the "Little Red Book." Mao realized early on that the peasantry could carry forward the ideals of communism, even when the workers' movement was destroyed by Jiang Jieshi. Mao was determined to eliminate "foreign dogmatism" and was against copying the Soviet blueprint for communism. His unique application of Marxism to China's needs gave rise to a cult following.

When Mao joined the party he began organizing workers in the industrial plants of the Wuhan region, but in 1925 he was re-assigned to peasant organization in his native Hunan. Despite the orthodox Marxist doctrines of Comintern advisors, Mao in Hunan came to see the Chinese peasantry, rather than the proletariat, as China's revolutionary vanguard. In terms of technology, he abandoned the emphasis on large-scale industrial planning and sought instead local solutions to local problems through locally developed, appropriate rural technologies. Mao's enthusiastic and influential, but polemical and doctrinaire, 1927 report on the Hunan peasant movement updated Li's more rural emphasis:

the broad peasant masses have risen to fulfill their historic mission … the democratic forces in the rural

The Communist Revolution in China Chinese Communists and Nationalists (GMD) initially united to consolidate the warlord factions which emerged after the collapse of the Manchu (Qing) dynasty, and to counter Japanese aggression. After 1927 Nationalist repression forced the Communists to retreat to remote areas, focussing in the north after the Long March of 1934–35, where a guerrilla war developed. With the outbreak of war with Japan (1937), the Nationalists were confronted with two enemies, and after the Japanese defeat in 1945, the Communists turned to driving out the GMD as well.

areas have risen to overthrow the rural feudal power. The patriarchal-feudal class of local bullies, bad gentry, and lawless landlords has formed the basis of autocratic government for thousands of years, the cornerstone of imperialism, warlordism and corrupt officialdom. To overthrow this feudal power is the real objective of the national revolution. … The leadership of the poor peasants is absolutely necessary. Without the poor peasants there can be no revolution. (de Bary, p. 869)

This revolution required violence: the peasants had to use their strength to overthrow the authority of the landlords.

Mao's enemy had its own tools of violence. While Mao was organizing peasants in the 1920s, Jiang was massacring the core of the revolutionary proletariat in Shanghai, Wuhan, and Guangzhou. As Jiang completed the northern expedition and consolidated his control over the warlords, he turned, in alliance with the international business community and without excessive objection from the Comintern, to murdering thousands of communist industrial workers in the spring of 1927. In Changsha, local military leaders joined with the GMD and local landlords to slaughter thousands of peasants who had recently expropriated the land they worked from its legal owners. By the summer of 1928, according to Zhou Enlai, one of the most sophisticated Communist leaders, only 32,000 union members in all of China remained loyal to the Communist Party. By 1929, only 3 percent of the Party members could be counted proletarians. Mao's peasant alternative was, of necessity, the communists' last resort.

When the GMD put down the Hunan Autumn Harvest Uprising in 1927, Mao's core group retreated to the Jinggangshan border area between Hunan and Jiangxi. Other communist leaders, driven from the cities, joined them. They built up a **soviet**, a local communist government, redistributing land, introducing improved farming methods, and instituting new educational systems spreading literacy and dispensing political indoctrination. They recruited and trained a guerrilla army. Mao himself formulated its tactics: "The enemy advances, we retreat; the enemy camps, we harass; the enemy tires, we attack; the enemy retreats, we pursue." (Spence, p. 375)

The guerrillas could exist only with the cooperation of the peasantry whom they wished to mobilize. Appropriate, rather revolutionary rules were established to govern soldiers' behavior: "prompt obedience to orders; no confiscations whatever from the poor peasantry; and prompt delivery directly to the Government, for its disposal, of all goods confiscated from the landlords." (Snow, p. 176). These were later elaborated to include: "Be courteous and polite to the people and help them when you can. … Be honest in all transactions with the peasants. … Pay for all articles purchased." (Snow, p. 176)

GENDER ISSUES

Mao's principles of women's rights recognized the changes already taking place. Feminism had begun to flourish in China by the 1920s with the formation of such organizations as the Women's Suffrage Association and the Women's Rights League. Its constituency was mostly Western-influenced urban intellectuals. *New Youth* magazine, for example, often critical of Confucius for his emphasis on patriarchy and obedience to authority, had translated and published Ibsen's *A Doll's House* in 1918 (see p. 549). Pa Chin's novel *Family*, one of the key works of China's reformist New Culture Movement, transplanted Ibsen's advocacy of women's equality and independence into a modern Chinese setting. Margaret Sanger, feminist and advocate of contraception, had toured and lectured throughout China in 1922. There were also some 1,500,000 women working outside their homes for pay in light industrial factories, mostly textiles, in China's cities. Now Mao refocused feminist attention on the countryside and the peasantry:

> the authority of the husband … has always been comparatively weak among the poor peasants, because the poor peasant women, compelled for financial reasons to take more part in manual work than women of the wealthier classes, have obtained more right to speak and more power to make decisions in family affairs. In recent years the rural economy has become even more bankrupt and the basic condition for men's domination over women has already been undermined. And now, with the rise of the peasant movement, women in many places have set out immediately to organize the rural women's association; the opportunity has come for them to lift up their heads, and the authority of the husband is tottering more and more every day. (de Bary, p. 872)

Communist policies took two complementary directions. The first, and more effective, restructured

Women of Shanghai with tiny bound feet working at frames for sorting tea leaves. From the early years of the twentieth century urban women had begun to leave the confines of home to work in light industry. The move from home to workplace gave women more status, which was further strengthened by the reforms of the Communist government when it came to power. The abandonment of footbinding in all but the most outlying areas of China did much to enhance the freedom of women.

the labor and military forces, giving more scope and power to women. Building the Chinese soviet and fighting guerrilla battles required the support of every available resource. While women did not usually participate in warfare directly, the increased need for production and personnel brought them out of the house into new jobs, effectively raising their status. Second, the communists issued a new marriage law forbidding arranged marriages, stopping all purchase and sale in marriage contracts and encouraging free choice of marriage partners. This law met strong resistance. Men who had already bought their wives objected; so did mothers-in-law, who ruled over each household's domestic labor force. The traditional Chinese family provided for old age security, child care, medical facilities, and the production and consumption of food, clothing, and shelter. The new communist marriage law seemed to threaten this structure without providing any alternative. The law was not widely enforced. In *The Unfinished Liberation of Chinese Women, 1949–1980* Phyllis Andors points out that this pattern would continue in China for decades: Restructuring of the labor force to include more women working for remuneration outside the home would raise women's status and be accepted if it was part of the task of building the nation; direct restructuring of the family as an end in itself would meet resistance. The leadership of the Party remained conspicuously male.

THE LONG MARCH AND THE RISE TO POWER 1934–49

Jiang sent five successive military expeditions against the Jiangxi soviet, beginning with 100,000 men and leading up to one million. By 1934, the communists could no longer hold out. Mao led some 80,000 men and thirty-five women out of the siege and began the Long March, a 370-day, 6000-mile (9650-kilometer) strategic retreat, by foot, under constant bombardment and attack from Jiang's forces, across rivers, mountain ranges, marshes, and grasslands, westward to Guizhou and then northward to a final new base camp in Yan'an. Some 20,000 men finally arrived in Yan'an, of whom about half had marched since the beginning, the rest having joined *en route*. The courage, comradeship, commitment, and idealism of this march, in the face of seemingly insurmountable natural obstacles and human opposition, was the formative experience of a generation of Chinese communist leaders. At the front, Mao now became the unquestioned leader of the movement, party, and army.

Mao established his capital at remote, impoverished Yan'an and rebuilt his soviet structure, nurturing his army, inducting its soldiers into agricultural assistance work, redistributing land, encouraging handicrafts, establishing newspapers and schools, an arts and literature academy, and medical programs for training paramedical "barefoot doctors." The Chinese communist program developed more fully here: a peasant-centered economy, administered and aided by guerrilla soldiers, capped by a dictatorial but comparatively benevolent communist leadership, encouraging literacy accompanied by indoctrination in communist ideology. These principles continued to characterize Chinese communism and the government it established after 1949, at least until the death of Mao in 1976. So, too, did the tension between visionary goals and concrete implementation, between being "Red" and being "expert."

Although Yan'an was remote from the main fighting, and was subject to GMD attacks, the communists launched guerrilla action against the Japanese after their invasion of China proper in 1937. By comparison, Jiang seemed less nationalistic. He appeared willing to compromise with the Japanese and more eager to pursue the Chinese communists than to fight the foreign invaders. Mao, on the other hand seemed willing to join forces with Jiang to unite China against the foreigner. Following the "Xi'an incident," the bold kidnap of Jiang by dissident generals in 1936, Jiang moved toward cooperation with the Communists.

At first, the Japanese had hoped to rule China with the help of Chinese collaborators, as they had Manchuria, but their cruelty after the capture of Nanjing in December 1937 ended those hopes (see p. 631). The Chinese vowed to fight back. The communists fought a rearguard guerrilla war from their northern base in Shaanxi, while Jiang led a scorched-earth retreat to a new headquarters far up the Yangzi River in Chongqing. Soldiers and civilians suffered catastrophically.

By the early 1940s, nationalist cooperation began to unravel as Communists and GMD forces jockeyed for temporary power and future position. After a temporary respite in 1945, full-scale civil war resumed. America, entering the Pacific war after Japan's bombing of Pearl Harbor in 1941, supported the GMD but not the communists. After Japan was defeated in 1945, the USA extended help to Jiang in training his troops, airlifting them to critical military locations, and turning over to them war material. The Soviet Union, fighting for its life against Germany, observed neutrality with Japan until the very last week of the war. Then it entered Manchuria, stripping for itself a great deal of that region's military and industrial equipment, while turning over some of it to the Chinese communists. As China's civil war continued after 1945, communist forces, well disciplined and warmly backed by peasants in many parts of the country, defeated the ill-disciplined and ill-provisioned GMD forces, whose rations and materials were often sold off for private profit without ever reaching them. By the fall of 1949, the communists had driven the GMD completely out of mainland China to the island of Taiwan. The Communist People's Republic of China was born.

THE GREAT LEAP FORWARD: ECONOMIC REVOLUTION 1949–66

For Mao and the guerrilla veterans who dominated the new government, the principal fears were for-eign domination, internal chaos, and the lingering power of the wealthy classes and the large-scale landholders. The extraordinary human drama of the Long March and the Yan'an soviet were formative experiences in their ability to cope with these threats. The new rulers modeled much of their new government on those experiences and returned to them for inspiration in difficult times as long as they lived, even up to the early 1990s. Important policies included:

- redistribution of land;

- women's rights to hold land;

- appropriate technology;

- production and equal distribution of basic necessities for everyone;

- universal literacy (reaching 81 percent by 1997, 73 percent for females and 90 percent for males)

The government mobilized tight-knit, local, social networks for suppressing such vices as opium addiction and prostitution but also for enforcing rigid political indoctrination and conformity, including the informing by one family member against another and semi-coerced personal confessions of political deviance.

The state immediately cracked down on private ownership. In 1949, on the eve of the completion of the revolution, Mao had declared: "Without the socialization of agriculture, there will be no complete and consolidated socialism. And to carry out the socialization of agriculture a powerful industry with state-owned enterprises as the main component must be developed" (de Bary, p. 894). In 1950, threats, expropriation, and accusations of espionage—sometimes justified—against businessmen and Christian missionaries forced almost all foreigners to leave China by the end of the year. Numerous campaigns against counter-revolutionaries; the confiscation and redistribution of private property; hundreds and even thousands of executions; intensive public, group pressure to elicit confessions from those perceived as enemies of the revolution; and regular confrontations between workers and owners, now incorporated into the processes of labor relations, destroyed the large capitalist sector in China. Many countries, led by the United States, refused to recognize the new government. The Russian communist government, on the other hand, maintained a strong alliance and helped to draft and implement China's first five-year plan between 1952 and 1957.

Communist policies on urbanization and industrialization were more ambivalent. The communists had come to power as an anti-urban, peasant movement. The large cities, especially Shanghai, had fostered the foreign enclaves, extraterritorial law, and colonial behavior which flagrantly insulted the Chinese in their own country, but they also housed China's industrial base, military technology, administration, and cultural life. As the communists began to capture the nation's cities, Mao began to re-evaluate their potential:

> From 1927 to the present the center of gravity of our work has been in the villages—gathering strength in the villages, using the villages in order to surround the cities, and then taking the cities. The period for this method of work has now ended. The period of the city leading the village has now begun. (Spence, p. 508)

Policies and results, however, were both uneven. To restrain urban growth, the government promulgated severe limitations on internal migration, but movement from the countryside continued steadily,

MAO ZEDONG AND THE CULTURAL REVOLUTION

1921	Mao is a founder member of the Chinese Communist Party (CCP) and soon emerges as its leader
1927	Leads a peasant uprising in Hunan after the party splits
1931	Elected as chairman of the Soviet Republic of China
1934–5	When Guomindang (former Communist allies) attack his base in Jiangxi, he leads his followers to the remote northeast in the Long March
1935	During the March Mao is elected chairman of the CCP
1937–45	Organizes armed struggle against Japanese invaders
1945	Leads guerilla warfare against forces of Jiang Jieshi (Chiang Kai-shek)
1949	Guomindang expelled, and Mao becomes first chairman of the People's Republic, suppressing all opposition to his rule
1956	Soviet aid is withdrawn when Mao denounces Khrushchev's rapprochement with the West
1957	"100 Flowers Campaign" permitted some liberalism
1958–60	Mao initiates "Great Leap Forward" experiment
1966–9	Mao launches the Cultural Revolution, a "rectification" campaign, directed against liberal "revisionist" forces
1969	Cultural Revolution ends, having caused bureaucratic and economic chaos
1970	Period of reconstruction begins, during which Mao works with Zhou Enlai
1976	After Mao's death, the threat from the "gang of four" (one of whom his widow) who had promoted the Cultural Revolution is averted by their arrest and punishment

Trial of a landlord during the Cultural Revolution. Most such trials ended with a confession and a promise to reform; some with a bullet for the accused. In its first moves toward collectivization, the Communist government instituted a number of land reforms that gave the arable land to the peasants who worked it, and did away with the landlords—literally.

if slowly. China's population, which had been 10.6 percent urban in 1949 and 16.3 percent in 1958, reached 23.5 percent urban in 1983. In sheer numbers this was an increase from 57 million to 241 million people. As time went by, the cities once again challenged communist ideological purity— Guangzhou promoted capitalism; Beijing political protest; Shanghai internationalism. Chinese leaders had to balance conflicting claims on behalf of urban, bureaucratic, strong-state, "expert," industrialization against those for rural, grass-roots, "Red" populism. To some degree, the leaders contended among themselves, with a group around Liu Shaoqi and Deng Xiaoping in the former camp; Mao and Lin Piao in the latter. Some, like Zhou Enlai, sought compromise and synthesis.

Militarily, the communists extolled the spirit of the guerrilla warrior over high-tech weaponry, and taunted America, the world's most heavily armed

country, as a "paper tiger." Indeed, China itself fought the United States to a draw in Korea, 1950–53 (see p. 602), and then saw the American superpower withdraw in defeat from Vietnam in 1973. Nevertheless, China bought, produced, or purloined up-to-date military technology. In 1964, China exploded its first atomic bomb; in the mid-1970s it followed with hydrogen bombs; in 1980 it tested missiles with a range of 7000 miles (11,200 kilometers) and in 1981 launched three space satellites. It began to manufacture and sell sophisticated missiles, submarines, and chemical weapons to other developing countries by the 1980s. Nevertheless, its military expenditure dropped from 12 percent of its total gross national product in 1960 to 2.7 percent in 1994. China was betting its future power on a developed economy leading its military rather than vice versa. (Kennedy, p. 384; Sivard 1991, p. 52; Sivard 1996, p. 46)

Economically, China adopted a five year plan based on the USSR model. It called for multiplying the value of industrial output between 1952 and 1957 almost two and one-half times, and claimed at the end to have overachieved the target by 22 percent. By the end of the plan, even democracy seemed a possibility. In 1956–7, Mao's call, "Let a hundred flowers bloom, let a hundred schools of thought contend," opened the gates of public expression and even criticism of government. In Beijing, students and others posted their thoughts on what became known as Democracy Wall, but by late 1957, fearing excessive protest, the government shifted its policies and jailed, exiled, and killed protesters. Economically, it responded with the Great Leap Forward, grouping virtually all of rural China into communes, sending city people back to the villages, virtually terminating whatever small private enterprises had survived, and attempting to downscale and disperse industry by establishing local, small-scale enterprises, referred to generically as "backyard steel mills."

THE CULTURAL REVOLUTION
1966

The economic disaster that followed the Great Leap Forward, administered by powerful, distant government officials, crippled the country and led to millions of deaths by starvation. The government relaxed for a few years, but reinstated similar and perhaps even more extreme ideological and economic policies in the Great Proletarian Cultural Revolution in 1966. Mao sought through this revolution to purge the party of time-serving bureaucrats and to reignite revolutionary fervor. Those who responded most enthusiastically were the army and students, who, with Mao's encouragement, organized themselves into the Red Guard. Teachers were denounced by their students and party officials; professors and intellectuals were exiled to remote villages and forced to undertake hard labor. For two years, 1966–8, militant, committed anarchy reigned.

The Long March was now thirty years in the past, yet its ideological commitment still motivated the leadership. Mao was venerated as the last hope to restore the intensity of those days. Key quotations from his statements were published in millions of copies of *The Living Thoughts of Chairman Mao*, often called the Little Red Book, because of its size and the color of its cover. These were circulated and read publicly throughout the country.

ECONOMIC RECOVERY
1970–1990s

Now that economic chaos and starvation on the one hand and the total stifling and destruction of intellectual and academic life on the other had brought China to a standstill, the internal party struggle returned to power more conservative and bureaucratic leaders, headed by Deng Xiaoping (1904–97). By the mid-1970s, and especially after Mao's and Zhou's deaths in 1976, the new leadership called for a restoration of economic, cultural, and educational interchange with the outside world; an economy more attuned to market principles; and greater freedom of expression. Imports and exports, which had held roughly flat for several years at slightly over $2 billion each through the late 1960s, rose steadily until, in 1978, each registered $10 billion. One fourth of the imports were machinery and equipment, including complete plants, 6,934 of them in 1978, built entirely by foreigners (Spence, p. 641). These were almost entirely in heavy industries, especially petrochemicals and iron and steel. By 1980, China was producing more steel than Britain or France. It was producing 5 percent of all the world's manufactures, up from 3.9 percent in 1973 (Kennedy, p. 420). In 1980, China joined the World Bank and the International Monetary Fund.

Maurice Meisner, Professor of History at the University of Washington, Seattle, in his assessment, *Mao's China and After*, underlines the ironic imbalance in strong support for industry and weak agricultural results under Mao, the leading apostle of peasant revolution. "Between 1950 and 1977 industrial output grew at an average annual rate of 13.5 percent … the highest rate of all developing or developed major nations of the world during the time and a more rapid pace than achieved by any country during any comparable period of rapid industrialization in modern world history" (pp. 436–7). Industrial growth was supported relatively lavishly by state re-investment of between 23 and 33 percent of the national product each year. Meanwhile, agriculture was upended, collectivized, de-collectivized, and relatively neglected in terms of investment. As Meisner points out, the agonizingly slow growth of agriculture at 2.3 percent a year from 1952 to 1977 could barely keep pace with population growth of 2 percent a year. Deng and the new leadership continued the industrial emphasis, but shifted more investment to agriculture, ended collectivization, and introduced a "private responsibility system," unleashing enormous productivity gains of 9 percent a year in the early 1980s. The Deng era, not the Maoist, Meisner concludes, "undoubtedly will be recorded as the most economically successful period in the history of modern Chinese agriculture" (p. 475).

The new leaders faced directly the problems of population growth. Earlier arguments in favor of a more populous China faded as the population, already the world's largest, continued to multiply.

POPULATION OF THE PEOPLE'S REPUBLIC OF CHINA

1964	695 million
1971	852 million
1982	1,008 million + 24 million in Taiwan, Hong Kong and Macao
1997	1,210 million (estimated)

Government programs for "small family happiness," beginning in 1974, culminated in the 1980 policy of one family, one child. Fertility rates dropped to 2.3 per hundred women in the 1980s, indicating considerable success. But once again, the enormous coercive power of the state evoked massive unrest, evasion, and, in some case, female infanticide, as couples preferred their one child to be male. The smaller families, however, led to a dramatic reduction in the responsibilities of child care and encouraged greater freedom for women in the home and greater equality and participation in work and public life outside.

While the communist government spoke proudly of its accomplishments in the "four modernizations" of agriculture, science and technology, industry, and defense, critics called for the "fifth modernization"—democracy. In 1989, tens of thousands of demonstrators, mostly students, assembled in Tiananmen Square, demanding democracy as the antidote to a government ruled by old men, infested with corruption, and no longer in touch with the grass roots. The government called in the army to clear the square. In the process, as many as 2000 demonstrators were killed, and more injured. The students' protests were tragically validated, but their proposed solution would have to wait.

In terms of international relations, also, China has implemented a series of dramatic turnabouts. In the first decade of independence, its chief ally was the USSR, which helped the new communist

Tiananmen Square, June 5, 1989. Tanks traveling down Changan Boulevard, in front of the Beijing Hotel, are confronted by a brave Chinese man who pleads for an end to the killing of demonstrating students. This photograph has come to symbolize the struggle of the Chinese people to reassert their dignity and gain democracy in the face of the huge and powerful communist regime.

state design its five-year plan, train and provision its armed forces, and build factories, transportation facilities, urban neighborhoods, and administrative centers. But in the mid-1950s, the USSR under Khruschev began to moderate its own militant policies both domestically and internationally. China, however, remained more "Red," and the two countries quarrelled bitterly over ideology, as they had in 1927. In China's border disputes with India, which would subsequently spill over briefly into warfare in 1962, the USSR backed India's claims and entered into defense alliances with China's opponent. In the summer of 1960, the USSR recalled all of its technical advisors in China, including those working on atomic energy projects. Diplomatic relations were severed in 1961.

Armed conflicts arose over borders in northern Manchuria and Xinjiang province. Fighting in 1969 caused about 100 Russian and 800 Chinese casualties. At considerable expense, China then concentrated its defense forces in these border areas. Only after 1985, under Gorbachev's new policies of *glasnost* (political and cultural openess) and *perestroika* (economic restructuring) in the Soviet Union, were diplomatic relations between the two countries normalized. Still, the two powers remain wary and armed across thousands of miles of shared borders.

Relations with the United States also oscillated. For almost two decades, America lamented and resented the "loss" of China and continued to support Jiang's **irredentist** forces on Taiwan after 1949. Communist policies thoroughly alienated capitalist business people and Christian religious communities, both of which had invested in China. The Chinese government's use of "brain washing" tactics to convert their internal opponents through unremitting propaganda, group pressure, and official coercion, scandalized Americans. China's "liberation" of Tibet

in 1950, and the ruthless suppression of the Tibetan Buddhist revolt in 1959, seemed to confirm the militaristic, brutal nature of the government, although no one moved to aid the Tibetan resistance. The Korean War, provoked by North Korea's invasion of the South in 1950, led to the three-year engagement of American and United Nations forces against those of China, fought to a deadlock. Against the advice of its closest overseas allies, the USA lobbied to keep the People's Republic of China out of the United Nations; the Chinese people were represented by the government of Taiwan.

In the early 1970s, however, the diplomatic scene changed dramatically. Mao and his new advisors, retreating from the economic catastrophe of the Cultural Revolution, sought assistance from abroad. President Nixon and his Secretary of State, Henry Kissinger, also favored more pragmatic policies. In 1971, the USA did not stand in the way of China's joining the United Nations, and in the next year, Nixon visited China, advancing the normalization of relations between the two countries. While the USA still formally protests the 1989 Tiananmen Square crackdown on democracy, relations are improving and top-ranking American government officials visit Beijing regularly, on Chinese terms. Concern for trade with China seems to outweigh concern for human rights abuses.

Within its own area of the world, China for 2000 years has viewed itself as the dominant, central power, and has sought that recognition from its neighbors with mixed success. In many of these

President Nixon meets with Communist Party Chairman Mao Zedong in Beijing, during his groundbreaking 1972 visit to China. The Chinese government, clearly worried by aggressive Soviet policy in Czechoslovakia, took steps to improve relations with the United States. Four years after the Sino-Western rapprochement, begun in 1971, foreign trade with China had trebled, and by 1980 China had joined the International Monetary Fund and the World Bank.

countries, China was a feared and resented neighbor, not an uncommon relationship for a regional superpower. China invaded and colonized Tibet. It backed the murderous Khmer Rouge Party and its leader Pol Pot in the vicious civil wars in Cambodia, even committing troops briefly to combat. In several neighboring states, Chinese minorities were viewed with suspicions as possible fifth column infiltrators, both for the Chinese nation and the Communist Party. In anti-Chinese and anticommunist riots in Indonesia in 1965 thousands of Chinese were murdered, and hundreds of thousands more were exiled. The startling economic success of Korea and Taiwan, not to mention that of Japan, has challenged both China's regional supremacy and its communist path of development. In 1997 the island of Hong Kong, and the tiny strip of adjacent territories on the mainland, which had been a tiny colony of the British empire since 1842 reverted to Chinese sovereignty. Commercial and political observers wait and watch to see the policies that China will implement in this historic outpost of capitalism in its shadow.

Finally, and perhaps most interesting, has been China's relationship with India, the other major nation of the third world. When India became independent in 1947 and China completed its revolution in 1949, they chose dramatically different social, political, and economic paths, and both saw themselves as leading the third world in new patterns of development. At the Bandung Conference in 1955, both offered leadership to newly independent nations. China became a model for agrarian guerrilla revolt throughout Southeast Asia, while India's non-violent path inspired others, especially in Black Africa. India did not protest China's takeover of Tibet in 1950, and consistently backed China's petition to enter the United Nations. But differences over border demarcations in the mountainous regions of Leh and Ladakh finally led to open warfare in 1962. The Chinese decisively defeated Indian troops, penetrated through the mountain passes to within striking distance of India's heartland, and then withdrew voluntarily to the borders they had claimed. In this war, the concept of third world solidarity suffered a mortal blow, which rhetoric would later try to cover but could not.

China demonstrated the inevitability of each huge nation of the world finding its own developmental path. China might for a time take guidance from one foreign ideology or another, and it might enter into alliances with various powers at one time or another, but finally it sought a path appropriate to its own size, geography, power, technology, and historical experience. Chinese at home and abroad, including many who disapproved of current government policies, took pride in the newfound unity, power, and independence of the Central Kingdom. China might make mistakes, but they would be its own mistakes. Leaving behind a century of humiliating colonialism and devastating civil war, today's China would kowtow to no one.

INDIA
1914–1990s

At the end of World War I, India's demand for independence ignited a mass movement that bore many similarities to China's. With the vast majority of its population in rural areas, India, like China, was rooted in agriculture and its peasantry. Like China's Mao Zedong, India's Mohandas Karamchand Gandhi (better known as Mahatma or "great soul" 1869–1948) mobilized this rural constituency. Both leaders created new social and economic institutions for greater equity and also emphasized the need for new technologies appropriate to their agrarian, impoverished societies. Both saw their methods and solutions as models for others to copy.

Fifty years after ending colonialism, both countries could point to significant accomplishments including: cumulative and growing, if slow, economic expansion; political cohesion; social transformation, in accord with their differing agendas; and dominance in the politics of their separate regions of the world. They also shared the similar challenge of maintaining national agreements on common agendas after the unifying enemy of colonialism had been defeated.

The differences between the two mammoth countries were at least equally significant. Unlike China, which had no functioning central government between 1912 and 1949 and had been carved into numerous European and Japanese spheres of influence, India had a central government, which was under British colonial control until independence in 1947. Political disputes evolved through generally peaceful, constitutional processes. India's nationalist leaders, unlike those of China, welcomed businessmen and professionals along with the peasantry in their struggle. Unlike China, in its independence movement India pursued an extraordinary strategy of non-violent mass civil resistance.

It fought no civil war nor did World War II significantly touch its borders. When Independence came, relationships with colonial Great Britain continued harmonious, and India retained membership in the Commonwealth of Nations. Even the partition of the subcontinent into two, India and Pakistan, in 1947, followed constitutional processes, although the subsequent transfers of population were enormously violent. The 1971 creation of the independent country of Bangladesh on the land of east Pakistan was the product of civil war, in which India aided Bangladesh against west Pakistan, but violence was usually contained.

After 1947, as an independent country, India chose a pattern of political democracy and a mixed economy, balancing a "socialist pattern of society," with considerable allowance for private ventures. India confronted enormous, persistent challenges from both its own social structure and the colonial heritage: hierarchical caste restrictions, especially discrimination against ex-untouchables; conflict between religious communities, especially Hindus and Muslims; tensions among regional and linguistic groups; renewed oppression of women; hunger and poverty in an economy of scarcity; and continuing massive population growth. In these struggles, India followed its own unique policies for development, including technological policies of great diversity.

THE INDEPENDENCE STRUGGLE 1914–47

Throughout World War I, resistance to British rule generally took the form of constitutional protest and was concentrated in the hands of men who were educated in British ways, through British-run schools, sometimes in Britain itself. The Indian National Congress, established in 1885 at British initiative as a vent for Indian nationalist criticism, had become the focal institution for nationalist organization. Somewhat more than a third of its membership was trained in the legal profession. In 1835, T.B. Macaulay, law member of the British Government of India, had declared the intent of the government's educational policies to create a class "Indian in blood and colour, but English in taste, in opinions, in morals, and in intellect" (Hay, p. 31) ; the Congress leadership reflected the results.

In 1917, the Secretary of State for India, Edwin Montagu, announced the goal of British policy to be "increasing association of Indians in every branch of the administration, and the gradual development of self-governing institutions, with a view to the progressive realisation of responsible government in India as an integral part of the British Empire." A series of constitutional reforms had already created official councils with substantial Indian membership, elected by very limited elites, to advise the government. The Government of India Act, 1919, expanded provincial and central legislatures and created a dual government, or **dyarchy**, transferring powers over agriculture, public works, education, local self-government, and education to Indian elected legislators at the provincial level.

This half-way house proved unstable; Britain had trouble deciding whether it wished India to be a democracy or a colony. Each new issue revealed the contradiction. When commodity prices rose sharply, virtually doubling between 1914 and 1920, the government seemed unable or unwilling to control them. When the post-war years increased the demands for political independence, the government responded with repression. Against the advice of all of the elected Indians in the Imperial Legislative Council, in 1919 the government cracked down on freedom of the press and assembly by passing the Rowlatt Acts. In Amritsar, Punjab, a British general, Reginald Dyer, ordered his troops to fire, to disperse an unarmed protest rally. Blocking the only exit, they turned the outdoor meeting-place of Jalianwala Bagh into a gruesome shooting gallery, killing 379 people and wounding 1100. The government forced the general to resign, but a popular outpouring of support for him in England thoroughly alienated Indian moderates. World War I had already exposed a murderous brutality within European civilization; now it appeared in India as well, thoroughly laced with racism. From this point onward in the eyes of even moderate Indians, British colonial rule had forfeited its legitimacy.

NEW POLITICAL DIRECTIONS AND REFORM: GANDHI

At this juncture Mohandas Karamchand Gandhi—Mahatma Gandhi—emerged as a leader offering new political directions, new moral perspectives, and new programs of internal reform as well as anti-colonial mobilization. Gandhi called India to find strength and courage in its own peasant roots and spiritual traditions. His success had limitations, but all political activity until well past independence, almost to the present, would revolve around the Congress, which he now reconstructed into a mass movement.

Gandhi's family had been advisors to local rulers in western India for several generations, and his uncle felt that if Mohandas were to maintain the family tradition under British rule, he must travel to Britain to study law. Gandhi emerged from three years of study in London with a deeply considered re-affirmation of his Indian heritage in Hinduism, in religious openness, and in an appreciation of localized, small-scale organizations. Two days after completing his legal training and one day after being admitted to the bar, Gandhi returned to India. He practised law without distinction for a year and then accepted the case of an Indian emigrant business firm in South Africa. There, apparently for the first time, Gandhi suffered racist persecution repeatedly.

The Indian community in South Africa had mostly come to work as indentured laborers. The South African government, which wanted them to return home at the end of their service, instituted many laws to make their long-term status untenable. Indians were required to carry identification cards at all times and to pay heavy head taxes. Then the government nullified all marriages not performed by Christian clergy, rendering illegitimate the children of almost all the Indian immigrants. Although he had arrived as the lawyer for a wealthy Indian Muslim client, Gandhi identified with the pain and humiliation of his less privileged countrymen and, indeed, suffered it himself, as he was physically evicted from public facilities and threatened with beatings and even death for asserting his rights. Heretofore a rather private person, Gandhi began to organize a protest movement.

$\mathcal{G}$ANDHI'S FIRST EXPERIENCE WITH RACISM IN SOUTH AFRICA

Mahatma Gandhi published his *Autobiography* originally as a series of newspaper articles. Many of the episodes also carried a moral message for readers. The story of his first encounter with racism in South Africa implies that he had not experienced such severe discrimination in neither colonial India nor during his law school days in London.

On the seventh or eighth day after my arrival, I left Durban. A first class seat was booked for me. … The train reached Maritzburg, the capital of Natal, at about 9 P.M. … A passenger came next, and looked me up and down. He saw that I was a "colored" man. This disturbed him. Out he went and came in again with one or two officials. They all kept quiet, when another offical came to me and said, "Come along, you must go to the van compartment."

"But I have a first class ticket," said I.

"That doesn't matter," rejoined the other. "I tell you, you must go to the van compartment."

"I tell you, I was permitted to travel in this compartment at Durban, and I insist on going on in it."

"No you won't," said the offical. "You must leave this compartment, or else I shall have to call a police constable to push you out."

"Yes, you may. I refuse to get out voluntarily."

The constable came. He took me by the hand and pushed me out. My luggage was also taken out. I refused to go to the other compartment and the train steamed away. I went and sat in the waiting room, keeping my hand bag with me, and leaving the other luggage where it was. …

It was winter, and winter in the higher regions of South Africa is severely cold. Maritzburg being at a high altitude, the cold was extremely bitter. My overcoat was in my luggage, but I did not dare to ask for it lest I should be insulted again, so I sat and shivered. There was no light in the room. A passenger came in at about midnight and possibly wanted to talk to me. But I was in no mood to talk.

I began to think of my duty. Should I fight for my rights or go back to India, or should I go on to Pretoria without minding the insults, and return to India after finishing the case? It would be cowardice to run back to India without fulfilling my obligation. The hardship to which I was subjected was superficial—only a symptom of the deep disease of color prejudice. I should try, if possible, to root out the disease and suffer hardships in the process. (Jack, p. 29–30)

SPOTLIGHT

Appropriate-scale Technologies?

What are appropriate technologies for third world countries? How should their governments balance the desire for high levels of productivity through advanced technology with the need to create jobs for all the population, usually at low-technology levels? With their very limited financial and technological resources, what level of technology can they afford and sustain? If they do not introduce as much modern techology as possible, will they not fall farther behind? On the other hand, will not advanced, labor-saving technologies increase unemployment? Finally, to the extent that new technologies are introduced, can the ecological harm experienced in already industrialized countries be avoided?

The massive use of raw human labor has certain virtues. In **picture 2** multitudes of Chinese student volunteers help to construct a road on a people's commune in the 1960s. During

Picture 1 Narmada Dam, Manibeli, India, 1994.

this period of China's Cultural Revolution, known as the Great Leap Forward, everyone was to make a contribution to national development: having a job was both a right and an obligation. There were, however, drawbacks. Machinery, if it was affordable, would get more work done, faster, and might, in the long run, create more jobs at higher levels of skill. The great Cultural Revolution, however, was not just an attempt to provide jobs for all. It sent trained personnel, especially university faculty, into rural areas to perform manual labor in order to break down their separation from the masses. This policy wreaked havoc on China's universities, but it remained in place until the death of Mao Zedong in 1976.

The dam on the Narmada River, under construction in western India in the mid-1990s (**picture 1**), represents another extreme in the use of resources. Although manual labor is also used in its construction, the size and complexity of the project, one of the largest dams in the world, requires high-tech engineering and massive uses of machinery. Moreover, it creates enormous ecological problems. Narmada, like many enormous dams recently constructed or under construction—such as the Aswan Dam in Egypt, the Three Gorges Dam in China, and dams along the Mekong River in southeast Asia—creates enormous lakes up-river, displacing millions of villagers. The dams interfere with natural processes of siltation and may ultimately harm the quality of the soil. On the other hand, these enormous dams promise to provide flood control, so much water for drinking and irrigation, and so much hydroelectrical power that governments and huge majorities of populations have usually welcomed them. In the case of the Narmada Dam, for example, when the World Bank withdrew its financial support, citing ecological concerns, the Indian government mobilized its own resources for the project and moved it forward. The dam is reaching completion at the end of the twentieth century.

Picture 2 Students helping a people's commune to build a road, Guangxi, 1965.

Instead of leaving at the end of his year's employment, Gandhi remained in South Africa for twenty-one years, 1893–1904, inventing new methods of resistance: *satyagraha*, "truth force," manifested in self-sacrificing, non-violent mass demonstrations, demanding that the persecutors recognize the immorality of their own position and redress the suffering of the oppressed; *ahimsa*, non-violence in the face of attack; civil disobedience against unjust laws, with a willingness to suffer the legal consequences, including imprisonment, and frequently illegal consequences, such as beatings; the establishment of a headquarters, modeled on the Hindu religious *ashram*, providing living and working quarters for himself, family, and closest allies in his campaigns; the creation of a press for publishing the principles of his movement. Because he renounced violence, Gandhi, in accord with his

Hindu caste status, called these methods "passive resistance," but they were actually systems of "militant non-violence." These techniques were later adopted, in greater or lesser degree, and with greater or lesser success, by leaders of resistance movements around the world from Martin Luther King (1929– 68) in the USA, to Kwame Nkruma (1909–72) in Ghana, to Nelson Mandela (b. 1918) in South Africa itself.

In South Africa, working with Indians from across the regional, linguistic, religious, and caste diversity of the subcontinent, Gandhi gained a breadth of experience of India that would have been difficult for a leader from within a single Indian region. Concurrently his reputation also spread throughout India.

In 1909, Gandhi published *Hind Swaraj, or Indian Home Rule*. Banned in India, it championed India's

Ɋ̲NDIAN INDEPENDENCE—KEY FIGURES

Rabindranath Tagore
(1861–1941) Indian poet, painter, and musician from Bengal, who translated his own verse into English. He received the Nobel prize for literature in 1913. An ardent nationalist and advocate of social reform, he resigned his knighthood (granted in 1918) as a gesture of protest against British repression in India.

Mohandas Karamchand Gandhi
(1869–1948) Indian political and spiritual leader, who fought against anti-Indian discrimination in South Africa before returning to India in 1915. He became leader of the Congress Party in the 1920s. Gandhi attempted to maintain non-violent ideals through civil disobedience campaigns and was imprisoned in 1922, 1932, 1933, and 1942 for anti-British activities. He played a crucial part in the negotiations leading to partition and Independence.

Muhammad Ali Jinnah
(1876–1948) The founder of Pakistan. A member of the Indian National Congress, he advocated cooperation between Hindus and Muslims. He transformed the Muslim League from a cultural to a political organization. In 1940 Jinnah demanded the partition of British India into separate Muslim and Hindu states. In 1947, after terrible riots in Calcutta, Jinnah had to accept a smaller state than he had demanded. He became governor-general of Pakistan in 1947 and died in office.

Jawaharlal Nehru
(1889–1964) Indian nationalist politician, who was prime minister from 1947. Before partition, he led the socialist wing of the Congress Party and was regarded as second only to Gandhi. Between 1921 and 1945 he was imprisoned by the British nine times for political activities. As prime minister he developed the idea of non-alignment (neutrality toward the major powers), established an industrial base, and founded a parliamentary democracy based on the rule of law.

Subhas Chandra Bose
(c. 1897–?1945) Indian Nationalist leader (known as "Netaji"—"Respected Leader"), who called for outright Indian independence. Frequently imprisoned, he became president of the All-India Congress (1938–9). He supported the Axis powers (Germany, Italy, and Japan) during World War II and became commander-in-chief of the Japanese-sponsored Indian National Army. He was reported killed in Formosa.

own civilization, exhorting Indians to conquer the feelings of fear and inferiority inherent in their colonial situation and to attack British hegemony courageously.

> We have hitherto said nothing because we have been cowed down … it is our duty now to speak out boldly. We consider your schools and law courts to be useless. We want our own ancient schools and courts to be restored. The common language of India is not English but Hindi. You should, therefore, learn it. We can hold communication with you only in our national language. …
>
> We cannot tolerate the idea of your spending money on railways and the military. We see no occasion for either. … We do not need any European cloth. We shall manage with articles produced and manufactured at home. You have great military resources. … You may, if you like, cut us to pieces. You may shatter us at the cannon's mouth. If you act contrary to our will, we shall not help you; and without our help, we know that you cannot move one step forward. (Jack, pp. 118–9.)

Gandhi's success in South Africa was limited to short-term compromises with the government, but he earned the esteem of his countrymen in both South Africa and India. They eagerly awaited his political initiatives when he returned home and established a new *ashram* in Ahmedabad in 1915.

Popular discontent with British rule already existed; Gandhi gave it new leadership and direction. By 1907, the extremist wing of Congress, led by Bal Gangahdar Tilak (1856–1920), called for the British to leave India immediately. *Swadeshi* (the use of indigenous products) campaigns, especially after 1905, had demonstrated the degree to which voluntary boycotts of imports could spur Indian industrial productivity and profits. How much more effective legal control over tariffs would be once the British left! Businessmen and industrialists also resented British reluctance to share industrial secrets, restrictions on industrial and infrastructural investment, removal of tax monies from India back to Britain in the form of "home charges," and limits on career advancement for Indians.

Several peasant movements which Gandhi would come to direct began with local organization, as in Champaran in Bihar, (1917), and in Kheda (1917) and Bardoli, (1922 and 1928) in Gujarat. Peasants from these areas asked Gandhi to provide more sophisticated and effective leadership to advance their own initial activities.

Millworkers in Ahmedabad had already organized their union, too (against local employers, not against the British), when they asked Gandhi to take charge of their strike in 1919. Gandhi recognized India's smoldering grass-roots anger, inflamed by post-war economic conditions and political repression. He reconstituted the Congress into a mass organization with millions of dues-paying members, a standing executive committee to keep the organization functioning between annual meetings, and a program of mass civil disobedience, *satyagraha*.

Identifying with the multitudes, Gandhi chose an ever simpler and more basic public presentation. Already a vegetarian and owning few possessions, he now rejected Western dress and reduced his clothing to a bare minimum, usually wearing just a loincloth and, in cold weather, a shawl, and simple wooden sandals—a very powerful fashion statement. To his nation and to his wife, without discussion, he announced his choice of celibacy at the age of thirty-seven. Oppressed peoples throughout the world have historically feared that their leaders might sell them out, but Gandhi's ascetic and quasi-religious idiom re-assured and captured India's masses. He lived his *satyagraha* and *ahimsa* principles of self-suffering and militant non-violence through fasting, "courting" arrest, and putting his life on the line in leading his public protest movements. Although his countrymen began calling him Mahatma, "great soul," Gandhi said that he was not a saint trying to work in politics, but rather a politician trying to become a saint. Many of his British opponents, and some Indian opponents as well, nevertheless saw him as a canny politician manipulating the symbols of sainthood. Winston Churchill scornfully dismissed Gandhi as a "half-naked fakir."

Gandhi knit together India's enormous size and diversity by cultivating personal and political alliances with the major regional leaders. His most analytic and thorough biographer, Judith Brown, praises his skill in winning the allegiance of such regional giants as C. Rajagopalachari (1879–1972) in Madras; Rajendra Prasad (1884–1963) in Bihar, later the first president of independent India; and, most critically, Vallabhbhai Patel (c. 1873–1933) in Gujarat, who went on to become chairman of the entire Congress Party before and after Independence, and Jawaharlal Nehru (1889–1964) in Uttar Pradesh (then called United Provinces), who became the first prime minister of independent India in 1947, a post he held until his death.

Gandhi and Nehru. Mahatma Gandhi, wearing his customary dhoti, and Jawaharlal Nehru are deep in conversation at the All India Congress Committee Meeting in Bombay, July 6, 1946, where Nehru took office as President of the Congress. Gandhi and Nehru were the charismatic figures who led the Indian National Congress, a broad-based political organization which was the vehicle for the nationalist movement for independence.

Gandhi was not successful everywhere, however. He did not capture the leadership nor the rank and file of the large eastern state of Bengal. In Calcutta, Subhas Chandra Bose often opposed Gandhi as too ascetic in his personal life, too narrow in his intellectual interests, too dictatorial in his political authority, and too compromising with business and landlord interests in consolidating his power. Left-wing socialists throughout India also found Gandhi too cozy with big business and landlord interests. When the Congress socialists advocated land redistribution in the 1930s, Gandhi successfully won over the highly respected, usually socialist, Nehru, and the issue was deferred until after Independence. Despite valiant efforts, Gandhi failed to capture the most important Muslim leadership. Mohammed Ali Jinnah (1876–1948), leader of the movement for a separate Pakistan, found Gandhi's style both too ascetic and too Hindu. As Independence neared, Jinnah did not trust Gandhi's Congress to deal equitably with Muslims.

INTERNAL PROBLEMS

Nevertheless, across India, key leaders praised Gandhi for redirecting them back to the rural, peasant center of Indian life. At the opposite end of the political/moral spectrum from Mao in his evaluation of means and ends, Gandhi nevertheless paralleled the Chinese leader in pointing to the problems, and the potentials, of the peasantry. When the Mahatma spoke of *swaraj*, self-rule, he intended not only freedom from colonialism, but internal self discipline as well. He stressed five principal domestic programs, each fundamental to India's twentieth-century development:

Hindu–Muslim Unity

Gandhi attempted to hold Hindus and Muslims together in a secular, egalitarian India. After World War I, he supported Muslim international religious concerns through the the Khilafat Movement, supporting the Muslim Caliphate of the Ottoman Empire against British designs, even after the fall of the Ottoman Empire. In 1924, Gandhi fasted for twenty-one days to promote Hindu–Muslim unity. During the partition riots in 1947, Gandhi walked through violence-torn areas to advocate peace. Muslims, however, doubted their fair treatment in a majority Hindu country and saw even Gandhi's political idiom as excessively Hindu. The partition of India into two nations, India led by Gandhi and the Congress and Pakistan led by Jinnah and the Muslim League, was his greatest failure, Gandhi felt, and he refused to participate in independence celebrations. In 1948, Gandhi was assassinated by a Hindu fanatic who found him soft on Muslims. The Hindu– Muslim breach continues to be a problem today, both in tensions across the international border between India and Pakistan and in domestic conflict between Hindus and Muslims.

Abolition of Untouchability

Gandhi worked to end untouchability. He was not opposed to the general concept of the caste system, seeing differences among people, even by birth, as a part of reality, but he fought the designation of about 15 percent of India's Hindu population as outcasts, humiliated and oppressed. Declaring, "It has always been a mystery to me how men can feel themselves honored by the humiliation of their fellow beings," Gandhi coined for the **untouchables** a new name, *harijan*, "children of God." In 1932, Gandhi undertook a fast-unto-death against separate electorates for the "depressed classes." He approved of reserving places in elected assemblies—even more places than the untouchables had asked and the government had been willing to allocate. But he wanted all voters to select from among the untouchable candidates lest the untouchables begin to form a political nation-within-a-nation, as Muslims were beginning to do. After a week, the untouchables' leader, B. R. Ambedkar (1893–1956), a lawyer trained partly at Columbia University, acceded in Gandhi's demands. At the same time Hindu leaders, their consciences touched, began to push for an end to restrictions on untouchables and even opened many Hindu temples to them.

The effects of Gandhi's campaign were mixed. Though he appeared far ahead of public opinion, many untouchable leaders thought Gandhi patronizing and restrictive, offering too little, too late. They called *harijan* a euphemism and preferred the more blunt designation *dalit*, oppressed. In 1955 the

government began a policy of protective discrimination, reserving a limited percentage of places in government jobs, universities, and elected offices only for the "scheduled castes," those castes that were listed on an official schedule as formerly untouchable. The issue of reservations for scheduled castes has continued as a hot topic since Independence. But over the years the question of how many places should be reserved, for whom, under what categories, and for how long has not been resolved. These disputes have evoked violent protests on both sides. In 1990 they led to the fall of the government of Prime Minister V.P. Singh.

Cultural Policies

In developing pride in India's heritages, fostering the development of regional languages and literatures, and encouraging more efficient schooling through the vernacular, Gandhi rejected the use of English in India's public life and schools. In his first major address after returning to the subcontinent Gandhi argued:

> Suppose that we had been receiving, during the past fifty years, education through our vernaculars … we should have today a free India, we should have our educated men, not as if they were foreigners in their own land but speaking to the heart of the nation; they would be working among the poorest of the poor, and whatever they would have gained during the past fifty years would be a heritage for the nation. (Jack, p. 131)

Over the years since Independence, Indian vernaculars have increasingly displaced English as the language of instruction in India's educational institutions all the way through to university level. Yet English remains one of the two official languages of India; the other is Hindi. Parents who have aspirations for their children's career prospects usually encourage them to study English, and the widespread knowledge of English among India's educated classes has kept the country in touch with world developments.

Prohibition

Gandhi led a temperance movement to ban alcoholic drinks. His argument was based primarily on concern for the effects of alcohol abuse on working-class families, especially when the husband/breadwinner spent his earnings on drink. After

Independence, many states of India chose to restrict or prohibit the use of liquor, but by the later 1980s only Gandhi's home state of Gujarat retained almost total prohibition—and it had enormous problems of bootlegging and of complicity between politicians and bootleggers.

Technology

Because of Gandhi's concern for appropriate technology, the Congress Party made the spinning wheel its emblem; hand-spun, hand-woven cloth its dress; and the production of a daily quota of hand-spun yarn a requirement for membership. Gandhi expressed his early denunciation of modern machinery in *Hind Swaraj* in a mystical religious idiom. Later he demanded small-scale, labor-intensive, alternative technologies for economic and humanitarian reasons:

> Hunger is the argument that is driving India to the spinning wheel. … We must think of millions who are today less than animals, who are almost in a dying state. The spinning wheel is the reviving draught for the millions of our dying countrymen and countrywomen. … I do want growth. I do want self-determination. I do want freedom, but I want all these for the soul. … A plea for the spinning wheel is a plea for recognizing the dignity of labor.

THE DEBATE OVER TECHNOLOGY

Again, not everyone agreed with Gandhi. His most politically powerful disciple, Jawaharlal Nehru (1889–1964), argued equally adamantly the importance of modern machinery and technology. Despite his western education and biases, Nehru could see both sides of the technological debate because Gandhi had introduced him—as he had introduced a generation of India's leaders—to the reality of India's 500,000 villages, where 85 percent of its population lived a technologically simple, generally impoverished existence:

> He sent us to the villages, and the countryside hummed with the activity of innumerable messengers of the new gospel of action. The peasant was shaken up and he began to emerge from his quiescent shell. The effect on us was different but equally far-reaching, for we saw, for the first time as it were, the villager in the intimacy of his mud-hut, and with the stark shadow of hunger always

pursuing him. We learnt our Indian economics more from these visits than from books and learned discourses. (Nehru, p. 365)

But, in the end, Nehru came down unequivocally in favor of large-scale industry:

> It can hardly be challenged that, in the context of the modern world, no country can be politically and economically independent, even within the framework of international inter-dependence, unless it is highly industrialized and has developed its power resources to the utmost. … Thus an attempt to build up a country's economy largely on the basis of cottage and small-scale industries is doomed to failure. It will not solve the basic problems of the country or maintain freedom, nor will it fit in with the world framework, except as a colonial appendage. (p. 414)

Nehru, a socialist from his study at Harrow, Cambridge, and the Inns of Court law school, advocated the need for planning to guide proper uses of high technology, and in 1938, the Congress appointed its own National Planning Commission, the forerunner of the official planning commission established after Independence.

Gandhi is praised by most Indians as the father of the new nation, but his influence on the actual winning of independence and of new policies of the new government has been widely questioned. India's transformation into an independent state was no simple moral victory, but an exercise in *realpolitik*, a response by Britain to enormous losses in the global economic depression and World War II, as much as to Gandhi's politics. Gandhi led three massive, nationwide *satyagraha* campaigns. The non-cooperation campaign of 1920–22 boycotted British colonial schools, law courts, administrative positions, manufactures, and imports. In a few localities, Indians refused to pay taxes. The Congress began to construct a parallel government. A decade later, in the salt march campaign of 1930–32, Gandhi mocked the government salt monopoly by marching to the sea and manufacturing salt from sea water. This simple action initiated a nationwide campaign of civil disobedience and law breaking, which focused world attention on the government's lack of authority and respect in the eyes of most Indians. After another ten years, the "Quit India" campaign of 1942 refused Indian political support to Britain's efforts in World War II unless Independence was granted. (The Indian

The Salt March. Mahatma Gandhi begins the symbolic walk from Ahmedabad to Dandi on the coast, where he collected sea salt and thus technically broke the salt law—the Government's monopoly on salt production. Civil disobedience did not win independence immediately, but it did discredit the moral and political authority of the colonial government.

army, however, did fight loyally under British command.) Despite these three massive, nationwide campaigns, the British did not finally concede independence until 1947.

INDEPENDENCE AND AFTER

At Independence, despite Gandhi's efforts to maintain unity, the subcontinent was partitioned into Hindu-majority India, governed by a generally secular Congress Party, and Muslim-majority Pakistan, under an officially Muslim government. The creation of Pakistan responded to Muslim cultural-religious claims, like those of the poet Muhammad Iqbal, for a nation governed according to Islamic principles, and to Muslim political-economic claims, like those of Muhammad Ali Jinnah, Pakistan's first president, for an equitable distribution of national positions and patronage. Pakistan's peculiar geography, with two wings, east and west, separated by some 800 miles (1280 kilometers) of hostile Indian territory, reflected the distribution of Muslim majorities in the subcontinent. An estimat-

ed 12 million people shifted their homes—6 million Hindus and Sikhs from east and west Pakistan, 6 million Muslims from India. In the process, between 200,000 and one million people were killed. Nevertheless, a sizeable Muslim minority, 10 percent of India's population, remained within India. While Hindus and Muslims mostly cohabit the land peacefully, under a secular constitution, tensions between them remain.

Relations between India and Pakistan have remained tense since partition, and have been further inflamed by disputes over the proper political affiliation for the Kashmir region They broke into open war in 1947, 1965, and 1971. The 1971 war was triggered by the break-up of the two wings of Pakistan and the formation of the new nation of Bangladesh in the east. India had always maintained that religion alone could not be the basis of a state, and, with everyone else, found the union of Urdu-speaking, arid, west Pakistan, with 800 mile (1280 kilometer) distant, Bengali-speaking, marshy, east Pakistan peculiar and unstable. When civil war broke out in 1971, India chose to ally itself with the newly emerging nation of Bangladesh, an impoverished, densely populated, deltaic country of 125 million people.

Despite Gandhi's quixotic vision of transforming the Congress into a non-official, social service institution, the party members quickly took over the new government of India. Although often called a "soft-state," not always able to implement its will and legislation, early moves by the independent government quickly consolidated the country. Britain had governed about one-third of India's landmass indirectly, through local rulers. Legally, these 562 "princes" maintained direct relations with the British Crown and at Independence had the (theoretical) power to declare merger with India, or Pakistan, or independence. Fears of a **Balkanization** of the subcontinent, its break-up into numerous, separate, small states, were countered by the carrot-and-stick offers of the Home

Minister, Vallabhbhai Patel, who prevailed on the princes within India's borders to accede. Dispute over the legitimacy of Kashmir's accession has remained the sole, but very contentious, exception.

Other threatened Balkanization was also averted. Gandhi had organized the Congress by linguistic regions, which did not correspond to the more random administrative divisions of the British. After Independence, the Congress government created new states in accordance with these linguistic borders. Despite fears of separatism, the states have stayed together in the Indian union. Strong separatist movements continue, however, in Punjab, based on discontent within the Sikh religious community; in Muslim-majority Kashmir; and in the far distant and ethnically Mongoloid northeast Himalayan regions of Assam. But thus far, a combination of political bargaining and armed force has kept the country together.

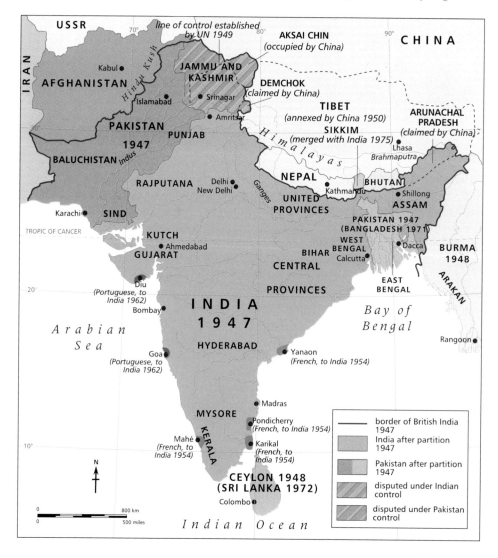

Political change in South Asia after 1947 At Independence in 1947, British India was partitioned into secular, but Hindu-majority, India and Muslim Pakistan amid enormous violence and migration. Disputes over Kashmir continue until today. In 1971 the east wing of Pakistan fought, with Indian assistance, a war of independence with the west and became Bangladesh.

Mass migration. The partition of India at independence created an unprecedented transfer of population in two directions: Hindus fled Pakistan for the safety of India, and Muslims living in India struggled to get safely over the border into their new homeland. This packed train, groaning with refugees from Pakistan, arrives in Amritsar, just over the Indian border, on October 16, 1947.

Gandhi's Congress generally respected constitutional process, and the democracy proposed by British rulers has become a reality in India since Independence. With the exception of two years of "Emergency Rule," 1975–7, during which Prime Minister Indira Gandhi (1917–84) asserted dictatorial powers, India has functioned democratically and constitutionally as a union of some thirty states and territories, with universal adult franchise and guaranteed freedoms of press, assembly, speech, religion, and an independent judiciary. Despite imperfections, India prides itself on being the world's largest democracy. It also has seen numerous freely elected state communist governments functioning within a democratic framework, first in Kerala in 1957 and later in West Bengal.

Since the 1950s, small groups of revolutionary guerrillas, named Naxalites, for the village of Naxalbari in Bihar where they began their activities, have also been a presence. But India has not given strong support to communism. The reasons may be India's generally religious orientation, skepticism about a philosophy and organization so tied to foreign governments, and recognition of communism's origin as a proletarian rather than a peasant movement.

Until recently, capitalism fared even less well. Only one party ever directly espoused a capitalist philosophy of development, and it had limited success and a short life. Indians, including much of the business community, seemed to view capitalism as excessively individualistic and materialistic, based on a philosophy of self-interest often seen as greed, and associated with colonialism in the past and the return of a neo-colonial economic dominance in the present. Despite a large free-enterprise sector in the economy, especially in agriculture, most major Indian parties have advocated socialism, on the grounds of its stated concern for the common good. Nehru, in particular, espoused "a socialist pattern of development." A change in this policy began in 1991 as India moved to open its economy to international markets. Prime Minister P.V. Narasimha Rao, with Finance Minister Manmohan Singh, lowered tariffs and began to welcome foreign investments, perhaps in light of the successes of the more open economies of the "Asian Tigers" of east Asia (see pp. 640–2). India's involvement in the global market continues, with some restraints.

Through the first four decades of Independence, India's democracy was dominated by one party, the Congress, and the party's leadership was dominated by one family, the Nehru dynasty. Jawaharlal Nehru, prime minister from Independence until his death in 1964, was soon succeeded by his daughter, Indira Gandhi (no relation to the Mahatma), who was prime minister in 1967–77 and from 1980 until her assassination in 1984, and she was followed by her son, Rajiv, in 1984–9. With Rajiv's assassination in 1991, India has moved clearly into a period of multi-party maneuvering and coalition governments. The fastest growing party emphasized Hindu nationalism, rather than the secularism of the earlier Nehru period, but it is unclear how far the pendulum will swing towards favoring the majority religion in politics.

GENDER ISSUES

With Mrs. Gandhi as prime minister, and such prominent women as Mrs. Vijayalakshmi Pandit as India's United Nations representative in the 1950s, Indian women have participated prominently in public life at the highest political levels. The struggle for Independence actively recruited women and thus opened public life to increasing female participation, although after 1947 many returned to a less public life. In 1988, women held forty-six seats out of 537 in the lower house of Parliament, twenty-eight out of 245 in the upper, indicating a slowly increasing proportion. State government ratios are similar. With Independence, India instituted universal adult suffrage, and in each national election approximately 55 percent of women have voted, compared with about 60 percent of men.

The 1955 Hindu Marriage Act assured Hindu women of the right to divorce and raised the age of marriage for Hindu women to fifteen (eighteen for males). The Hindu Succession Act of 1956 gave daughters equal rights with sons in inheriting their father's property. On the other hand, Parliament did not legislate new personal law for non-Hindus, and other religious communities continue under their traditional laws. The issue disturbs many feminists but they tread lightly here because of the complex inter-mixture of Hindu–Muslim communal sensitivities.

Because family structures in India, especially north India, are both **patrilineal** and **patrilocal**, the birth of a female child is often regarded as a financial and even emotional burden. Years of childhood care and expense culminate in the girl's leaving home for marriage into another family, somewhat distant, with restricted ties to the family of origin. The sex ratio in India, about 930 women to 1000

Indira Gandhi, prime minister of India (1966–77; 1980–84), inspects the guard at an Independence Day celebration, August 23, 1967. Mahatma Gandhi did much to encourage women's participation in public life during the years leading to Independence. Although many women are well-educated, the great number of girls whose education is of short duration or non-existent is cause for concern.

men, is one of the lowest in the world, and it suggests the systematic neglect of females, especially young girls. Suicide rates for Indian women are very high: the practice of *sati* (suttee), in which a widow throws herself on her husband's funeral pyre, continues, albeit rarely. As amniocentesis becomes more widely available, allowing parents to know the sex of unborn children, abortion of females may result. The literacy rate (1997) among females is 38 percent as compared with 66 percent for males; but this is up from 8 percent and 25 percent, respectively, in 1951. South India's treatment of women is widely regarded as more egalitarian, perhaps because of different local traditions, including some influence of matrilineal systems.

Disconcerting results from Syracuse University anthropologist Susan Wadley's 1984 re-study of Karimpur village, about 100 miles (160 kilometers) from Delhi, suggest that the position of poor, rural women may deteriorate as a result of increasing general prosperity in the new economic system and of increasing urbanization.

There were several factors affecting women's work, all producing a marked decline in employment opportunities of women. First, with the relative decline of male employment in agriculture and the shift of landless men to urban-based jobs, women who had worked in agriculture alongside their male kin were displaced. Second, women traditionally employed in caste-based occupations as servants through *jajmani* [family patronage systems] were no longer so employed. Third, mechanization had replaced female labor in a variety of arenas. Finally, changes in cropping patterns had made female help in the fields less necessary. These factors all contributed to the marginalization of poor women, giving them less voice in their families and ultimately devaluing them. (p. 287)

An encouraging contrary development is the organization of working women into effective unions, which provide both economic opportunity and political representation. In cities such as Bombay, Madras, and Ahmedabad, voluntary organizations of tens of thousands of working women have begun to gain access to capital for working-class women who carry on their own small businesses; to incorporate cooperatives, which help them secure raw materials and market finished products; lobby government for workers' safety, health, insurance, maternity, and job protection in non-unionized, small-scale shops; develop new educational models for job training; and create new systems of health delivery, especially for women. One of the most important of these organizations is the Self-Employed Women's Association (SEWA) in Ahmedabad, a daughter organization of the Textile Labour Union, which had been founded with the help of Mahatma Gandhi.

ECONOMIC, SOCIAL, AND TECHNOLOGICAL CHANGE SINCE INDEPENDENCE

Economically and technologically, India has accomplished the once seemingly impossible feat of producing enough food to feed its growing population. At Independence, India had 361 million people; today, it has 950 million. Mass-starvation during droughts in 1964–6 was averted only by the importation of 12 million tons of food grains each year, primarily from the United States. Then, in the late 1960s, the "green revolution" began in India. New strains of wheat, developed in Mexico under the auspices of the Rockefeller Foundation, were introduced. They increased India's productivity even faster than her population. India, almost miraculously, proved able to feed itself, raising annual grain production by 1990 to about 175 million tons, compared with about 50 million tons at Independence. Further breakthroughs were sought in rice production, the country's other major crop. Meanwhile, a "white revolution" in dairy production and distribution was also taking place. Dairy cooperatives were formed throughout India, enabling village farmers to pool and ship their highly perishable products to urban markets—as fresh milk in refrigerated train cars, and as processed cheese and dairy products in conventional shipping—thus providing incentives for increasing production.

Women workers in a textile factory in Calcutta hand-embroider designs on cotton fabric. Kamaladevi Chattopadhyaya, active in the women's movement from the 1930s, was an early advocate of education and better working conditions for women. Today, although conditions have improved greatly, and despite the relatively high profile of women in India, they remain at a disadvantage in the workplace.

The revolutions in agriculture were not without their problems. First, ecologically, many questions were raised about relying so exclusively on so few new strains of "miracle wheat." Were too many seeds coming from too few genetic baskets? Would the massive new quantities of chemical fertilizers needed to support the new seeds ultimately ruin the ecology? Second, economic growth increased disparities and tensions between haves and have-nots and between those who worked more entrepreneurially and those who did not. The new productivity benefited most those who already had the economic resources to afford the new seeds, fertilizers, and requisite irrigation water. The rich were getting richer and social tensions increased. Similarly, disparities between rich and poor states grew. The Punjab, in particular, progressed dramatically in transforming both its agriculture and small industries. The small northern state became the richest in India, the country's breadbasket.

Control of land and its redistribution is a matter for each state in India, and different states have enacted different policies. In general, redistribution has been accompanied by compensation paid by new owners to old, and the process has been peaceful but slow. Government implementation of family planning, rejected overwhelmingly in the wake of Indira Gandhi's program of forced sterilization in 1975–7, has been soft-pedalled ever since, yet birth rates have fallen to about twenty-six per thousand (1997), down from about forty-four per thousand at Independence. Life expectancy at birth has risen from about thirty years at Independence in 1947 to fifty-nine years for men and sixty years for women in 1996.

Industrial productivity increased, but the structure of the workforce did not change—exactly the process Gandhi had feared. New machinery produced more goods more efficiently, but did not provide more jobs. The business and industrial sectors had contributed only 5 percent to the nation's income in 1947; slightly more than 30 percent by the mid-1980s (Hardgrave, p. 20). Industrial production multiplied almost five times between 1951 and 1980 (Hardgrave, p. 325). In the 1980s it was increasing almost 8 percent a year, achieving "a new growth trajectory" (Adams, pp. 77–100). Urbanization increased to just under 30 percent, up from 17 percent at Independence. On the other hand, the percentage of workers in industry had essentially stagnated: about 10 percent in 1951; about 13 percent in 1991. Unemployment stayed steady at 8 percent.

Until the 1980s, industrial policy derived from Gandhi's and Nehru's philosophies. Gandhi had urged austere consumption levels, handicraft production, and national self-sufficiency through import substitution. Nehru implemented socialism, central planning, government control and development of the "commanding heights" of the economy—energy, steel, petroleum, banking—and regulation of the large-scale capitalist sector. Both Gandhi and Nehru stressed internal self-sufficiency in production. These policies were increasingly challenged by a new international political-economic wisdom in the 1980s based on the economic successes of the East Asian countries and the political successes of President Reagan in the USA and Prime Minister Thatcher in Britain. Increased consumption has spurred increased productivity, and a consumer society has began to appear in India. Readers wishing to sense this development, as well as others in present-day India, might browse through the advertising as well as the news reports in *India Today*, a weekly news magazine published in India as well as in foreign editions.

High-tech innovation for both home and foreign markets has increased productivity, and India began to manufacture submarines, computer software and hardware, machine tools, and even prepared to export nuclear power plants adapted to Third World conditions.

There is widespread appreciation that India now has an impressive scientific and technological establishment and the capacity to assimilate the newest technological advances occurring elsewhere in the world. Securing access to world-class technologies has been the most important element of India's foreign economic policy in recent years. (Adams, p. 85)

The political scientist Myron Weiner has pointed out the extraordinary imbalance in India's educational expenditures, which strongly favors higher education while starving the primary schools. These policies, rooted in traditional hierarchical attitudes and interests, have produced a very skewed society, in which the highly educated elites compare with the best anywhere in the world, but overall literacy is only 52 percent. Again, Mahatma Gandhi's fears were coming true.

A new economic world, based on greater international trade, wider scope for domestic capitalist competition, and more efficient and competitive administration of government enterprises, was

People throng a main street in Benares. Although the streets of India's cities are crowded, and the problems created by huge numbers of people living within the confines of a city are great, the bulk of the country's population, some 70 percent, is located in non-urban areas.

superpower. Since 1974, only India has tested nuclear weapons, although Pakistan also seems to be capable of producing them. India's military expenditures have risen from US$ 1.7 billion in 1960 to US$ 9.8 billion in 1987, where it has remained about level (in constant dollars).

In the larger world arena, India was the first major colony to win independence after World War II, and it served as a leader to other newly emerging countries. Nehru, in particular, provided articulate, innovative direction. In 1997, with abundant human and institutional resources in absolute terms, India remains a model of democratic political stability and gradual economic growth in a nation of unparalleled heterogeneity. But its leadership role may have peaked. India's border war with, and defeat by, China in 1962 crippled its claim to third world harmony and leadership, and, in any case, political colonialism is no longer a major global issue. Economically, attention is flowing toward more open, more liberalized, and more expansive economies than India's, and India's persistent poverty and illiteracy make it a questionable model for others.

India today is occupied primarily in cultivating its own garden; coping with the tensions of religious, regional, linguistic, and caste diversity; dominating its region; searching at both the grass-roots and large-scale levels for new technologies appropriate to its degree of economic development, pressures of population, and the need to create full

beckoning by the 1990s. Mahatma Gandhi's concern for the basic needs of the poor was de-emphasized, and Nehru's policies of a commanding government were criticized for placing bureaucratic obstructions in the way of economic growth. Foreign investors continued to complain of India's foot-dragging in opening markets, but the country was, in part, unwilling to jettison too quickly its concern for *swaraj*, internal self-sufficiency, which had motivated its struggle for independence. Internally, Indian businessmen also chafed, but India was moving decisively into active participation in the world economy.

INTERNATIONAL RELATIONS SINCE 1947

Finally, India's international stature has both grown and diminished from the time Nehru provided leadership to the third world movement as leader of the first "new nation" just after Independence. In its own region, especially after the division of Pakistan into two separate countries, India has become an unchallenged, sometimes resented,

employment; and struggling with a heritage of hierarchical practices difficult to overcome. Experimenting democratically with numerous alternative solutions to political, economic, social, religious, and regional problems, India seems to have moved away from the clear directions provided by Gandhi and Nehru in fighting colonialism and establishing a new state. Today's problems, and constituencies, are far more complex and diverse, in a land of amazing diversity, and India eclectically, democratically, and reasonably successfully, muddles through.

BIBLIOGRAPHY

Adams, John, "Breaking Away: India's Economy Vaults into the 1990s," in Bouton and Oldenburg, eds. *India Briefing, 1990*, 77–100.

Andors, Phyllis. *The Unfinished Liberation of Chinese Women 1949–1980* (Bloomington: University of Indiana Press, 1983).

Andrea, Alfred and James Overfield, eds. *The Human Record* (Boston: Houghton, Mifflin, 1990).

Blunden, Caroline and Mark Elvin. *Cultural Atlas of China* (New York: Facts on File, 1983).

Bouton, Marshall M. and Philip Oldenburg, eds. *India Briefing, 1990* (Boulder, CO: Westview Press, 1990).

Brown, Judith M. *Modern India: The Origins of an Asian Democracy* (New York: Oxford University Press, 1984).

de Bary, W. Theodore *et al., Sources of Chinese Tradition* (New York: Columbia University Press, 1960).

Desai, Meghnad, "Economic Reform: Stalled by Politics?" in Oldenburg, ed., *India Briefing: Staying the Course*, 75–95.

Ebrey, Patricia Buckley, ed. *Chinese Civilization: A Sourcebook* (New York: The Free Press, 1993).

Fairbank, John King. *The Great Chinese Revolution: 1800–1985* (New York: Harper & Row, 1986).

Fitzgerald, C.P. *The Birth of Communist China* (Baltimore: Penguin Books, 1964).

Hardgrave, Robert L. and Stanley Kochanek. *India: Government and Politics in a Developing Nation* (San Diego: Harcourt Brace Jovanovich, 4th ed., 1986).

Hay, Stephen, ed. *Sources of Indian Tradition*, Vol. 2 (New York: Columbia University Press, 2nd ed., 1988).

India Today (news magazine).

Jack, Homer, ed. *The Gandhi Reader*, no. 1 (New York: Grove Press, 1956).

Kennedy, Paul. *The Rise and Fall of the Great Powers* (New York: Random House, 1987).

Meisner, Maurice. *Mao's China and After* (New York: The Free Press, 1986).

Naqvi, Hameeda Khatoon. *Urban Centers and Industries in Upper India 1556-1803* (New York: Asia Publishing House, 1968).

Nehru, Jawaharlal. *The Discovery of India* (Bombay: Asia Publishing House, 1960).

Oldenburg, Philip, ed. *India Briefing, 1991* (Boulder, CO: Westview Press, 1991).

—, ed. *India Briefing: Staying the Course* (Armonk, NY: M.E. Sharpe, 1995)

Pa Chin. *Family* (Garden City, N.Y.: Doubleday & Company, 1972).

Raychaudhuri, Tapan and Irfan Habib, eds. *The Cambridge Economic History of India, Vol 1 c. 1200–c. 1700* (Cambridge: Cambridge University Press, 1982).

Roach, James R., ed. *India 2000: The Next Fifteen Years* (Riverdale, MD: The Riverdale Co., 1986)

Rudolph, Lloyd I. and Susanne Hoeber Rudolph. *In Pursuit of Lakshmi* (Chicago: University of Chicago Press, 1987).

Shadow of the Dictators (Alexandria, VA: Time-Life Books, 1989)

Sievers, Sharon L., "Women in China, Japan, and Korea," in *Restoring Women to History: Asia* (Bloomington, IN: Organization of American Historians, 1988).

Sivard, Ruth Leger. *World Military and Social Expenditures 1991 and 1996* (Washington, D.C.: World Priorities, 14th ed., 1991 and 16th ed., 1996).

Snow, Edgar. *Red Star over China* (London: Victor Gollancz, 1968).

Spence, Jonathan D. *The Search for Modern China* (New York: W.W. Norton & Company, 1990).

Wadley, Susan, "The Village in 1984," in William H. Wiser and Charlotte Viall Wiser. *Behind Mud Walls 1930–1960* (Berkeley: University of California Press, 1989).

Weiner, Myron. *The Child and the State in India* (Princeton: Princeton University Press, 1991).

Wolf, Eric R. *Peasant Wars of the Twentieth Century* (New York: Harper & Row, 1969).

Wolpert, Stanley. *A New History of India* (New York: Oxford University Press, 3rd ed., 1989).

21

CHAPTER

THE ARAB WORLD AND ITS NEIGHBORS

"The High Aswan Dam ... has become a symbol of the will and determination of the people to fashion their lives."

GAMAL ABDEL NASSER

1880s–1990s

NATIONALISM AND TECHNOLOGY IN WEST ASIA AND NORTH AFRICA

China and India are giant countries of subcontinental geographical size ruled by powerful central governments. In this chapter and the two chapters that follow, we turn toward three very different regions of the world—the Middle East, Sub-Saharan Africa, and Latin America. Each of these regions has common cultural features and is composed of numerous separate countries, which often seek to act as a bloc in regard to common problems. Each country has a relatively small population, ranging from one two-hundredth to one-tenth of the size of China and India. The countries within each region are very diverse, in resource bases, ecology, culture and history, and even language and religious beliefs and practices. This makes an integrated narrative account of each region difficult. So here we turn to a more overtly analytical account of key issues in each of the three regions within a general chronological framework.

THE MIDDLE EAST AND NORTH AFRICA

The Middle East and North Africa includes the entire Arab world, Iran (which although not an Arab country shares concerns over oil, the Persian Gulf, and the significance of Islam), and Israel. It covers a vast geographical area, stretching from Morocco, Algeria, and Tunisia in North Africa—the Maghreb or western reaches of Islam—to Iraq in the east. Long called the "Middle East," because of its geographical relationship to Western Europe, the region is often also referred to as West Asia and North Africa, a less Eurocentric designation. The outstanding issues in this area in the twentieth century and those on which we will focus in this chapter include:

- nationalist struggles against colonialism and neo-colonialism ;

- attempts to maintain government stability;

- the impact of abundant oil resources on income distribution, urbanization, education, internal and international migration, and technology;

- differing philosophies and methods of regional development;

- the search for regional cooperation;

- the place of religion in the cultural and political life of the state.

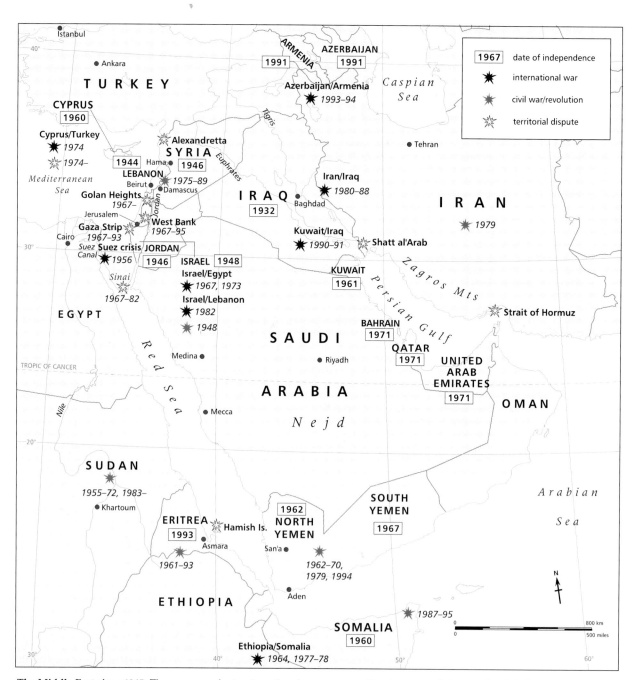

The Middle East since 1945 The presence of extensive oil and gas reserves, disputes over religious and political programs, the establishment of a Jewish homeland state of Israel in Palestine (1948), and the intervention of outside states have dominated the politics of the region. In addition to Arab–Israeli woes, an eight-year conflict between Iran and Iraq, a war over Iraq's invasion of Kuwait, and a multitude of civil wars and revolutions have kept the region in turmoil.

KEY VARIABLES IN THE MIDDLE EAST/NORTH AFRICA

	Turkey	Egypt	Iraq	Iran	Saudi Arabia	Algeria	Israel
Population (thousands)							
1960	27,509	25,922	6,847	20,301	4,075	10,800	2,114
1994	62,484	63,575	21,422	66,094	19,409	29,183	5,421
Per capita income, based on Gross Domestic Product (GDP) (US$)							
1960	584	261	2,261	2,083	2,685	1,794	3,419
1994	4,910	2,490	2,000 (GNP)	4,720	9,510	3,480	13,880
Urban dwellers (percentage)							
1965	32	41	51	37	39	38	81
1994	63	44	70	58	79	50	90
Female literacy (percentage)							
1970	35	20	18	17	2	11	–
1994	72	39	45	59	50	49	93
Oil reserves (billion barrels)							
	0.1	4	100	92	255	4.8	0.7
Military expenditure (US$million)							
1960	828	375	1,346	1,916	619	397	212
1994	5,292	1,819	1,860	2,240	16,539	1,435	6,590

Sources: World Almanac 1997 for all 1994 data; Sivard, *World Military and Social Expenditures* 1996 for female literacy 1994, per cap. income, 1960, and data for estimating military expenditure; World Bank, World Development Report, 1987 for percent urban 1965; UNICEF, *State of the World's Children*, 1984 for female literacy, 1970, reprinted in Richards and Waterbury, p. 88.

TURKEY

Turkey faces in many directions. Its dominant population of Turkish peoples and its eastern Anatolian geography recall its ancient, central Asian ethnic origins. Its dominant religion, Islam, and the geography of its predecessor Ottoman Empire orient it to the Arab world. Its northern border with Russia ties it to eastern Europe. Its toe-hold in Thrace through Istanbul, its recent modernizing heritage through Atatürk, its secularism, and its current political alignments with NATO and the Organization for Economic Cooperation and Development turn it toward Europe.

THE END OF THE OTTOMAN EMPIRE 1914–23

Turkey was born as a nation from the victory of the French and British in World War I that finally destroyed the sprawling, faltering, 500-year-old Ottoman Empire. According to the 1920 Treaty of Sèvres, one of the treaties ending World War I, the heartland of the Empire, Turkey, was to be carved into spheres of control and influence parceled out among France, Italy, and, most provocatively, Greece, the centuries-old Christian enemy of the Muslim Turks. An independent Armenian state was to be established in eastern Turkey on the shores of the Black Sea.

Turkish General Mustafa Kemal, later Atatürk (1881–1938), led a rebellion against the terms of the

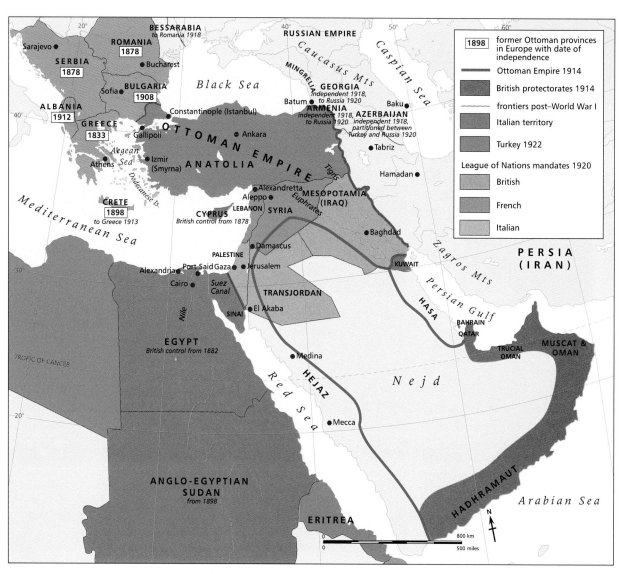

The end of the Ottoman Empire The last decades of the nineteenth century saw the Ottoman presence in Europe decline as Austria–Hungary, Russia, and several aspiring new nations challenged its power. Arab revolt and internal dissent, combined with the Turkish defeat in World War I, brought to an end 600 years of Ottoman domination. Turkey was the core residual state, while several other regions were mandated to British and French control.

treaty and drove out the foreign troops stationed in Turkey. In eastern Anatolia, age-old hatreds inflamed further fighting, and thousands of Armenians were butchered. These murders followed the massacres of Armenians by the Ottomans in 1894, and the genocidal murder of hundreds of thousands of Armenians—estimates run as high as 1.8 million—as potential sympathizers with the enemy in 1915. The proposed Armenian state died in the carnage. In confrontations among Turks, Greeks, and Armenians in the Aegean coastal city of Izmir, in the final battles of the war, as many as 100,000 people died and half

the city, including all of the Armenian and Greek quarters, was burned to the ground. In 1922, Kemal forced the last sultan of the Ottoman Empire to abdicate, leaving Turkey as a constitutional republic. The 1923 Treaty of Lausanne recognized full Turkish sovereignty over virtually all of the new Turkish national state.

RISE OF SECULAR NATIONALISM 1923–1990s

As a military officer, Kemal understood Western technology and believed that Turkey should adopt western ways because they were valuable and because Turkey would otherwise be crushed by the Western powers, just as the Ottoman Empire had been. In his years as president, from 1923 until his death in 1938, Mustafa Kemal curbed the power of religion in his overwhelmingly Muslim state. Declaring "Religion is like a heavy blanket that keeps the people of Turkey asleep," he abolished the office of caliph, the chief Muslim religious authority of the state, and abandoned all claims to leadership of the Muslim world. He abolished both Islamic law and polygamy. He introduced the Western calendar, adopted the metric system, granted universal adult suffrage (although he himself ruled as a dictator), replaced Arabic script with the Roman alphabet, established schooling which raised literacy dramatically, banned the fez hat and encouraged Turks to wear Western clothes, a plan that succeeded more among men than among women, many of whom continued to wear veils. He ordered official Turkish placenames, such as Istanbul and Ankara, to replace older forms such as Constantinople and Angora. He abolished Arabic personal titles and demanded that each Turk take a surname, Western style. Mustafa Kemal himself became Atatürk, Father of the Turks.

Atatürk promoted the armed forces as a pillar of the state. In 1931 he proclaimed:

> The Turkish nation has … always looked to the military … as the leader of movements to achieve lofty national ideals … when speaking of the army, I am speaking of the intelligentsia of the Turkish nation who are the true owners of this country. …

> The Turkish nation … considers its army the guardian of its ideals. (cited in Richards and Waterbury, p. 369)

For Atatürk, modernity was synonymous with technological modernization and cultural innovation. Economically, he began by relying on the private sector and agricultural growth rather than a government-led economy and heavy industrialization. But in 1931, in the midst of the world depression, he moved to have "the Government ensure the welfare of the nation and the prosperity of the state." In 1932 he negotiated a loan of $8 million from the Soviet Union, which may well have been the first loan of its kind to a developing country, and used it to buy Soviet equipment for sugar refineries and a textile mill. In 1934, Atatürk instituted Turkey's first five-year plan, which included nationalizing banks and extending electricity to remote areas. With financing provided by the nationalized banks, the government promoted new industries: textiles, basic chemicals, cement, iron, paper and cellulose, synthetic fabrics, and hemp. A second five-year plan, adopted in 1938, just before Atatürk's death, included programs for power generation, engineering, marine transport, and a heavy industrial center based on coal, steel, and cement at a new port on the Black Sea.

Turkey became a model for some of the larger, more secular new states emerging from the Ottoman Empire. An Iraqi army officer attending Atatürk's funeral wrote: "I saw signs of progress which amazed me … a social revolution in education and economics, and in cultural and spiritual

President Mustafa Kemal Pasha (later, Atatürk) inspects troops at the Officers' Training School in Constantinople (Istanbul). Behind him are the prime minister and the minister of war. Because of widespread support by the elite (comprised in the main by officers and top civil servants), the Republican People's Party, formed by Mustafa Kemal, was able to implement policies unpopular with the masses.

	TURKEY	IRAN (*known as Persia until 1935*)	IRAQ
1900	∎ Young Turk revolution (1908) attempts – but fails – to halt decline of "Sick Man of Europe"	∎ Revolutions (1905, 1909) lead to establishment of parliamentary regime ∎ Oil struck (1908)	
1910	∎ Alliance with Germany drew country into World War I ∎ Treaty of Sèvres: imposed humiliating terms on Turkey ∎ War of Independence (1919-22): Mustafa Kemal (Atatürk) defeats French, Italian, and Greek forces; Kemal becomes president (1923-38) and starts process of westernization	∎ During World War I country occupied by Russia and Britain	∎ Becomes British League of Nations protectorate
1920	∎ Treaty of Lausanne (1923): Turkey established as independent republic ∎ Religious courts abolished (1924) ∎ Islam no longer state religion (1928)	∎ Colonel Reza Khan becomes minister of war (1921) and is crowned as shah (1925); begins program of modernization	∎ Hashemite dynasty established with Faisal I (r. 1921-33) ∎ Oil struck (1927)
1930	∎ Women get vote (1934) ∎ Kemal succeeded by Ismet Inönü (1938-50) who continues program of modernization; keeps Turkey out of World War II	∎ During World War II occupied by Britain, US and Soviet Union, leading to growth of anti-US sentiment	∎ Independence from Britain (1932)
1940		∎ Muhammad Reza Pahlavi is shah (1941)	∎ Baath Party founded (1940)
1950	∎ Free elections (1950): Adnan Menderes prime minister ∎ Turkey admitted to NATO (1952)	∎ Oilfields nationalized (1951) by prime minister Muhammad Mussadeq, who is deposed (1953); shah, with US backing, takes control	∎ Monarchy overthrown (1958); Iraq becomes a republic
1960	∎ Military coup (1960) Inönü prime minister (1961-5) ∎ Suleyman Demirel prime minister (1965-71)	∎ Shah modernizes with US help; offends many interests (1963) ∎ Ayatollah Khomeini exiled for criticizing secular state (1964)	∎ Salem Aref heads joint Ba'athist-military coup (1963) ∎ Hassan Al-Bakr in power after military coup (1968)
1970	∎ Army forces Demirel from power (1971) ∎ Civilian rule under Bulent Ecevit (1971-5, 1977-9) ∎ Demirel returns to power (1975-7, 1979-80)	∎ Single-party system introduced (1975) ∎ Opposition to shah organized from France by Ayatollah Khomeini ∎ Shah flees (1979) and Khomeini returns to create Islamic state ∎ Revolutionaries hold US hostages at embassy, leading to US trade embargo	∎ Sadam Hussein replaces Al-Bakr (1979)
1980	∎ Army intervenes as economic difficulties compound factional violence; imposes new constitution (1982) ∎ Turkey applies to join EEC but is rejected (1989)	∎ Shah dies in exile (1980) ∎ Iran-Iraq war (1980-8) ∎ US hostages released (1981) ∎ Khomeini proclaims *fatwa* (death sentence) on British writer Salman Rushdie	∎ Iran-Iraq war (1980-8); Iraq uses chemical weapons against Kurdish rebels; peace treaty favouring Iran agreed
1990	∎ Earthquake claims thousands of lives (1992) Kurdish separatists active	∎ Kurds arrive from Iraq, fleeing persecution	∎ Iraq invades and annexes Kuwait (1990); defeated in Operation Desert Storm by coalition (mostly US) forces

affairs. I saw the pride of the Turks in their fatherland, pride in their nationalism, their self-reliance and their independence" (cited in Richards and Waterbury, pp. 187–8).

Turkey remained neutral for most of World War II, siding with the Allies toward the end. The war temporarily interrupted the modernization plans, but also ensured that Turkey would continue to build up its industries in conjunction with the war effort and later, as part of the Cold War. In general, Turkey's industrialization has been oriented to its internal market, but when its economy deteriorated in the 1970s, the military coup of 1980 redirected industrial production towards export growth, and the restored civilian government after 1983 has continued that policy.

Atatürk's secular nationalism drew the censure of more religious nationalists like Muhammad Iqbal (1877–1938), the poet of Pakistani nationalism: "The country is the darling of their hearts. ... Politics dethroned religion." After Atatürk's death, however, religion re-negotiated a more flexible balance with secularism in Turkey's official life. Especially during the decade 1950–1960, under the Democrat Party, state radio began to broadcast on religious themes; thousands of mosques were built; all Muslim children had compulsory instruction in religion; schools were established to train *ulama* once again.

The government of Turkey has alternated between democratic elections and military dictatorships. Through the years, the armed forces have intervened periodically in politics when they judged the elected government too chaotic or too religious, or incompetent. Sometimes they took over direct rule as in 1960 and 1980. After the 1960 coup, the government again became more secular, but with significant recognition of Islam in politics and public life. Democratic rule was regained in 1983 after the military coup in 1980. In 1997, as the Turkish government seemed to institutionalize some Islamic practices, the military considered taking action.

Turkey is now in the middle ranks of economic development with an average life expectancy of 65 years; per capita income of $1,360; literacy 90 percent; urbanization rate of 55 percent; but with 56 percent of its workforce in agriculture, only 14 percent in industry and commerce. Programs of dispersal of industry as a means of developing Anatolia, including the designation of Ankara as national capital, have provided an important counter-magnet to the dominance of Istanbul. With a huge foot in western Asia and a toe in eastern Europe, Turkey has been actively courted economically and militarily by western European powers and the United States. Sharing their fear of Russian expansion, especially through the Black Sea and the Dardenelles, Turkey joined the North Atlantic Treaty Organization (NATO) in 1952 and the Baghdad Pact in 1955.

Turkey continues to demonstrate the diversity of its orientations. In 1991 it joined with Allied forces under the United States in expelling Iraqi forces from Kuwait (see p. 693). In the aftermath of this Persian Gulf war, millions of Kurdish people fled as refugees from northern Iraq into Turkey, and called for the creation of a Kurdish state, a demand deeply opposed by Turkey. In 1993 Turkey elected Tansu Cillar, its first woman prime minister. In 1996 Turks elected a more religiously oriented Islamic party, but also began military negotiations with the Jewish state of Israel, presumably to stand against a perceived common threat from Islamic Syria. Turkey fits no simple political nor cultural category.

EGYPT

Egypt has roughly the same population as Turkey, about 63 million, but it is somewhat less developed economically and industrially. While Turkey charts a course for itself alone, Egypt is the largest of the Arab countries and is usually considered the most culturally sophisticated, both because of its long experience with modern politics, and the range and depth of its cultural institutions.

BRITISH RULE 1882–1952

Despite nominal rule by the Ottomans, the military governor Muhammad Ali (1805–48) won effective autonomy for Egypt but, from the time the British first intervened militarily in 1882 until 1956, Egypt fell under British hegemony. Britain expanded its economic interests in Egyptian cotton exports, lucrative interest on loans, and, most importantly, the Suez Canal, which opened in 1869 and facilitated intercontinental trade by shortening the route between Europe and Asia. When nationalists began

Tourism in Turkey. Copper pots gleam, enticing tourists to stop and buy, in Bodrum, Turkey, on the Aegean Sea. Turkey's image as a stable nation, allied with both West and East, has assured its success with the worldwide tourist industry. Just as importantly for Turkey's long-term economic well-being, recent years have seen a growth of heavy industry and the introduction of high-technology.

	ALGERIA	EGYPT	SAUDI ARABIA	ISRAEL
1900				
1910		▌Becomes British protectorate (1914)	▌Sharif Husain aids British in World War I (1914–18)	▌Balfour Declaration that Britain would support Jewish homeland in Palestine (1917)
1920		▌Fuad I (r. 1922-36)		
1930		▌Independence from Britain (1936) ▌Farouk (r. 1936-52) ▌Muslim Brotherhood formed (c. 1935)	▌Ibn Saud (r. 1932-53) brings territories of central Arabia under his rule, including Hejaz and Nejd ▌Oil discovered near Riyadh (1937)	
1940		▌League of Arab States (1945)		▌Independent state declared (1948) with David Ben-Gurion as prime minister ▌Attacked by Arab nations, but Israel wins war of independence; displaced Arabs settle in refugee camps in Gaza Strip and West Bank
1950	▌National Liberation Front (FLN) leads war for independence from France (1954)	▌Farouk overthrown in coup and Egypt declared a republic, with General Neguib as president (1952) ▌Nasser replaces Neguib (1956) and announces nationalization of Suez Canal; Egypt attacked by Britain, France, and Israel; cease-fire agreed after US intervention ▌Brief merger of Egypt and Syria as United Arab Republic (1958-61)	▌Saud II (r. 1953-64)	▌Egypt blockades ports and supports Arab guerillas in Gaza (1952) ▌Israel invades Sinai and Gaza (1956) ▌Egypt renews blockade of Israel trade through Suez Canal (1959)
1960	▌Independence achieved (1962); Ahmed Ben Bella elected prime minister (1962) and president (1963-5)	▌Six-Day War with Israel (1967); Egypt defeated	▌Saud II forced to abdicate; replaced by his bother Faisal (r. 1964-75)	▌Palestine Liberation Organization (PLO) founded (1964)

to threaten the formal ruler, the *khedive*, Britain entered Egypt militarily at his request, propping up his government, securing their own investments, and becoming the unofficial power lying behind the throne.

Until 1952, attempts to free Egypt of this British rule were stalled not only by British military power, but also by deep and fundamental internal divisions. Egypt's first mass-nationalist party, the Wafd, for example, won limited national independence in 1922 and the withdrawal of British forces, except from the Suez Canal, in 1936. But Wafd policies of constitutional government, secularism, elective democracy, and public education antagonized the traditional religious *ulama*. Paradoxically, the *ulama* preferred to maintain their religious protection under British rule rather than take their chances with the secular Wafd. The still more conservative and militant Muslim Brotherhood organization opposed both the Wafd and the *ulama*. Formed in

the 1930s and 1940s and continuing as a powerful influence even today, when it has been outlawed, the Brotherhood proposed a **theocratic** Islamic government, to be established by violence if necessary. Its founder, Hasan al-Banna, rallied the membership thus:

> You are a new soul in the heart of this nation to give it life by means of the Qur'an. ... When asked what it is for which you call, reply that it is Islam, the message of Muhammad, the religion that contains within it government, and has as one of its obligations freedom. If you are told that you are political, answer that Islam admits no such distinction. If you are accused of being revolutionaries, say, "We are voices for right and for peace ... If you rise against us or stand in the path of our message, then we are permitted by God to defend ourselves against your injustice."
> (cited in Hourani, p. 348)

	ALGERIA	EGYPT	SAUDI ARABIA	ISRAEL
1960	▌Ben Bella deposed (1965) by military coup led by Houan Boumédienne (1925-78), who continues policy of land reform, introduces national health services and socialist domestic policies		▌Saudi Arabia joins with Jordan and Iraq against Israel in Six-Day War (1967)	▌Six-Day War (1967): Israel occupies West Bank, east Jerusalem, Golan Heights, Sinai, and Gaza ▌Golda Meir (1898-1978) founds Israel Labour Party (1968); becomes prime minister (1969-74)
1970	▌Oil fields nationalized (1971) ▌New constitution establishing a socialist state approved (1976) ▌Benjedid Chadii president (1979-92)	▌High Aswan Dam opened (1970) ▌Nasser succeeded by Anwar al-Sadat (1970) ▌Expels Soviet advisers (1972) ▌Attempt (1973) to regain territory lost to Israel in 1967; cease fire arranged by US ▌Sadat visits Israel to address Israeli parliament (1977); criticized by Arab neighbors ▌Camp David talks in US (1978-9) result in treaty between Egypt and Israel; Egypt expelled from Arab League	▌Oil embargo on West imposed (1973) ▌Faisal assassinated (1975) and succeeded by his half-brother, Khalid (r. 1975-82) ▌Muslim fundamentalists seize Grand Mosque in Mecca	▌Yom Kippur War (1973) ▌Yitzak Rabin prime minister (1974-7) ▌Suez Canal re-opened (1975) ▌Menachem Begin prime minister (1977-83) ▌Camp David talks (1978) lead to Israel-Egypt agreement; Israel withdraws from Sinai (1979)
1980	▌Algeria helps negotiate release of US hostages in Iran (1981) ▌Chadii re-elected but riots protesting at government policies break out (1988) ▌Constitutional changes to permit pluralism proposed (1989)	▌Sadat assassinated (1981) and succeeded by Hosni Mubarak who improves relations with rest of Arab world and is readmitted to Arab League (1987)	▌Fahd ibn Abdul Aziz succeeds his half-brother as king (1982) ▌Rioting by Iranian pilgrims cause 400+ deaths in Mecca (1987); diplomatic relations with Iran broken ▌Saudi signs non-aggression pact with Iraq (1989)	▌Jerusalem declared capital of Israel (1980) ▌Golan Heights formally annexed (1981) ▌Peace treaty with Lebanon not ratified ▌PLO acknowledges Israel's right to exist (1988)
1990	▌Fundamentalist Islamic Salvation Front (FIS) win first round of elections (1991); Chadii resigns (1992); military takes control; new democratic elections (1995)	▌Participates on US-led side in Gulf War (1991) ▌Militant campaign by Islamists designed to undermine state (1993 onward)	▌Fahd asks for help from US and UK when Iran invades Kuwait; provides military and financial support to allies	▌Rabin prime minister again (1992-5); assassinated by Israeli extremist (1995) ▌Israel builds on land held by Palestine ▌Palestinian extremists plant suicide bombs in Israel

Dismantling of the blockade of the Suez Canal, set up during the Suez Crisis, 1956. The Egyptian frigate *Abukir*, loaded with explosives to form part of an effective blockade of the Suez Canal, is raised between two German salvage ships, the *Energie* and the *Ausdauer*. The *Abukir* was the last of a series of obstructions in the canal, and once it was raised and disposed of, the waterway could be reopened to navigation.

THE ARAB WORLD AND ITS NEIGHBORS (1880s–1990s)   687

Less extreme nationalists and less militant Muslims, alarmed by these hardline policies, preferred the modernizing British alliance as a lesser obstacle to their programs.

During World War II, the British put the government in the hands of the Wafd as the most effective political force in the country. The new government used the increasingly sophisticated communication and transportation networks generated by warfare to convene and create the League of Arab States in 1945, consolidating Egypt's own role at the center of the Arab world. After the war, an army coup in 1952 drove Khedive (King) Farouk out of Egypt and cut many ties with the British.

The leader who finally emerged from the coup, Gamal Abdel Nasser (1918–70), played both sides in the developing Cold War to increase Egypt's leverage. In 1955 he joined with Tito of Yugoslavia and Nehru of India to convene in Bandung, Indonesia, the first major meeting of non-aligned states. In 1956 he nationalized the Suez Canal. When Britain, France, and Israel launched a concerted military attack to reclaim it, the United States supported Nasser and forced its own allies to withdraw. Nasser's bold program of anti-imperialism, unfettered independence, non-alignment, Arab unity, Arab socialism, and a strong reliance on a modernizing military establishment brought him enormous acclaim. He was achieving his goal of moving Egypt to a position of leadership in three circles: "the First Circle—the Arab Circle … the Second Circle—the African Continent Circle … the Third Circle—the circle encompassing continents and oceans—the Circle of our Brethren in Islam" (cited in Sigmund, pp. 154–5).

TECHNOLOGICAL INNOVATION 1956–1990s

Nasser recognized the importance of technological innovation both to break colonial dependency and to cope with Egypt's massive population growth: from 25,922,000 in 1960 to 63,575,000 in 1994. His greatest showcase project, the building of a massive high dam on the upper Nile at Aswan, promised to multiply Egypt's hydroelectric power seven times; to store up to a year's water of the Nile, ensuring a reliable, constant supply of irrigation water; and, most of all, to irrigate new land which could be distributed to the masses. While Nasser wanted the state to control large-scale, major industry, he wanted small farmers to have their own private lands. He declared:

> The revolutionary solution to the land problem in Egypt is to increase the number of land owners. This was the aim of the land reform laws of 1952 and 1961.
> It was also—in addition to the aim of raising

Egypt's engineering feat. The High Aswan Dam, which spans the River Nile at one of its narrowest points in Egypt, was built jointly by the United Arab Republic and the Soviet Union, after the United States withdrew from the project for political reasons. The dam was officially opened by Egyptian president Anwar Sadat and Soviet premier Alexei Kosygin in late 1970. The dam created Lake Nasser, and is situated 4 miles (6.4 kilometers) upstream of the smaller Aswan Dam. It is 364 ft (111 m) high and almost 3280 ft (1000 m) long, with a capacity to generate 2100 megawatts of hydroelectricity.

The Camp David peace accords. In Maryland, September 1978, President Jimmy Carter, Israeli prime minister Menachem Begin and Egyptian president Anwar Sadat relax during the historic Camp David peace talks that resulted in the 1979 treaty between Israel and Egypt. The Camp David Accords, documents signed by the leaders of Israel and Egypt, were a preliminary to the signing of the formal peace treaty between the two nations. The treaty returned the Sinai to Egypt.

production—one of the reasons for the great irrigation projects, the powerful symbol of which is the High Aswan Dam, for which the people of Egypt have suffered all kinds of military, economic, and psychological hardships. The dam has become the symbol of the will and determination of the people to fashion their lives. It is also a symbol of their will to provide the right of land ownership to large numbers of farmers for whom this opportunity was never provided through centuries of continuous feudal rule. (Sigmund, p. 164)

The USA first promised to fund the Aswan Dam project but then withdrew in opposition to state-ownership of the dam and to Nasser's international non-alignment. Nasser secured the support of the USSR in 1958 and went ahead. The project has had the difficulties of many similar gigantic dams, especially the problems of relocating people (and historic monuments) displaced by the dam and its new Lake Nasser; of inadequate drainage downriver; and of not releasing the vital silt of the Nile that fertilized Egypt's fields. Yet, on balance, thus far the project has helped satisfy many of Egypt's immediate food needs.

In 1957 Nasser launched a five-year plan for industry, and in 1960 a five-year plan for the entire economy. With a decree of socialism in 1961, the state took over most large-scale industry, all banking, foreign trade, utilities, marine transport, airlines, and new desert reclamation projects (p. 195). It had already undertaken a gigantic fertilizer plant

at Aswan and an iron and steel complex at Helwan, 40 miles (65 kilometers) south of Cairo.

Many of the industrial gains were counter-balanced, however, by the catastrophic loss of the 1967 Six Day War to Israel. Nasser had challenged the Jewish state by ordering the United Nations peace-keeping forces to leave their buffer positions in the Sinai and then blockading Israeli shipping through the Gulf of Iran. When diplomacy failed, Israel responded with a pre-emptive air strike, which destroyed the entire Egyptian airforce, and then proceeded to capture the Sinai, with its medium-sized oil fields; the Suez Canal, with its revenues; and, after Jordan joined Egypt, the West Bank of the Jordan River, including Jerusalem. In six days Israel scored a massive victory; Egypt and her allies suffered a humiliating defeat.

Nasser lived on for three years, but he had lost most of his charismatic appeal. The decision by his successor, Anwar Sadat (1918–81), to negotiate peace with Israel, following another war in 1973 in which Egypt attacked and held its own against Israel, was undertaken largely for economic reasons. Egypt could no longer afford the costs of military confrontation. Sadat, boldly, flew to Jerusalem in 1977 personally to negotiate peace with the Israelis. When finally achieved through the mediation of US President Jimmy Carter, the peace agreement of 1979 returned to Egypt the Sinai peninsula with its oil wells and the Suez Canal, and gained US assistance of more than US$1 billion a year to rebuild the peace-time Egyptian economy.

Sadat, Carter, and Israeli Prime Minister Menachem Begin were collectively awarded the Nobel Peace Prize. Other Arab nations, and many Egyptians, nevertheless viewed the accords as a betrayal, especially of Palestinian claims against the Israelis (see p. 704), and ejected Egypt from the Arab League. Internally, Sadat's crackdown on dissident students, politicians, and religious leaders, and his inability to cope with continuing economic difficulties loosened his grip on the country. In October 1981 he was assassinated by a splinter group of the Muslim Brotherhood. His successor, Hosni Mubarak (b. 1928), however, maintained Sadat's general policies, including the peace agreements, and became one of the Middle East's most adroit negotiators between East and West, Arab and Israeli, and within the Arab bloc. Islamic militants continue to challenge his authority, and Mubarak has responded with a balance of some concessions and considerable official suppression. In 1991 Egypt was restored to its position as principal member of the Arab League.

Technologically and economically, three elements mark Egypt since Sadat. First, with female literacy at only about 39 percent, attempts to reduce the rate of population growth are hampered. Second, job opportunities in the oil-rich Persian Gulf states have attracted from 1 to 3 million (estimates vary widely) temporary emigrants from Egypt. A job in the Saudi oil fields paid an estimated thirty times the income of a peasant in the Nile valley. In 1984 these migrants sent a record US$4 billion in remittances back to Egypt, one-third of the nation's total imports. New patterns of interaction are forming between Egypt and the oil states, among the multitude of emigrants abroad, and between emigrants and stay-at-homes, especially since the Gulf War of 1991. The effects are not yet clear. Third, a new policy of "economic opening," *infitah*, began to reduce the government role in the economy and give greater encouragement to private business, part of a worldwide trend. The results of this new policy in terms of productivity and the distribution of wealth are not yet known.

THE PERSIAN GULF

With the overthrow of the Ottoman Empire that had ruled them, the Arabic-speaking nations of the Persian Gulf region, especially the large countries of Iraq, Iran and Saudi Arabia, looked forward to becoming independent, as had Turkey and Egypt. They also found that they would have to struggle against new imperial powers.

POLITICAL AND ECONOMIC BACKGROUND 1914–39

In 1916 the Sharif Husain, of the Hashemite family that ruled Mecca, joined with the British in defeating the Ottomans in World War I. When Arab and British forces captured Damascus in 1918, the Sharif's son Faisal established a new, independent Arab government there. Albert Hourani, a leading historian of the Arab world wrote: "The political structure within which most Arabs had lived for four centuries had disintegrated … for the first time the claim that those who spoke Arabic constituted a nation and should have a state had been to some extent accepted by a great power" (pp. 316–17).

The British and French, however, had other plans. In the Sykes–Picot agreement of 1916, they agreed to divide up between themselves the area that today includes Iraq, Syria, Lebanon, Jordan, and Israel. League of Nations mandates in 1922 generally confirmed the agreement. The French, therefore, deposed Faisal and divided his territory into two states, Syria and Lebanon, which they ruled more or less directly. The British acted more circumspectly. They established Faisal as the king of Iraq, where he reigned as Faisal I from 1922 until

A mosque in Hasan Fathy's mud brick village of New Gourna near Luxor, Egypt, completed in 1948. Although meticulously planned in every detail by Fathy, the project was totally rejected by the people it was intended to house, and they twice flooded the new village to prevent their forced relocation there. The project was not a complete failure, however, as Fathy used the example to explain his principles and methods of architectural theory, the most important aspect being the need for modern architectural planning and implementation of policy for social housing.

1933. The Anglo-Iraqi Treaty of 1930 granted Iraq formal independence; and the country was accepted as a member of the League of Nations in 1932. But Iraq's foreign policy remained under British surveillance and its military facilities open to British use. In Jordan, the British established Abdullah, another of the Sharif's sons, as ruler but retained considerable power over his government and its international trade.

Iran, an Islamic but not an Arabic-speaking nation nor a part of the Ottoman Empire, asserted greater independence vis-à-vis Britain, and greater secularism vis-à-vis the *ulama*. A colonel in the Cossack Brigade, Reza Khan, seized power in 1921 and declared himself shah in 1926, bringing both central authority and Western-style modernization, under army tutelage, to Iran. Following the example of Atatürk, the shah implemented secular education and law, curtailed the power of the *ulama*, ordered the men, except the *ulama*, to wear Western dress, and, after 1936, had women go without veils. Police were ordered to rip off veils from any women who defied the order. These reforms, however, failed to keep the British at bay; when the shah announced his neutrality in World War II, the British, with Soviet agreement, invaded Iran and forced his abdication in favor of his son.

In its desert isolation, Saudi Arabia established greater independence, and held more tenaciously to Islamic law—within limits. King ibn Saud (1880–1953) began to build a power base in central Saudi Arabia. He conquered Riyadh in 1902 and dispatched *ulama* of the Wahabi sect, the Ikhwan, or brotherhood, to establish some 200 ascetic communities at oases throughout the central part of the peninsula. In 1924 they captured Mecca, taking Medina and its surroundings in 1925. But as the king began to introduce such modern innovations as automobiles and telephones, the Ikhwan turned against him. In the decisive battle of Sabila in 1929, most of the Ikhwan were killed, as ibn Saud consolidated his rule.

DISCOVERY OF OIL

The discovery of oil pushed the entire Persian Gulf region ineluctibly to the center of world struggles for power and wealth. The first commercially valuable strike was drilled at Masjid-i-Suleiman in Iran in 1908. Subsequently, oil was discovered in Iraq in 1927 and in Kuwait and Saudi Arabia in 1938. Exploration and discovery has continued unabated ever since. As of January 1990, the Persian Gulf

States hold about 60 percent of all the world's known reserves of one trillion barrels of crude oil. Saudi Arabia alone has 260 billion barrels; Iraq, 100; Iran, 93; Kuwait, 97. (The USA, by comparison, holds 26 billion; Japan almost none at 26 million) (cited in Richards and Waterbury, p. 59).

Oil increased profoundly the international significance of the Persian Gulf region, on the one hand making it a focus for international rivalry and control, but, on the other, providing a resource with which the region could fight to assert its own independence and chart its own destiny. Oil invested the state, as custodian of underground natural resources, with enormous wealth and power. It provided the potential for the complete restructuring of national economic, social, and political life. It financed record military expenditures. All five of the nations of the world that devote the highest percentages of their budget to military expenditures, from 20 to 30 percent, are Persian Gulf, oil-rich states. As a highly capitalized industry under government control, oil drilling and refining creates much wealth but few jobs, and no clear direction for distribution or investment of profits. Policies for using the new wealth varied from country to country and ruler to ruler.

IRAQ 1939–1990s

Iraq's politics have been tumultuous and brutal. During World War II, Iraq joined the Axis powers. The British defeated the Iraqi army and turned it against the Axis. After the war, however, the weakened European powers began to extricate themselves from Middle Eastern politics, while America began to play a more central role. In the Baghdad Pact of 1955, Iraq joined Pakistan, Iran, Britain, and the USA in military opposition to Russian threats. Meanwhile, internal revolts overthrew successive Iraqi governments in 1948, 1952, and 1958. The last revolt, led by army officers, inspired in part by Nasser's Egyptian revolution, killed King Faisal and Prince Abdul Ilah, declared Iraq a republic, and terminated the military alliances with the West. Internal coups, among army officers and leaders of the Baath Party—an Arab Socialist Party founded in 1940 with pan-Arab nationalist aims—continued until Ahmad Hasan al-Bakr won out in 1968 and established a military government. It followed the Baath Party theories of Michel Aflaq, a Christian from Damascus, who advocated a single Arab nation, and, later, secular "Arab socialism." Al-Bakr ruled until he was succeeded by his second-in-command, Saddam Hussein, in 1979.

Under the Baath leaders, the state consolidated its economic and technological powers. With a birth rate of forty-five per thousand through much of this period, Iraq's population more than tripled from 6,847,000 in 1960 to 21,422,000 in 1994. Iraqis streamed from the villages to the cities, raising the percentage of the urban population from 43 in 1960 to 70 in 1994. Baghdad, the capital, grew to 4 million, almost one-fifth of Iraq's population. In 1969 the Baath government nationalized all banks and some thirty-two major industrial and commercial firms. In the early 1970s it nationalized the oil fields. At the same time, OPEC was raising prices and, as a result, the state came to control 75 percent of Iraq's gross domestic product, of which 50 percent was oil. Including all workers in nationalized industry, government bureaucracy, the armed forces, public schools, and pensioners, the state employed almost a quarter of all the workers in Iraq.

War with Iran and the West

Political consolidation was also a challenge. Many Middle Eastern borders are artificial creations of European colonizers. Most states include minority ethnic groups which have been feared and often persecuted by the majority.

In light of all such political/demographic realities, Saddam Hussein sought first to eliminate challenges to Iraq and to himself, and then to extend the powers and the boundaries of the state. He regarded the Kurds, about 15 percent of Iraq's population, and largely resident in its northern, oil-rich regions, as potential rebels seeking their own separate state. He has repeatedly attacked them on the ground and from the air, sometimes with chemical weapons. Almost all the population of Iraq are Muslims, but they are divided by sect: 60 percent are Shi'ite, especially in the south, while Saddam is a Sunni. He has often attacked the Shi'ites, perhaps fearing a potential alliance with the Shi'ites of Iran. In coming to power, Saddam systematically

Tel Aviv after a Scud missile attack by the Iraqis on January 22, 1991. Iraq tried to draw Israel into the Gulf War in an attempt to split the Western–Arab alliance, but Israel bowed to pressure from the US not to retaliate, while retaining the right to defend their country. Americans dispatched Patriot anti-missile systems to protect Israel, but some casualties were sustained when undetected missiles slipped through the defense. Meanwhile, the Allies bombarded Baghdad day and night in an attempt to bring Saddam Hussein into submission.

murdered potential opponents within the government and the military.

Saddam's rival, Hafez al-Assad of neighboring Syria, acted with similar brutality in murdering between 10,000 and 25,000 Sunni Muslims in Hama, Syria, in 1982. Thomas Friedman, the *New York Times* Middle East correspondent, characterizes the political methods of both Saddam and Hafez:

> The real genius of Hafez Assad and Saddam Hussein is their remarkable ability to move back and forth among all three political traditions of their region, effortlessly switching from tribal chief to brutal autocrat to modernizing President with the blink of an eye. (p. 103)

In 1980, fearful of the appeal of religiously militant Shi'ite Iran to Iraq's Shi'ite majority and jealous of his neighbor's oil wealth, Saddam attacked and invaded Iran. An eight-year war ensued. Iran is not an Arab nation, and most Arab nations supported Iraq with weapons or money. (Syria, because of its own disputes with Iraq, sided with Iran.) The United Nations ceasefire, arranged in 1988, left the nations about where they had begun in terms of territory, but some 900,000 Iranians and 300,000 Iraqis had been killed. During the course of the war, Iraq's military expenditure reached one-third of its entire gross national product, the highest of any country in the world.

In 1990, Saddam invaded Kuwait, a tiny country in the Persian Gulf with vast oil resources. A massive United Nations response, orchestrated by the United States, drove the Iraqis from Kuwait and destroyed much of their huge store of armaments, including chemical weapons and materials for nuclear weapons manufacture. In a war fought mostly through aerial bombardment followed by land sweeps, the allied forces lost relatively few forces while Iraq lost perhaps 100,000 soldiers and suffered enormous civilian damage and death as the technological infrastructure of urban life was destroyed. The long-term political effects of the war are not clear, but in the short term, the United States gained recognition in the Arab world as an active, significant power once again; the Kuwaiti royal family was restored to rule; Iraq had been humbled, but Saddam Hussein remained in power despite some US efforts to topple him; the military alliance of Saudi Arabia and Syria with the USA against Iraq over-rode long standing enmities and enabled peace talks to begin between Israel and her Arab neighbors, as well as with Palestinians.

"Desert Storm" memorial. The soaring Liberation Tower, a monument to the Gulf War, stands above central Kuwait. Although very small in land area, Kuwait has vast wealth derived from its oil resources, and in 1990 Iraq attacked and attempted to annex the tiny nation. Saddam Hussein and the Iraqis were rebuffed by a huge UN initiative, and Kuwaiti sovereignty was re-established.

IRAN 1970–1990s

Iran's transformation during the twentieth century has wavered dramatically. Periodic change within the government, especially revolutionary change in 1979, frequently reordered the priorities of the nation and often appeared to threaten the stability of the entire Persian Gulf region. The reformist administration of Shah Reza Khan after 1921 and his forced abdication in favor of his pro-British son, Muhammad Reza Pahlavi, in 1941, during World War II, together with the increased exploitation of Iran's oil resources at about this time had begun to bring new wealth to the kingdom. In 1951, prime minister Muhammad Mussadeq nationalized the Iranian oil industry against the shah's wishes. In response, Britain and the US conspired with the Iranian army in a coup that supported the shah and overthrew Mussadeq.

Deeply indebted to the West, the shah joined the American-inspired Baghdad Pact, invited additional Western oil investment, and proceeded to use Iran's oil wealth to fund deep and massive—but convulsive, erratic, and uneven—Westernization of the country. By the mid-1970s, about 150,000 foreigners came to the country to run the new high-technology industries and to live a luxurious lifestyle in secluded "colonies." Opponents of the shah's system of modernization, including much of the student community, were pursued, jailed, and often tortured, by SAVAK, the shah's secret police.

Anthony Parsons, who was the British ambassador to Teheran at the time, describes the dislocations of the middle and later 1970s, when

> serious inflation and a fall in the real value of the oil revenues necessitated a policy of economic retrenchment. ... [T]he alarming dislocations and disruptions of the boom were clear. The ports and railways were choked; skilled manpower had proved grossly inadequate and huge numbers of foreigners had been brought in to meet this deficiency; there had been a massive influx of the rural population into the capital, creating grim problems of inadequate housing and social deprivation. The distribution system was overstrained and local shortages of foodstuffs and other supplies were commonplace. The scale of corruption in the Court and the government, and in the entrepreneurial class and bureaucracy, had become a scandal even to the tolerant Iranians. (cited in Netton, p. 117)

THE RISE OF AYATOLLAH KHOMEINI

Opposition to the shah's forced modernization included *ulama* on the right who lamented the suppression of traditional religion; students and intellectuals on the left who were deprived of freedoms of expression; and farmers, new urban migrants, and many urban residents who were squeezed by inflation, recession, unemployment, and a loosening of what they felt to be the moral foundations of the society. In 1963 a religious leader, the Ayatollah Khomeini (1902– 89), had led an abortive uprising against the shah. The army killed 15,000 rebels and exiled Khomeini. But from Paris the Ayatollah kept in contact with dissidents in Iran via tape recordings and telephone, and in 1979 he returned to lead popular demonstrations of as many as 5 million people. The shah was forced into exile: Islamic law, the **shari'a**, became the law of the land and Islamic government was introduced. Women were ordered to return to draping themselves in the *chador* as Iran became a theocracy. Khomeini explained:

Women dressed in the traditional black chador undergo weapons training northeast of Tehran, Iran, in 1986. Although females in Iran have benefited from improvements to their daily lives (more girls are entering primary school; contraception is more widely used), nevertheless they remain severely restricted by Islamic dress codes and laws governing their daily lives.

Islamic government is a government of divine law. The difference between Islamic government and constitutional government—whether monarchical or republican—lies in the fact that, in the latter system, it is the representatives of the people or those of the king who legislate and make laws. Whereas the actual authority belongs exclusively to God. No others, no matter who they may be, have the right to legislate, nor has any person the right to govern on any basis other than the authority that has been conferred by God. ... It is the religious expert and no one else who should occupy himself with the affairs of the government. (Robinson, p. 171)

The religious fervor of the revolution astonished many Western observers.

Strategically located, rich in oil, religiously militant, and internally secure, Khomeini's revolutionary government terrified its neighbors and wrecked havoc on many others more distant. In its first two years, it executed 8000 people and exiled thousands. When America offered refuge to the exiled shah, who was suffering from cancer, Khomeini seized the American embassy in Teheran and held fifty-two of its staff hostage. President Carter failed to secure their release through negotiations. He then launched a guerrilla air rescue, which was aborted in humiliating failure. Carter's defeat in the 1980 election was due in part to these failures to cope with Iran.

Khomeini's militance inspired Saudi religious dissidents to attempt to trigger a revolt against their government by attacking the Great Mosque in Mecca during the *hajj* period in 1979. Three hundred were killed, and the Saudi government drew closer to the Americans. In Egypt, in 1981, Islamic militants, linked to Iran, assassinated President Anwar Sadat. In 1989, following the publication of the novel *The Satanic Verses*, the Indian-born British author, Salman Rushdie, was judged a heretic and marked for execution. A bounty of $5 million was placed on his head, and he was forced into hiding under the protection of the British government. In Beirut and other Middle Eastern centers, Western hostages were seized. Iraq's attack on Iran was inspired in part by fear that its Shi'a religious revolution would spill across the border. With Khomeini's death in 1979, more moderate leaders have come to power in Iran, seeking greater interchange with the rest of the world and limited political liberalization at home.

Legal restrictions on women, based on interpretations of religious principles, continued, calling for Islamic dress codes and Islamic legal authority over marriage, divorce, child custody, and the right to work. Many reports from Iran indicated that women generally accepted these restrictions as a stand against Western culture and imperialism. Women's literacy continued to rise to 59 percent, with 95 percent of girls of primary school age attending classes. Birth rates dropped from forty-nine per thousand under the shah to thirty-nine per thousand under Khomeini, and to thirty-four by 1996. The percentage of families using some kind of contraception rose from 3 to 23 in 1987 to 65 in 1994 (*World Resources*, 1987, p. 257; Sivard, 1996, p. 51). Feminism, nationalism, and religion in Iran were intertwined in a unique configuration that did not fit any stereotype.

SAUDI ARABIA

Until oil was discovered in 1938, Saudi Arabia could remain isolated from global currents of technological change. Thereafter, as guardian of the holy cities of Mecca and Medina, King Ibn Saud began to employ his newfound resources for the propagation of Islam and for his family. He helped to create such pan-Islamic groups as the World Muslim League, headquartered in Mecca, to spread Islam, adjudicate on Islamic issues, and support pan-Islamic causes; the Islamic Conference, to finance Islamic projects and economic development around the world; and the Arab League, set up in 1945 to represent Arab political positions in international forums.

Saudi Arabia has also counseled moderation in international politics. As early as 1945, King Ibn Saud had met with President Franklin Roosevelt of the United States to discuss threats to the peace in the Gulf area. Historians are just now uncovering agreements reached after World War II for US military protection in exchange for Saudi moderation in Middle Eastern affairs, especially in opposition to Israel; US access to military bases in Arabia; and guaranteed access to oil.

The oil revenues elevated Ibn Saud's family to unparalleled power among the desert rulers of Arabia. Ibn Saud's son, Faisal, who ruled from 1964 until his assassination by a nephew in 1975, forged from oil an international weapon for Arab political and economic as well as religious causes. In 1973, during the War with Israel, he and his oil minister, Shaikh Ahmed Yamani, instituted an embargo on all shipments of oil to the United States, and the

SPOTLIGHT
Islamic Architecture
FOR CONTEMPORARY TIMES

Architects regularly confront the dilemma of conserving traditional, long-accepted forms of building while meeting the requirements of new functions. Sometimes they simply choose to break with the past, for example by constructing the skyscraper, a radically new form of building which takes advantage of new technologies to meet new needs. Sometimes they stay closer to tradition. The challenge has been especially severe in Islamic countries. For clearly religious buildings, such as mosques, traditional architecture may seem most appropriate, yet some modern variation is also welcome to accommodate both new building materials and new religious sensibilities. For buildings serving commercial purposes, a new architecture meeting the needs of hot climates may be necessary.

The Al-Ghadir Mosque (**picture 1**), opened in suburban Tehran, Iran, in 1980, retains in the interior the key features of a mosque: the open prayer hall with a pronounced inset in one wall of the mihrab, or architectural denotation of the direction

Picture 1 Jahangir Mazlum Yazdi, Al-Ghadir Mosque, Tehran, Iran, 1980.

toward Mecca. It is adorned inside and out with calligraphy of verses from the Koran. Moreover, the twelve sides of the prayer hall, and the repeating motif of twelve-sided designs, symbolize the twelve imams who defined early Shi'ism (see Chapter 11). But the ocher-colored brickwork and blue ceramic tiles that dress the walls actually cover a technologically modern steel and reinforced concrete structure. In addition the architect, Jahangir Mazlum Yazdi, withstood intense public pressure to add minarets and adopt a more traditional form for the dome. Sherefuddin's White Mosque in Visoko, Bosnia, (**picture 2**), also opened in 1980, presents an even more dramatic break with the past. It, too, includes the key elements of a traditional mosque, but its image breaks entirely with the historic Ottoman mosques, like those of

Sinan (Chapter 11). The style resonates more strongly with the values of Modernist industrial architecture in the West such as that of Le Corbusier. In replacing an earlier mosque which had burned down, the architect, Professor Zlatko Ugljen, built the mosque of reinforced concrete covered with plastered concrete painted white. Highlighting includes the use of pine wood, travertine tiles, and green carpeting.

Picture 2
Zlatko Ugljen, Sherefuddin's White Mosque, Visoko, Bosnia, 1980.

The National Commercial Bank (**picture 3**), completed in Jeddah, Saudi Arabia, in 1983, responds not to religious but to climatic needs. The key problem was to create an international building to serve as the headquarters for a huge bank in Jeddah's very hot, humid environment, where the glare of the sun is oppressive. Because Jeddah is built on the Red Sea, traditional architecture had allowed more windows than in desert regions, but even those windows were heavily shaded and shuttered. The first large commercial office buildings in the city had paid no attention, simply using a conventional glass curtain wall exterior designed for temperate climates. Here, however, the chief architect, Skidmore, Owings, & Merrill of Chicago, designed a 27-storey "glass box" skyscraper turned inside-out. Light enters through the huge openings in the blank wall to gray-tinted glass interior curtain walls and a central triangular courtyard below.

Picture 3
Skidmore, Owings, & Merrill, National Commercial Bank, Jeddah, Saudi Arabia, 1983.

other Arab states followed suit. (Libya acted one day ahead of Saudi Arabia.) With the end of the war, the embargo also ended, but Saudi Arabia transformed the Organization of Petroleum Exporting Countries (OPEC) into a cartel, raising prices and lowering production to gain control over world petroleum sales. The price of oil leaped from $1.80 a barrel in 1970 to $11.65 in December 1973. The combined earnings of the petroleum exporters rose from $23 billion in 1972 to $140 billion by 1977.

The ruling family began to use the fortune for new development projects. The budget for development rose from $40 billion in 1977 to $70 billion in 1980 and funded the construction of an industrial infrastructure and the growth of many cities. It led to an enormous influx of foreign workers from Yemen, Oman, Egypt, and Pakistan. In that year assistance to poorer countries rose to $5.6 billion, almost 8 percent of its gross national product, and military expenditure reached $20.6 billion, over one-fifth of the nation's gross national product, the second highest ratio in the world.

With the influx of foreign workers, the population of Saudi Arabia began to shift in location and composition. In 1960, about 30 percent of the country was urban, but by 1996 the figure was about 79 percent urban. An estimated 43 percent of the population in 1975 consisted of foreign workers. There was also a revolution in education with approximately one million children attending schools by 1980. Literacy rose from 2 percent in 1960 to 61 percent in 1994. Increasingly Saudis were being trained for technical work in the petroleum industry, agriculture, commerce, communications, finance and the military.

Following the 1973 oil price and availability shocks, Saudi Arabia counselled moderation in OPEC's international market policies and lowered its prices, increasing its immense production to ensure the lower levels. There were several reasons. A worldwide recession among industrialized countries in the 1970s demonstrated that excessive oil price rises could destroy the world economy. If that happened, the oil producers would suffer as well. Not only would they lose markets, but, ironically, the profitability of their international investments would decline. The profits from oil had become so overwhelming that some of the oil-rich countries, notably Saudi Arabia and, even more, the tiny kingdoms like Kuwait, could not invest it all internally. Their populations were too small—Saudi Arabia had only about 15 million people, Kuwait only about 2 million—and their economies were so undeveloped that they could not absorb all the oil income. Therefore, they invested their profits heavily in developed countries, and they did not want to see these investments founder. By the 1980s, Kuwait was earning more from its overseas investments than from its oil.

By the 1980s, the discovery of additional oil supplies in the North Sea, Alaska, Mexico, Venezuela,

THE OIL CRISES 1960–1990S

1960 Organization of Petroleum Exporting Countries (OPEC) is formed by major oil exporters (excluding Canada and the USSR) to control development, output and prices, to regulate Western oil companies, and to improve position of third-world countries by forcing Western countries to open their markets

1967–8 Middle East and North African oil-producing countries formed Organization of Arab Petroleum Exporting Countries (OAPEC) and imposed an embargo on the US, Britain, and West Germany for supporting Israel in the 1967 war, with grave results for European economies

1973 Yom Kippur War (Egypt and Syria attack Israel) is followed by OPEC's concerted action in restricting oil supplies, which led to worldwide recession; this has unlooked-for effect of reducing demand and thereby lessening power of OPEC

1980 Price of oil has risen to $30 a barrel from $3 in 1973, encouraging search for alternative fuels and non-OPEC suppliers

1986 Price of oil falls within the year from $28 to $10 a barrel, reflecting increased reliance on alternative sources, including Norway, Britain, and Mexico

1991 OPEC members are Algeria, Ecuador, Gabon, Indonesia, Iran, Iraq, Kuwait, Libya, Nigeria, Qatar, Saudi Arabia, the United Arab Emirates, and Venezuela

the USSR, and China, and the inability of the cartel to hold its internal line on production, sales, and price did bring a sharp slump in OPEC oil revenues. The reductions forced Saudi Arabia, as well as almost all the oil-producing states, to cut back on programs of economic modernization.

In the late 1970s the modernizing, secularizing, and socialist policies spreading in Egypt, Syria, Iraq, and Iran frightened the conservative Saudis. Jobs in the oil fields brought 1,500,000 immigrant workers from the Arab world alone to the heretofore isolated kingdom, as they did throughout the Gulf region, and with them at least a taste of different, sometimes threatening ways of life. After 1979, the Iranian revolution presented a threat from the other side, from radical religious militants. Saudi Arabia also felt very threatened by Iraq's 1990 invasion of Kuwait. So the Saudis, a small nation, very rapidly emerging from centuries of pastoral nomadism, conservative and committed to *shari'a* law and government, under an absolute monarchy, and possessed of one-fourth of the world's reserves of petroleum, sought further business and political accommodation with the United States and the West in international relations. They asked for, and hosted, American military assistance in driving Iraq out of Kuwait, further splitting the Arab world. Explosions at United States military installations in Saudi Arabia in 1995 and 1996 demonstrated, however, that internal opposition forces continued to be resentful of the Saudi-American accords.

NORTH AFRICA: ALGERIA

In the Maghreb, "the West" in Arabic, the countries of Morocco, Algeria, and Tunisia had experienced settler colonialization, different from the more remote colonialism of the Middle East. They emerged from it a little later, and, in the case of Algeria, only through violence and civil war. Independence for Morocco and Tunisia came relatively easily and peacefully in 1956.

Algeria had the largest European settler community, and these settlers had become quite prosperous and comfortable. They were not eager to leave. The French in Algeria numbered one million, about 12 percent of the population, and they held one-third of the cultivable land. For them, Algeria was home. By the early 1950s, 80 percent of them had been born in Algeria. Officially Algeria was not a colony, but an integral part of France with constitutional representation.

THE MOVEMENT TOWARD INDEPENDENCE

The Algerians themselves moved only slowly toward seeing themselves as separate and independent from France. In the 1930s, the leader of the French-educated elite, Farhat Abbas, maintained, "I have questioned history; I have questioned the living and the dead; I have visited the cemeteries. The empires of the Arabs and Islam are in the past; our future is decisively linked to that of France" (Lapidus, p. 687). But reformists were moving to create a more powerful Arab-Islamic nationalism, fostering social unity, distinct national consciousness and sense of destiny, and solidarity with other Arabs against foreign rule. The reform leader, Ben Badis, replied as follows to Farhat Abbas, "This Muslim nation is not France, it is not possible for it to be France. It does not want to become France, and even if it wanted to, it could not" (cited in Lapidus, p. 690).

THE ALGERIAN REVOLUTION

The Algerian revolution led by the National Liberation Front (FLN) in the mid-1950s was met by French repression. The two sides became increasingly entrenched. The violence ratcheted upward and spread not only throughout Algeria but to France as well. The governmental system of France, the Fourth Republic, was weak, and it fell as civil war seemed to threaten. The hero and leader of the French resistance in World War II, Charles De Gaulle, was called into power under a new, more powerful constitution. Despite an apparent mandate to continue the war, De Gaulle chose to negotiate a settlement and finally granted independence in 1962, but only after 300,000 Algerians and 20,000 Frenchmen had been killed.

Virtually all the one million French residents left Algeria. Of the Algerians, only 7000 were in secondary school, and as of 1954, only seventy living native Algerians had had a university education. The leaders of the new state, hardened by their years of guerrilla warfare, and ideologically committed to centralized control, took over the tasks of development. They instituted a four-year plan in 1969, and nationalized the petroleum and natural gas resources that had been discovered only in 1956. They encouraged industrialization through one of the world's highest rates of investment, one-third of the national income. Oil revenues formed the base of this income, bringing in 30 percent of

SOCIAL REALITIES OF COLONIALISM: TWO VIEWS

In the late 1930s and during World War II, the independence movement began to take shape. The French, and especially the colonists living in Algeria, prepared to fight politically and militarily to maintain their control. They dominated the coastal cities of Algiers and Oran. Frantz Fanon (1926–61), a psychiatrist practising in Algeria, wrote a trenchant and bitter description of the urban situation, based largely on Algeria but widely applicable across the third world. *The Wretched of the Earth* became a classic account of the segregation and cruelty of urban colonialism:

> The settlers' town is a strongly built town, all made of stone and steel. It is a brightly lit town; the streets are covered with asphalt, and the garbage cans swallow all the leavings, unseen, unknown and hardly thought about. The settler's feet are never visible, except perhaps in the sea; but there you're never close enough to see them. His feet are protected by strong shoes although the streets of his town are clean and even, with no holes or stones. The settler's town is a well-fed town, an easygoing town; its belly is always full of good things. The settler's town is a town of white people, of foreigners.
>
> The town belonging to the colonized people, at least the native town, the Negro village, the medina, the reservation, is a place of ill fame, peopled by men of evil repute. They are born there, it matters little where or how; they die there, it matters not where, nor how. It is a world without spaciousness; men live there on top of each other, and their huts are built one on top of the other. The native town is a hungry town, starved of bread, of meat, of shoes, of coal, of light. The native town is a crouching village, a town on its knees, a town wallowing in the mire. (Fanon, p. 39)

At the same time, hundreds of thousands of North Africans worked as laborers in Europe, a sign of the lack of opportunity at home. A touching poem by a Moroccan woman lamenting the departure of her husband tells the human as well as political dimensions of the emigration for employment:

Germany, Belgium, France
and Netherlands
Where are you situated?
Where are you?
Where can I find you?
I have never seen your countries, I do not
speak your language.
I have heard it said that you are beautiful,
I have heard it said that you are clean.
I am afraid, afraid that my love forgets
me in your paradise.
I ask you to save him for me.
One day after our wedding he left,
with his suitcase in his hand, his eyes looking
    ahead.
You must not say that he is bad or aggressive;
I have seen his tears, deep in his heart, when he
    went away.
He looked at me with the eyes of a child;
He gave me his small empty hand and asked me:
"What should I do?"
I could not utter a word; my heart bled for him.

Germany, Belgium, France
and Holland:
I ask you to save him for me, so I can see him
    once a year.
I knew him in his strength which could break
    stones
I am afraid, jealousy is eating my heart.
With you he stays one year, with me just one
    month
to you he gives his health and his sweat,
to me he only comes to recuperate.
Then he leaves again to work for you, to beautify
you as a bride, each day anew.
And I, I wait; I am like a flower that
withers more each day.

He gives you his health and his power,
with you he stays one year,
with me only one month.
I am afraid that he forgets me.

I ask you: give him back to me.
(Johnson and Bernstein, pp. 173–4.)

Charles de Gaulle visits Algiers in June, 1958. Algeria had been agitating for independence since 1954, and in 1956 Ben Bella, one of the main Algerian leaders, was arrested. Two years later a political crisis in France, precipitated by continuing Algerian frustration and pressure for independence, put de Gaulle into office as the new president of the Republic. De Gaulle maintained French rule in Algeria as long as possible, while he prepared the French people for the inevitable shift in power. Finally, in 1962, Algerians achieved independence and the French withdrew.

Algeria's GNP after the oil price rises of 1973. The government built good roads and basic metal and machine industries. As much as 27 percent of the workforce was employed in industry. Education also received attention, expenditure rising from 2.2 percent of GNP in 1960 to 10 percent in 1987. Literacy rose to 52 percent; with female literacy climbing rapidly from 11 percent in 1970, to 24 percent in 1980, to 49 percent in 1994. Agriculture, however, was neglected, and Algeria imports two-thirds of its food; rural migrants have streamed toward the cities, which now hold 50 percent of the population. Hundreds of thousands have migrated to France. The birth rate and population growth rate remain extremely high. Algeria had 10,800,000 citizens in 1960; 29,183,000 in 1996.

The new government and its successors were largely secular and dominated by professional army officers, but in Algeria, too, Islamic religious forces persisted beneath the surface. As the new government did not seem to do enough to redis-

tribute land, to end absentee landlordism, to redistribute income, and to increase the productivity of the economy, opposition arose, rallying around Islam, which again served as the voice of the poor. In 1989, a multiple party system and free elections were promised, but as Islamic militants seemed likely to win, the military government cancelled the 1992 national elections, promising to reschedule them later. Civil war continues in Algeria, with the death toll to date estimated at 50,000.

ISRAEL

Of all issues in the modern Middle East, Israeli–Arab relations have been the most discussed by historians. In Chapter 17 we have seen the emergence of Zionism—the Jewish quest for a homeland—as one of the many nationalist movements of nineteenth century Europe. The British government recognized this movement by issuing the Balfour

Declaration in 1917, proposing their support for the establishment of a national homeland for the Jews in Palestine. In 1920, however, there were only about 60,000 Jews and ten times that number of Arabs living in the area. Jewish settlement increased between the two world wars, but with it came increasing conflict. Nazi persecution of Jews throughout World War II and the atrocities of the Holocaust (see p. 592), demonstrated a desperate need for a political state and refuge for the Jewish people which no nation had provided. Following the war, in 1947, a United Nations resolution agreed to the (re)establishment of an independent Jewish state in Palestine on land currently occupied by Arabs. The state of Israel was created in 1948.

ISRAEL AND THE ARAB WORLD: WHAT DO WE KNOW? HOW DO WE ASSESS SIGNIFICANCE?

The relationships between Israeli and Arab combine and confront so many compelling issues and tell so many intertwined stories that collectively they have touched the imagination of much of the world. Historians recognize that the narrations through which they tell their stories—the plots, as historian Hayden White calls them—present the underlying structure of their understanding of the past. Each plot frames the historical story in a fundamentally different way. In considering Arab–Israeli relations, let us consider the variety of separate stories, "emplotments," that have been narrated and that need to be brought together in order for the "whole story" to begin to emerge.

Readers may begin to make their own choices as to which plot, or mix of plots, most accurately captures the complexity, drama, and passion of this historical relationship. Readers will also see how participants in the drama have understood and plotted their own roles, and how this analysis of emplotment can be employed in understanding historical disputes generally.

A Contest of Religions

The first emplotment, and perhaps the one told most frequently, sees Israeli–Arab relationships as a conflict between two historically competitive religious groups. Ever since 135 C.E., when the Jews were exiled by the Romans from Judaea (Israel), a land promised to them by God in the Bible, they sought to return. A few managed to remain throughout the ensuing 2000 years; all, everywhere, were to recite in formal prayers morning, afternoon, and night, and after all meals, a reminder to God of his promise. The recreation of a modern Israel seemed to many Jews a partial fulfillment of those prayers.

When they arrived in the late nineteenth century, however, they found the land already occupied. The hundreds of thousands of Arabs resident in Palestine understood the return of Jews to Israel as a challenge to the religious supremacy they had themselves established throughout the Middle East since the time of Muhammad. The Muslims chanted Quranic verses telling of the Jews' rejection of Muhammad as God's special prophet, and they resented and opposed the Jewish resurgence on land that Muslims nowoccupied. This religiously based narrative reprised a religious conflict dating back at least 1300 years.

A Clash of Nationalisms

The second emplotment tells of two secular nationalisms on a collision course. Nineteenth-century European nationalism inspired Jews in Europe to seek a homeland of their own once again. At first, the goal was expressed in cultural terms: to restore Hebrew as a living language of everyday national life; to work the land again after centuries of urban ghettoization; to live as a "normal" people with a land and culture of its own. Then, as **pogroms** against Jews resumed with unprecedented ferocity under Russian Czar Alexander III after 1881, the movement of Jewish nationalism became far more urgent and far more political.

Assimilated Jews, living more contentedly in the USA and Western European countries, generally discounted this argument. Even the Jews fleeing Russian pogroms headed mostly to the USA; only a comparative handful chose the more difficult, nationalistic route to Palestine. But then anti-Semitism re-surfaced strongly in the 1890s in France. Assimilated Jews of Western Europe were shocked. The Austrian-Jewish journalist Theodor Herzl founded the modern political Zionist movement—"Zion" is a Biblical designation for Jerusalem—to restore to Jews a political homeland in their ancestral land of Palestine. At this time, with the Ottoman Empire still in place, and the period of the mandates far in the future, Arab nationalism had not yet surfaced. But, as we have seen above, by the 1920s, conditions had changed. The two nascent nationalisms, Arab and Zionist,

Salting fish at Kibbutz Ein Gev, situated on the east side of Lake Kinneret, Israel. Much of the food-processing in Israel is conducted by kibbutzim, agricultural cooperatives that serve as both defensive unit in case of outside attack and a socialist solution for pooling resources. Kibbutzim blossomed in the 1950s as part of the Israeli drive toward self-sufficiency.

grew up together, and were soon fighting for control of the same land.

The Struggle against Neo-colonialism

According to a third emplotment, Jews and Arabs were both incidental players in a story of European colonialism. In 1917, the British government issued the Balfour Declaration, re-allocating parts of the conquered Ottoman Empire:

> His Majesty's Government view with favour the establishment in Palestine of a national home for the Jewish people, and will use their best endeavours to facilitate the achievement of this objective, it being clearly understood that nothing shall be done which may prejudice the civil and religious rights of existing non-Jewish communities in Palestine.

Through this declaration Britain inserted a foreign, Western-oriented political entity into the Middle East, fostering a politics of divide-and-rule. Zionists reading the declaration have emphasized "the establishment ... of a national home for the Jewish people," while Arabs have stressed "nothing shall be done which may prejudice the civil and religious rights of existing non-Jewish communities." In this version of the story, Britain wrote the script; Arabs and Jews simply followed through, performing their assigned, antagonistic roles.

The nature of early Zionist settlement in the early twentieth century reinforced this colonial reading in Arab eyes. The Jewish immigrants, "pioneers" as they called themselves, came mostly from cities and small towns in eastern and central Europe. They had European educations, philosophies, technologies, and attitudes, and they usually viewed the Arabs among whom they settled as educationally backward and technologically primitive nomadic and farming peoples. Many of the Jewish settlers built egalitarian collective farms, **kibbutzim**, to maximize agricultural efficiency, achieve a social vision, and provide for their common defense. By contrast, they saw the local agricultural arrangements between *effendi* (landlords) and *fellahin* (tenants) as exploitative. The Zionists argued, with a kind of colonial paternalism, that they could help reform and modernize the land and the people. To some degree, with new medicine, farming, education, and industrial technology they were correct, but they took little account of the displacement of local society caused by their arrival and the anger it evoked. Armed Arab uprisings attempted unsuccessfully to halt and drive out Jewish immigration from the 1920s onward.

THE CREATION OF ISRAEL 1948

All three "stories," established by 1920, also influenced subsequent interpretations. For example, a central factor in the creation of Israel in 1948 was the Holocaust. For Jews, that catastrophe reaffirmed the desperate need for a political state and refuge, and they redoubled their efforts to achieve it. They tended to (mis)interpret the efforts of Arabs to block the creation of Israel, not as a struggle over control of land, but as a new Nazism, intent on root-and-branch destruction. This portrayal increased Jewish fear of, and opposition to, Arab concerns, and an Arab rhetoric of violence reinforced their apprehension. For Arabs the creation of Israel raised the haunting question of why Christian guilt over a Holocaust in Europe should be expiated by assigning to Jews lands held by Muslims in the eastern Mediterranean. Surely this was just European colonialism parading as humanitarianism at Arab expense.

ARAB–ISRAELI CONFLICT

Another ironic reconstitution of the core stories grew out of the displacement of Palestinians from their homes in Israel. With the establishment of the State of Israel in 1948, and later with Israeli occupation of the West Bank of the Jordan River after the 1967 war, many Palestinians left, becoming the "wandering Jews" of the Middle East. Palestinians generally argue that they were forced out by armed intimidation; Jews claim that Palestinians followed their leaders' advice that they leave temporarily in order to return later in armed triumph. A great outpouring of revisionist historical writing by Israeli authors such as Benny Morris has provided documentary evidence on both sides. Whatever the immediate cause, some 600,000 Palestinians fled the borders of Israel at the time of the establishment of the State and the 1948 war. During and after the 1967 war still more left. Over the decades their numbers have multiplied to several millions.

Israelis apparently believed that the neighboring Arab states would absorb these exiles as Israel absorbed more than a million Jews who immigrated from Arab states after 1948, either pulled by the attraction of a Jewish homeland or pushed by fear of future reprisals by Arabs. But the Arab states chose to leave the Palestinians in refugee status, living in refugee camps, or seeking employment in the oil fields, or leaving the area. The result has been a bitter irridentism, a desire to reclaim their homeland, represented among Palestinians primarily by the Palestine Liberation Organization (after 1996 the Palestine National Authority); militant hostility towards Israel; and unsettled refugee groups which threaten the stablility of neighboring states.

Israel's 1967 conquest of the West Bank and Gaza strip inflamed the tensions by placing one and a half million Palestinians under direct Israeli military occupation. The Palestinians wanted to establish a state of their own in this land. Fearing these territorial ambitions for a Palestinian state, the Israelis refused to end the occupation. In effect, the Israeli–Arab conflict now had two inter-related dimensions. The first was the internal struggle between two nations—Israel and a Palestine-striving-to-be-born—inhabiting a single geographical land. The second was the international strife between Israel and the surrounding Arab states. Through the 1970s and early 1980s, attacks within Israeli borders and terrorist attacks against international travellers, especially in airports and airplanes, and against the Israeli participants in the 1972 Munich Olympics, expressed Palestinian anger; Israeli bombings of refugee camps were a common response. In 1987 Palestinians in the West Bank and Gaza regions began the *intifada* (uprising), employing both civil disobedience and low-intensity violence in a pattern of continuous demonstrations to disrupt Israeli control. Israel cracked down and hardened its positions.

A major breakthrough in the external warfare came with the Egyptian peace treaty of 1979 (see p. 689). Further possibilities seemed to open in the early 1990s as the Soviet Union dissolved, ending the superpower rivalries that had helped militarize

Israelis claim Jerusalem. On June 1, 1967, five Israeli soldiers look into the Jordanian sector of Jerusalem from their high perch on the Israeli side of the city. A week after this picture was taken, the Israeli armed forces had liberated the old city from Jordanian troops, and for the first time in nearly 2000 years, Jerusalem was entirely under Jewish rule.

the Middle East, and as the war against Iraq led to divisions and re-alignments among Arab states, perhaps allowing new openings toward Israel, too.

A breakthrough in the internal Israeli–Palestinian conflict came in 1993, when the government of Israel and the Palestine Liberation Organization signed an agreement to recognize each other, to cease fighting, and to extend at least limited self-rule to the Palestinians in Gaza and the West Bank. The assassination of Israeli Prime Minister Yitzhak Rabin by a Jewish extremist in 1995, followed by Arab militant attacks on Israeli buses later in the year, crippled the movement toward peace and indicated just how fragmented were the forces on both sides. Dialogues are continuing. The peace agreements between Israel and the Palestinians opened the way for other Arab nations to normalize their relations with Israel. Jordan signed a peace treaty in 1995, but no one knows how external relations will be affected by problems in the internal Israel–Palestinian negotiations.

Israel itself had many internal problems: continuing social tensions among the amazingly diverse immigrant groups which have come to the country since 1948, especially between the Ashkenazic half from Europe and the Sepharadic half from the Arab states themselves; assimilation of the hundreds of thousands of eastern European Jews seeking refuge

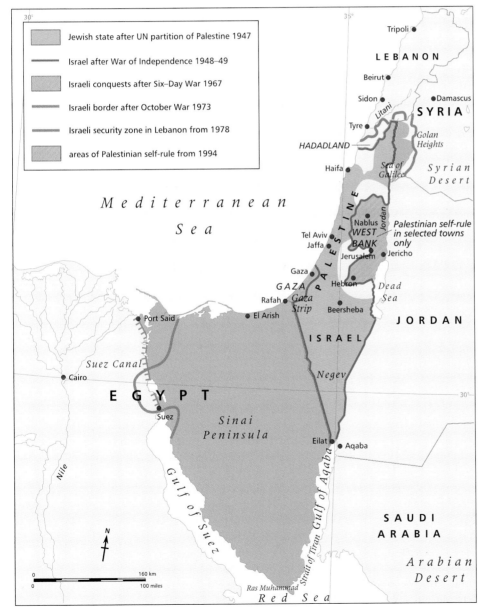

Legend:
- Jewish state after UN partition of Palestine 1947
- Israel after War of Independence 1948–49
- Israeli conquests after Six–Day War 1967
- Israeli border after October War 1973
- Israeli security zone in Lebanon from 1978
- areas of Palestinian self-rule from 1994

Israel and its neighbors
The creation, with Western support, of a Jewish homeland in Palestine in 1947 occurred at a time of increasing Arab nationalism. Israel's birth in 1948 was attended by war and more followed in 1956, 1967, 1973, and 1982. Peace treaties exist only with Egypt, which regained the Sinai peninsula, and Jordan (1996). Beginning in the 1970s, an *intifada* (uprising) by Palestinians has forced more attention on Israeli–Palestinian relations—an extremely vexed issue.

after the USSR and its allies opened their gates to emigration in the 1980s; continuing religious antagonism between the small minority of orthodox Jews and the vast majority who are secular; and wary apprehension between the 85 percent of Israel's population who are Jews and the 15 percent who are Arabs.

Israel had accomplished much of its nationalist, Zionist agenda, providing a home to 4.7 million Jews (as well as 750,000 Arabs), almost all of them immigrants or the immediate descendants of immigrants who had arrived within the last century. Culturally they had taken the ancient Hebrew language and recreated it as a vehicle for everyday life, and for modern literature as well. They had done all this within a democratic framework, although Arab citizens received second-class treatment in terms of education, public services, and access to land, water, and jobs.

To make the land a liveable home they had introduced state-of-the-art farming technology, including methods of arid land agriculture which were a model for others. They had created light industries, notably the processing of industrial diamonds and, more recently, the production of computer software. Continuously at war, they had developed an arms industry, with the Uzi—one of the hand weapons—known throughout the world. The armed forces had become critical in the nation's life. Conscription was and remains universal: three years for men, two for women, with reserve service continuing for men to age 55. Israel's army had become the most powerful in the region and one of the most powerful in the world. Although not acknowledged officially, the state almost certainly had developed nuclear weapons. Fearful of terrorism within the country, soldiers were on constant deployment. The annual expenditure on the armed forces was a staggering $1,216 per capita, partly defrayed by assistance from the United States.

All of these developments in technology, culture, economics, and politics tended to reinforce Israel's identity as more European than Middle Eastern. Its many ties to Western nations, and especially to the United States, further affirmed that identity. These contrasts between Israel and its Arab neighbors, in addition to the religious differences, and the bitter struggle of hostile nationalisms each claiming the same land, create a situation filled with tension, in a part of the world already beset by national and international tensions.

BIBLIOGRAPHY

American Historical Review XCVI No. 5
(December 1991), 1363–1496. Special Issue on the Historiography of the Modern Middle East.

Avishai, Bernard. *The Tragedy of Zionism*
(New York: Farrar Straus Giroux: New York, 1985).

Fanon, Frantz. *The Wretched of the Earth*, trans. by Constance Farrington (New York: Grove Press, 1963).

Friedman, Thomas L. *From Beirut to Jerusalem*
(New York: Farrar, Straus and Giroux, 1989).

Hourani, Albert. *A History of the Arab Peoples*
(Cambridge: Belknap Press, Harvard University, 1991).

International Institute for Environment and Development and the World Resources Institute. *World Resources 1987* (New York: Basic Books, 1987).

Johnson, Hazel and Henry Bernstein, eds.
Third World Lives of Struggle
(London: Heinemann Educational Books Ltd., 1982).

Lapidus, Ira M. *A History of Islamic Societies* (Cambridge: Cambridge University Press, 1988).

Laqueur, Walter and Barry Rubin, eds. *The Israeli--Arab Reader* (New York City: Penguin, 5th ed., 1995).

Morris, Benny. *The Birth of the Palestinian Refugee Problem 1947–1949*
(Cambridge: Cambridge University Press, 1988).

Netton, Ian Richard, ed. *Arabia and the Gulf: From Traditional Society to Modern States*
(London: Croom Helm, 1986).

Richards, Alan and John Waterbury. *A Political Economy of the Middle East*
(Boulder, CO: Westview Press, 1990).

Robinson, Francis. *Atlas of the Islamic World since 1500*
(New York: Facts on File, 1982).

Sachar, Howard M. *A History of Israel*
(New York: Alfred A. Knopf, 1985).

Sigmund, Paul E., ed. *The Ideologies of the Developing Nations* (New York, Praeger, 2nd rev. ed., 1972).

Sivard, Ruth Leger. *World Military and Social Expenditures 1991* (Washington, DC: World Priorities, 14th ed., 1991, 16th ed., 1996).

Toubia, Nahid, ed. *Women of the Arab World*
(London: Zed Books, 1988).

Yergin, Daniel. *The Prize*
(New York: Simon and Schuster, 1991).

22
CHAPTER

"What other countries have taken three hundred years to achieve, a once dependent territory must try to accomplish in a generation if it is to survive."

KWAME NKRUMAH

SUB-SAHARAN AFRICA

1914–1990s

COLONIALISM, INDEPENDENCE, AND THEIR AFTERMATH

The second largest continent, Africa stretches from 35° south of the equator to 37° north, with the Sahara extending all the way across, west to east, at a latitude of about 20° north. The countries of this vast continent are dramatically different from one another in ecological, economic, demographic, and political terms. In population, the largest, Nigeria, has 104 million inhabitants, while many have fewer than 5 million. The GDP of Botswana, which has a population of 1.4 million, is $2,750; that of the Congo, with a population of 2.5 million, is $460; while for Nigeria it is $300. Size, however, is not the deciding factor: Mozambique, with 16.6 million citizens, has a GNP of $70, the poorest sizeable country in Africa. Female literacy varies from 80 percent in Zimbabwe to 7 percent in Niger and 9 percent in Burkina Faso (Sivard, p. 52). Life expectancy is forty-six years in Angola, Malawi, Mali, Mozambique, and Niger; it is fifty-six years

in Cameroon, Ghana, and Kenya. Infant mortality in Kenya is fifty-nine per thousand live births; in Angola 112; in Mali 149. In geographical area, the Sudan has 966,757 square miles (2,500,000 square kilometers), the largest country in Africa, one-fourth the size of the United States; the Gambia has 4,127 square miles (10,700 square kilometers). Some of Africa's countries are rich in raw materials: South Africa with gold and diamonds, the Congo with copper and cobalt, and Nigeria with oil. Some produce abundant quantities of tropical vegetation and crops: coffee and cocoa on the Côte d'Ivoire, coffee in Kenya, and peanuts in Senegal. Some, such as Mali and Chad, have few natural resources.

In 1914, sub-Saharan Africa was governed by Europeans, who ruled through the power of their technology, especially steamboats and machine guns and military and administrative organization. Forty-three years later, in 1957, Ghana became the first

	ANGOLA	GHANA	NIGERIA
1900			▌British Protectorate of Northern Nigeria established (1900)
1910			▌Nigeria and South Nigeria united (1914)
1920			▌Women's protests at Aba (1925, 1929)
1930			▌Azikiwe launches populist journalism (1935)
1940		▌United Gold Coast convention (1947)	
1950	▌Becomes overseas territory of Portugal (1951) ▌People's Movement for the Liberation of Angola (MPLA) formed (1956); supported by communist states, notably Cuba and Soviet Union	▌Becomes independent within British Commonwealth, with Kwame Nkrumah as president (1957), who embarked on a policy of "African socialism" ▌All Africa People's Conference, Accra (1958)	▌Becomes a federation (1954)
1960	▌Unsuccessful rebellion for independence (1961) ▌National Front for the Liberation of Angola (FNLA) formed (1962); backed by "non-left" countries in southern Africa ▌National Union for the Total Independence of Angola (UNITA) formed (1966); supported by Western powers	▌Becomes republic (1960) ▌Becomes one-party state (1964) ▌Economy begins to fail and Nkrumah deposed and replaced by Joseph Ankrah (1966) ▌Ankrah replaced by Akwasi Afrifa (1969), who instigates return to civilian government	▌Achieves independence within the British Commonwealth (1960) ▌Becomes a republic (1963) ▌Military coup quickly followed by counter-coup led by Yakubu Gowon (1966) ▌Conflict over oil revenues leads to declaration of independent Ibo state of Biafra (1967)
1970	▌Revolution in Portugal (1974) ▌Independence from Portugal (1975); traditional government formed from representatives of MPLA, FNLA, UNITA, and Portuguese government ▌MPLA proclaim People's Republic of Angola with Agostino Neto as president (1975) ▌FNLA and UNITA proclaim People's Democratic Republic of Angola ▌MPLA gain control of most of country (1976); South African troops withdraw but Cuban forces remain	▌Edward Akufo-Addo elected as president (1970) ▌Military coup puts Colonel Acheampong at head of government (1972) ▌Bloodless coup puts Frederick Akuffo in power, but he is almost immediately replaced by Jerry Rawlings (1978) ▌Hilla Limann brings return to civilian rule (1979)	▌Civil war ends and Biafra surrenders (1970) ▌Military coup puts Olusegun Obasanjo in power (1975) ▌Shehu Shagan becomes civilian president (1979)
1980	▌Constitution amended to provide for elected assembly (1980); UNITA guerillas (aided by South Africa) continue raids against government and bases of South West Africa People's Organization (SWAPO) ▌Lusaka Agreement (1984) set up commission to supervise South Africa's withdrawal (1985); further raids occur (1986) ▌Peace treaty with South Africa and Cuba (1988), but UNITA rebels begin guerilla activity again	▌Rawlings seizes power again (1981) ▌Coup against Rawlings fails (1989)	▌Military coup led by Muhammad Buhari (1983) ▌Bloodless coup led by Ibrahim Babangida (1985), who promises return to democracy
1990	▌Peace agreement signed (1991)		▌Nine new states created; Babangida confirms commitment to democracy (1991) ▌Elections won by Babangida (1992) ▌Results of presidential elections suspended following charges of malpractice; Babangida resigns; replaced by Sani Abacha, who restores military rule and dissolves all military parties (1993 ▌Ken Saro-Wiwa and other Ogoni protesters executed (1995)

black African colony to gain its independence. By the mid-1970s European direct political control of Africa was ended. Independence arrived with high hopes and aspirations for Africa's ability to establish effective democratic governments and prosperous economies. By the mid-1990s, however, neither the political nor the economic developments in the continent had lived up to these expectations. How was independence won? After independence, what political, economic, and social systems did African

	SOUTH AFRICA	UGANDA	CONGO
1900	▌Boer War (1899-1902)		▌Congo Free State annexed to Belgium (1908)
1910	▌Union of South Africa formed from two British colonies and two Boer republics (1910) ▌African National Congress formed (1913) ▌Native Land Acts (1913)		
1920			
1930	▌Independence within Commonwealth (1934)		
1940	▌Apartheid system imposed by Daniel Malan of National Party (1948)		
1950	▌ANC adopts Freedom Charter (1955) Hendrik Verwoerd becomes prime minister (1958); implements policy of Apartheid		▌Rioting in Leopoldville (1959) ▌Belgium suddenly announces it will withdraw in one year (1959)
1960	▌Sharpeville Massacre; ANC banned (1960) ▌South Africa withdraws from Commonwealth and becomes republic (1961) ▌Nelson Mandela and other ANC leaders sentenced to life imprisonment (1964) ▌Verwoerd assassinated; B.J. Vorster becomes prime minister (1966)	▌Independence within Commonwealth; Milton Obote prime minister (1962) ▌Becomes federal republic with King Mutesa II as president (1963) ▌Mutesa ousted in Obote-led coup; federal status ended; Obote president (1966) ▌Opposition parties banned (1969)	▌Independence as Republic (1960) ▌Civil war between central government and Katanga province; UN intervenes (1960-63) Belgian troops help quell risings in east and center of country ▌New constitution adopted (1967)
1970	▌Soweto uprising (1976) ▌Vorster replaced by P.W. Botha (1978)	▌Idi Amin-Dada leads coup against Obote (1971); ruthless dictatorship follows in which 49,000 Ugandan Asians expelled and 300,000+ opponents of regime killed ▌Amin forced to flee by opponents backed by Tanzanian troops; Usuf Lule president in provisional government, soon replaced by Godfrey Binaisa (1978) ▌Fighting against Tanzanian forces (1978-9)	▌Joseph-Désiré Mobutu elected president (1970) ▌Country renamed as Republic of Zaire (1971) ▌Popular Movement of the Revolution province renamed Shaba; names "Africanized" (1972) ▌Mobutu seizes foreign-owned businesses and plantations, which are given in patronage (1974) ▌Original owners of confiscated property invited back; Mobutu re-elected (1977) ▌Zairians invade Shaba province from Angola; repulsed with Belgian help (1977-8)
1980	▌New constitution gives segregated representation to Asians and Coloreds (1984) ▌Township violence increases (1985) ▌Commonwealth and US Congress impose sanctions (1986) ▌Agrees to withdraw from Angola and recognize independence of Namibia (1988) ▌F.W. de Klerk becomes president; ANC activists released; public areas desegregated (1989	▌Binaisa overthrown by army; Obote returns to power after elections (1980) ▌Obote ousted in military coup led by Tito Okello; power-sharing agreement with National Resistance Army leader Yoweri Museveni (1985) ▌Museveni becomes president at head of broad-based coalition (1986)	▌Increasing unrest and foreign criticism of civil rights violations (1986-1990) Potential rift with Belgium avoided (1988)
1990	▌Ban on ANC lifted; Mandela released (1990) ▌Mandela elected president of ANC; de Klerk repeals remaining apartheid laws (1991) ▌New constitution agrees to majority rule (1992) ▌Free elections; Mandela becomes president (1994)	▌East African cooperation pact with Kenya and Tanzania to be revived (1992) ▌King of Baganda reinstated as formal monarch (1993)	▌Mobutu announces end of ban on multi-party politics following internal dissent (1990) ▌Zaire seeks international help to deal with refugees flooding into country from Rwanda (1995) ▌Laurent Kabila overthrows government of Mobutu (1997) ▌Mobutu dies of cancer (1997)

peoples implement to rule themselves, develop their economies, and formulate the appropriate technologies which they advocated? How were these systems working—or not working and why? This chapter looks at the years during which Europeans carved up Africa into their own colonies; the period of colonial rule; and events since independence. Although most of its focus is on government, economics, and technology, it also considers cultural life and creativity. A segment of the chapter examines the special case of South Africa and its apartheid system, which was finally overthrown in the early 1990s.

TO WORLD WAR I: COLONIALISM ESTABLISHED

As we have seen in Chapter 16, after the slave trade was outlawed in the early 1800s Europeans intensified their search for alternative sources of profit from Africa. Some wished to transfer plantation economies to Africa while others sought to cultivate and export tropical products such as tea, coffee and palm oil. Still others wanted to explore for yet unknown potential riches. To pursue commercial and religious goals and to expand geographical explorations, national governments, churches, and business groups sponsored the expeditions of explorers such as David Livingstone (1813–73), Heinrich Barth (1821–65), Henry Morton Stanley (1841–1904), and Pierre Savorgnan de Brazza (1852–1905). European technology enabled the explorers to penetrate Africa. The steamboat facilitated their movement, quinine gave them some protection from malaria, and the Maxim gun gave them military power.

In the second half of the nineteenth century, as European countries became more nationalistic and more competitive in economic development and armaments, the countries of Africa provided a new arena for competition and an opportunity to defuse competition by moving it to a peripheral area. To lay down ground rules for European activity and boundaries in Africa, Otto von Bismarck convened the Berlin Conference of 1884–5, where Europeans staked and negotiated claims among themselves peacefully. Meanwhile, within Africa representatives of these governments signed treaties by which African rulers ceded to them huge estates. The

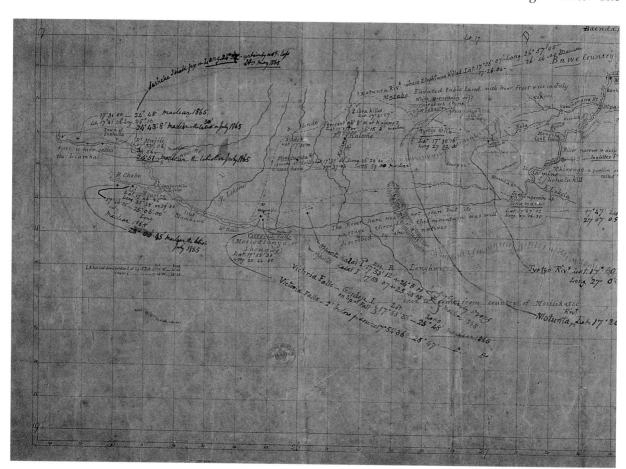

Chart of the Zambezi River, drawn by the explorer Dr David Livingstone, c.1865. As the first European into the heart of the African interior, Livingstone's explorations had a major impact on cartographers of the day. Already hailed in England for his discoveries of the Zambezi River and the Victoria Falls, by 1866 he was intent on finding the sources of the Nile, that most intriguing of problems for nineteenth-century explorers. In the event, it was the Congo River, not the Nile, that he found and explored. When Livingstone died, the Africans buried his heart beneath a favorite tree before sending the body for burial in Westminster Abbey, London.

Africans signing the treaties were often unauthorized and uncomprehending. Nevertheless, the Europeans enforced the treaties with soldiers and guns. When Africans resisted these one-sided agreements, Europeans responded with force. Between 1884 and 1898, the French put down the rebellion of the Mande peoples under the Muslim Samori Toure. The British finally quelled a series of Asante revolts in the Gold Coast in 1900. The Germans crushed perhaps the greatest of the unsuccessful rebellions, the Maji-Maji revolt of 1905–7 in Tanganyika. Led by Kinji-kitile Ngwele, who claimed to have magic water (*maji*), which would turn German bullets to water, the rebels had refused to perform forced labor on the cotton plantations. The uprising ended with 70,000 dead, including those who succumbed to disease and malnutrition. Other less spectacular revolts were similarly suppressed with violence.

Ethiopia was alone in defending its independence successfully. King Menelik II (r. 1889–1913) had purchased sufficient guns and trained his forces well enough to defeat Italy at the Battle of Adowa in 1896.

Many states had flourished prior to the European arrival—the Asante and Oyo in west Africa, the Luba in central Africa, and the Baganda and Bunyoro in the east—but only Ethiopia was still independent in 1914. (Liberia held nominal independence, but the indigenous peoples were actually subordinate to the control of an immigrant American-Liberian elite.) By 1914, the European

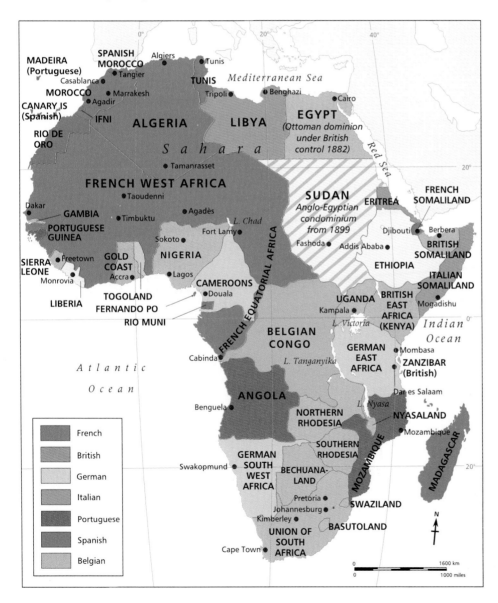

Africa in 1914 By the end of the nineteenth century, Africa presented European imperialists with their last chance to claim a "place in the sun." In an ignoble scramble for territory, Belgium, Germany, and Italy joined Spain, Portugal, Britain, and France in carving up the continent, riding roughshod over native concerns with brutal insensitivity. Conflict between the colonists was common, the Boer War between the British and Dutch in South Africa being the most bloody.

powers had "partitioned" Africa, carved it up among themselves; "pacified" the continent; implanted limited doses of European technologies of transportation, communication, and international commodity trade; and introduced a light veneer of western education, often in the form of missionary schools.

ECONOMIC INVESTMENT

Economically, the Europeans invested in the extension of cash cropping in the lands they had seized, cultivating especially palm oil, peanuts, cotton, coffee, and cocoa. They instituted patterns of continuous **monoculture** (the growing of a single commercial crop for sale) that were quite different from both of the more traditional patterns of mixed cropping and slash-and-burn agriculture primarily for food. Ultimately, the extension of monoculture, in peanuts for example, especially onto the fringes of the Sahara desert, depleted and eroded the soil. The local Tuareg and Fulani residents then migrated northward into increasingly precarious desert enclaves, where they were tragically vulnerable to killing droughts. European strategies for exploiting the natural environment pushed the limits of Africa's resources for human life, and for animal life as well. For example, the hunt for ivory, which

was popular in Europe and Asia for billiard balls and piano keys as well as for ornaments and jewellery, depleted the elephant population.

As commercially valuable deposits of metals and minerals, including gold and diamonds, were discovered, Europeans initiated mining enterprises, especially in South Africa, Zimbabwe, the Gold Coast, and the Congo. During the years of the slave trade, the Europeans had remained mostly along the coast. Now, to oversee, harvest, mine, and bring to market their new investments they steamed upriver in boats, laid new railway track—8000 miles (12,800 kilometers) in British Africa by 1946; 2600 miles (4100 kilometers) in French West and Equatorial Africa (Fieldhouse, p. 35)—and constructed feeder roads.

Africans had the worst jobs. Import-export activities, banking, and administration and ownership were kept entirely in European hands. Some foreign labor was imported under indenture contracts, and some workers chose to immigrate in search of new job opportunities within the colonial economy. By the beginning of World War I, communities of Indian immigrants had established themselves in East and South Africa. Although blocked from the "commanding heights" of the economy, the Indian immigrants gradually moved into significant positions in local trade and com-

Building the Uganda Railway, from Mombasa, Kenya, into the interior. The workers are laying track at the base of the Kikuyu Escarpment at Mile 363, c. 1900. The very steep sides of the escarpment, which form the walls of the Rift Valley, presented builders with the most difficult section of the route. Some 32,000 laborers were imported from India to build the railway, which helped Britain to maintain a presence in Uganda by its direct link with the port of Mombasa.

merce. Africans, with very little formal education, generally did not enter into careers in business, and the resulting economic imbalance between immigrants and natives sowed a bitter harvest of dispossession and jealousy.

ADMINISTRATION

To administer their lands and investments, the British and French placed in each of their new colonies a governor, a council of advisers, law courts, police forces, army installations, and hospitals. Cities were built to house the administrative centers, introducing a pattern of favoritism of the city over the countryside that has persisted until today. To keep costs low, the colonizers coopted Africans into the administration, following two distinctly different patterns. In some places they coopted local chiefs—or men whom they designated as local chiefs—to serve as their administrative officials. This pattern of indirect rule, associated most strongly with Frederick Lugard, 1st Baron Lugard (1858–1945), who adapted it from British methods in India and introduced it into Nigeria in the early 1900s, was designed to keep Africans loyal to the colonizers by making the local rulers dependent upon the British, and by supporting these local rulers against any popular resistance. The alternative system was to educate in European fashion a **cadre** of less conservative leaders who would share European outlooks, values, and urban residence, and in some places, especially in urban areas, this plan was also implemented. The response to new educational and administrative opportunities was not uniform. Some groups, especially the Fulbe in Nigeria, the Swahili in Tanganyika, and the Baganda in Uganda, showed considerable interest. These groups tended to ally themselves with the new administration and economic innovations of the colonizers.

In some areas of Africa, particularly western Africa, Europeans did not come as settlers, but as administrators and business agents on temporary postings. But in other regions, most notably southern and eastern Africa, Europeans came in greater numbers and took possession of the best lands for themselves, sometimes through dubious contracts, more often by force. As we saw on pp. 531–3, the European colonizers coerced the Africans to work on their plantations through levying taxes and restricting land ownership. The harsh employment policies of the Europeans created a part-time, uncommitted labor force reluctantly engaged in mines, plantations, administration, and urban occupations. Whenever they could, the Africans returned to working their own lands, mostly in subsistence farming.

All the European powers ruled their African colonies in order to make profits, to claim prestige, and, as they saw it, to civilize the Africans. They differed in the degree of force they used to achieve these goals, with the British generally considered the least physically coercive. King Leopold II of Belgium, who had personal control of the Congo, was so brutal toward the Congolese, treating them little better than domesticated animals, that in 1908 the Belgian government decided to take over authority from him.

COLONIALISM CHALLENGED 1914–57

After 1914, the political power of European nations was challenged and their philosophy changed. Two world wars and an intervening worldwide economic depression weakened European hegemony and devastated its confidence in its *"mission civilizatrice"* and "white man's burden." During World War I, the leaders of the European Allies declared their commitments to "making the world safe for democracy," and these proclamations could not be entirely jettisoned when the war was over. Indeed the Ghanaian historian Adu Boahen believes the turning point in colonial authority in Africa came with the Italian invasion of Ethiopia in 1935, through which Mussolini sought to avenge the humiliating defeat the Italians had suffered at the Battle of Adowa in 1896 and to start the restoration of the Italian Empire. The conquest of this last remaining independent African state shocked public opinion not only in Africa but even in Europe and the United States—though not enough to prevent it (Boahen, pp. 90–91). It was no longer considered proper for European countries to establish new colonies.

By the end of World War II, the apparent inevitability and the moral sanction of European colonialism had been undermined. The South Asian countries of India, Pakistan, Sri Lanka, and Burma won their independence between 1947 and 1948. China's communist revolution expelled foreign interests in 1949. Military power and political leadership passed from the European colonizing powers to the United States and, to a lesser extent, the Soviet Union. Both took strong public stands against overseas colonialism, although Russia was taking over control of the countries of eastern Europe, and America's wealth and military commanded enormous power around the globe.

As we have seen in previous chapters on the ending of colonialism in other regions, many critics feared that the new order was not so much post-colonial as **neo-colonial**. During their years in power in their colonies, Europeans had succeeded

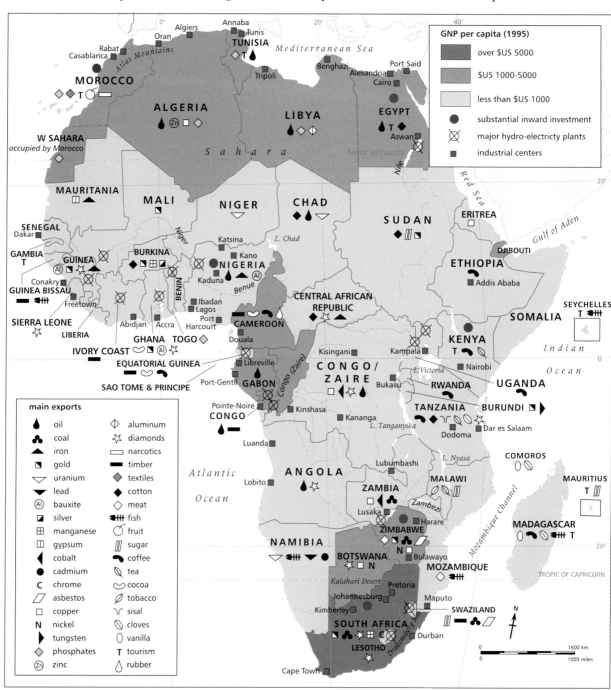

The economic development of Africa The legacy of European colonialism has determined Africa's economic development, with a persistent reliance upon primary products, mainly mineral wealth and cash crops. Both are widely exploited by multinational franchises, bringing little real economic benefit to local economies. Political instability, corruption, and natural disaster combine with low investment in education and health to create a general condition of underdevelopment and overpopulation. The northern tier of Arab states and South Africa stand out with greater wealth compared with the central part of the continent.

in molding leaders who were amenable to participating as partners in a global political and economic order set by the Europeans. The colonial rulers could grant formal independence while still maintaining economic, cultural, and even political influence, or **hegemony**. They had no further need to support the expense and burden of formal political colonization. Those critics, like Frantz Fanon, whose fierce critiques of colonialism we have already encountered in Algeria (see p. 699), waited and watched, apprehensively, to examine the substance as well as the form of the new independence. How deeply had it taken root, and how strong would it be in practice?

THE ORIGINS OF THE INDEPENDENCE MOVEMENTS

The African quest for independence had ripened through the years. It had passed to men newly educated in European ideals, including concepts of nationalism and democracy, and no longer willing to suffer in silence the arrogance of European domination. Very few, however, received this formal education. In 1960 only about 16 percent of adults in Africa were literate, and the average enrollment in secondary schools was only 3 percent of the age group. So few universities had been established in Africa that students were far more likely to study abroad than at home. In 1960 396 Kenyans were studying at Makerere University College in neighboring Uganda, the closest African university, while 1655 studied at universities abroad. Training

in industrial and managerial skills was practically non-existent.

The tiny group of educated elites had disproportionate influence. They claimed to have supplanted the leadership of the traditional chiefs and asserted their right to represent their nations.

Newspapers became an important vehicle in mobilizing literate opinion as early as 1890. In 1935, the Nigerian Nnamdi Azikiwe (b. 1904) first edited the Accra *African Morning Post*, and in 1937 he founded in Lagos the *West African Pilot*, thereby introducing populist, revolutionary journalism to Africa. Azikiwe learned his journalism in the United States, where he also experienced at first hand American racism and the efforts of radical journalists to combat it. Returning to Africa, he helped to launch political movements and parties through his newspapers (July, p. 434).

Education in values and skills takes place outside schools, too, and military service in two world wars provided a significant training ground. In World War I, the British recruited 26,000 Africans to serve under arms, and the French 180,000 (July, pp. 361–2); in World War II, 80,000 African soldiers fought inside France until the country was conquered by Germany in 1940; the British recruited 280,000 soldiers from East Africa and 167,000 from the West (Davidson, pp. 57–8). These soldiers travelled far from home and learned new ways of life. They learned the advantages of new technologies of organization and machinery, but they also saw the murder of whites by whites, and indeed were ordered by white Europeans to kill other white

German East Africa Campaign, World War I. Drafts of Nigerians for the Nigerian Brigade disembark at Lindi, December 1917. Although the men have been issued with regulation hats and items of uniform, their feet are bare below the leg strappings. A great number of porters was needed for the campaign in German East Africa to conquer the German colony of Tanganyika. British East Africa provided up to one million conscripts for the war effort, many of whom died from disease rather than war wounds.

Europeans. They came to understand the underside of European treatment of other Europeans. At army bases they mingled with white women. Racial myths tumbled. After each war, soldiers returned home, expecting and demanding political rewards for their military service. Frustrated at the end of World War I, they were received more respectfully following World War II.

SEEDS OF DISCONTENT

Labor organization in the mines, plantations, railroads, and docks also introduced new perspectives. Although the percentage of Africans at work in these European-controlled installations was small

—1 percent of the population of French West Africa, for example—the sheer numbers (167,000 in this case) were substantial. Moreover, seasonal and migrant laborers carried back to their villages stories of industrial life.

Strikes further helped to consolidate African feeling against European economic control and racial supremacy. The Sierra Leone Railway Workers Union struck in 1920 and again in 1926. In 1925–6, the year of the "great strikes," mechanics, dock workers, and railway workers in West Africa went on strike. In 1935, the Zambian copper belt was affected, and in 1938–9, there were strikes in the diamond mines in Sierra Leone. From October 10, 1947 to March 19, 1948 workers struck the

South African miners' strike. Huge crowds of white miners demonstrate over pay and conditions in Bree Street, Johannesburg, during a strike of 1913. One striker was killed by police during these demonstrations. White and black workers had different unions to represent them, because the whites wanted to ensure they were on different pay scales and firmly separated from the blacks. Diamonds and gold were the mainstays of South Africa's economic development, so miners' strikes presented an unwelcome threat to the wealth and smooth running of the colony.

Dakar–Niger railway line and docks, a confrontation commemorated in Sembene Ousmane's novel *God's Bits of Wood*. In 1947, 15,000 workers struck in Mombasa, Kenya. The mines of South Africa and the Belgian Congo, where conditions were especially severe, endured more numerous strikes. In order to secure higher wages for themselves and to discourage the employment of black strikebreakers, white workers formed separate unions. Striking blacks were on their own from the first organized strike of 9000 miners in 1913.

OUR ONLY HOPE FOR A NEW LIFE LIES IN THE MACHINE

Ousmane's novel, *God's Bits of Wood*, tells of the workers' strike on the Dakar–Niger railway in west Africa from October 1947 to March 1948. Ousmane describes the workers' realization that they have developed a commitment to their new industrial jobs. They have become new men:

> Like rejected lovers returning to a trysting place, they kept coming back to the areas surrounding the stations. Then they would just stand there, motionless, their eyes fixed on the horizon, scarcely speaking to each other. Sometimes a little block of five or six men would detach itself from the larger mass and drift off in the direction of the tracks. For a few minutes they would wander along the rails and then, suddenly, as though seized with panic, they would hasten back to the safety of the group they had left. Then again they would just stand there, or squat down in the shade of a sand hill, their eyes fixed on the two endless parallels, following them out until they joined and lost themselves in the brush. Something was being born inside them, as if the past and the future were coupling to breed a new kind of man, and it seemed to them that the wind was whispering a phrase they had often heard from Bakayoko: "The kind of man we were is dead, and our only hope for a new life lies in the machine, which knows neither a language nor a race." They said nothing, though, and only their eyes betrayed an inner torment brought on by the mounting terror of famine and inconsolable loneliness for the machine. (p. 76)

Other new organizations also found their activities spilling over into politics. African churches provided safe spaces in which politics could be discussed free from European censorship. Independent churches—called Ethiopian, Zionist, and Watchtower Churches—filled this need, and frequently opposed the missionary activities of white European churches. The black churches often supported the labor union activities of their members.

Gender also played a role. In 1929, at Aba in Nigeria, some 10,000 women gathered, with another 6000 assembling at Owerrinta, to protest new market taxes and market license requirements. These women felt more vulnerable than men since they had fewer alternatives to their market jobs. Some relief was offered, but only after sixty women were killed in confrontation with colonial authorities. Women had gathered before at Aba in 1925 to preserve their religion, which they felt to be under attack by Christians. Elsewhere and at other times women seem to have played a strong role in support of other protest movements.

Social clubs, literary circles, welfare associations, youth movements, and ethnic associations multiplied throughout Africa, becoming vehicles for political expression and protest. Some were from the outset overtly political, most notably the National Congress of British West Africa, which was founded in 1920. Like almost all the others, it wanted a voice in colonial policies, an end to racial discrimination in government hiring, an expansion of educational opportunities, and greater opportunities for Africans in the economy. But most members still saw themselves as loyal subjects of the British crown, ending their resolutions with affirmations of "their attachment to the British connection and their unfeigned loyalty and devotion to the throne and person of His Majesty the King Emperor" (Boahen, p. 83).

PAN-AFRICANISM 1918–45

Bringing these groups together was a long-held dream that began to find its realization in five pan-African meetings between the end of World War I and the end of World War II. Race was the binding issue of these meetings, yet the Eurocentric transportation and communication systems available at the time required that all five congresses meet in Europe, or the United States; not until 1958 did an All-African People's Conference convene in Africa. (The very first meeting of representatives of the African diaspora had been held in London in 1900, but its participants came mostly from the West Indies and the USA rather than Africa.)

The 1919 congress was convened by W.E.B. Du Bois (1868–1963), the great American scholar and publicist, to coincide with the Versailles peace conference (see p. 585). Participants called on the assembled powers to attend to the racial, economic, and political concerns of Africa. They also asked that Germany's African colonies be turned over to an international body, a kind of precursor of mandatory power. The request was not accepted. A second conference, convened in 1921, met sequentially in London, Brussels, and Paris. Its final manifesto called for an end to racism and inequality:

> The absolute equality of races—physical, political, and social—is the founding stone of world peace and human advancement. … It is the shame of the world that today the relation between the main groups of mankind and their mutual estimate and respect is determined chiefly by the degree to which one can subject the other to its service, enslaving labor, making ignorance compulsory, uprooting ruthlessly religion and customs, and destroying government, so that the favored Few may luxuriate in the toil of the tortured Many. (Andrea and Overfield, pp. 471–3)

African-Americans formed the majority at the first four of the Congresses. Some Africans, led by Blaise Diagne of Senegal, rejected American advocacy of independence for Africa:

> We Frenchmen of Africa wish to remain French. … None of us aspires to see French Africa delivered exclusively to the Africans as is demanded, though without any authority, by the American Negroes. (July, p. 378)

But many representatives felt that Diagne had sold out his earlier militancy to consolidate his own position in France. The third Congress, convened by Du Bois in London and Lisbon in 1923, and the fourth, in New York in 1927, continued the debate on Africa's proper relationship to Europe.

The Fifth Congress convened in Manchester, England, in 1945 under very different conditions, with European empires about to crumble and African leadership more self-confident and militant. A new generation of African leaders, notably Kwame Nkrumah of Ghana and Jomo Kenyatta of Kenya, joined together in Manchester and demanded independence for Africa.

The British and French were prepared to be responsive, investing greater financial and devel-opment resources in Africa than ever before. Perhaps the new investments would encourage the colonies to remain within the imperial structures, or at least to accept post-independence cooperation with the former colonizers. Britain already had adopted these policies in 1940 by establishing the Colonial Development and Welfare Act, and in 1945 it added further legislation that chaneled funds for development. France provided its colonies with similar, and slightly larger, funding known as FIDES.

Investment patterns suggested the importance ascribed to technology both in the development of Africa and in establishing the balance between Europe and Africa. Major hydroelectric schemes were introduced on the Nile at Jinja in Uganda, at Kariba on the Zambesi, between the Rhodesias, in the Gold Coast on the Volta River at Akasombo, and in Guinea at the Fria and Kimbo Rivers. Construction of the Inga dam on the lower Congo was interrupted by warfare and civil war. Agricultural, veterinary and fishing technology, and education were extended. Transportation networks were extended and improved. Education was expanded; teacher training schools were established; between 1945 and 1949 four university colleges were established by the British. (French higher education was still available only in France.) Local self-government was made more representative through election.

Even so, the African economies were very weak, their educational systems minuscule, and participation in electoral politics virtually non-existent, even in the British and French colonies. In the Belgian Congo and the Portuguese colonies of Angola and Mozambique, Africans were generally even more impoverished, less powerful, and treated with even less dignity. A brief overview of the winning of independence in a few of the major colonies will indicate some of the differences, both in the policies of the colonizers and the resources and mobilization of the colonized.

WINNING INDEPENDENCE 1945–75

THE BRITISH COLONIES

The Gold Coast was the first black African country to win independence and, like several others, immediately chose a new name—Ghana—symbolically linking itself with historical traditions of earlier African empires. Ghana specialized in growing cash crops, like coffee, cocoa, and peanuts. It had mineral resources, generally untapped, in bauxite, gold, and manganese. It had few European settlers. In 1947, the United Gold Coast Convention organized to represent the political opinions of educated Ghanaians. It invited Kwame Nkrumah (1909–72), recently returned from higher education in the United States, to serve as secretary. Nkrumah, more radical than most of the delegates, began by insti-

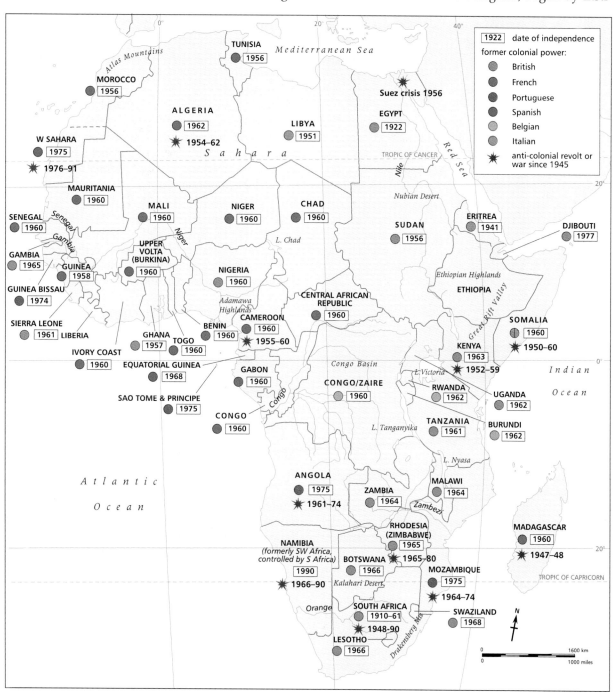

The decolonization of Africa Ethiopia had been colonized only briefly by Italy, Liberia had been established as an independent state, and Egypt had nominal independence from 1922, but most African states gained their independence after World War II, first those in North Africa, and then, following Ghana in 1957, those of Sub-Saharan Africa. Each colonial power had its own pattern for granting independence. The British and French hoped to establish amicable relations, generally, while the Portuguese and Belgians left more bitterly.

Ghana's independence. Prime minister (later president) Kwame Nkrumah waves to a celebrating crowd as the Gold Coast colony becomes the newly independent country of Ghana on March 6, 1957. Although Nkrumah made much of the release from British rule, shouting "Freedom! Freedom! Freedom!"in speeches, he formed a one-party state in 1964, and his regime was ended by a military coup in 1966 during his absence on a trip to China.

gating riots and then splintered the organization by founding the more militant Convention People's Party in 1949 and organizing a general strike in 1950. Jailed, Nkrumah was released when he won elected office in 1951. He entered into continuing negotiations with the British until independence was won in 1957. Always a pan-Africanist, Nkrumah in 1958 convened the All-Africa People's Conference at Accra, transferring the geographical locus of the movement to Africa, and inspiring national leaders throughout the continent.

In terms of education, resources, and political mobilization, Nigeria was as prepared for independence as Ghana; with 42 million people in 1960, it was the most populous country in Africa, seven times Ghana's size. Its borders, like those of most African nations, had been drawn rather arbitrarily by its colonizers, yoking together unrelated, and often hostile, groups within the same country and separating related and often congenial groups by new international boundaries. Nigeria was composed of three distinct regions: the Muslim majority in the more desertlike north; the Yoruba-controlled southwest; and the Ibo-dominated southeast. Creating a federal constitution that could harness these regions into a single nation delayed Nigeria's independence from Britain to 1960. (The fit was imperfect and civil war broke out in 1967.)

Despite the relatively high educational levels of the leading Kikuyu and Luo ethnic groups, and their relatively high levels of politicization, Kenya's road to independence was blocked by a sizeable European settler community, which continued militantly to claim its privileges, especially its land holdings in the rich highlands area. Six years of armed revolt led to the deaths of thirty-two European civilians, fifty-three European soldiers, and 11,503 Africans until independence from Great Britain was finally achieved in 1963.

THE FRENCH COLONIES

In contrast to the British, who had always thought of their African subjects as "other," different from themselves (compare Spotlight, p. 412), the French proposed to assimilate Africans into the culture and politics of France. In 1956, France turned over local self-government to its colonies in West and Equatorial Africa, but kept external affairs in its own hands. In 1958, it offered each of its colonies the choice between complete independence, with neither ties to nor assistance from France, and more limited internal autonomy in a French-controlled federation. At first, only Guinea opted for independence, but by 1960, all but French Somaliland declared for independence.

Strong ties still continue between France and many of its former African colonies. The French reserve some rights of military intervention, and the former colonies seem to feel free to invoke such intervention as in Chad, where the French maintain a military presence, and in the Central African Republic, where French assistance was requested for overthrowing an unpopular dictator. Many African currencies are tied to the French franc through agreements that give France power over African central banks and financial policies. The number of French expatriates in high-ranking African governmental positions remains significant. In 1986, Côte d'Ivoire (the Ivory Coast) contained three times more French nationals than it had at the height of the colonial era. Through the Yaoundé Convention of 1963, extended by the Lomé Convention of 1975, France's former colonies receive preferential trading rights within the European Union. Some critics see the relationship as neo-colonial, especially in such countries as Côte d'Ivoire under Felix Houphouet-Boigny (1905–93), the head of state from independence in 1960 until his death.

THE BELGIAN COLONIES

Independence for the Belgian Congo, which renamed itself Zaire, was not planned and triggered catastrophe. As neighboring countries moved towards independence, Congolese nationalists began to agitate as well. Rioting broke out. Belgium, which had done little to prepare the way for independence, envisioning it at least thirty years away, suddenly decided in 1959 to depart in the next year, leaving the country in chaos that soon descended into civil war. Zaire had virtually no graduates of institutes of higher education and no administrative cadres trained to administer a modern nation. The Belgian government had been one of the most cruel and exploitative, and at the independence ceremony transferring power from Belgium to Zaire, June 30, 1960, the new prime minister, Patrice Lumumba (1925–61), revealed the extent of Zairean bitterness:

> We are no longer your monkeys. … We have known the back-breaking works exacted from us in exchange for salaries which permit us neither to eat enough to satisfy our hunger, nor to dress and lodge ourselves decently, nor to raise our children as the beloved creatures they are.
>
> We have known the mockery, the insults, the blows submitted to morning, noon, and night because we were *nègres* [blacks]. We have known that our lands were despoiled in the name of supposedly legal text which in reality recognized only the right of the stronger. … And, finally, who will forget the hangings or the firing squads where so many of our brothers perished, or the cells into which were brutally thrown those who escaped the soldiers' bullets—the soldier whom the colonialists made the instruments of their domination?
> (Andrea and Overfield, pp. 507–8)

The two present-day countries of Rwanda and Burundi were administered as the single territory of Ruanda-Urundi by Belgium under a League of Nations Mandate and then under United Nations Trusteeship. During Belgian rule, Ruanda-Urundi was dominated by the ethnic Tutsi minority (about 15 percent of the population). After independence in 1962, and separate statehood for each country,

Aerial view of rioting in Leopoldville, Belgian Congo, January 6, 1959. The shot shows Congolese streaming through the streets, pillaging and burning the Portuguese shops in the village. Riots raged for two days in the Congo capital, leaving thiry-five dead. Many more Congolese and Europeans were injured in the conflict, which began when Abakos, members of the first Congo political party, gathered and demanded to hear the report of the Congolese burgomaster, Arthur Pinzi, after his return from Belgium.

rivalries and tensions between Tutsi and Hutu peoples became more intense and finally broke out in bitter civil war in 1993.

THE PORTUGUESE COLONIES

At least the Belgians left of their own accord. Portugal, ruled at home by a dictator, was not about to give up control of its large overseas colonies of Angola and Mozambique. It governed harshly, with repressive labor policies that forced some 65,000 to 100,000 Mozambiquans to travel each year to work in the mines of South Africa's Rand. Each person had to keep an identification passbook at all times. The press was rigidly censored. The police were ruthless. Most of all, Portugal, alone among the European colonizers, believed that its own future greatness depended on its continuing control over African colonies. Supported by South Africa, Portugal fought fiercely against guerrilla freedom fighters. Troops were dispatched from the USSR and Cuba to aid the guerrillas, and the struggle became thoroughly internationalized. In 1974, however, a domestic revolution at home overthrew Portugal's dictatorship, and a year later Portugal freed its colonies.

SOUTHERN RHODESIA

White southern Rhodesians refused to grant equality to blacks, though that was the condition Britain demanded before granting the country's independence. Instead, southern Rhodesia, under white control, declared its own independence unilaterally in 1965. United Nations and bilateral sanctions, adopted to force the country to reconsider, were not seriously implemented, and were in any case easily avoided through collusion with neighboring Portuguese Mozambique and Angola, and white-dominated South Africa. When the Portuguese departed, however, southern Rhodesia reconsidered its opportunities and agreed to majority, black rule in 1977. In 1980 the country was granted its independence and renamed Zimbabwe for the eleventh- to fifteenth-century people who had built cities and developed crafts in the region.

SOUTH AFRICA

After 1980, South Africa remained the only white-ruled country south of the Sahara. South Africa's whites—some 8 million out of a total population of

Seaside segregation. South African apartheid manifests itself on a beach in Durban, in 1985. The sign, written in English and Afrikaans, proclaims that the beach "is reserved for the sole use of the members of the white race group." Apartheid (Afrikaans for "apartness"), the policy of separate development and segregation of the races of South Africa, was supported and encouraged by the Nationalist Party when it came to power in 1948. With the African National Congress in power in South Africa, the country is emerging from the constraints of its racial policies and building a more united nation.

almost 40 million in 1990—had come to view themselves as Africans. The first major group, settlers from the Netherlands called Afrikaners or Boers, were pushed by later immigrants from Britain into a "great trek" north of the Orange River. The South Africans of British descent defeated the Boers in three years of warfare, 1899–1902, but the two groups finally came together to form the Union of South Africa in 1910, and they adopted the Afrikaners' harsher policies toward the black majority. Wages and conditions in the European mines were so abysmal that Africans would not work them. Chinese contract laborers were imported. The 1913 Native Land Acts restricted African residence and purchase of land to only 13 percent of the surface of the country, effectively forcing black Africans into service as landless laborers in white-controlled farming and industry. The labor market had two impermeable tiers, the top with better conditions and pay for whites, the lower for blacks. Nonwhites had no political rights.

Still more restrictive laws after 1948 established **apartheid** (segregation of the races). Blacks working in the cities could not legally live there, but had to commute long distances each day from black residential areas or stay in dormitory settings, leaving their families behind in the village areas.

Black African frustration, resentment, and anger at first expressed itself principally through independent Ethiopian Churches as early as the 1870s and 1880s. The African National Congress (ANC), formed in 1913, grew steadily over several decades as a constitutional party of protest. As other African nations began to win independence, Europeans urged South Africa to liberalize its racial policies. British Prime Minister Harold Macmillan made this point at Cape Town in February 1960: "The wind of change is blowing through the continent, and whether we like it or not this growth of national consciousness is a political fact, and our national policies must take account of it" (Oliver and Atmore, p. 273).

But the government of South Africa stubbornly resisted the "wind of change." It confronted unarmed political protest in March 1960 at Sharpeville with a massacre in which sixty-nine were killed and many were wounded. The African National Congress now shifted to strikes and armed protest, although limiting itself to sabotage of property and renouncing attacks on people. The South African government crackdown sentenced ANC leader Nelson Mandela (b. 1918), a 39-year-old lawyer, to life imprisonment and continued its apartheid policies.

𝒩ELSON MANDELA'S SPEECH TO THE COURT AT THE RIVONIA TRIAL, 1964

The African people were not part of the Government and did not make the laws by which they were governed. We believed in the words of the Universal Declaration of Human Rights, that "the will of the people shall be the basis of authority of the Government". ... The ANC refused to dissolve but instead went underground. ... All lawful modes of expressing opposition ... had been closed by legislation, and we were placed in a position in which we had either to accept a permanent state of inferiority or to defy the Government. ...

The Whites enjoy what may well be the highest standard of living in the world, whilst Africans live in poverty and misery. Forty percent of the Africans live in hopelessly overcrowded and, in some cases, drought-stricken Reserves, where soil erosion and the overworking of the soil makes it impossible for

them to live properly off the land. Thirty percent are laborers, labor tenants, and squatters on white farms and work and live under conditions similar to those of the serfs of the Middle Ages. The other 30 percent live in towns where they have developed economic and social habits which bring them closer in many respects to White standards. Yet most Africans, even in this group, are impoverished by low incomes and high cost of living ... the laws which are made by the Whites are designed to preserve this situation. ...

I have fought against white domination. I have cherished the ideal of a democratic and free society in which all persons live together in harmony and with equal opportunities. It is an ideal which I hope to live for and to achieve. But if needs be, it is an ideal for which I am prepared to die. (Andrea and Overfield, pp. 522–6)

The ANC and the general movement for racial justice were crippled but not killed off by this action. As Zambia and Zimbabwe, Angola and Mozambique won independence and majority rule, the attention of the African nations and of the community of nations focussed on South Africa as the last remaining center of white, minority rule. In addition, the newly independent, **front-line** nations sheltered members of the ANC and other movements for majority rule, including some dedicated to guerrilla warfare. Through the United Nations as well as through unilateral actions, many nations adopted sanctions against South Africa, restricting or stopping trade; "disinvesting" or withdrawing economic investments; and ending diplomatic, cultural, and sports exchanges. South Africa was to be treated as a pariah nation, cut off from intercourse with much of the rest of the world until it moved towards racial equality.

Enforcing the sanctions proved difficult. South Africa was a regional economic powerhouse, with significant bargaining chips of its own. The country has rich resources: 85 percent of the world's known platinum; two-thirds of its chromium; half its gold; half its manganese; and substantial proportions of its gem-quality diamonds. Its GNP, which had been 30 percent of all of sub-Saharan Africa's in 1960, increased to 35 percent by 1987. Geo-politically, 90 percent of Europe's oil passes by its waters. Many large and powerful nations saw sanctions as self-destructive and did not fully comply. The front-line states had tens of thousands of workers who subsisted only through jobs in the South African mines and industries; these states continued surreptitious trade and diplomatic relationships. In addition, to withstand guerrilla threats, South Africa increased its military personnel from 24,000 in 1960 to 97,000 in 1987, and its military expenditures from US$243 million to US$3,292 million, equal to about 50 percent of the military expenditures of all of black Africa combined (Sivard, p. 53).

Nevertheless, the sanctions did gradually exact their toll; isolation was painful, culturally and diplomatically as well as economically. The continuing expansion of independence among the African states brought black rule ever closer to South Africa's borders, and unrest within the country continued. In

A new and democratic dawn for South Africa. South African president Nelson Mandela and second deputy president F.W. de Klerk address a huge crowd in front of the Union Building in Pretoria, after the inauguration ceremony on May 10, 1994. Only a few years earlier it would have been inconceivable that the imprisoned Nelson Mandela could ever attain high office in a country so firmly wedded to the policies of apartheid.

First-time voters. Residents of Soweto, a black African township in Transvaal, linked by rail to Johannesburg, queue to vote for the first time in South Africa's elections on May 10, 1994. Soweto has frequently been a scene of unrest, most notably in 1976 when several hundred students, protesting against the teaching of Afrikaans in the township's schools, were mowed down by police.

1976 protests against government educational policies began in Soweto, a black township outside Pretoria, and led to nationwide riots, in which 600 people were killed. Some liberalization was granted: black labor unions were legalized, the prohibition of interracial sex was abolished, segregation in public transportation ended. Finally in 1990, the new government of President F.W. de Klerk (b. 1936) lifted its ban against the ANC and freed Nelson Mandela after twenty-seven years in prison. It repealed apartheid laws and began wary and difficult negotiations with the ANC for transition to majority rule. In 1993, de Klerk's National Party and the ANC under Mandela's leadership agreed on the principle of a new constitution.

In 1994 elections, open equally to all races on the principle of one person-one vote, the ANC won 62 percent of the vote. The National Party won 20 percent and the Inkatha (Freedom) Party 11 percent, mostly in the Zulu province, which was its ethnic stronghold. Despite extensive, murderous conflict between the ANC and the Inkatha Party, largely based on ethnic rivalry, the two began to negotiate

workable compromises on governance, as did the National Party. Since 1995 a national Truth Commission has been investigating abuses under apartheid in the past in an effort to clear the air for further inter-racial cooperation in the future.

EVALUATING THE LEGACY OF COLONIALISM

Colonialism brought ambiguous, paradoxical configurations to Africa. On the one hand it brought Africa into the world economy, opening markets, building infrastructure, and tapping mineral and industrial wealth. On the other hand it geared Africa's economy not to the needs of Africans, but rather to those of the economic and political leaders of the outside world, leaving much of Africa with an ecologically and economically vulnerable monoculture, and with mines, industry, and plantations in the hands of foreigners. African economies were, for example, oriented to European demands, while

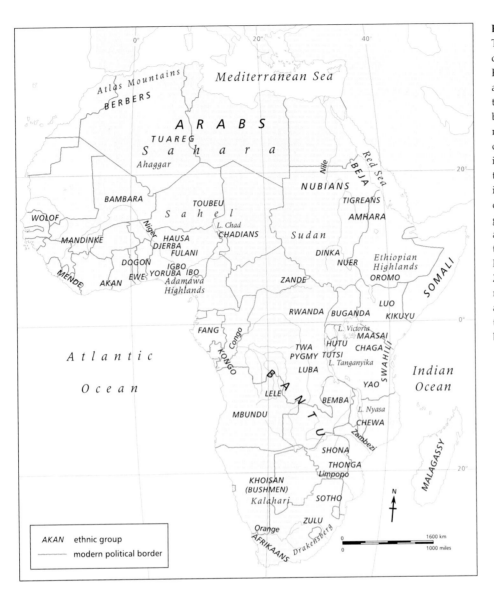

Ethnic groups in Africa
The insensitivity to local conditions of many European colonial administrators created a template of territorial boundaries which failed to match the underlying cultural map of Africa and its peoples. The results of this were seen in post-independence internecine conflicts between ethnic groups hemmed into artificial national territories: Congo (Zaire), Nigeria, Uganda, Angola, Zimbabwe, Sudan, and, more recently, Rwanda and Burundi are among those that have reaped this bitter harvest.

the commercial and transportation links within Africa itself were neglected. Critics such as Walter Rodney, Samir Amin, and Andre Gunder Frank wrote of Europe's intentional "development of underdevelopment" in Africa. Cities grew on the basis of government's administrative needs, drew rural people away from their roots and culture, and developed a "colonial mentality," which valued European urban forms over African patterns of settlement. The vast majority of the population continued in a subsistence economy of simple technology. A large number remained pastoralists.

The colonizers introduced and facilitated the spread of Christian missionaries and educators. (The improved transportation and communication systems facilitated the spread of Islam as well.) Many Africans joined the newly growing Ethiopian Church movement, which espoused Christianity without its European bias.

The official languages of administration and public life were also European. Since different, unrelated ethnic groups with different languages were brought together, "in a large majority of the forty-seven African countries, excluding the Mediterranean tier, no one language is spoken as the first language, or mother tongue, by a majority of the people" (Sklar, p. 100–1). So the European languages of the colonizers became the link languages, even though the vast majority of the population could not speak, read, or write these foreign, official languages. Among the elites, however, colonialism created the seeds of modern national identity and of pan-Africanism. Previous identifications had been far more localized.

INDEPENDENCE AND AFTER

Kwame Nkrumah had told the people of Ghana and of all Africa: "Seek first the political kingdom and everything else shall be added to you" (Salvatore, p. 56). Expectations at independence were commensurately high in 1957 as Ghana became the first newly independent nation in black Africa. Dozens of nations soon followed. But within a few years many of the expectations were dashed. Various observers blamed the problems on the colonial legacy, the continuing intervention by former colonial powers and the United States and USSR, the price system of the international marketplace, and the inability of Africans themselves to surmount the problems.

INTERNAL POLITICS

In one area, however, despite enormous conflict and civil war, the promise of independence was sustained: almost all of the African states maintained their national unity. National borders had been drawn arbitrarily and artificially by the European colonizers with little regard to African social and political groupings. Very diverse, and sometimes hostile, ethnic groups had been thrown together. In Nigeria, for example, Hausa, Yoruba, and Ibo peoples each constituted about 20 percent of the population, with other smaller groups making up the rest. In Kenya, the Kikuyu were about 20 percent of the population; Luo, Luhya, Kelenjin, and Kamba each 10–15 percent, with an admixture of Asians, Arabs, and Europeans completing the demographic picture. Uganda included such diverse groups as the Buganda, Langi, Acholi, and Lugbara ethnic groups of the south and west, with Nilotic ethnic groups stronger in the north, and a substantial community of South Asians, mostly in the cities. In Zaire, the main groups were the Kongo, the Luba, the Mongo, and the Rwanda. In Senegal it was the Wolof, Serer, Peuhl, Diola, Toucouleur, and Mandingo; in Côte d'Ivoire, the Baule, Bete, Senufo, and Malinke. In light of the internal diversity of the states, the ability to retain unity was remarkable.

TRADITIONAL INSTITUTIONS AND NATIONAL GOVERNMENTS

In many countries, the state incorporated traditional ethnic and religious leaders into the administration in order to encourage their loyalty to the new institution. The participation of tribal chieftains, at least informally, was often critical. In the areas near the Sahara, where Islam is a very powerful religious presence, the support of the organizations of pious men, *sufis,* became important to the cohesion of the state, in patterns we have explored for earlier times and other places in Chapter 11. The political scientist Conor Cruise O'Brien describes the importance of a *sufi* lodge in Senegal both to the welfare of its inhabitants and to governmental stability:

> The lodge is sited at the tomb of a revered saint, and apart from pious pilgrimage, it exists for the task of sacred instruction. But the social purposes of the *zawiya* are wonderfully varied, a true functionalist's utopia; an inn to accommodate the pious traveller, a school to instruct the faithful, a court to arbitrate differences sacred or profane, a market place and farm to provide for the material sustenance of the believers, a miniature welfare state for the distribution of alms, as well as a church and a final resting place for the bones of the devout. The conventional label of lodge seems inadequate to cover such a social range which, if anything, brings to mind the glories of the medieval Christian monastery. In political terms the *zawiya* can accommodate to hard times, to a surrounding anarchy or civil war, by a self-encapsulating autarchy; all the tasks of government are after all already included within its purposes. Under a secure state authority the *zawiya* can develop an intermediary political role and convert the faithful into a negotiable clientele. The sacredly sanctioned hierarchy of the sufi *zawiya* then becomes a parallel hierarchy of government, valuable to state authority as resting on a true popular devotion. In multiparty situations one can even see the *zawiya* converted to the political purposes of a party cell. (cited in Sklar, pp. 92–3)

In some cases, however, unity was preserved only by the use of military force in civil wars. The revolt and secession of the Ibo peoples in the Biafra region of Nigeria, Africa's largest country demographically, precipitated 1 million deaths between 1967 and 1970 in one of the first, and worst, of these civil wars. Yet, in the long run, the decision to re-align Nigeria into twelve states conforming more closely to ethnic borders, and the relatively compassionate terms of the peace settlement, ultimately helped to foster national unity.

In the sprawling Sudan, the largest country in Africa geographically, ethnic, regional, and religious conflicts between the more Arabic, Islamic north, and the more Nilotic, Christian and **animist** south were, again, built into the fabric of the artificially created nation. The south began guerrilla warfare in 1961, and this continued and grew into a civil war that lasted until 1972. Armed conflict has re-appeared intermittently thereafter and continues until today. Neighboring Chad had very similar ethnic, religious, and linguistic divisions, but here the southern, black, Christian and animist factions have thus far proved more powerful than the northern, more Islamic groups. External forces entered the combat, with Libya backing the northerners and France entering on the side of the south. The potential for further conflict remains.

In Uganda, the dominant Buganda and their king, the Kabaka, were attacked by coalitions of other ethnic groups in 1966. Continuing fighting in Uganda, especially after General Idi Amin was in power (1971–9), saw up to 300,000 people killed, and the entire community of Asian origin, mostly Indians, driven out of the country. In all these cases, however, national borders remained intact.

EXCEPTIONS: ALTERING BORDERS

In the Horn of Africa, the constituent units of Ethiopia—Eritrea, Tigre, and Ogaden—and neighboring Somalia fought for years. Here, a new state and new borders were created. Eritrea, which had been absorbed by Ethiopia in 1962, fought for its independence continuously, until achieving it in 1993. Tigreans also seek independence. Somalia fought against Ethiopia primarily for control of the Ogaden region. Intervention by Americans, Russians, Cubans, and others exacerbated the warfare throughout the 1970s and 1980s, which ended with the end of the Cold War. In 1988, a peace agreement was reached between Somalia and Ethiopia, but in 1991, Somalia dissolved into civil warfare so severe that the United Nations declared Somalia to be a country without a government. Armed forces of the United Nations and of the United States, attempting to alleviate famine and restore order, were drawn into the civil war, suffered casualties, and withdrew in 1994–5. Continuing fighting has spread as far as Zaire, destabilizing that country. In 1997 guerilla forces

Problems in dispensing aid. A US Marine restrains Somalis while supplies are unloaded at Mogadishu airport, Somalia. In recent years, agencies dispensing aid have not always been given a cordial reception by the warring parties. The aid workers have not been exempted from war conditions. More than one aid worker has been killed, and others have been kidnapped and harassed. Often food and other supplies meant for distribution to the needy have been stolen by the truckload.

led by Laurent Kabila captured the capital, Kinshasa, overthrowing the dictatorship of Mobutu Sese Seko and renaming the country the Democratic Republic of Congo.

Both of the tiny, contiguous states of Rwanda and Burundi (see p. 721) have been wracked by conflict between the formerly dominant Tutsi people, and their former underlings, the Hutu. In both countries the Hutu have now become dominant, but only after brutal ethnic warfare has left some 750,000 people dead. Hundreds of thousands of refugees, fleeing to neighboring Zaire, have internationalized the conflict. Uganda, to the north has also entered the factional and ethnic fighting. This situation is still in flux. Resolution of the Hutu–Tutsi fighting has not been concluded.

African Independence

(The colonial power at the outbreak of World War I and, where appropriate, colonial names are shown in brackets)

1934 South Africa (Britain)

1936 Egypt (Britain)

1946 Réunion (France; now overseas department of France)

1951 Libya (Italy)

1956 Morocco (France); Sudan (Britain); Tunisia (France)

1957 Ghana (Britain, Gold Coast)

1958 Guinea (France)

1960 Benin (France, Dahomey); Burkina Faso (France, Upper Volta); Cameroon (French Cameroon); Central African Republic (French Equatorial Africa); Chad (French Equatorial Africa); Congo (French Equatorial Africa); Côte d'Ivoire (France); Gabon (French Equatorial Africa); Madagascar (France); Mali (French Sudan); Mauritania (France); Niger (France); Nigeria (Britain); Senegal (French West Africa); Somalia (British Somaliland/Italian Somaliland); Togo (Germany, Togoland); Congo (Belgian Congo, Zaire)

1961 Sierra Leone (Britain); Tanzania (Germany, Tanganyika)

1962 Algeria (France); Burundi (German East Africa); Rwanda (German East Africa); Uganda (British East African Protectorate)

1963 Kenya (British East African Protectorate); Tanzania (Britain, Zanzibar)

1964 Malawi (British Central African Protectorate/Nyasaland); Zambia (Britain, Northern Rhodesia)

1965 Gambia (Britain)

1966 Botswana (Britain, Bechuanaland); Lesotho (Britain)

1968 Equatorial Guinea (Spain); Mauritius (Britain); Swaziland (Britain)

1974 Guinea-Bissau (Portuguese Guinea)

1975 Angola (Portugal); Cape Verde (Portuguese Guinea); Comoros (France); Mozambique (Portugal); São Tomé and Principe (Portugal); Western Sahara (Spain; unresolved)

1977 Djibouti (French Somaliland)

1980 Zimbabwe (Britain, Southern Rhodesia)

1990 Namibia (Germany)

REFUGEES

Ethnic, religious, and regional strife, combined with poverty and dictatorship, and inflamed by foreign intervention has encouraged persecution and flight in many regions of Africa. In 1979 Africa held 2 million refugees; in 1989, 4 million; in 1996, 5 million, with Congo (Zaire) alone holding more than a million, and Guinea and Tanzania sheltering more than a half million each.

DICTATORSHIP AND CORRUPTION

Throughout Africa the search for an appropriate form of government, and for appropriate government leaders, has been tortuous. Consider Ghana. Kwame Nkrumah, the leader of Ghana's independence struggle and its first prime minister in 1957 and first President in 1960, declared Ghana a one-party state in 1964. By 1966, Nkrumah was considered so dictatorial that the Ghanaian military overthrew him in a coup while he was out of the country. Despite his downfall, many Ghanaians continue to revere Nkrumah's memory for his dedication and his early successes.

Following the example of Ghana, one-party states, and coups launched to displace them, began to characterize African politics. By about 1980, some forty African states were ruled by military or quasi-military administrations. In the Central African Republic, Jean-Bédel Bokassa (b. 1921) spent $22 million, one quarter of his nation's annual revenues, in a ceremony installing himself as emperor. Later, in 1979, when he was deposed, Bokassa was convicted of numerous murders of soldiers, civilians, and students.

Although some states, like Malawi, Mali, and Zambia, had moved toward more fully democratic government by the mid-1990s, most of Africa had not. Blaine Harden, the *Washington Post* bureau chief in sub-Saharan Africa, reported a total of at least seventy coups in sub-Saharan Africa between 1957 and 1990, with six in Nigeria and five each in Ghana and Benin. His book *Africa: Dispatches from a Fragile Continent* decries the rise to power of "Big Men" as dictators in many African states, focusing on Mobutu Sese Seko of Congo, Samuel Doe of Liberia, and Daniel arap Moi of Kenya. He sees them as power-hungry, ruthless, greedy, and corrupt. He calls Mobutu's government, especially, a "kleptocracy," and estimates Mobutu's personal wealth from the sale of Congo's assets at $5 billion.

Harden implicates many foreign governments in supporting these "Big Men." He accuses especially the USA of helping to create Mobutu's power in Congo and sustaining Doe until he was killed in a civil war in 1990. In choosing its clients in the Cold War, America was creating monsters.

ECONOMIC ISSUES

Africa's economic record since independence has been as discouraging as its politics to which it is related. Again, there are numerous targets at which to point fingers—Africa's political leadership, Africa's choices of economic policy, the international economic system, and foreign intervention. We have already touched on the corruption, greed, and theft among some of Africa's individual leaders.

In the first years after independence, in many African countries, capitalism was widely condemned for its association with the colonial rulers and as a philosophy that stressed personal gain, seen as greed, rather than community welfare (compare Chapters 13 and 16 for similar views elsewhere and earlier). A variety of socialist alternatives were favored, including: local, collective ownership; large-scale collectivization; state ownership; and state planning. President Nyerere of Tanzania chose the first two, linking them to African conditions, and called for the reconstruction of *ujamaa*, the village community:

> In the old days, the African had never aspired to the possession of personal wealth for the purpose of dominating any of his fellows. He had never had laborers or factory hands to do his work for him. But then came the foreign capitalists. ... Our first step, therefore, must be to re-educate ourselves; to regain our former attitude of mind. ... And in rejecting the capitalist attitude of mind which colonization brought into Africa, we must reject also the capitalist methods which go with it. One of these is individual ownership of land. (cited in Sigmund, rev. ed., p. 291)

Kwame Nkrumah of Ghana, in language reminiscent of Trotsky, stressed the need for state control to achieve

> a total mobilization of brain and manpower resources. What other countries have taken three hundred years to achieve, a once dependent territory must try to accomplish in a generation if it is to

survive. Unless it is, as it were, "jet-propelled," it will lag behind and thus risk everything for which it has fought. (cited in Sigmund, 1st ed., p. 186)

Such policies, no matter how congenial with the African past or promising for the future, did not lead to growth. "By 1980, the per capita output of foodstuffs had fallen by more than 20% below the 1960 level ... between 1965 and 1989 sub-Saharan Africa had registered a disappointing annual growth rate of 0.3%" (July, p. 481).

The most successful economy seemed to be that of Côte d'Ivoire, a country that vigorously promoted individual enterprise and participation in the global economy, especially through the production and sale of coffee and cocoa, and through links with French expertise. From 1965 to 1980 Côte d'Ivoire experienced a 6.8 percent annual growth rate. Then, in the 1980s, prices for coffee and cocoa plunged. In the decade 1980–90, Côte d'Ivoire's growth rate dropped to 0.5 percent. (*World Development Report 1992*, p. 220). Dependence on the volatile international market now crippled the economy.

Many African countries concentrated on producing just one or two major exports, almost always raw materials from agriculture or mining, which rendered them similarly vulnerable. In 1986, the total manufactured exports from all of sub-Saharan Africa were only $3.2 billion. The rapid jump in oil prices, the oil shocks of the 1970s which triggered a world economic slump, only added to the difficulties.

International debts multiplied. By the end of 1988 for sub-Saharan Africa these had reached nearly $135 billion, eighteen times the 1980 figure and equal to the region's total gross domestic product. By the early 1990s they had reached $180 billion. Foreign investors were frightened away. Private international investment had been $6 billion in 1980; in 1985 it registered a disinvestment of $1 billion. The combination of unstable international market prices, growing international debt, and disinvestment demonstrated Africa's economic dependency and vulnerability.

When the World Bank of the United Nations offered desperately needed investment capital, it demanded that borrowers adopt more market-oriented policies (as in Latin America, see p. 768). Such policies included a reduction or ending of subsidies in the domestic prices of basic commodities, the devaluation of inflated currencies, and the enforced schedules for repayment of debt. Greater domestic economic efficiency was also demanded, which often meant firing the excess workers who padded government employment roles. The World Bank wanted to end **statism**, government policies to control the economy so as to siphon off capital for the state and its own officials. The Bank's policies made sense on the yearly economic balance sheet, but they created great pain. Government employees lost their jobs; the price of subsidized food went up. Riots often followed these reforms, testing the political will of leaders, who, naturally enough, questioned the wisdom of the World Bank. Was the Bank simply a new form of colonial control, a new mechanism for telling Africans how to conduct their business so that Western businessmen could make greater profits?

Some countries preferred to withdraw from the world market economy, which they saw as neo-colonial, and to concentrate on internal development. The Lagos Plan of the Organization of African Unity, approved in 1980, had encouraged this route.

> Africa was to 1) utilize and mobilize its resources principally for its own development, and more precisely for the well-being of its populations, rather than for the foreign market; 2) expand industry and production for internal consumption and only secondarily for export; 3) rely on technologies of African origin or those which could be controlled by Africans; 4) recommend models and types of consumption suitable for the stage of development reached by African society and African culture; encourage inter-African trade by removing existing trade barriers and introducing preferential areas. (Salvatore, p. 67)

Despite the Lagos Plan, in the 1990s most of Africa, like most of the developing world, sought increasing participation in the world economy. At the same time, the World Bank was becoming less strict in the belt-tightening conditions it imposed, recognizing the need for governments to continue to provide certain fundamental services, such as education, medical assistance, and sometimes food subsidies, to their people.

ROOTS OF THE ECONOMIC PROBLEMS: AN ECONOMIC AND HISTORIOGRAPHIC DEBATE

Many observers found the roots of Africa's economic problems in its colonial legacy. Giampaolo Calchi-Novati, of the University of Pisa, blamed the

SPOTLIGHT
Refugees and Exiles

The wars and political instability of the twentieth century have forced millions of people to flee their homes as refugees. Earlier in the century, World Wars I and II triggered mass exoduses as people were driven from their homes by invading troops, or chose to flee battlefields. At the end of World War II, the United Nations established international and regional commissions to help settle the millions of displaced persons of the war. The Partition of India and Pakistan in 1947 created an estimated 12 million refugees, about half of them Muslims fleeing India, half Hindus and Sikhs fleeing East and West Pakistan (later Bangladesh) for India (see picture, p. 673). In 1948 and after, warfare between Israelis and Arabs created several hundred thousand Palestinian refugees. In the last decades of the century, the largest numbers of refugees, millions of them, have been from Africa.

Picture 1 shows one section of the 250,000 refugees from civil war in Rwanda crossing the border into Tanzania in 1994. They travel by foot and by bicycle, taking with them whatever personal possessions they can carry. In part, Africa's refugee problems remain so intractable because the political situation has not stabilized. Ethnic groups, such as the Hutu and Tutsi, continue to fight, and national governments attempt to consolidate their own borders and to encroach on others. The borders between Rwanda, Burundi, Zaire, Kenya, and Tanzania continue to witness

Picture 1 Rwandan refugees at Rusomo, Tanzania, May 1, 1994.

Picture 2 Eritrean refugee in Bethnal Green, London, 1995.

Picture 3 Wole Soyinka at UNESCO, Paris, October 16, 1986.

streams of refugees at the end of the twentieth century. The United Nations, individual nations, churches, and numerous voluntary associations such as Oxfam and Médecins sans Frontières (Doctors without Borders), have provided food, makeshift shelter, and medical treatment for these refugees, as they did earlier with others. The numbers and the suffering are, however, overwhelming.

Refugees move not only *en masse*, but also as individuals. Often an initial mass flight is followed by individuals seeking homes for themselves. **Picture 2** shows a woman from Eritrea now living in Bethnal Green, London. From the picture alone we cannot tell whether she thinks of herself as a refugee far from home, radically disoriented, and eager to return, or as a new immigrant beginning to make her way in a new setting, or as some mixed combination of both.

Picture 3 of Nigerian playwright Wole Soyinka celebrating his Nobel Prize for Literature in 1986 presents a very different face of refugee status.

Soyinka had fallen foul of the Nigerian government in 1967 and had been held in political detention for two years. In 1995 he was exiled from Nigeria and its highly corrupt administration. Soyinka is now a refugee living in the United States, although his specific location has not been disclosed for security reasons. Like many other refugees of conscience, and very much unlike the streams of refugees in picture 1, Soyinka's economic and social conditions may be excellent, but he, too, at least at present, cannot go "home."

lack of a capitalist class on the patterns of European capitalist colonialism, which had stunted the growth of African entrepreneurship:

> The ancient self-sufficiency of African society was lost forever. As the continent was opened up and transport improved, European products were able to penetrate into Africa, also at the expense of the newly born African industry. At the same time it spelled the end of any proto-capitalistic class already existing in the various African states since no local organization had the capacity to stand up to competition from the colonial power and from the companies. (cited in Salvatore, p. 57)

Few Africans had been educated in modern business, technology, and organization. Again, this was a product of the lack of educational systems introduced under colonial rule.

But some observers found deeper indigenous reasons for Africa's lagging economy. John Ravenhill of the University of Sydney wrote: "Beyond a handful of countries like Kenya and Nigeria which have nascent capitalist classes, the prospects for successful capitalist development in Africa are … remote" (p. 28). Ravenhill's observation, that capitalism was necessary to development but that Africa lacked a capitalist class, was only the obverse of Nyerere's argument against capitalism,

A giant AIDS poster in Lusaka, Zambia, where the disease is rife. AIDS has been a severe problem in many African countries, with rates of infection up to 25 percent of the adult, sexually active population. It is an enormous task to educate people about the dangers of unprotected sex.

cited above (p. 730). Interestingly Ravenhill separated Africa's largest country, Nigeria, from the rest. He felt that a capitalist class was gradually emerging in Nigeria.

D.K. Fieldhouse, of Cambridge University, put the problem in more critical terms: "African governments have never, despite their protestations, been primarily concerned with economic growth but rather with maintenance of political power and the distribution of wealth to themselves and their supporters" (p. 94).

Despite the dismal economic results, the population of sub-Saharan Africa continued to grow, and at a rising rate of increase: 2.7 percent a year, 1965–80, and 3.1 percent a year in 1980–90. With the Middle East and North Africa, these were the highest rates in the world (*World Development Report 1992*, p. 269). In 1990 46 percent of the population had not yet reached fifteen years of age (*WDR 1992*, p. 269). Growth was fastest in the urban enclaves—the cities had held 14 percent of the population in 1965 but 29 percent in 1990; the rate of growth was 5.9 percent (*WDR 1992*). Yet black Africa had the lowest life expectancy—fifty years at birth—of any major region.

The status of women, increasingly seen as a barometer of development, continued low, although some steps were made to improve it. Female literacy was 44 percent, compared with a male literacy rate of 35 percent. While other areas of the world cut their fertility rates dramatically—China, for example, from 6.4 in 1965 to 2.5 in 1990, and India from 6.2 to 4.0—sub-Saharan Africa barely changed at all, dropping only from 6.6 to 6.5 over the quarter century (*WDR 1992*, p. 270–71). Infant mortality declined in the same period, from 157 per 1000 live births to 94 in 1994 (Sivard, p. 53), but was still the highest in the world. In 1994, Africa had only one physician for 11,788 people (*WDR 1992*, p. 273), four times the ratio in the next worst-off area, South Asia. (Sivard, p. 50–53).

By the late 1980s, and with increasing virulence into the 1990s, Africa was suffering the greatest toll of victims of AIDS of any region on earth. Unlike the United States, where the disease was transmitted primarily through homosexual contact and through the sharing of infected needles in the use of drugs, in Africa AIDS was transmitted primarily through heterosexual contact. In several countries, infection rates as high as 25 percent of the population were common. By the mid-1990s Africa had about two-thirds of all the world's people recorded as HIV positive and suffered 75 percent of the AIDS-related deaths. The full consequences of this widespread plague in Africa are not yet known. Although some medical treatments to combat AIDS were being discovered in the wealthier countries, their cost was still far too high for widespread use in Africa.

ECONOMIC SOLUTIONS?

What might be a way out of the economic morass? Both inside and outside Africa, answers were being suggested. Many focused on appropriate scale technology, thinking small and locally, avoiding government show projects, and relying upon manual laborers. Such viewpoints, often drawing their inspiration from E.F. Schumacher's classic text on small-scale development economics, *Small Is Beautiful*, pointed out the failures of large-scale projects designed overseas and unsuited to Africa's human and natural environment. They gave many examples. European cattle-raising in the 1890s inadvertently introduced the rinderpest plague, which killed off a sizeable proportion of African cattle; the mould-board plow, again introduced from Europe, led to severe soil erosion; agriculture based on machinery, in a region without mechanical experience, led to broken-down tractors; large-scale irrigation projects often led to soil erosion; introduction of cash crops led to excessive reliance on monoculture, which was vulnerable to world price fluctuations; and cultivation that extended into unsuitable soils soon depleted them. Franke and Chasin, in their book *Seeds of Famine*, blame the post-1970 collapse of the ecology of the arid Sahel region adjoining the Sahara Desert on the European introduction of peanut monoculture into the Sahelian fringes, forcing animal grazing ever closer to the desert, and ultimately destroying the soil's natural fertility.

Instead, much new thought focussed on small, local, more easily monitored projects, such as new forms of oil presses introduced into Ghana and Tanzania, windmills, solar energy, more efficient cook stoves, sheet metal water tanks, and agroforestry, which integrates forest products in the overhead canopy with ground crops below. All these programs, however, call for step-by-step incremental change, bringing local people and resources into the development process. They reject the concept of large-scale, leap-frog development. The debates over the proper plan, or mix of plans, will continue.

CULTURAL LIFE

In cultural terms, Africa did not forget its own heritage in music, art, and architecture. Even during the high tide of colonialism, African forms remained potent, even influencing the colonizing countries, as the art of Picasso, Matisse, Brancusi, and others testifies (see p. 596). But indigenous traditions were deeply threatened and in large part destroyed by Western formal education administered through foreign governments and churches, and by the foreign cultural values that reigned supreme, especially in the newly constructed urban centers of trade and rule. Nigerian geographer Akin Mabogunje argues in *Urbanization in Nigeria* that the physical forms of these cities and the European-designed plantations and industrial and mining centers, with their European architecture, gridiron street plans, and barracks structures for African workers, destroyed the traditional housing and family patterns of Africans who came to live and work there.

In part, the traditional forms endured because they were so deeply a part of Africa: the legends and history of the *griot*; the music of the stringed *mbira* and the various forms of drumming; the

Léopold Sédar Senghor, Senegal's poet-statesman. He retired from the presidency in 1980, after serving in that capacity for twenty years. He had been a member of the French Constituent Assembly in 1945, and the deputy for Senegal in the French National Assembly for ten years from 1948. He has been widely respected for his wise leadership, and in addition, has won several literary awards for his poetry.

"PRAYER TO MASKS"

Senghor's poem "Prayer to Masks," written after World War II, and looking forward to independence, addresses the masks that represent his, and Africa's, ancestors, and prays that their ancient wisdom and rhythms may be able to repair the destruction the world has suffered. War-devastated Europe is in need of the wisdom and the rhythm of Africa.

Prayer to Masks

Masks! Masks!
Black mask red mask, you white-and-black
   masks
Masks of the four points from which the Spirit
   blows
In silence I salute you!
Nor you the least, the Lion-headed Ancestor
You guard this place forbidden to all laughter of
   women, to all smiles that fade
You distil this air of eternity in which I breathe
   the air of my Fathers.
Masks of unmasked faces, stripped of the marks
   of illness and the lines of age

You who have fashioned this portrait, this my
   face bent over the altar of white paper
In your own image, hear me!
The Africa of the empires is dying, see, the agony
   of a pitiful princess
And Europe too where we are joined by the
   navel.
Fix your unchanging eyes upon your children,
   who are given orders
Who give away their lives like the poor their last
   clothes.
Let us report present at the rebirth of the World
Like the yeast which white flour needs.
For who would teach rhythm to a dead world of
   machines and guns?
Who would give the cry of joy to wake the dead
   and the bereaved at dawn?
Say, who would give back the memory of life to
   the man whose hopes are smashed?
They call us men of coffee cotton oil
They call us men of death.
We are the men of the dance, whose feet draw
   new strength pounding the hardened earth.

           (cited in Okpewho, p. 134)

dances of Africa; the grace and function of the residential compound and its several huts for different family members and for storage. These forms endured more strongly in the countryside than in the city. But in the 1930s these traditions began to assert themselves among the Western-educated elites as well. The movement for **Negritude,** was born among Africans resident in Europe itself. Negritude was defined by Léopold Sédar Senghor (b. 1906), one of its principal exponents, as "the whole complex of civilized values—cultural, economic, social, and political—which characterize the black peoples, or, more precisely, the Negro-African world" (cited in Sigmund, rev. ed., p. 249).

The movement was strongest in French-speaking Africa, where cultural assimilation was taken more seriously than in the more politically oriented British areas. Wole Soyinka (b. 1934), Nobel Prize winning playwright from Nigeria (see p. 733), has described Negritude as "a revolt against the successful assimilative strategy of French and Portuguese colonialism" and it "held undisputed sway in the formulation of creative sensibilities for the next two decades" even in Anglophone Africa (cited in Boahen, p. 564). The leading exponents of the worldwide movement, Léopold Sédar Senghor (b. 1906) of Senegal, Aimé Cesaire (b. 1913) of Martinique in the French-speaking West Indies, and Léon Damas of French Guiana, asserted the link between cultural and political nationalism. Indeed, Senghor, author and editor of several volumes of poetry and one of the founders, with Alioune Diop, in 1947, of the seminal literary journal *Présence Africaine* (Oliver and Atmore, p. 231), was also the leader of the independence movement in Senegal and later (1960–80) its first president.

Some African critics complained that Negritude glossed over class struggle and formal politics, but the movement raised African consciousness in other, perhaps equally fundamental ways.

African art and music have emphasized continuity of tradition rather than innovation, and vernacular products of the group rather than new forms of the individual artist. Artists worked within received canons rather than creating new ones, so African art tends to recreate the wooden, bronze, and terracotta sculpture and reliefs; the baskets and woven containers; the decorated calabashes and gourds; and the ivory, stone, and beaded jewellery of tradition. Paradoxically, leading Western artists, like Picasso (see p. 596), considered African traditional art "modern." Some innovation, nevertheless, linked past and present, as in the Oshogbo artists of Nigeria, who introduced new techniques and materials, including aluminum, to carry out traditional themes.

African music and dance of thousands of years ago are represented in archaeological finds of bells and parts of musical instruments and in rock paintings in the Sahara. Technology has meant that instruments and the styles have spread and interacted throughout Africa more rapidly in modern times. Gerhard Kubik, of the University of Vienna, traces the spread of the *likembe*, now one of Africa's most popular and widely used instruments. Invented in Zaire, it was carried upriver by porters and colonial servants in the late nineteenth century, spreading to non-Bantu areas. By the beginning of

An *mbira,* or thumb piano, from the Kalibar tribe in Nigeria. This particular example was collected by the explorer Mary Kingsley in the 1880s. The spread of this type of musical instrument, which has a different name in every culture where it is found, has been phenomenal. Another name for this instrument, in Zaire, is *likembe*.

MAJOR AFRICAN POLITICIANS

Jomo Kenyatta (1894–1978) The first president of Kenya from 1964 until his death. In London in 1931, he helped Kwame Nkrumah found the Pan-African Congress. Returning to Kenya in 1946, he was elected president of the Kenya African Union, but was tried and imprisoned, later exiled, by the British in 1953 on suspicion of masterminding the Mau Mau rising in 1952. As the first president of Kenya, he developed the, albeit temporary, stability and prosperity of his country.

Kwame Nkrumah (1909–72) Ghanaian statesman, prime minister (1957–60), and president (1960–6). Called "the Gandhi of Africa," Nkrumah fought against white domination and for pan-African solidarity, and presided over the independence of Ghana (formerly, Gold Coast).

Nelson Mandela (b. 1918) Imprisoned in 1964 as an organizer of the then proscribed African National Congress, he became a symbol for the worldwide anti-apartheid movement. Released from prison in 1990, he was elected, unopposed, in 1991 to the presidency of the ANC and was later sworn in as South Africa's first post-apartheid president in May 1994.

Jean-Bédel Bokassa (1921–96) President of the Central African Republic (1966–79) and self-proclaimed emperor. Bokassa's regime was characterized by arbitrary state violence and cruelty, and a lavish life-style his impoverished nation could ill afford.

Julius Nyerere (1922–) Tanzanian statesman and president (1962–85). After studying at Edinburgh, he reorganized the nationalists into the Tanganyika African National Union (1954) and became president on independence (1962). He united Zanzibar with the country and led (the renamed) Tanzania—with little success—on a path of socialism.

Idi Amin (1925–) In charge of the armed forces, Amin staged a coup against prime minister Milton Obote in 1971 and established a military dictatorship. Asians and many Israelis were expelled, and foreign-owned businesses and land were seized. He was ousted after attempting to annex part of Tanzania and fled to exile.

the twentieth century it had been adopted in Uganda. By the 1950s it had also spread even to the !Kung of southeastern Angola.

African music and dance had spread with slavery to the Western hemisphere, especially to Latin America, where the group life of the slaves remained more intact than in the United States, partly because slavery and the slave trade continued so much longer there. Interaction between African music and dance and that of the diaspora continue actively today. The music of the Congo (Zaire), for example, influences, especially, the music of the West Indies and Brazil, and vice versa, and it has become popular in Europe and the United States as well. New beats, syncopations, and even musical instruments flow freely throughout Africa and through the diaspora. Reggae flourishes everywhere as a medium of political protest as well as popular dance and artistic creativity, from Bob Marley in the West Indies to Alpha Blondy in West Africa. Ballets Africains, the national dance troup of Guinea, performs throughout the world.

When Paul Simon, the American pop singer, traveled to South Africa in 1985 to work and perform with black musicians there, some criticized his going into that country while apartheid was still in effect. Simon argued, however, that infusing more mainstream American popular music with that of such groups as Tao Ea Matsekha, General M.D. Shirinda and the Gaza Sisters, the Boyoyo Boys Band, Ladysmith Black Mambazo and the Soweto Rhythm Section, and such individual artists as Youssou N'dour, Joseph Shabala, and Chikapa "Ray" Phiri, would help all the musicians and would invigorate all international popular music. Simon's *Graceland* album, 1986, demonstrated the wisdom of his choice, and his 1990 *Rhythm of the Saints*, which added Brazilian diaspora influences, pushed the fusion further. Modern technology transports the sounds, the sights, and the performers themselves back and forth across the oceans.

CINEMA

Cinema production began in Africa as part of the colonial enterprise. In 1935 Britain established in Tanganyika (later Tanzania) the Bantu Educational Cinema Experiment, which later grew into the Colonial Film Unit, to spread British conceptions of appropriate colonial life to their African subjects. The Belgians established a Film and Photo Bureau in the Congo in 1947, and Catholic missions established their own film production centers for propagating religious doctrines. Almost all these activities shut down after independence.

More recently, however, France established a Consortium Audio-visuel International in the 1960s to help its former colonies develop their own films, and they have been a great success. The distinguished Senegalese social-realist novelist Ousmane Sembene (b. 1923) helped lead the way. For more than a quarter century he has told stories of modern Africa through a series of films from *La Noire de …* (1966) to *Guelowaar* (1993). The film festival in Ouagadougou, Burkina Faso, has become one of the most important annual cultural events of today's Africa. Of special interest to historians, Dani Kouyate of Burkina Faso has produced *Keita: the Heritage of a Griot*, which depicts an urban schoolboy suddenly confronted by the arrival from the countryside of a distant relative, a *griot* or traditional custodian of folk history. Through his stories, the *griot* shows the young boy that historical knowledge has more dimensions and interpretations than are taught in school. The movie theaters of Africa continue to screen more films from the United States and India than indigenous productions, bringing many charges of cultural imperialism, an issue in itself, but the African film industry continues to grow and to make its own significant contribution to local, and international, culture.

LITERATURE

African literature has also flourished in poetry, essays, plays, and novels. Frequently, this creativity blends traditional African rhythms in word and song mixed with a profound sexuality, confusion over the loss of an old identity and the search for a new, and despair over the bitter politics of both colonial and post-colonial life. Consider this poem of Negritude from Senghor's student days in Paris. He tells of his homesickness for Africa, evoked by the vision of a beautiful black woman:

Relentlessly She Drives Me

[For two balafongs]
Relentlessly she drives me through the thickets of
    Time.
My black blood hounds me through the crowd to the
    clearing where white night sleeps.
Sometimes I turn round in the street and see again
    the palm tree smiling under the breeze.
Her voice brushes me like the soft lisping sweep of a
    wing and I say

"Yes it is Signare!" I have seen the sun set in the blue
    eyes of a fair negress.
At Sèvres-Babylon or Balangar, amber and gongo,
    her scent was near and spoke to me.
Yesterday in church at the Angelus, her eyes shone
    like candles burnishing
Her skin with bronze. My God, my God, why do
    you tear my pagan senses shrieking out of me?
I cannot sing your plain chant that has no swing to
    it, I cannot dance it.
Sometimes a cloud, a butterfly, raindrops on my
    boredom's window pane.
Relentlessly she drives me across the great spaces of
    Time.
My black blood hounds me, to the solitary heart of
    the night.

(cited in Okpewho, p. 52)

For John Pepper Clark of Nigeria, dance and the dancer evoke the magic and power of traditional Africa, from which he, as an intellectual trained in European ways, a "lead-tether'd scribe," may be irrevocably cut off:

Agbor Dancer

See her caught in the throb of a drum
Tippling from hide-brimmed stem
Down lineal veins to ancestral core
Opening out in her supple tan
Limbs like fresh foliage in the sun.

See how entangled in the magic
Maze of music
In trance she treads the intricate
Pattern rippling crest after crest
To meet the green clouds of the forest.

Tremulous beats wake trenchant
In her heart a descant
Tingling quick to her finger tips
And toes virginal habits long
Too atrophied for pen or tongue.

Could I, early sequester'd from my tribe,
Free a lead-tether'd scribe
I should answer her communal call
Lose myself in her warm caress
Intervolving earth, sky and flesh.

(cited in Okpewho, p. 66)

Finally Dennis Brutus, of South Africa, condemns the masters of apartheid in his country. He reflects that all people, we ourselves, may be capable of wishing "arbitrary exercise of power," but not on the obscene scale enforced by the masters of apartheid:

Their Behaviour

Their guilt
is not so different from ours:
—who has not joyed in the arbitrary exercise of
     power
or grasped for himself what might have been
     another's
and who has not used superior force in the moment
     when he could,
(and who of us has not been tempted to these
     things?)—
so, in their guilt,
the bared ferocity of teeth,
chest-thumping challenge and defiance,
the deafening clamour of their prayers
to a deity made in the image of their prejudice
which drowns the voice of conscience,
is mirrored our predicament
but on a social, massive, organised scale
which magnifies enormously
as the private déshabillé of love
becomes obscene in orgies.

(Okpewho, p. 63)

Africa's best-known novelist is probably Chinua Achebe (b. 1930) of Nigeria. In a series of novels, from *Things Fall Apart* through *No Longer at Ease* and *A Man of the People*, to *Anthills of the Savannah*, Achebe depicts and laments the cultural uprooting of his people under colonialism and finds that independence brings new problems. The indigenous rulers are as greedy and ruthless for power in their own way as were the foreigners.

Wole Soyinka, also a novelist, poet, essayist, and translator, and also of Nigeria, brings into his work not only the political and cultural issues of the day, but also the ancestors, gods, and spirits of the past and present who act upon them. He has written the autobiography of his childhood, *Ake*, alive with humor and fantasy, and the play *The Lion and the Jewel*, filled with what he calls a "total artwork" of spectacle, music, and choreography in celebration of the vitality of traditional culture. In more somber plays, such as *Kongi's Harvest* and *The Road*, Soyinka confronts death, both physiological and cultural. A political activist for democratic values, Soyinka was imprisoned by the Nigerian government in 1967–9,

and in the 1990s was living in European exile. In 1986 he was awarded the Nobel Prize for Literature, suggesting that regardless of Africa's political, economic, and technological difficulties, its artistry has succeeded in capturing the twentieth-century world.

AFRICAN HISTORY: HOW DO WE KNOW?

In another cultural dimension, the formal study, preservation, and transmission of history took on new vigor and new directions. Africans argued that their history, from ancient times to the present, had been hidden from view by European colonials. With independence it would be recovered. Significant examples of this evolution are the eight-volume *Cambridge History of Africa* and the parallel eight-volume *UNESCO General History of Africa*, edited by African historians. In volume I of the UNESCO series, Philip Curtin explained the significance of the new history:

> A recovery of African history has been an important part of African development over recent decades, not an expensive frill that could be set aside until more pressing aspects of development were well in hand. ... The fact that African history was seriously neglected until the 1950s is only one symptom of a large phenomenon in historical studies. The colonial period in Africa left an intellectual legacy to be overcome, just as it had in other parts of the world. ... African history had been more neglected than that of other non-European regions and ... African history had been even more distorted by racist myths. ... It takes a long time to uproot prejudice ("Recent Trends," pp. 54–71)).

New paths in the study of African history opened. The recording and analysis of oral history, a crucial approach in a region where written records were very limited, opened a fruitful new method. Cheikh Anta Diop of Senegal, who argued for the prominence of Africa, especially Egypt, in the early history of Greece and Mediterranean Europe, helped popularize revisionist anti-Eurocentric perspectives. And the construction and expansion of new historical and anthropological museums in many cities across Africa encourages the formation of a new African consciousness that includes national and ethnic dimensions.

BIBLIOGRAPHY

Accelerated Development in Sub-Saharan Africa
(Washington: The World Bank, 1981).

Amin, Samir. *Unequal Development*
(Delhi: Oxford University Press, 1979).

Andrea, Alfred and James H. Overfield, eds.
The Human Record: Sources of Global History, 2 vols.
(Boston: Houghton Mifflin, 1990).

Bates, Robert H., V.Y. Mudimbe, and Jean O'Barr, eds.
Africa and the Disciplines
(Chicago: University of Chicago Press, 1993).

Berry, Sara, "Economic Change in Contemporary
Africa," in Martin and O'Meara, eds. *Africa,* 359–74.

Boahen, A. Adu, ed. *Africa under Colonial Domination
1880–1935: [UNESCO] General History of Africa,* VII
(Berkeley: University of California Press, 1985).

Cambridge History of Africa (New York: Cambridge
University Press, 6 vols., 1975–86).

Coquery-Vidrovitch, Catherine. *Africa: Endurance and
Change South of the Sahara,* trans. by David Maisel
(Berkeley: University of California Press, 1988).

Curtin, Philip, Steven Feierman, Leonard Thompson,
and Jan Vansina. *African History from Earliest Times to
Independence* (New York: Longman, 2nd ed., 1995).

Curtin, Philip D. "Recent Trends in African
Historiography and Their Contribution to History in
General," in *[UNESCO] General History of Africa,* Vol.
1, 54–71.

Davidson, Basil. *Modern Africa*
(London: Longman, 1983).

Diawara, Manthia. *African Cinema*
(Bloomington: University of Indiana Press, 1992).

Fieldhouse, D.K. *Black Africa 1945–1980*
(London: Allen and Unwin, 1986).

Frank, Andre Gunder. *Dependent Accumulation
and Underdevelopment*
(New York: Monthly Review Press, 1979).

Franke, Richard W. and Barbara H. Chasin.
Seeds of Famine (Totowa, NJ: Rowman and Allanheld
Publishers, 1980).

Gulhati, Ravi. *The Making of Economic Policy in Africa*
(Washington: The World Bank, 1990).

Harden, Blaine. *Africa: Dispatches from a Fragile Continent*
(Boston: Houghton Mifflin, 1990).

Harrison, Paul. *The Greening of Africa*
(London: Palladin, 1987).

Jegede, Dele, "Popular Culture in Urban Africa," in
Martin and O'Meara, eds. *Africa,* 273–94.

July, Robert W. *A History of the African People*

(Prospect Heights, IL: Waveland Press, 4th ed. 1992).

Mabogunje, Akin L. *Urbanization in Nigeria*
(New York: Africana Publishing Corporation, 1968).

Martin, Phyllis M., and Patrick O'Meara, eds. *Africa*
(Bloomington: University of Indiana Press, 1995).

Okpewho, Isidore, ed. *The Heritage of African Poetry*
(Harlow, Essex: Longman Group, 1985).

Oliver, Roland and Anthony Atmore. *Africa since 1800*
(Cambridge: Cambridge University Press, 3rd ed.,
1981).

Ousmane, Sembene. *God's Bits of Wood,* trans. by Francis
Price (London: Heinemann, 1970).

Pacey, Arnold. *Technology in World Civilization: A
Thousand Year History* (Oxford: Basil Blackwell, 1990).

Ravenhill, John, ed. *Africa in Economic Crisis*
(London: Macmillan Press, 1986).

Rodney, Walter. *How Europe Underdeveloped Africa*
(Washington: Howard University Press, 1982).

Salvatore, Dominick, ed. *African Development Prospects:
A Policy Modelling Approach*
(New York: Taylor and Francis, 1989).

Sigmund, Paul E. *The Ideologies of the Developing Nations*
(New York: Praeger Publishers, 1st ed., 1963; rev. ed.,
1967; second rev. ed., 1972).

Sivard, Ruth Leger. *World Military and Social Expenditures
1996* (Washington: World Priorities, 16th ed., 1996).

Sklar, Richard L. "The African Frontier for Political
Science," in Bates, *et al., Africa and the Disciplines,*
83–110.

Smillie, Ian. *Mastering the Machine: Poverty, Aid, and
Technology* (Boulder, CO: Westview Press, 1991).

Stryker, Richard and Stephen N. Ndegwa, "The African
Development Crisis," in Martin and O'Meara, eds.
Africa, 375–95.

Time-Life Books. *The Colonial Overlords: TimeFrame AD
1850–1900* (Alexandria, VA: Time-Life Books, 1990).

—. *The Nuclear Age: TimeFrame AD 1950–1990*
(Alexandria, VA: Time-Life Books, 1990).

[UNESCO] General History of Africa
(Berkeley: University of California Press, 8 vols.,
1981–92).

Winchester, N. Brian, "African Politics since
Independence," in Martin and O'Meara,
eds. *Africa,* 347–88.

World Almanac and Book of Facts 1997
(Mahwah, NJ: World Almanac Books, 1996).

World Bank. *World Development Report, 1992*
(New York: Oxford University Press, 1992).

CHAPTER 23

LATIN AMERICA

1870–1990s

"Poor Mexico:
So far from God,
so close to the
United States."

PORFIRIO DÍAZ

THE SEARCH FOR AN
INTERNATIONAL POLICY
ON ECONOMICS AND
TECHNOLOGY

The countries of Latin America are different from one another, and yet they have much in common with each other and with many newly independent countries of the world. They were the first of the developing countries to gain their independence, and they have been struggling with colonial and postcolonial legacies and the complex problems of economic development and technological change since the 1820s. Revolutions and counterrevolutions have led to new political realities in many of these countries, affecting internal relationships between the elites, the masses, and the military. In this chapter we examine these issues in broad terms and consider in more detail the experiences of four countries—Mexico, Brazil, Argentina, and Cuba—in the twentieth century.

LATIN AMERICAN
DIVERSITY TODAY

Including the independent island states of the Caribbean, Latin America consists of twenty-seven independent countries with a total population of just under a half billion people, a total that has risen, astonishingly, from about 38 million in 1900 and 166 million in 1950. About one out of every three Latin Americans is Brazilian (165 million people) and one out of five Mexicans (about 100 million people). The next largest countries, Colombia and Argentina, have approximately 35 million people each.

The vast majority of Latin Americans—about 300 million people—speak Spanish, but most of Brazil's population speaks Portuguese. In addition, about 100 million people speak indigenous Indian languages, although most of them also speak Spanish or Portuguese. A few small groups in the Caribbean and in the eastern Brazilian state of Bahia continue to speak Yoruba as their mother tongue, thereby sustaining a link with cultures in Africa, from where their ancestors were brought as slaves in the nineteenth century. Most Latin Americans, reflecting their colonial heritage, are Catholic (about 90 percent), but the percentage is declining as more people turn to evangelical Protestantism.

The economic development of Latin America Following the Great Depression and World War II, the nations of Latin America sought to move beyond their dependence upon the export of primary goods—minerals, timber, and food. Investment from North America and Europe allowed some industrial development in Chile, Argentina, Brazil, and Mexico, but was often undermined by political instability. Development throughout the region is diverse as are economic policies.

	ARGENTINA	BRAZIL	CHILE
1870	∎ First refrigerated ship takes beef to Europe (1977) ∎ Pampas Indians almost exterminated in war (1878-83)		∎ War of the Pacific (1879-83): Chile gains land from Peru and Bolivia with rich nitrate reserves
1880		∎ Pedro II abolishes slavery (1888); landowners and military oppose him; monarchy abolished and republic established (1889)	
1890	∎ Jorge Luis Borges (1899-1986)	∎ Constitution for a federal state agreed (1891)	∎ Parliamentary republic ends with increasing political chaos (1891-1924)
1900			∎ Pablo Neruda (1904-73)
1910	∎ Hipolito Irigoyen president (1916-22, 1928-30) after first democratic elections		
1920		∎ Working classes and intellectuals call for democratic government	
1930	∎ Military coup upsets republican constitution (1930) Roberto M. Ortiz president (1938-42); pursues reformist radical policies but power continues to reside with army and land owners	∎ Coffee prices collapse; Getúlio Vargas becomes president (1930) and sets up pro-fascist, totalitarian state, *Estado Novo*	∎ Communist, Radical, and Socialist parties unite to form Popular Front coalition (1936-46)
1940	∎ Coup (1943) supported by urban working class brings Juan Perón to power (1946); he organizes trade unions	∎ Brazil declares war on Germany (1942) ∎ Vargas deposed in military coup (1945) ∎ New constitution adopted (1946)	∎ Chile backs US in World War II ∎ Right-wing presidents marginalize all left-wing parties (1946-70)
1950	∎ Evita Perón (1919-52) dies ∎ Perón overthrown and civilian administration restored (1955); inflation and unemployment begin to get out of control	∎ Vargas returns to power (1951-4) but US opposes his program, including minimum wage, and he is deposed in military-backed, right-wing coup ∎ Juscelino Kubitschek president (1956-60) and attracts foreign investment	
1960	∎ Coup brings return to military rule (1966)	∎ Jânio da Silva Quadros president (1960-61) and tries to free country of US influence ∎ Brasilia built (1960-63)	∎ Eduardo Frei president (1964-70)

Latin Americans are on the move. In the late nineteenth and early twentieth centuries, labor-hungry Latin America countries welcomed more immigrants—particularly from Europe—in proportion to their populations than any other region of the world, including the United States. Today, the movement is more internal. People are moving, especially out of villages, "pulled" by the attraction of greater opportunities elsewhere. Cities seem to promise job possibilites, "bright lights," and necessities, such as schools and doctors. Other people are "pushed" out of their current locations because of the scarcity of opportunities. The enormous population growth over the last forty years has filled up the countryside. Moreover, as farming is mechanized, agricultural work diminishes, creating a "push" factor. In 1900, perhaps 20 percent of Latin America's people lived in cities. By 1950, four out of every ten people lived in cities, and today about three out of four people do so. The two largest cities, Mexico City and São Paulo (Brazil), have between 15 and 20 million inhabitants each—as many as all the cities of the continent held in 1900. Nevertheless, because of the immense population growth, the rural population has remained steady at 100 million throughout the second half of the twentieth century.

Governments also offered new land to settlers. Brazil, in particular, has attempted to satisfy the land hunger of its population by opening vast tracts in the Amazon River basin and inviting millions of immigrants into these virgin lands. As we shall see (p. 769), these new invasions solved some problems but created new ones as well. Spanish-speaking peoples have also emigrated to the United States in sizeable numbers, and today, between 25 and 30 million Hispanic-Americans live in the continental United States.

	ARGENTINA	BRAZIL	CHILE
1960		∎ João Goulart president (1961-3) ∎ Castelo Branco brought to power in coup; he acts as dictator and bans political parties (1964-7) ∎ New constitution brings Da Costa e Silva to power (1967-9); he is replaced by military junta	
1970	∎ Peronist party wins presidential and congressional elections; Perón returns from exile in Spain as president with his wife Isabel as vice-president (1973) ∎ Perón dies (1974) and is succeeded by Isabel ∎ Military coup (1976) puts General Jorge Videla in power; congress is dissolved and hundreds detained ∎ "Dirty war" (1976-83) in which at least 10,000 people vanish ∎ Roberto Viola promises a return to democracy (1978)	∎ Oil crisis ends economic growth (which had been accompanied by ruthless suppression of left-wing radicals) ∎ Ernest Geisel president (1974-8) ∎ João Baptista de Figueriredo president (1978-85) ∎ Political parties legalized (1978)	∎ Salvador Allende is first democratically elected Marxist president (1970-73) and embarks on program of nationalization and social reform ∎ Augusto Pinochet, with US backing, becomes president (1973); Allende killed; policy of repression begins during which opposition put down and political activity banned; opponents imprisoned, tortured, or "disappeared"
1980	∎ Viola dies and Leopoldo Galtieri in power (1981) ∎ To boost popularity with economy ailing, Galtieri invades Falklands (1982) ∎ War is lost and Reynaldo Bignone replaces Galtieri ∎ General election brings Peronist Raúl Alfonsin to power; constitution of 1953 is revived (1983); Alfonsin introduces austerity program	∎ Popular calls for return to democratic government (1984) ∎ Tancredo Neves becomes first civilian president since 1964 (1985) but dies before taking office ∎ Neves succeeded by José Sarney (1985) ∎ Constitution transfers power to Congress (1988) ∎ Measures to halt burning of Amazonian rainforest announced ∎ Chico Mendes (leader of rubber-tappers' union and environmentalist) murdered (1988) ∎ Forest Protection Service and Ministry for Land Reform abolished (1989) ∎ Fernando Collor president (1989) promising free-market economics	∎ Opposition to Pinochet growing from all sides and a referendum on whether he should serve again results in clear "no" (1988) ∎ Constitutional changes agreed (1989) and Patricio Aylwin is elected president, although Pinochet remains as commander of army
1990	∎ Carlos Menem president (1989-92) and begins to bring inflation down ∎ Menem re-elected (1995)	∎ Collor charged with corruption and replaced by Itamar Franco (1992) ∎ Earth Summit held in Rio de Janeiro (1992)	∎ Aylwin achieves end of junta (1990) ∎ Pinochet is censured and some military officers jailed for civil rights abuse (1995)

A few figures on living standards help to fill out the picture of the overall conditions and of the diversity within the continent today. The average life expectancy at birth is sixty-eight years (compared with seventy-six years in USA), but it varies from a high of seventy-six years in Barbados and Costa Rica, to fifty-six years in Haiti. In the two largest countries, Brazil and Mexico, it is sixty-six and seventy-one years, respectively. Female literacy is 85 percent overall (99 percent in USA), ranging from 98 percent in Guyana and Uruguay, to 42 percent in Haiti, with Brazil at 83 percent and Mexico at 87 percent. The gross national product per capita averages $3400 (that of the USA is $25,500), with a range from $8140 in Argentina to $230 in Haiti. Both Brazil and Mexico are at about $3900. In world terms, Latin American countries lie about the middle range, not nearly as rich as the developed countries of Europe and North America, but not nearly as poor as most regions of Africa, or East or South Asia. They are at about the same standard as Eastern Europe.

TECHNOLOGY, INDUSTRIALIZATION, AND LATIN AMERICAN ELITES 1870–1916

Through the late nineteenth and early twentieth centuries, Latin America began to industrialize, largely with investments from overseas. At first, Britain was the principal investor, but after World War I the United States assumed that role. Between 1870 and 1919, Argentina alone received $10 billion in foreign investments, about half of which came from Britain. At the time of the Great Depression in

	CUBA	GUATEMALA	MEXICO
1870	▪ Ten Years' War (1868-78) against Spain for independence		▪ Porfirio Díaz president (1877-80) and country enjoys period of economic growth, including railway system built
1880			
1890	▪ Second war of independence; thousands die in Spanish concentration camps ▪ Spain gives up claim after US supports Cuba (1898) ▪ US installs military interim government (1899)		
1900	▪ US granted intervention rights and military bases, including Guantanamo Bay (1901) ▪ Tomás Estrada Palma becomes first president of the republic (1902) ▪ US withdraws (1902) but intervenes in 1906-9 ▪ Miguel Goméz president (1909): economy prospers under liberal regime; US invests in sugar and gambling		▪ First oil production (1901)
1910	▪ US intervenes again (1919-24)		▪ Revolution begins (1910) in response to excessive exploitation by foreign companies and desire for land reform ▪ Civil war claims 250,000 lives (1913) ▪ New constitution designed to establish permanent democracy introduced; also limits power of church and reserves mineral and subsoil rights for nation (1917)
1920	▪ Gerardo Machado dictator (1925-33)		▪ Cristero rebellion of militant priests (1926-9) ▪ National Revolutionary Party (PRI) founded 1929; has been in power almost ever since
1930	▪ Fulgencio Batista seizes power (1933)		▪ Cárdenas president (1934-40); land reforms accelerated and cooperative farms established; railways nationalized and US and UK oil companies expelled
1940	▪ Nationalist, social-democratic constitution agreed, including universal suffrage and state rights over subsoil (1940) ▪ Batista retires (1944)	▪ Democratically elected Juan José Arévalo president (1944); began program of socialist reforms, including land redistribution	▪ Economy grows with help of US war effort (1940s)
1950	▪ Batista seizes power and begins oppressive regime (1952)		

the 1920s and 1930s, United States private investments in Latin America had reached $3.5 billion, 40 percent of all the investments in the region, and these investments paid for new railway lines, mining, agriculture, and ocean shipping, including the refrigerated compartments that enabled Argentinians to ship their beef profitably to Europe. This, in turn, made it possible to fence off the *pampas*, the great Argentinian plains, and turn them into ranches. The **gauchos**, the emblem of Argentina, were reduced in status from free-ranging cowboys to employees of the ranches.

For the most part, these economic and technological innovations were initiated by foreigners in search of profits. Most of the investments were concentrated in primary production—that is, farming and mining—rather than in industrial manufacturing. At the time of World War I, for example, the United States was buying about one-third of Brazil's exports, mostly coffee, rubber, and cocoa. (Half of Brazil's export was coffee.) Members of the creole elites, who saw that they too could share in the new earnings and win some acceptability among Europeans, joined in the new commerce. But for the most part the initiatives came from outside, and most of the creole elites were content to treat their nations as private estates. Control and patronage mattered—money and profits were means to an end, not the end in itself. In an essay, *Ariel*, written in 1898, the Uruguayan philosopher

	CUBA	GUATEMALA	MEXICO
1950	▮ Fidel Castro leads two unsuccessful coups (1953, 1956) ▮ Castro overthrows Batista (1959); constitution of 1940 replaced by "Fundamental Law" making Castro prime minister	▮ Jacobo Arbenz president (1954); continued program of reforms, including nationalizing United Fruit Company's land, leading to US-backed coup ▮ Carlos Castillo president (1954); land reforms halted	
1960	▮ All US-owned businesses appropriated without compensation; US breaks off diplomatic relations (1960) ▮ US sponsors unsuccessful invasion of Bay of Pigs (1961) ▮ Castro announces that Cuba will be Marxist-Leninist state ▮ Soviet missiles installed but removed on US insistence (1963)	▮ Enrique Peralta president after military coup (1963) ▮ Military rule (1963-6) ▮ Cesar Méndez elected president (1966) ▮ Counter-insurgency war sees first use of "disappearances" as a state weapon (1966-8)	
1970	▮ Socialist constitution approved; Castro institutes (with Soviet money) social and economic program ▮ Cuba joins Comecon (1972)	▮ Series of military governments begins with election of Carlos Araña as president (1970) ▮ Kjell Laugerud becomes president (1974), but widespread violence follows discovery that election returns had been falsified ▮ Guatemala City severely damaged by earthquake (1976) ▮ Fernando Romeo becomes president (1978)	
1980	▮ Cuban troops withdrawn from Angola	▮ Anti-government guerilla movement gains momentum (1981) ▮ Angel Anibal becomes president (1982) but military coup installs Rios Montt as head of junta and then as president; Montt begins to fight corruption but anti-government violence continues ▮ Meija Victores removes Montt in coup and offers amnesty to guerillas (1983) ▮ New constitution adopted and Vinicio Cerezo elected president (1985) ▮ Coup against Cerezo fails (1989) ▮ Army (funded and trained by US) responsible for more than 100,000 civilian deaths (1980-9)	▮ Financial crisis and Mexico unable to repay foreign debt; IMF insists on economic reforms; restrictions on foreign investment relaxed (1982-4) ▮ Earthquake in Mexico City claims 7000 lives (1985) ▮ PRI returned to power (1985) ▮ IMF loan agreement (1986) ▮ Carlos Salinas Gotari elected president and debt reduction negotiated with US (1988)
1990	▮ Withdrawal of all Soviet forces (1995)	▮ Jorge Serrano Elias elected president but flees from country (1991-5) ▮ President Arzú elected and seeks meeting with guerillas to end civil war (1995)	▮ PRI wins in general election (1991) ▮ Guerilla rebellion in Chiapas state ruthlessly suppressed (1994-5) ▮ PRI reduced to minority in national government

José Enrique Rodó (1872–1917) analyzed Latin America's move in the direction of an industrial democracy, on the United States model, and rejected it. He saw that path as barbaric and inconsistent with the more leisurely, elitist, civilized world of the creole rulers of Latin America. In the absence of democratic systems, most governments in Latin America were still in the hands of *caudillos*, strongmen who governed on their own authority. In 1896, a revolt among the peasants in Canudos, northeast Brazil, raised another fundamental issue: Could the economic and industrial changes that were beginning to affect Latin American cities and the rural regions where commercial agriculture was practiced, also reach the peasantry?

Not everyone was content with a system of control by *haciendado* and *caudillo* elites. Businessmen who were participating in the new commerce and industry began to think of new goals—more education, more industrialization, more independence from foreign investors and more consistent, less arbitrary government, with a larger, formal voice in politics for themselves. Toward the end of the nineteenth century, a huge influx of immigrants from Europe, especially from Italy, brought with them ideas of industrial development and union representation, and by the early years of the twentieth century, important labor unions were in place in the larger nations of Latin America. Another group advocating reform and national pride was the

Steaming into the Americas. The Central Railway, Peru, was constructed with great feats of engineering, during the 1870s and 1890s. Here, the train *San Francisco* waits at the official opening of the Verrugas Bridge on the Transandine Railway (the early name of the Central Railway). Flags were raised in honor of the American construction and British ownership of the railroad. In the Andes, a railroad was needed to transport the copper from Cerro de Pasco, but there were few links between coastal towns. Today most railroads are nationalized.

army, especially its junior officers. Often drawn from middle-class urban families and aware of modern technology through their knowledge of weaponry, army officers were more used to the importance of education, industrialization, business, and stable government.

In some countries these groups worked together and achieved their goals, notably in Uruguay. Under newspaper editor José Batlle (1856–1929), who served as president in 1903–7 and 1911–15 and who remained influential until his death, Uruguay succeeded in providing social welfare, separating church from state, and enacting a constitution that limited the powers of the president by sharing them with a National Council of Administration. Like the rest of Latin America, however, Uruguay failed to undertake perhaps the most influential reform of all. It did not restructure the land-holding patterns that left wealthy landlords in charge of impoverished peasants. As elsewhere in Latin America, the reformers were urban people, and they were frequently related to landlords; they had little practical sympathy for the agricultural laborers and little thought of sharing power with them. In 1916, similar limited political and economic reforms, with similar successes and shortcomings, were instituted in Argentina by urban interests united behind Hipólito Yrigoyen, who was president in 1916–22.

THE MEXICAN REVOLUTION 1910–20

In 1910, in Mexico, the most economically advanced of all the Latin American countries at the time, urban and rural leaders rose up against the dictatorship of Porfirio Díaz (1830–1915), who had been ruling the country since 1876. At the age of eighty in 1910, Díaz seemed poised to retire from the presidency. Under his leadership Mexico had seen the development of mining, oil drilling, and railways, in addition to increasing exports of raw agricultural products, especially henequen fibers used in making rope. The middle-class urban creole elite had prospered, but the salaries of the urban workers had declined, and rural peasants had fared even worse. Ninety-five percent of the rural peasantry owned no land, while fewer than 200 Mexican families owned 25 percent of the land, and foreign investors owned another 20–25 percent. One hacienda spread over 13 million acres (5.3 million hectares) and another over 11 million acres (4.5 million hectares). Huge tracts of land lay fallow and unused, while peasants went hungry. Finally, on a political level, no system of orderly succession had been worked out for Mexico. The reins of power rested in the hands of Díaz and his allies alone.

Democratic participation in voting existed for a few in law but not in fact, and when Díaz changed his mind and did run again for president, he imprisoned his principal challenger, Francisco Madero (1873–1913). Díaz won, but several rebellions against his continuing rule broke out across Mexico, and he soon resigned and went into exile in Paris. A number of regional leaders rose up to assert their influence on whatever future government would be formed, and Mexico became convulsed in years of civil war. In part, the warfare was both personal and factional. It concerned differences in policy among the factions, and it was fought over the appropriate division of power between the central government and the states.

Many of the leaders who contested for power were *mestizos*, people of mixed race and culture (see Chapter 15), who were offering a dramatic break with the past control by the creole elite. The two most radical, Francisco "Pancho" Villa (1878–1923), who was from the northern border region, and Emiliano Zapata (1879–1919), who was from the state of Morelos, just south of Mexico City, advocated significant land reform, and even carried it out in the areas they captured during the civil war. Farm workers, agricultural colonists, former soldiers, unemployed laborers, cowboys, and delinquents joined under Villa's banner. In November 1911 Zapata declared the revolutionary Plan of Ayala, which called for the return of land to Indian *pueblos* (villages). Tens of thousands of impoverished peasants followed him, heeding his cry of "Tierra y Libertad"—"Land and Liberty" and accepting his view that it was "Better to die on one's feet than to live on one's knees." Zapata's supporters seized large sugar estates, haciendas with which they had been in conflict for years. By including previously scorned groups and taking their agendas seriously, the revolution became more radical and agrarian.

With Díaz in exile, Francisco Madero became president, but he was removed by a coup and then assassinated in 1913. General Víctoriano Huerta (1854–1916) then attempted to take over and to re-establish a repressive government like that of Díaz. Opposed by all the other major leaders—Venustiano Carranza, Álvaro Obregón, Plutarco Elias Calles, Villa, and Zapata—and also by President Woodrow Wilson of the United States, who sent American troops into Veracruz to express his displeasure with Huerta, the general was forced from power in March 1914. Álvaro Obregón, another general, who understood the uses of the machine gun, won out militarily, but he agreed to serve under Carranza, who had himself installed as provisional president.

Villa invited Zapata, Obregón, and others to the town of Aguascalientes in Central Mexico, where they approved Zapata's radical plan for redistributing land to the peasants. They then removed Carranza from office temporarily as civil war continued, and Villa and Zapata entered Mexico City. The city changed hands several times, but ultimately Carranza and Obregón won, Villa and Zapata were forced out, and Carranza became president in 1916.

Mexican revolutionaries. General Francisco "Pancho" Villa and Emiliano Zapata (right), sporting his flamboyant moustache, sit together with their Mexican revolutionary army, men who had come from many different occupations and walks of life to join the ranks. Even the radical leaders hailed from different parts of the country, Zapata from south of Mexico City and Villa from the northern border, but they shared common goals.

SPOTLIGHT

Diego Rivera:

MURALIST PAINTER
OF MEXICO'S HISTORY

The early, conventional artistic training which Diego Rivera (1866–1957) received in Mexico and in France gave no indication that he would create an entirely new way of understanding and representing the history of his people. But by the time he returned to Mexico in 1921 his country had passed through a decade of revolution and civil war that had seen more than a million people killed, a new system of government installed, and a new cultural policy proclaimed to celebrate the history of Mexico's *mestizo* peasants and workers. Three great muralists accepted this challenge: Rivera, Jose Clemente Orozco (1883–1949), and David Alfaro Siqueiros (1894–1974). Each filled vast public spaces with their murals, telling the history of Mexico in presentations which could be understood even by illiterate peasants, and yet win the recognition of sophisticated critics as an

important new art form.

Rivera, being the most prominent of the three, was assigned the most prominent spaces, first the Ministry of Education and later the National

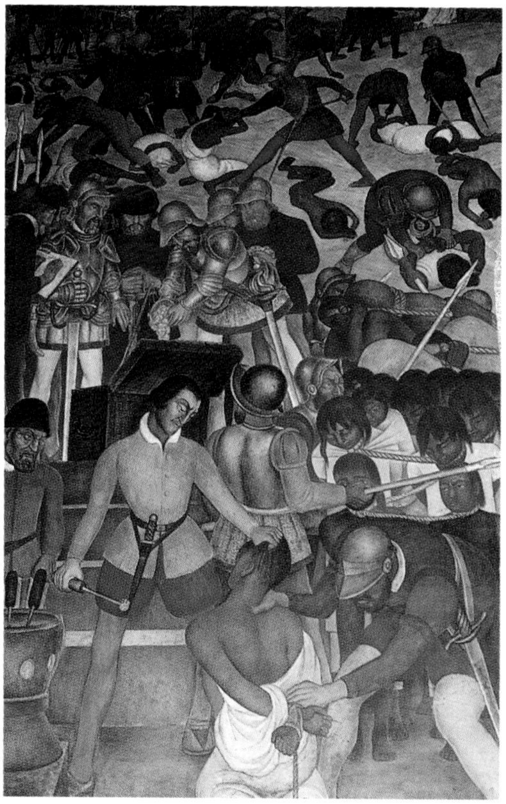

Picture 1 Diego Rivera, *The Conquest of Mexico* (detail), 1929–30.

Palace, both in the heart of Mexico City. Here he first painted a set of enormous murals depicting the history of Mexico from the time of the arrival of Hernán Cortés and the *conquistadores* through the revolution of Rivera's own time, on to a proposed future of industrialization under a Marxist philosophy. At about the same time, 1929 to 1930, he painted a similar history of the conquest at the Cortés Palace in Cuernavaca. **Picture 1** is a detail from Cuernavaca focussing on *The Conquest of Mexico*. Rivera is unsparing in his representation of Spanish brutality and greed. Although soldiers do the dirtiest work, noblemen supervise and participate while priests look on greedily and make records of the spoils.

Picture 2 was painted in 1945 in another corridor of the National Palace. In this mural of *The Great City of Tenochtitlán*, Rivera reconstructs the life of the

Picture 2 Diego Rivera, *The Great City of Tenochtitlán* (detail), 1945.

native Americans before the arrival of the Spanish. The background cityscape reminds the viewer of the majesty, power, and order of this earlier urban civilization, while the foreground represents the everyday lives of its inhabitants, from the ruler on his throne to the laborers who constructed the buildings. Rivera captures the pulse of life: women selling food in the marketplace, parents inspecting a child's teeth, merchants negotiating prices, artisans creating and selling their handicrafts, peasants bearing their agricultural products to the city, and, in the right foreground, a young woman seducing older men, with apparent success. He does not, however, touch on Aztec imperialism nor its human sacrifice of captured subjects.

Picture 3 Diego Rivera, *Man at the Crossroads* (detail), 1934.

Rivera was invited to the United States to paint murals of workers' lives and struggles in the San Francisco Stock Exchange, the Detroit Institute of Arts, and New York's Rockefeller Center, although the last was canceled when Rivera insisted on painting Lenin into the mural. **Picture 3**, a detail from *Man at the Crossroads* was to be part of the Rockefeller Center mural, but when John D. Rockefeller himself stopped the painting and had it destroyed, Rivera copied it at the Palace of Fine Arts in Mexico City. This segment of the mural shows the communist leader Trotsky unfurling a banner with the motto "Workers of the World Unite" in the midst of an assembly of workers. Engels and Marx look on.

When Carranza convened the constituent assembly in 1917, he was forced by Obregón and others to accept more radical policies. The final document, the Mexican Constitution of 1917, promised land reform and the imposition of restrictions on foreign economic control, including limits on the ownership of mineral and water rights. It protected Mexican workers by passing a labor code, with minimum salaries and maximum hours, and enacted a code enshrining workers' rights, including accident insurance, pensions, social benefits, and the right to unionize and strike. It placed severe restrictions on the church and clergy, denying them the rights to own property and to provide primary education. (Most of the revolutionaries were anti-clerical. Zapata was an exception in this, as the peasantry who followed him were extremely devoted to the church.) The constitution also decreed that no foreigner could be a minister or priest, vote, hold office, or criticize the government.

Enacting the new laws was easier than implementing them, but having the new constitution in place set a standard of accountability for government and served as a beacon for the continuing revolution. On the material level, not much changed at first. With the killing of Carranza in 1920, Obregón became president and distributed 3 million acres (1.2 million hectares) of land to peasants, 10 percent

MEXICAN REVOLUTION—KEY EVENTS

1907	Recession in US leads to economic crisis compounded by poor harvests
1908	Francisco Madero (1873–1915) calls for democracy and criticizes capitalist dictatorship of Porfirio Díaz (1830–1915)
1910	Díaz imprisons Madero and wins election Pascual Orozco and Francisco "Pancho" Villa (1877–1923) lead insurrection of farm laborers in Chihuahua Emiliano Zapata (1879–1919) leads rising of Indian pueblos in Morelos
1911	Madero leads military rising and captures Ciudad Juárez, where he establishes a capital Díaz gives way to Madero, who, as president (1911–13), re-establishes a more liberal regime Zapata issues the revolutionary Plan de Ayala, calling for wholesale return of land to the pueblos, while industrial workers take opportunity to organize themselves into trade unions and began to call strikes
1913	Víctoriano Huerta (1854–1916) campaigns against Madero's ineffectual government with rebellion that sees street fighting in Mexico City Madero is deposed and later murdered, and Huerta becomes provisional president (1913–14), but is faced with revolts of Venustiano Carranza (1859–1920), Álvaro Obregón (1880–1924), Villa, and Zapata; 250,000 killed in subsequent civil war;
1914	Huerta forced into exile in Europe and US (1914–16) and Carranza is proclaimed "First Chief" by revolutionary bands, when he adopts social and economic reform program, although he is attacked by forces of Villa and Zapata
1915–17	Carranza becomes provisional president Unsuccessful US expedition to kill Villa
1917	Carranza accepts new constitution limiting church power while reserving mineral and subsoil rights for nation
1920	Obregón forces Carranza to flee capital and becomes president
1923–4	Obregón puts down revolt of Adolfo de la Huerta
1924	Obregón re-elected president but is soon assassinated by militant Catholic, and Plutarco Calles (1877–1945) becomes president (1924–8), carrying out a program of agrarian reforms
1926–9	Militant Catholic priests lead Cristero rebellion
1929	National Revolutionary Party (later PRI) formed by Calles; has been in power almost ever since

Mexican women revolutionaries in fighting form. A group of rebel women and young girls, wearing traditional dress, practice their shooting skills for the Mexican Revolution in 1911. Those people opposed to the government in power were drawn from many different factions, but all fought together for a common cause.

of whom benefited. This redistribution helped to establish the principles of the revolution, demonstrating good faith on the part of the state and putting new land into production, but the state did not provide the technical assistance needed to improve productivity. Politically, Obregón began to include new constituencies in his government, including the labor movement, represented by a Labor Party, and the peasants, represented by a National Agrarian Party. The institutionalization of their presence in government promised new stability through wider representation. The representation, everyone recognized, was not only by social class but also by ethnicity and culture. *Mestizos* and even indigenous Indians now had achieved a place in government.

Warfare continued, however, partly in the form of factional struggles among the various leaders, partly between the government and the church. Obregón was assassinated in 1924, and Plutarco Elías Calles (1877–1945) became president. The new ruling *caudillos* were anti-clerical, seeing the church as a rival for power, and as the government began to extend and enforce its anti-clerical policies in the mid-1920s, many of the clergy went on strike, refusing to perform services. The peasantry supported the clergy, and as many as 50,000 armed peasants confronted the government in the War of the Cristeros. Calles backed down, allowing the anti-clerical legislation to lapse, and beginning a more sensitive accommodation between church and state, which has remained, and deepened, until the mid 1990s.

In 1928 Calles also institutionalized a new, more comprehensive party, the National Revolutionary Party, which was the forerunner of today's Party of Revolutionary Institutions (PRI). This national party, with its broad internal representation, elevated the party above the individual, solved the problem of succession in leadership, and brought an institutional stability to Mexico that has endured until today. Rule by *caudillos* was largely ended. Calles observed the rule of a one-term limit on the presidency, although he remained an influential figure in the background.

Under Lázaro Cárdenas (1895–1970), president from 1934 to 1940, the PRI pushed forward the reforms still further. Cárdenas resdistributed 45 million acres (18.2 million hectares) of land, starting a process by which 253 million acres (102.4 million hectares) would be redistributed by 1984. (Nevertheless, a rapidly expanding population has left several million peasants still landless—in absolute terms more than at the time of the revolution.) Cárdenas understood not only the political need for the redistribution of land to the peasants, but also the economic need to base Mexico's industrial development on a solid agricultural foundation. Cárdenas also stood up to foreign control in Mexico, nationalizing Mexico's oil industry in 1938. Seventeen foreign oil companies had refused to accept a pro-union ruling of an arbitration council upheld by Mexico's Supreme Court. Cárdenas defied the foreign owners, deriding their arrogance and disregard for the Mexican workers:

Who is not aware of the irritating discrimination governing construction of the company camps? Comfort for the foreign personnel; misery, drabness, and insalubrity for the Mexicans. Refrigeration and

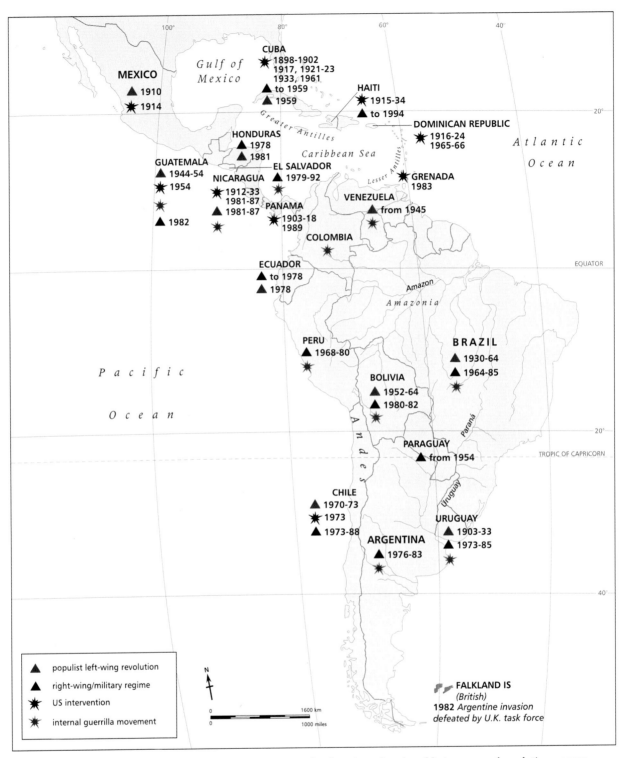

Latin American politics in the twentieth century Latin America has been beset by a bewildering range of revolutions, coups, insurrections, and foreign interventions by the United States. The map cannot do justice to the variety of revolutions, from Communist in Cuba, to right-wing military in Chile and Argentina. It does, however, present a picture of a continent with vibrant, often unstable, politics.

protection against tropical insects for the former; indifference and neglect, medical services and supplies always grudgingly provided, for the latter; lower wages and harder, more exhausting labor for our people. (Andrea and Overfield, p. 462)

Cárdenas offered compensation to the companies. Foreign governments, especially the United States, did not intervene and Cárdenas established a new level of national pride in Mexico.

The PRI envisioned a one-party state, in which a single party would include all the major interest groups and the contest for political power would take place within the party. The party, it argued, could institutionalize the revolution. Most analysts have been skeptical of both claims, arguing that a single party cannot balance all major factions and that revolution cannot be institutionalized. They find the Cárdenas presidency the last to attempt fundamental reforms on a nationwide scale. Nevertheless, only in the 1960s did opposition parties begin seriously to challenge PRI rule. The PRI has won every national election until 1997, although the integrity of the election process has sometimes been challenged. In 1997 the PRI was reduced to a minority in the national legislature, and it lost the mayoralty of Mexico City to opposition leader Cuauhtemoc Cárdenas, Lázaro's son.

CULTURE AS A TOOL OF REVOLUTION

On the cultural level, as well as the political, the revolution transformed Mexico. Obregón appointed the noted author José Vasconselos (1882–1959) as minister of education with a mandate to establish schools—especially among the indigenous population—to combat illiteracy, which was then at 80 percent. Vasconcelos believed that the future of Mexico lay in the fusion of all of the nation's diverse ethnic streams into a single "cosmic race," and he fostered this ideal of unity. Vasconselos arranged state patronage for new artists, in particular a school of mural painters—Diego Rivera (1886–1957), David Alfaro Siqueiros (1896–1974), and José Clemente Orozco (1883–1949)—whose enormous, bold, and powerful murals brought a new, unifying, national image to Mexico and achieved recognition throughout the world. Although trained in European art schools, they returned to Mexico to develop art forms entirely different from European models in both content and form. Their huge murals, painted in some of Mexico's most honored public spaces,

gave prominence to the Indians and working classes of Mexico in a new visual history of the country. The Mexican Union of Technical Workers, Painters, and Sculptors issued a militant manifesto: "Art must no longer be the expression of individual satisfaction, but should aim to become a fighting educative tool for all."

REVOLUTIONARY POLITICS IN THE 1920s AND 1930s

The wealthy grew wealthier, and in Mexico the poor began to believe that the revolution might improve their situation. In most of Latin America, however, the poor became poorer and more restive. In Peru, for example, critics from all levels of society denounced the triple problems of racial discrimination against Indians, economic discrimination against the poor, and the denial of both problems behind a façade of political rhetoric. José Carlos Meriátegui, an Indian, was raised by his mother, a seamstress, and went to work when he was fourteen years old as a printer's assistant in Lima. He taught himself to read and write and became a journalist, poet, and novelist. Exiled temporarily for his writings, he returned to Peru to write and to organize for socialist solutions to his country's problems, until his death of cancer in 1930, at the age of thirty-five. At the same time, the far wealthier and more formally educated Víctor Raúl Haya de la Torre (1895–1979) was creating a new party, the American Popular Revolutionary Alliance (APRA) in 1924. He spoke of the technological and cultural disparities in Latin America:

In [Central and South] America, we have living together and at the same time in opposition, within the frontiers of our continent or even within the frontiers of each country, all forms of social organization and every level of economic development—savagery, barbarism, and civilization, communal primitive agriculture, feudalism, manufacturing, industrialism, and imperialism. Indians who have never known the use of a wheel as a means of locomotion see swift airplanes in the skies above their mountains. The young gentleman of Buenos Aires who plays golf and visits London has as a compatriot and fellow citizen the half-naked Indian in the Chaco. The same thing is true in Peru and Mexico and Colombia and Central America. (Sigmund, p. 383)

He then called for an economic, political, and social revolution:

> The new revolution in Latin America will be a revolution with an Indian base and orientation, with the native conscience and subconscious expressed in an economic and social renaissance. The Mexican revolution is a symptom of this great movement. (Sigmund, p. 385)

APRA mobilized mass support among urban workers and rural peasants, but it did not achieve its goals. When it seemed to be winning power, as in the Peruvian election of 1931, the government imprisoned Haya de la Torre and killed many of his followers. At other times APRA was manipulated by middle-class and military leaders, who siphoned off its energies without effecting reform. By the time APRA gained political office in 1985, conditions had become much worse than even in the early days of disillusionment in the 1930s.

THE MARKET CRASH AND IMPORT SUBSTITUTION 1929–60

Nationalism appeared to inspire the countries of Latin America, but often national sentiment was manipulated by the upper classes to allow the lower classes a voice but little actual political or economic power. The response to the worldwide stock market crash in 1929 (see p. 586), and the call for new economic and technological policies of import substitution revealed this cynicism. In the 1920s, the foreign exchange earnings of most Latin American countries were based on the export of raw materials. In many countries, just one or two products were the key: coffee from Colombia, Brazil, and Costa Rica; bananas from Central America and Ecuador; tin from Bolivia; copper from Chile and Peru; sugar from Cuba. Through the 1920s, demand for many of these products began to wane, and during the Great Depression, the market declined by as much as 80 percent. Latin American economists argued for a new economic and technological policy, later called import substituting industrialization (ISI). This concept of industrialization rested on two premises. First, Latin American countries must diversify their productivity, thus reducing their dependency on exports of a very few raw materials. Second, they must become internally more self-sufficient, thus reducing their dependence on international markets and the kind of catastrophe they had experienced when those markets collapsed.

Latin American countries began to industrialize further during World War II, when world markets could not provide their necessities. The trend continued after the war, with industrial growth exceeding agricultural. In Brazil, between 1945 and 1960,

Coffee remains a principal export of Latin American countries. In this 1933 photograph, two Colombian workers proudly display the tools of their trade, including cultivating spades, heavy machetes, pruning spears, and an unusual step-cut bamboo ladder. In the background are the fermentation tanks in which the outer pulp of the twin coffee beans is loosened before removal. To the right is one of the many washing canals in which clear water from mountain streams washes the coffee before it is marketed.

Brazil's revolutionary president. Dr Getúlio Vargas, surrounded by Brazilian admirals and generals, assumes office at the Cattete Palace (the Brazilian equivalent of the White House in Rio de Janeiro). After seizing power by revolution, he was sworn in as the provisional president of Brazil on November 19, 1930. As president, Vargas was able to play off the different political factions against each other, enabling his own rise to great power.

industry grew at an average of 9.4 percent per year and agriculture at 4 percent. In Venezuela, where oil was becoming a major export, industry grew at 8.5 percent compared with 4.7 percent in agriculture. But two elements of the policy were not working: Latin America was not becoming self-sufficient. The development of new industries actually required, at least in the early years, more imports of machines and technology than the new industries exported in the form of finished products. Second, the profits of the new industries went predominantly to the urban middle classes. They did not reach the rural workers. Class and cultural tensions intensified. Workers and peasants protested, and governments repressed the protests, often employing violence.

Frequently, the military, a very powerful force in most countries, intervened to restore order. By social background and occupational training, the military often favored technological modernization combined with social order. These policies continued in practice at least into the 1960s. In effect, public policy and the state itself were fractured. The interest groups that sought technological modernization did not take to heart the needs of the workers and peasants; at the same time, the workers and peasants did not appreciate the economic costs of their demands. Frequently split along cultural lines, neither side had much sympathy for the other. To understand more fully this split between opposing sides and the role of the military, it is instructive to study two other countries in more detail—Brazil and Argentina.

MILITARISM AND DEMOCRACY IN BRAZIL 1930–1990s

Getúlio Vargas (1883–1954) seized power by revolution in 1930 and for the next fifteen years was president of Brazil. The economy, which was dependent on coffee, had been deeply wounded by the market crash, and Vargas moved to strengthen Brazil's central government at the expense of the states. He put down revolts, especially that of the São Paulo militia, and attempted coups by communists in 1935 and fascists in 1937. In 1937, he also proclaimed a new constitution, declaring an *Estado Novo*, or "new state." He committed the state to an active role in developing mining, oil, steel, electricity, chemicals, motor vehicles, and light aircraft, soliciting investment from both the United States and Germany, at a time when those two nations saw each other as enemies. Brazil's industrialists, entrepreneurs, and military supported him. At the same time, Vargas understood that he had to gain the support of urban labor, so he created a Ministry of Labor, charging it with establishing new unions under governmental supervision. In bringing these disparate groups together, Vargas was following the German and Italian models of the corporate state (see p. 589). He organized the Brazilian Labor Party, and his government passed wide-ranging social legislation, introducing a minimum wage, a 48-hour working week, annual vacations, maternity benefits and child care, retirement and pension plans—but it did not allow strikes. The reforms did not touch the peasantry.

The army, fearing, on the one hand, the growing power of the urban workers and, on the other, Vargas's strong-arm methods of stifling opposition, deposed him in 1945. A spectrum of three new parties emerged, a new constitution was enacted, and free elections were held every five years from 1945 through 1960. A literacy test was required for voting, and as literacy improved, the percentage of adults, male and female (female suffrage was enacted in 1932), registered to vote rose from 15 percent in 1945 to 25 percent in 1962. Vargas was re-elected in 1951 with the support of many conflicting interest groups of Brazil, but he could not satisfy them all. He could not invest Brazil's resources in industrialization while at the same time satisfying the demands of the working classes for higher pay and more benefits. In his relationships with the United States, Brazil's largest external source of investment capital, he could not simultaneously satisfy those in

OPINIONS FROM AND ABOUT "EVITA"

*I*n 1951, age thirty-two, at the height of her public powers but suffering from terminal cancer, Eva Perón published her autobiography, *My Mission in Life*, which was divided into three parts: "The Causes of My Mission," "The Workers and My Mission," and "Women and My Mission." Devotees and critics divided sharply on their evaluations of her presentation.

I was not, nor am I, anything more than a humble woman … a sparrow in an immense flock of sparrows … but Perón was and is a gigantic condor that flies high and sure among the summits and near to God. … That is why neither my life nor my heart belongs to me, and nothing of all that I am or have is mine. All that I am, all that I have, all that I think and all that I feel, belongs to Perón.

Memories of injustices against which I rebelled at every age still rankle. I remember very well how sad I was for many days when I first realized that there were poor and rich in the world; and the strange thing is that the fact of the existence of the poor did not hurt me so much as the knowledge that, at the same time, the rich existed. … One day I heard for the first time, from the lips of a workingman, that there were poor because the rich were too rich; and that revelation made a strong impression on me.

Evita believed that the home was the most important place for a woman, and that she should be paid by the society for her work there.

The mother of a family is left out of all security measures. She is the only worker in the world without a salary, or a guarantee, or limited working hours, or free Sundays, or holidays, or any rest, or indemnity for dismissal, or strikes of any kind. All that, we learned as girls, belongs to the sphere of love … but the trouble is that after marriage, love often flies out of the window, and then everything becomes "forced labor" … obligations without any rights! Free service in exchange for pain and sacrifice!

I think one should commence by fixing a small monthly allowance for every woman who gets married, from the day of her marriage. A salary paid to the mothers by all the nation and which comes out of all the earnings of all the workers in the country, including the women. … That allowance could be, for a start, half the average national salary, and thus the woman, housekeeper, mistress of the home, would have an income of her own apart from what the man wishes to give her. Later increases for each child could be added . … I do not yet wish to carry this idea into the field of action. It would be better for everyone to think it over. When the time comes, the idea should be ripe.

She had hospitals and clinics, with first-rate equipment and medical personnel, built for poor people. Each day she herself spent hours in public audience with poor people. A young Catholic poet, José Maria Castineira de Dios, reported in admiration:

There were human beings in that room with dirty clothes and they smelt very bad. Evita would place her fingers into their suppurating wounds for she was able to see the pain of all these people and feel it herself. She could touch the most terrible things with

Brazil who approved of foreign investment and those who criticized it as anti-national. In the end, pulled in conflicting directions, implicated in corruption charges leveled against his government, and under attack for the assassination of an opponent by a member of his own bodyguard, Vargas committed suicide in 1954. His successors continued his administration of limited democracy, a policy consistent with most other countries in Latin America. In 1961 Vargas's former Minister of Labor, João Goulart, became president. He was also unable to balance the conflicting interest groups, and in

1964 he moved decisively to the left, nationalizing the oil industry, expropriating large estates, granting the right to vote to enlisted soldiers, and legalizing the Communist Party. The army deposed him and remained in power for the next twenty years.

Brazil's fall to military rule was also consistent with events elsewhere. In 1959, only four Latin American states were ruled by the military. Between 1962 and 1964, however, the same fate befell eight additional countries in Latin America. In Brazil the military interpreted the national motto *ordem e progresso*, order and progress, aggressively.

a Christian attitude that amazed me, kissing and letting herself be kissed. There was a girl whose lip was half eaten away with syphilis and when I saw that Evita was about to kiss her and tried to stop her, she said to me, "Do you know what it will mean when I kiss her?"

On the other hand, Argentina's most distinguished man of letters, Jorge Luis Borges (1899–1986) publicly referred to Evita as a "whore," and he was not alone. Perón dismissed Borges from his government job in a library and shifted him to inspecting chickens in a public market. (Winn, p. 148). Many in the upper classes and in the military feared in her the potential

for revolution. British journalist Richard Bourne reported in 1967:

As a crusade Eva's feminism was logically entwined with an attack on the oligarchy and a drive for industrialization and labour benefits: for the countryside, to the traditional eye of the rural landowners, was a man's world, and increasing industrialization must call on female labour which must itself get near to equal rights if male labour was not to suffer. The virulent dislike of Eva among wealthy women, though it focused on superficialities like her opulent jewellery and her décolleté dresses, testified, along with the latent hostility to her in the officer class, to the revolutionary nature of her role. (all quotations cited in Hanke and Rausch)

Eva Perón in Buenos Aires, Argentina, April 8, 1952. Eva, wife of Juan Perón, speaks the closing words in the final meeting of the National Congress of Rural Workers in Buenos Aires. She is pale and drawn, after a long illness that began shortly after she withdrew as a candidate for the vice-presidency of Argentina. It was reported that the Army had "requested" her to step down. Eva Perón remains a charismatic figure beyond the boundaries of South America.

When confronted with guerrilla opposition in the cities, the generals used torture and death squads to suppress it. By 1968 Brazil's "economic miracle" was underway. The Brazilian economic rate of growth between 1968 and 1974 averaged 10–11 percent. Even after the oil shocks of 1973 (see pp. 695 and 698), it remained at 4–7 percent per year. But income distribution was one of the least equitable in the world. The richest 10 percent saw their share of the nation's income rise from 40 percent in 1960 to 50 percent in 1980. By that time, the poorest 50 percent received only 13 percent of the national income. In addition, in order to sustain its investments, Brazil borrowed on a large scale externally and printed money at home. Rates of debt and of inflation skyrocketed.

POPULISM AND NATIONALISM IN ARGENTINA 1920–80

In the 1920s, the wheat and beef of the *pampas* dominated Argentina's export economy. Industrial production was small but growing, providing some 10 percent of the national income, and industrial workers, many of them immigrants, especially from Italy, were demanding rights. In 1919, a metalworkers' strike had developed into a general strike of all workers. The police responded by seeking out anarchists and radicals and by shooting demonstrators, and sometimes innocent passers-by, on the streets.

In 1929 the economy crashed. Argentina, because of the vulnerability of its food exports, suffered perhaps more than anywhere else in Latin America. Already the nation's politics had been split between the industrial interests in the cities and the rich landlords of the *estancias*, the estates of the *pampas*. Argentina had no better policies for reconciling these diverse interests than had Brazil. In 1930 a military coup ousted President Yrigoyen and took power. The new government did institute ISI in the 1930s and saw the industrial sector grow to almost 20 percent of the national product by 1940. It expanded still further during World War II, when foreign supplies and markets were cut off. Because Argentina remained neutral during the war (until March 1945), the United States refused to supply the country with weapons, so the state began to manufacture its own armaments. Each increase in industrialization increased the tensions between industrialists, workers, and landlords of the estates.

In 1943 the army staged another coup, and soon Colonel Juan D. Perón (1895–1974) emerged as its leader, basing his power on the urban laboring classes, which he had organized and rewarded with benefits when he had been Minister of Labor from 1943 to 1945. Trade unions quadrupled in size. When other military leaders jailed Perón, workers from the whole country converged on Buenos Aires in mass demonstrations, forcing his release. In the election of 1946, Perón, campaigning with and for the **descamisados**, "shirtless" workers, was elected president with 56 percent of the vote. But could he, or anyone, rule this politically fractured country? Identfying himself with the common people of Argentina, Perón promoted populism and nationalism, calling for sacrifices on behalf of the nation, and calling on the nation to serve the workers. He nationalized foreign-owned (British) railways, telephone companies, and oil resources. He paid off the foreign debt. He granted higher pay, better conditions, vacations, and other benefits to urban workers and kept them in state-sponsored unions. He crushed independent labor unions that challenged him, especially when the economy experienced a downturn after about 1949.

Perón was controversial, and his wife, María Eva Duarte Perón (1919–52), was even more so. A beautiful actress, born out of wedlock to an impoverished mother, she was accused of sleeping her way to the top of Argentina's power structure. Even more than Perón, however, Evita, as she chose to be called, identified closely with the masses. She implemented her own programs through a Social Aid Foundation, and she led the Peronist Women's Party, which won equal rights for women, including the vote, in 1947. Her presence, and her radio broadcasts on behalf of her husband and herself, encouraged popular support for Perón's government. Her death from cancer in 1952 at the age of thirty-three seriously reduced Perón's power and effectiveness.

Economic problems multiplied, interest groups clashed, and Perón could not solve the intractable conflicts. He clamped down decisively and violently, outlawing alternative unions on both the right and left, closing newspapers, jailing his opposition, and taking control of radio broadcasting. In 1955 anti-Perónist military officials drove him from office. Perón's popularity remained so strong among the masses, however, that he was recalled to Argentina in 1973 and won election as president, with his new wife Isabel as vice-president. Perón died the next year, and Isabel took over the presidency until ousted by a military coup in 1976. The military remained in power until 1984.

THE UNITED STATES AND LATIN AMERICA

As Latin Americans were creating new political, economic, social, and cultural strategies, they usually had to keep in mind, to some degree, the background presence of the United States in the region. The Monroe Doctrine of 1823, issued just as revolutions had won for Latin American countries their independence from the Spanish, declared the Americas out-of-bounds for European military intervention or colonization. The American declaration was backed by the approval of the more powerful British government. The Doctrine has been called ineffective, inasmuch as Spain did intervene peripherally in the region. Yet the most significant European intervention in Latin America, France's military seizure of Mexico and its (temporary) placement of Maximilian of Austria on the throne, took place in 1862, when the United States was involved in its own civil war. However, as we have seen, the United States did intervene in Latin America on its own. It encouraged Texas' independence from Mexico in 1836 and annexed Texas in 1845. In the Mexican–American war of 1846-8, the United States seized territory from Mexico, and in 1898 won Puerto Rico and Cuba in the Spanish–American War. The United States annexed Puerto Rico and, through the Platt Amendment of 1898, the United States also established a kind of protectorate over Cuba. In 1903, the United States encouraged Panama to secede from Colombia, and immediately recognized Panamanian independence and negotiated for the right to build the Panama Canal.

The United States became the principal trade partner and source of investment capital for many Latin American countries. In the mid-1910s, it bought 75 percent of Mexico's exports, and 67 percent of Central America's. In exchange, the United States sold Mexico 50 percent of its imports, and 75 percent of Central America's. "Dollar diplomacy" was considered appropriate. President William Howard Taft (1908–12) declared that he stood ready for "active intervention to secure our merchandise and our capitalists' opportunity for profitable investment" (Burns, p. 174). By 1929, 40 percent—$3.5 billion—of all United States foreign investment was in Latin America.

Between 1898 and 1934, the United States sent troops into Latin American countries more than thirty times, including Colombia, Cuba, the Dominican Republic, Guatemala, Haiti, Honduras, Mexico, Nicaragua, and Panama. Most frequently the purpose was to collect debts owed to the American government or to American or European investors. The nations of Central America, in particular, were sometimes referred to, negatively, as "banana republics," connoting not only their reliance on single tropical fruits as the basis of their economies, but also their domination by the United States and their lack of effective control over their own politics. United States intervention in Nicaragua lasted from 1909 to 1933 almost without a break. The United States marines trained the Nicaraguan National Guard and its commander Anastasio Somoza (1896–1956). In 1934 Somoza

An anti-American poster from the time of the Sandinista revolution, Nicaragua, 1979. Note the various drawings on the figure: military helicopters on the hat; a peace sign ("paz") among the little egghead representations of people massed together demonstrating; an ironic dollar bill with "In God we trust" on the leg. The final touch is the cowboy boot resting firmly on Uncle Sam's hat to keep him in check. Uncle Sam is even a sickly gray color in contrast with the brightly colored cowboy. The stripes of the American flag serve as a backdrop.

assassinated Augusto César Sandino (1893–1934) who had been the leading guerrilla fighter against the United States, and in 1936 he seized control of the national government, turning the presidency into a family dynasty. That dynasty, supported by the United States, was brought down in 1979 by guerrilla fighters calling themselves "Sandinistas."

In 1933 President Franklin Roosevelt inaugurated the "Good Neighbor Policy," to limit United States intervention. During the administration of Lázaro Cárdenas in Mexico, Roosevelt refused to act militarily when Cárdenas nationalized United States oil companies in 1938 and redistributed millions of acres of land in promoting "Mexican socialism." Cárdenas ultimately compensated the oil companies and resolved to improve church–state relations. United States–Latin American relations gradually improved, and following World War II, the United States sought Latin American backing in the Cold War and in 1948 took the lead in establishing the Organization of American States (OAS) to address hemispheric issues.

GUATEMALA 1951–1990s

Latin American critics of United States economic power were branded communists, and the United States often condemned as communist Latin American attempts to make their societies more egalitarian. In Guatemala,the world's second largest producer of bananas, Colonel Jacobo Arbenz (1913–71) won election as president in an open, free election in 1951. Arbenz proceeded to seize some 400,000 acres (161,880 hectares) of fallow land held by the United Fruit Company, a private company owned mostly by United States citizens. He offered compensation according to the value of the land declared for tax purposes by the company, but the company found this insufficient. Arbenz also wanted to build a highway from his capital to the Atlantic Ocean, which would have broken the company's transportation monopoly, and he proposed building a hydroelectric power plant which would free Guatemala from its dependence on a foreign supply. Finally, fearing an attack by exiles training in neighboring countries, Arbenz sought to buy arms from the United States. When they turned him down, he bought from Poland, which was then a communist country. A small Guatemalan army-in-exile of some 150 soldiers, equipped by the United States, attacked almost immediately from Honduras. The Arbenz government fell, virtually without defenders. Arbenz's successor, Carlos Castillo

Armas (1914–57) returned the lands taken from the United Fruit Company, abolished several political parties, disenfranchised all illiterates, about half the adult population, and had those who opposed him jailed, tortured, exiled, or executed. Castillo Armas was assassinated in mid-1957, and soon Guatemala plunged into a civil war in which 100,000 people died before a negotiated resolution was achieved in the 1990s.

CHILE 1970–90

From 1964 to 1970, Eduardo Frei (1911–81) led a Christian Democratic government in Chile, which began a program of agrarian reform and nationalized, with compensation, copper mines owned by United States private companies. Considered moderate, Frei had good relations with the United States government. In 1970, seeking more radical reform, the voters in Chile elected the socialist Salvador Allende (1908–73). The United States government and major transnational corporations were apprehensive and opposed his appointment. Once in office, President Allende confirmed their fears. He continued the nationalization of the foreign-owned copper industry, which produced three-fourths of Chile's exports, increased agrarian reform, and purchased control of most banks. Allende increased the salaries of government workers, and expanded medical and housing programs. The usual conflict between the desire to improve economic and social benefits, on the one hand, and the problem of finding resources to pay, on the other, arose. Shortages and inflation resulted. The United States government sharply reduced loans and aid to Allende's government, and international banks also cut loans. The United States Central Intelligence Agency, with a mandate to overthrow Allende, covertly financed strikes and opposition parties. Finally, the middle class, and especially women, who found the economic situation intolerable, persuaded the military to act. In September 1973 they attacked and bombed the presidential palace, and Allende was killed.

General Augusto Pinochet (b. 1915), who headed the new government, immediately killed or detained thousands of Allende supporters, men and women. He ruled until 1988, feared and hated for his violence towards the opposition, but effective in restoring the economy, with the aid of advisers from the United States. In a plebiscite in 1988, however, he was rejected by Chile's voters, and the government passed to the opposition. Chile had returned to democracy.

CUBA 1950–1990s

The greatest confrontation between any Latin American country and the United States followed the Cuban revolution of 1959. Fidel Castro (b. 1926), received his law degree in 1950 and, two years later, sued in Cuba's Constitutional Court to have the government of Cuban dictator Fulgencio Batista (1901–73) ruled unconstitutional. Batista had ruled Cuba from 1934 to 1944, and he returned as president, seizing power in 1952. Castro's suit was unsuccessful, and he took to the mountains to organize a guerrilla movement. On July 26, 1953 (celebrated in Cuba as the origin of the revolution), Castro, with a few allies, attacked the Moncada military barracks in Santiago de Cuba. The attack was unsuccessful, and he was captured and sentenced to fifteen years in prison. At his sentencing, Castro declared "History will absolve me," and laid out his own six-point plan for Cuba:

- extensive land redistribution and collectivization, with common use of expensive equipment;

- limits on foreign investment and mobilization of Cuba's own capital through the national bank to invest in industrialization;

- housing policies that would enable each Cuban family to own its own home;

- full employment;

- full literacy in an educational system appropriate to an agrarian society;

- and health care facilities for all.

He further claimed that adequate funding was already available within Cuba and could be mobilized by ending graft and scaling back military expenditures.

Released from jail in the general amnesty of 1955, Castro fled initially to the United States and Mexico, returning to Cuba and resuming guerrilla warfare in 1956. On January 1, 1959, he captured Havana, the capital, and declared a new government for Cuba. Contrary to his promises, Castro did not hold elections, declaring that "the intimate union and identification of the government with the people," made elections unnecessary. Although Castro denied that he was a communist and did, for a time, try to negotiate military and economic agreements with the United States, he soon established close military and economic ties with the Soviet bloc. In the Cold War environment of the time, the United States viewed Castro as a communist and ended the special quota of sugar purchases it had guaranteed to Cuba since the 1930s. In December 1961, Castro announced his allegiance to Marxism-Leninism. From that time, Cuba became dependent upon the Soviet Union, replacing Batista's earlier dependence on the United States with this new alignment.

Castro then proceeded to carry out his announced program. He expropriated foreign assets, including $1 billion in North American property and investments. He collectivized farms, and centralized control of the economy in the hands of the government. He took human development issues most seriously, and devoted money and energies to health, education, and cultural activities. Education and all medical services were free. Between 1958, the year before the revolution, and 1983, a quarter of a century later, life expectancy rose from fifty-eight years to over seventy-three years. The number of doctors rose from 6250 to 17,000; nurses from 400 to 32,000; and medical technicians from 500 to 29,000. Medical facilities began to reach the countryside. Both male and female literacy rates reached about 95 percent. The publication of books rose from 100 titles per year in 1958 to 800 titles in 1973, with the actual numbers of books increasing from 900,000 to 28 million. The living standards of most Cubans improved sharply. Most of the elites fled, however, with the acquiescence of the government, which was pleased to have them gone. These exiles were received with open arms in the United States, where they formed a new large community and lobbied heavily for the United States to take action against Castro.

Two confrontations between Cuba and the United States followed. The American government agreed to arm and support a group of Cuban exiles who wanted to invade the island on the assumption that Cuba's people would welcome the opportunity to overthrow Castro. When the exiles did invade, on April 17, 1961, at the Bay of Pigs, they were immediately defeated by Cuban armed forces. In the next year, Cuba was the focus of the most direct confrontation of the Cold War between the United States and the Soviet Union. The Soviet Union had positioned nuclear missiles in Cuba. They denied the existence of these missiles, but American reconnaissance aircraft obtained photographic evidence. President Kennedy demanded that they be with-

CHE GUEVARA AND GUERRILLA WARFARE

With the success of Mao's communist, agrarian revolution in China (see p. 655) and Castro's in Cuba, and continuing peasant uprisings around the world, including Vietnam, the 1960s were especially alive with rural guerrilla warfare. Usually led by young, vigorous, brave, and single-minded revolutionaries, the guerrilla movements had a powerful mystique, and a number of successes. Technologically, they demonstrated the potential of very simple technologies in conflict against the most sophisticated modern weapons. One of the most charismatic of the guerrilla warriors was Ernesto "Che" Guevara, who was born in Argentina in 1928, and was captured and killed while organizing a guerrilla movement in Brazil in 1967. He participated in Castro's revolution in Cuba and was later appointed head of the national bank. But Guevara chose life as a full-time revolutionary, helping to establish guerrilla *focos*, revolutionary outposts, in many locations.

Nuclei of relatively few persons choose places favorable for guerrilla warfare, sometimes with the intention of launching a counterattack or to weather a storm, and there they begin to take action. But the following must be made clear: At the beginning, the relative weakness of the guerrilla fighters is such that they should endeavor to pay attention only to the terrain, in order to become acquainted with the surroundings, establish connections with the population, and fortify the places that eventually will be converted into bases. The guerrilla unit can survive only if it starts by basing its development on the three following conditions: constant mobility, constant vigilance, constant wariness. ...

We must carry the war into every corner the enemy happens to carry it—to his home, to his centers of entertainment: a total war. It is necessary to prevent him from having a moment of peace, a quiet moment outside his barracks or even inside; we must atack him wherever he may move. ...

Our every action is a battle cry against imperialism, and a battle hymn to the people's unity against the great enemy of mankind: the United States of America. Wherever death may surprise us, let it be welcome, provided that this, our battle cry, may have reached some receptive ear and another hand may be

extended to wield our weapons and other men be ready to intone the funeral dirge with the staccato singing of the machine gun and new battle cries of war and victory.

(Sigmund, pp. 370, 381)

Ernesto "Che" Guevara, photographed in 1963 with his ever-present cigar during his tenure as Minister of Industry. He was born in Argentina, but joined Fidel Castro's revolutionary troops in Cuba. Together they launched the Cuban Revolution, from 1956 to 1959. Castro then appointed Che Minister of Industry, a post he held until 1965. That year Che left Cuba to organize revolutionary warfare elsewhere in Latin America. It was at Waucakwazu in the Bolivian jungle, on October 8, 1967, that he and a group of rebel troops were tracked down by Bolivian government troops and shot.

drawn, even threatening nuclear warfare over the issue. As the world watched, the Soviet Union backed down and removed the missiles, but the United States agreed not to invade Cuba. In the mid-1970s, the military-political interests of the United States also collided as Cuba sent thousands of troops to Ethiopia and Angola to fight, along with Russian troops, in aiding left-wing governments. The Cuban troops remained until the agreement to end the fighting in Angola in 1988.

These events of the early revolution caught the attention and imagination of the world. They test-

Castro, victorious, en route to Havana. Fidel Castro embraces a child amongst a crowd of well-wishers in a small town, shortly after taking power. In January 1959, Cuban dictator Fulgancio Batista was ousted by Castro and his popular revolutionary army. The revolutionaries had been hiding in the mountains since December 1956, fighting against Batista's regime. Their fight to overthrow the dictator was called the "26th July Movement," after the date of their first insurrection against Batista.

ed the ability of a new revolutionary administration to establish a communist government just 90 miles (145 kilometers) off the mainland of the United States and to spread the revolution, establish an independent foreign policy, and to carry out a radical restructuring of the politics, economics, culture, and social life of the country. The achievements were mixed, and problems multiplied after the end of the Cold War. Castro's government did not allow free and open nationwide elections, but it did permit and even encourage its enemies to leave the island. Almost one million people departed, mostly for the United States. Cuba's health and welfare measures were models for the entire developing world. It did not succeed in industrializing and diversifying the economy, but has remained dependent on sugar as its principal export crop. While it was no longer dependent on the United States, it had developed an equal dependency on the Soviet Union. With the disintegration of the Soviet Union, Cuba remains one of the last outposts of communist government, and with the end of subsidies from the communist bloc, Cuba's economy has deteriorated.

CURRENT ISSUES AND TRENDS

THE MILITARY IN POWER 1960–90

Seeking to contain the Cuban revolution in 1961, President John F. Kennedy committed the United States to a new program—the Alliance for Progress. Begun with considerable fanfare and spending about $10 billion in the next decade, the Alliance, nevertheless, seemed not to achieve any lasting structural changes in Latin America, and after some years the program dropped from public attention. Within many countries, the military decided to take charge. Acquainted with modern technology through their weapons systems, viewing themselves as acting for the good of the nation as a whole, uneasy with the threat of revolutionary change from below, and with a long tradition of intervention, the generals seized control in many countries.

In Brazil, for example, the military overthrew the democratically elected constitutional president João Goulart in 1964 and stayed in power for the next twenty-one years. Argentina was in the hands of its military almost continuously from the time of its first coup against Juan Perón in 1955 until 1982, when they tried to capture by force the Malvina (Falkland) Islands from the British. They failed and stepped down from office, allowing democratic elections in 1983. Uruguay, too, came under military rule in 1973. The military in Brazil, Argentina, and Uruguay all used repression and torture to stay in power. In Argentina especially, the military crushed opposition brutally and illegally in a "dirty war." Thousands of people "disappeared," kidnapped, tortured, and killed by the government. Women took the lead in protesting these disappearances. Meeting regularly for public demonstrations, the Mothers of the Plaza de Mayo kept alive the memory of their relatives and focussed national and international attention on their fate.

In the 1980s, many of the military administrations returned to civilian rule: Peru in 1980; Argentina in 1983; Brazil in 1989. Mexico, a one-party democracy since the revolution, found new parties arising and contesting for power. In the 1990s, these parties began to win local and state elections and built popular support for continuing challenges at the national level.

ECONOMICS AND TECHNOLOGY

To what degree will Latin American countries adjust their economic policies toward "development"—that is, an increase in living standards for all their peoples—rather than just "growth"—that is, increasing national productivity with the benefits going to a small elite? This question of the politics of the economy has occupied Latin America's thinking for 200 years and it remains unresolved.

THE POLITICAL ECONOMY OF LATIN AMERICAN DEVELOPMENT

*R*aul Prebisch (1901–85) of Argentina, one of Latin America's most distinguished economists, served in many important positions concerned with Latin American development, including Secretary General of the United Nations Conference on Trade and Development. His recommendations, formulated mostly in the 1960s and still influential, include: agrarian and tax reform, government planning, economic integration within the country, international price agreements on primary commodity exports, and some preferences for goods from developing countries:

> The social structure prevalent in Latin America constitutes a serious obstacle to technical progress and consequently to economic and social development. ... The social structure is largely characterized by a situation of privilege in the distribution of wealth and therefore of income ... extravagant patterns of consumption in the upper strata of society, in contrast with the unsatisfactory living conditions of the broad masses of the population. ... The test of a system's dynamic strength lies in its ability to accelerate the rate of development and progressively improve the distribution of income. ... Such a rate of growth is not feasible without substantial restriction of the consumption of the higher income brackets. ...

> Latin America must quicken its rate of economic development and redistribute income in favor of the broad masses of the population. ... State action is indispensable as a means of progressively remedying the marked disparities in income distribution by virtue of the increase in income accompanying the changes. ... The goal must be a social order free from privilege, and not only economic privilege, but also the baneful privilege by which some men usurp dominion over the ideas of the rest, over the creative forces of the spirit, and over the deepest feelings of the heart.

> Without prejudice to measures aimed at eliminating or reducing these barriers to trade, it is a matter of urgent necessity to explore with the utmost diligence the possibilities for trade with other regions of the world. . .

> There is no doubt that the most stubborn bottleneck in the whole of Latin America's development process is generally to be found in agricultural production. Several factors are jointly responsible for this: the system of land tenure, which makes it difficult for modern techniques to be assimilated; inadequate state aid in the work of adapting and diffusing these techniques; and the unsatisfactory investment saturation. (Sigmund, pp. 424–38)

Latin American economies had suffered throughout the 1980s because of the enormous debts that were incurred in the 1970s. Development possibilities had appeared robust in that decade, especially with the success of oil production in Mexico, and creditors had extended enormous loans. Pay-back time came in the 1980s, and the burdens were too great. The World Bank offered assistance in rescheduling the debts, but the Bank required rigorous schedules of repayment, and it required nations to restructure their economies to achieve these repayments. The World Bank remedies required cut-backs in subsidies of food to the poor, in social programs, and in state employment. As governments attempted to implement these policies, they were often met by rioting in the streets. World Bank policies might be economically sound, but they were politically and socially destabilizing. The old conflict between economic necessity and social wishes resurfaced. Nevertheless, in the 1990s, the Bank and various national governments were attempting to reach compromises acceptable to both.

A dramatic shift in international economic relations occurred in 1992–3, as Mexico joined the United States and Canada in the North American Free Trade Agreement (NAFTA). After years of aggressive nationalism on both sides of the Rio Grande, the United States and Mexico were agreeing that free, open trade would be the best policy. The early results of NAFTA are still being assessed. Meanwhile in the "southern cone," Argentina, Brazil, Paraguay, and Uruguay were establishing a similar free-trade agreement among their 200 million people and almost $500 million economies into a single free-trade zone called MERCOSUR.

The structures of production and of marketing were undergoing massive change as producers, consumers, and governments adjusted to the new possiblities of the movement of goods across borders. For example, another initiative between the United States and Mexico on free trade has led to the development of large urban production centers at the border. Here, parts of manufactured products are brought to Mexico from the United States, assembled, and then shipped back to the United States. The assembly plants, *maquiladores*, have increased employment possibilities and swelled the populations of border cities like Tijuana to over a million inhabitants.

Borders were not, however, supposed to be open for trade in drugs. Nevertheless, billions of dollars in illegal drugs were being grown and processed in Latin American countries, notably Colombia, and shipped to the United States and Europe. The trade brought enormous wealth to those who

Latin American drugs trade. Processing coca leaves in Colombia, the first step to manufacturing the illegal drug cocaine. The farmers who grow the crop see but a fraction of the money gained from their labors. Drugs remain a lucrative business for the criminal barons of Latin America, and it is unlikely that manufacture will be forcibly stopped in the near future, despite increasing pressure from Western governments.

controlled it, but it corrupted governments by purchasing their complicity, or by murdering leaders who opposed the traffic. Colombia suffered years of internal warfare, partly over the control of the drug trade. In the late 1990s, the murders of government officials and of drug traffickers suggested that citizens of Mexico, too, were involved in the trade. In addition, millions of people in the United States, Europe, and Latin America, had become addicted. The trade flourished, and still flourishes, on the demand of consumers in the developed world and on the need for an economic cash crop among the peasantry in Latin America. Actions to control the trade within Latin America have had some limited effect, but the industry will continue until demand is reduced, and this problem is centered in the United States and Europe.

Another problem of the economic growth of the 1970s was its impact on the ecology. Mexico City, Santiago, and São Paulo are among the most polluted cities in the world, with a constant blanket of smog lying over them. Dangerous pesticides—banned in the United States—are in widespread use. International attention has focussed especially on the destruction of two-thirds of Latin America's tropical rainforests, and the loss of thousands of plant and animal species. In the Amazon rainforest Brazil targeted massive projects of economic development, including oil and mineral exploration, and of settlement for its rapidly multiplying population. The regional capital of Manaus is now teeming with oil refineries, metal works, lumber mills—and pollution.

Latin American countries, especially Brazil, which have been heavily criticized by the United States and others for destroying the rainforests, have replied with cries of hypocrisy. North America, too, was once covered with forests that were long ago cut down by development. Latin Americans argue that they are being criticized only for coming to the process late. Moreover, they argue, they "develop" the Amazon basin because they need its wealth. If outsiders were serious in their criticisms, they would propose alternative schemes that would allow economic development without ecological harm.

AMERINDIANS—OPPRESSION AND RESPONSE

In the 1970s, the Trans-Amazon highway opened the rainforest to new settlement, and millions of peasants migrated in search of free land. They were followed by ranches and big business corporations. The soil itself proved to be unsuitable for agriculture and was soon eroded and abandoned, although many immigrants stayed on in the new cities. Meanwhile, indigenous populations of the Amazon were unable to defend themselves or their lands in the face of these commercially driven invasions. They were often pushed off ancestral lands and reduced to jobs at low wages in difficult conditions. Many have contracted new diseases, or, like the Yanomami Indians of the Amazon, have been poisoned by the mercury poured into the Amazon by gold miners, or by the waste products of the new industries. Some of the Indians of the Amazon, following patterns established by the Shuar of Ecuador, are forming themselves into federations to maintain their land rights.

In the mountainous regions of the Andes, which run all the way from central America to Chile, the Amerindians have also been extremely ill-treated. Rigoberta Menchu, a Quiche Indian woman, spoke for the millions who suffered in her autobiography, *I, Rigoberta Menchu: An Indian Woman in Guatemala*, which was published in 1983, when she was twenty-three years old. This international bestseller served to focus attention on the brutal repression of Guatemala's indigenous communities that was carried out by the Guatemalan state during the civil war of the 1980s. In 1992, Menchu was awarded the Nobel Prize for Peace for her efforts at negotiating a settlement to this conflict, a process that continues in the mid-1990s.

The autobiography is anything but peaceful as Menchu describes the living and working conditions on the agricultural estates, **fincas**, of Guatemala where Indian workers die early deaths from the burden of the work and the lack of food and medical attention. Her younger brother died, as a child, from such fundamental poverty. When the Indian workers do not submit to the will of the **ladinos**, *mestizos* who own and run the *fincas*, they are beaten and tortured, and the women are raped. Those who protest the conditions on the *fincas* are murdered, often after brutal torture. Menchu witnessed the torture and murder of her brother, saw the raped and disfigured body of her dead mother, and knew of the murder of her father. The Indians began to organize against these conditions and marched on, and occupied, the Spanish embassy in Guatemala City. In January 1981, during a march led by her father Vicente, the Indians were massacred, but others then began to organize a Peasant Unity Committee (CUC).

RIGOBERTA MENCHU AND INDIAN POLITICAL ORGANIZATION

*T*he story of the Latin American Indians, especially in the Andean regions, was not often told in the world outside the mountains, partly because of suppression, partly because their languages were not widely understood. Understanding this difficulty, Rigorberta Menchu learned Spanish, despite the great opposition of the Quiche to cultural assimilation:

> I'm an Indianist, not just an Indian. I'm an Indianist to my fingertips and I defend everything to do with my ancestors. But I didn't understand this in the proper way, because we can only understand when we start talking to each other. And this is the only way we can correct our ideas. Little by little, I discovered many ways in which we had to be understanding towards our ladino [*mestizo*] friends and in which they had to show us understanding too. Because I also knew companeros, ladinos with whom we shared the worst conditions, but who still felt ladino, and as ladinos they didn't see that our poverty united us. But little by little, both they and I began discussing many very important things, and saw that the root of our problems lay in the ownership of the land. All our country's riches are in the hands of the few. ...
>
> In Guatemala the division between Indians and ladinos has contributed to our situation. And it's certain that in our hearts this has affected us very badly. Ladinos are mestizos, the children of Spaniards and Indians who speak Spanish. But they are in the minority. There is a larger percentage of Indians. Some say it is 60 percent, others that it's 80 percent. We don't know the exact number for a very good reason—there are Indians who don't wear Indian clothes and have forgotten their languages, so they are not considered Indians. And there are middle-class Indians who have abandoned their traditions. They aren't considered Indians either. However this ladino minority thinks its blood is superior, a higher quality, and they think of Indians as a sort of animal.
>
> (Menchu, pp. 166-67)

Rigoberta Menchu, a Guatemalan Indian, won the Nobel Peace Prize in 1992 for her efforts to reach a settlement in Guatemala's civil war. Her book, *I, Rigoberta Menchu: An Indian Woman in Guatemala*, was published in 1983 and became a bestseller.

RELIGION AND HOPE FOR THE POOR

The social and economic changes of the twentieth century have also transformed religious belief and practice. Spanish and Portuguese colonialism brought Catholicism to Latin America, and it became an important cultural influence. In the nineteenth century a schism occurred between conservatives, who favored the maintenance of the traditional privileges of the Catholic Church, and liberals, who were often deeply anti-clerical. In the twentieth century, the influence of Catholicism at the popular level has been challenged by urbanization, migration, and the spread of evangelical Protestantism. Within Catholicism, substantial transformations have also occurred.

In March 1980, Archbishop Oscar Romero of El Salvador was assassinated as he was officiating at the mass in a San Salvador chapel. The right-wing assassin had perhaps opposed the archbishop's message: "When all peaceful means have been exhausted, the church considers insurrection moral and justified" (Keen, p. 571). Romero had also advised soldiers that it was morally just to refuse to follow unjust orders. Romero was only one of about 850 church leaders who had been assassinated during the previous fifteen years, since the assassination of Camilo Torres, a priest and sociologist in Colombia. An outstanding scholar and teacher, Torres gave up on peaceful reform and joined Colombia's communist-led guerrillas. He was killed in a battle with government forces in February 1966. In December 1980, three American nuns and a lay missionary, who had gone to work with poor refugees in El Salvador, were also murdered by security officers of the state. Many members of the church had moved toward a position of active involvement on behalf of the poor.

The church's identification with the poor was part of an international reassessment addressed by the Second Vatican Council (1962–5) in Rome, which called for much greater concern with issues of material welfare and the mal-distribution of wealth throughout the world. At the 1968 second conference of Latin American bishops at Medellín, Colombia, the bishops further supported this reorientation, and reaffirmed that point of view in 1979 at their meeting in Mexico.

In the late 1960s and 1970s a new school of thought, called **liberation theology**, took shape.

Identifying with Jesus' ministry to the poor, it began to establish grass-roots organizations in poor neighborhoods of cities and in rural pockets of poverty. These *comunidades de base* combined study, prayer, and active efforts to identify, define, and solve the problems of their localities by directly confronting them and the local leaders who had power to effect change. Dom Helder Camara, Archbishop of Recife, Brazil, stated its central perspective thus:

> Come, Lord, do not smile and say you are already with us. Millions do not know You and to us who do, what is the difference? What is the point of Your presence if our lives do not alter? (Lernoux, p. 449)

As this movement threatened the state and the wealthy, it confronted powerful opposition and was willing to engage in violence if necessary.

The pope since 1978, John Paul II, did advocate for the poor:

> The voice of the Church, echoing the voice of human conscience … deserves and needs to be heard in our time when the growing wealth of a few parallels the growing poverty of the masses. (Lernoux, p. 409)

But he backed away from commitments that were so deeply political and so radically confrontational. The advocates of liberation theology claim to combine Christian ethics with Marxist politics, and the

Radical religion. A priest holds hands with members of the Base Christian Community in Panama. Proponents of liberation theology, which originated in Latin America in the 1960s, typically aligned themselves with left-wing, revolutionary movements, such as the Sandinistas in Nicaragua. When influential priests and bishops espoused a Marxist view of society and argued that the church's role was to assist the oppressed, they came into conflict with established Catholic authorities as well as political leaders.

Pope, who had grown up in communist Poland, rejected the Marxist part of the orientation, and has appointed mostly conservative clergy as new posts opened. The clergy in Latin America have been deeply split. About 20 percent, especially in Brazil, have aligned themselves with liberation theology; the overwhelming majority have rejected this level of activism.

The most rapidly growing religious movement in Latin America, however, has been evangelical Protestantism. Its popularity has increased for several reasons: the long-term missionary effort from the United States, the identification of the Catholic Church with the powerful elites, and the movement's suitability for the now largely urban and industrial environment. Evangelical Protestantism claims between 30 and 50 million adherents throughout Latin America, perhaps 10 percent of the population. The missionaries work among the poor, especially the immigrants to the cities, and

Mexican painter Frida Kahlo's *Marxism Will Give Health to the Sick*, **1954.** Kahlo, who was married to Diego Rivera, the famous revolutionary muralist, mainly produced self-portraits that focussed on the physical pain, caused by an accident, which was a chronic feature of her life.

CARIBBEAN AND LATIN AMERICAN NOBEL LAUREATES

St. Lucia:	Derek Walcott (b. 1950; literature 1992)
Argentina:	Carlos Saavedra Lamas (1878–1959; peace 1936) Luis Federico Leloir (1906–87; chemistry 1970) Adolfo Pérez Esquivel (peace 1980)
Chile:	Gabriela Mistral (1899–1957; literature 1945) Pablo Neruda (1904–73; literature 1971)
Colombia:	Gabriel García Márquez (b. 1928; literature 1982)
Costa Rica:	Oscar Arias Sánchez (peace 1987)
Guatemala:	Miguel Angel Asturias (1899–1974; literature 1967) Rigoberta Menchu (peace 1992)
Mexico:	Alfonso García Robles (1911–91; peace 1982) Octavio Paz (b. 1914; literature 1990) Mario Molina (chemistry 1995)

most eschew violence, condemn communism, and promise salvation in the next lifetime rather than here and now. Some also work actively for agrarian reform and social change.

THE "UNORGANIZED" SECTOR

Finally, the enormous cities of Latin America, exploding with the growth of new immigrants, demonstrate new ways in which citizens cope with poverty and urbanization. Academics have come to distinguish between "slums of hope" and "slums of despair," and they have found far more hope than previously thought. We have already discussed this phenomenon in other regions of the world, but Latin America, which experienced rapid urbanization earlier than other third world regions, also experienced these grass-roots problems and solutions first. As immigrants entered the cities, many of them found, or seized, their own parcels of land for housing.

Frequently they acted together as communities, finding strength in numbers. Sometimes government intervened and bulldozed their dwellings. Often, however, in deference to the numbers of people involved, they left the squatter settlers alone. As immigrants from rural areas, the settlers were accustomed to building their own housing, and they now proceeded to improve their housing with whatever materials they found available. Over the years, squatter settlements have often transformed themselves into middle-class housing colonies. The squatters gained reputations as upwardly mobile citizens, working to build a place for themselves in the face of enormous difficulties. Their slums were slums of hope.

Finding, and creating, jobs also became a do-it-yourself project. Governments offered little if any help in finding work, and existing large-scale enterprises preferred to hire more established workers. So the immigrants began to develop enterprises in the "unorganized" sector; they became self-employed. They took on jobs in local construction, sold goods door-to-door, pushed carts, created and peddled handicrafts. In short, in order to survive they used their own ingenuity. The ingenuity and creativity of these common people created a different kind of hope for the poor than the political confrontation of liberation theology. Hernando de Soto's study of this movement, *The Other Path*, emphasizes the initiative and dynamism of Peru's underground economy. Although many observers saw the political and the entrepreneurial routes to change as opposing one another, they might, in fact, well provide complementary approaches to improving the position of Latin America's people. We have seen in Latin America a deep, continuing disjuncture between political wishes and economic realities. These grass-roots movements so characteristic of Latin America in the late 1990s promised a way of combining both.

BIBLIOGRAPHY

Andrea, Alfred J. and James H. Overfield, eds. *The Human Record* (Boston: Houghton Mifflin, 2nd ed., 1994).

Azuela, Mariano. *The Underdogs*, trans. by E. Munguia, Jr. (New York: Signet Classic, 1963).

Berryman, Phillip. *Liberation Theology* (Philadelphia: Temple University Press, 1987).

Borges, Jorge Luis. *Borges: A Reader*, ed. by Emir Rodriguez Monegal and Alastair Reid (New York: E.P. Dutton, 1981).

Burns, E. Bradford. *Latin America: A Concise Interpretive History* (Englewood Cliffs, NJ: Prentice Hall, 5th ed., 1990).

Freire, Paulo. *Pedagogy of the Oppressed* (New York: Seabury Press, 1968).

Fuentes, Carlos. *The Death and Life of Artemio Cruz* (New York: Farrar, Straus and Giroux, 1964).

Gárcia Márquez, Gabriel. *One Hundred Years of Solitude*, trans. by Gregory Rabasa (New York: Harper and Row, 1970).

Gilbert, Alan and Joséf Gugler. *Cities, Poverty and Development: Urbanization in the Third World* (Oxford: Oxford University Press, 2nd ed., 1992).

Hanke, Lewis and Jane M. Rausch, eds. *People and Issues in Latin American History* (New York: Markus Wiener, 1990).

Keen, Benjamin. *A History of Latin America* (Boston: Houghton Mifflin, 5th ed., 1996).

Lernoux, Penny. *Cry of the People* (New York: Penguin, 1982).

Mallon, Florencia E. *Peasant and Nation* (Berkeley: University of California Press, 1995).

—. "The Promise and Dilemma of Subaltern Studies: Perspectives from Latin American History," *American Historical Review*, XCIX No. 5 (December 1994), 491–515.

Menchu, Rigoberta. *I, Rigoberta Menchu: An Indian Woman in Guatemala*, trans. by Elisabeth Burgos Debray (London: Verso, 1984).

Sigmund, Paul, ed. *The Ideologies of the Developing World* (New York: Praeger, 2nd ed. revised, 1972).

Sivard, Ruth Leger. *World Military and Social Expenditures 1996* (Washington: World Priorities Inc., 16th ed., 1996).

Soto, Hernando de. *The Other Path* (New York: Harper and Row, 1989).

Winn, Peter. *Americas: The Changing Face of Latin America and the Caribbean* (Berkeley: University of California Press, 1992).

AFTERWORD

*"Society also expects
an interpretation of
the past which is
relevant to the present
and a basis for
formulating decisions
about the future."*

JOHN TOSH

SO WHAT?
MAKING SENSE OF IT ALL

SITUATING ONESELF
IN HISTORY

Historians typically claim that history is more than just interesting. They claim it provides a necessary preparation for life by enriching human understanding and thus providing a basis for action. In his quotation introducing this afterword John Tosh sets out what he calls "the proper social role of historical knowledge" (p. 21). P.B. and J.S. Medawar reinforce this expectation from their point of view as biologists:

> Human behavior can be genuinely purposive because only human beings guide their behavior by a knowledge of what happened before they were born and a preconception of what may happen after they are dead; thus only human beings find their way by a light that illumines more than the patch of ground they stand on. (cited in Boorstin, p. 557)

History provides this guidance. As Tosh points out: "History trains the mind, enlarges the sympathies, and provides a much needed historical perspective on some of the most pressing problems of our times" (p. 24). It teaches "practical lessons in public affairs." But the lessons are not simple, nor

are they the same for all students. Each of us interprets the "lessons of history" according to an individual system of values. Tosh continues: "Different conceptions of the social order produce rival histories ... History is a political battle ground" (p. 8). Our closing section addresses these diverse calls to action, making suggestions for practical, local engagement with today's global issues.

UNDERSTANDING
THE WORLD THROUGH
HISTORICAL METHOD

Throughout *The World's History* we have stressed history as a disciplined method of understanding the processes of change in human life, an understanding which helps in forming contemporary policy. The discipline begins by asking questions, posing problems, and addressing themes. In the case of world history these are big questions, global problems, and universal themes.

By touching on virtually every region of the world and providing readers with a wide sampling of peoples and the societies they have built, this text has emphasized global coverage. Constant comparison and contrast among these societies have prepared readers to ask important questions: How have various societies coped with similar problems? What can be learned from their experience? By following a chronology of events and examining institutions and processes of global importance readers are able to understand more clearly how people work within their past heritage to create a new future. Studies of the interactions of individuals and societies in the past also provide examples for understanding these relationships today. The exploration of domestic life and gender and class relations in earlier societies enables readers to consider alternate possibilities for the future.

These explorations have employed all the social science disciplines as tools of understanding: anthropology, economics, geography, political science, and sociology. They have relied on the humanities—art and literature—to uncover the feelings and attitudes of people. Fundamental skills in reading and analyzing texts and artifacts underlie all these studies.

From beginning to end *The World's History* has emphasized multiple perspectives. What is important and consequential to one person may be less so to someone else. What appears beneficial to one may seem less so, or even harmful, to another. The historical characters have their differing perspectives; historians studying them have their own perspectives; and the study of these layers of perspectives helps readers to develop their own value systems.

The study of history can also encourage change. In so far as we find the present imperfect and seek to change it, we may find in the past some guidance to alternate institutions and practices, and to methods employed in achieving them. In demonstrating that human arrangements have not always been as they are today, nor need they be the same in the future, history may even be subversive. In all cases, the study of history beckons us to consider the kind of future we might like, and to make personal commitments to bringing it into existence.

UNDERSTANDING THROUGH CONTENT AND INFORMATION

The study and the teaching of history do carry with them civic responsibilities, although each person may interpret them in his or her own way. Some readers may find a place in science or technology, others in the military, some in economics and business, others in education or social work, still others in the creative and applied arts, some raising families in the home, others in the workplace earning a livelihood. Most of us will engage in several of these activities. The study of history encourages us to see our work in broader perspective—to see ourselves as part of the global, millennia-old pattern of human life.

A brief review of the contents of *The World's History* enables us to understand this global perspective and gives an opportunity to consider some possible world futures and possible commitments to encouraging those futures.

An understanding of early hominid life, for example, provides insight into contemporary human behavior (Part 1). Human evolution points to a need to sustain human roots in nature, and therefore a concern for the ecology of the globe. The establishment of small, kin-based bands and their relationships to one another indicate a need to nourish small-group relations, and to achieve satisfying inter-group relationships.

The earliest settlements demonstrate the need for leadership, government, and protection (Part 2). Composed 5000 years ago, *The Epic of Gilgamesh* points out the suffering of citizens under tyranny, and their need to curb excessive, arbitrary power. Hammurabi's *Code* demonstrates the critical importance of law to society. Large-scale armed battles, and the need for defense, had begun. Literature and the arts flourished, suggesting the importance of self-expression as a basic human characteristic. Jewelry, sometimes dazzling in its beauty, marked an early concern for personalized adornment. Intense concern with the afterlife exhibited the human quest for some transcendent meaning and a sense of purpose in life beyond everyday existence.

An examination of empires shows that from earliest times observers believed the desire for conquest was natural—as was the desire to be free (Part 3). Conquest and resistance coexisted. Empires rose and fell. Valuable lessons from these early experiences include: an understanding of the impermanence of conquest, a distrust of imperial power, a deeper sense of humility and compassion, and a recognition of people's ultimately unquenchable desire to be free from rule by others. Nevertheless, political/military/economic power is real, and we must decide when and how to build it, resist it, compromise with it, attempt to negotiate its benevolent application. Some readers may look forward to some form of global political structure which might bring greater order and stability to these relationships.

An exploration of five religious belief systems dating back thousands of years reveals these faiths to be still very much alive, although in modified forms, in today's world (Part 4). These systems have inspired some of the most noble artistic creations and humane teachings—as well as some of the most cruel persecutions. They again remind us that it is a part of being human to seek some understanding of one's place in the cosmos; that people create and join organizations locally and globally to find guidance and companionship in that quest; and that each person's search is unique and deserving of respect. People resist the imposition of unwelcome spiritual authority just as they resist political and military authorities that are imposed against their will. In every age some people have modified older religious systems and created new ones. Some have rejected supernatural teachings in favor of more humanistic perspectives.

By studying the beginnings of world trade and the emergence of a capitalist system (Part 5) we can gain greater insight into the principal economic system of the modern world—one in which business communities have achieved great power, asserting the belief that private gain is beneficial and will ultimately serve the public good. Other, earlier, alternate systems that vested power in other groups in society, especially religious, political, and military authorities, were also examined. These systems, typically, were unwilling to put their trust in the benevolence of entrepreneurs. Readers who are pleased with the capitalist system as it exists today will applaud and attempt to conserve it. Skeptics may advocate the return of earlier systems or the creation of new ones. All will recognize that the size and power of modern business enterprise modify the structure of the economy and require constant monitoring, although they will differ on the significance of the results.

Historians may not be able to study individual life stories of everyday people who did not leave personal records, but they may be able to understand a great deal from the study of mass movements (Part 6). Waves of migration, for example, affect masses of population in both the sending and the receiving areas, just as they transform the individual migrants themselves. Readers might give greater attention to large scale movements in our own day, including the tragic uprooting of tens of millions of refugees, and the displacement of indigenous peoples as "civilization" encroaches on their homelands. They may also consider the world's enormous population growth, which has restructured life everywhere on the planet and left virtually no empty frontiers for new settlements.

A consideration of the stated goals of revolutions and a comparison of them to actual results demonstrates that humans have only limited control of the spin of events (Part 7). It also shows the need for skepticism in assessing revolutionary claims. In our examination of the industrial revolution (Chapter 16) we stressed the need to consider the consequences of technological change, and to evaluate the social and ecological consequences of technology as well as its productive potential. We also explored personal and group identities based on urbanization, nationalism, and gender—identities which remain central today. Most people today understand their place in the world, to an important degree, through their neighborhood and civic participation, their citizenship in a specific nation, and their gender. These identities are so ingrained that they are often taken for granted. But this afterword asks that we evaluate the kinds of cities and neighborhoods in which we wish to live and the kind of nation we wish to inhabit.

Our survey of how the major geographical/cultural regions of the world have used technology in the twentieth century (Part 8) invites readers to consider mechanisms by which immensely diverse peoples of the world can live together creatively. Such a survey raises many questions which are important to us as we enter a new millennium. What is an appropriate technology? Are some technologies so dangerous that they should be banned? What is the role and purpose of science in society? How can technology best serve human needs? What is an equitable balance between wealth and poverty among nations and individuals? How can individuals and groups best plan for the long-term future rather than just for the immediate present? Should nations begin to attempt to construct a "social contract" which binds them into an international system just as citizens of individual countries are bound by national laws?

MAKING COMMITMENTS BASED ON VALUES

Understanding of the present and the past, in preparation for the future, is unified through the value system of the interpreter. On which story from the past shall we focus? Whom shall we choose to highlight as our heroes and as our villains? The choice depends in part on our agenda for the future. Are we most interested in ecology? Gender, class or national identity? Our neighborhood, university, work, or religious community? Success in international business and politics? Current interests will help determine which pieces of the past we choose to engage with and studies of the past will guide us toward issues in the present.

In our era it may be difficult to make commitments. We live in an age of relativism. The laws of relativity discovered in the physical world by Einstein demonstrate that we can understand the placement of objects only in their relationships to others. Historians today make the same argument about events. Events all around the globe are interrelated, but formulating a value system which provides global coherence, stability, creativity, and justice seems a far-distant goal.

The certainties of an age of triumphant empire are not ours. We seem to be in a world of constant international competition, although cooperation is also evident and abundant. Old truths are constantly challenged. Some philosophers of history, such as Michel Foucault and Jacques Derrida, argue that historical change cannot be guided at all; power is so diffused throughout society that no levers for effecting change are there to be grasped.

Yet we do choose and we do make commitments, for intuitively we know that we wish at least some small space on this planet to be "home," to reflect values and ways of life with which we feel comfortable, a place where people who share our values are our companions, and where people who endanger them are kept at some safe distance. This does not mean that we seek a boring uniformity; quite the contrary, we recognize that diversity fosters creativity, and we seek diversity and even disagreement, but without unnecessary antagonism. Changing the entire world may be beyond us, but we can work in our own space. We may, as the phrase goes, "Think globally; act locally." By transforming our immediate environment we set an example which others might follow, if they choose.

WHAT TO DO?

In concluding this course of study in world history, we hope that you will be prepared to pay increased attention to activities from places around the globe, and from other times in history—to listen to diverse forms of music, read world literature, travel, visit archaeological digs. Beyond this generalized concern for broadening your horizons, you should be prepared to become involved with specific activities, organizations, and individuals active in those world affairs you find most interesting. An abundance of organizations awaits those who wish to get involved. For example, most religious denominations have some overseas involvement; Oxfam, a secular organization, supports and promotes development projects among poor people around the world; ecological groups with international concerns include the World Wildlife Fund and Greenpeace; and Amnesty International campaigns actively on behalf of prisoners of conscience around the world, putting pressure on dictatorial governments by exposing their activities. These organizations and many more keep their members and volunteers informed of international developments in their area of service, so the more you do the more you learn. You should not wait for the perfect organization or the perfect leader but should begin now by searching out an organization which addresses your own concerns and try to accomplish as much as you can within the limits of your time and energy. As Rabbi Tarfon stated in the Talmud 2000 years ago, "It is not your duty to complete the task, but neither may you exempt yourself from undertaking it." (Aboth, II:21)

BIBLIOGRAPHY

Bennington, Geoffrey and Jacques Derrida. *Jacques Derrida*, trans. by Geoffrey Bennington (Chicago: University of Chicago Press, 1993).

Bloch, Marc. *The Historian's Craft*, trans. by Peter Putnam (New York: Vintage Books, 1964).

Boorstin, Daniel. *The Discoverers* (New York: Random House, 1983).

Bradley Commission on History in the Schools. *Building a History Curriculum* (Washington: Educational Excellence Network, 1988).

Carr, E.H. *What is History?* (Harmondsworth, Middlesex: Penguin Books, 1964).

"Aboth: Sayings of the Fathers," in Joseph H. Hertz, ed. Daily Prayer Book, rev. ed., pp. 610-721 (New York: Bloch Publishing, 1954).

Foucault, Michel. *The Archaeology of Knowledge*, trans. by A.M. Sheridan Smith (London: Tavistock, 1974).

Laqueur, Walter and Barry Rubin. *The Human Rights Reader* (New York: New American Library, 1989).

McNeill, William H. *Mythistory and Other Essays* (Chicago: University of Chicago, 1986).

Tosh, John. *The Pursuit of History*, 2nd ed. (New York: Longman, 1991).

White, Hayden. *Metahistory* (Baltimore: Johns Hopkins University Press, 1973).

GLOSSARY

animist One who believes that the world is permeated by spiritual beings who have an interest in human affairs and may intervene in them. Animism is characteristic of most tribal peoples.

apartheid An Afrikaans word meaning "apartness," referring to racial segregation and implying white supremacy. The policy was officially implemented in South Africa in 1948, when increasingly restrictive laws against blacks were introduced. The establishment of the Bantu "homelands" effectively disenfranchised blacks from the South African body politic. Internal opposition and international censure, particularly the sanctions imposed by Britain and the United States in 1985, led to shifts in policy and enfranchisement, culminating in the election of a coalition government with a black majority in 1994.

asiento A contract between the Spanish crown and a private individual or sovereign power, by which the latter was granted exclusive rights to import a stipulated number of slaves into the Spanish American colonies in exchange for a fee. The British South Sea Company was granted a monopoly at the Treaty of Utrecht of 1713, a privilege that was relinquished for a lump sum in 1750.

Balkanization The process by which a large political or geographical unit is broken into smaller ones, with the implication that hostilities may ensue. The term was coined to describe the fragmentation of the Ottoman Empire in the nineteenth and early twentieth centuries; it has also been applied to the emergence of independent states in post-colonial Africa and to the break-up of the former Soviet Union.

bourgeoisie A French word that originally applied to the inhabitants of walled towns, who occupied a socio-economic position between the rural peasantry and the feudal aristocracy; with the development of industry, it became identified more with employers, as well as to other members of the "middle class," professionals, artisans, and shopkeepers. In Marxist theory, it refers to those who do not live by the sale of their labor, as opposed to the **proletariat**.

cadre A nucleus of key personnel. Cadre was originally a French military term denoting the officers of a regiment; it is also applied to an organized group of political activists.

caravanserai In Middle Eastern countries, a public building for the use of travelers and caravans, usually situated outside the walls of a town. It comprises an arcaded two-storied courtyard with storerooms, stabling, and areas for food preparation on the ground floor and lodgings above. Massive walls with small, high windows and a single barred gateway provide protection at night.

cartel An association of independent producers or businessmen whose aim is to control the supply of a particular commodity or group of commodities in order to regulate or push up prices.

caudillismo In Spanish America, a system of rule through *caudillos* (leaders), men with a strong personal following who wield almost absolute authority. It emerged during the nineteenth-century wars of independence, at a time when there was little social or political stability.

chasidic (hasidic) A pietistic strand of orthodox Judaism that stresses the indwelling of God in all creation. Founded in Poland in the eighteenth century, it spread throughout eastern Europe; huge numbers of chasidic Jews perished under the Nazis during World War II. There are now communities in Israel, the United States, and Britain.

Cheka The secret police of early Soviet Russia, established by the Bolsheviks after the Revolution of 1917 to defend the regime against dissidents. Criticized for its severe brutality, the agency was reorganized in 1922.

collectivization A policy that aims to transfer land from private to state or communal ownership. It was adopted by the Soviet government in the 1920s and implemented with increasing brutality; by 1936 almost all the peasants had joined the *kolkhozy* (large collective farms), although many resisted violently. The integration of agriculture into the state-controlled economy helped to supply the capital required for industrialization.

comprador (Portuguese: "buyer") A Chinese merchant hired by Western traders to assist with their dealings in China. The comprador provided interpreters, workers, guards, and help over currency exchange.

Concordat A public agreement, subject to international law, between the Pope as head of the Roman Catholic Church and a temporal ruler regulating the status, rights, and liberties of the church within the country concerned.

counterurbanization A shift in population from metropolitan areas to the country or smaller towns, a phenomenon of advanced industrial nations first identified in the 1970s. Since it tends to be the more affluent citizens who migrate, the process creates poor and decaying inner-city areas.

Creole In the sixteenth to eighteenth centuries, a white person born in Spanish America of Spanish parents. Excluded from the highest offices under the Spanish colonial administration, the Creoles became the leaders of revolution, and then the ruling class of the new independent nations. The term creole is also used more loosely, with a wide range of applications.

daimyo The feudal lords of Japan, who by the sixteenth century controlled almost the entire country. Their constant warfare was finally ended in 1603 under the Tokugawa **Shogunate**; they subsequently served as local rulers, joined to the **shogun** by oath. In 1868, when imperial rule was restored, their domains and **han** were surrendered to the emperor; in 1871 they were given titles and pensioned off.

descamisados The "shirtless ones," the urban poor of Argentina, who supported Juan Perón (1895–1974) and his wife Eva. They organized mass protests at his arrest in 1945; Perón had gained popular support through his wage and welfare measures while a minister in the government of 1943–5.

developed world Those countries that enjoy considerable wealth, derived largely from sophisticated industrialization, and characterized by high standards of living, healthcare and literacy, advanced technological development, democratic constitutions, and world influence, as well as high labor costs and energy consumption. They comprise most of Europe, the United States, Canada, Japan, Australia, and New Zealand, the first areas to be industrialized.

developing world Those countries lacking advanced industrial development and money for investment, and with a low *per capita* income. Their economies are largely agrarian, often relying on one crop, with low yields. Labor is plentiful, cheap, and unskilled; levels of literacy are low; poverty, disease, and famine have not been eliminated. They include most Asian countries, as well as Africa and Latin America. (*See* **third world**.)

development of underdevelopment A theory developed by Latin American social scientists in the mid-1960s; also known as dependency theory. It argues that, despite the end of colonialism, wealthy nations such as the United States and members of the European Community continue to exercise great political control over **third world** countries through their domination of the global economy.

divine right of kings A political doctrine influential in the sixteenth and seventeenth centuries. It held that the monarch derived his or her authority from God and was therefore not accountable to earthly authority. James I of England (1603–25) was a foremost exponent.

duma The Russian parliament established by Nicholas II in response to the Revolution of 1905. Its powers were largely restricted to the judicial and administrative areas; the czar retained control over the franchise. The first two dumas (1906, 1907) were radical and soon dissolved; the third (1907–12) was conservative; the fourth (1912–17) became a focus of opposition to the czarist regime, particularly over its conduct of World War I, and enforced Nicholas's abdication in 1917.

dyarchy A system of provincial government in British India introduced under the Government of India Act (1919). Crown-appointed councillors retained control of law and order, justice, and revenue, but Indian ministers, chosen by the governor from elected legislators, took over local government and such matters as education, health, public works, and agriculture. Dyarchy was superseded by full provincial autonomy in 1935.

econometrics The use of statistical techniques and mathematical models to analyze economic relationships. Econometrics may be applied by a government or private business to test the validity of an economic theory or to forecast future trends.

encomienda A concession from the Spanish crown to a Spanish American colonist, giving him permission to exact tribute – in gold, in kind, or in labor – from a specified number of Indians living in a certain area; in return he was to care for their welfare and instruct them in the Catholic faith. The system was designed to supply labor for the mines, but it was severely abused and later abolished.

enlightened despotism A benevolent form of absolutism, a system of government in which the ruler has absolute rights over his or her subjects. It implies that the ruler acts for the good of the people, not in self-interest.

Eurocentricity A concentration on the history and culture of Europe, often disregarding other areas and influences.

existentialism A philosophical and literary movement that came to prominence after World War II, particularly associated with French intellectuals, notably Jean-Paul Sartre. It rejects metaphysics and epistemology, and is concerned with being rather than knowing; it stresses the uniqueness of each individual, and the need to find one's own authenticity.

extraterritoriality In international law, the immunities enjoyed by the official representatives of a sovereign state or international organization within a host country; they are in effect "foreign islands," and thus exempt from prosecution, interference, or constraint.

feudal Refers to a social, military, and political system organized on the basis of land tenure and the manorial system of production. Property (the fief) was granted to a tenant (vassal) by a lord in exchange for an oath of allegiance and a promise to fulfill certain obligations, including military service, aid, and advice; in return, the lord offered protection and justice. Originally bestowed by investiture, the fief later became hereditary. Within the system, each person was bound to the others by a web of mutual responsibilities, from the king or emperor down to the **serfs**. Feudalism is particularly associated with medieval Europe, and with China and Japan. (*See* **manorial economy**.)

finca A Spanish farm, country estate, or coffee plantation.

first world The advanced capitalist nations of the **developed world**, as opposed to the second world (countries with socialist state systems, particularly the former Soviet bloc) and the **third world**.

free market economy An economic system in which the means of production are largely privately owned and there is little or no government control over the markets, which operate according to **supply and demand**. The primary aim is to maximize profits, which are distributed to private individuals who have been encouraged to invest capital in an enterprise. The system is also known as a free enterprise economy or capitalism.

front-line A state that is bordered by a country engaged in armed conflict, and often drawn into the conflict.

garden city A planned town combining work, residential, agricultural, and recreational facilities, and surrounded by a rural belt. This influential idea was the British planner Ebenezer Howard's solution to rural depopulation and the urban overcrowding of the industrial age. Letchworth (1903) in southeast England was the first example.

gaucho A nomadic cattle-herder, of any race, in the grasslands of South America, noted for his fearless riding and distinctive dress. Heroic figures in the colonial wars of independence, the gauchos became

employees of the ranchers when the pampas were enclosed in the nineteenth century.

gazi A warrior or war leader in Islam, sometimes used as a military title among the Turks.

geo-politics The analysis of the effect of geographic environment on national policy and on the power relationships between nations. The theory that geography determines a nation's area of struggle was particularly influential on Germany in the 1920s, and on the Nazis.

Girondins A French revolutionary group formed largely from the middle classes, many of them originally from the Gironde region. They were prominent in the Legislative Assembly (1791), urged war against Austria (1792), opposed the more radical **Montagnards**, and were overthrown in 1793.

glasnost A Russian word meaning "openness," adopted as a political slogan by the Soviet leader Mikhail Gorbachev in 1986. It encouraged greater freedom of expression and genuine debate in social, political, and cultural affairs; with **perestroika**, it heralded greater democracy and improved relations with the West.

guild A sworn association of people who gather for some common purpose. In the towns of medieval Europe, guilds of craftsmen or merchants were formed in order to protect and further the members' professional interests and for mutual aid. Merchant guilds organized trade in their locality and had important influence on local government. Craft guilds were confined to specific crafts or trades; they set and maintained standards of quality, regulated production and controlled recruitment through the apprenticeship system; they also had important social and religious functions. In India the guilds were associations of businessmen and producers who regulated weights and measures and prices and enforced quality control.

hacienda A large rural estate in Spanish America, originating with Spanish colonialization in the sixteenth century. The laborers, usually Indians, were in theory free wage earners, but in practice many became bound to the land through indebtedness to the owner. The owners (*haciendados*) controlled local, and sometimes national government.

han In Japan, the territory or feudal estate controlled by a **daimyo** under the Tokugawa **Shogunate** (1603–1868). Although legally subject to the central government, each *han* formed an autonomous and self-sufficient economic unit, with its own military forces. They were abolished in 1871.

harijan A Hindu term meaning children of God, applied by Mahatma Gandhi to the poorest classes of Indian society, including the **untouchables**.

hegemony The predominance of one unit over the others in a group, for example one state in a confederation. It can also apply to the rule of an empire over its subject peoples, when the foreign government is exercised with their substantial consent (as opposed to dominance, the imposition of alien government through force). Hegemony usually implies exploitation but, more positively, it may connote leadership.

heliocentric A system in which the sun is

assumed to be at the center of the solar system – or of the universe – while Earth and the planets move around it. Ptolemy of Alexandria's geocentric or Earth-centered system dominated scientific thought in the Western world from the second century C.E. until the publication of Copernicus's *De revolutionibus orbium coelestium* in 1543. There was much religious and scientific controversy before his thesis was shown to be essentially correct.

humanism A term applied to the intellectual movement initiated in Western Europe in the fourteenth century by such men as Petrarch and Boccaccio and deriving from the rediscovery and study of Classical, particularly Latin, literary texts. The humanist program of studies included rhetoric, grammar, history, poetry, and moral philosophy (the humanities); the humanist scholar aimed to emulate Classical literary achievements. The examination of Classical civilization formed the inspiration for the **Renaissance**. Although humanism attached prime importance to human qualities and values, unlike its twentieth-century counterpart it in no way involved the rejection of Christianity.

indulgences In the Roman Catholic Church, the remission from the temporal penalty of an absolved sin, obtainable through good works or special prayers and granted by the Church through the merits of Christ and the saints. The financial value often attached to indulgences in the late medieval church led to widespread abuse.

infitah An Arabic term meaning liberality and receptiveness to new ideas and arguments. In commerce, it implies expansion and freedom from restrictive rules and regulations.

irredentist An individual or group that seeks to restore territory to the state that once owned it.

Jacobins A French revolutionary party founded in 1789; the word derives from the popular name for the former Dominican convent in Paris, where meetings were held. It later became the most radical party of the Revolution, responsible, under Robespierre, for implementing the Reign of Terror and the execution of the king (1793).

janissary A member of the elite corps of Ottoman footsoldiers. Originally, in the late fourteenth century, they were Christian conscripts from the conquered Balkans who were forcibly converted to Islam and subjected to strict rules, including celibacy. Highly trained, they later became very powerful, frequently engineering palace coups; they were massacred after their insurrection in 1826.

keiretsu Alliances of independent Japanese firms, either between large corporations in different industries or between a large corporation and sub-contractors. They are successors of the pre-war **zaibatsu**.

khedive The title granted by the Ottoman sultan Abdulaziz to the hereditary pasha (viceroy) of Egypt in 1867. In 1904, when Egypt became a British protectorate, the title was replaced by that of Sultan.

kibbutz An Israeli settlement, usually agricultural but sometimes industrial, in which wealth and property are held in common, profits are reinvested in the enterprise and decisions are made democratically. Work and meals are organized collectively and children housed away from their parents.

kulak A prosperous peasant in late czarist and early Soviet Russia. The leaders of local agricultural communities, kulaks owned sizeable farms and could afford to hire labor. They vigorously opposed Stalin's **collectivization** policy and were regarded as class enemies; large numbers were deported or executed, and their property confiscated.

ladino A Spanish-speaking inhabitant of Central America of predominantly Spanish descent, distinguished by their Western dress and habits. They are often engaged in small-scale commerce and agriculture, where they tend to use more modern farming methods than the Indians, and to concentrate more on cash crops.

laissez-faire An economic policy of non-interference by government in the working of the market and the economic affairs of individuals. Proponents of the theory, which was developed in the eighteenth century, argued that an unregulated economy would work "naturally" at maximum efficiency and that the pursuit of self-interest would ultimately benefit society as a whole.

lateen A triangular sail affixed to a long yard or crossbar at an angle of about 45 degrees to the mast, with the free corner secured near the stern. The sail was capable of taking the wind on either side. The rig, which was developed by the Arabs, revolutionized navigation because it enabled vessels to tack into the wind and thus to sail in almost any direction; with a square sail, ships could only sail with the wind behind them.

liberation theology A movement in the Roman Catholic Church in Latin America that stresses the importance of translating religious faith into active political involvement in order to redress social wrongs. It views the church as belonging especially to the poor, and has been responsible for the establishment of local Christian groups or *communidades de base* to serve members' spiritual and physical needs.

madrasa (pl.: **medresses**) A traditional Islamic school of higher education, principally of theology and law, literally a "place of study." The madrasa usually comprised a central courtyard surrounded by rooms in which the students resided and with a prayer room or mosque, where instruction took place. Tuition, board, and lodging were free. Studies could last for several years and primarily consisted of memorizing text books and lectures.

mahdi An Arabic word meaning "the right-guided one." According to Islamic tradition, a messianic leader will appear to restore justice, truth, and religion for a brief period before the Day of Judgment. Some Shi'a Muslims believe that the twelfth imam (ninth century C.E.) will reappear as the Mahdi. Several impostors have claimed the title.

maidan An open space or square in an Iranian town or city.

mandate The authority given to a member power from the League of Nations – the organization set up in 1919 to settle international disputes through arbitration – to govern the former colonies of the German and Ottoman empires. Mandate also referred to the area of jurisdiction itself. In 1946 the system was replaced by the United Nations trusteeship system.

mangonel An upright armed catapult worked by torsion. Mangonels of various types were used in China and the ancient world, as well as by the Mongols and in medieval Europe.

manorial economy An economic system based on the manor, or the lord's landed estate, the most common unit of agrarian organization in medieval Europe. The manor comprised the lord's own farm (the demesne) and the land farmed by peasant tenants or **serfs** who were legally dependent on the lord and owed him or her **feudal** service on the demesne. The manor was not completely self-contained but it aimed more at self-sufficiency than at the market and supported a steady increase in population up to the fourteenth century.

maroonage A situation of slaves in the West Indian islands in the early eighteenth century. They organized their escape and sometimes lived in communities in inaccessible mountainous regions or forests.

mazombo A direct descendant of Portuguese settlers in the Americas.

medresses (See **madrasa**.)

mercantilism An economic policy pursued by many European nations between the sixteenth and eighteenth centuries. It aimed to strengthen an individual nation's economic power at the expense of its rivals by stockpiling reserves of bullion, which involved government regulation of trade. Measures included tariffs on imports, the passing of sumptuary laws to keep demand for imported goods low, the promotion of thrift, and the search for new colonies, both as a source for raw materials and as a market for the export of finished goods.

mestizo A person of mixed race. In Central and South America it usually denotes a person of combined Indian and European descent.

mfecane A period of strife (1818–28) among the Bantu peoples of southern Africa, initiated by Zulu expansion under the warrior king Shaka and leading to the displacement of other tribes. It facilitated white colonial expansion in the area.

mir A self-governing community of peasants in pre-revolutionary Russia having control over local forests, fisheries, and hunting grounds; arable land was allocated to each family according to size, in return for a fixed sum. The communes had elected officials and were responsible for the payment of taxes.

mita A system of forced labor in Peru, begun under Inca rule and continued by the Spanish colonists, by which Indian communities were required to contribute a set number of laborers for public works for a given period. Conditions were appalling, particularly in the mines, and many Indians perished. The system was abolished in 1821. (*See* **repartimiento**.)

monoculture A farming system devoted to the cultivation of a single crop, often a cash crop. Although monoculture can be more efficient, it is susceptible to the spread of disease and price fluctuations.

monopoly The exclusive control over the production or supply of a particular commodity or service for which there is no substitute. Because there is no competition, the supplier can fix the price of the product and maximize profits.

Montagnards Members of a radical French revolutionary party, closely associated with the **Jacobins** and supported by the artisans, shopkeepers, and **sansculottes**. They opposed the more moderate **Girondins** and controlled the Legislative Assembly and National Convention during the climax of the Revolution in 1793–4.

mulatto In the Americas, a person of mixed race, usually with parents of European and African origin.

nabob A British employee of the East India Company who made a huge fortune in India, often through corruption, in the eighteenth century.

Negritude A mid-twentieth-century literary movement originating among French-speaking writers from Africa and the Caribbean in protest against French colonial rule and its policy of assimilation, which they felt assumed European cultural superiority. They emphasized the special qualities of African traditions and peoples, and hoped to inspire readers with a desire for independence.

neo-colonialism The control exercised by a state or group of states of the **developed world** over the economies and societies of the **developing world**. Although the latter countries may be legally independent, investment and economic control are often accompanied by political manipulation.

patrilineal The tracing of ancestry and kinship through the male line only.

patrilocal Residence by a couple in or near the home of the male's family or group.

perestroika A Russian word meaning "restructuring," used, like **glasnost**, to describe the reforms introduced by the Soviet leader Mikhail Gorbachev after 1985. It marked the development of a more flexible socio-economic system, distinguished by a move to a market-oriented economy, increased private ownership, and decentralization.

philosophes A group of eighteenth-century French writers and philosophers who emphasized the supremacy of human reason and advocated freedom of expression and social, economic, and political reform. They included Voltaire, Montesquieu, Rousseau, and Diderot, editor of the *Encyclopédie* (1751–72), which manifested their ideas. The *philosophes* influenced the ideals of the French Revolution and the American Declaration of Independence.

plebiscite A direct vote by the people of a district or country on a specific issue. The term usually refers to a choice of nationality, but it may also concern a matter of national policy or a selection of ruler or government.

pogrom (Russian: "devastation") A violent attack on a minority group. The term is usually applied to attacks on Jews and Jewish property, particularly those that took place in the Russian Empire after the assassination of Alexander II in 1881 as a result of the government's anti-Semitic policy. There were further pogroms in eastern Europe, forcing many Jews to emigrate, and in Nazi Germany.

proletariat In Marxist theory, those who live solely by the sale of their labor, as opposed to the **bourgeoisie**. The term is usually applied to the wage workers engaged in industrial production.

raja An Indian king or princely ruler.

realpolitik A German term meaning practical politics, that is, a policy determined by expediency rather than by ethical or ideological considerations.

Renaissance Literally "rebirth," a French term applied to the cultural and intellectual movement that spread throughout Europe from the fourteenth century. It was characterized by a new interest in Classical civilization, stimulated by the Italian poet Petrarch, and a response to the challenge of its models, which led to pride in contemporary achievement and renewed vigor in the arts and sciences. The new concept of human dignity found its inspiration in **humanism**.

reparations Payments due from defeated powers to the victors of war in compensation for their losses, also known as war indemnities.

repartimiento A system by which the Spanish crown allowed Spanish American colonists to employ Indians for forced labor, whether in agriculture or the mines. This had to be for the production of essential food or goods, and was for limited periods, but there was much abuse. (*See* **mita**.)

sahel "Shore" – the northern and southern edges of the Sahara Desert. A semi-arid region of Africa, extending from Senegal eastwards to the Sudan and forming a transitional zone between the Sahara desert to the north and the belt of **savanna** to the south. The area is dry for most of the year, with a short and unreliable rainy season, and is subject to long periods of drought. Low-growing grasses provide pasture for camels, pack oxen, cattle, and sheep.

samurai A member of the warrior class of feudal Japan, who became vassals of the **daimyo**. Characterized by their military skills and stoical pride, they valued personal loyalty, bravery, and honor more than life. During the peaceful years of the Tokugawa **Shogunate** (1603–1867) they became scholars, bureaucrats, and merchants. The class was officially abolished in 1871.

sansculottes (French: "without knee-breeches") In the French Revolution, members of the militant, generally poorer classes of Paris, so-called because they wore trousers rather than the knee-breeches of affluent society. The dress was also adopted by political activists. The name was proscribed after the fall of Robespierre in 1794.

sati (suttee) An ancient Hindu custom that requires widows to be burned on the funeral pyre of their husbands, or soon afterwards. The practice of self-immolation was officially abolished in British India in 1829.

satyagraha A Hindi expression meaning "truth force," applied to Gandhi's policy of non-violent opposition to British rule in India.

savanna The grassland areas of the tropics and sub-tropics adjacent to the equatorial rain forests in each hemisphere and bordered by arid regions of desert. Savannas cover extensive parts of Africa, South America, and northern Australia. The natural vegetation is mainly grass with scattered shrubs and trees, the latter low and often flat-topped. The land is particularly suitable for cattle rearing.

serf An agricultural worker or peasant bound to the land and legally dependent on the lord, characteristic of the **manorial economy** and the **feudal** system. Serfs had their own homes, plots, and livestock but they owed the lord labor, dues, and services. These services could be commuted to rent, but serfs remained chattels of the lord unless they were emancipated by him or her, or escaped. Serfdom declined in western Europe in the late medieval period, but persisted in parts of eastern Europe until the nineteenth century.

shari'a The "road" or sacred revealed law of Islam, based on the Quran and the traditional teachings of Muhammad. Since Islam does not distinguish between the religious and the secular spheres, Islamic law applies to every aspect of life. It covers such matters as marriage, divorce, inheritance, diet, and civil and criminal law.

Shogun The military dictator of Japan, a hereditary title held by three families between 1192 and 1867. Although they were legally subservient to the emperor, their military power gave them effective control of the country, and they also took on judicial and administrative functions. The Tokugawa Shogunate (1603–1867) established a powerful centralized government at Edo (Tokyo). Imperial rule was restored in 1868.

Shogunate The government of the **shogun**.

signares African concubines of French traders in the Senegambia.

soviet A council, the primary unit of government in the Soviet Union at local, regional, and national levels, also adopted by other Communist regimes. Committees of workers' elected deputies first appeared in 1905 to coordinate revolutionary activities; they sprang up throughout the Russian Empire and were a crucial agent in the Revolution of 1917, forming the basis of Soviet administration thereafter.

Sufi In Islam, a member of one of the orders practicing mystical forms of worship that first arose in the eighth and ninth centuries C.E. Sufis interpret the words of Muhammad in a spiritual rather than a literal sense. Their goal is direct personal experience of God, achieved by fervent worship.

supply and demand In economics, the relationship between the amount of a commodity that producers are able and willing to sell (supply), and the quantity that consumers can afford and wish to buy (demand). The price fluctuates according to a product's availability and its desirability. Supply and demand thus controls a **free market economy**. In practice it is usually subject to some degree of regulation.

swadeshi "Of one's own country," a Hindi word used as a slogan in the Indian boycott of foreign goods, part of the protest against Britain's partition of Bengal in 1905. The Indian people were urged to use indigenous goods and to wear garments of *khadi*, homemade cloth.

swaraj A Hindi word meaning "self-government" or "home rule," used as a slogan by Indian nationalists in their campaign for independence from British rule.

syncretism The mixture of different religious traditions. The term is also used to refer to hybridity in other areas, such as art and culture.

technopolis A town or geographical area devoted to technological research and development.

theocracy A system of government administered by priests or other religious body, in which God is regarded as the immediate ruler.

third world The countries outside the **first world** and the second world (countries with socialist state systems); more loosely, the **developing world**, which contains more than 70 percent of world population. The twenty-five least developed countries are sometimes characterized as "fourth world."

transhumance A form of pastoralism or nomadism organized around the seasonal migration of livestock, practiced in areas that are too cold or wet for winter grazing. The animals are moved to mountain pastures in warm seasons and to lowland ones in winter, or between lower and upper latitudes, or between wet- and dry-season grazing areas.

trebuchet A military engine for hurling heavy missiles, operated by counterpoise, on the principle of the seesaw. Developed in China, the trebuchet first appeared in Europe in the twelfth century.

untouchables Members of the lowest castes of traditional Indian society or those outside the caste system; the "untouchable" groups were those engaged in "polluting" activities.

voodoo The popular religious cult of Haiti, as well as other areas of the Caribbean. It combines ritual elements from Roman Catholicism with theological and magical elements of West African origin. Voodoo ritual centers on animal sacrifice, drumming, and dance, and contact with a populous spirit world through trance.

warlord A local Chinese despot with a private army. The warlords attempted to seize power after the death of Yuan Shihkai, first president of Republican China, in 1916; their civil war was ended when Chiang Kai-shek unified the country in 1928. They continued to exert power until the Communist government took over in 1949.

yurt A portable dwelling used by the nomadic peoples of Central Asia, consisting of a tentlike structure of skin, felt or hand-woven textiles arranged over wooden poles, simply furnished with brightly colored rugs.

zaibatsu (Japanese: "wealthy clique") A large Japanese business corporation, usually under the control of a single family. A *zaibatsu* was a form of cartel, engaging in all important areas of economic activity and funded by its own bank. They emerged under the modernizing Meiji government (1867–1912) and were dissolved by the Allies in 1946 after World War II.

zemstvo A rural council in the Russian Empire, established by Czar Alexander II in 1864 and abolished in 1917. The assemblies, which operated at both district and provincial level, comprised the representatives of individual landed proprietors and village communes (**mir**). They were concerned with such matters as primary education, road building, agricultural development, and public health.